Jewi
Travel Guide
2009

INTERNATIONAL EDITION

Published in association with
the *Jewish Chronicle*, London

VALLENTINE MITCHELL
LONDON • PORTLAND, OR

First published in 2009 by

VALLENTINE MITCHELL & CO. LTD

920 NE 58th Avenue, Suite 300
Portland, Oregon 97213 3786,
USA

Suite 314, Premier House
112-114 Station Road
Edgware, Middlesex HA8 7BJ, UK

Email: jtg@vmbooks.com
www.vmbooks.com

Copyright © 2009 Vallentine Mitchell & Co. Ltd and Jewish Chronicle Ltd

ISBN 978 0 85303 880 1
ISSN 0075 3750

British Library Cataloguing in Publication Data

Jewish travel guide 2009
1. Jews - Travel - Guidebooks
910.8'8296

Printed by Bell and Bain Ltd, Glasgow, Scotland

Contents

Publisher's Note

WE NEED YOUR ASSISTANCE TO KEEP
THIS GUIDE UP TO DATE

The 2009 edition of the Jewish Travel Guide, in addition to the usual extensive corrections, now has two new features. These comprise:

- A new section added in 2007 that includes details of Jewish heritage tours and kosher holidays and cruises worldwide. This will assist the Jewish traveller whether visiting sites of Jewish interest, researching a family tree or interested in the depth and history of Jewish culture around the world. The kosher holiday and cruise information will allow the kosher traveller to see at a glance, the spread and variety of options available to them worldwide, whether they are looking for a kosher safari, skiing trip or climbing a mountain.

- Maps. In 2008 the inclusion of a selection of 17 maps covering parts of Eastern Europe and the former USSR. These will assist travellers in planning their trips. The maps are in the public domain and reproduced by courtesy of the University of Texas.

The Publishers have made every effort to ensure that the guide is as accurate and up to date as possible.

As in previous years, an update form is included at the back of the book for those who become aware of additions they would like considered for inclusion. In addition, of course, we wish to be notified of any errors that may have occurred in the preparation of this book. **For advertising, updates, new entries or to purchase copies please contact Toby Harris at the address below:**

Jewish Travel Guide Updates
Suite 314, Premier House, 112-114 Station Road, Edgware, Middlesex HA8 7BJ, UK
T: +44(0)20 8952 9526 F: +44(0)20 8952 9242 E: jtg@vmbooks.com W: www.vmbooks.com

Please include a contact email address whenever possible. Potential advertisers, or those who wish to stock and sell copies of the Jewish Travel Guide, may use any of the above means to contact us for details of advertising rates and trade terms. Orders for 5 or more copies will be supplied at trade terms.

Please include a contact email address whenever possible

Tips for Kosher Travellers

Travel has never been more popular with many exotic cruising destinations being added each year to the existing 'portfolio' of the Mediterranean and Caribbean.

But unless you travel on an exclusively kosher cruise how easy is it to keep kosher?

Here frequent traveller Rabbi Dr Avraham Abrahami gives his expert advice – and it's easier than you think.

As many cruises involve a flight to your port of departure and, sometimes, an overnight hotel stay on your outward or inward journey, Rabbi Abrahami has covered that aspect of the journey too.

If you wish to keep kosher while you travel without your kosher deli or kosher butcher close by, it will be a challenge, but it can be done. Here is my step-by-step guide.

AIR TRAVEL AND HOTEL STAY

Kosher meal. Ensure you order your kosher meal and verify it was actually ordered and confirm with the airline at least five days before flying.

Contingency. As a precaution, in case your kosher meal does not turn up after all, take with you some kosher food.

Just in case. In case you do not get your kosher meal on the flight and you forgot to bring with you some kosher food, you may eat some fruit, plain yoghurt (if it contains no gelatine), and you may also eat any other product that you are familiar with, which appears on the list of kosher products in your own country.

Kosher products. Unless you stay in a kosher hotel or in case you will be on the go most of the time, check before you leave home the range of products available in the country in which you are staying. You can do so via the Internet, or contact the local Orthodox rabbi at your destination and he should be able to e-mail or fax to you the relevant information about what you can buy in local supermarkets and/or the restaurants available.

Plates and cutlery. Make sure that before you leave home you take with you, or immediately after you land at your destination, you purchase paper or plastic plates and plastic cutlery.

Kosher labels. As a general rule it's much easier and more practical to live on preserved kosher fish, fruit and vegetables, while you travel. However, particularly in the USA, in main cities, you should be able to find a variety of kosher products, including meat, sold in supermarkets. The best-known kosher label is OU, although there are numerous other kosher labels. The following website is an excellent source of information: www.kashrut.com

What to do if ... you do not have plastic plates and cutlery, you may eat breakfast cereals with a fruit juice or non-supervised cow's milk, using the hotel crockery and cutlery but *only for non-cooked, cold food.* If you travel to countries where their cow's milk may contain milk from non-kosher animals, e.g. Spain, you cannot rely on the authorities and therefore you may not drink this milk.

Hot drinks. It is better to drink from plastic or glass cups but if unavailable, glazed china/porcelain cups are acceptable.

SEA TRAVEL AND CRUISE SHIPS

General. The general advice in the previous section concerning air travel and hotel stay applies also in this case; however, it is less challenging to keep kosher on a cruise ship, if you travel five-star.

Kosher food. Although kosher food is available anyway on most luxury liners, make sure you order it at the time of your booking. You may find that the kosher food on board the cruise ship is not what you expected. I found that the highest quality travel kosher food comes from the UK in a pre-packed airline style, to be heated in a microwave oven or served cold.

And if not ... If you are unable to eat the pre-packed kosher meal then you may ask the restaurant staff to cook for you in a double-packed aluminium foil a kosher fish (e.g. haddock, mackerel, cod, salmon, halibut, carp etc.). Although according to Jewish Law, cooking by a non-Jew is not permitted, if there is no other choice, this may be allowed.

Vegetarian food. Eating a vegetarian meal cooked in the ordinary kitchen utensils – even if all the ingredients are kosher - is not permitted, according to Jewish Law, except in exceptional circumstances, ill health etc. I visited high-class cruise ship kitchens and found them spotless, generally well above the cleanliness standards of most hotels and restaurants. Usually, these luxury cruise ships have a separate vegetarian kitchen and their salads are OK, as well as a boiled egg.

Speak to the restaurant manager. Make sure that unless it is a kosher cruise, whereby the kosher food is supervised and cooked fresh on board the ship in a separate kosher kitchen, you introduce yourself on day one to the restaurant manager and explain to him/her your kosher food needs. Also ensure that other managers on other shifts are likewise informed about your needs. I cannot over-emphasise how important this is, do not be embarrassed and do it as soon as you settle into your cabin or stateroom.

For glatt kosher cruising, I highly recommend www.kosherica.com You may not embark or disembark the ship during Shabbat or Yom Tov, except in an emergency

GENERAL COMMENT AND TIPS

Wine without a kosher label may not be drunk, but whisky, vodka, rum and fruit liqueurs (containing no grape product) are acceptable.

If you do not have kosher wine, you can make Kiddush and Havdala on most other alcoholic drinks, including beer, but not on tea, coffee or a soft drink. Any kitchen or food store would have spices for Havdala.

Vegetable and fruit salads are generally alright but it's better to avoid broccoli and ordinary lettuce, which are not easy to clean from bugs. Carefully check any salad dressing. Whole fruit or vegetable may be provided on request.

Most smoked salmon, sardines and tuna are OK but check the label carefully first and if in doubt ask.

If you have no choice and there is no kosher bread to eat, you may eat French bread that is made from flour and water only.

Ryvita and Jacob's crackers are OK but many places outside the UK do not stock them, so you may take them with you.

It's advisable to take with you some Matza and as many *sealed* kosher food items as you can carry to ease off your journey at least until you locate an appropriate kosher food store.

In most countries, including the USA and Israel, fresh fruit and vegetables and meat and fish are *not allowed* to be taken into the country, only sealed snacks (e.g. crisps, biscuits etc.) and possibly some tinned food. *If in doubt check beforehand.*

Most chocolates are OK, but you may not eat cheese unless it has a kosher label or it appears on the list of kosher products (e.g. Philadelphia).

Be particularly careful with biscuits, sweets and ice creams (except Haagen Dazs, Ben & Jerry's etc.).

La Bruite kosher meals (pre-packed) contain a patented, flameless food heater made of magnesium and iron. Website: www.labriutemeals.com

Hermolis kosher meals (pre-packed). Web site: www.hermolis.com

Remember to pack your Shabbat candles, prayer book, Tzitzit, Tefillin etc.

Kosher and Heritage Tours, Holidays and Cruises

Planning a holiday? Listed below are tour companies and private individuals who offer services to the Jewish and kosher traveller. We have gathered information which will help you, whether you wish to book a kosher safari, tour Australia, go skiing or even climb Kilimanjaro. If you would prefer to discover your historical roots, or would like to arrange a Bar or Batmitzvah in Israel or China, help is also at hand. Many of the operators listed can help you book kosher Passover or summer holidays in America and Europe. Don't forget to check out all the listings, as some operators offer their services in many different countries. You will also find a separate listing of companies offering kosher cruises at the end of this section. International dialling codes are listed at the beginning of each country section in the main Guide.

ARGENTINA
Jewish Tours
Telephone: 11-4544 8984
Email: info@jewish-tours.com.ar
Website: www.jewish-tours.com.ar
Tours of Jewish Buenos Aires.

Travel Jewish
PO Box 6771, Ithaca, NY, 14851
Email: info@traveljewish.com
Website: www.traveljewish.com
Half and full day tours Buenos Aires.

AUSTRALIA
Jewish Journeys
Telephone: 888-273 9384 / 212-682 5995
Email: JewishJourneys@yahoo.com
Kosher tours of Australia.

Jewish Sydney Tours
Telephone: (2) 9328 7604
For information about tours of Jewish Sydney, contact the Great Synagogue or Karl Maehrischel on (2) 9267 2477

BELARUS
Kosher Tours
Email: belshtetl@yahoo.com
A Kosher guided 7-day tour of Jewish interest sights in Belarus.

BELGIUM
Visit Antwerpen
Toerisme Antwerpen, Grote Markt 15 2000
Telephone: (3) 232 0103
Fax: (3) 231 1937
Email: visit@antwerpen.be
Website: www.visitantwerpen.be
Historical tours of Antwerp.

BOLIVIA
Jewish School and Tour Info
Calle Canada, Stronguest 1846,
PO Box 2198, La Paz

BRAZIL
Carmel Tur
Rua Xavier de Toledo 121/10
Telephone: (11) 257 2244

Sao Paulo Jewish Tour
Email: Paulo@jewishbrazil.com
Website: www.jewishbrazil.com
Tours of Jewish Sao Paulo with kosher meals.

Sharontur
Rua Sergipe 475/607- 608 Higienpolis 01243-001
Telephone: (11) 3826 8388
Fax: (11) 3825 3828
Rua Correa de Melo, Bom Retiro 01125-001
Telephone: (11) 3223 8388
Fax: (11) 3331 5036
Email: sharontur@sharontur.com.br
Website: www.sharontur.com.br

Rio Tours
Email: patricia@inriotur.com.br
Website: www. Inriotur.com.br
Tours of Jewish sites.

Travel Jewish
PO Box 6771, Ithaca, NY, 14851
Telephone: 949-307 9231
Fax: 949-861 7497
Email: info@traveljewish.com
Website: www.traveljewish.com
Half and full day tours of Rio.

Verticetur
Vertice Rua Sao Bento 545/10 01011-100
Telephone: (11) 3115 1970
Fax: (11) 3115 1970
Email: verticetur@terra.com.br

CANADA
Panorama Travel & Tours Ltd.
46 Niagara St. Unit #3, St. Catharines, ON L2R 4K9
Telephone: 905-682 5819
Toll Free: 1-800-216 9316
Fax: 905-682 4492
Email: info@panoramatours.ca
Jewish heritage tours to Poland.

CHILE
Travel Jewish
PO Box 6771, Ithaca, NY, 14851
Telephone: 949-307 231
Fax: 949-861 7497
Email: info@traveljewish.com
Website: www.traveljewish.com
Half and full day tours of Chile.

CHINA
China Direct
109-110 Ferguson Close, Ferguson's Wharf,
London E14 3SJ United Kingdom
Telephone: 020 7538 2840
Fax: 020 7536 9088
Email: info@chinadirect-travel.co.uk
Website: www.chinadirect-travel.co.uk

IAT Heritage Tours
P.O. Box 1936, Livingston, N.J. 07039-7536
Telephone: (866) 878-1600 (800) 963-6610
Fax: 973-228 0005
Email: israeladvantage@hotmail.com

Heritage tours of China. Bar or Bat Mizvahs can be arranged at Kaifeng Synagogue site.

Pacific Delight Tours
3 Park Avenue, 38th Floor, New York, NY 10016-5902
Tel: 1-800 221 7179 / 212 818 1781
Website: www.pacificdelighttours.com
China and Yangtze River Jewish Heritage Tour.

COSTA RICA
Kosher Expeditions
Telephone: 1-800-923 2645
Toll Free: 404-634-9206
Email: info@kosherexpeditions.com
Website: www.kosherexpeditions.com
Kosher tours of Costa Rica.

CZECH REPUBLIC
Kosher Prague Jewish Tours
Telephone: (2) (731) 108 744
Email: info@kosherprague.com
ww.Kosherprague.com
Includes Jewish Prague Tour, General Prague Tour and special Kivreu Tzadikim Tour.

Precious Legacy Tours
Kaprova 13, Prague 1, Josefov
Telephone: (+420) 222 321 951/4
Fax: (+420) 222 321 954
Weekends (+420) 602 214 088
Website: www.legacytours.net
Tours in Prague, Kutna Hora, Kolin, Vienna, Budapest.

Wittmann Tours
Manesova 8, 120 00 Prague 2
Telephone: (02) 2225 2472
Fax: (02) 2225 2472
Email: Sylvie@wittmann-tours.com
Website: www.wittmann-tours.com
Guided visits to Jewish sites.

DENMARK
Copenhagen Walking Tours
Telephone: 4081 1217
Website: www.copenhagen-walkingtours.dn
Walking tours of sites of Jewish interest in the old city.

FINLAND
Jewish Heritage in Finland
Malminkatu 38 D 46, Helsinki
Telephone: 9-694 7756
Fax: 9-694 7756
Email: zweig@jewish-heritage-finland.com
Website: www.jewish-heritage-finland.com
3 hour tour of Helsinki

FRANCE
Ideal Tours
Telephone: 972-2-5868717
Email: goski@idealtours.co.il
Website: www.idealtours.co.il
Kosher skiing holidays in France.

Paris Tours
Telephone: 6 85 71 03
Fax: 1 60 72 35 04
Email: chanoon2000@yahoo.fr
Private tours of Jewish Paris and France.

GERMANY
Tours of Berlin
Contact: Iris Weiss
Telephone: (30) 4535304
Email: iris.weiss@snafu.de
Website: www.berlin-judentum.de
Over twenty different tours on Jewish history
and Jewish life.

GIBRALTAR
Holyland Travel Ltd
21 Bell Lane
Telephone: 75965

HUNGARY
Aviv Travel
Telephone: (1) 317 2754
Email: aviv@aviv.hu
Website: www.aviv.hu.
A walking tour of Jewish Budapest, arranged by
the Municipality.

Chosen Tours
Telephone: (1) 185 9499
Fax: (1) 166 5165
Tours of Jewish sites are provided by telephone
arrangement.

Heritage Tours
Mazsike (Hungarian Jewish Cultural Association
VI. Révay Street 16, Budapest
Phone: 1 311 6665
Email: mazsike@gmail.com
Website: www.mazsike.hu

Jewish Visitors' Service.
Andrea Medgyesi
Phone: 309 428 215
Fax: 1326 24 72
Email: andrea@jewishvisitorsservice.com
Website: www.jewishvisitorsservice.com
Jewish tours of Budapest and Hungary.

INDIA
ORT India 68 Worli Hill Estate, PO Box 6571
400018
Telephone: (22) 496 2350 / 8423
Fax: (22) 364 7308
Email: jhirad@giasbm01.vsnl.in.
The Travel and Tourism Department arranges
tours in Mumbai and Raighad District Tours.

Tov Jewish India Tours
96 Penso Villa, 1st Floor, Mbraut Rd., Shivaji Park
400028
Telephone: (22) 244 50134
Email: indoisr@hotmail.com
118 Citadel Palace Orchard, Rdindhari, Green
Forest
Telephone: (20) 693 1488

Unlimited India Tours
Uniglobe Total Travel based in Edgware, UK
Telephone: 208 731 2111
Website: www.unlimitedindia.co.uk
Jewish heritage tours in India.

ISRAEL
Bar or BatMitzvah in Israel
P.O. Box 217 Gilboa, Israel 18120
Telephone: 054-4617-677
Website: www.barmitzvahinisrael.com
Clients in the U.S. and Canada can now reach us in
Israel, by calling our new U.S. phone number. This
number operates Sunday-Thursday from 10 AM-6
PM and Friday from 10 AM-2 PM (Israeli time)
Telephone: 1-617-848 2011

Kosher Holidays
Telephone: 9 7484846
Fax: 9 7464740
Website: www.kosherholidays.net
An excellent selection of worldwide kosher
holidays.

Kosher Travelers
Telephone: 2 992 9801
Fax: 2 992 9802
Email: info@koshertravelers.com
Website: www.koshertravelers.com
Worldwide kosher tours and cruises.

Peylim Student Union
10 Shoarim Street
Telephone: (2) 653 2131
Free tours of Jewish Quarter and free
accommodation in the hostel quarters.

Keshet Educational Tours
Telephone: 1 877 481 8065
Toll Free: 2 671 3518
Fax: 2 671 3624
US: 1-646-358-4058
Email: info@keshetisrael.co.il
Website: www.keshetisrael.co.il
Educational tour programmes in Israel.

Knesset (Parliament)
Telephone: (2) 675 3416
Fax: (2) 561 1201
Website: www.knesset/gov.il
Call to book tours, Sunday & Thursday 8.30am
and 2.30pm.

Synagogue Travel
64 Hashalom Street, Mevasseret Zion, Israel
Telephone: 2 534 0964
Fax: 2 534 0965
Website: www.syngagouetravel.com
Specialists in Bar and Bat Mitzvahs in Israel.

Tours of Israel Company
Telephone: (4) 867 4342
Bahai shrine and gardens, Druse villages,
Muchraka, the Moslem village of Kabair, the
Carmelite monastery and Elijahs cave,
Wednesday, 9.30am. Mt Carmel, Druse villages,
Kibbutz Ben Oren and Ein Hod artists colony.

ITALY
Amalfi Life
Telephone: 718 797 9300.
Email: Laurie@AmalfiLife.com
Website: www.amalfilife.com
Jewish heritage tours in Southern Italy by
arrangement.

Grape Adventures/Mariner Tours
PO Box 16564, Stamford, CT 06905-8564
Telephone and Fax: 781-658-2211
Email: gail@marinertours.com
Website: www.grapeadventures.com/jewish
_heritage _tours

Jewish Italy
Telephone and fax: 0577 660290
Mobile: 339 3716872
Email: info:jewishitaly.net
Website: www.jewishitaly.net
Kosher tours of Italy.

Jewish Rome Tours
Micaela Pavoncello
Telephone: 328 863 8128
Email: info@jewishroma.com
Website: www. Jewishroma.com

Smileservice
Via Valdirivo 19 34132
Telephone: (40) 348 1631
Fax: (40) 348 7023
Website: www.smileservice.it
Smile Tech organises tours around the Jewish
sites of Friuli, Venezia and Guilia.

LITHUANIA
Visit Lithuania – The Jewish Heritage Trail
Phone: (370 5) 2625 241
Fax: (370 5) 2625 242
Email: incoming@VisitLithuania.net
Website: www.tourslithuania.com

MEXICO
Website: www.jewishtours.com.mx
Walking tours to get to know more about the
Jewish presence in Mexico City.

NETHERLANDS
Easy Rider Excursions
POB 9086 1180 MB Amstelveen
Telephone: (20) 297 527 444

Mobile Phone: 0611292616
Email: maxmeron@hotmail.com
Website: www.easyriderexcursions.nl
Walk through the Jewish history of Amsterdam.
Licensed tour guides.

Footstep Tours
Admiralengracht 42 3 1057 EZ
Telephone: (20) 612 5252
Fax: (20) 689 3276
Email: info@footsteptours.nl
Website: www.footsteptours.nl
Dutch and Jewish destinations from Amsterdam
throughout the Netherlands, licensed tour guides
relate history on site, walking & museum tours, city
& country tours all year round, by reservation only.

Jeanette Loeb
Buitenzagerij 37 Amsterdam 1021 NP
Email: info@jewishhistoryamsterdam.com
Jeanette Loeb has studied Jewish history and
culture at the University of Amsterdam (UvA).
She organises guided tours and lectures in the
Jewish field.
In a personal consult you can develop your own
programme

NEW ZEALAND
Jewish Journeys
Tel: 888-273-9384 / 212-682-5995
Email: JewishJourneys@yahoo.com
Kosher tours of Australia.

PERU
Peru4you Tours
Av. del Ejercito 2154, Dpt. 302, San Isidro, Lima
27, Peru
Telephone and fax: (511) 264 0324
Email: elena@peru4youtours.com
Website: www.peru4youtours.com
Tours of Peru with Glatt kosher meals.

POLAND
European Legacy Tours
ul. Miodowa 26, 31-055 Kraków
Telephone and Fax: 12 422 24 35
Telephone: 12 423 26 62
Mobile phone for urgent inquiries and
emergency 601 52 52 26
Email: info@eltours.com
Website: www.eltours.com
Jewish heritage tours of Poland.

Panorama Travel & Tours Ltd.
46 Niagara St. Unit #3, St. Catharines, ON L2R 4K9
Telephone: 905-682 5819
Toll Free: 1-800-216 9316
Fax: 905-682 4492
Email: info@panoramatours.ca
Jewish heritage tours to Poland.

Shalom Travel Service
Twarda Street 6 00 105
Telephone: (22) 652 2802
Fax: (22) 652 2803

PORTUGAL
Jewish Tours Jewish Heritage Tours
Avenida 5 de Outubro, 321 1649 015
Telephone: (21) 791 9954
Fax: (21) 791 9959
Website: www.jewishheritage.pt
Tours to explore Jewish ancestral roots in
Portugal and to meet the descendants of the the
secret Jews.

Mouriscas Tours
Telephone: 1 963 857 776
Fax: 1 289 813 690
Email: geral@mouriscastours.com
Website: www.mouriscastours.com
Jewish heritage tours in Lisbon and Portugal.

RUSSIAN FEDERATION
All Russia Tours
Website: www.allrussiatours.com
The website has links to local tour operators
who can arrange your tour. Jewish heritage tours
of Russia.

**Zekher Avoteinu, Jewish Tourist and
Genealogical Agency**
Nastavnikov Av., 26 1 318 195298
Telephone: (921) 945 0874
Fax: (812) 325 2264
Can be contacted in the USA, telephone +01 718
236 6037
Website: www.zekhera.hypermart.net

SOUTH AFRICA
African Kosher Safaris
PO Box 51380, Raedene 2124
Telephone: (11) 485 4635
Email: yoni@aksafaris.com
Website: www.aksafaris.com

Kosher tours, safaris and youth camps in Southern Africa for all budgets and interest groups run by Rabbi Yoni Isaacson. Victoria Falls, Cape Town, Garden Route, St Lucia Wetlands, Kruger, Blyde River Canyon etc.

African Safaris Experience
26 Kings Road, Bedfordview
Telephone: (11) 832 5652
Email: ase@cgs.co.za
Website: www.asesouthafrica.co.za

Celafrica Tours
PO Box 357, Highlands North, 2037
Telephone: (11) 887 5262
Fax: (11) 885 3097
Mobile Phone: +27 82 320 5525
Email: celeste@celafrica.com
Website: www.celafrica.com
The company specialises in kosher safaris and tours to southern Africa.

Lion of Africa
PO Box 64189, Highlands North 2037
Telephone: (11) 640 1608
Fax: (11) 640 1608
Mobile Phone: (82)331 8412
Email: lion@roary.com
Website: www.roary.com

Unlimited Africa
Uniglobe Total Travel based in Edgware, UK
Telephone: 0208 731 2111
Website: www.unlimitedafrica.co.uk
Travel and safaris in South Africa.

SPAIN
Jewish Heritage Tours in Spain - Toledo Private Tours
Mobile Phone: 607 716 642
Email: koteltravel@hotmail.com
www.puertademadrid.es/jewishspain
Specialise in Toledo and Cordoba Tours.

Circa Tours
division of Circa Terras, Inc.
30919 Brassie Ln.
Temecula, California 92591, USA
Tel: 1-951-676-6117
Jewish Spain – The Sephardic Route.

Jewish Travel Agency
Viajes Morava, Consejo de Ciento 380
Telephone: (93) 246 0300

Urban Cultours Project
Telephone: (93) 417 1191
Fax: (93) 417 1191
Website: www.urbancultours.com
Walk of the Calle (Jewish Quarter) by a Jewish American architect. Visits to other places of Jewish interest in Catalonia can also be arranged.

SWITZERLAND
Ideal Tours
Telephone: 972-2-5868717
Email: goski@idealtours.co.il
Website: www.idealtours.co.il
Kosher skiing holidays in Switzerland.

Maagalim Tours
Telephone: 972-3-6166177
Fax: 972-3-6166188
London Tel/Fax: 0208 8001725
Email: maagalim@maagalimtours.com / maagalim@btopenworld.com
Website: www.maagalimtours.com
Kosher skiing holidays in Switzerland.

TANZANIA
Travel Jewish
PO Box 6771, Ithaca, NY, 14851
Telephone: 949 307 9231
Fax: 949 861 7497
Email: info@traveljewish.com
Website: www.traveljewish.com
Kosher climbing – reach the summit of Kilimanjaro.

TURKEY
TravelShop Turkey
Cevat Sakir Mah Bitez Sk No:15, Gumbet, Bodrum
Telephone: 0090 252 316 2127
Mobile: 0090 537 304 3488
Fax: 0090 252 316 8931
Email: info@travelshopturkey.com
Website: www.travelshopturkey.com
Jewish heritage tours of Turkey (5 and 13 day tours).

Turkey Package Tours

Akbiyik Cad. No : 61 Sultanahmet, Istanbul
Telephone: (212) 638 0276
Fax: (212) 638 0283
Mobile 241 0592
Email: info@turkeypackagetour.com
Website: www.turkeypackagetour.com
The Quincentennial - Jewish Heritage full day
tour. The Story of Turkish Jews 500 Years of Peace
& Harmony.

UNITED KINGDOM
China Direct

109-110 Ferguson Close, Ferguson's Wharf,
London E14 3SJ
Telephone: 020 7538 2840
Fax: 020 7536 9088
Email: info@chinadirect-travel.co.uk
Website: www.chinadirect-travel.co.uk
Kosher holidays in China.

LestAir Services

80 Highfield Avenue, Golders Green, London
NW11 9TT
Telephone: 020 455 9654
Email: family.schleimer@ukgateway.net
Promoting Jewish Heritage Tours to Eastern Europe.

London Jewish Tours

Website: www.londonjewishtours.com
Unique customised walking tours of the historic
Jewish East End of London.

Jewish Heritage Trails in Manchester

190 Cheetham Hill Road, Manchester M8 8LW
Telephone: 0161 834 9879.
Fax: 0161 832 7353.
Two hour tours of the old northern Jewish
Quarter of Manchester. Please phone for tour
times. Groups up to 20 are welcome but must be
booked in advance.

Manchester Tours

Louise Kane
Telephone: 0161-428 6708.
Email: jaandlu@freenet.co.uk
Jewish Manchester

A Jewish Trail of Leeds

Telephone: 0870 800 8532
Individuals can join our walking tours (Sundays
at 2.30) whilst groups can be catered for at
mutual convenience.

Uniglobe Total Travel

Edgware, UK
Telephone: 0208 731 2111
Website: www.unlimitedindia.co.uk /
www.unlimitedafrica.co.uk
Jewish heritage tours in India and safaris in
South Africa.

Yorkwalk

3 Fairway, Clifton YO30 5QA
Telephone: 01904 622 303
Fax: 01904 656 244
Email: admin@yorkwalk.fsnet.co.uk
Website: www.yorkwalk.co.uk
The Jewish Heritage Walk, recalling the Jewish
contribution to Yorks history. The walk finishes at
Cliffords Tower, the site of a dreadful massacre in
1190.

UNITED STATES OF AMERICA
Florida Jewish Travel

Email: info@floridajewish.com
Website: www.floridajewish.com

Heritage Tours Online

121 West 27 Street, Suite 1201
New York, NY 10001
Telephone: (800) 378 4555
Toll Free: (212) 206 8400
Fax: (212) 206 9101
Email: info@heritagetoursONLINE.com
Website:
www.heritagetoursonline.com/jewish_heritage
Jewish heritage tours to Morrocco, Turkey, Spain
and South Africa.

Jewish Hassidic Walking Tours

The Chassidic Discovery Welcome Center, 305
Kingston Avenue, Brooklyn, NY 11213
Telephone: (718) 953-5244
Fax: (718) 771-6315
Email: tours@jewishtours.com
Website: www.jewishtours.com

Jewish heritage tours in Italy

Telephone: 707 963 8930
Fax: 707 963 2301
Email: info@jewishitaly.net
Website: www.jewishitaly.net
Kosher tours of Italy.

Jewish Journeys
Telephone: (888) 273-9384 / (212) 682-5995
Email: JewishJourneys@yahoo.com
Kosher tours to exotic destinations.

Jewish Travel Agency
Telephone: 877-466 2934
Toll Free: 203-363 0015
Fax: 203-653 5586
Email: info@JewishTravelAgency.com
Website: www.JewishTravelAgency.com
Jewish heritage tours worldwide.

Jewish Tours of New York in Lower East Side
Telephone: (212) 374 4100
Website: www.nycjewishtours.org

Kesher Tours
Telephone: 800-847 0700 (toll free)
Website: www.keshertours.com
Worldwide kosher tours.

Kosher Expeditions
1779 S Shenandoah St, Ste11, Los Angeles, CA 90035
Telephone: 800-923 2645
Toll Free: 310-237 0122
Fax: 770-234 5170
Email: info@kosherexpeditions.com
Website: www.kosherexpeditions.com
Jewish/kosher travel programmes and vacations worldwide.

Matzafun Tours
Email: info@matzafun.com
Website: www.matzafun.com
Passover holidays in the US.

New York Tours
Email: drphil@newyorktalksandwalks.com
Website: www.newyorktalksandwalks.com
A variety or walks and tours from Jewish heritage to Jewish gangsters.

European Jewish Tours
5 Chestnut Street
Medford, Mass. 02155 USA
Telephone and Fax: + 33 (0)1 45 77 01 63
Email: kaplan@club-internet.fr
Website: www.europeanjewishtours.com
Jewish heritage tours in Europe.

Passover Vacations
Telephone: 800 950 1240 / 718 332 3900 (NY and outside USA)
Email: info@passovervacations.com
Website: www.passovervacations.com
Passover vacations in Mexico and the USA.

Synagogue Travel
752A Hempstead Turnpike, Suite 203, Franklin Square, NY 11010
Telephone: (516) 489-6586 or (800) 448-0399
Fax: (516) 489-6949
Website: www.synagoguetravel.com
Specialists in Bar and Bat Mitzvahs in Israel.

KOSHER CRUISES

The following travel companies operate kosher cruises:

Amazing Journeys
733 Valleyview Road, Pittsburgh, PA 15243
Telephone: 412-571 0220
Fax: 412-344 3937
Email: info@amazingjourneys.net
Website: www.amazingjourneys.net
Cruises for Jewish singles.

Chosen Voyage by Intrav
Telephone: (800) 990-0890
Toll Free: (314) 655-6800
Email: chosenvoyage@intrav.com
Website: www.chosenvoyage.com

Jewish Singles Kosher Cruises
Email: infosinglescruise@yahoo.com
Website: www.jsinglescruise.com

Kosher Cruise Enterprise
1924 Clairmont Road, Suite 10, Atlanta, GA 30033
Telephone: (800) 303-6393
Toll Free: (404) 634-9206
Email: info@kcecruises.com
Website: www.kcecruises.com

Kosherica Kosher Cruises
Telephone: (305) 695-2700 / (877) 724-5567
Fax: (305) 695-8151
Email: information@kosherica.com
Website: www.kosherica.com

Le Voyage Travel
Email: info@levoyagetravel.com
Website: www.levoyagetravel.com
Specialise in group travel for fund raising.
Glatt kosher tours and cruises.

Suite Life Kosher Cruises
1492 Pine Park Avenue, Lakewood, NJ 08701
Telephone: (866) 604 9838
Toll Free: (732) 367 2029
Fax (732) 2437
Website: www.slkosher.com

Please check that you are satisfied with the level of kashrut and the services offered before you book. The Jewish Travel Guide 2009 and Vallentine Mitchell Publishers cannot be held responsible for any holidays booked.

ALBANIA

There have been Jews living in the area now known as Albania since Roman times, and there are remains in Dardania, in the north, of an ancient synagogue. The community was re-established by Jews from Iberia escaping the Spanish Inquisition in the fifteenth and early sixteenth centuries.

By 1930, the Jewish population had grown to 204, but was soon augmented by refugees escaping the Nazis. Most Jews were helped to hide from Italian occupiers, and then from the Nazis.

Post–war communism isolated Jews until the regime fell. In 1991 almost the entire community, about 300, was airlifted to Israel. The few Jews who remained in Albania live in the capital Tirana.

The Albanian–Israel Friendship Society will be happy to provide any further information.

GMT +1 hours
Country calling code: **(355)**
Total population: **3,738,000**
Jewish population: **Under 100**
Emergency telephone: **(police–19; 24445)**
(fire–18; 23333) (ambulance–17; 22235)
Electricity voltage: **220**

TIRANA
CONTACT INFORMATION
Albanian–Israel Friendship Society
Rruga 'Barrikatave' 226
Telephone: (42) 22611

ALGERIA

Jews first settled in Algeria soon after the start of the Diaspora following the destruction of the Second Temple. A later influx occurred when Jews were escaping from Visigothic Spain.

In the twelfth and thirteenth centuries, Islamic conversion was forced on the Jews. Many Jews, however, crossed the Mediterranean from Spain during the time of the Inquisition, and these included some famous scholars. In 1830 the French occupied the country and, in due course, granted the Jews French citizenship.

Algerian Jews suffered anti-semitism from both the local Muslim population and the wartime Vichy government. After the Allied landings in 1942, the anti-Jewish laws were slowly lifted. In the late 1950s 130,000 Jews lived in Algeria, but after the civil war, which led to independence from France in 1962, most of the community moved to France, with some to Israel, leaving very few behind. The present-day community, centred in Algiers, has a synagogue but no resident rabbi.

GMT +1 hours
Country calling code: **(+213)**
Total population: **29,050,00**
Jewish population: **Under 100**
Emergency telephone: **(police–17) (fire–14)**
(ambulance–21606666)
Medical assistance by telephone 115
Electricity voltage: **117/220**

BLIDA
COMMUNITY ORGANISATIONS
Consistoire d'Algerie
29 rue des Martyrs 4120
Telephone: (3) 492 657

ANDORRA

Andorra, which is governed by two co - princes – the Bishop of Urgel in Spain and the President of France – does not have a Jewish history. There are currently, however, around 15 Jewish families.

A synagogue was established in 1997 in Escaldes and is the first in Andorra's 1,100-year history. While its liturgy leans towards Sephardism, it is also influenced by its Ashkenazi members. There is a community centre in Escaldes.

GMT +1 hours
Country calling code: **(+376)**
Total population: **66,000**
Jewish population: **under 100**
Emergency telephone: **(police–110) (fire–118)**
(ambulance–118)
Emergency medical assistance 825; 225

ANDORRA
CONTACT INFORMATION
Dr David ben-Chayil or Dr David Bezold
Francesco B.P. 244, Andorra la Vella
Telephone: 333 567
For visits to the synagogue contact Isaac Benisty tel 860 758

ARGENTINA

The first Jewish arrivals (*Conversos*, or 'secret Jews') came in the sixteenth and seventeenth centuries from Portugal and Spain. They assimilated quickly. A more significant Jewish immigration occurred in the middle of the nineteenth century from western Europe, and at the end of the nineteenth century many Jews arrived from eastern Europe, taking advantage of the 'open-door' policy towards immigrants. The new arrivals set up some Jewish agricultural settlements, under the auspices of the *Alliance Israelita Universelle*, and on the whole mixed with the local population.

The largest Jewish community is in Buenos Aires, with smaller communities in provincial centres. There are also some Jewish families remaining in the Jewish agricultural colonies, with Moiseville, Rivera and General Roca being the three most important.

There are Jewish newspapers, restaurants and other institutions. The Delegation of Argentine Jewish Associations (DAIA) represents all Jewish organisations.

GMT -3 hours
Country calling code: (+54)
Total population: 35,672,000
Jewish population: 395,000
Emergency telephone: (police–101) (fire–100) (ambulance–107)
Electricity voltage: 226

BAHIA BLANCA
Beit Jabad or Beith Chabad
Chiclana 763 8000
Telephone: (291) 453 6582
Fax: (291) 456 5596
Email: rbjabad@yahoo.com
Supervision: Chabad Lubavitch
Central organisation: Chabad Lubavitch
For details of Mikvah please phone

BUENOS AIRES
The first recorded Jewish event in Buenos Aires was a wedding in 1860. Around 220,000 Jews live in Buenos Aires. There are fifty or so synagogues in the city and kosher food is widely available. The most interesting synagogues for visitors are in Once although few Jews live there now.

Enytour
Dr.J.F.Aranguren 2915, Ciudad Autonoma de Buenos Aires 1406
Telephone: (11) 4611 1400

Fax: (11) 4613 6704
Website: www.enytour.com
Contact: Nisim Daniel Minian
BAKERIES
Confitería Aielet
Aranguren 2911, Flores
Telephone: (11) 4637 5419
Confitería Ganz
Pasco 752, Once
Telephone: (11) 4961 6918
Confiteria Helueni
Tucumán 2620, Once
Telephone: (11) 4961 0541
Confitería Mari Jalabe
Bogota 3228, Flores
Telephone: (11) 4612 6991
Panaderia Malena
Av. Pueyrredón 880, Once
Telephone: (11) 4962 6290

BOOKSELLERS
Kehot Lubavitch Sudamericana
San Luis 3281 1186
Telephone: (11) 4865 0625
Fax: (11) 4865 0625
Libreria Editorial Sigal
Av. Corrientes 2854 C1193AAN
Telephone: (11) 4861 9501
Fax: (11) 4865 7208
Email: info@libreriasigal.com
Website: www.liberiasigal.com

COMMUNITY ORGANISATIONS
AMIA (Central Ashkenazi community)
Pasteur 633
Telephone: (11) 4953 9777 / 2862
The community centre has now been reopened following the terror bomb attack in 1964.
Asociacion Israelita Sefaradi Argentina (CAISA)
Paso 493
Telephone: (11) 4952 4707
DAIA (Political representative body of Argentine Jewry)
Pasteur 633, 7th Floor
Telephone: (11) 4378 3200
Fax: (11) 4378 3200

CONTACT INFORMATION
Asociacion Shuva Israel
Paso 557, Once
Telephone: (11) 4962 6255

Beit Chabad Belgrano
O'Higgins 2358, Belgrano 1428
Telephone: (11) 4781 3848
Fax: (11) 4783 4573

Beit Chabad Villa Crespo
Serrano 69
Telephone: (11) 4855 9822

Beith Chabad West Area
Sarmiento 933 Moron 1708
Telephone: (11) 4627 3563

Chabad Lubavich Argentina
Agüero 1164, Flores 1425
Telephone: (11) 4963 1221

Congregacion Israelita de la Republica
Libertad 785, Centro
Telephone: (11) 4372 2474
Fax: (11) 4372 2474

International Youth Organization for the spreading of Judaism
Camargo 870 Capital Federal C1414HR
Telephone: (11) 4855 6945
Fax: (11) 4855 9377
Email: intinfo@menora.org.ar
Website: www.menora.org.ar

Sephardic Community of Buenos Aires
Camargo 870 C1414AHR
Telephone: (11) 4855 6945
Fax: (11) 4855 9377
Website: www.acisba.org.ar
The total number of synagogues in Buenos Aires where there is minyan at least on Friday night and shabbat morning exceeds fifty. Call any of the above numbers to locate the synagogue nearest you.

EMBASSY
Embassy of Israel
Avenida de Mayo 701-10° 1084
Telephone: (11) 4338 2500
Fax: (11) 4338 2624
Email: pedidoscidipal@buenosaires.mfa.gov.il

GROCERIES
Almacén Behar
Campana 347, Flores
Telephone: (11) 4613 2033

Almacén Shalom
San Luis 2513, Once
Telephone: (11) 4962 3685

Autoservicio Ezra
Ecuador 619, Once
Telephone: (11) 4963 7062

Autoservicio Siman Tov
Helguera 474, Flores
Telephone: (11) 4611 4746

Azulay
Helguera 507, Flores

Battías
Pasco 706, Once

Kahal Jaredim
Argerich 386, Flores
Telephone: (11) 4612 4590

Kaler
San Luis 2810, Once

Kol Bo Brandsen
Brandsen 1389, Barracas

Kol Bo I
Ecuador 855, Once
Telephone: (11) 4961 3838

Kol Bo II
Viamonte 2537, Once
Telephone: (11) 4961 2012

Kosher Delights
La Pampa 2547, Belgrano
Telephone: (11) 4788 3150

La Esquina Casher
Aranguren 2999, Flores
Telephone: (11) 4637 3706

La Quesería
Viamonte 2438, Once
Telephone: (11) 4961 3171

La Tzorja
Ecuador 673, Once
Telephone: (11) 4961 1096

Lidia's Macolet
Ecuador 586, Once
Telephone: (11) 4863 5595
Fax: (11) 4932 4443

Yehuda Kosher Foods
Moldes 2452, Belgrano
Telephone: (11) 4637 1465

JEWISH CENTRE
Yeshiva & Kollel "Jafetz Jaim"
Boulogne sur Mer 966 1213
Telephone: (11) 4961 3553
Fax: (11) 4961 3883
Email: info@jafetzjaim.edu.ar
Website: www.jafetzjaim.edu.ar
social aid giving clothes, meals and medicines to needy people. It is part of the International   Vaad Hatzdokoh Committee and holds up the espiritual performance of A.M.I.A. (Asociación Mutual Israelita Argentina).

KASHRUT INFORMATION
The Central Rabbinate of Vaad Hakehillot
Ecuador 1110, Once
Telephone: (11) 4961 2944
The Orthodox Ashkenazi Chief Rabbi of Argentina is Rabbi Shlomo Benhamu Anidjar

LIBRARIES
Sociedad Hebraica Argentino
Sarmiento 2233
Telephone: (11) 4952 5570
Also has an art gallery

Museum
Fundación IWO/YIVO Library
Ayacucho 483 1026
Telephone: (11) 4953 0293/9614
Fax: (11) 4953 9614
Email: archivos@iwo.org.ar
Website: www.iwo.org.ar
Public opening hours: Mon to Thu 11am to 6pm, Fri 11am to 3pm

MEDIA
Newspapers
Mundo Israelita
Pueyrredón 538 1° B 1032
Telephone: (11) 4961 7999
Fax: (11) 4961 0763

MIKVAOT
Mikva
Moldes 2431, Belgrano 1428
Telephone: (11) 4783 2831
Fax: (11) 4786 8046

MUSEUMS
Museo Judio de Buenos Aires
Libertad 769 1012
Telephone: (11) 4123 0832/33
Website: www.judaica.org.ar
Hours: Tuesday and Thursday 3pm to 6pm

RESTAURANTS
Dairy
Soultani Café
San Luis 2601, Once
Telephone: (11) 4961 3913

Meat
Al Galope
Tucumán 2633, Once
Telephone: (11) 4963 6888

Mama Jacinta
Tucumán 2580 C-P 1052
Telephone: (11) 4962 9149
Fax: (11) 4962 7535
Supervision: Gran Rabino Josef Chehebar

McDonald's
Shopping Abasto, (Corrientes and Anchorena), Once
Supervision: Rav Oppenheimer–Ajdut Israel
There are two MacDonalds, only one is kosher

Sucath David
Tucumán 2349
Telephone: (11) 4952 8878
Fax: (11) 4953 9656

SYNAGOGUES
Ashkenazi
Baron Hirsh
Billinghurst 664
Telephone: (11) 4862 2624

Beit Chabad Once "Litvishe Shul"
Jose Evaristo Uriburu 348
Telephone: (11) 4952 7968
Fax: (11) 4952 7968
Bet Rajel
Ecuador 522
Telephone: (11) 4862 2701
Brit Abraham
Antezana 145
Telephone: (11) 4855 6567
Etz HaJaim
Julian Alvarez 745 (between Loyola and Castillo), Villa Crespo 1414
Telephone: (11) 4857 0984 (synagogue) / 4854 6870 (secretary)
Mobile Phone: 15 6547 5191
Email: jabadjulianalvarez@yahoo.com.ar
Website: www.jabadvc.com.ar
Supervision: With Rabbinical help from Jabad Lubavitch
Central organisation: Jabad Lubavitch Argentina
Torah Vaaboda
Julian Alvarez 667
Telephone: (11) 4854 0462
Zijron le David
Azcuenaga 736
Telephone: (11) 4953 0200

Conservative
Beit Hilel
Araoz 2854, Palermo
Telephone: (11) 4804 2286
Benei Tikva
Vidal 2049
Telephone: (11) 4781 9392; 4786 9374
Fax: (11) 4781 9392; 4786 9374
Website: www.beneitikva.AR
Colegio Wolfson, Comunidad Or-El
Amenabar 2972
Telephone: (11) 4544 5461
Comunidad Bet El
Sucre 3338
Telephone: (11) 4552 2365
Dor Jadash
Murillo 649, Villa Crespo
Telephone: (11) 4854 4467
Nueva Comunidad Israelita
Arcos 2319
Telephone: (11) 4781 0281
Or Jadash
Varela 850, Flores
Telephone: (11) 4612 1171

German Orthodox and Sephardic
Ajdut Yisroel
Moldes 2449 1428
Telephone: (11) 4783 2831
Fax: (11) 4781 6725
Website: www.adjut.com.ar; www.kosher.org.ar

Reform
Templo Emanu-El
Tronador 1455
Telephone: (11) 4552 4343
Fax: (11) 4555 4004

Sephardi
Centro Comunitario Chalom
Olleros 2876
Telephone: (11) 4552 2720
Fax: (11) 4552 6730
Website: www. chalom.org.ar

Sephardi Orthodox
Aderet Eliahu
Ruy Diaz de Guzman 647 1267
Telephone: (11) 4303 1320
Fax: (11) 4303 1320

Agudat Dodim
Avellaneda 2874
Telephone: (11) 4611 0056

Asociacion Comunidad Israelita Sefaradi de Buenos Aires
Camargo 870
Telephone: (11) 4855 6945
Fax: (11) 4855 9377

Bajurim Tiferet Israeil
Helguera 611
Telephone: (11) 4611 3376

Etz Jaim
Carlos Calvo 1164
Telephone: (11) 4302 6290

Jaike Grimberg
Campana 460
Telephone: (11) 4672 2347

Kehal Jaredim
Helguera 270, Once
Telephone: (11) 4612 0410

Kehila Shaare Sion
Helguera 453 1406
Telephone: (11) 4637 5897/98/99
Fax: (11) 4637 6704
Email: director@shaaresion.org.ar
Website: www.shaaresion.org.ar

Od Yosef Jai
Tucumán 3326
Telephone: (11) 4963 2349

Or Misraj
Ciudad de la Paz 2555
Telephone: (11) 4784-5945

Shaare Tefila
Paso 733
Telephone: (11) 4962 2865

Shuba Israel
Ecuador 627
Telephone: (11) 4862 0562

Sinagoga Rabino Zeev Grinberg
Felipe Vallese 3047, Ciudad Autonoma de Buenos Aires
Telephone: (11) 4611 3366

Templo la Paz (Chalom)
Olleros 2876
Telephone: (11) 4552 6730

Yeshurun
Republica de la India 3035
Telephone: (11) 4802 9310

Yesod Hadat
Lavalle 2449
Telephone: (11) 4961 1615

TOURS
Jewish Tours Argentina
Telephone: (11) 4544 8984
Mobile Phone: (54911) 15 4410 1423
Email: info@jewish-tours.com.ar
Website: www.jewish-tours.com.ar
Tours of Buenos Aires

Travel Jewish
Website: www.traveljewish.com
Full and half day tours of Buenos Aires.
Based in New York, PO Box 6771, Ithica NY 14851

CORDOBA
CONTACT INFORMATION
Jabad Lubavitch Cordoba
Sucre 1380, Barrio Cofico 5000
Telephone: (351) 471 0223
Fax: (351) 474 0358
Website: www.chabadcordoba.org

GROCERIES
Almacén
Sucre 1378, Barrio Cofico 5000
Telephone: (351) 4471 0223

ROSARIO
CONTACT INFORMATION
Beit Jabad Rosario
S. Lorenzo 1882 P.A. 2000
Telephone: (341) 425 2899

GROCERIES
La Granja Kasher
Montevideo 1833
Telephone: (341) 449 6210

TUCUMAN
CONTACT INFORMATION
Beit Jabad Tucuman
Lamadrid 752 4000
Telephone: (381) 424 8892
Fax: (381) 424 8893
Supervision: Rabbi Daniel Levy
Kosher supermarket tel: (381) 420 2147

GROCERIES
Almacén y Carnicería
9 de Julio 625
Telephone: (381) 431 0227

ARMENIA
Jews have lived in Armenia for many hundreds of years. Nowadays, nearly all Armenian Jews live in Yerevan, with only a few families living in Vanadzor (Kirokavan) and Gjumri (Leninakan). A handful are scattered throughout other small towns and villages.

GMT +2 hours
Country calling code: **(+3741)**
Jewish population: **500**
Emergency telephone: **(police–102) (fire–101) (ambulance–103)**

YEREVAN
SYNAGOGUES
Yerevan
Nar-Dosa Street 23, Yerevan, Armenia 375018
Telephone: 571 677
Fax: 554 132

AUSTRALIA
The first Jews in Australia arrived with the first convict ships from the United Kingdom in 1788, and regular, organised worship started in the 1820s. The first free Jewish settler arrived with her husband, a deported convict, in 1816. The community grew in the nineteenth century, with the first synagogue being established in the mid-1840s. Events such as the gold rush and pogroms in eastern Europe were catalysts for more Jewish immigration.

The Jewish contribution to Australian life has been prominent, with the commander of the ANZAC forces in the First World War being a practising Jew, Sir John Monash. The twentieth century saw some 7,000 Jewish refugees from Nazi Europe settling in Australia, and the community contains the largest percentage of Holocaust survivors in the world. They are a major influence on the present community, which is expanding and predominately religious. There have also been two Jewish Governors-General; one being Sir Issac Issacs, who was the first Australian-born to hold that position.

The community is led by the Executive Council of Australian Jewry. 75 per cent of primary and 55 per cent of secondary Jewish school children attend Jewish schools, and there is a low level of intermarriage. Melbourne has the largest community, (42,000), with 35,000 in Sydney. There are Jewish newspapers, radio programmes of Jewish interest and museums on Jewish themes.

GMT +7 to +10 hours
Country calling code: **(+61)**
Total population: **19,105,000**
Jewish population: **100,000**
Emergency telephone: **(police–000) (fire–000) (ambulance–000)**
Electricity voltage: **240/250**

Australian Capital Territory

CANBERRA
EMBASSY
Embassy of Israel
6 Turrana Street, Yarralumla 2600
Telephone: (2) 6273 1309
Fax: (2) 6273 4279

SYNAGOGUE
The A.C.T. Jewish Community Synagogue
National Jewish Memorial Centre, corner Canberra Avenue & National Circuit, Forrest 2603
Telephone: (2) 6295 1052
Fax: (2) 6295 8608
Website: www.actjewish.org.au
Postal address: POB 3105, Manuka 2603

New South Wales

NEWCASTLE
SYNAGOGUES
Newcastle Synagogue
122 Tyrrell Street 2300
Telephone: (49) 262 820
Contact: Dr L.E. Fredman, 123 Dawson Street Cooks Hill 2300 N.S.W.

SYDNEY

The first Jewish convict settlers were generally illiterate in both English and Hebrew, and there was no Jewish organisation until a Chevrah Kadishe was formed in 1817 and services were held under the leadership of former convict Joseph Marcus.

Most of Sydney's Jews are now settled outside the city centre in two suburban areas: the eastern suburbs, including Bondi, and the North Shore.

BAKERIES
Carmel Cake Shop
14 O'Brien Street, Bondi
Supervision: NSW Kashrut Authority

BOOKSELLERS
Gold's World of Judaica
9 O'Brien Street, Bondi 2026
Telephone: (2) 9300 0495
Fax: (2) 9389 7345
Email: sydney@golds.com.au

BUTCHERS
Eilat
173 Bondi Road, Bondi
Telephone: (2) 9387 8881
Supervision: NSW Kashrut Authority

Hadassa
17 O'Brien Street, Bondi
Telephone: (2) 9365 4904
Fax: (2) 9130 4760
Supervision: NSW Kashrut Authority

COMMUNITY ORGANISATIONS
Executive Council of Australian Jewry
146 Darlinghurst Road, second floor, Darlinghurst 2010
Telephone: (2) 9360 5415
Fax: (2) 9360 5416

EMBASSY
Embassy of Israel
6 Turrana Street, Yarralumla 2600
Telephone: (2) 6273 1309
Fax: (2) 6273 4273
Website: www.canberra.mfa.gov.il

HOSPITAL
Wolper Jewish Hospital
8 Trelawney Street, Woollahra
Telephone: (2) 9328 6077
Fax: (2) 9327 5973
Email: info@wolper.com.au
Website: www.wolper.com.au

KASHRUT INFORMATION
Kosher Consumers Association
PO Box 2013, Rose Bay North 2030
Telephone: (2) 9388 1158

Mobile Phone: 0414 388 851
Email: KCA_Sydney-owner@yahoogroups.com
Website:
www.groups.yahoo.com/group/KCA_Sydney
A grass roots organisation whose work includes assisting locals and visitors to find kosher food in Australia and kosher eateries in Sydney.

Kashrut Supervision
The Kashrut Authority
PO Box 7206, 2/58 Chambers Ave, Bondi Beach 2026
Telephone: (2) 9365 2933
Fax: (2) 9365 0933
Website: www.ka.org.au
Supervision: Sydney Beth Din Yeshiva Rabbinate

MEDIA
Newspapers
Australian Jewish News
Level 1, 10-14 Waterloo Street, Surry Hills 2010
Telephone: (2) 8218 1600
Fax: (2) 8218 1655
Website: www.ajn.net.au

MUSEUMS
Sydney Jewish Museum
148 Darlinghurst Road, Darlinghurst 2010
Telephone: (2) 9360 7999
Fax: (2) 9331 4245
Email: admin@sjm.com.au
Website: www.sydneyjewishmuseum.com.au
Displays depicting the history of the Holocaust with survivor guides describing their experiences during the Holocaust. Also exhibits of Australian Jewish history, tradition and culture.
Has a kosher(dairy) cafe.

RESTAURANTS
Dairy
The Museum Café
148 Darlinghurst Road, Darlinghurst 2010
Telephone: (2) 9360 7999
Fax: (2) 9331 4245
Website: www.sydneyjewishmuseum.com.au
Supervision: Sydney Kashrut Authority
Kosher dairy cafe situated in the Sydney Jewish Museum, open 11am to 3pm, Sunday to Thursday.
Toovya the Milkman
379 Old South Head Road, North Bondi 2026
Telephone: (2) 9130 4016
Supervision: NSW Kashrut Authority
Not Cholov Yisrael. Vegetarian and vegan food. Eat in or take away. Delivery to eastern suburbs, including to hotel room. Hours: Sunday to Thursday, 5pm to 10pm; Saturday, after Shabbat to midnight.

Meat
Beaches Kosher Restaurant
11 O'Brien Street 2026
Telephone: (2) 9365 5544
Fax: (2) 9365 5577
Supervision: NSW Kasrut Authority
Lunch is only Pareve. Delivery to all Sydney addresses.

Katzy's Food Factory
Shop 2, 113-115 Hall Street, Bondi Beach
Telephone: (2) 9130 6743
Fax: (2) 9130 6742
Supervision: NSW Kashrut Authority
Also take-away.

Tibby's Kosher Restaurant at Jaffa
61-67 Hall Street, Bondi Beach 2026
Telephone: (2) 9130 5051
Supervision: NSW Kashrut Authority
Open Saturday to Thursday for dinner. Continental, Chinese, Sephardi and Israeli food. Glatt kosher.

Meat and parve
Lewis' Continental Kitchen
2 Curlewis Street, corner Old South Head Road, Bondi 2026
Telephone: (2) 9365 5421
Fax: (2) 9300 0037
Website: www.lewiskosher.com
Supervision: NSW Kashrut Authority Inc
Glatt Kosher. Specialises in assisting tourists with their meals in Australia.

SYNAGOGUES
Adath Yisroel
243 Old South Head Road, Bondi
Telephone: (2) 9300 9447

Coogee Synagogue
121 Brook Street, Coogee
Telephone: (2) 9315 8291
Since April 2005 temporarily re-located to Emanuel School, 20 Stanley Street, Randurch

Illawarra Synagogue
502 Railway Parade, Allawah
Telephone: (2) 9587 5643

Paramatta Synagogue
116 Victoria Road, Paramatta 2150
Telephone: (2) 9683 5626
Website: parramattasynagogue.com
Only synagogue in Sydney's western suburbs.
Youth programs/social events centre

South Head & District Synagogue
662 Old South Head Road, Rose Bay 2029
Telephone: (2) 9371 7300
Fax: (2) 9371 7416
Website: www.southhead.org

Strathfield & District Synagogue
19 Florence Street, PO Box 466, Strathfield 2135
Telephone: (2) 9642 4803
Fax: (2) 9642 4803

Orthodox
Bondi Mizrachi Synagogue
339 Old South Head Road, Bondi 2026
Telephone: (2) 9365 3838
Fax: (2) 9365 3838
Website: www.mizrachi.org.au
Mailing address: 101/60 Blair Street, North Bondi 2026

Cremorne Synagogue
12a Yeo Street, Neutral Bay
Telephone: (2) 9908 1853
Fax: (2) 9908 1853
Email: cremornesyn@telstra.com
Website: www.cremornesynagogue.com
Postal address is PO Box 126, Neutral Bay Junction, 2089

Great Synagogue
166 Castlereagh Street
Telephone: (2) 9267 2477
Fax: (2) 9264 8871
Email: admin@greatsynagogue.org.au
Website: www.greatsynagogue.org.au
One of the most beautiful and historic synagogues in the world. It houses the Rabbi L.A. Falk Memorial Library and the A.M. Rosenblum Jewish Museum. (Entrance for services: 187 Elizabeth Street.) There are synagogue tours on Tuesdays and Thursdays.

Kehillat Masada
9-15 Link Road, St Ives 2075
Telephone: (2) 9988 4417
Fax: (2) 9449 3897
Email: k_masada@optusnet.com.au

Maroubra Synagogue (K.M.H.C.)
635 Anzac Parade, Maroubra 2035
Telephone: (2) 9344 6095
Fax: (2) 9344 4298
Email: admin@maroubrasynagogue.org.au

Newtown Synagogue
20 Georgina Street, Newtown 2042
Telephone: (2) 9550 1192
Fax: (2) 9550 1192
Mobile Phone: 417 462 870
Email: newtownsynagogue@yahoo.com
Website: www.newtown.shul.org.au
Sydney's second oldest synagogue.

North Shore Synagogue
15 Treatts Road, Lindfield
Telephone: (2) 9416 3710
Fax: (2) 9416 7659
Email: nss@bigpond.com

The Central Synagogue
15 Bon Accord Avenue, Bondi Junction 2022
Telephone: (2) 9389 5622
Fax: (2) 9389 5418
Website: www.centralsynagogue.com.au

Yeshiva Synagogue
36 Flood Street, Bondi 2026
Telephone: (2) 9387 3822
Fax: (2) 9389 7652

Progressive

North Shore Temple Emanuel
28 Chatswood Avenue, Chatswood 2067
Telephone: (2) 9419 7011
Fax: (2) 9413 1474
Website: www.nste.org.au

Shearit Yisrael
146 Darlinghurst Road, Darlinghurst 2010
Telephone: (2) 9365 8770

Temple Emanuel
7 Ocean Street, Woollahra 2025
Telephone: (2) 9328 7833
Fax: (2) 9327 8715
Website: www.emanuel.org.au

Sephardi

Sephardi Synagogue
40-44 Fletcher Street, Woollahra 2025
Telephone: (2) 9389 3982
Fax: (2) 9369 2143
Email: mail@sephardi.org.au

Sephardim

Beth Yosef
243 Old South Head Road,, Bondi 2026
Fax: (2) 9264 8941
Mobile Phone: (61) 411869431
Email: info@betyosef.org.au

TOURS

Jewish Sydney Tours
Telephone: (2) 9328 7604
For information about tours of Jewish Sydney, contact the
Great Synagogue or Karl Maehrischel on (2) 9267 2477.

Queensland

BRISBANE

COMMUNITY ORGANISATIONS

Jewish Communal Centre
2 Moxom Road, Burbank 4156
Telephone: (7) 3349 9749

MIKVAOT

Queensland Mikvah
46 Bunya Street, Greenslopes 4120
Telephone: (7) 3848 5886

RELIGIOUS ORGANISATIONS

Chabad House of Queensland
43 Cedar Street, Greenslopes 4120
Telephone: (7) 3848 5886
Fax: (7) 3848 5886

SYNAGOGUES

Brisbane Hebrew Congregation
98 Margaret Street 4000
Telephone: (7) 3229 3412

Givat Zion
43 Bunya Street, Greenslopes 4000
Telephone: (7) 3397 9025
Fax: (7) 3397 9025

South Brisbane Hebrew Congregation
46 Bunya Street, Greenslopes 4120
Telephone: (7) 3397 9025
Fax: (7) 3397 9025

Progressive

Beit Knesset Shalom
13 Koolatah Street, Camp Hill 4152
Telephone: (7) 3398 8843/3391 2579
Fax: (7) 3391 2579

GOLD COAST

BAKERIES

Goldstein's Bakery
509 Olsen Avenue, Ashmore City 4214
Telephone: (7) 5539 3133
Fax: (7) 5597 1064
Website: www.goldsteinsbakery.com.au
Supervision: Rabbi Gurevitch, Gold Coast Hebrew
Congregation
Under the umbrella of the NSW Kashrut Authority. Challah
and kosher breads available at seventeen stores along the
Gold Coast.

SYNAGOGUES

Progressive

Temple Shalom
25 Via Roma Drive, Isle of Capri 4217
Telephone: (7) 5570 1716
Fax: (7) 5570 1716
Email: ts_gcenquiries@hotmail.com
Website: www.templeshalomgoldcoast.org.au

SURFERS PARADISE

Ashkenazi/Orthodox

Surfers Central Synagogue
4 Rivers Terrace 4217
Telephone: (7) 5570 6143
Fax: (7) 5570 6143

Orthodox

Gold Coast Hebrew Congregation
34 Hamilton Avenue 4217
Telephone: (7) 5570 1851
Fax: (7) 5538 6712
Website: www.goldcoasthc.org.au

South Australia

ADELAIDE

BAKERIES

Bakers Delight
Frewville Shopping Centre, Glen Osmond Road

GROCERIES
Kosher Imports
c/o Hebrew Congregation, 13 Flemington Street,
Glenside 5065
Telephone: (8) 8338 2922
Fax: (8) 8379 0142
Website: www.adelaidejewish.com
Kosher and Judaica products available

SYNAGOGUES
Orthodox
Adelaide Hebrew Congregation
13 Flemington Street, Glenside 5065
Telephone: (8) 8338 2922
Fax: (8) 8379 0142
Website: www.adelaidejewish.com
Mikva on premises. Mailing address: PO Box 320, Glenside 5065.

Progressive
Beit Shalom
41 Hackney Road, Hackney 5000
Telephone: (8) 8362 8281
Fax: (8) 8362 6260
Email: bshalom@bshalomadel.com
Website: www.bshalomadel.com
Mailing address PO Box 47, Stepney 5069

Tasmania
Established as a penal colony in 1803. Jewish names first appeared in 1819, one being Ikey Solomons, a famous Jewish convict who was said to be the model for Dicken's Fagin in Oliver Twist. The community remained small. The Launcerlin synagogue was closed in 1871 and not reopened until 1939.

HOBART
The Jewish Centre
93 Lord Street 7005
Telephone: (3) 6223 7116
Mobile Phone: 0427 237 116
Email: jwc@eftel.net.au

CONTACT INFORMATION
Jewish Centre
Chadbad House, 93 Lord Street, Sandy Bay 7005
Telephone: (3) 6223 7116
Mobile Phone: 04272 37116
Email: jwc@eftel.net.au
Contact in advance for Shabbat hospitality and mikvah.

SYNAGOGUES
Progressive
Hobart Hebrew Congregation
59 Argle Street 7000
Telephone: (3) 6234 4720
Email: Shule@hobart.org
Website: www.hobartsynagogue.org
The oldest continuously functioning synagogue in

Australia, having been consecrated in July 1845. Orthodox Shabbat services every Saturday (10.30am); for Progressive services please visit our website.

LAUNCESTON
CONTACT INFORMATION
Chabad House of Tasmania
5 Brisbane Street 7250
Telephone: (3) 6344 9960
Mobile Phone: 0409770 515
Email: yygordon@gmail.com

SYNAGOGUES
Jewish Synagogue
St. John Street 7250
Telephone: (3) 6343 1143
The synagogue in St John Street is the second oldest in Australia, founded in 1846. It is shared by Reform and Orthodox congregations and still has the original convict benches.

Victoria
BALLARAT
Synagogue
211 Drumond Street North 3350
Telephone: (353) 326 330

BENTLEIGH
Progressive
Bentleigh Progressive Synagogue
549 Centre Road 3204
Telephone: 9563 9208
Fax: 9557 9880
Website: www.bps.org.au
Supervision: Rabbi Aviva Kipen
Central organisation: Union for Progressive Judaism

CAULFIELD
RELIGIOUS ORGANISATIONS
Council of Orthodox Synagogues of Victoria
c/- 234 Balaclava Rd, PO Box 2197 3161
Fax: (61) 9509 2302
Email: yaron@jewishnews.net.au
Website: www.cosv.org.au
President M Trebish. (61) 3 9509 7033
Exec Officer Yossi Aron (61) 4 1951 1772

MELBOURNE
With 42,000 Jews, Melbourne has the largest Jewish community in the country, and the largest Jewish school in the world (the Mount Scopus).

BAKERIES
Big K Kosher Bakery
316 Carlisle Street, Balaclava 3183
Telephone: (3) 9527 4582
Supervision: Rabbi A.Z. Beck, Adass Israel

Glicks Cakes and Bagels
330a Carlisle Street, Balaclava 3183
Telephone: (3) 9527 2198
Supervision: Melbourne Kashrut

Haymishe Bakery
320 Carlisle Street, Shop 4 3183
Telephone: (3) 9527 7116
Supervision: Rabbi A.Z. Beck, Adass Israel

Kosher Delight Bakery
75 Glen Eira Road, Ripponlea
Telephone: (3) 9532 9994
Supervision: Rabbi A.Z. Beck, Adass Israel

Lowy's Cakes & Catering
59 Gordon Street, Elsternwick
Telephone: (3) 9530 0246
Supervision: Rabbi A.Z. Beck, Adass Israel

Meal-Mart
251 Inkerman Street, St Kilda 3182
Telephone: (3) 9525 5077
Fax: (3) 9525 4230
Supervision: Rabbi A.Z. Beck, Adass Israel
Pies, salads, pre-cooked and frozen foods.

BOOKSELLERS
Judaica Store
Golds World of Judaica
3-13 William Street, Balaclava 3183
Telephone: (3) 9527 8775
Fax: (3) 9527 6434
Email: info@golds.com.au
Website: www.golds.com.au
Trading Hours: Sunday 10am to 4pm, Monday to Thursday 9am to 5.30pm, Friday 9am to 3pm

BUTCHERS
Continental Kosher Butchers
155 Glenferrie Road, Malvern 3144
Telephone: (3) 9509 9822
Fax: (3) 9509 9099
Email:
Supervision: Rabbi J.S. Cohen and Rabbi M. Gutnick, Melbourne Kashrut

Melbourne Kosher Butchers
251 Inkerman Street, East St Kilda
Telephone: (3) 9525 5077
Fax: (3) 9525 4230
Supervision: Rabbi A.Z. Beck, Adass Israel.
Sells other kosher products as well. Hours: 10am to 5.30pm; Tuesday to Thursday, 7am to 5.30pm; Friday 7am to 3pm. Winter 2pm.

Solomon Kosher Butchers
140-144 Glen Eira Road, Elsternwick 3185
Telephone: (3) 9532 8855
Fax: (3) 9532 8896
Website: www.solomon.com.au
Supervision: Rabbi Y.D. Groner, Agudas Chabad Kashrut Committee. Hours: Monday to Thursday, 7am to 5.30pm; Friday 7am to 3pm

Yumi's Kosher Seafoods
29 Glen Eira Road, Ripponlea 3183
Telephone: (3) 9523 6444
Fax: (3) 9532 8189
Supervision: Rabbi A.Z. Beck, Adass Israel
Also suppliers of kosher fresh fish.

CHOCOLATE SHOPS
Kosher
Alpha Kosher Chocolates
17 William Street, Balaclava
Telephone: (3) 9527 2453
Australia's only kosher chocolate factory. Handmade chocolates. Visitors welcome. Open Sunday mornings.

COMMUNITY ORGANISATIONS
Jewish Community Council of Victoria Inc.
306 Hawthorn Road, South Caulfield 3162
Telephone: (3) 9272 5566
Fax: (3) 9272 5560
Email: community@jccv.org.au
Website: www.jccv.org.au
Peak body of Melbourne Jewish community

CONTACT INFORMATION
Mizrachi Hospitality Committee
81 Balaclava Road, Caulfield 3161
Telephone: (3) 8317 2555
Fax: (3) 9527 5665
Email: office@mizrachi.com.au
Mailing address: PO Box 2247, Caulfield Junction, Victoria 3161

DELICATESSEN
Eshel Take-Away Foods & Catering
59 Glen Eira Road, Ripponlea 3161
Telephone: (3) 9532 8309
Fax: (3) 9532 8089
Supervision: Rabbi A.Z. Beck, Adass Israel

GROCERIES
Dainty Foods (Kraus)
62 Glen Eira Road, Elsternwick 3185
Telephone: (3) 9523 8463
Fax: (3) 9532 4033
Email: daintyfood@bigpond.com
Kosher Food Importers and Distributors

Rishon Foods Party Ltd.
23 William Street, Balaclava 3183
Telephone: (3) 9527 5142

Tempo Kosher Supermarket
5/320 Carlisle Street, St. Kilda 3182
Telephone: (3) 9527 5021
Manufacturers of a range of kosher foods, including cheese, butter and juice drinks.

Liquor
Gefen Liquor Store
328 Carlisle Street, Balaclava 3183
Telephone: (3) 9527 1100
Fax: (3) 9527 1244
Selling a wide range of kosher wines and spirits produced locally and from around the world. Open Sunday to Friday.

Retail
Kraus Foods
62 Glen Eira Road, Elsternwick 3185
Telephone: (3) 9523 8463
Fax: (3) 9532 4033
Mobile Phone: 0418 288 875
Email: daintyfood@bigpond.com
Website: www.krausfoods.elocal.com.au
Kosher Food Retailer, Importer and Distributor

HOTELS
Quest East St Kilda
441 Inkerman Street, St Kilda East 3183
Telephone: (3) 9526 3888
Fax: (3) 9525 9691
Email: questeaststkilda@questapartments.com.au
Website: www.questeaststkilda.com.au
Central organisation: Quest Serviced Apartments
Strictly Glatt Kosher

JUDAICA
The Antique Silver Co.
253 Carlisle Street, Balaclava 3183
Telephone: (3) 9525 8480
Fax: (3) 9525 8479
Large selection of Judaica and ritual objects.

KASHRUT INFORMATION
Kashrut Authority
Kosher Australia Pty Ltd
81 Balaclava Road, Caulfield 3161
Telephone: (3) 8317 2500
Fax: (3) 9527 5665
Email: info@kosher.org.au
Website: www.kosher.org.au
Kosher Certification
Mailing address: PO Box 2247 Caulfield Junction, Victoria 3161

LIBRARIES
Kadimah Jewish Cultural Centre & National Library
7 Selwyn Street, Elsternwick 3185
Telephone: (3) 9523 9817
Hours: 9.30am to 2.30pm

Makor Jewish Community Library
306 Hawthorn Road, South Caulfield 3162
Telephone: (3) 9272 5611
Fax: (3) 9272 5629
Email: info@makorlibrary.com
Website: www.makorlibrary.com

MEDIA
Newspapers
Jewish News
PO Box 1000, South Cantfield 3185
Telephone: (3) 9507 2320
Publishes weekly newspaper Yiddishe Gesheften,

Yiddishe Gesheften The Jewish Community Advertiser
PO Box 1031 Elsternwick, Victoria 3185
Telephone: (3) 9507 2320
Published quarterly

MIKVAOT
Caulfield Mikva
9 Furneaux Grove, East St Kilda 3183
Telephone: (3) 9528 1116; 9525 8585
Contact: Mrs C. Sofer

Lubavitch Mikva
38 Empress Road, East St Kilda 3183
Telephone: (3) 9527 7555
Fax: (3) 9525 8838

MUSEUMS
Jewish Holocaust Centre
15 Selwyn Street, Elsternwick 3185
Telephone: (3) 9528 1985
Fax: (3) 9528 3758
Email: admin@jhc.org.au
Website: www.jhc.org.au
Hours: Monday- Thursday 10 am to 4 pm; Friday 10 am to 2 pm & Sunday 12 noon to 4 pm

Jewish Museum of Australia
26 Alma Road, St Kilda 3182
Telephone: (3) 85343600
Fax: (3) 9534 0844
Email: info@jewishmuseum.com.au
Website: www.jewishmuseum.com.au
Cutting edge exhibitions open a window into the Jewish world to explore 4000 years of tumultuous history and showcase the unique expression of contemporary Australian Jewish culture.

RELIGIOUS ORGANISATIONS
Melbourne Beth Din
Synagogue Chambers, 572 Inkerman Road, North Caulfield 3161
Telephone: (3) 9527 8337
Fax: (3) 9527 8072

Rabbinical Council of Victoria
c/o Honorary Secretary, Rabbi Mordechai Gutnick
7 Meadow Street, East St Kilda 3183
Telephone: (3) 9525 9542
Fax: (3) 9525 9546

Progressive
Victorian Union for Progressive Judaism
78 Alma Road, St Kilda 3182
Telephone: (3) 9510 1488
Fax: (3) 9521 1229

RESTAURANTS

Dairy

Sheli's Coffee Shop
306 Hawthorn Road, South Caufield
Telephone: (3) 9272 5607

Meat

Delishes Restaurant
8-10 Glen Eira Avenue, Ripponlea
Telephone: (3) 9523 1801

Klein's Kosher Gourmet
19 Glen Eira Road, Ripponlea 3185
Telephone: (3) 9528 1200
Fax: (3) 9528 1300
Email: kleinsgourmetfoods@hotmail.com
Website: www.kleinsgourmetfoods.com
Supervision: Kosher Australia

SYNAGOGUES

Independent

Bet Hatikva Synagogue
233 Nepan Highway, Gardenvale 3185
Telephone: (3) 9576 9755

Orthodox

Brighton Hebrew Congregation
132-136 Marriage Road, East Brighton 3187
Telephone: (3) 9592 9179
Fax: (3) 9593 1682
Email: brightonshule@iprimus.com.au
Office hours: Monday to Friday 9am to 1pm. PO Box 202
Bentleigh 3204. Visitors welcome.

Burwood Hebrew Congregation
38 Harrison Avenue 3125
Telephone: (3) 9808 3120

Caulfield Hebrew Congregation
572 Inkerman Road, Caulfield 3161
Telephone: (3) 9525 9492
Fax: (3) 9527 8463
Email: admin@caulfieldshule.com
Website: www.caulfieldshule.com
Rabbi S. Gutnick

Chabad House Malvern
316 Glenferrie Road, Malvern 3143
Telephone: (3) 9822 4985
Fax: (3) 9822 1093
Website: www.chabad.com.au

East Melbourne City Synagogue
488 Albert Street, East Melbourne 3002
Telephone: (3) 9662 1372
Email: office@melbournecitysynagogue.com
Website: www.melbournecitysynagogue.com
The only synagogue in the inner city area. A historically
significant synagogue classified by the National Trust of
Victoria. It celebrated its 125 year anniversary in 2002.

Elwood Talmud Torah Congregation
39 Dickens Street, Elwood 3184
Telephone: (3) 9531 1547

Fax: (3) 9531 6063
Email: elwoodshule@netspace.net.au
Website: www.elwoodshule.com

Kew Hebrew Congregation
53 Walpole Street, Kew 3101
Telephone: (3) 9853 9243
Fax: (3) 9853 1354
Email: office@khc.org.au
Website: www.khc.org.au

Kollel Beth Hatalmud-Yehuda Fishman
362a Carlisle Street, East St Kilda 3183
Telephone: (3) 9527 6156
Fax: (3) 9527 8034

Melbourne Hebrew Congregation
Corner Toorak & St Kilda Roads, South Yarra 3141
Telephone: (3) 9866 2255
Fax: (3) 9866 2022
Email: mhc@melbournesynagogue.org.au
Website: www.melbournesynagogue.org.au

Mizrachi
81 Balaclava Road, Caulfield 3161
Telephone: (3) 8317 2555
Fax: (3) 9527 5665
Email: administrator@barnetsynagogue.org.uk
Mailing address: PO Box 2247, Caulfield Junction, Victoria
31761

Moorabbin & District Synagogue
960 Nepan Highway, Moorabbin 3189
Telephone: (3) 9553 3845

South Caulfield Synagogue
47 Leopold Street, South Caulfield 3161
Telephone: (3) 9578 5922
Fax: (3) 9578 5299

St Kilda Hebrew Congregation Inc.
12 Charnwood Grove, St Kilda 3182
Telephone: (3) 9537 1433
Fax: (3) 9525 3759
Email: office@stkildashule.org
Website: www.stkildashule.org.au

Yeshiva Shule
92 Hotham Street, St Kilda 3183
Telephone: (3) 9522 8222
Fax: (3) 9522 8266

Progressive

Leo Baeck Centre for Progressive Judaism
31-37 Harp Road, Kew East 3102
Telephone: (3) 9819 7160
Fax: (3) 9859 5417
Email: office@lbc.org.au
Website: www.lbc.org.au
PO Box 430, East Kew 3102

Temple Beth Israel
76–83 Alma Road, St Kilda 3182
Telephone: (3) 9510 1488
Fax: (3) 9521 1229
Website: www.tbi.org.au

Victorian Union for Progressive Judaism
78 Alma Road, St Kilda 3182
Telephone: (3) 9510 1488
Fax: (3) 9521 1229

Sephardi
The Sassoon Yehuda Sephardi Synagogue
79 Hotham Street, East St Kilda 3183
Telephone: (3) 9527 8863
Email: rylco@optusnet.com.au
Sephardi Kiddush follows Saturday service. Monday,
Thursday and Sunday services followed by breakfast.

TOURIST SITES
North Eastern Jewish War Memorial Centre
6 High Street, Doncaster 3108
Telephone: (3) 9816 3516
Fax: (3) 9857 4430
Email: nejc@bigpond.com
Website: www.nejc.com.au

Western Australia
PERTH
BUTCHERS
W.A. Kosher Butcher & Bakery
4 Bayley Street, Dianella
Telephone: (8) 9276 2525

COMMUNITY ORGANISATIONS
Jewish Community Council of Western Australia
PO Box 659, North Perth 6006
Email: jccwa@bigpond.com

KOSHER FOODS
Aviv Catering
The Jewish Centre, 61 Woodrow Avenue, Yokine 6060
Telephone: (8) 9276 6030
Fax: (8) 9276 6030
Supervision: KAWA Open 10am to 2pm.

Kosher Food Centre
Perth Synagogue Carpark, Plantation Street,
Menora WA 6050
Telephone: (8) 9271 1133/9370 3311
Fax: (8) 9371 1717
Mobile Phone: 0410 558 383
Email: info@kosherfoodcentre.com.au
Website: www.kosherfoodcentre.com.au
Supervision: KAWA
Kosher butchery, bakery, patisserie, deli and grocer

SYNAGOGUES
Orthodox
Chabad House
396 Alexander Drive, Dianella 6059
Telephone: (8) 9275 2106
Fax: (8) 9275 1601
Website: www.chabadwa.org

Dianella Shule
68 Woodrow Avenue, Yokine 6060
Telephone: (8) 9375 1276

Northern Suburbs Congregation
4 Vernon Street, Noranda 6062
Telephone: (8) 9275 5932
Perth Hebrew Congregation
Freedman Road, Menora 6050
Telephone: (8) 9271 0539
Fax: (8) 9271 9455
Email: phc@theperthshule.asn.au
Website: www.theperthshule.asn.au
Also has a mikvah

Reform
Temple David
34 Clifton Crescent, Mount Lawley 6050
Telephone: (8) 9271 1485
Fax: (8) 9272 2827
Website: www.templedavid.org.au

AUSTRIA

The arrival of Jews in this area of Europe was more than one thousand years ago. The community was expelled from Austria between 1420 and 1421, but Jews were allowed to return in 1451. The Jews were granted their own quarter of Vienna in 1624, but were expelled again in 1670. The economy declined after the expulsion, and so they were asked to return.

It was not until 1782 that the situation became more stable when Joseph II began lifting the anti-Jewish decrees that his mother, Maria Theresa, had imposed on her Jewish subjects. The Jews received equal rights in 1848 and, in 1867, legal and other prohibitions were lifted.

Anti-semitism did continue, however, and many influential anti-semitic publications were available in Vienna and were keenly read by many people, including the young Adolf Hitler. After the First World War Austria lost its empire (which included Czech lands and Galicia, which had a very large Jewish community), and the Jewish population fell accordingly. At the time of the Nazi take-over in 1938, 200,000 Jews lived in the country. Some 70,000 were killed in the Holocaust, the rest having escaped or hidden.

Today there are several synagogues in Vienna. The city has an active Ultra-Orthodox community and kosher food is available. There are prayer rooms in some provincial cities.

Visitors to Vienna should not miss the new Jewish Museum opened in 2001. It combines Rachel Whiteread's memorial, the Museum of Medieval Jewish life and details of the excavation of a medieval synagogue built around the middle of the thirteenth century.

GMT +1 hours
Country calling code: **(+43)**
Total population: **8,086,000**
Jewish population: **10,000**
Emergency telephone: **(police–133) (fire–122) (ambulance–144)**
Electricity voltage: **220**

BADEN
CEMETERIES
Jewish Cemetry
Halsriegelstrasse 4 2500
Telephone: (2252) 2525 300
Fax: (2252) 2525 3030
Mobile Phone: 0664 210 6767
Website: www.jewish community.at
Supervision: Chewra Kadischa Baden
Contains some 2,200 graves. Keys to be obtained from the Jewish Community.

SYNAGOGUES
Bethaus Baden
Grabengasse 14 2500

Orthodox
Juedische Gemeinde Baden Bei Wien
Grabengasse 14, POB 149A-2500 2500
Telephone: (2252) 210 6767
Fax: (2252) 217 0768
Website: www.juedischegemeinde.at;
www.jewishcommunity.at
Community and cultural center, administration and synagogue; keys to the Jewish cemetary at 2 Halsriegelstr. can be obtained with the administration (Monday-Friday 9.00am to 1.00pm)
Kosher meals are provided by the Jewish community on Shabbatot and Chagim.

EISENSTADT
CEMETERIES
Old Cemetery
Unterbergstrasse 6
The old cemetery, closed around 1875, contains the grave of Rav Meir Eisenstaat (Maharam Esh), who died in 1744. To this day it is the scene of pilgrimages, particularly on the anniversary of his death. Keys to the cemetery are with the porter of the local hospital, which adjoins the old cemetery.

MUSEUMS
Austrian Jewish Museum
Unterbergstrasse 6
Telephone: (2682) 65145
Fax: (2682) 65145; 65144
The museum now also comprises the restored private synagogue of Samson Wertheimer, Habsburg Court Jew and Chief Rabbi of Hungary (1658–1724). The museum is open daily except Monday from 10am to 5pm. The Eruv Arch, spanning Unterbergstrasse, is at the end near the Esterhazy Palace. The road chain was used in former times to prevent vehicular traffic on Shabbat and Yom Tov.

GRAZ
Graz is considered one of the oldest Jewish communities in Austria. There has been a self-contained Jewish quarter in Graz since 1142. In November 1938 (Kristallnacht) the synagogue was burnt and the Jewish community was expelled.

The new synagogue, consecrated in November 2000, was partially rebuilt using bricks from the old synagogue.

SYNAGOGUES
Jewish Religious Community Synagogue
David-Herzog-Platz 1 A-8020
Telephone: (316) 712 468
Fax: (316) 720 433
Website: www.ikg-graz.at

HINTERGLEMM
HOTELS
Hotel Knappenhof
Dorfstrasse 140 A574
Telephone: (6541) 6497
Fax: (6541) 64976

INNSBRUCK
COMMUNITY ORGANISATIONS
Jewish community for Tyrol and Vorarlberg
Sillgasse 15 A-6020
Telephone: (512) 586 892
Fax: (512) 586 892
Website: www.ikg-innsbruck.at

KOBERSDORF
CEMETERIES
Jewish Cemetery
Waldgasse
The keys of the cemetery on the Lampelberg are with Mr Piniel , Waldgasse 25 and Mr Grässing, Haydngasse 4.

LINZ
COMMUNITY ORGANISATIONS
Community Centre
Bethlehemstrasse 26
Telephone: (732) 779 805

SYNAGOGUES
Liberal
Synagogue der Israelitischen Kultusgemeinde Linz
Bethlehemstrasse 26 A-4020
Telephone: (732) 779 805
Website: www.ph-linz.at/LuF.be/synagogue

SALZBURG
The Salzburg community dates back to 803 AD when Archbishop Arno summoned a Jewish doctor to set up a practice in the town.

COMMUNITY ORGANISATIONS
Synagogue and Mikva
Lasserstrasse 8 A-5020
Telephone: (662) 872 228
Fax: (662) 872 228; 820 175
Website: www.ikg-salzburg.at
Community synagogue and mikva are to be found at the same address

HOTELS
Kosher
Knappenhoh and Tirolerhof
5754 Hinterglemm
Website: www.kosher-hotel.at
Supervision: Kashrus Komitee Khal Yisroel

ST. POELTEN
MUSEUM
Institute for Jewish History in Austria
Dr. Karl Renner Promenade 22 3100
Telephone: (2742) 771 710
Fax: (2742) 771 7115
Email: office@infoest.ac.at
Website: www.injoest.ac.at/english/index.html
Open Mon to Fri 9am to 1pm and on appointment. Entrance Ledererergasse 12

VIENNA
Vienna was in the past the most important centre for Central European Jews. From 180,000 Jews in the 1930s, there are about 1,000 Jews (mainly elderly) in Vienna today. Doctor Freud's clinic is a popular attraction, and the Jewish Museum of Vienna gives much information on the history of the Jews.

BED AND BREAKFAST
Pension Lichtenstein
Grosse Schiffgasse 19 1020
Telephone: (1) 216 8498
Fax: (1) 214 7690
Website: www.pension-lichtenstein.at
The pension consists of suites. Visits should be arranged in advance as there is no front desk reception.

BOOKSELLERS
Books & Bagels
Ruprechtsplatz 4-5 1010
Website: www.booksnbagels.com
This year our Books&Bagels online store will be active on www.booksnbagels.com
Opening hours: Monday to Thursday 8am to midnight, Friday 8am to 4pm, Sunday 10am to 11pm.

Chabad Simcha Center
Hollandstrasse 10 1020
Telephone: (1) 216 2924

Hamifgash
Karmeliterplatz 2 / Kleine Sperlgasse 1020
Telephone: (1) 219 5370
Fax: (1) 219 5370
Opening hours: Monday to Thursday 2pm to 6.30pm, Friday 9am to 2pm.

BUTCHERS
B. Ainhorn
Stadtgutgasse 7 1020
Telephone: (1) 214 5621
Fax: (1) 214 0392
Supervision: Rabbi David Grunfeld
Also supplies fast food

Khassidov Sinchaiva
Volkertplatz 4, Stand 61, 64
Telephone: (1) 214 9650

Rebenwurzel
Grose Mohrengasse 19 1020
Telephone: (1) 216 6640
Supervision: Rabbi Chaim Stern

CEMETERIES
Floridsdorfer Cemetery
Ruthnergasse 28 1210
Those wishing to visit must first obtain a permit from the community centre.

Rossauer Cemetery
Seegasse 9 1090
This is the oldest Jewish cemetery in Vienna, dating from the sixteenth century. It has now been restored after being devasted by the Nazis and is open daily from 8am to 3pm. Access is via the front entrance of the municipal home for the aged at Seegasse 9–11, but a permit must first be obtained from the community centre.

Vienna Central Cemetery
Simmeringer Haupstrasse 244 A-1110
Telephone: (1) 767 6252
Fax: (1) 767 6252
Email: a.pollack@ikg-wien.at
Website: www.ikg-wien.at
Central organisation: Jewish Community of Vienna
The Jewish section (the only one still in use) is at Gate 4 and there is an older Jewish section at Gate 1.

Währinger Cemetery
Semperstrasse 64a 1180
Those wishing to visit must first obtain a permit from the community centre.

CONTACT INFORMATION
Jewish Community Centre
Seitenstettengasse 4
Telephone: (1) 5310 4104
Fax: (1) 5310 4108

Jewish Welcome Service Vienna
Stephansplatz 10 1010
Telephone: (1) 533 2730
Fax: (1) 533 4098
Mobile Phone: 6645 034 656
Email: jewish.welcome@verkehrsbuero.at
Website: www.jewish-welcome.at
Open Monday to Friday 9am to 5.30pm

DOCUMENTATION CENTRE
Documentation Centre of Austrian Resistance
Old City Hall, Wipplingerstrasse 8 1010
Telephone: (1) 228 9469-319
Fax: (1) 228 9469-319
Email: teva.kriss@doew.at
Website: www.doew.at
Hours of opening:Thursday 9am to 7pm

Documentation Centre of Union of Jewish Victims of the Nazis
Salztorgasse 6 A-1010
Telephone: (1) 533 9131
Fax: (1) 535 0397

EMBASSY
Embassy of Israel
Anton-Frankgasse 20 1180
Telephone: (1) 4764 6500

GROCERIES
Koscherland
Kleine Sperlgasse 6 1020
Telephone: (1) 219 6886
Fax: (1) 219 7291
Email: office@kosherland.at
Website: www.kosherland.at
Opening hours: Monday to Thursday 7.30am to 7pm, Friday 7.30am to 2pm.

Kosher Supermarket & Shatnes Laboratory
Hollandstrasse 7 1020
Telephone: (1) 269 9675
Supervision: Rabbi Abraham Yonah Schwartz

Ohel Moshe Kosher Supermarket
Hollandstrasse 10 A-1020
Telephone: (1) 216 9675
Fax: (1) 214 8708
Opening times: Monday to Thursday 8am to 6.30pm, Friday 8am to 2pm.

Rafael Malkov
Tempelgasse 6, Ferdinandstrasse 2 A-1020
Telephone: (1) 214 8394

HOTELS
Hotel Stefanie (member of WorldHotels)
Taborstrasse 12 1020
Telephone: (1) 211 500
Fax: (1) 2115 0160
Mobile Phone: 211 50 160
Email: stefanie@schick-hotels.com
Website: www.schick-hotels.com
Central organisation: Schick Hotels
Four star hotel with kosher breakfast on request

Pension Liechtenstein
Grosse Schiffgasse 19 1020
Telephone: (1) 216 8498
Website: www.pension-liechtenstein.at

JUST–ISRAEL WINE SHOP
Gross–Import–Wien
Nicklegasse 1 A-1020
Telephone: (1) 214 0607
Fax: (1) 214 7690
Website: www.gross-weine.at

MEDIA
Newspapers
Die Gemeinde
Seitenstettengasse 4 1010
Telephone: (1) 5310 4271
Fax: (1) 5310 4279
Website: www.ikg-wien.at
Bi-monthly

MIKVAOT
Agudas Yisroel
Tempelgasse 3, entrance: Czerningasse 4 1020
Telephone: (1) 216 9973

MONUMENT
Nameless Library
Judenplatz
Rachel Whiteread's monument, opened in 2001, depicts shelves of 9,000 books with their spines turned to the inside. The names of the concentration camps in which Austrian Jews were killed are engraved around the base. Underneath the memorial one can view the ruins of a synagogue razed in 1421.

MUSEUMS
Jewish Museum Vienna
Dorotheergasse 11 A-1010
Telephone: (1) 535 0431 ext. 112
Fax: (1) 535 0424
Email: info@jmw.at
Website: www.jmw.at
Hours: Sunday to Friday, 10am to 6pm, Cafeteria and bookshop on site. The cafeteria is not supervised

Museum Judenplatz
Judenplatz 8 A-1010
Telephone: (1) 535 0431
Fax: (1) 535 0424
Email: info@jmw.at
Website: www.jmw.at
A memorial to the Austrian victims of the Holocaust. A
place of remembrance was created that is unique in
Europe. It combines Rachel Whiteread's memorial
(Nameless Library, see above) and the excavations of a
medieval synagogue with the Museum on Medieval Jewish
Life to form a commemorative whole. Opening hours 10am
to 6pm, Friday 10am to 2pm. Special guided tours for
groups by prior arrangement only.

Sigmund Freud Museum
Berggasse 19 1090
Telephone: (1) 319 1596
Fax: (1) 317 0279
Website: www.freud-museum.at
Hours: March–June 9am to 5pm, July–September 9am to 6pm

RESTAURANTS
Kosherland
Kleine Sperlgasse 7
Telephone: (1) 218 0565
Fax: (1) 219 7291

Simchas
Taborstrasse 47 1020
Telephone: (1) 218 2833
Fax: (1) 218 2893
Website: www.s-catering.at

Dairy
Milk 'n' Honey
KL Sperlgasse 7 1020
Telephone: (1) 212 8169
Fax: (1) 219 7291
Website: www.kosherland.at
Supervision: Rabbi R.J. Schartz
Opening times;Monday to Thursday 11am to 3pm and 6pm
to 10pm.

Kosher
Bachur Tov
Taborstrasse 19 1020
Supervision: Sephardic Rabbinate of Vienna

Hadar Koscher Lebensmittel
Krummbaumgasse 12 1020
Telephone: (1) 958 0774

Meat
Restaurant Alef- Alef
Seitenstettengasse 2 A-1010
Telephone: (1) 535 2530
Fax: (1) 535 2533
Website: www.alef-alef.at

Meat-Kosher
Alef Alef
Seitenstettengasse 4 1010
Telephone: (1) 535 2530
Fax: (1) 535 2533

Website: www.alef-alef.at
Supervision: Othodox of Vienna

Snack Bar
Berl Ainhorn Koscher Fleisch und Imbiss
Gross Stadtgutgasse 7 1020
Telephone: (1) 214 5621
Supervision: Orthodox of Vienna

RESTAURANTS/SHOP
Kosher
Abraham Davidov
Karmelitermarkt 29-39
Telephone: (1) 214 5023
Meat and snacks

SITE
Mauthausen Memorial Site
Telephone: (1) 7238 2269
Fax: (1) 7238 3696
Those wishing to visit the site should contact the Jewish
Welcome Service.

SNACK BAR
Dairy-Kosher
Bäckerei Malkov
Tempelgasse 8 1020
Telephone: (1) 214 8394

SUPERMARKET
Koscherland
Kleine Sperlgasse 7 1020
Telephone: (1) 219 6886

SYNAGOGUES
Orthodox
Agudas Jescurun
Riemergasse 9 1010

Agudas Yisroel
Grünangergasse 1 1010
Telephone: (1) 512 8331
Tempelgasse 3 1020
Telephone: (1) 216 9973

Bet hamidrasch Torah Etz Chayim
Grosse Sciffgasse 8
Telephone: (1) 216 3699
Supervision: Rabbi Michael Pressburger

Central Synagogue
Seitenstettengasse 4 1010
Telephone: (1) 5310 4111
Fax: (1) 5310 4108
Website: www.ikg-wien.at
Built in 1824–26, the inside was destroyed during the Nazi
period. This beautiful synagogue was restored by the
community after the Holocaust. For more information
about guided tours contact the community centre offices.

Machsike Haddas
GroBe Mohreng 19 A-1020
Telephone: (1) 216 0679

Misrachi
Judenplatz 8 1010
Telephone: (1) 214 8011
Email: info@misrachi.at
Website: www.misrachi.at

Ohel Moshe
Lilienbrunngasse 19 1020
Telephone: (1) 216 8864
Supervision: Rabbi Abraham Y Schwartz

Rambam
Bauernfeldgasse 4 A-1190
Telephone: (1) 368 1655

Shomre Haddas
Glasergasse 17 1090

Thora Etz Chayim
Grosse Schiffgasse 8 1020
Telephone: (1) 214 5206
Fax: (1) 216 2032

Progressive
Or Chadasch
Robertgasse 2 1020
Telephone: (1) 219 6302
Fax: (1) 219 6302
Email: info@orchadasch.at
Website: www.orchadasch.at

Sephardi
Sephardi Centre
Tempelgasse 7 1020
Telephone: (1) 214 3097

AZERBAIJAN

Azerbaijan has a remarkable Jewish history, which can be better explored now that the country is independent from the former Soviet Union. The Tats (mountain Jews) believe that their ancestors arrived in Azerbaijan at the time of Nebuchadnezzar. They lived in several mountain villages and adopted the customs of their non-Jewish neighbours. They spoke a north Iranian language known as Judeo-Tat, to which they added some Hebrew words. The Soviets clamped down on their way of life after 1928, changing the alphabet of their language from Hebrew to Latin, and then in 1938, to Cyrillic. Some of their synagogues were also closed down. Zionist feeling is high, with almost 30,000 emigrating to Israel since 1989.

The other strand in Azerbaijan's Jewish population are the Ashkenasis who arrived in the nineteenth century from Poland and other countries to the west.

The largest synagogue in Baku is the Tat synagogue, but there are also Ashkenazi and Georgian synagogues. Synagogues are found in other towns.

GMT +5 hours
Country calling code: (**+994**)
Total population: **7,625,000**
Jewish population: **10,000**
Emergency telephone: (**police–02**) (**fire–01**) (**ambulance–03**)

BAKU
EMBASSY
Embassy of Israel
Stroiteley Prospect 1

SYNAGOGUES
Mountain Jews
Dmitrova Street 39 370014
Telephone: (12) 892 232 8867

Ashkenazi
Synagogue
Pervomoskaya Street 271
Telephone: (12) 892 294 1571

KUBA
Kuba Synagogue
Kolkhoznaya Street 46

BAHAMAS

Luis de Torres, the official interpreter for Columbus, was the first Jew in the Bahamas, as well as being one of the first Europeans there. He was a *converso*. The British arrived in 1620 and eventually gained control of the islands. Although there was a Jewish Attorney-General and Chief Justice in the islands in the eighteenth century, few Jews settled there until the twentieth century, coming from Eastern Europe and the UK after the First World War, and settling in the capital Nassau.

There are approximately 300 Jewish residents in the Bahamas. However, it is estimated that about 350,000 Jews visit the islands each year as tourists. There are congregations in Nassau and Freeport. Both cities have Jewish cemeteries, that in Nassau being more historic.

GMT -5 hours
Country calling code: **(+1242)**
Total population: **289,000**
Jewish population: **300**
Emergency telephone: **(police–919) (fire–919) (ambulance–919)**
Electricity voltage: **120**

FREEPORT
SYNAGOGUES
Freeport Hebrew Congregation
Luis de Torres Synagogue, East Sunrise Highway
Telephone: 373 2008 / 1041 / 4025
Fax: 871-5528
President: Geoff Hurst

NASSAU
Progressive
Bahamas Jewish Congregation
POB CB-11002
Telephone: 363 2305

BARBADOS

Jewish history in Barbados starts in 1628, a year after the British first settled there. Jewish settlers came from Brazil, Surinam, England and Germany, and were mainly Sephardi. The first synagogue was established in the capital Bridgetown in 1654. Early settlers were engaged in cultivating sugar and coffee.

The Jewish population was well treated, and in 1831 Barbados was the first British possession in which Jews were granted full political emancipation. Despite a largely favourable climate the community suffered losses from hurricanes, which destroyed sugar plantations, and the Jewish population fell to 70 by 1848. In 1925 no Jews remained, but a new influx (30 families escaping Nazism) came shortly after.

The synagogue was restored in 1987, and postage stamps were produced which commemorated its restoration. The Jewish population remains small, but it was a group of Barbadian Jews who founded the Caribbean Jewish Congress. The Jewish

cemetery, one of the oldest in the Americas, is now back in use.

GMT -4 hours
Country calling code: **(+1246)**
Total population: **262,000**
Jewish population: **Under 100**
Emergency telephone: **(police–462 0125) (fire–999) (ambulance–462 0251)**
Electricity voltage: **110**

BRIDGETOWN
COMMUNITY ORGANISATIONS
Barbados Jewish Community
PO Box 651, Bridgetown
Telephone: 427 0703
Fax: 436 8807

Caribbean Jewish Congress
PO Box 1331, Bridgetown
Telephone: 436 8163
Fax: 437 4992

Synagogue Restoration Project
PO Box 256, Bridgetown
Telephone: 432 0840
Fax: 432 2147
Local inquiries to Henry Altman, Little Mallows, Sandy Lane, St James. Tel: 432 0840.

SYNAGOGUES
Nidhe Israel
Synagogue Lane
Telephone: 432 7114
Services are held Friday evenings at 7pm at True Blue, Rockley New Road, Christ Church, during the summer, and at the Nidhe Israel synagogue, Bridgetown at 7.30pm in winter. This synagogue includes a newly open museum dedicated to the Jewish history of Barbados

Shaare Tzedek
Rockley New Road, Christ Church
Email: sharon@sheratonmall.com
Friday 7.30pm

BELARUS

For the adventurous traveller who has a keen interest in Jewish history, Belarus (also known as White Russia) makes an interesting and unusual destination. Situated on the western side of the former Soviet Union, this largely flat country borders Poland and Lithuania to the west, Ukraine to the south and Russia to the east. Belarus finally achieved independence in 1991, and within its present borders are many towns and villages of Jewish interest, such as Minsk, Pinsk and Grodno. One of the most famous villages in Belarus is Lubavitch, a hamlet in the far east of the country, near the Russian border, where the worldwide Lubavitch movement had its origins.

During WW11 over 800,000 Belarusian Jews were massacred, and in the following years emigration to Israel was very high. However, the community has slowly started to rebuild itself and in the late 1980s an Ulpan (classed to study Hebrew) and a Jewish Sunday School were opened. In 1992 there was the arrival of the first Rabbi to Belarus and the community continued to flourish with the publication of the first Jewish newspaper and openings of the first Kindergarten, Secondary school and an Israeli Embassy.

GMT +2 hours
Country calling code: (+375)
Total population: 10,179,000
Jewish population: 55,000
Emergency telephone: (police–03) (fire–03) (ambulance–003)
Electricity voltage: 220

BARANOVICHI
COMMUNITY ORGANISATIONS
Jewish Community of Baranovichi
President, Lubov Lvova, 58-48 Kurova Street 285320

BOBRUISK
Jewish Community of Bobruisk
President, Boris Gelfand, 31 Komsomolskaya Street 213826
SYNAGOGUES
Bobruisk Synagogue
Engels Street

Synagogue
Prolitarskaya 17/65
Telephone: (29) 699 1770

BORISOV
COMMUNITY ORGANISATIONS
Jewish Community of Borisov
President, Boris Gitlin, 1-37 Stekolnaya Street 222120
SYNAGOGUES
Borisov Synagogue
Trud Street

BREST
COMMUNITY ORGANISATIONS
Jewish Community of Brest
President, Arkady Blyacher, 23-30 Sovetskoy Konstitutzi Street 224032
Telephone: (162) 419 209
SYNAGOGUES
Brest Synagogue
Narodnaya Street
Synagogue
Khalturina Street 2/1
Telephone: (29) 610 2770
Fax: (162) 216 834

GOMEL
COMMUNITY ORGANISATIONS
Jewish Community of Gomel
President, Mikchael Shechtman, 21a-27 Pobedi Street 246017
CONTACT INFORMATION
Rosa Sorkina
Telephone: (23) 252 5808
SYNAGOGUES
Gomel Synagogue
13 Sennaya Street

GORKI
COMMUNITY ORGANISATIONS
Jewish Community of Gorki
President, Vladimir Livshitz, 4-41 Sovetskaya Street 213410

GRODNO
Jewish Community of Grodno
President, Yuri Boyarski, 59aB. Troizkaya Street 230023
Telephone: (15) 233 3305
CONTACT INFORMATION
Mishas Kemerov
Telephone: (15) 231 3798

SYNAGOGUES
Menorah Jewish Community
Block 43, Flat 37 230009
Telephone: (15) 231 3798

Synagogue
B. Troizkaya 59a 230023
Telephone: (15) 274 3270

KALINKOVITCH
COMMUNITY ORGANISATIONS
Jewish Community of Kalinkovitch
President, Yaakov Erenburg, 8-31 Komsomolskaya
Street 24771

KORBIN
Jewish Community of Korbin
President, Elenora Sacharuk, 38-4 Trudovaya Street
225860

MINSK
**Jewish Community of Minsk (Chabad
Lubavitch Or Avner)**
Chief Rabbi of Minsk Yossef Gruzman, 22 Kroptkina
Street 220002
Telephone: (17) 234 2273
Fax: (17) 223 679

**Union of Jewish Communities and
Organisations of Belarus**
22 Kroptkinav Street 220002
Telephone: (17) 234-22-73

CONTACT INFORMATION
**Union of Belarusian Cultural Organizations
and Communities**
Skorina Prospekt 137-6
Telephone: (17) 264 3083

EMBASSY
Embassy of Israel
Partizanski Prospekt 6A 220002
Telephone: (17) 230 4444

MEMORIAL
Minsk Jewish Memorial
Yama
This memorial, devoted to 5,000 Jews killed by the Nazis
on Purim 1942, was erected in 1946 and is the only one in
what was the USSR devoted to the Holocaust which
displays Yiddish writing.

SYNAGOGUES
Minsk Synagogue
22 Kropotkina Street
Telephone: (17) 255 8270
13b Daumana Street

Progressive
**Association of Progressive Jewish
Congrations in Belarus**
Per K Chyornogo 4, apartment 18, Simach 220012
Telephone: (17) 284 6089
Fax: (17) 266 2928

MOGHILEV
Synagogue
38/121 Kobrinskaya Street 212030
Telephone: (222) 237 270

COMMUNITY ORGANISATIONS
Jewish Community of Moghilev
President, Naum Yoffei, 28-11 30 Let Pobedi Street
221011

SYNAGOGUES
Moghilev Synagogue
1 2nd Krutoy Lane

MOZIR
COMMUNITY ORGANISATIONS
Jewish Community of Mozir
President, Grigory Skolnukov, 30-4 Prititzkova
Street 247760

ORSHA
Jewish Community of Orsha
President, Ysaak Gurevitsh, 20-20 pr. Tekstilshikov
210030

SYNAGOGUES
Orsha Synagogue.
Nogrin Street

Synagogue
Tekstilchikov 3/8
Telephone: (21) 623 0486

OSIPOVITSHI
COMMUNITY ORGANISATIONS
Jewish Community of Osipovitshi
President, Sarra Utevskaya, 43-2 Tshumakova
Street 213760

PINSK
Jewish Community of Pinsk
President, Aleksander Lapidus, 140-22 Parkovaya
Street 225710

POLOTOSK
Jewish Community of Polotosk
President, Filip Zavt, 18-32 Gogolya Street 211401

RECHITZA
Jewish Community of Rechitza
President, Alla Shkon, 22-113 Naumova Street
247500
Telephone: (029) 734 8261
Fax: (2340) 35555

SYNAGOGUES
Rechitza Synagogue
120 Lunacharsky Street

SLOTSK
COMMUNITY ORGANISATIONS
Jewish Community of Slotsk
President, Raisa Titshina, 11-27 Parizhskoy
Kommuni Street 223610

VITEBSK
Jewish Community of Vitebsk
President, Arkady Shulman, 4-167 pr. Probedi
Vitebsk 210038

BELGIUM

Jewish settlement in the area now called
Belgium dates back to the thirteenth century, and suffered a similar fate to other
medieval European Jewish communities,
taking the blame for the Black Death and
suffering expulsions. The Sephardim were
the first to resettle in Belgium, mainly in
Antwerp. After independence in 1830, conditions for the Jews improved and more
Jews began to settle there. The diamond
centre of Antwerp later developed rapidly,
attracting many Jews from Eastern Europe.

By 1939 the Jewish population had grown
to 100,000, a large proportion of whom
were refugees hoping to escape to America.
Some succeeded, but many became
trapped after the German invasion. Some
25,000 Belgian Jews were deported and
killed in the Holocaust. A national monument listing the names of the victims
stands in Anderlecht in Brussels.

The present Jewish population includes a
large Hassidic community in Antwerp,
where there are some 30 synagogues.
There are also more than ten synagogues
in Brussels. There are Jewish schools and
newspapers in Antwerp and Brussels.

GMT +1 hours
Country calling code: (+32)
Total population: **10,188,000**
Jewish population: **33,000**
Emergency telephone: (**police–101**) (**fire–101**)
(**ambulance–101**)
Electricity voltage: **220**

ANTWERP
Seen by some as the 'last shtetl in Europe',
Antwerp is a well-known Hassidic centre.
Antwerp's Jewish population (15,000) has one
of the highest numbers of Ultra-Orthodox in the

Diaspora. Served by 30 synagogues (many of
them small shtiebels), there are also kosher
restaurants and food shops.

BAKERIES
Kleinblatt
Provinciestraat 206
Telephone: (3) 233 7513; 226 0018
Fax: (3) 232 0920
Steinmetz
Lange Kievitstraat 64
Telephone: (3) 234 0947

BOOKSELLERS
I. Menczer
Simonstraat 40
Telephone: (3) 232 3026
N. Seletsky
Lange Kievitstraat 70
Telephone: (3) 232 6966
Fax: (3) 226 9446

BUTCHERS
Berkowitz
Isabellalei 9
Telephone: (3) 218 5111
Supervision: Machzike Hadass
Fruchter
Simonstraat 22
Telephone: (3) 233 1811 / 1557
Fax: (3) 231 3903
Kosher King
Lange Kievitstraat 40
Telephone: (3) 233 6749
Fax: (3) 239 6380
Kosher King
Isabellalei 7
Telephone: (3) 239 4189
Mandelovics
Isabellalei 96
Telephone: (3) 218 4779
Moszkowitz
Lange Kievitstraat 47
Telephone: (3) 232 6349
Fax: (3) 226 0471

CONTACT INFORMATION
Machsike Hadass (Israelitische Orthodoxe Gemeente)
Jacob Jacobsstraat 22 2018
Telephone: (3) 233 5567
Shomre Hadass (Israelitische Gemeente van Antwerpen)
Terliststraat 35 2018
Telephone: (3) 232 0187
Fax: (3) 226 3123
Email: info@shomre-hadas.be
Website: www.shomre-hadas.be

DELICATESSEN
Weingarten
Lange Kievitstraat 124
Telephone: (3) 233 2828

GROCERIES
Braun's Grocery
Terliststraat 28
Telephone: (3) 232 4626
Fax: (3) 232 3346

Col-Bo
Jacob Jacobsstraat 40
Telephone: (3) 234 1212

Stark
Mercatorstraat 24
Telephone: (3) 230 2520

Super Discount
Belgielei 104-108
Telephone: (3) 239 0666

Superette Lamoriniere
Lamboriniere Straat 199
Telephone: (3) 239 3110
Fax: (3) 281 3205

MEDIA
Newspapers
Belgisch Israelitisch Weekblad
Pelikaanstraat 106-108 2018
Telephone: (3) 233 7094
Fax: (3) 233 4810

MIKVAOT
Machsike Hadass
Steenbokstraat 22
Telephone: (3) 239 7588

MUSEUMS
Museum Plantin-Moretus/Prentenkabinet
Vrijdagmarkt 22 2000
Telephone: (3) 221 1450
Fax: (3) 221 1471
Website:
www.museum.antwerpen.be/plantin_moretus
Open: Tuesdays to Sundays 10am to 5pm. (Open on Easter Monday and Whit Monday). Closed on Mondays and 1 and 2 January, 1 May and Ascension Day, 1 and 2 November, 25 and 26 December.

The Plantin-Moretus house, workshop and museum complex is included on the UNESCO list of immovable World Heritage. Contains examples of early Jewish printing, such as the famous Polyglot Bible.

RESTAURANTS
Dairy
USA Pizza
118a Isabellalei
Telephone: (3) 281 2300
Supervision: Machzikey Hadas
Take away option

Dairy/kosher
Creamshnit
Lang Lemme 144
Telephone: (3) 04848 89100
Fax: (3) 0323 96380
Also pizzeria and bakery. Special prices for groups.

Meat
Blue Lagoon
Lange Herentalsetraat 70
Telephone: (3) 226 0114
Supervision: Machsike Hadass
Also sells chocolates

Hoffy's
Lange Kievitstraat 52
Telephone: (3) 234 3535
Fax: (3) 226 0282

Jacob
Lange Kieitstraat 49
Telephone: (3) 233 1124

Lamalo
Appelmanstraat 21
Telephone: (3) 213 2200

Vegetarian
Time Out
Lange Herentalse Straat 58 2018
Telephone: (3) 281 2300
Fax: (3) 281 2300

SYNAGOGUES
Great Synagogue Romi Goldmuntz
Van Den Nestlei 1
Telephone: (3) 232 0187

Sephardic Synagogue
Hovenierstraat 31
Telephone: (3) 232 5339

Orthodox
Machsike Hadass
Jacob Jacobsstraat 22 2018
Telephone: (3) 232 0021; 233 5567
Fax: (3) 233 8797

Oosten Synagogue
Oostenstraat 43
Telephone: (3) 230 9246

TOURS
Toerisme Antwerpen
Grote Markt 15 2000
Telephone: (3) 232 0103
Fax: (3) 231 1937
Website: www.visitantwerpen.be

ARLON
SYNAGOGUES
Arlon Synagogue
Rue St Jean 6700
Telephone: (63) 217 985

Fax: (63) 217 985
Email: jeanclaude.jeanC1@skynet.be
Website: www.site.voila.fr/synagogarlon
Established 1863. The secretary, J.C. Jacob, can be reached
at 11 rue des Martyrs, 6700 Arlon. A monument has been
erected in the new Jewish cemetery to the memory of the
Jews of Arlon deported and massacred by the Nazis. The old
Jewish cemetry is the oldest in Belgium an can be visited.

BRUSSELS

The capital of Belgium has fewer kosher
facilities than Antwerp, although there are
23,000 Jews living in the city. The headquarters
of the European Union of Jewish Students is
based there. The Anderlecht area has a
monument to the Belgian Holocaust victims
and a memorial to Jews who fought in the
Belgian Resistance.

BOOKSELLERS
Menorah
12 Avenue J. Voldens 1060
Telephone: (2) 537 5073

COMMUNITY ORGANISATIONS
Centre Communautaire Laic Juif
Yitzhak Rabin Center, 52 rue Hotel des Monnaies
1060 Brussels
Telephone: (2) 543 0270
Fax: (2) 543 0271
Website: www.cclj.be

EMBASSY
Embassy of Israel
40 Avenue de l'Observatoire 1180
Telephone: (2) 373 5500
Fax: (2) 373 5617
Website: www.ambisrael.be

KOSHER STORES
Colbo
Chee d'Alsemboerg 1190
Telephone: (2) 346 8161
Bread, milchiks, meats and other kosher items available.

Library
Shoresh
rue Henri Wafelaerts 12 1060
Telephone: (2) 343 1848
Fax: (2) 343 8669
Website: www.shoresh.be
Bread, milchiks, meats and other kosher items available.

MEDIA
Newspapers
Centrale
91 Avenue Henri Jaspar
Telephone: (2) 538 8036
Monthly

Fax de Jerusalem
68 Ave Ducpétiaux
Telephone: (2) 538 5673

Fax: (2) 534 0236
Weekly
Regards
52 rue Hotel des Monnaies, 1060
Telephone: (2) 543 0281
Fax: (2) 537 5565
Website: www.cclj.be/Regards
Fortnightly

Radio
Radio Judaica (Jewish Radio)
FM 90.2
Jewish interest programs 24-hours a day

MIKVAOT
Machsike Hadass
67a rue de la Clinique
Telephone: (2) 537 1439

MUSEUMS
Jewish Musem
rue des Minimes 21 1000
Telephone: (2) 512 1963
Fax: (2) 513 4859
Email: info@mjb-jmb.org
Website: www.mjb-jmb.org
Hours: Sunday to Friday and Sunday 10am to 5pm.
Saturday and Jewish Holidays closed.

RELIGIOUS ORGANISATIONS
Communaute Israelite de Bruxelles
2 rue Joseph Dupont B-1000
Telephone: (2) 512 4334
Fax: (2) 512 9237

**Machsike Hadass (Communauté Israélite
Orthodoxe de Bruxelles)**
67a rue la Clinique
Telephone: (2) 524 1486; 521 1289

RESTAURANTS
Meat
Pil Pel
82 Avenue De Fre 1180
Telephone: (2) 374 5300
Bassari with community hechsher. Bread, milchiks, meats
and other kosher items available.

SITE
**National Monument to the Jewish Martyrs of
Belgium**
Corner rue Emile Carpentier and rue Goujons,
Square of the Jewish Martyrs, Anderlecht
This monument commemorates the Jews of Belgium who
were deported to concentration camps and killed by the
Nazis during the Second World War. The names of all
23,838 are engraved on the monument.

SYNAGOGUES
Beth Habad
Avenue du Roi 87, Avenue Ducpetiaux 141
1060
Telephone: (2) 534 1850
Fax: (2) 534 7343
Mobile Phone: 477 531217
Email: yentylasker@hotmail.com
Website: http://chabadbrussels.com/default.aspx
Are happy to invite for Shabbat people passing through
Brussels.

Brussels Airport
Transit lounge

Conservative
**Communaute Israelite Liberale de Belgique
Synagogue Beth Hillel**
Rue des Primeurs 80 1190
Telephone: (2) 332 2528
Fax: (2) 376 7219
Email: info@beth-hillel.org
Website: www.beth-hillel.org

Orthodox
Adath Israel
126 rue Rogier 1030
Telephone: (2) 241 1664
Email: cios@skynet.be

Ahavat Reim
73 rue de Thy
Telephone: (2) 648 3837

Beth Itshak
115 Avenue du Roi 1060
Telephone: (2) 538 3374; 520 1359

Communaute Israelite d'Uccle-Forest
11 Avenue de Messidor 1180
Telephone: (2) 344 6094
Fax: (2) 344 6094
Website: www.maale.org

The Great Synagogue
32 rue de la Regence 1000
Telephone: (2) 512 4334
Fax: (2) 512 9237
The synagogue, built in 1878, survived the occupation

Sephardi
Synagogue Simon and Lina Haim
47 rue du Pavilion 1030
Telephone: (2) 215 0525
Fax: (2) 215 0242
There is a memorial to the Jews deported from Rhodes,
Greece

CHARLEROI
COMMUNITY ORGANISATIONS
Community Centre
56 rue Pige-au-Croly

GHENT
CONTACT INFORMATION
Jacques Bloch
Okkernootsteeg 1 9000
Telephone: (9) 224 3889
The treasurer of the community will be happy to meet
English-speaking visitors. As the community is very small,
there is no permanent synagogue. Services are held on the
High Holy Days.

KNOKKE
SYNAGOGUES
Knokke Synagogue
30 Van Bunnenlaan
Telephone: (50) 610 372
Also has a mikva

LIÈGE
COMMUNITY ORGANISATIONS
Community Centre
12 Quai Marcellis 4020

MUSEUMS
Musee Serge Kruglanski
19 rue L. Frédéricq 4020
Telephone: (4) 343 8043
Fax: (4) 224 4360

SYNAGOGUES
Liège Synagogue
19 rue L. Frédéricq 4020
Telephone: (4) 436 106

MONS
CONTACT INFORMATION
SHAPE
Telephone: (65) 445 808; 444 809
Nearby, at Casteau, the International Chapel of NATO's
Supreme Headquarters Allied Powers Europe, includes a
small Jewish community, established 1951, that holds
regular services. Call for further information.

OSTEND
SYNAGOGUES
Israelitic Community Ostend
Filip Van Maestrichtplein No. 3 8400
Telephone: 059 707 493
Fax: 059 707 493
Mobile Phone: (0) 496 53 91 83
Services during July and August, also Rosh Hashana and
Yom Kippur at 9am and 8pm. Inquiries to Mrs Liliane
Wulfowicz, Parklaan 21, B-8400, Tel: 59 802 405, Mr
Armand Benizri 477 277 223 or Jacques Ketels 59 70 74
93/496 5391 83.

WATERLOO
Traditionalist
Communaute Isralite de Waterloo et du Brabant Sud (CIWABS)
140 Avenue Belle-Vue, 1410
Telephone: (2) 354 6833
Fax: (2) 514 5977
Regular services Shabbat and festivals; English speaking visitors very welcome; tel 351 3631 (evenings).

BERMUDA

Jews have lived in Bermuda since the seventeenth century, but the first formal congregation was not established until the twentieth century.

The resident Jewish population is very small, but the transient population (of tourists largely from the USA, Britain and Canada) is much greater. There is a Jew's Bay, but whether this is merely named to balance a nearby Christian Bay or has some other origin is not known.

GMT -4 hours
Country calling code: **(+1 441)**
Total population: **60,000**
Jewish population: **Under 100**
Emergency telephone: **(police–112) (fire–113) (ambulance–115)**
Electricity voltage: **110**

HAMILTON
COMMUNITY ORGANISATIONS
Jewish Community of Bermuda
PO Box HM 1793 HM05
Telephone: 291 1785
Website: www.jcb.bm

BOLIVIA

The history of the Jews of Bolivia dates back to the Spanish colonial period. *Conversos* came with the Spaniards in the seventeenth century.

The main influx of Jews occurred in 1905 with immigrants from Eastern Europe, but the number entering Bolivia was much smaller than that going to other South American countries. In 1933 there were only some 30 Jewish families. At the end of the decade, however, there was a small increase in Jewish immigration as German

and Austrian Jews fled from Europe. Ironically, the Jewish community did not grow very much, even though the government granted every Jew an entry visa.

Many Jews started to leave Bolivia in the 1950s because of political instability and the apparent lack of educational opportunities. The present-day community has a central organisation known as the Circulo Israelita de Bolivia.

GMT -4 hours
Country calling code: **(+591)**
Total population: **8,140,000**
Jewish population: **500**
Emergency telephone: **(police–110) (ambulance–118)**
Electricity voltage: **110/220**

COCHABAMBA
Associaciacion Israelita de Cochabamba
PO Box 349, Calle Valdivieso

SYNAGOGUES
Synagogue
Calle Junin y Calle Colombia, Casilla 349

LA PAZ
CONTACT INFORMATION
Jabad Lubavitch Bolivia
Calle 16 #8, Second Floor, Achumani
Telephone: (2) 214 0963

SYNAGOGUES
Circulo Israelita de Bolivia
Obrajes, Calle 1 No 307, PO Box 1545
Telephone: (2) 278 5083
Fax: (2) 278 5371
Representative body of Bolivian Jewry. All La Paz organisations are affiliated to it. Service Shabbat morning only.

Communidad Israelita Synagogue
Calle Canada Stronguest 1846, PO Box 2198
Friday evening services are held here.

SANTA CRUZ
COMMUNITY ORGANISATIONS
Centre Cruceño
PO Box 469

WIZO
Castilla 3409

BOSNIA-HERCEGOVINA

Sephardi Jews were the first to arrive in the area in the late sixteenth century. They established a Jewish quarter in Sarajevo, and this was home for poorer Jews until the Austrians conquered the area in 1878. It was the Turks, however, who emancipated the Jews in the nineteenth century when Bosnia-Hercegovina was under Ottoman rule.

When Bosnia-Hercegovina became part of the newly formed Yugoslavia, after the First World War, the community maintained its Sephardi heritage and joined the all-Yugoslav Federation of Jewish Religious Communities. The Jewish population numbered 14,000 in 1941. This number dropped sharply after the Germans conquered Yugoslavia.

After the war the survivors were joined by many who had decided to return. The Sephardi and Ashkenazi communities became unified. La Benevolencija, founded 100 years ago, is a humanitarian organisation which supported the plight of the community and became well known in the early 1990s at the time of the civil war. After the Yugoslav civil war, many made aliyah to Israel, reducing the community still further.

GMT +1 hours
Country calling code: (+387)
Total population: 3,784,000
Jewish population: 400
Emergency telephone: (police–664 211) (fire–93) (ambulance–94)
Electricity voltage: 220

SARAJEVO

CEMETERIES
Kovacici
Kovacici-Debelo-Brdo
This historic Jewish cementery is in town. Not far from the centre of town, on a hill called Vraca, there is a monument with the names of the 7,000 Jews from the area who fell victim to the Nazis.

COMMUNITY ORGANISATIONS
Jewish Cultural-Educational and Humanitarian Society "La Benevolencija" Sarajevo
Hamdije Kresevljakovica 59 71000
Telephone: (33) 229 666
Fax: (33) 229 667
Email: la_bene@open.net.ba
Website: www.benevolencija.eu.org

MUSEUMS
Jewish Museum
Velika Avlija b.b.
This historic museum is in the oldest synagogue in Bosnia-Herzegovina, with priceless relics dating back to the expulsion from Spain.

SYNAGOGUES
Synagogue and Community Centre
Hamdije Kresevljakovica 59
Telephone: (33) 663 472
Fax: (33) 663 473
Email: la_bene@open.net.ba
Website: www.benevolencija.eu.org

TOURIST SITES
The National Museum of Bosnia and Herzegovina
Zmaja od Bosne 3
Telephone: (33) 668 027 / 025
Fax: (33) 668 025; 262 710
Email: z.muzej@zemaljskimuzej.ba
Website: www.zemaljskimuzej.ba
The world famous Sarajevo Haggadah, written around 1314 as a wedding gift to a young couple, has now been fully repaired and restored. It is in a secure climate-controlled room.

BRAZIL

The first Jewish settlers in Brazil came with the Portuguese in 1500. They were mainly *Conversos* escaping persecution in Portugal, and initially worked on the sugar plantations. In due course they played important roles as traders, artisans and plantation owners. The huge area which is called Brazil today was in the process of being conquered by the Dutch and the Portuguese. Two synagogues were opened in Recife during the 1640s when many Jews came from Holland. When the Dutch left Brazil in 1654 one of the terms of surrender allowed the Jews who had been on their side to emigrate. Many fled and some went on to found the first Jewish community in New York, then known as New Amsterdam. A seventeenth-century Mikvah was discovered in 2000 in the basement of the Tsur Israel Synagogue in Recife.

With Brazilian independence in 1822, conditions became more favourable for Jews and many came from North Africa and Europe. The majority of Jews in Brazil today, however, originate from the immigration of East European Jews in the early twentieth century. From about 6,000 Jews in 1914, the community grew to 30,000 in 1930. After 1937 Brazil refused to allow Jewish immigrants into the country, but some limited immigration managed to continue despite the restrictions.

A central organisation was established in 1951 (the CONIB), and this includes 200 various Jewish organisations. Brazilian Jews live in an atmosphere of tolerance and prosperity, and assimilation is prominent.

There are synagogues in all the major cities.

GMT -3 to -5 hours
Country calling code: (**+55**)
Total population: **159,884,000**
Jewish population: **110,000**
Emergency telephone: (**police–147**) (**fire–193**) (**ambulance–192**)
Electricity voltage: **220/100**

Amazonas
MANAUS
Comite Israelita Amazonas
R. Leonardo Malcher, 630 69010-170
Telephone: (92) 3234 9558
Fax: (92) 3233 6361
Email: comiteisraelita@gmail.com
Website: www.comiteisraelita.com.br

Bahia
SALVADOR
SYNAGOGUES
Sociedade Israelita da Bahia
Rue Alvaro Tiberio 60
Telephone: (71) 3321 4204

Fax: (71) 3321 6412
Community centre and Zionist organisation are at the same address

Goiás
BRASILIA
EMBASSY
Embassy of Israel
Avenida das Nacoes Sul, Lote 38
Telephone: (61) 244 7675 / 7875
Fax: (61) 244 6129

SYNAGOGUES
ACIB
Entrequadras Norte 305-306, Lote A
Telephone: (61) 273 855
Fax: (61) 366 3651
Community centre is at the same address

Minas Gerais
BELO HORIZONTE
COMMUNITY ORGANISATIONS
Associacao Israelita Brasileira
Rua Rio Grande do Norte 477
Telephone: (31) 3224 2129
Fax: (31) 3224 2129
Supervision: Henry Katina

União israelita de Belo Horizonte
Rua Pernambucco 326
Telephone: (31) 3213-7759
Fax: (31) 3226-7848
Email: uibh@hotmail.com

CONTACT INFORMATION
Lojinha do Beit Chabad
Av. Serzedelo Corrêa 276
Telephone: (31) 241 2250

MIKVAOT
Mikvaot
Rua Rio Grande do Norte 477
Telephone: (31) 3224 2129

SYNAGOGUES
Reform
Congregacao Israelita Mineira
Rua Rio Grande Norte 477
Telephone: (31) 3224 2129
Fax: (31) 3224 2129

Para
BELÉM
COMMUNITY ORGANISATIONS
Community Centre
Travessa Dr. Moraes 37
Telephone: (91) 222 3184

SYNAGOGUES
Eshel Avraham
Travessa Campos Sales 733
Shaar Hashamaim
Rua Alcipreste Manoel Theodoro 842

Parana
CURITIBA
COMMUNITY CLUB AND JEWISH FEDERATION
Centro Israelita do Parna
Rua Mateus Leme 1431 80530
Telephone: (41) 338 7575
Fax: (41) 338 7922

SYNAGOGUES
Orthodox
Francisco Frischmann
Rua Cruz Machado 126
Telephone: (41) 224 5218
Fax: (41) 224 8172

Pernambuco
RECIFE
COMMUNITY ORGANISATIONS
Community Centre
Rua da Gloria 215

SYNAGOGUES
Synagogue Israelita do Recife
Rua Martin Junior 29 51011-000
Telephone: (81) 3222 0431
Supervision: Dr Jacques Ribemboim

Rio de Janeiro
CAMPOS
COMMUNITY ORGANISATIONS
Community Centre
Rua 13 de Maio 52

GREATER RIO DE JANEIRO
The old Jewish area is situated around Rua Alfandega. The country's first Ashkenazi Synagogue (Grande Templo Israelite) is an imposing building which was renovated in 1986.

BUTCHERS
Frigorifico
Rua Ronald Carvalho 265, Copacabana 22021-020
Telephone: (21) 295 7341
Supervision: Rav Stauber

Meat
Kosher House
Rua Anita Garibaldi 37A, Copacabana
Telephone: (21) 255 3891

COMMUNITY ORGANISATIONS
Confederacao Israelita de Brazil (CONIB)
Avenida Nilo Pecanha 50
Telephone: (21) 240 0034
Fax: (21) 240 2717
Organizaco Israelita do Eatado do Rio de Janeiro
Rua Tenente Possolo 8
Rabinado do Rio de Janeiro
Rua Pompeu Loureiro 40, Copacabana 22061
Telephone: (21) 2256 3587
Fax: (21) 2256 358
Email: rabinatorio@uol.com.br

CULTURAL ORGANISATIONS
ASA–Associacao Scholem Aleichem
Rua Sao Clemente 155, Botafogo 22260
Telephone: (21) 2539 7740
Fax: (21) 2266 1980
Website: www.asa.org.br
The institution is dedicated to promoting cultural events (seminars, debates, video exhibitions, etc.)

EMBASSY
Consul General of Israel
Avenida Copacabana 680
Telephone: (21) 255 5432

GROCERIES
Kosher House
Rua Antia Garibaldi 37 lj.A, Copacabana
Telephone: (21) 255-3891

MIKVAOT
Kehilat Yaakov
Rua Capelao Alvares da Silva 15, Copacabana 22041
Telephone: (21) 2236 3922

MUSEUMS
Museu Judaico do Rio de Janeiro
Rua México 90, sala 110, Cep:20031-141
Telephone: (21) 2524 6451
Fax: (21) 2240 1598
Email: presidente@museujudaico.org.br

RESTAURANTS
Cafeteria in Rabinate Paladar Judaico
Rua Pompeu Loureiro 40, Copacabana
Telephone: (21) 2256 3587
Hours: 10am to 5pm Sunday to Thursday

SYNAGOGUES
Liberal
Associaca Religiosa Israelita
Rua General Severiano 170, Botafogo 22290
Telephone: (21) 2543 6320; 2542 5598
Fax: (21) 2542 6499

Orthodox
Aqudat Israel
Rua Nascimento Silva 109, Ipanema 22421-020
Telephone: (21) 2267 5567
Fax: (21) 2267 5567

Beith Chabad of Rio de Janeiro
Rua Pompeu Loureiro No 40, Copacabana
Telephone: (21) 2256 3587

Grande Templo Israelita
Rua Tenente Possolo 8, Centro 20230
Telephone: (21) 232 3656

Kehilat Yaakov
Rua Capelao Alvares da Silva, Copacabana 22041

NITEROI
COMMUNITY ORGANISATIONS
Centro Israelita
Rua Visconde do Urugui 255 24030

Sociedade Hebraica
Rua Alveres de Azevedo 185, Icarai 24220

PETROPOLIS
RELIGIOUS ORGANISATIONS
Machane Israel Yeshiva
Rua Duarte de Silveira 1246 25600
Telephone: (242) 454 952

SYNAGOGUES
Sinagoga Israelita Brasileira
Rua Aureliano Coutinho 48 25600

Rio Grande do Sul
ERECHIM
Erechim Synagogue
Avenida Pedro Pinto de Souza 131

PASSO FUNDO
Passo Fundo Synagogue
Rua General Osório 1049

PELOTAS
Pelotas Synagogue
Rua Santos Dumont 303

PORTO ALEGRE
BUTCHERS
Kosher Butcher
Rua Fernandes Viera 518
Telephone: (51) 250 441

CULTURAL ORGANISATIONS
**Instituto Cultural Judaico Marc Chagall
Projeto Memoria**
Rua Dom Pedro II, 1220, sala 216
Telephone: (51) 343 5748

MIKVAOT
Mikva
Rua Francisco Ferrer 170
Telephone: (51) 3335 1264
Fax: (51) 3335 1264
Mobile Phone: 8119 3727 / 0349
Email: liberowpoa@hotmail.com
Supervision: Rabbi Mendel Liberow, Chabad Rabbi

MUSEUMS
Museu Judaico
Rua Joao Telles 329
Telephone: (51) 226 0379

RELIGIOUS ORGANISATIONS
City Rabbinate
Rua Henrique Dias 73
Telephone: (51) 219 649

SYNAGOGUES
Liberal
**SIBRA - Sociedade Israelita Brasileira de
Cultura e Beneficência**
Mariante 772 90430-180
Telephone: (51) 3331 8133
Fax: (51) 3330 4305
Email: sibrars@terra.com.br
Website: www.sibra.org.br
Supervision: Prof. Guershon Kwasniewski
Services on Shabbat and Holidays

Orthodox
Beit Chabad
Rua Felipe Camarao 748
Telephone: (51) 3335 1264
Mobile Phone: 8119 0349
Email: liberowpoa@hotmail.com
Website: www.seminary.com.br
Daily services

Centro Israelita Porto Alegrense
Rua Henrique Dias 73
Telephone: (51) 228 1935
Daily services

Linath Ha-Tzedek
Rua Bento Figueredo 55
Telephone: (51) 3013 8526
Fax: (51) 3392 1922
Mobile Phone: (51) 9999 5631
Email: presmad@vol.com.br
Supervision: Daniel Presman
Daily services
Food (kosher)

Poilisher Farband
Rua Joao Telles 329
Telephone: (51) 226 0379
Daily services

Uniao Isralita Porto Algrense
Rua Dr Barros Cassal 750
Telephone: (51) 3311 6515; 3312 4713
Fax: (51) 3311 5886
Supervision: Rabino Prof. Ruben Najmanovitch
Daily services

Sephardi
Centro Hebraico Riograndense
Rua Cel. Machado 1008
Services on Shabbat only

Sao Paulo

CAMPINAS
Beth Yacob Campinas
Rua Barreto Leme 1203
Telephone: (19) 231 4908

GUARUJA
Beit Yaacov
Avenida Leomil 628
Telephone: (13) 387 2033

MOGI DAS CRUZES
COMMUNITY ORGANISATIONS
Jewish Society
Rua Dep. Deodato Wertheiner 421
Telephone: (11) 469 2505

SANTO ANDRE
SYNAGOGUES
Beit Chabad
Rua 11 de Junho 172
Telephone: (11) 449 1568

SANTOS
COMMUNITY ORGANISATIONS
Club
Rua Cons. Neblas 254
Telephone: (13) 329 016

SYNAGOGUES
Beit Sion
Rua Borges 264

Sinagoga Beit Jacob
Rua Campos Sales 137

SAO CAETANO DO SUL
Sociedade Religiosa S. Caetano do Sul
Rua Para 67
Telephone: (11) 442 3514

SAO JOSE DOS CAMPOS
Beit Chabad - Assibrave - São José dos Campos
Rua Republica do Ira 91 12.216-600
Telephone: (12) 3951-0014
Email: assibrave@gmail.com
Supervision: Rabino Natan Stulman

SAO PAULO
Many *conversos* came to Sao Paulo to escape the Inquisition, which was centred in northern Brazil. A number rose to positions of importance.

By 1972 the Jews of Sao Paulo built the Albert Einstein hospital as a contribution to the public health service.

BAKERIES
Matok Bakery
Al. Barros 921
Telephone: (11) 667 514
Supervision: Rabbi I. Dichi

Mazal Tov
Rua Peixoto Gomide 1724 01409-001
Telephone: (11) 3061 0179
Fax: (11) 3061 0358

BOOKSELLERS
Livraria Sêfer
Alameda Barros, 893 01232-001
Telephone: (11) 3826 1366
Fax: (11) 3826 4508
Website: wwww.sefer.com.br
Bookseller and Judaica

BUTCHERS
Casa de Carnes Casher
Rua Fortunato 241
Telephone: (11) 221 2240
Supervision: Rabbi Elyahu B. Valt

Kosher Express
Rua Tupi No 506, Higienopolis 01233-000
Telephone: (11) 3367 0863
Fax: (11) 3825 4986

Mehadrin
Rua Sao Vicente de Paulo
Telephone: (11) 679 090
Supervision: Rabbi M.A. Iliovitz

Mehadrin
Rua Prates 689
Telephone: (11) 228 1771
Supervision: Rabbi M.A. Lliovitz

EMBASSY
Consul General of Israel
Rua Luis Coelho 308, 7th Floor
Telephone: (11) 257 2111/2814

GROCERIES
All Kosher
Rua Albuquerque Lins 1170
Telephone: (11) 3825 1131

Casa Santa Luzia
Al. Lorena 1471 01424001
Telephone: (11) 3897 5000
Fax: (11) 3088 0663
Website: www.santaluzia.com.br

Casas Menora
Rua Guarani 114
Telephone: (11) 228 6105

Kosher Mart
Rua Tenente Pena 187, Bom Retiro
Telephone: (11) 221 7299
Website: www.koshermart.com.br

Mazal Tov
Rua Peixoto Gomide 1724 01409-001
Telephone: (11) 3061 0179
Fax: (11) 3061 0358

Zilanna
Rua Itambé 506
Telephone: (11) 257 8671

MEDIA
Newspapers
O Hebreu
Rua Cunha Gago 158 05421-000
Telephone: (11) 3819 1616
Fax: (11) 3819 1616
Website: www.brasiljudaico.com.br
Monthly

Tribuna Judaico
Rua Tanabi 299 05002-010
Telephone: (11) 3871 3234/3873 3020/3862 9074
Fax: (11) 3871 3234
Weekly

Periodical
Morashá Magazine
Rua Dr Veiga Filho 547, Higienópolis 05607-000
Telephone: (11) 3825 9784
Fax: (11) 3030 5630
Email: morasha@uol.com.br
Website: www.morasha.com
Instituto Morashá de Cultura

MIKVAOT
Beit Yaacov Synagogue
Rua Dr Veiga Filho 547, Higienópolis 01229-000
Telephone: (11) 3662 2154
Fax: (11) 3662 2154
Email: morasha@uol.com.br

Congregacao Monte Sinai
Rua Piaui 624, Higienópolis 01241-000
Telephone: (11) 3824 9229
Fax: (11) 3824 9229

Micre Taharat Menachem-Perdizes
Rua Dr. Manoel Maria Tourinho 261
Telephone: (11) 3865 0615
By appointment only

Mikva Maayanei Esther
Rua Melo Alves 580 01417-010
Telephone: (11) 3081 3081
Fax: (11) 3060 9778
Website: www.chabad.org.br

Orthodox
Congregacao Mekor Haim
Rua Sao Vicente de Paulo 276 01229-010
Telephone: (11) 3662 6238; 3826 7699
Fax: (11) 3666 6960
Email: revista_nascente@hotmail.com
Supervision: Rabbi Yitschak Dichi Shelita

RELIGIOUS ORGANISATIONS
Comunidade Israelita Ortodoxa de Sao Paulo
Rua Haddock Lobo 1091 01414-003
Telephone: (11) 3062 1562; 3082 1562
Fax: (11) 3064 0302
Rabbi M A Iliovits

Rabanut- Rabino Elyahu Baruch Valt
Rua Corre de Melo 84 cj 308
Telephone: (11) 3331 5642
Fax: (11) 3064 9054
Email: ravvalt@hotmail.com
Office hours: 9am to 1pm weekdays

RESTAURANTS
Hebraica Kosher Restaurant and the Buffet Mosico
Rua Hungria 1000
Telephone: (11) 3815 6788; 3818 8831
Fax: (11) 3815 6980
Supervision: Rabbi Elyahu B. Valt
Buffet Mosaico inside the Hebraica Sao Paulo club. Closed Mondays, open Saturday night 90 minutes after Shabbat.

Restaurante Kosher Delight
Rua Baronesa de Ita 436
Telephone: (11) 3661 3106

Meat
Bero
Rua Peixoto Gomide 2020
Telephone: (11) 3086 2808
Fax: (11) 3086 2809

Milk
Cantina Do Bero
Rua Pe. Joao Manoel, 881
Telephone: (11) 3064 9022
Open from Sunday to Thursday, 6pm until 11.30pm. Also delivers.

Milk and Parve
Jacky Gourmet Café
Rua Rosa e Silva 146, Higienópolis
Telephone: (11) 3823 3537
Fax: (11) 3664 7034
Supervision: Ha Rav Y.D. Horowitz Shlita.

SYNAGOGUE
Synagogue Beit Yaacov - Bela Cintra
Rua Antonio Carlos, 550 Consolação 01309-010
Telephone: (11) 3258-7931
Email: morasha@uol.com.br
Central organisation: Congregação e Beneficência Sefardi Paulista

SYNAGOGUES

Conservative
Comunidade Shalom
Rua Coronel Joaquim Ferreira Lobo 195 04544-150
Telephone: (11) 3849 1477
Fax: (11) 3849 1477

Hasidic
Uniao Ortodoxa Judaica
Rua Mamore 597
Telephone: (11) 3224 8639
Fax: (11) 3224 9029

Liberal
Congregacao Israelita Paulista
Rua Antonio Carlos 653 01309-011
Telephone: (11) 2808 6299
Fax: (11) 2808 6260
Email: cip@cip.org.br
Website: www.cip.com.br

Orthodox
Beit Chabad Augusta
Rua Augusta 259 01305-000
Telephone: (11) 258 7173

Beit Chabad Central
Rua Melo Alves 580 01417-010
Telephone: (11) 3081 3081
Fax: (11) 3060 9778
Website: www.chabad.org.br

Beit Chabad Perdizes
Rua Man. Maria Tourinho, 261
Telephone: (11) 3865 0615

Beit Yaacov
Rua Dr Veiga Filho 547, Higienópolis 01229-000
Telephone: (11) 3662 2154
Fax: (11) 3662 2154
Email: morasha@uol.com.br
Central organisation: Congregação e Beneficência Sefardi Paulista

Congregacao Mekor Haim
Rua Sao Vicente de Paulo 276 01229-010
Telephone: (11) 3826 7699
Fax: (11) 3666-6960
Email: revista_nascente@hotmail.com
Supervision: Rabbi Yitschak Dichi Shelita

Sephardi
Templo Israelita Brasileiro Ohel Yaacov
Rua Abolicao 457
Telephone: (11) 606 9982
Fax: (11) 227 6793

TRAVEL AGENCIES
Sharontur
Rua Sergipe 475/607~608 Higienópolis 01243-001
Telephone: (11) 3826 8388
Fax: (11) 3825 3828
Website: www.sharontur.com.br

Open: 8am to 6pm. Closed Shabat and Sunday.
International & domestic tickets. Car rental, exchange, hotel reservations. Languages spoken: English, Hebrew, Spanish. Contact person: Mr Dov Smaletz

Sharontur
Rua Correa de Melo, Bom Retiro 01125-001
Telephone: (11) 3223 8388
Fax: (11) 3331 5036
Website: www.sharontur.com.br
Open 8am to 6pm. Closed Shabat (Saturday) & Sunday.
International and domestic tickets. Car rental, exchange, hotel reservations. Contact: Dov Smaletz

Vertice
Rua Sao Bento 545/10 01011-100
Telephone: (11) 3115 1970
Fax: (11) 3115 1970

SOROCABA
SYNAGOGUES
Community Centre
Rua Dom Pedro II 56
Telephone: (11) 313 168

BULGARIA

Dating back to the Byzantine conquest, the community in Bulgaria was established by Greek Jews in Serdica (Sofia, the capital). The Jewish community grew when the Bulgarian state was founded in 681. Czar Ivan Alexander (1331–71) had a Jewish wife who converted to Christianity.

The community has included eminent rabbinic commentators, such as Rabbi Dosa Ajevani and Joseph Caro, the codifier of the Shulchan Aruch who escaped to Bulgaria after the expulsion from Spain. The various Jewish groups joined to form a unified Sephardi community in the late seventeenth century.

About 50,000 Jews lived in Bulgaria in 1939. Bulgaria joined the war on the side of Germany but, despite much pressure from the Nazis, the government and general population refused to allow Bulgarian Jews to be deported. Only Jews from Macedonia and Thrace, then occupied by Bulgaria, were deported. Despite being saved, most of the community emigrated to Israel after the war. The 10 per cent who remained were then under the control of the communists and had little contact with the outside world.

Since the fall of communism, the community has been reconstituted and now has synagogues in Sofia and Plovdiv. The community is ageing, although 100 children attend a Sunday school run by the Shalom Organisation, the central Jewish organisation for Bulgaria.

GMT +2 hours
Country calling code: (+359)
Total population: 8,306,000
Jewish population: 3,000
Emergency telephone: (police–166) (fire–160) (ambulance–159)
Electricity voltage: 220

PLOVDIV
LIBRARIES
Library and House of Culture
Vladimir Zaimov Street 20
Telephone: (32) 761 376

SYNAGOGUES
Sephardi
Zion Synagogue
Tsar Kalojan Street 15
In the courtyard of a large apartment complex

ROUSSE
Community Centre
Ivan Vazoz Square 4
Telephone: (82) 270 540

SOFIA
About half of Bulgarian Jewry lives in Sofia. The Great Synagogue of 1878 ranks among the largest of Sephardi synagogues.

CEMETERIES
Jewish Cemetery
Orlandovtzi suburb
Take a tram (No2, 10 or 14) to the last stop for this large Jewish cemetery.

COMMUNITY CENTRE
The Rohr Chabad Jewish Community Centre
38 Stara Planina Street 1504
Telephone: (2) 944 3380/3562/3538
Fax: (2) 944 3380/3562/3538

COMMUNITY ORGANISATIONS
Social & Cultural Organisation of Bulgarian Jews
Shalom, Alexander Stambolisky Street 50
Telephone: (2) 870 163
Publishes a periodica *Evreiski Vesti* and a yearbook. It also maintains a museum devoted to the rescue of Bulgarian Jews, 1941–1944. At the same address are the offices of El Al, the Joint and the Jewish Agency.

EMBASSY
Embassy of the State of Israel
1 Bulgaria Square, NDK-Admin. building, 7th Floor 1463
Telephone: (2) 951 5044
Fax: (2) 952 1101
Website: www.sofia.mfa.gov.il
Hours of opening: Consular Section Mon to Fri 9.30am to 12.30pm

RELIGIOUS ORGANISATIONS
Central Jewish Religious Council
Ekzarh Josef Street 16 1000
Telephone: (2) 983 1273
Fax: (2) 983 5085
Website: www.sofiasynagogue.com

RESTAURANTS
Kosher Restaurant
Sofia Synagogue, Ekzarh Josef St. 16
Telephone: (2) 400 6355

SYNAGOGUES
Sofia Synagogue
Ekzarh Josef Street 16
Telephone: (2) 983 5085/1273
Fax: (2) 985 5085
Website: www.sofiasynagogue.com
The Sofia synagogue is the third largest in Europe and was designed by Austrian architect Grunanger in a Spanish-Moresque style to resemble the Vienna synagogue destroyed by the Nazis. It dates back to 1909, when Tsar Ferdinand attended its opening ceremony
Religious services are held each day at 8am and on Shabbat at 10am. The synagogue offers kosher meat, butter and various Sephardic dishes at its restaurant.

CANADA

The Jewish settlement of Canada began with the British expansion into Canada. In 1760, the Shearith Israel synagogue was founded in Montreal, and in 1832 Jews received full civil rights. In the 1850s the community began to spread from Montreal to Toronto and Hamilton.

The community grew throughout the early twentieth century from 16,000 in 1900 to 126,000 in 1921. After the Second World War Jewish immigration increased, and by 1961 the population was 260,000.

The headquarters of the Canadian Jewish Congress is in Montreal. This is the main national organisation for Canadian Jewry, and the community is provided with a full range of services, with Jewish schools, yeshivot, newspapers and the unique (in the Americas) Montreal Jewish Library. There are also several kosher restaurants.

GMT -3 to -8 hours
Country calling code: (+1)
Total population: 30,491,000
Jewish population: 365,000
Emergency telephone: (police–911) (fire–911) (ambulance–911)
In remote area calls have to be made via the operator.
Electricity voltage: 110

Alberta
CALGARY
BAKERIES
Barel's Bakery & Nosh
131, 2515 - 90th Avenue SW T2V 0L8
Telephone: (403) 238 5300
Fax: (403) 238 3023
Email: barels@shaw.ca
Website: www.barelsbakery.com
Supervision: Calgary Kosher
Hours of operation: Sunday 10am to 2pm, Monday to Wednesday 9am to 6pm, Thursday 9am to 7pm, Friday 8am to 5pm (winter 8am to 4pm). Closed Shabbat. Completely nut free and Parve.
Completely nut free & Parve. A wide range of breads, pastries, prepared meals, dry goods and fresh made pareve meals by order. Please contact to discuss your needs.
COMMUNITY ORGANISATIONS
Calgary Jewish Community Council
1607 90th Avenue S.W. T2V 4V7
Telephone: (403) 253 8600
Fax: (403) 253 7915
Website: www.jewishcalgary.org

DELICATESSEN
Izzy's Kosher Meats and Deli
2515 90th Avenue S.W. T2V 0L8
Telephone: (403) 251 2552
Fax: (403) 281 3322

HOTELS
Carriage House Inn
9030 Macleod Trail South
Telephone: (403) 253 1101
Supervision: Vaad Hakashrus of Calgary

RELIGIOUS ORGANISATIONS
Calgary Kosher
1607-90 Avenue SW T2V 4V7
Telephone: (403) 444 3158
Fax: (403) 253 7915
Email: calgarykosher@cjcc.ca
Regional kosher agency. Founded in 1980. Supervises 20 companies.

RESTAURANTS
Karen's Café
Calgary Jewish Centre, 1607 90th Avenue S.W.
Telephone: (403) 255 5311
Hours: Monday to Thursday, 10am to 7pm; Friday, 10am to 1pm. Closed on Sunday.

SYNAGOGUES
Conservative
Beth Tzedec Congregation
1325 Glenmore Trail S.W. T2V 4Y8
Telephone: (403) 255 8688
Fax: (403) 252 8319
Email: info@bethtzedec.ca
Website: www.bethtzedec.ca/

Orthodox
Congregation House of Jacob-Mikveh Israel
1613 92nd Avenue, SW T2V 5C9
Telephone: (403) 259 3230
Fax: (403) 259 3240
Website: www.hojmi.org

Orthodox Chabad
Chabad Lubavitch of Alberta
28-523 Woodpark Boulevard T2W 4J3
Telephone: (403) 238 4880
Fax: (403) 281 0338
Website: www.chabadalberta.org

Reform
Temple B'nai Tikvah
Calgary Jewish Centre, 1607 90th Avenue S.W. T2V 5C9
Telephone: (403) 252 1654
Fax: (403) 252 1709

EDMONTON
COMMUNITY ORGANISATIONS
Edmonton Jewish Federation
7200 156th Street T5R 1X3
Telephone: (780) 487 0585
Fax: (780) 482 1854
Contact Gayle Tailman, Director, for additional information

Shoshana Szlachter
B'nai Brith, Western Region Director, 7200-156
Street T5R 1X3
Telephone: (780) 481 6939
Fax: (780) 481 1854

MEDIA
Newspapers
Edmonton Jewish Life
7200 156th Street T5R 1X3
Telephone: (780) 488 7276
Fax: (780) 484 4978

Edmonton Jewish News
#330, 10036 Jasper Avenue T5J 2W2
Telephone: (780) 421 7983
Fax: (780) 424 3951

SYNAGOGUES
Conservative
Beth Shalom
11916 Jasper Avenue T5K 0N9
Telephone: (780) 488 6333
Fax: (780) 488 6259
Website: www.bethshalomedmonton.org

Orthodox
Beth Israel Synagogue
131 Wolf Willow Road T5T 7T7
Telephone: (780) 488 2840
Fax: (780) 482 2470
Website: www.edmontonbethisrael.org

Chabad Lubavitch
502 Wolf Willow Road
Telephone: (780) 486 7244
Fax: (780) 486 7243
Email: chabad@shaw.ca
Website: www.chabadedmonton.org
Mailing address: 84 Westridge Road Edmonton Alberta. T5T
1B6

Reform
Temple Beth Ora
7200 156th Street T5R 1X3
Telephone: (780) 487 4817
Fax: (780) 481 1854
Email: tboffice@shaw.ca
Website: www.templebethora.org
Central organisation: Union for Reform Judaism
Services: Every Friday evening, First Saturday morning of
the month.

British Columbia

COQUITLAM
Sha'arei Mizrah
2860 Dewdney Trunk Road V3C 2H9
Telephone: (604) 552 7221
Fax: (604) 552 7201
Website: www.burquest.org
Mailing Address: B3-1410 Parkway Boulevard, #14
Coquitlam, BC V3E 3J7

KELOWNA
Traditional
Beth Shalom Sanctuary
OJCC, 102 Glenmore Road North V1V 2E2
Telephone: (250) 862 2305
Fax: (250) 862 2365
Email: shalom@shawcable.com
Website: www.ojcc.ca

RICHMOND
BAKERIES
Garden City Bakery
#360-9100 Blundell Road
Telephone: (604) 244 7888

SYNAGOGUES
Conservative
Beth Tikvah
9711 Geal Road V7E 1R4
Telephone: (604) 271 6262
Fax: (604) 271 6270
Website: www.bitikvah.ca

Hasidic
Chabad of Richmond
200-4775 Blundell Road
Telephone: (604) 277 6427
Fax: (604) 263 7934
Website: www.chabadrichmond.com

Orthodox
Eitz Chaim
8080 Fraces Road V6Y 1A4
Telephone: (604) 275 0007
Fax: (604) 277 2225

SURREY
Chabad
The Center for Judaism of the Lower Fraser Valley,
2351 128th Street V4A 3W1
Telephone: (604) 542 5454
Website: www.centerforjudaism.org

VANCOUVER
The most famous of early Jewish settlers were
the Oppenheimer brothers who settled there the
year the city was founded. David Oppenheimer
was the city's second mayor. The city's first
synagogue was built in 1912, although of
course services had been held much earlier.

BAKERIES
Sabra Bakery
3844 Oak Street
Telephone: (604) 733 4912

CONTACT INFORMATION
Shalom BC - Jewish Information, Referral, Welcome Centre & Volunteer Centre
950 West 41st Avenue V5Z 2N7
Telephone: (604) 257 5111 ext 238
Fax: (604) 257 5119
Email: info@shalombc.org
Website: www.shalombc.org
Hours: Monday to Thursday 9am to 4pm, Friday 9am to Shabbat Closing
Languages: English, French, Russian, Hebrew, Spanish.
Provides current information about Jewish resources, practices and activities in BC and will make referrals to appropriate agencies and/or organizations. We also assist newcomers to Vancouver to integrate into the community.

RESTAURANTS
Green V Organics
2936 West Fourth Avenue
Telephone: (604) 730 1808
Supervision: British Columbia Kosher Council

Pinis Pizza
729 West 16th Avenue
Telephone: (604) 879 7100
Fax: (604) 733 4911
Mobile Phone: 778 8617 464

Dairy
Nava Creative Kosher Cuisine
950 West 41st Avenue V5Z 1Z2
Telephone: (604) 676 7579
Fax: (604) 676 7633
Email: nhi@shaw.ca
Supervision: BCK
Take out with pre-order Tel: 604 676 7632

Meat
Omnitsky Kosher B.C.
5866 Cambie Street
Telephone: (604) 321 1818
Fax: (604) 321 1817
Email: kosher@telus.net
Supervision: BCK
Glatt Kosher delicatessen with a full line of prepared foods and groceries

Sabra Kosher Restaurant and Bakery
3844 Oak Street V6H 2M5
Telephone: (604) 733 4912
Fax: (604) 733 4911
Website: www.sabrakosherestaurant.com
Take-out, eat-in and catering

SYNAGOGUES
Chabad of Downtown
1260 Howe Street
Telephone: (778) 371 9508; 688 1273
Email: rabbi@chabadcitycentre.com
Website: www.chabadcitycentre.com
The Downtown Synagogue is located in the heart of Downtown Vancouver, within walking distance from all the major hotels.

Schedule of Shabbat services: Friday Evening: 7pm - Kabbalat Shabbat Shabbat Morning: 10:00 am - Shacharit A Kiddush & light refreshments follow Shabbat Morning services. For more information, please visit our website at www.chabadcitycentre.com

Conservative
Beth Israel
4350 Oak Street V6H 2N7
Telephone: (604) 731 4161
Fax: (604) 731 4989
Website: www.bethisrael.ca

Congregation Har El
1305 Taylor Way, West Vancouver V7T 2Y7
Telephone: (604) 925 6488
Fax: (604) 922 8245
Website: www.harel.org
Friday 6pm; Shabbat 9.30am (seasonal). Visitors welcome.

Hasidic
Chadbad-Lubavitch
5750 Oak Street, V6M 2V9
Telephone: (604) 266 1313
Fax: (604) 263 7934
Website: www.lubavitchbc.com
Hours: Daily 7am; Shabbat 10am; Sunday 9am. Wheelchair access.

Jewish Renewal
Or Shalom
710 East 10th Avenue V5T 2A7
Telephone: (604) 872 1614
Fax: (604) 872 4406
Website: www.orshalom.bc.ca
Family Kabbalat Shabbat and potluck dinner monthly; Shabbat 10am. Wheelchair access.

Orthodox
Louis Brier Home
1055 West 41th Avenue V6M 1W9
Telephone: (604) 261 9376
Fax: (604) 266 8172

Schara Tzedeck
3476 Oak Street V6H 2L8
Telephone: (604) 736 7607
Fax: (604) 730 1621
Email: gabriella@scharatzedeck.com
Website: www.scharatzedeck.com
Central organisation: Affiliated with the OU
Hours: Monday and Thursday 7am; Tuesday, Wednesday and Friday 7.15am; Sunday 8:30 am; weekday sunset; Friday 7.30pm; Shabbat 9:00 am followed by Kiddush

Torat Hayim Community
483 Eastcot Road
Telephone: (604) 984 4168
Fax: (604) 984 4168
Website: www.hayim.com/sposor
Shabbat 10.30am followed by Kiddush

Reform
Temple Sholom
7190 Oak Street V6P 3Z9
Telephone: (604) 266 7190
Fax: (604) 266 7126
Email: templesholom@telus.net
Website: www.templesholom.ca
Hours: Monday and Wednesday 7.15am; Friday 8.15pm;
Shabbat 10am. Also has a gift shop.

Sephardi Orthodox
Beth Hamidrash
3231 Heather Street V5Z 3K4
Telephone: (604) 872 4222
Fax: (604) 872 4222

Traditional
Shaarey Tefilah
785 West 16th Avenue V5Z 158
Telephone: (604) 873 2700
Website: www.shaareytefilah.com
Friday evening, call for time, Shabbat and Sunday 9am.
Wheelchair access.

VICTORIA
COMMUNITY ORGANISATIONS
Victoria Jewish Community Centre
3636 Shelbourne Street
Telephone: (250) 477 7184
Fax: (250) 477 6283

SYNAGOGUES
Conservative
Congregation Emanu-El
1461 Blanshard V8W 2J3
Telephone: (250) 382 0615
Fax: (250) 380 3553
Email: office@congregation-emanu-el.org

Manitoba
WINNIPEG
BAKERIES
City Bread
238 Dufferin Avenue R2W 2X6
Telephone: (204) 949 2480

Gunn's
247 Selkirk Avenue R2W 2L5
Telephone: (204) 582 2364

BUTCHERS
Omnitsky's Kosher Foods
1428 Main Street R2W 3V4
Telephone: (204) 586 8271
Fax: (204) 586 8270
Website: www.omnitsky.com

COMMUNITY ORGANISATIONS
Asper Jewish Community Campus
C300- 123 Doncaster Street R3N 2B2
Telephone: (204) 477 7400
Fax: (204) 477 7405
Website: www.jewishwinnipeg.org
Home to Rady Jewish Community Centre, Winnipeg Jewish
Theatre, the Jewish Federation of Winnipeg, the, Jewish
Heritage Centre, and Schmoozer's Cafe

MIKVAOT
Herzlia-Adas Yeshurun
620 Brock R3N 0Z4
Telephone: (204) 489 6262
Fax: (204) 489 5899

MUSEUMS
Jewish Heritage Centre of Western Canada
C140-123 Doncaster Street R3N 2B2
Telephone: (204) 477 7460
Fax: (204) 477 7465
Website: www.jhcwc.org

RESTAURANTS
Garden Café
146 Magnus Avenue R2W 2B4
Telephone: (204) 586 9781

Dairy
Mariner Neptune
472 Dufferin
Telephone: (204) 589 5341

Schmoozer's Café
123 Doncaster Street R3N 2B2
Telephone: (204) 477 7418
Fax: (204) 477 7418
Located at the Asper Jewish Community Campus

SYNAGOGUES
Egalitarian Conservative
Beth Israel
1007 Sinclair Street R2V 3J5
Telephone: (204) 582 2353

Congregation Shaarey Zedek
561 Wellington Crescent R3M 0A6
Telephone: (204) 452 3711
Fax: (204) 474 1184
Website: www.shaareyzedek.mb.ca

Orthodox
Chabad Lubavitch
2095 Sinclair Street R2V 3K2
Telephone: (204) 339 8737
Fax: (204) 586 0487

Traditional
Chevra Mishnayes Synagogue
700 Jefferson Avenue R2V 0P6
Telephone: (204) 338 8503
Email: chevra@shaw.ca

New Brunswick
FREDERICTON
GROCERIES
Scoop & Save
934 Prospect
Telephone: (506) 459 7676

SYNAGOGUES
Orthodox
Sgoolai Israel
Westmorland Street E3B 3L7
Telephone: (506) 454 9698
Fax: (506) 452 8889
For information on availability of kosher food, call Rabbi
Yochanan Samuels: (506) 454 2717

MONCTON
Tiferes Israel
56 Steadman Street E1C 8L9
Telephone: (506) 858 0258
Fax: (506) 859 7983
Mikva on premises

SAINT JOHN
MUSEUMS
Saint John Jewish Historical Museum
29 Wellington Row E2L 3H4
Telephone: (506) 633 1833
Fax: (506) 642 9926
Email: sjjhm@nbnet.nb.ca
Website: www.personal.nbnet.nb.ca/sjjhm
Mid-May to late October 10am to 4pm Monday to Friday.
Also, during July and August, Sunday 1pm to 4pm or by
appointment. This is the only Jewish museum in the
Atlantic Provinces of Canada. There are eight display areas
as well as a library and archives. Guided tours available.

Please note that the museum will be relocating in 2009 -
unfortunately the new address is not available at this time,
however, updated information will be available on our
website or through the local tourist bureaus.

Newfoundland
ST. JOHN'S
SYNAGOGUES
Conservative
**Hebrew Congregation of Newfoundland &
Labrador (Beth El)**
Elizabeth Avenue A1B 1S3
Telephone: (709) 726 0480
Fax: (709) 777 7054.
Email: mpaul@mun.ca

Nova Scotia
GLACE BAY
Orthodox
Sons of Israel
1 Price Street B1A 3C8
Telephone: (902) 849 8605

HALIFAX
COMMUNITY ORGANISATIONS
Atlantic Jewish Council
5670 Spring Garden Road, Suite 508 B3J 1H6
Telephone: (902) 422 7491
Fax: (902) 425 3722
Email: atlanticjewishcouncil@theajc.ns.ca
Website: www.theajc.ns.ca
Covers Jewish communities in Nova Scotia, New
Brunswick, Prince Edward Island, Newfoundland and
Halifax. Also at this address: Canadian Jewish Congress,
Atlantic Region, Canadian Zionist Federation, United
Jewish Appeal, Canadian Young Judea, Hadassah, Jewish
National Fund, JSA (Jewish Student Association) for
Atlantic Canada.

GROCERIES
Barrington Meat Super Store
1145 Barrington
Telephone: (902) 492 3240
Sobeys
1120 Queen
Telephone: (902) 422 9884

SYNAGOGUES
Conservative
Shaar Shalom
1981 Oxford Street B3H 4A4
Telephone: (902) 423 5848
Fax: (902) 422 2580

Orthodox
Beth Israel
1480 Oxford Street B3H 3Y8
Telephone: (902) 422 1301
Fax: (902) 422 7251
Email: info@thebethisrael.com
Website: www.thebethisrael.com
Mikva on premises

TOURIST SITES
Pier 21 Canada's Immigration Museum
1055 Marginal Road B3H 4P6
Telephone: (902) 425 7770
Fax: (902) 423 4045
Website: www.pier21.ca
This newly restored award-winning National Historic Site
tells the stories of 1.5 million immigrants, war brides,
displaced people, evacuee children and Canadian military
service personnel who passed through its doors between
1928 and 1971. Now Canada's last surviving ocean
immigration shed, Pier 21 promises a dramatic exploration
of a critical part of our heritage through interactive exhibits,
multimedia presentations and activities for all ages.

SYDNEY
SYNAGOGUES
Conservative
Temple Sons of Israel
PO Box 311, Whitney Avenue B1P 6H2
Telephone: (902) 564 4650

YARMOUTH
CONTACT INFORMATION
R & V Indiq
13 Parade Street B5A 3A5
Will be happy to provide details of the local Jewish community

Ontario
BELLEVILLE
SYNAGOGUES
Conservative
Sons of Jacob
211 Victoria Avenue K8N 2C2
Telephone: (613) 962 1433
Website: www.iks.net/-soj

CHATHAM
Children of Jacob
29 Water Street N7M 3H4
Telephone: (519) 352 3544

HAMILTON
BUTCHERS
Hamilton Kosher Meats
889 King Street West L8S 1K5

COMMUNITY ORGANISATIONS
Hamilton Jewish Federation
1030 Lower Lions Club Road, Ancaster L9G 3N6
Telephone: (905) 648 0605
Fax: (905) 648 8350
Website: www.jewishhamilton.org

DELICATESSEN
Westdale Deli
893 King Street West L8S 1K5
Telephone: (905) 529 2605
Fax: (905) 529 2605

MEDIA
Newspapers
Hamilton Jewish News
PO Box 7528, Ancaster L9G 3N6
Telephone: (905) 648 0605
Fax: (905) 648 8388

SYNAGOGUES
Conservative
Beth Jacob
375 Aberdeen Avenue L8P 2R7
Telephone: (905) 522 1351

Orthodox
Adas Israel
125 Cline Avenue South L8S 1X2
Telephone: (905) 528 0039
Fax: (905) 528 0544
Email: office@adasisrael.ca

Website: www.adasisrael.ca
Supervision: Rabbi Daniel Green
Reform
Anshe Sholom
215 Cline Avenue North L8S 4A1
Telephone: (905) 528 0121
Fax: (905) 528 2994

KINGSTON
COMMUNITY ORGANISATIONS
B'nai B'rith Hillel Foundation
26 Barrie Street
Telephone: (613) 542 1120

SYNAGOGUES
Orthodox
Beth Israel
116 Centre Street K7L 4E6
Telephone: (613) 542 5012
Fax: (613) 542 9071
Website: www.members.kingston.net/bethisrl

Reform
Temple Iyr Hamelech
331 Union Street West K7L 2R3
Telephone: (613) 789 7022

KITCHENER
Orthodox
Beth Jacob
161 Stirling Avenue South N2G 3N8
Telephone: (519) 743 8422
Fax: (519) 743 9252

Reform
Temple Shalom
543 Beechwood N2T 2S8
Telephone: (519) 746 2234

LONDON
COMMUNITY ORGANISATIONS
London Jewish Federation
536 Huron Street N5Y 4J5
Telephone: (519) 673 3310

SYNAGOGUES
Conservative
Or Shalom
534 Huron Street N5Y 4J5
Telephone: (519) 438 3081
Fax: (519) 439 2994
Website: www.london.uscjhost.net

Orthodox
Congregation Beth Tefilah
1210 Adelaide Street North N5Y 4T6
Telephone: (519) 433 7081
Fax: (519) 433 0616
Website: www.bethtefilah.org
Mikva on premises

Reform
Temple Israel
605 Windermere Road N5X 2P1
Telephone: (519) 858 4400
Fax: (519) 858 2070
Website: www.uahc.org/congs/cd/cdool

MISSISSAUGA
Solel Congregation
2399 Folkway Drive L5L 2M6
Telephone: (905) 820 5915
Fax: (905) 820 1956

NIAGARA FALLS
B'nai Tikvah
5328 Ferry Street L2G 1R7
Telephone: (716) 354 3934

NORTH BAY
Conservative
Sons of Jacob
302 McIntyre Street West P1B 2Z1
Telephone: (705) 497 9288
Fax: (705) 497 9812
Friday evening services

OAKVILLE
Reform
Shaarei-Beth El Congregation
186 Morrison Road L6J 4J4
Telephone: (905) 849 6000
Fax: (905) 849 1134
Email: bobbie.sbe@bellnet.ca
Website: www.sbe.ca

OSHAWA
Orthodox
Beth Zion
144 King Street East L1H 1B6
Telephone: (905) 723 2353

OTTAWA
Ottawa is the capital of Canada and its fourth largest city. The first Jewish settler came in 1858 when Ottawa was still known as Bytown. Ottawa has always been strongly traditional, and has a growing community presently numbering around 13,000.

BAKERIES
Coffee Bar Dairy
Rideau Bakery
384 Rideau Street K1N 5Y8
Telephone: (613) 789 1019
Fax: (613) 789 2962
Supervision: Ottawa Vaad Ha'ir
Also serves dairy food

COMMUNITY ORGANISATIONS
Canadian Jewish Congress National Office
100 Sparks Street, Suite 650 K1P 5B7
Telephone: (613) 233 8703
Fax: (613) 233 8748
Email: canadianjewishcongress@cjc.ca
Website: www.cjc.ca

Jewish Federation of Ottawa.
21 Nadolny Sachs Private K2A 1R9
Telephone: (613) 798 4696
Fax: (613) 798 4695
Website: www.jewishottawa.org
Vaad Hakashruth located here for all kashrut information

EMBASSY
Embassy of Israel
Suite 1005, 50 O'Connor Street K1P 6L2
Telephone; (613) 567 6450
Fax: (613) 237 8865

MEDIA
Ottawa Jewish Bulletin
Telephone: (613) 798 4646
Fax: (613) 798 4730

RESTAURANTS
Dairy
Rideau Bakery
1666 Bank Street
Telephone: (613) 737 3356
Fax: (613) 789 2962
Supervision: Ottawa Vaad Hair
Also serves dairy food

Viva Pizza
Soloway JCC, 21 Nadolny Sachs Private
Telephone: (613) 798 9818

SYNAGOGUES
Young Israel of Ottawa
627 Kirkwood Avenue K1Z 5X5
Telephone: (613) 722 8304

Conservadox/Traditional
Beth Shalom
151 Chapel Street K1N 7Y2
Telephone: (613) 789 3501
Fax: (613) 789 4438
Website: www.bethshalom.ca
In our 2nd century of service to the community we may be the oldest synagogue structure in Ottawa, but we take a modern yet traditional approach to our faith. We are a shul for all ages and stages; there are plenty of reasons to join us in prayer, study and simcha. Currently celebrating its 50th year anniversary.

Conservative
Agudath Israel
1400 Coldrey Avenue K1Z 7P9
Telephone: (613) 728 3501
Fax: (613) 728 4468
Website: www.agudathisrael.net

Adath Shalom Congregation
31 Nadolny Sach Private K2A 1R9
Telephone: (613) 240 4564
Website: www.adath-shalom.ca
Central organisation: United Synagogue of Conservative Judaism
A Conservative Egalitarian congregation, an equal role for women and men in all aspects of ritual aspects is recognised. Regular services are member-led and a visiting Rabbi provides Rabbinical leadership at High Holy Day services and special Shabbat on weekends. Newcomers always welcome.

Orthodox
Beth Shalom West
15 Chartwell Avenue K2G 4K3
Telephone: (613) 723 1800
Fax: (613) 723 6567
Website: www.bethshalomwest.org

Machzikei Hadas
2310 Virginia Drive K1H 6S2
Telephone: (613) 521 9700
Fax: (613) 521 0067
Email: machzikei@magma.ca
Website: www.machzikeihadas.com
Opening hours: Monday-Thursday 9-4.00pm, Friday 9-2.00pm

Orthodox Community Ohev Yisroel
516 Rideau Street K1N 5Z6
Telephone: (613) 321 6200/565 6194
Email: heshel@science.uottawa.ca
Website: www.ohevyisroel.ca

Ottawa Torah Center Chabad
416 Amar Lane, Nepean K2J 0C2
Telephone: (613) 823 0866
Fax: (613) 823 7540
Website: www.ottawatorahcenter.com
Mailing address: 79 Stradwick Avenue, Nepean, Ontario K2J 2Z2

Reconstructionist
Ottawa Reconstructionist Havurah (ORH)
Suite 136, 99 Fifth Avenue K1S 5P5

Reform
Temple Israel
1301 Prince of Wales Drive K2C 1N2
Telephone: (613) 224 1802
Fax: (613) 224 0707
Website: www.templeisraelottawa.ca

Sephardi
Sephardi Association of Ottawa
PO Box 23111, 2121 Carling Avenue K2A 4E0
Telephone: (613) 729 2104

OWEN SOUND
Conservative
B'nai Ezekiel
313 11th Street East N4K 1V1
Telephone: (519) 376 8774

PETERBOROUGH
Beth Israel
Waller Street
Telephone: (705) 745 8398

RICHMOND HILL
Beth Rayim
9711 Bayview Avenue L4C 9X7
Telephone: (905) 770 7639

ST CATHARINE'S
Traditional
B'nai Israel
190 Church Street L2R 3E9
Telephone: (416) 685 6767
Fax: (416) 685 3100

SUDBURY
Shaar Hashomayim
158 John Street P3E 1P4
Telephone: (705) 673 0831

THORNHILL
BOOKSELLERS
Matana Judaica Inc.
180 Steeles Ave. W # 2B L4J 2L1
Telephone: (905) (905) 731 6543
Fax: (905) (905) 882 6196
Website: www.matanajudaica.ca

Judaica Giftware
Israel's the Judaica Centre
441 Clark Avenue West L4J 6W7
Telephone: (905) 881 1010
Fax: (905) 881 1016
Email: israelsjudaica@yahoo.ca
Website: www.israelsjudaica.com
Religious and secular books, Hebrew learning tools and books, giftware, Israeli art and Judaica, music, DVDs and computer software, kosher candy and honey.ds

RESTAURANTS
Cafe Sheli
7700 Bathurst Street
Telephone: (905) 762 0640
Website: www.cafesheli.com

Cookoos Inc.
7241 Bathhurst Street L4J 3W1
Telephone: (905) 886 8686

Dairy
King David Pizza, Bourekas, Falafel
531 Atkinson Avenue, Unit 3 L4J 8L7
Telephone: (905) 771 7077

My Zaidy's Pizza
441 Clark Avenue West L4J 6W8
Telephone: (905) 731 3029

Yehudale's Falafel & Pizza
7241 Bathurst Street
Telephone: (905) 889 1400

Meat
Miami Grill
441 Clark Avenue West L4J 6W7
Telephone: (905) 709 0096

THUNDER BAY

SYNAGOGUES

Orthodox
Shaarey Shomayim
627 Grey Street P7E 2E4
Telephone: (807) 622 4867

TORONTO

There have been over one and a half centuries of organised Jewish life in Toronto since its start in 1849. The Jewish population increased significantly during the 1980s, and now Toronto is home to almost half of Canada's Jews. There is a good range of Jewish facilities in the city.

BAKERIES
Carmel Bakery
3856 Bathurst Street
Telephone: (416) 633 5315

Dairy Treats Bakery
3522 Bathurst Street
Telephone: (416) 787 0309
Fax: (416) 787 1935
Website: www.dairytreats.com

Richman's Kosher Bakery
4119 Bathurst Street M3H 3P4
Telephone: (416) 636 9710
Email: jonah@richmansbakery.ca
Website: www.richmansbakery.ca
Supervision: COR Kasruth Council of Canada

BAKERIES AND RESTAURANT

Dairy
Isaac's Bakery & Cafe
221 Wilmington Avenue
Telephone: (416) 630 1678

Isaac's Bakery & Cafe
3390 Bathurst Street M6A 2B9
Telephone: (416) 789 7587
Fax: (416) 789 7620

BOOKSELLERS
Aleph Bet Judaica
3453 Bathurst Street M6A 2C5
Telephone: (416) 781 2133
Fax: (416) 781 1311

Israel's Judaica Centre
870 Eglinton Avenue West M6C 2B6
Telephone: (416) 256 1010

Email: israels@israelsjudaica.com
Website: www.israelsjudaica.com
Negev Importing Co Ltd
3509 Bathurst Street M6A 2C5
Telephone: (416) 781 9356
Toll free: 1 888 618 9356
Fax: (416) 781 0071
Website: www.negevjudaica.com

Judaica Giftware
Israel's the Judaica Centre
870 Eglinton Ave West M6C 2B6
Telephone: (416) 256 1010
Fax: (416) 256 0391
Email: israelsjudaica@yahoo.ca
Website: www.israelsjudaica.com
Religious and secular books, hebrew learning tools and books, giftware, Israeli art and Judaica, music, DVDs and computer software, kosher candy and honey.

CAFETERIA
Rachel's Centre Cafe
BJC 4588 Bathurst Street M2R 1W6
Telephone: (416) 638 0526

Second Cup (Baycrest)
3560 Bathurst Street M6A 2E1
Telephone: (416) 785 2500

Second Cup (BJC)
4588 Bathurst Street M2R 1W6
Telephone: (416) 636 1880

Dairy
Amazing Donuts
3772 Bathurst Street M3H 3M6
Telephone: (416) 398 7546
Fax: (416) 771 6253

Kosher
Oasis Cafe & Health Bar
130 King Street, Exchange Tower M5X 1A6
Telephone: (416) 368 8805
Website: www.oasiscafe.ca

COMMUNITY ORGANISATIONS
Bernard Betel (Seniors' Community Centre)
1003 Steeles Avenue West M2R 3T6
Telephone: (416) 225 2112
Fax: (416) 225 2097
Website: www.betelcentre.org
Centre operates a Conservative Synagogue and has two Sephardi congregations on site - Beth Yosef and Tehillat Yerushalayim

Kashruth Council of Canada-COR
3200 Dufferin Street, #308 M6A 3B2
Telephone: (416) 635 9550
Fax: (416) 635 8760
Website: www.cor.ca
Supervision: Kosher Supervisory Agency
All enquiries about kashrut here

CONTACT INFORMATION

Jewish Information Service of Greater Toronto – Centre for Jewish knowledge & Heritage of UJA Federation
4600 Bathurst Street, 4th floor M2R 3V2
Telephone: (416) 635 5600
Fax: (416) 849 1005
Email: jinfo@ujafed.org
Website: www.jewishtoronto.com
Information about the Jewish community in the Greater Toronto area, Canada including synagogues, kosher restaurants, sites of interest. Tourist information.

EMBASSY

Consul General of Israel
180 Bloor Street West, Suite 700 M5S 2V6
Telephone: (416) 640 8500
Fax: (416) 640 8555
Israel Government Tourist Office: (416) 964 3784.

MEDIA

Newspapers
Jewish Tribune
15 Hove Street, Downsview M3H 4Y8
Telephone: (416) 633 6224
Fax: (416) 633 6224

MEMORIAL

Holocaust Education & Memorial Centre
4600 Bathurst Street, Willowdale M2R 3V2
Telephone: (416) 635 2883
Fax: (416) 635 0925

MUSEUMS

The Morris & Sally Justein Heritage Museum
Baycrest Centre for Geriatric Care, 3560 Bathurst Street M6A 2E1
Telephone: (416) 785 2500 Ext 2802
Fax: (416) 785 4228
Email: pdickinson@baycrest.org
Website: www.baycrest.org/museum
One of the few Judaica museums in Canada. It has an active exhibit program.

RESTAURANT/COFFEE SHOP

Dairy
King David Pizza
219 Wilmington Avenue M3H 5K1
Telephone: (416) 636 3456

RESTAURANTS

Chinese
King Solomon's Table
3705 Chesswood Drive M3J 2P6
Telephone: (416) 630 1666
Fax: (416) 975 0987
Email: joe@glanelm.com
Website: www.kingsolomonstable.com
Supervision: COR
Open Monday to Thursday 12 to 10pm. Sunday 4pm to 10pm. Closed Friday and Saturday.

Dairy
Brooklyn Pizza
3016B Bathurst Street M6B 3B6
Telephone: (416) 789 4085

Dairy Treats Cafe
3522 Bathurst Street M6A 2C6
Telephone: (416) 787 0309
Fax: (416) 787 1935

King David Pizza
3020 Bathurst Street M6B 3B6
Telephone: (416) 781-1326

King Kosher Pizza & Sushi
3774 Bathurst Street M3H 3M6
Telephone: (416) 633 5678
Website: www.kingkosherpizza.com

Milk 'n' Honey
3457 Bathurst Street, Downsview M6A 2C5
Telephone: (416) 789 7651
Fax: (416) 789 4788

Not just Yogurt
7117 Bathurst Street
Telephone: (416) 764 2525

Not Just Yogurt
2997 Bathurst Street M6B 3B3
Telephone: (416) 782 2424

Omni Jewels & Java
2793 Bathurst Street
Telephone: (416) 783 2091
Fax: (416) 783 9026

Tov Li Pizza
5982 Bathurst Street, Willowdale M2R 1Z1
Telephone: (416) 650 9800

Kosher
Bistro Grande
1000 Eglington Avenue W M6C 2C5
Telephone: (416) 782 3302
Fax: (416) 782 3261
Website: www.bistrogrande.com

Marron
948 Eglinton Avenue M6C 2C2
Telephone: (416) 784 0128

Unami Fusion Dining
288 Eglinton Avenue W M4R 1B2
Telephone: (416) 483 9018
Fax: (416) 483 9016

Meat
Colonel Wong Restaurant
2825 Bathurst Street M6B 3A4
Telephone: (416) 784 9664
Supervision: COR
Authentic Chinese cuisine

Gladstones Bar
398 Eglinton Avenue W M5N 1A2
Telephone: (416) 487 9500

Hakerem Restaurant
3030 Bathurst Street M6B 3B6
Telephone: (416) 787 6504

Jerusalem One
3028 Bathurst Street M6B 3B6
Telephone: (416) 631 9602

Marky's Deli & Restaurant
280 Wilson Avenue M3H 1S8
Telephone: (416) 638 1081
Fax: (416) 636 0807
Supervision: C.O.R.
Family, full menu restaurant open till 1am

The Chicken Nest
3038 Bathurst Street M6B 4K2
Telephone: (416) 787 6378
Email: info@chickennest.ca
Website: www.chickennest.ca
Supervision: Glatt Kosher

Vegetarian
Tov-Liv Pizza & falafel
3519 Bathurst Street M6A 2C7
Telephone: (416) 784 9900

SYNAGOGUES
Conservative
Beth Tzedec Street
1700 Bathurst Street M5P 3K3
Telephone: (416) 781 3514
Fax: (416) 781 0150
Website: www.beth-tzedec.org

Orthodox
Anshei Minsk
10 St Andrew Street M5T 1K6
Telephone: (416) 595 5723
Fax: (416) 595 9586
Email: reachus@theminsk.com
Website: www.theminsk.com

Kiever Congregation
25 Bellevue Avenue M5T 2N5
Telephone: (416) 593 9956
Shabbat and Holiday services

Shaarei Shomayim
470 Glencairn Avenue M5N 1V8
Telephone: (416) 789 3213
Fax: (416) 789 1728
Email: info@shomayim.org
Website: www.shomayim.org
Supervision: Jessica Pelt

The Village Shul-Aish Hatorah Learning Centre
1072 Eglington Avenue West M6C 2E2
Telephone: (416) 785 1107
Fax: (416) 783 9870
Website: www.aishtoronto.com

Reform
Holy Blossom
1950 Bathurst Street M5P 3K9
Telephone: (416) 789 3291
Fax: (416) 789 9697
Website: www.holyblossom.org

WINDSOR
COMMUNITY ORGANISATIONS
Jewish Community Council
1641 Ouellette Avenue N8X 1K9
Telephone: (519) 973 1772

MEDIA
Periodical
Windsor Jewish Community Bulletin
Telephone: (519) 973 1774

SYNAGOGUES
Orthodox
Shaar Hashomayim
115 Giles Boulevard East N9A 4C1
Telephone: (519) 256 3123
Fax: (519) 256 3124

Shaarey Zedek
610 Giles Boulevard East N9A 4E2
Telephone: (519) 252 1594

Reform
Congregation Beth-El
2525 Mark Avenue N9E 2W2
Telephone: (519) 969 2422

Quebec

MONTREAL
1760 saw the arrival of the first Jews in Montreal as civilians attached to the British army. In the 1920s and 1930s the Boulevard St-Laurent was equivalent to London's East End or New York's Lower East Side. There are now just over 100,000 Jews in the city. Twenty percent of them are North African Sephardim.

BAKERIES
Adir Bakery
6795 Darlington
Telephone: (514) 342 1991

Andalos
266 Lebeau
Telephone: (514) 856 0983

Biscuit Adar
5458 Westminister
Telephone: (514) 484 1198

Cheskie
359 Bernard West
Telephone: (514) 271 2253

Cite Cashere
4747 Van Horne
Telephone: (514) 733 2838

Delice Cashere
4655 Van Horne
Telephone: (514) 733 5010

Montreal Kosher
7005 Victoria H4P 2N9
Telephone: (514) 739 3651
Fax: (514) 739 7278
Website: www.montrealkosherbakery.com
Supervision: Vaad Ha'ir

Montreal Kosher
2765 Van Horne, Widerton Shopping Centre
Telephone: 737 0393
Fax: 737 2427
Website: www.montrealkosherbakery.com
Supervision: Vaad Ha'ir

Montreal Kosher
2135 St. Louis, St. Laurent
Telephone: 747 5116
Website: www.montrealkosherbakery.com
Supervision: Vaad Ha'ir

New Homemade Kosher Bakery
6915 Querbes H3N 2B3
Telephone: (514) 270 5567
Fax: (514) 270 5041
6685 Victoria
Telephone:(514) 733 4141
5638 Westminister
Telephone: (514) 486 2024
Website: www.homemadekosher.com
Supervision: Vaad Ha'ir

Patisserie Chez Ma Souer
5095 Queen Mary
Telephone: (514) 737 2272

Renfels Bakery
2800 Bates
Telephone: (514) 733 5538

Take Away
Kosher Quality Bakery
5855 Victoria N3W 3R6
Telephone: (514) 731 7883
Fax: (514) 731 0205
Supervision: Glatt Kosher MK

BOOKSELLERS
Kotol Book & Gift Store
6414 Victoria Avenue H3W 2S6
Telephone: (514) 739 4142
Fax: (514) 739 7330

Rodal's Hebrew Book Store & Gift Shop
4689 Van Horne Avenue H3W 1H8
Telephone: (514) 733 1876
Fax: (514) 733 2373

COMMUNITY ORGANISATIONS
Federation CJA
5151 ch, de la Côte Ste-Catherine H3W 1M6
Telephone: (514) 735 3541
Operates the Jewish Information and Referral Service
(JIRS), Tel: 737 2221

Jewish Community Council of Montreal
6825 Decarie Boulevard H3W 3E4
Telephone: (514) 739 6363
Fax: (514) 739 7024
Email: semanuel@mk.ca
Website: www.mk.ca
Visitors requiring additional information about kosher
establishments should contact the Vaad Ha'r at the above
numbers. Also apply to them for a list of kosher butchers,
bakeries, caterers and restaurants.Rabbi Saul Emanuel
Executive Director

HOTELS
The Quality Hotel Midtown
6445 Decairie
Telephone: 1866 465 3800
Fax: (514) 739 3800
Mobile Phone: 514 739 3800
Email: sales@tac.ca
Website: www.qualityhotelmidtown.com

JUDAICA
Victoria Gift Shop
5875 Victoria Avenue H3W 2R6
Telephone: (514) 738 1414
Fax: (514) 737 6518

LIBRARIES
Archives
Jewish Public Library
1 Carre Cummings Square H3W 1M6
Telephone: (514) 345 2627
Fax: (514) 345 6477
Email: info@jplmontreal.org
Website: www.jewishpubliclibrary.org
Central organisation: Federation CJA
Public library: with primary focus on Judaica

MEDIA
Newspapers
The Canadian Jewish News
6900 Decarie Boulevard Suite 341 H3W 2T8
Telephone: (514) 735 2612
Fax: (514) 735 9090
Email: montreal@cjnews.com
Website: www.cjnews.com
Paid circulation weekly newspaper for the Canadian Jewish
population.Covers local, national and international and is
important to the Jewish community

RESTAURANTS

Cummings Jewish Centre for Seniors Cafeteria
5700 Westbury Avenue H3W 3E8
Telephone: (514) 342 1234
Fax: (514) 739 6899
Website: www.cummingscentre.org

Dairy
Bistrot Casa Linga
5095 Queen Mary H3W 1X4
Telephone: (514) 737 2272

Foxey's
5987A Victoria Avenue
Telephone: (514) 739 8777
Supervision: Vaad Ha'ir

Pizza Pita
5710 Victoria Avenue
Telephone: (514) 731 7482
Supervision: Vaad Ha'ir
Open 9.30am to 11.30pm daily, Saturday night until
2.30am

Tatty's Pizza
6540 Darlington
Telephone: (514) 734 8289
Fax: (514) 734 5046
Supervision: Vaad Ha'ir

Meat
El Morocco II
3450 Drummond Street
Telephone: (514) 844 6888 / 0203
Fax: (514) 844 1204
Supervision: Vaad Ha'ir
Open for lunch and dinner until 10pm

Ernie's & Ellie's Place
6900 Decarie Boulevard H3X 2T8
Telephone: (514) 344 4444
Fax: (514) 344 0001
Supervision: Vaad Ha'ir

Exodus Restaurants
5395 Queen Mary
Telephone: (514) 483 6610
Fax: (514) 483 6810
Supervision: Vaad Ha'ir

SYNAGOGUES

**Canadian Jewish Congress National
Headquarters**
Samuel Bronfman House, 1590 Docteur Penfield
Avenue H3G 1C5
Telephone: (514) 931 7531
Fax: (514) 931 0548
Contact to find out which of the many synagogues in
Montreal is nearest

QUEBEC CITY
Orthodox
Beth Israel Ohev Shalom
1251 avenue de Merici G1R 1Y2
Telephone: (418) 688 3277
Email: rabbi@jquebec.com
Website: www.jquebec.com
Kosher catering service:www.kosherquebec.com

TOURIST SITES
Beth Israel Ohev Shalom
Boulevard Rene Levesque, Saint-Foy
Telephone: (418) 688 3277
This is an official monument and historic site

STE. AGATHE DES MONTS
A resort in the Laurentian Mountains known as
the 'Catskills of Montreal' where members of
the Montreal community spend their summer
months.

SYNAGOGUES
Orthodox
House of Israel Congregation
31 rue Albert J8C 1Z6
Telephone: (819) 326 4320
Fax: (819) 326 8558
Mobile Phone: 514 918 9080
Website: www.houseofisrael.org
Supervision: Rabbi Emanuel Carlebach

Saskatchewan
REGINA
Conservative
Beth Jacob
4715 McTavish Street S4S 6H2
Telephone: (306) 757 8643
Fax: (306) 353 3499
Email: bethjacob@accesscomm.ca
Website: www.bethjacobsynagogue.com

Reform
Temple Beth Tikvah
Box 33048, Cathedral Post Office S4T 7X2
Website: www.uahc.org/cd/cd012

SASKATOON
Shir Chadash
610 Clarence South S7H 2E2
Telephone: (306) 242 3756

Conservative
Agudas Israel
715 McKinnon Avenue S7H 2G2
Telephone: (306) 343 7023
Fax: (306) 343 1244

CAYMAN ISLANDS

In addition to a very small permanent Jewish community there are a number of Jews who spend part of the year on the Islands.

GMT -5 hours
Country calling code: **(+1 345)**
Total population: **30,000**
Jewish population: **15**
Emergency telephone: **(police–911)** **(ambulance–555)**
Electricity voltage: **110**

GRAND CAYMAN
CONTACT INFORMATION
Jewish Community of the Cayman Islands
PO Box 72 KY1-1102
Telephone: 949 7739
Contact: Harvey De Souza

HOTELS
Britania-A Hyatt Beac, Villa & Golf Resort
30735 Seven Mile Beach
Telephone: 949 7440
Fax: 949 8032
Kosher meals are available-please request in advance if possible.

The Hyatt Regency Grand Cayman
Seven Mile Beach
Telephone: 949 1234
Fax: 949 8528
The hotel provides kosher foods; however, it is necessary to inform that kosher food is required

CEUTA

KASHRUT INFORMATION
Ceuta Kashrut Information
Calle Sargento Coriat 8

SYNAGOGUE
Ceuta Synagogue
Calle Sargento Colat 8

CHILE

The original Jewish settlers in Chile were *Conversos*. Rodrigo de Organos, a *Converso*, was the first European to enter the country in 1535. The Inquisition, however, curtailed the growth of the community.

The first legal Jewish immigration, albeit small, occurred only after Chile's independence in 1810. In 1914 the Jewish community numbered some 500, but this increased in the late 1930s with those refugees from Nazism who were able to avoid the strict immigration laws. Anti-semitism, however, also grew, and the *Comite Representativo* was formed to respond to it.

There is an umbrella organisation and a large Zionist body in Chile. Most of the community is not religious, but some keep kosher and there are several synagogues in the capital Santiago, and a few kosher shops. There are two Jewish schools and several Jewish newspapers are published.

GMT -4 hours
Country calling code: **(+56)**
Total population: **14,622.000**
Jewish population: **21,000**
Emergency telephone: **(police–133)** **(fire–132)** **(ambulance–131)**
Electricity voltage: **220**

ARICA
COMMUNITY ORGANISATIONS
Sociedad Israelita
Dr Herzl, Casilla 501

IQUIQUE
Comunidad Israelita
Playa Ligade 3263, Playa Brava

LA SERENA
Community Centre
Cordovez 652

SANTIAGO
The majority of Chilean Jews live in Santiago. The city has a couple of notable features in connection with its Jewish community. The Circulo Israelita Synagogue has an interesting stained glass design in its interior, and the 'Bomba Israel' is a fire service manned by volunteers who include a few Rabbis. Two of their fire engines carry the Chilean and Israeli flags.

BUTCHERS
Kosher Deli
Avenida Las Condes 8400
Telephone: (2) 251 3145; 848 6921
Fax: (2) 251 3149
Supervision: Jabad

EMBASSY
Embassy of Israel
San Sebastian 2812, Casilla 1224
Telephone: (2) 246 1570

RESTAURANTS
Meat
Mi Refugio
14345 Camino Farellones Street
Telephone: (2) 475 0948
Fax: (2) 325 4180
Email: shemtovkosher@yahoo.com
Supervision: Rabbi Shoshan Ghoori
Delivery 24 hours a day

SYNAGOGUES
Ashkenazi
Communidad Israelita de Santiago
Serrano 214-218

German
Sociedad Cultural Israelita B'nei Jisroel
Mar Jonico No 8860
Telephone: (2) 663 3300
Fax: (2) 663 3309
Website: www.bneisrael.cl

Hungarian
Maze
Pedro Bannen 0166
Telephone: (2) 274 2536

Orthodox
Bicur Joilim
Avenida Matte 624
Jabad (Chabad) Lubavitch
Los Catus 1575, La Dehesa
Telephone: (2) 228 2240

Sephardi
Maguen David
Avenida R. Lyon 812

TEMUCO
COMMUNITY ORGANISATIONS
Comunidad Israelita
General Cruz 355, P.O.Box: 38 47 90907
Telephone: (45) 210582

CHINA

There is archaeological evidence of a Jewish presence in China in the eighth century,but it is believed that their existance as a community only dates from the twelth century. The largest established community of around 1,000 was in Kaifeng. The first Kaifeng synagogue was built in 1163.

The Treaty of Nanking in 1842 opened Shanghai to trade. In 1845 Elias Sassoon pioneered the Jewish settlement of Shanghai. Many Baghdadi Jews followed and were under the protection of the British government. In due course they were in the forefront of the development of the city. A second community was formed later, mainly by Russians and Poles fleeing religious persecution. The final influx was refugees from Nazi oppression in the period 1933-39. Almost all the community left Shanghai after the Second World War. In 1999 a community was again established.

Hong Kong, previously listed as a separate entity but, since July 1997, again a region of China is included here.

GMT +8 hours
Country calling code: **(+86)**
Total population: **1,284,100,000**
Jewish population: **2,100**
Emergency telephone: **(police–110) (fire–119)**
Electricity voltage: **220/240**

BEIJING
COMMUNITY CENTRE
Mikvah
Rohr Family Chabad Community Centre
Grand Hills #262 Jing Shun Lu Chao Yang District
100015
Telephone: (10) 8470 8239 ext.200
Fax: (10) 8470 8221
Email: info@chabadbeijing.cn
Website: www.chabadbeijing.com
Shabbat, Kings Garden Villa, 18 Xiao Yun Rd, F1 Chao Yang
Dist. Beijing 100016,

EMBASSY
Embassy of Israel
1 Jianguo Menwai Da Jia 100004
Telephone: (10) 6505 2970/1/2
Fax: (10) 6505 9561

KOSHER FOODS
Mrs Shanen's Bagel's
5 Kaifa Jie, Xibaixin Zhuang Shunyi District
Telephone: (10) 8046 4301
Ask for kosher bagels

RESTAURANTS
Chabad of Ya Bao LU
Asia Pacific Building, Apartment 907, Ya Bao Lu

Kosher
Dini's Kosher Restaurant
Nuren Jie Xingba Lu Jiuba Jie, Chaoyang 100016
Telephone: (10) 6461 6220
Fax: (10) 6461 3735
Website: www.kosherbeijing.com

SYNAGOGUES
Chabad Lubavitch of Beijing China
Kings Garden Villa, 18 Xiao Yun Road, F1, Chao
Yang District 100016 100016
Telephone: (10) 6468 1321
Fax: (10) 6468 1322
Email: info@chabadbeijing.cn
Website: www.chabadbeijing.com
2nd location at Jian Guo Men Diplomatic Building, Building
3, 2F, Room 23 category 2:
Kosher restaurant Nuren Jie Super Bar Street, No. 32 Tianze
Lu, Chaoyang District, Beijing
Weekday minyan on Friday and Sunday mornings and Rosh
Chodesh as well as Shabbat services on Friday night.
Shabbat Friday night dinners and Shabbat lunches. All are
welcome.

GUANGZHOU
Chabad of Guangzhou
31 He Ping Lu, Overseas Village
Telephone: (20) 8376 7070
Mobile Phone: 137 1050 5049
Email: info@chabadgz.org
Website: www.chabadgz.org

KAIFENG
MUSEUMS
Kaifeng Museum
The Kaifeng museum documents the ancient history of
Kaifeng Jewry. The most significant artifact is a 15th
century etched stone with inscriptions describing Kaifeng's
Jewish history and customs 'from the times of Abraham.

SHANGHAI
Shanghai was opened to foreign trade in 1843.
A flourishing Jewish community built up
including Jews of many nationalities. There
were three synagogues; one of which, the Ohel
Rachel built in 1917, was designated in 2001 as
an endangered site. The current community is
planning to raise money for its restoration.

RESTAURANTS
Meat
Kosher Café
Shangmira Garden, Villa #2, 1720 HongQuiao Road
Telephone: (21) 6278 0225
Fax: (21) 6278 0223
Website: www.chinajewish.org
Supervision: Rabbi Shalom Greenberg
Daily 10am to 8pm

SYNAGOGUES
Chabad Jewish Center of Pudong
Apt. 2B, building 11, Alley 99, Puming Road,
Pudong 200120
Telephone: (21) 5878.2008
Fax: (21) 5879.3689
Entrance via Yanlord Garden from Puming Road entrance,
and make a right turn. After 20 feet turn left in to a roofed
walkway, then turn right. The third building is no. 11.

Orthodox
Chabad of Shanghai
Villa #1, Shang-Mira Garden 1720 HongQiao Road
200336
Telephone: (21) 6278 0225
Fax: (21) 6278 0228
Website: www.chinajewish.org
Services and kosher meals available as well as some kosher
products. Contact for reservations and more information.

Shanghai Jewish Center
Shanghai-Mira Garden Villa #2, 1720 HongQiao
Road 200336 200336
Telephone: (21) 6278 0225
Fax: (21) 6278 0223
Website: www.chinajewish.org
Shabbat meals are available. Kosher restaurant

SHENZHEN
Chabad of Shenzen
ist Floor B, 9 Xinbafeng, Jiabin Road Cai Wu Wei
Bldg 518001
Telephone: (755) 8207 0712

HONG KONG

Although there were some Jewish merchants trading out of Hong Kong over the
centuries, the first permanent community
consisted of Jews who came from Baghdad
in the early nineteenth century. The first
synagogue was not established until 1901,
the early settlers preferring to organise
communal events from their homes. The
majority of the community were Sephardi,
but Nazi persecution led to more Ashkenazi
settlers arriving in Hong Kong, via
Shanghai. Since the Second World War
many Chinese Jews have emigrated through
Hong Kong to Australia and the USA,
although some have remained in Hong
Kong. Following the reversion to Chinese
control in mid-1997, the Jewish community
is still thriving, and the mood is optimistic.

The Jews have contributed greatly to the
building of the infrastructure of Hong Kong
and, since the 1960s, many Western Jews,
attracted by the success of this major financial centre, have made their homes there.
The first communal hall was founded in
1905, but a new, multi-purpose complex
(the Jewish Community Centre) has
recently been opened, which is one of the
most luxurious in the world. This centre

includes everything from a library and a strictly kosher restaurant to a swimming pool and sauna.

GMT +8 hours
Country calling code: **(+852)**
Emergency telephone: **(police–999) (fire–999) (ambulance–999)**

HONG KONG
CEMETERIES
The Jewish Cemetery
Located in Happy Valley
Telephone: (852) 2589 2621
Fax: (852) 2548 4200

COMMUNITY ORGANISATIONS
Hong Kong Jewish Community Centre
One Robinson Place, 70 Robinson Road, Mid-Levels
Telephone: (852) 2801 5440
Fax: (852) 2877 0917
Website: www.jcc.org.hk
Two glatt kosher restaurants and one coffee bar under the supervision of a full-time Mashgiach. Regular Shabbat and festival dinners. Kosher supermarket, full banquet facilities, library, swimming pool and leisure facilities and a full programme of activities and classes. Visitors are welcome. Charge to visitors for admission.

CONSULATE
Consul General of Israel
Room 701 Admiralty Centre, Tower 2, 18 Harcourt Street
Telephone: (852) 2821 7500
Fax: (852) 2865 0220
Website: http://hongkong.mfa.gov.il

MEDIA
Jewish Times Asia
Asia Publishing Group Ltd, Suite 2207-2209, Twr 2, Lippo Centre, Admiralty,
Telephone: (852) 2530 8177
Email: info@jewishtimesasia.org
Website: www.jewishtimesasia.org
RESTAURANTS
Shalom Grill
2/F Fortune House, 61 Connaught Road, Central
Telephone: (852) 2851 6300
Fax: (852) 2851 7482
Email: shuva-israel@darvick.com.hk
Website: www.shuva–israel.com
Glatt kosher restaurants under full-time Mashgiach supervision. Meals on Shabbat after services, take-away and delivery servce available. There is also a kosher supermarket, Sunday to Friday 10am to 3pm and from Sunday to Thursday 6.30pm to 10pm. Sunday to Thursday lunch 12pm to 2.30pm, dinner 6.30 pm to 9.30 pm, Friday 12.30pm to 2.30 pm.

SUPERMARKET
Kosher
Great
Seibu-Pacific Olace
Telephone: (852) 2918 9986
A section in this gourmet supermarket is devoted exclusively to kosher products.

SYNAGOGUES
Hong Kong Jewish Community Centre
One Robinson Place, 70 Robinson Road, Mid-Levels
Telephone: (852) 2801 5440
Fax: (852) 2877 0917
Website: www.jcc.org.hk

Orthodox
Chabad of Hong Kong
Chabad House, 1/F Hoover Court, 7 Macdonell Road, Midlevels
Telephone: (852) 2523 9770
Fax: (852) 2845 2772
Website: www.chabadhk.org
Shabbat Minyan & meals in Central District.

Ohel Leah Synagogue
70 Robinson Road, Mid-Levels
Telephone: (852) 2801 5440
Website: www.jjc.org.hk
Built in 1902 and carefully restored in 1998, the Orthodox Ohel Leah Synagogue, known by some as the 'crown jewel' of Asian Jewery, still remains the region's most vibrant centre of Jewish religious activity. Classes, daily services, a Beth Din, and a mikva operate on the premises. Gourmet catered shabbat meals-Friday eve is by reservation and shabbat community kiddush luncheon is complimentary following services. Book nearby hotels at discounted rates through the synagogue office.

Zion Congregation
21 Chatham Road, Kowloon
Telephone: (852) 2366 6364
Corner of Mody Road (opposite to Kowloon Shangri-La Hotel)

Sephardi
Beth Midrash Shuva Israel and Community Centre
3/F Fortune House, 61 Connaught Road, Central
Telephone: (852) 2851 6218; 2851 6300
Fax: (852) 2851 7482
Email: shuva-israel@darvick.com.hk
Website: www.shuva–israel.com
Daily Shacharit at 7am and Mincha-Ma'ariv twenty minutes before sunset. Shabbat services are followed by Shabbat meals. Full day kollel. Shabbat Shacharit at 8am.

KOWLOON

RESTAURANTS
Kosher
Mul Hayam
62 Mody Road
Breakfast served after morning services (free of charge)
lunch 1pm to 2.30pm, dinner 6pm to 10pm. Takeaway
available after 12pm.

SYNAGOGUES
Kehilat Zion
Hechal Ezra, 1st floor, unit 105, 62 Mody Road, Tsim
Sha Tsui East
Telephone: (852) 2366 6364
Fax: (852) 2367 0139

COLOMBIA

The first Jews in Colombia were *Conversos*,
as was common in South America.
However, they were soon discovered by the
Inquisition when it was established in
Colombia.

The next influx of Jews came in the nineteenth century, followed by mass immigration from eastern Europe and the Middle
East after 1918. Jews were banned from
entering after 1939, but this restriction was
eased after 1950.

The present community is a mix of
Ashkenazi and Sephardi elements, each
having their own communual organisations. There are also youth and Zionist
organisations. There is a central organisation for Colombian Jewry in the capital
Bogota. There are also Jewish schools and
synagogues, and Jewish publications and
radio programmes.

GMT -5 hours
Country calling code: **(+57)**
Total population: **36,612,000**
Jewish population: **5,000**
Emergency telephone: **(police–112) (fire–119)
(ambulance–132)**
Electricity voltage: **110/120**

BARANQUILLA

COMMUNITY ORGANISATIONS
Centro Israelita Filantropico
Carrera 43, 85-95, Apartado Aereo 2537
Telephone: (53) 342 310; 351 197

BOGOTA

EMBASSY
Embassy of Israel
Calle 35, No 7-25, Edificio Caxdax
Telephone: (1) 245 6603; 245 6712

RELIGIOUS ORGANISATIONS
Union Rabinica Colombiana
Tranversal 29, No 126-31
Telephone: (1) 625 4377
Fax: (1) 274 9069

SYNAGOGUES
Congregacion Adath Israel
Carrera 7a, No 94-20
Telephone: (1) 257 1660; 257 1680
Fax: (1) 623 9069
Mikva on premises

Ashkenazi
Centro Israelita de Bogota
Traversal 29, No 126-31
Telephone: (1) 625 4377
Fax: (1) 274 9069
Kosher meals available by prior arrangement with Rabbi
Goldschmidt, 218 2500

Orthodox
Comunidad Hebrea Sefaradi
Calle 79, No 9-66
Telephone: (1) 256 2629; 249 0372
Mikva on premises

Jabad House
Calle 92, no 10, Adt. 405
Rabbi's Tel: (1) 257-4920

CALI

Ashkenazi
Sociedad Hebrea de Socoros
Avenida 9a #10-15, Apartado Aereo 011652
Telephone: (2) 668 8518
Fax: (2) 668 8521

German
Union Cultural Israelita
Apartado Aereo 5552
Telephone: (2) 668 9830
Fax: (2) 661 6857

Sephardi
Centro Israelita de Beneficiencia
Calle 44a, Avenida. 5a Norte Esquina, Apartado
Aereo 77
Telephone: (2) 664 1379
Fax: (2) 665 5419

MEDELLIN

COMMUNITY ORGANISATIONS
Union Israelita de Beneficencia
Carrera 43B, No 15-150, Apartado Aereo 4702

COSTA RICA

The first Jews arrived in Costa Rica in the nineteenth century from nearby islands in the Caribbean such as Jamaica. The next wave of immigrants came from eastern Europe in the 1920s. Thereafter Costa Rica did not welcome new Jewish immigrants, and passed laws against foreign merchants and foreign land ownership. However, the Jewish community in Costa Rica established a communual organisation in 1930. There is a monthly newsletter, and a synagogue in San Jose. Most Jewish children attend the Haim Weizmann School, which has both primary and secondary classes.

It is interesting to note that the Costa Rican embassy in Israel is in Jerusalem and not Tel Aviv, where most other embassies are situated.

GMT -6 hours
Country calling code: **(+506)**
Total population: **3,464,000**
Jewish population: **2,500**
Emergency telephone: **(police–911)** **(fire–911)** **(ambulance–911)**
Electricity voltage: **110/220**

SAN JOSE

CONTACT INFORMATION
Centro Israelia Sionista de Costa Rica
PO Box 1473-1000
Telephone: 233 9222
Fax: 233 9321
Website: www.centroisraelita.com

EMBASSY
Embassy of Israel
Edificio Centro Colon, Piso 11, PO Box 5147-1000
Telephone: 221 6011; 221 6444
Fax: 257 0867

GROCERIES
Little Israel Pita Rica
Pavas Rd. 1055-1200
Telephone: 290 2083
Fax: 262 5425
Website: www.kosherfoodcostarica.co
The only kosher bakery and mini-market in Costa Rica. Delivers to hotels.

HOTELS
Barcelo San Jose Palacio
Apdo 458-1150
Telephone: 220 2034; 220 2035
Fax: 220 2036

Hotel has separate kosher kitchen, with the key in the Mashgiach's (Rabbi Levkovitz) hands. The hotel is about a half hour walk to the synagogue.
Camino Real
Prospero Ferandezy, Camino Real Boulevard
Telephone: 289 7000
Fax: 231 5834
Hotel has separate kosher kitchen, with the key in the Mashgiach's (Rabbi Levkovitz) hands
Melia Confort Corobici
PO Box 2443-1000
Telephone: 232 8122
Fax: 231 5834
There is no separate kosher kitchen, but it is fairly close to the Orthodox synagogue. The hotel has two separate storage rooms for kosher cookware.

RESTAURANTS
Meat
Delight-Sabor Mediterraneo
Costado Sur de Perifericos, San Rafael de Escazu, San Jose
Telephone: 288 2707
Cuisine: Israeli - Meat

SYNAGOGUES
B'nai Israel Synagogue
700 meters West of Pops in the Sabana, (on the old road to Escazu, corner building at your left)
Telephone: 231 5243
Fax: 2315787
Website: www.bnei-israel.org
Cogregación B'ni Israel-Judaismo Reformista en Costa Rica
Old Road to Escazu.
Telephone: 231 5243
Fax: 231 5787
Website: www.bnei-israel.org
A Liberal Synagogue affiliated with World Union of Progressive Judaism Liberal Congregations of Central America and the Caribbean.

Orthodox
Shaarei Zion
De la Torre Medica en Paseo Colon
Website: www.centroisraelita.com

CROATIA

Jews were in the land now known as Croatia before the Croats themselves. The Croats arrived in the seventh century, the Jews some centuries before with the Romans: there are remains of a third-century Jewish cemetery in Solin (near Split).

The first Jewish communites were involved in trade with Italy across the Adriatic Sea, and also in trade along the River Danube. Their success was brief, however, and they

were expelled in 1456, only returning more than 300 years later. The area became part of the newly formed Yugoslavia after the First World War, and the Jewish community became part of the Federation of Jewish Communities in Yugoslavia.

The Croatian Jews suffered greatly under the German occupation in the Second World War when the local *Ustashe* (Croatian Fascists) assisted the Germans. Despite their efforts some Jews survived and even decided to rebuild their community when peace returned.

Today, after the civil war, there are synagogues in towns across the country. There are some Hebrew classes and newsletters are published. There are also many places of historical interest, such as Ulicia Zudioska (Jewish Street) in Dubrovnik. This street has recently been renamed Jewish Street.

GMT -1 hours
Country calling code: **(+385)**
Total population: **4,498,000**
Jewish population: **2,000**
Emergency telephone: **(police–92)** **(fire–93)**
Other emergenc-94)
Electricity voltage: **220**

DUBROVNIK
MUSEUMS
Jewish Museum
Zudioska Street 3
The first Jewish museum in Croatia opened in May 2003. It is located in the Dubrovnik Synagogue and has Torah scrolls dating back to the 13th century.

SYNAGOGUES
Dubrovnik Synagogue
Zudioska Street 3
Telephone: (20) 321 028
Zudioska means 'Street of the Jews'. This is the second oldest synagogue in Europe and is located in a very narrow street off the main street-the Stradun or Placa. The Jewish community office is in the same building. Zudioska Street is the third turning on the right from the clock tower. There are about thirty Jews in the city. Tourists help to make up a minyan in the synagogue on Friday night and High Holy Days.

OSIJEK
COMMUNITY ORGANISATIONS
Community Building
Brace Radica Street 13
Telephone: (31) 211 407
Fax: (31) 211 407
The community building contains objects from the synagogue that was destroyed during the Second World War. The community numbers about 150 members and has two cemeteries. No regular services are held. A former building of the pre-war synagogue in Cvjetkova Street is a Pentecostal church today. There is a plaque at the site of the destroyed synagogue in Zupanijska Street.

RIJEKA
SYNAGOGUES
Rijeka Synagogue
Filipovieva ul. 9, PO Box 65 51000
Telephone: (51) 425 156; 336 032
The community numbers about sixty. Services are held in the well maintained synagogue on Jewish holidays.

SPLIT
COMMUNITY ORGANISATIONS
Jewish Community of Split
Zidovski Prolaz 1 21000
Telephone: (21) 345 672
The synagogue at Split is one of the few in Yugoslavia to have survived the wartime occupation. The Jewish community numbers about 200. There is a Jewish cemetery, established in 1578. More information from the community offices at the above number.

ZAGREB
The Bet Israel Jewish Community of Croatia
Mazuranicev Trg 6/II 10000
Telephone: (1) 4851 008
Fax: (1) 4851 376
Email: ured@bet-israel.com
Website: www.bet-israel.com
Supervision: Kashrut by Chief Rabbi Dr. Kotel Da-Don
Before the War Zagreb had 11,000 Jews. There are now only 1,500, but they remain very active in Jewish communal life. Services are held in the community synagogue in Radiceva Street 26 on Shabbats and holidays.

MONUMENT

Central Synagogue
Praska Street 7
There is a plaque on the spot of this pre-war synagogue

Mirogoj Cemetery
There is an impressive monument in this cemetery to the Jewish victims of the Second World War

SYNAGOGUES

Chabad of Croatia
Zerjaviceve 9
Telephone: (1) 485 6786; (98) 974 7966
Contact: Rabbi Pinchas Zaklas

TOURIST SITES

National Museum
Features an Ashkenazi prayerbook from the 18th century

CUBA

The first Jew to set foot in Cuba (1492) was Luis de Torres. Although hundreds arrived following the Spanish Inquisition they were prohibited from practising their religion. This changed in 1898 following Cuba's liberation from Spain. With the end of Spanish colonial rule in that year, Jews from nearby areas, such as Jamaica and Florida, and Jewish veterans of the Spanish American War, began to settle in Cuba. A congregation was established in 1904. Later, Turkish Sephardim formed their own synagogue. The community was then augmented by immigrants from eastern Europe who had decided to stay in Cuba, which was being used as a transit camp for those seeking to enter America. A central committee was established for all Jewish groups in the 1930s. Cuba imposed severe restrictions on immigration at that time, and the story of the German ship St Louis (full of Jewish refugees), which was refused entry into Cuba, is well known.

About 12,000 Jews lived on the island in 1952. Havana had by far the largest community, and 75 per cent of the Cuban community was Ashkenazi. Although the Cuban revolution did not target Jews, religious affiliations were initially discouraged and many Jews emigrated (as did many non-Jews). The remaining community has synagogues and a Sunday school. Kosher food and Judaica are imported, mainly

from Canada and Panama. Cuba broke off diplomatic relations with Israel in 1973, although in 1998/99 a number of Jews were allowed to emigrate to Israel.

GMT -5 hours
Country calling code: (+53)
Total population: **11,509.000**
Jewish population: **600**
Emergency telephone: (**police–82 0116**) (**fire–81 115**) (**ambulance–404 551**)
Electricity voltage: **110/220**

HAVANA

COMMUNITY ORGANISATIONS

Jewish Community in Cuba
Casa de la Communidad Hebrea de Cuba, Calle 1, #259, Esquina de la Habana 10400
Telephone: (7) 832 8953
Fax: (7) 833 3778

SYNAGOGUES
Conservative

Patronado de la Casa de la Comunidad Hebrea de Cuba
Calle 13 el, Vedado
Telephone: (7) 832 8953
This is also the location of a modern community centre

Orthodox
Comunidad Religiosa Hebrea Adath Israel de Cuba
Acosta No. 357 Esq., Picota
Telephone: (7) 861 3495
Fax: (7) 860 8242
Website: www.adathcuba.com
Kosher Food. Dan Heller provides a photo essay and material on Cuba's Jewish community

Hadath Israel
Calle Picota 52 Habana Vieja
Telephone: (7) 861 3495

Sephardi
Centro Sefardi (Conservative)
Calle 17 Esquina E Vedado, La Habana 10400
Telephone: (7) 832 6623
Jose Levy Tur President

CYPRUS

During the Roman Empire, Jewish merchants made their home on Cyprus. However, after a revolt that destroyed the town of Salamis, they were expelled. In medieval times small Jewish communities were established in Nicosia, Limassol and other towns, but the community was never large.

It is interesting to note that Cyprus was seen as a possible 'Jewish Homeland' by the early Zionists. Agricultural settlements were established at the end of the nineteenth century, but they were not successful. Herzl himself tried to persuade the British government to allow Jewish rule over Cyprus in 1902, but met with failure.

Some German Jews managed to escape to Cyprus in the early 1930s. After the war, many Holocaust survivors who had tried to enter Palestine illegally were deported to special camps on the island. Some 50,000 European Jews were held there. Since the establishment of the state of Israel, the Jewish community on the island has become small; the Israeli embassy serves as a centre for community activities.

GMT +2 hours
Country calling code: **(+357)**
Total population: **766,000**
Jewish population: **Under 100**
Emergency telephone: **(police–112) (fire–112) (ambulance–112)**
Electricity voltage: **240**

LARNACA
COMMUNITY ORGANISATIONS
Cyprus Jewish Community Centre - Chabad Lubavitch of Cyprus
Mikvah Mei Menachem, Diogenous 7, 6020 PO Box 42461 6534
Telephone: (24) 828 770
Fax: (24) 828 771
Mobile Phone: 99 931 679
Email: office@jewishcyprus.com
Website: www.jewishcyprus.com
Supervision: Rabbi Arie Zeev Raskin, Chief rabbi and Emissary of Cyprus
: Kosher meals by arrangement, religious services, Synagogue, Judaica store, Torah classes and Mikvah

NICOSIA
Committee of the Jewish Community of Cyprus
Po Box 24784 1303
Telephone: (99) 694 758
Fax: (22) 662 077
Email: amiyes@spidernet.com.cy

EMBASSY
Embassy of Israel
4 Grypari Strret
Telephone: (22) 369 500/549
Fax: (22) 666 338

Website: www.nicosia.mfa.gov.il
Contact Mrs Z. Yeshrun for information

CZECH REPUBLIC

Prague, the capital of this small central European country, has become a major tourist attraction. It is one of the few cities to actively promote its Jewish heritage, which dates from early medieval times. The oldest (still functioning) synagogue in Europe is there (the Altneuschul), as well as other interesting Jewish sites.

After the arrival of the first Jews in the country, in the tenth century, they suffered similar tragedies to those of other medieval Jewish communities; forced baptism by the Crusaders and expulsions, together with some tolerance. Full emancipation was reached in 1867 under the Habsburgs. The celebrated Jewish writer, Franz Kafka, lived in Prague and did not neglect his Judaism, unlike many other Czech Jews who assimilated and intermarried.

The German occupation led to 85 per cent of the community (80,000 people) perishing in the Holocaust. Further difficulties were faced in the communist period after the war, but since the 1989 'Velvet Revolution', Judaism is being rediscovered. The community (mostly elderly) has several synagogues around the country, a kindergarten and a journal, and there are kosher restaurants in the old Jewish Quarter in Prague.

GMT +1 hours
Country calling code: **(+420)**
Total population: **10,304,000**
Jewish population: **5,000**
Emergency telephone: **(police–158) (fire–150) (ambulance–155)**
Electricity voltage: **220**

BOSKOVICE

MUSEUMS
Jewish Town of Boskovice - Medieval Ghetto
680 01
Telephone: (516) 452 077
Fax: (516) 454 607
Website: www.boskovice.cz/muzeum
Seventeenth-century Jewish town, synagogue and cemetery

BRNO

SYNAGOGUES
Brno Synagogue
Skorepka 13

HOLESOV

MUSEUMS
Schach Synagogue
Dating from 1650, this synagogue is now a museum. Open in the mornings. At other times the curator will show visitors around, if contacted. The old cemetery is close by

KARLOVY VARY

Carslbad (as it was then called) was popular among Jews as a spa and resort. The beautiful synagogue, destroyed on Kristallnacht, is recorded by a plaque on the wall of the Bristol Hotel.

SYNAGOGUES
Jewish Community of Karlovy Vary (Chabad)
Bezrucova 8
Telephone: (353) 230 658

LIBEREC

Community Centre
Matousova 21, Reichenberg 46001
Telephone: (48) 510 3340
Each weekday 9 am to 11 am

MIKULOV

SITE
Cemetery and partly restored Synagogue
Only one synagogue, still being restored, remains of the many which flourished here when the town was the spiritual capital of Moravian Jewry and the seat of the Chief Rabbis of Moravia. The cemetery contains the graves of famous Rabbis.

OLOMOUC

SYNAGOGUES
Community Centre
Komenskeho 7 77900
Telephone: (68) 522 3119
Website: www.kehila-olomouc.cz

PILSEN

The Jewish Community of Pilsen
Smetanovy Sady 5, Pilsen 30137
Telephone: (0042) 03 772 35749
Fax: (0042) 03 772 35749
Services Friday evenings. The Great Synagogue is now closed.

POLNA

MUSEUMS
Museum
A museum was opened in 2000 in a reconstructed seventeenth century synagogue. It charts the spread of anti-Semitism in Central Europe.

PRAGUE

Most of the Jews in the Czech Republic live in Prague, which has had a thousand-year history of Jewish settlement. The impact of the Jews in Prague has been great, the Golem has entered Prague folklore, and the Altneushul is the oldest functioning synagogue in Europe. The Jewish Quarter in the old town contains many historical sites.

Terezin is some forty miles from Prague and is easily visited. On the way is the town of Lidice, destroyed in June 1942 by the Nazis in retaliation for the assassination of Reinhard Heydrich.

Bejt Simcha
Mánesova 8 120 00
Telephone: 22 252 472
Fax: 22 252 472
Website: www.bejtsimcha.cz
Bejt Simcha meets every Friday to celebrate Kabalat Shabbat; it is usually combined with a lecture, a discussion or a cultural program. We use our own Hebrew-Czech siddur for the service. At least once a month there is a Saturday morning service as well. There is a small synagogue, library, room for social and cultural events, bar

CEMETERIES
New Jewish Cemetery
Praha 3, Vinohradská
Telephone: (02) 7274 1893
Founded in 1890 this is larger but less visitied than the Old Jewish Cemetery.
Franz Kafka is buried at grave N°137.

Old Jewish Cemetery
U Stare Skoly 1 11000
Telephone: (02) 2171 1511
Fax: (02) 2171 1584
Website: www.jewishmuseum.cz
The oldest Jewish cemetery in Europe, containing the graves of such famous Rabbis & scholars as Avigdor Karo (1439), Yehuda Low ben Bezalel (1609), David Gans (1613), David Oppenheim (1736).

CONTACT INFORMATION
Federation of Jewish Communities
Maislova 18 11001
Telephone: (02) 481 0130
Fax: (02) 481 0912
Website: www.kehilaprag.cz
Houses the Federation of Jewish Communities in the Czech Republic as well as The Jewish Community of Prague. It has the world famous Hebrew clock. Also houses the Shalom Jewish community restaurant.

EMBASSY
Embassy of Israel
Badeniho 2, Prague 7 17076
Telephone: (02) 3309 7500
Fax: (02) 3309 7529
Website: www.praque.mfa.gov.il

GALLERIES
Robert Guttman Gallery
U Staré školy 1
Open: 10am-5pm daily (until 6pm in summer months).
Closed Saturdays and on Jewish holidays
Part of the Jewish Musuem

HOTELS
President Hotel
Namesti Curieovych 100 110-00
Telephone: (02) 3461 4100
Fax: (02) 3461 4110
Email: reservations@hotelpresident.cz
Website: www.hotelpresident.cz
A few minutes walk from the old Jewish quarter

MUSEUMS
Jewish Museum in Prague
U Stare Skoly 1, 3 110 00
Telephone: (02) 2481 9456
Fax: (02) 2481 9458
Website: www.jewishmuseum.cz
The Jewish Museum, founded in 1906, is the largest
museum of its kind in Europe. The museum contains almost
40,000 articles and 100,000 books.

RESTAURANTS
Shalom Restaurant
18 Maislova Marianskolazenska
Telephone: (02) 232 104

Delicatessen
Shelanu Cafe Deli
Brehova 8, Jewish Quarter 110 00
Telephone: 2166 5141
Email: shelany.deli@gmail.com
Website: www.shelanu.cz
Supervision: Chabad of Prague
Open daily for breakfast, lunch and dinner. Shabbat meals
by reservation.

Meat
Chabad Centre
3 Parizska
Telephone: (2) 2232 0200

King Solomon Restaurant
Siroka 8 110 00
Telephone: (02) 2481 8752
Fax: (02) 7486 4664
Email: solomon@kosher.cz
Website: www.kosher.cz
Supervision: Rav Michael Yerochim
Accomodation available at synagoge at daily or weekly

basis. Please contact:
Mrs Lilly Gabai +45 3332 5730

Meat and Parve
Bilkova
Josefov 12 11000
Telephone: (2) 2231 3308

SYNAGOGUES
Klausen Synagogue
U Starého hrbitova 3A
A baroque style building which houses a permanent
exhibition of Jewish customs and traditions. The
Ceremonial Hall is next door.

Maisel Synagogue
Maiselove 10
Home to a large collection of silverware, previously
confiscated from Jewish families by the Nazis and has a
permanent exhibition, The History of Jews in Bohemia and
Moravia.

Pinkas Synagogue
Siroka 3 1
Inside Pinkas Synagogue, the walls are covered with the
names of 77,297 Jewish Holocaust victims from Bohemia
and Moravia. There is also a permanent exhibition of
children's drawings from Terezin concentration camp,
drawn between 1942 and 1944.

The Spanish Synagogue
Vezenská 1
Originally constructed in 1868, the synagogue was restored
and reopened in 1998. Also houses an exhibition on Czech
Jews

Orthodox
Chabad Center Prague
3 Parizska Street 11000
Telephone: (02) 2232 0192
Fax: (02) 2232 0200
Email: chabadprague@gmail.com
Website: www.chabadpraque.cz

Old-New Synagogue
Corner of Maiselova St and Cervena St 1
Telephone: 224 800 849
Fax: 224 800 845
Email: rabinat@kehilaprag.cz
Website: www.kehilaprag.cz
Considered to be the most historic site in Josefov. Dates
back from the 13th century, this is one of the few remaining
medieval buildings in the Quarter. Still used for prayer. The
High Synagogue is next door.

TOURS
Kosher Prague
Telephone: (731) 108 744
Website: www.kosherprague.com
Includes Jewish Prague Tour, General Prague Tour and
special 'Kivreu Tzadikim Tour'

Precious Legacy Tours
Kaprova 13, Prague 1, Josefov
Telephone: (02) 2232 1951/4
Fax: (02) 2232 1954
Mobile Phone: 602 214 088
Website: www.legacytours.net
Tours in Prague, Kutna Hora, Kolin, Vienna, Budapest etc.
Shops also sells Judaica, books and souvenirs.

Wittmann Tours, spol. s.r.o.
Manesova 8, 120 00 2
Telephone: (02) 2225 2472
Fax: (02) 2225 2472
Email: sylvie@wittmann-tours.com
Website: www.wittmann-tours.com

TEPLICE
SYNAGOGUES
Community Centre
Lipova 25, Tepliz-Schönau
Telephone: (417) 26580

TEREZIN
MUSEUMS
The Terezin Museum
Thereseinstadt
There is a new museum in the town dedicated to the Jews who were deported from Theresienstadt to Auschwitz

Moravia
BRNO
COMMUNITY ORGANISATIONS
Jewish Community Centre
tr. Kpt. Jarose 3 60200
Telephone: (5) 4450 9622
Fax: (5) 4450 9623
Email: zob@zob.cz
Website: www.zob.cz
The community president can be reached on (6) 00420 7936

DENMARK

Jews were allowed to settle in Denmark in 1622, earlier than in any other Scandinavian country. Thereafter the community grew, with immigration largely from Germany. The Danish king allowed the foundation of the unified Jewish community of Copenhagen in 1684, and the Jews were granted full citizenship in 1849.

In the early part of the twentieth century many refugees arrived from eastern Europe, and Denmark welcomed refugees from Nazi Germany. When the Germans conquered Denmark and ordered the Jews to be handed over, the Danish resistance managed to save 7,200 (90 per cent of the community) by arranging boats to take them to neutral Sweden. Some Jews did, however, stay behind and were taken to the transit ghetto of Theresienstadt (Terezin), and many died.

After the war most of the Jews returned, and there is now a central Jewish organisation based in Copenhagen. There are also homes for the elderly, synagogues and a mikvah. Kosher food is available.

GMT +1 hours
Country calling code: (+45)
Total population: **5,284,000**
Jewish population: **8,000**
Emergency telephone: (**police–112**) (**fire–112**) (**ambulance–112**)
Electricity voltage: **220**

COPENHAGEN
With a Jewish population of almost 7,000, the vast majority of Danish Jews live in the capital. The Community Centre contains most of the offices of the Jewish community, and an old-age home run jointly with the Copenhagen Municipality. The Great Synagogue and the cemetery dating from 1693 are interesting sites.

BUTCHERS
Copenhagen Kosher
83 Lyngbyvej 2100
Telephone: 3918 5777
Mon to Thu 8am to 6.30pm, Fri 8am to 1pm

EMBASSY
Embassy of Israel
Lundevangsvej 4, Hellerup 2900
Telephone: 3962 6288
Fax: 3962 1938

LIBRARIES
The Royal Library, The National Library of Denmark and Copenhagen University Library
The Black Diamond, Søren Kierkegaards Plads 1
1016 K
Telephone: 3347 4747
Email: kb@kb.dk
Website: www.kb.dk
Postal address: The Royal Library, Post box 2149, 1016 Copenhagen K

MIKVAOT
Mikva
12 Krystalgade 1172
Telephone: 3324 9683; 3526 3540

Restaurant
Jewish Community Centre
Ny Kongensgade 6 1472 K
Telephone: 3312 8868
Fax: 3312 3357
Email: mt@mosaiske.dk
Website: www.mosaiske.dk
Hours: Mon to Thu 9am to 1pm and 2pm to 3.30.pm

MUSEUMS
Museum of Danish Resistance
Frihedsmuseet, Churchillparken 1263
Telephone: 33 7714
Website: www.natmus.dk

The Danish Jewish Museum
The Royal Library Garden, Proviantpassagen 6
1218 K
Telephone: 3311 2218
Email: info@jewmus.dk
Website: www.jewmus.dk
Winter: Tue to Fri 1pm to 4pm, Sat/Sun 12pm to 5pm.
1st June to 31st August tue to Sun 10am to 5pm

SANDWICH BAR
I. A. Samson
Roerholmsgade 3 1352
Telephone: 3313 0077
Fax: 3314 8277
Kosher grocery provisions and delicatessen. Catering for groups, twenty persons plus.

SYNAGOGUES
Copenhagen Synagogue
Granavenget 8
Telephone: 4220 0731
Open from Shavuot to Succot

Orthodox
Great Synagogue of Copenhagen
12 Krystalgade 1172 K
Telephone: 3312 8868
Website: www.mosaiske.dk
Shabbat morning service 9am. (Take your passport).

Machsike Hadass
Ole suhrsgade 12 1354
Telephone: 3332 5730
Fax: 49700731
Supervision: Raw Yitzi Löwenthal
Daily and Shabbat services

TOURS
Copenhagen Walking Tours
Telephone: 4081 1217
Website: www.copenhagen-walkingtours.dn
Walking tours of sites of Jewish interest in the old city

HORNBAEK
A resort and seaside town where many members of the Copenhagen community spend the summer months, or weekends. It is the area of the coast from which the Jewish community escaped in 1943.

Hornbæk, Elsinore, Copenhagen and Denmark

Hotel Villa Strand has a unique location right at one of Denmarks most popular beaches - Hornbæk Beach. Only a few minutes walk from the Harbour and a wide selection of shops.

The hotel has a private guest garden with two sun terraces and entrance directly to Sand dunes and the Beach. All the rooms have private toilet and shower. Our kitchen is international and specialised in Glat Kosher (Kosher meals).

Hotel Villa Strand lies in the picturesque harbour town of Hornbæk. Hornbæk has everything to offer, beautiful white beaches, a unique selection of excellent restaurants and a wide choice of shops and boutiques which remain open every day all year round.

Kystvej 12 | DK-3100 Hornbæk | Denmark | Phone: +45 49 700 088 | Fax: +45 49 701 100
Email: hotel@villastrand.dk Internet: www.villastrand.dk

HOTELS
Kosher
Hotel Villa Strand
Kystvej 12 3100
Telephone: 4970 0088
Fax: 4970 1100
Email: hotel@villastrand.dk
Website: www.villastrand.dk

DOMINICAN REPUBLIC

Jewish settlement in the Dominican Republic was comparatively late the oldest Jewish grave dates back to 1826. Descended from central European Jews, the community was not religious and many married Christians. President Francisco Henriquez y Carvajal (1916) traced his ancestry back to the early Jewish settlers.

In 1938 the republic decided to accept refugees from Nazism (one of the very few countries of the world that did so freely), and even provided areas where they could settle. As a result, there were 1,000 Jews living there in 1943. This number declined as, once again, the Jewish community assimilated and married the local non-Jewish population. Despite this, many non-Jewish husbands, wives and children take part in Jewish events.

Two synagogues and a rabbi who divides his time between them are features of Jewish life. There is also a Sunday school in Santo Domingo and a bi-monthly magazine is produced. There is a small Jewish museum in Sosua.

GMT -4 hours
Country calling code: **(+1 809)**
Total population: **8,097,000**
Jewish population: **150**
Emergency telephone: **(police–999) (fire–999) (ambulance–999)**
Electricity voltage: **220/240**

SANTO DOMINGO
COMMUNITY ORGANISATIONS
Consejo Dominicano de Mujeres Hebreas
PO Box 2189
Telephone: (809) 535 6042
Fax: (809) 688 2058

EMBASSY
Embassy of Israel
Av. Pedro Henriquez Urena 80 1404
Telephone: (809) 542 1635; 542 1548

SYNAGOGUES
Chabad Lubavitch
Email: chabaddominican@gmail.com
Contact: RABBI SHIMON PELMAN + 1 809 53 38 770

Traditional Conservative
Centro Israelita de la Republica Dominicana
Avenida Sarasota #21, Bella Vista
Telephone: (809) 535 6042
Fax: (809) 533 0168
Email: centroisraelitarepdom@gmail.com
We are a small but very active Congregation, not affiliated with any of the main ethnic or ideological orientations in contemporary Judaism; we strive to find a "Golden Path" in the practice of our faith, away from both extremes, be they liberalizing or restrictive.

SYNAGOGUE: Our ritual services are conducted in a traditional fashion, mostly in Hebrew; we do not use a PA system; although our Temple does not have a Mehitza (partition) we strictly abide by separate seating; we have a Minyan for Kabalat Shabat (Eve of Sabath) and Thursday mornings. Anniversary (yahrzeit) and other special occasions of the Jewish Life Cycle are observed. Guests are welcome to all our Services (for the High Holidays Services reservations are required

SOSUA
MUSEUM/SYNAGOGUE
Liberal
Parroquia Israelita de Sosus
Located in centre of Sosua village
Telephone: (809) 571 1386
Email: museojudiososua@codetel.net.do
Contact: Ms. IVONNE MILZ: + I 809 299 9825

ECUADOR

As in most Latin American countries, *Conversos* comprised the earliest Jewish settlers in Ecuador. It was not until 1904 that Eastern European Jews began to arrive, and numbers increased further following the Nazi take-over in Germany, as Ecuador granted refuge to more Jews than other neighbouring countries. About 3,000 Jews entered Ecuador in the 1930s. The Jewish population peaked in 1950 at 4,000, but this number declined owing to emigration. In recent years, some Jews have moved to Ecuador from elsewhere in South America.

EGYPT

There are no Jewish schools, but children do have access to Jewish education.

GMT -5 hours
Country calling code: **(+593)**
Total population: **11,937,00**
Jewish population: **1,000**
Emergency telephone: **(police–101) (fire–102) (ambulance–131)**
Electricity voltage: **110/220**

QUITO
COMMUNITY ORGANISATIONS
Communidad Judia del Ecuador
Calle Roberto Andrade, OE3 590 y Jaime, Roldos
Urbanizacion Einstein (Carcelen)
Telephone: (2) 2483 800/927
Fax: (2) 2486 755

EMBASSY
Embassy of Israel
Av. Eloy Alfaro 969, Casilla 2463
Telephone: (2) 547 322; 548 431

EGYPT

For more than 2,000 years there has been a virtually continuous Jewish presence in the vicinity of Cairo, and an even more ancient Jewish presence in Egypt is recounted in the Bible. After the exodus, Jews returned to Egypt during the time of Alexander the Great, and at that time the Ben Ezra synagogue was built. The Bible was translated into Greek during that period. In the first century CE, the Jewish presence declined, but a renaissance occurred with Moses Maimonides's arrival in Egypt in the twelfth century. Most of his books were written in Cairo and his yeshiva still exists in the Jewish quarter. From then on the Jewish community expanded and flourished, especially with the arrival of refugees from pogroms and during the First and Second World Wars.

Before 1948 there were about 70,000 Jews in Egypt. The 1956 Suez War and the 1967 Six Day War encouraged Jewish emigration. At present the community is small but the Jewish heritage, mostly synagogues classified as antiquities, represents an inestimable treasure worth visiting, as, for example, the recently restored Ben Ezra synagogue, home of the world-famous Genizah of some 400,000 documents (the majority of which are now in Cambridge, England).

GMT +2 hours
Country calling code: **(+20)**
Total population: **67,974,000**
Jewish population: **Under 100**
Emergency telephone: **(police–0) (fire–03180) (ambulance–0)**
Electricity voltage: **220**

ALEXANDRIA
SYNAGOGUES
Eliahu Hanavi
69 Nebi Daniel Street, Ramia Station
Telephone: (3) 492 3974; 597 4438

CAIRO
Cairo has had a long and important Jewish history. The community has however declined in line with the rest of Egyptian Jewry. There are a number of interesting sites, such as the recently restored Ben Ezra Synagogue where the Cairo Genizah used to be located.

COMMUNITY ORGANISATIONS
Community Organisation
13 Rue Sabyl El Kazindar, Abbassieh, Midan el Gueish
Telephone: (2) 824 613, 824 885
Website: www.geocities.com

EMBASSY
Embassy of Israel
6 Ibn Malek Street Gizeh
Telephone: (2) 361 0528
Fax: (2) 361 0414

SYNAGOGUES
Ben-Ezra
6 Harett il-Sitt Barbara, Mari Girges, Old Cairo
Telephone: (2) 362 2752
The synagogue was built in 1892 and is the oldest in Egypt. According to legend, under the building is the site where Pharaoh's daughter found Moses.

Meir Enaim
55 No. 13 Street, Maadi
Supervision: Jewish Community of Cairo
Can be visited on request

Shaare Hashamayim
17 Adly Pasha Street, Downtown Cairo
Telephone: (2) 393 5896
Website: www.geocities.com/rainforest/vines/5855
Services are held on high holidays. There is an interesting library withinthe synagogue which is only accessible with a key. Ask the librarian.

63

EL SALVADOR

The Jewish connection to El Salvador is not a strong one. It is believed that some Portuguese *Conversos* crossed the country a few hundred years ago. After that, some Sephardis from France moved to Chaluchuapa. Other Jews came from Europe, but in smaller numbers than those settling in other Latin American countries. There were only 370 Jews in 1976, a number reduced during the civil war, when many emigrated. Some returned, however, when the war was over.

An official community was set up in 1944 and a synagogue was opened in 1950. El Salvador is one of the few countries to have an embassy in Jerusalem, rather than Tel Aviv.

GMT -6 hours
Country calling code: (+503)
Total population: 5,928,000
Jewish population: 120
Emergency telephone: (police–123) (fire–123) (ambulance–123)
Electricity voltage: 110

SAN SALVADOR
EMBASSY
Embassy of Israel
Alameda Roosevelt y63 Avenida Sur, Centro, Finaciero Gigante Torre B, 11 o piso
Telephone: 211 3434
Fax: 211 3443
Website: www.elsalvador.com

SYNAGOGUES
Conservative
Comunidad Israelita de El Salvador
Boulevard del Hipodromo 626 #1, Colonia San Benito, PO Box 06-182
Telephone: 2263 8074
Fax: 2263 8074
Website: http://cies.syncdata.com.sv
Services Friday 18:30 hs, Shabbat morning 8am and Holy Days
Rabbi Pablo Berman rabpabloberman

San Salvador Synagogue
23 boulevard del Hipodromo 626, Colonia San Benito
Telephone: 2263 8074
Email: cisraelita@integra.com.sv
Website: www.comunidadisraelitadeelsalvador.org
Friday evening Kabalat Shabat 6:30pm
Shajarit Shabat 8am
Contact Rabbi Pablo Berman

ERITREA

GMT +5 1/2 hours
Country calling code: (+291)
Total population: 18,552,000
Jewish population: Under 100
Emergency telephone: (police–43 333) (fire–42 2222) (ambulance–42 2222)
Electricity voltage: 230/240

ASMARA
BAKERIES
Gottesfeld
Mercatorstraat 20
Telephone: (1) 230 0003

COMMUNITY ORGANISATIONS
Asmara Jewish Community
PO Box 1475, 34 Serae Street
Telephone: (1) 120 084/480
Fax: (1) 120 340
Email: samico@gemel.com.er

SYNAGOGUES
The Synagogue of Asmara
34 Serae Street
Telephone: (1) 120 480
The Synagogue of Asmara was built in 1906. It is a beautiful, serene building just off the main street. The wooden cornices and fittings are hand carved and the scrolls of the Torah are hand written.

ESTONIA

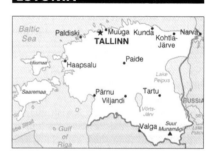

Despite being the only country officially declared 'Judenrein' (free of Jews) at the Wannsee conference in 1942, there is a Jewish community here today. The community has always been small, and is believed to have begun in the fourteenth century. However, most Jews arrived in the nineteenth century, when Czar Alexander II allowed certain groups of Jews into the area.

The first community was established in Tallinn in 1830. By 1939, the community had grown to 4,500 and was free from restraints. After the Soviet and Nazi occupations in the Second World War the Jews returned, mainly from the Soviet Union. Now that Estonia is independent, the Jewish community is able to practise its religion freely.

GMT +2 hours
Country calling code: (+372)
Total population: 1,454,000
Jewish population: 2,500
Emergency telephone: (police–002 in Tallinn, 02 elsewhere) (fire–001 in Tallinn, 01 elsewhere) (ambulance–003 in Talinn, 03 elsewhere)
Electricity voltage: 220

TALLINN
COMMUNITY CENTRE
Jewish Community of Tallinn
P.O. Box 961 EE 0034

RESTAURANTS
Vegetarian -Kosher
Ganga
(C-4) Tartu mnt. 23
Telephone: (6) 2515 5220

SYNAGOGUES
Synagogue
9 Magdalena Street
Telephone: (6) 0255 7154

Orthodox
Tallinn Synagogue
16A Karu Street, PO Box 3576 10120
Telephone: (6) 623 050
Fax: (6) 623 001
Website: www.ejc.ee

ETHIOPIA

The Falashas (*Ge'ez* for 'stranger', applied to the Ethiopian Jews) of Ethiopia became known world-wide in the early 1980s, when many were airlifted to Israel. The origins of the Beta Israel, as they call themselves, are unclear and little is known for certain. Historians have concluded that they may have become Jewish as early as the second or third century.

As the area became known to the West through nineteenth-century explorers, some Western Jews set up schools in the country. The Jewish population was believed to have been about 50,000 in 1934. After the establishment of Israel, more interest was taken in the Ethiopian community and the Ethiopian civil war was the catalyst for Operation Moses, when 10,000 people were airlifted to Israel in 1984–85. A further 15,000 left for Israel in 1991.

GMT +2 hours
Country calling code: (+251)
Total population: 63,495,000
Jewish population: 500
Emergency telephone: (police–91) (fire–93) (ambulance–92)
Electricity voltage: 220

ADDIS ABABA
COMMUNITY ORGANISATIONS
Community
PO Box 50
Telephone: (1) 111 725; 446 471

EMBASSY
Israel Embassy in Ethiopia
PO Box 1266 Higher 16 Kebela 22 House, #283
Telephone: (1) 612 456

FIJI

When Henry Marks, at the age of 20, moved to Fiji from Australia in 1881, he was the first recorded Jew on the island. Over the years, he developed a successful business across the region, and was later knighted.

Indian and other Jews later moved to Fiji but did not organise any official community. In recent years the Fiji Jewish Association has been created. The Israeli embassy organises an annual Seder.

GMT +12 hours
Country calling code: (+679)
Total population: 772,000
Jewish population: Under 100
Emergency telephone: (police–000) (fire–000) (ambulance–000)
Electricity voltage: 240

SUVA
Embassy of Israel
Joske Street, 69, Parade Building, PO Box 15249
Telephone: 303 420
Fax: 300 415

FINLAND

When Finland was occupied by Russia in the nineteenth century, many Jewish conscripts in the Russian army settled in Finland after their discharge. They were still subject to restrictions, but these ended after Finland's independence in 1917. In addition to these *'Cantonists'*, as they were known, immigrants came to Finland from eastern Europe. Finland proved a safe haven, as the government refused to hand over Finnish Jews to the Nazis, despite being allied to Germany in its war with Soviet Russia.

The community is keen to preserve a sense of Jewish identity among the young generation, who are encouraged to experience Jewish life in Israel. The community is also keen to help other Jews in the newly independent Baltic states across the sea to the south of the country. There is a central body for Jewish communities, and kosher food is available. There are also synagogues and a school.

GMT +2 hours
Country calling code: (**+358**)
Total population: **5,140,000**
Jewish population: **1,200**
Emergency telephone: (**police–10022**) (**fire–112**) (**ambulance–112**)
Electricity voltage: **220**

HELSINKI
Some 1,200 Jews (the majority of the Jewish population in Finland) live in Helsinki. The community centre is next to the synagogue. There is also a Jewish cemetery containing an area dedicated to the Jews who fought in the Finnish army in various wars, including the Russo-Finnish war.

BUTCHERS
Butcher/Deli
Kosher Deli
Malminkatu 24
Telephone: (9) 685 4584
Fax: (9) 694 8916
Website: www.jchelsinki.fi

COMMUNITY ORGANISATIONS
Community Centre
Jewish Community of Helsinki
Malminkatu 26 00100
Telephone: (9) 586 0310
Fax: (9) 694 8916

Website: www.jchelsinki.fi
Kosher meals by arrangement. The synagogue and community centre may be visited by arrangement with the office

EMBASSY
Embassy of Israel
Yrjonkatu 36A 00100
Telephone: (9) 681 2020
Fax: (9) 135 6959

MONUMENT
Memorial to Jewish Refugees–Hands Begging for Mercy
Laivasillankatu, Ullanlinna
A Monument was unveiled in 2000 in a park opposite the harbour where Jewish refugees were deported in 1942 to Germany.

SYNAGOGUE
Orthodox
Jewish Community Synagogue
Malminkatu 26 00100
Telephone: (9) 586 0310
Fax: (9) 694 8916
Email: srk@jchelsinki
Website: www.jchelsinki.fi
Built in 1906. Preserved in the synagogue is a wreath presented in 1944 by the then President of Finland in memory of Jews who died in the Russo–Finnish war. Services Monday and Thursday morning, 7.45 am, other weekdays 8 am: Friday evening 7pm (summer), 5pm (winter); Shabbat and Sunday mornings 9am.

TOURS
Jewish Heritage in Finland
Malminkatu 38 D 46 00100
Telephone: (9) 694 7756
Fax: (9) 694 7756
Email: zweig@jewish-heritage-finland.com
Website: www.jewish-heritage-finland.com
3 hour tour of Helsinki

TURKU
SYNAGOGUES
Orthodox
Turku Synagogue
Brahenkatu 17
Telephone: (2) 231 2557
Fax: (2) 233 4689
The secretary is always pleased to meet visitors

FRANCE

France now boasts the largest Jewish community in Europe. The Jewish connection with France is a long one: it dates back over 1,000 years as there is evidence of Jewish settlement in several towns in the first few centuries of the Jewish Diaspora. The community grew in early medieval times, and contributed to the economy of the region. Two great Jewish commentators, Rashi and Rabenu Tam, both lived in France. However, French Jewry suffered both from the Crusaders and from other anti-semitic outbursts in the medieval period.

Napoleon's reign heralded the emancipation of French Jewry and, as his armies conquered Europe, the emancipation of other communities began. Despite this, incidents such as the Dreyfus Affair highlighted the fact that anti-semitism was not yet dead. The worst case of anti-semitism in France occurred under the German occupation, when some 70,000 Jews were deported from the community of 300,000. After the war, France became a centre for Jewish immigration, beginning with 80,000 from eastern Europe, and then many thousands from North Africa, which eventually swelled the Jewish population to nearly 700,000.

The community is well served with organisations. Paris alone has 380,000 Jews, more than in the whole of the UK. There are many kosher restaurants, synagogues in many towns throughout the country, newspapers, radio programmes and schools in several cities. In Carpentras and Cavaillon there are synagogues which are considered to be national monuments.

GMT +1 hours
Country calling code: (+33)
Total population: **58,607,000**
Jewish population: **600,000**
Emergency telephone: (police–17) (fire–18)
(ambulance–15)
Electricity voltage: 220

North East

AMIENS
SYNAGOGUES
Amiens Synagogue
38 rue du Port d'Amont 8000

BAR-LE-DUC
Bar-Le-Duc Synagogue
7 Quai Carnot

BEAUVAIS
Beauvais Synagogue
Rue Jules Isaac 60000
Telephone: 03 44 05 46 90

BELFORT
COMMUNITY ORGANISATIONS
Community Publishers
27 rue Strolz, 6 rue de l'As de Carreau 90000
Telephone: 03 84 28 55 41
Fax: 03 84 28 55 41
Publishes *Notre Communaute*

SYNAGOGUES
Belfort Synagogue
6 rue de l'As de Carreau 90000
Telephone: 03 84 28 55 41
Fax: 03 84 28 55 41

BENFELD
Benfield Synagogue
7a rue de la Dime 67230
Telephone: 03 88 74 47 11

BESANCON
BUTCHERS
M. Croppet
18 rue des Granges 25000
Telephone: 03 81 83 35 93
Thursdays only

COMMUNITY ORGANISATIONS
Community
10 rue Grosjean 25000
Telephone: 03 81 80 82 82

SYNAGOGUES
Besancon Synagogue
23c Quai de Strasbourg 25000

BITCHE
Bitche Synagogue
28 rue de Sarreguemines 57230
Services Rosh Hashana & Yom Kippur

BOULAY
Boulay Synagogue
Rue du Pressoir 57220
Telephone: 03 87 79 28 34

BOULOGNE SUR MER
Orthodox
Boulogne Sur Mer Synagogue
43 rue des Abondances, Hauts de Seine 92100
Telephone: 01 46 03 90 63
Fax: 01 46 03 90 63

BOUXWILLER

MUSEUMS
Musee Judeo Alsacien
62a Grand Rue, (on Freeway to Paris) 67330
Telephone: 03 88 70 97 17
Fax: 03 88 70 97 17
Website: www.sdv.fr/juaisme
Visiting hours: from Easter to mid-September. Tuesday to Friday from 2pm to 5pm. Sunday from 2pm to 6pm. The museum, which is housed in an old synagogue, traces the history and culture of the Jews of Alsace.
English spoken and English guidebook

BOUZONVILLE

SYNAGOGUES
Bouzonville Synagogue
3 rue des Benedictins 57320

CHALON SUR-SAONE

Chalon Sur-Saone Synagogue
10 rue Germiny 71100

CHALONS SUR MARNE

Chalons Sur Marne Synagogue
21 rue Lochet 51000

CHAMBERY

Chambery Synagogue
44 rue St Real 73000
Services Friday 7 pm and festivals.

COLMAR

COMMUNITY ORGANISATIONS
Community Centre
3 rue de la Cigogne 68000
Telephone: 03 89 41 38 29
Fax: 03 89 41 12 96
Kosher food can be purchased in the community centre on Wednesdays and Thursdays. Kosher restaurant Wednesday noon during the school period.

SYNAGOGUES
Colmar Synagogue
3 rue de la Cigogne 68000
Telephone: 03 89 41 38 29
Fax: 03 89 41 12 96

COMPIEGNE

Compiegne Synagogue
4 rue du Dr. Charles Nicolle 60200

DIEUZE

Dieuze Synagogue
Avenue Foch 57260

DIJON

BUTCHERS
Albert Levy
25 rue de la Manutention 21000
Telephone: 03 80 30 14 42

SYNAGOGUES
Dijon Synagogue
5 rue de la Synagogue 21000
Telephone: 03 80 66 46 47
Mobile Phone: 0955 649757
Website: www.aci-dijon.org
Mikva on premises

TOURIST SITES
Archaelogical Museum
Has an important collection of old Jewish tombstones

DUNKIRK

SYNAGOGUES
Dunkirk Synagogue
19 rue Jean Bart 59140

EPERNAY

Epernay Synagogue
2 rue Placet 51200
Telephone: 03 26 55 24 44
Services Yom Kippur only

EPINAL

Epinal Synagogue
9 rue Charlet 88000
Telephone: 03 29 82 25 23

FAULQUEMONT CREHANGE

Faulquemont Crehange Synagogue
Place de l'Hotel de Ville 57380
Services Festivals & High Holy Days only.

FORBACH

Forbach Synagogue
98 Av. St. Remy 57600
Telephone: 03 87 85 25 57

GROSBLIEDERSTROFF

Grosbliederstroff Synagogue
6 rue des Fermes 57520

HAGONDANGE

Hagondange Synagogue
Rue Henri Hoffmann 57300

HAGUENAU

Haguenau Synagogue
3 rue du Grand Rabbin Joseph Bloch 67500
Telephone: 03 88 73 38 30

INGWILLER

Ingwiller Synagogue
Cours du Chateau 67340

INSMING

Insming Synagogue
Rue de la Synagogue 57670

LILLE
GROCERIES
Monoprix
Shopping Centre Euralille, rue du Molinel
Telephone: 03 20 06 81 25

SYNAGOGUES
Lille Synagogue
5 rue Auguste Angellier 59012
Telephone: 03 20 52 12 52
Fax: 03 20 31 35 46
Mikva on premises, phone 03 20 85 27 37

LUNEVILLE
Orthodox
Luneville Synagogue
5 rue Castara 54300
Telephone: 03 83 74 08 07
The synagogue built in 1785 has been listed as an historic monument.

MERLEBACH
Merlebach Synagogue
19 rue St Nicholas 57800

METZ
BUTCHERS
Claude Sebbag
22 rue Mangin, Moselle 57000
Telephone: 03 87 63 33 50
Supervision: Chief Rabbi of Moselle

GROCERIES
Atac
23 rue de 20e Corps Amèricain, Moselle 57000

Galaries Lafayette
4 rue Winston Churchill, Moselle 57000
Telephone: 03 87 38 60 60

MIKVAOT
Mikva
30 rue Kellerman
Telephone: 03.87.32.38.04
Mme Rivkah Elalouf,

SYNAGOGUES
Adass Yechouroun
41 rue du Rabbin Elie Bloch, Moselle 57000

Main Synagogue and Community Centre
39 rue du Rabbin Elie Bloch, Moselle 57000
Telephone: 03 87 75 04 44

MONTBELIARD
Montbeliard Synagogue
Rue de la Synagogue 25200

MULHOUSE
Mulhouse Synagogue
2 rue des Rabbins 68100
Telephone: 03 89 66 21 22
Fax: 03 89 56 63 49
Mikva on premises, the old cemetery is also worth a visit

NANCY
COMMUNITY ORGANISATIONS
Communal Centre
19 boulevard Joffre 54000
Telephone: 03 83 32 10 67

MIKVAOT
Mikva
53 rue Hoche
Telephone: 03 83 41 34 48
Mme Myriam Dahan

MUSEUMS
The Musee Historique Lorrain
64 Grand rue 54000
While Jewish buildings were plundered in 1944 an important Jewish collection in the museum survived.

RESTAURANTS
Restaurante Universitaire
19 boulevard Joffre 54000
Telephone: 03 83 32 10 67
Open weekdays at noon

SYNAGOGUES
Nancy Synagogue
17 boulevard Joffre 54000
Telephone: 03 83 32 10 67

OBERNAI
Obernai Synagogue
Rue de Selestat 67210
Telephone: 03 88 95 15 45

TOURIST SITES
Ruins
41 rue du General Gouraud
Remains of an old synagogue.

PHALSBOURG
SYNAGOGUES
Phalsbourg Synagogue
16 rue Alexandre Weill 57370

REIMS
Reims Synagogue
49 rue Clovis 51100
Telephone: 06 16 43 23 10/03 26 54 25 25
Website: http://cjreims.free.fr

SAINT AVOLD

CEMETERIES
The American Military Cemetery
Contains many graves of the USA servicemen who fell in the Second World War

SYNAGOGUES
Saint Avold Synagogue
Place Saint Nabor 57000
Telephone: 03 87 91 16 16

SAINT DIE
Saint Die Synagogue
Rue de l'Eveche 88100
Services, Festivals and Holy Days only.

SAINT LOUIS

CEMETERIES
The Hegenheim Cemetery
Fax: 33 89 67 67 20
Supervision: Rabbi Marc Meyer
Central organisation: Consistoire Israelite Du Ht Rhin 68000 Colmar
This cemetery dates from 1673

COMMUNITY ORGANISATIONS
Community Centre
19 rue du Temple 68300
Telephone: 03 89 70 00 48
Kosher products available

SYNAGOGUES
Orthodox
Saint Louis Synagogue
3 rue de General Cassagnou 68300
Telephone: 03 89 69 07 05
Fax: 03 89 70 15 15
Kosher shop tel: 03 89 70 00 48

SAINT QUENTIN
Synagogue
11 ter boulevard Henri Martin
Telephone: 03 23 08 72

SARREBOURG
Sarrebourg Synagogue
12 rue du Sauvage

SARREGUEMINES
Sarreguemines Synagogue
Rue Georges V 57200
Telephone: 03 87 98 81 40
Fax: 03 87 98 81 40
Mikva on premises

SEDAN CHARLEVILLE
Sedan Charleville Synagogue
6 avenue de Verdun 82000

SELESTAT
Selestat Synagogue
4 rue Ste. Barbe 67600

SENS
Association Cultuelle Israelite de Sens et de L'Yonne
14 rue de la Grande Juiverie 89100
Telephone: 03 86 95 16 65
Fax: 03 86 65 02 11

STRASBOURG
With a Jewish population of 16,000, this city,contested by France and Germany throughout history, currently has an important Jewish community,with several kosher restaurants, butchers and even a kosher vineyard. The earliest evidence of jewish life dates from 1188. In the heart of the Jewish quarter is a thirteenth century Mikvah. Discovered during excavations in the neighborhood, it is not yet completely restored and in a fragile state..

BAKERIES
Crousty Cash
4 rue Sellènick, Bas Rhin 67000
Telephone: 03 88 35 68 21

BOOKSELLERS
Fraenckel
19 rue du Marechal Foch 67000
Telephone: 03 88 36 38 39
Fax: 03 88 37 96 60

Judaica old books and antiquities
Librairie du Cedrat
15 rue de Bitche 67000
Telephone: 03 88 37 32 37
Fax: 03 88 35 63 11
Mobile Phone: 06 11 04 62 30
Email: librairie.cedrat@wanadoo.fr

BUTCHERS
Buchinger
63 rue du Faubourg de Pierre 67000
Telephone: 03 88 32 85 03
13 rue Wimpheling 67000
Telephone: 03 88 61 06 98
David
20 rue Sellenick 67000
Telephone: 03 88 36 75 01
FB Espace Casher
2 4 avenue Foret Noire 67000
Telephone: 03 90 41 18 68
Fax: 03 90 41 19 69

COFFEE SHOP
Coffee Shop
4 rue Strauss Durkheim 67000

DELICATESSEN
Dan Delicatessen
17 rue Finkmatt 67000
Telephone: 03 88 15 19 33

GROCERIES
Cash Center
22 rue Finkmatt 67000
Telephone: 03 88 35 12 38

MEDIA
Newspapers
Echs Unir
1a rue Grand Rabbin Rene Hirschler 67000
Telephone: 03 88 14 46 50
Fax: 03 88 24 26 69
Monthly publication

MUSEUMS
Musee Alsacien
23 quai Saint Nicolas 67000
Telephone: 03 88 52 50 01
Fax: 03 88 43 64 18
Email: mlschneider@cus-strasbourg.net
Website: www.musees strasbourg.org
Has a section on Jewish Art

RELIGIOUS ORGANISATIONS
Consistoire Israelite du Bas Rhin
23 rue Sellenick 67000
Telephone: 03 88 25 05 75
Fax: 03 88 25 12 65
Email: cibr1@libertysurf.fr
Website: http://www.cibr.fr

Regional Chief Rabbi, Rene Gutman
5 rue du General de Castelnau 67000
Telephone: 03 88 25 05 75
Fax: 03 88 25 12 65

RESTAURANTS
Restaurant Universitaire
ORT Laure Weil, 11 rue Sellenick 67000
Telephone: 03 88 76 74 76
Fax: 03 88 76 74 74
Website: www.strasbourg.ort.asso.fr

Dairy
Autre Part
60 boulevard Clemenceau
Telephone: 03 88 37 10 02

Meat
Le King
28 rue Sellenick 67000
Telephone: 03 88 52 17 71
Supplies food early on Friday to take to hotels

SYNAGOGUES
Esplanade
17 rue de Nicosie 67000

Etz-Haim
7 rue Turenne 67000
Telephone: 03 88 24 38 36
Fax: 03 88 24 38 36
Email: president@etzhaim.fr
Website: www.etzhaim.fr

Synagogue de la Paix
1a rue du Grand Rabbin Rene Hirschler 67000
Telephone: 03 88 14 46 50
Fax: 03 88 24 26 69
Website: www.cisonline.org

THIONVILLE
Thionville Synagogue
31 avenue Clemenceau 57100
Telephone: 03 82 54 47 89
Fax: 03 82 53 03 76

TOUL
Toul Synagogue
Rue de la Halle 54200

TROYES
MEMORIAL
Statue of Rashi
Central organisation:
A statue of Rashi stands in Place Jean Moulin

MIKVAOT
Mikvaot
15 rue Brunneval
Telephone: 03 25 73 34 44

SYNAGOGUES
Troyes Synagogue
5 rue Brunneval
The only half timbered shul in France.

VALENCIENNES
Valenciennes Synagogue
36 rue de l'Intendance 59300
Telephone: 03 27 29 11 07

VERDUN
Verdun Synagogue
Impasse des Jacobins 55100
Telephone: 03 83 41 34 48

VITTEL
Vittel Synagogue
211 rue Croix Perrot 88800
Telephone: 03 29 08 10 87
Open in July and August only

WASSELONNE
Wasselonne Synagogue
Ruedes Bains 67310

North West

ANGERS
Angers Synagogue
12 rue Valdemaine 49100

BISCHEIM SCHILTIGHEIM
Bischeim Schiltigheim Synagogue
9 place de la Synagogue 67800
Telephone: 02 38 33 02 87

BREST
Brest Synagogue
40 rue de la Republic 29200
Services Friday, at 7.30 pm

CAEN
BUTCHERS
Boucherie Marcel
26 rue de l'Engannerie 14000
Telephone: 02 31 86 16 25

SYNAGOGUES
Caen Synagogue
46 avenue de la Liberation 14000
Telephone: 02 31 43 60 54

CHATEAROUX
CONTACT INFORMATION
Michel Touati
3 allee Emile Zola, Montierchaume, Deols 36310
Telephone: 02 54 26 05 47

DEAUVILLE
SYNAGOGUES
Deauville Synagogue
14 rue Castor 14800
Telephone: 02 31 81 27 06

ELBEUF
Elbeuf Synagogue
29 rue Gremont 76500
Telephone: 02 35 77 09 11

LE HAVRE
GROCERIES
Super U Porte Oceane
Boulevard Francois 1er
Telephone: 02 35 21 31 35

SYNAGOGUES
Le Havre Synagogue
38 rue Victor Hugo 76600
Telephone: 02 35 21 14 59

LE MANS
Le Mans Synagogue
4-6 boulevard Paixhans 72000
Telephone: 02 43 86 00 96

LORIENT
Lorient Synagogue
18 rue de la Patrie 56100
Services,Friday nights, festivals & Holy Days only

NANTES
Nantes Synagogue
5 Impasse Copernic 44000
Telephone: 02 41 87 48 10
Fax: 02 41 37 11 79
Mikva on premises

ORLEANS
Orleans Synagogue
14 rue Robert de Courtenay (to the left of the cathedral) 45000
Information on services to be had from Marcus Sellem, tel: 02 62 89 18

RENNES
COMMUNITY ORGANISATIONS
Centre Edmond Safra
Rue de la Heronniere, 5 allee du Mont dol 35000
Telephone: 02 99 63 57 18
Services held telephone for times

ROUEN
SYNAGOGUES
Rouen Synagogue
55 rue des Bons Enfants 76100
Telephone: 02 35 71 01 44
The Jewish Youth Club can provide board residence for student travellers and holiday makers

TOURIST SITES
Old Jewish Quarter
Excavations in the 1970s uncovered the ruins of what is the only known medieval Jewish structure whose walls have survived. Now called ëThe house of the Jews' It is considered to most likely have been a yeshiva but it may in fact have been a synagogue.

TOURS
SYNAGOGUES
Tours Synagogue
37 rue Parmentier 37000
Telephone: 02 47 05 56 95

Paris Region

Orthodox
Community Centre and Synagogue
1 rue Sdèrot, angle 1, rue Barthèlèmy, Hauts de Seine 92160
Telephone: 01 46 66 19 17

ANTONY
RESTAURANTS
Pizza-Kosher
mi'Saada
81 avenue Kennedy 92160
Telephone: 01 46 66 80 86
Supervision: Beth Din of Paris

ASNIERES
MIKVAOT
Mikvaot
82 rue du R.P. Christian Gilbert, Hauts de Seine
92600
Telephone: 01 47 99 26 59

SYNAGOGUES
Orthodox
**Asnieres Synagogue ACIP Centre
Communautaire Asnieres-gennevilliers-Bois
Columbes**
73 bis rue des Bas, Hauts de Seine 92600
Telephone: 01 47 99 32 55
Email: yves.akoun@wanadoo.fr

ATHIS MONS
Athis Mons Synagogue
55 rue des Coquelicots, Essonne 91200
Telephone: 01 69 38 14 29

AUBERVILLIERS
RESTAURANTS
Bassari-Kosher
Deux Six
45 avenue Victor Hugo 93300
Telephone: 01 48 39 26 26
Supervision: Beth Din.

French/Bassari-Kosher
Migdal Ohr
17 rue du clos Bernard 93300
Telephone: 01 41 61 17 82
Supervision: Rabbinat Loubavitch de France

AULNAY SOUS BOIS
SYNAGOGUES
Orthodox
Aulnay Sous Bois Synagogue
80 rue Maximilien Robespierre, Seine Saint Denis
 93600
Telephone: 01 48 69 66 93

BAGNEUX
BUTCHERS
Isaac
188 avenue Aristide Briand, Hauts de Seine 92220
Telephone: 01 45 47 00 21

BAGNOLET
BAKERIES
Sonesta
27 rue Adèlaide Lahaye, Seine Saint Denis 93170
Telephone: 01 43 64 92 93
Fax: 01 43 60 51 26
Supervision: Beth Din of Paris

SYNAGOGUES
Orthodox
Bagnolet Synagogue
15 17 rue D. Vienot, Seine Saint Denis 93170
Telephone: 01 43 60 39 93

BOBIGNY
RESTAURANTS
Bassari-Kosher
Nina's Cafe
90 avenue Henri Gautier 93000
Telephone: 01 48 31 94 98
Supervision: Beth Din

Dairy
Cez Daryl
22 24 rue Henri Barbusse, Seine Saint Denis 93000
Telephone: 01 43 60 39 93
Supervision: Beth Din of Paris

North African-Kosher
Regalim
22-24 avenue Henri Barbusse 93000
Telephone: 01 41 71 06 25
Live music Thursdays and Saturdays.

BONDY
SYNAGOGUES
Orthodox
Maison Communautaire
28 avenue de la Villageoise , Seine Saint Denis
93140
Telephone: 01 48 47 50 79

BOULOGNE SUR SEINE
BAKERIES
Ariel
143 avenue J.B. Clèment, Hauts de Seine 92100
Telephone: 01 46 04 24 42
Supervision: Beth Din of Paris

GROCERIES
Ednale
28 rue Georges Sorel, Hauts de Seine 92100
Telephone: 01 46 03 83 37

PATISSERIE
Kosher
Bouogne Cachere
143 avenue J.B. Clement 92100
Telephone: 01 46 04 24 42
Supervision: Beth Din of Paris

RESTAURANTS
Fast Food-Kosher
Cafeteria
15 rue du Port 92100
Telephone: 01 46 04 30 74

Mille et un Buffets
65 rue d'Aguessau 92100
Telephone: 01 46 03 47 17
Supervision: Beth Din of Paris
Fast food for lunch only, delivers meals in Boulogne and 16th

Kosher
K85
85 avenue de la Republique 92100
Supervision: Beth Din of Paris

Pizza-Kosher
Lol Cafe
100 bis avenue Victor Hugo 92100
Telephone: 01 49 09 99 99
Supervision: Beth Din of Paris

Momento Cafe
46 rue de l'ancienne Mairie 92100
Telephone: 01 41 10 08 80
Supervision: Beth Din of Paris

CHAMPIGNY
SYNAGOGUES
Orthodox
Synagogue Beth David
25 avenue du Gènèral de Gaulle, Val de Marne 94500
Telephone: 01 48 85 72 29

CHARENTON LE PONT
PATISSERIE
Kosher
Patisserie Raphael Traiteur
52-54 quai des Carrieres 94220
Supervision: Beth Din

RESTAURANTS
Bassari-Kosher
Bagel Street
3 rue du General Leclerc 94220
Telephone: 01 43 96 20 77
Supervision: Beth Din

Chinese-Kosher
Au delices de Charenton
28 rue de Pris 94220
Telephone: 01 43 78 65 58
Supervision: Beth Din

Japanese-Kosher
Nissaia
172 rue de Paris 94220
Telephone: 01 53 66 26 26
Supervision: Beth Din

Kosher
Joseph
42 rue de Paris 94220
Telephone: 01 43 78 97 55
Supervision: Beth Din

CHELLES
SYNAGOGUES
Orthodox
Chelles Synagogue
14 rue des Anèmones, Seine et Marne 77500
Telephone: 01 60 20 92 93

CHOISY LE ROI
MIKVAOT
Mikvaot
28 avenue de Newburn, Val de Marne 94600
Telephone: 01 48 53 43 70; 02 48 92 68 68

SYNAGOGUES
Orthodox
Choisy Le Roi Synagogue
28 avenue de Newburn, Val de Marne 94600
Telephone: 01 48 53 48 27

CLICHY SUR SEINE
Clichy Sur Seine Synagogue
26 rue Mozart (Espace Clichy), Hauts de Seine 92210
Telephone: 01 47 39 02 43

CRÈTEIL
BAKERIES
La Nougatine
20 Esplanade des Abimes, Val de Marne 94000
Telephone: 01 49 56 98 56
Supervision: Beth Din of Paris

Quick Chaud
26 allèe Parmentier, Val de Marne 94000
Telephone: 01 48 99 08 30
Supervision: Beth Din of Paris

BUTCHERS
Boucherie Patrick
2 rue Edouard Manet, Val de Marne 94000
Telephone: 01 43 39 29 64

La Charolaise Julien
Cte Commercial Kennedy, Loge 13 rue Gabriel Peri,
Val de Marne 94000
Telephone: 01 43 39 20 43

CAFETERIA
Kosher
Kineret Cafe
17 avenue des Abymes 94000
Telephone: 01 43 99 26 26
Supervision: Beth Din

MIKVAOT
Mikvaot
Rue du 8 MMai 1945, Val de Marne 94000
Telephone: 01 43 77 01 70; 01 43 77 19 68

PATISSERIE
Kosher
Caprices et Delices
5 rue Edouard Manet, Val de Marne 94000
Telephone: 01 43 39 20 20
Supervision: Beth Din of Paris

Les Jasmins de Tunis
C.C. Kenndy, Val de Marne 94000
Telephone: 01 43 77 50 56
Supervision: Beth Din of Paris

My Cookies
66 avenue du General Billotte 94000
Telephone: 01 43 77 35 22
Supervision: Beth Din

Tov 'Mie
25 rue Dr Paul Casalis, Val de Marne 94000
Telephone: 01 48 99 00 39

RESTAURANTS
Bassari-Kosher
Chez Hanna
10 esplanade des Abymes 94000
Telephone: 01 43 77 25 97
Supervision: Beth Din

Chicken Tov
Centre Commercial Kennedy 94000
Telephone: 01 43 99 95 06
Supervision: Beth Din

Les Jardins de la Mediterrannèe
28 boulevard J F Kennedy 94000
Telephone: 01 43 77 05056
Supervision: Beth Din

Chinese-Kosher
Le Bamboo du Lac
20 esplanade des Abymes 9400
Telephone: 01 43 39 46 42
Supervision: Beth Din

Mexican-Kosher
Top Kafe
22 esplanade des Abymes 94000
Telephone: 01 43 99 00 39
Supervision: Rabbinat Loubavitch de France

Pizza-Kosher
Pizza Kash
15 esplanade des Abymes 94000
Telephone: 01 43 99 01 04
Supervision: Rabbinat Loubavitch de France

Pizza Yomi
Centre Commercial du Palais 94000
Telephone: 01 48 98 54 88
Supervision: Communautes orthodoxes de Paris

SYNAGOGUES
Orthodox
Consistorial Synagogue
Rue du 8 Mai 1945, Val de Marne 94000
Telephone: 01 43 77 01 70; 01 43 39 05 20
Fax: 01 43 99 03 60
Website: www.synadesvosges.com
Possibilities of Shabbat meals

ENGHIEN
MIKVAOT
Mikvaot
47 rue de Malleville, Val d'Oise 95880
Telephone: 01 34 17 37 11

SYNAGOGUES
Orthodox
Enghien Synagogue
47 rue de Malleville, Val d'Oise 95880
Telephone: 01 34 12 42 34

EPINAY SUR SEINE
PATISSERIE
Kosher
Petit Dejeuner et Cie
5 place des Arcades 93800
Telephone: 01 48 23 11 12
Supervision: Communautes orthodoxes de Paris

RESTAURANTS
Pizza-Kosher
Au grand Large
7 rue des poissommiers 93800
Telephone: 01 42 35 43 43
Supervision: Communautes orthodoxes de Paris

Croc Pizza
5 rue Lacepede 93800
Telephone: 01 42 35 42 42
Supervision: Communautes orthodoxes de Paris

FONTAINEBLEAU
SYNAGOGUES
Orthodox
Fontainebleau Synagogue
38 rue Paul Seramy, Seine et-Marne 77300
Telephone: 01 64 22 68 48
Website: www.consistoire.org/

FONTENAY AUX ROSES
Centre Moise Meniane
17 avenue Paul Langevin, Hauts de Seine 92660
Telephone: 01 46 60 75 94

FONTENAY SOUS BOIS
MIKVAOT
Haya Moussia
177 rue des Moulins, Val de Marne 94120
Telephone: 01 48 77 53 90
Mobile Phone: 06120 34471
Supervision: Beth Din of Paris
Hours: Winter till 7.45pm. Summer til 15 mins before night.
Mikve Vaisselle is open from 8am to 6pm

SYNAGOGUES
Orthodox
Fontenay Sous Bois Synagogue
79 boulevard de Verdun, Val de Marne 94120
Telephone: 01 48 77 38 67

GARGES LES GONESSE
BUTCHERS
Boucherie Berbeche
C.C. Pal de la Dame Blanche, Val d'Oise 95140
Telephone: 01 39 86 42 06

Chez Harry
1 rue J B Corot, Val d'Oise 95140
Telephone: 01 39 86 53 81

MIKVAOT
Mikvaot
15 rue Corot, Val d'Oise 95140
Telephone: 01 39 86 75 64

SYNAGOGUES
Orthodox
Maison Communautaire Chaare Ra'hamim
14 rue Corot, Val d'Oise 95140
Telephone: 01 46 48 34 49

ISSY LES MOULINEAUX
Issy Les Moulineaux Synagogue
72 boulevard Gallieni, Hauts de Seine 92130
Telephone: 01 46 48 34 49

LA COURNEUVE
La Courneuve Synagogue
13 rue Saint Just, Seine Saint Denis 93120
Telephone: 01 48 36 75 59

LA GARENNE COLOMBES
Synagogue and Community Centre of Courbevoie / La Garenne Colombes
13 rue L.M. Nordmann, La Garenne Colombes 92250
Telephone: 01 47 69 92 17; 01 49 05 43 64
Email: alaincohen1@frre.fr

LA VARENNE ST HILAIRE
La Varenne St Hilaire Synagogue
10 bis avenue du chateau, Val de Marne 94210
Telephone: 01 42 83 28 75

LE BLANC MESNIL
Le Blanc Mesnil Synagogue
65 rue Maxime Gorki, Seine Saint Denis 93150
Telephone: 01 48 65 58 98

LE CHESNAY
MIKVAOT
Mikvaot
39 rue de Versailles, Yvelines 78150
Telephone: 01 39 54 05 65; 01 39 07 19 19

LE KREMLIN BICETRE
SYNAGOGUES
Orthodox
Le Kremlin Bicetre Synagogue
41-45 rue J. F. Kennedy, Val de Marne 94270
Telephone: 01 46 72 73 64

LE PERREUX NOGENT
Synagogue Nogent/Le Perreux/Bry Sur Marne
165 bis avenue du Gal de Gaulle, Val de Marne 94170
Telephone: 01 48 72 88 65

LE RAINCY
MIKVAOT
Mikve du Raincy
67 boulevard du Midi, Seine Saint Denis 93340
Telephone: 06 19 30 15 68

PATISSERIE
Kosher
Le Ness
4 allee Victor Hugo 93340
Telephone: 01 43 81 39 36
Supervision: Beth Din

SYNAGOGUES
Orthodox
Maison Communautaire
19 allèe Chatrian, Seine Saint Denis 93340
Telephone: 01 43 02 06 11

LE VESINET

MIKVAOT
Mikvaot
29 rue Henri Cloppet, Yvelines 78110
Telephone: 01 30 53 10 45; 01 30 71 12 26

SYNAGOGUES
Orthodox
Maison Communautaire
29 rue Henri Cloppet, Yvelines 78110
Telephone: 01 30 53 10 45

LES LILAS

BUTCHERS
Boucherie Des Lilas
6 rue de la Republique, Seine Saint Denis 93260
Telephone: 01 43 63 89 15

PATISSERIE
Kosher
La Haloterie
68 rue de pris 93260
Telephone: 01 49 93 06 85
Supervision: Beth Din

RESTAURANTS
Bassari-Kosher
Li Shai
4 bis rue Jea Moulin 93260
Telephone: 01 43 60 49 57
Supervision: Beth Din

LEVALLOIS PERRET

CAFE/PATISSERIE
Cafe des Delicies
109 rue Louis Rouquier 92300
Telephone: 01 47 39 63 39
Supervision: Beth Din of Paris

RESTAURANTS
Cafe Joseph
70 rue Baudin 92300
Telephone: 01 55 90 92 19
Supervision: Beth Din of Paris

Twenty Six
69 rue Marius Aufan 92300
Telephone: 01 47 57 37 22
Supervision: Beth Din of Paris

Fast Food-Kosher
Ztov
34 rue Gabriel Peri 92300
Telephone: 01 47 57 59 08
Supervision: Rabbinat Loubavitch de France
Israeli, Bassari

Meat
Delicates Eden
102 rue Rivay, Hauts de Seine 92300
Telephone: 01 42 70 97 06
Supervision: Beth Din of Paris

Pizza-Kosher
Kotel Cafe
132 rue Louis Rouquier 92300
Telephone: 01 47 37 71 31
Supervision: Beth Din of Paris

Sushi-Kosher
Sushi Eden
9 rue Louise Michel 92300
Telephone: 01 47 48 90 63
Supervision: Beth Din of Paris

SYNAGOGUES
Orthodox
Jewish School
63 rue Louis Rouquier 92300
Telephone: 01 47 57 11 15
Fax: 01 47 57 39 12
Website: www.accil.org
Open hours: 7 am to 8 pm daily

MAISONS ALFORT

MIKVAOT
Mikvaot
92-94 rue Victor Hugo, Val de Marne 94700
Telephone: 01 43 78 95 69

SYNAGOGUES
Orthodox
Maisons Alfort Synagogue
68 rue Victor Hugo 94700
Telephone: 01 43 78 95 69

MASSY

MIKVAOT
Mikvaot
Allèe Marcel Cerdan 91300
Telephone: 01 42 37 48 24

SYNAGOGUES
Orthodox
Massy Synagogue
2 Allèe Marcel Cerdan 91300
Telephone: 01 69 20 94 21

MEAUX

Meaux Synagogue
11 rue P. Barennes, Seine et Marne 77100
Telephone: 01 64 34 76 58

MELUN

Melun Synagogue
Corner rues Branly & Michelet 77003
Telephone: 01 64 52 00 05

MEUDON LA FORET

MIKVAOT
Mikvaot
Rue de la Synagogue, Hauts de Seine 92360
Telephone: 01 46 32 64 82; 01 46 01 32

SYNAGOGUES
Orthodox
Maison Communautaire
Rue de la Synagogue, Hauts de Seine 92360
Telephone: 01 48 53 48 27

MONTREUIL

BAKERIES
Korcarz
134 bis rue de Stalingrad, Seine Saint Denis 93100
Telephone: 01 48 58 33 45
Supervision: Beth Din of Paris/Chief Rabbi Mordechai
Rottenberg

Le Relais Sucre
62 rue des Roches, Seine Saint Denis 93100
Telephone: 01 48 70 22 60
Supervision: Beth Din of Paris

Nat Cacher
21 rue Gabriel Pèri, Seine Saint Denis 93100
Telephone: 01 41 58 05 25
Supervision: Beth Din of Paris

BUTCHERS
Andre Volailles
62 rue des Roches, Seine Saint Denis 93100
Telephone: 01 41 58 58 58

Boucherie Andre
64 rue des Roches, Seine Saint Denis 93100
Telephone: 01 41 58 58 58

PATISSERIE
Kosher
L'abre de Vie
99 rue de Stalingrad 93100
Telephone: 01 48 70 59 77
Supervision: Beth Din

RESTAURANTS
Fast Food-Kosher
Mehorav Cafe
63 rue barbes 93100
Telephone: 01 48 70 07 07
Supervision: Beth Din Delivers

Mendel's
8 rue galvani 93100
Telephone: 01 43 63 17 17
Supervision: Rabbinat Loubavitch de France
Bassari, delivers

Kosher
Pizza Monte Carlo
129 rue Marcel 93100
Telephone: 01 48 59 55 15
Supervision: Beth Din
Halavi

MONTROUGE

MIKVAOT
Ismah Israel
90 rue Gabriel Pèri, Hauts de Seine 92120
Telephone: 01 42 53 08 54

RESTAURANTS
Bassari-Kosher
Aviva Grill
103 rue Gabriel Peri 92120
Telephone: 01 42 53 05 61
Supervision: Beth Din of Paris

Pizza-Kosher
La table de Yaacov
103 rue Gabriel Peri 92120
Telephone: 01 46 56 00 80
Supervision: V

SYNAGOGUES
Orthodox
**Centre Communautaire Regional Malakoff
Montrouge**
90 rue Gabriel Pèri, Hauts de Seine 92120
Telephone: 01 46 32 64 82
Fax: 01 46 56 20 49

NEUILLY

BUTCHERS
Neuilly Cacher
2/6 rue de Chartres, Hauts de Seine 92200
Telephone: 01 47 45 06 06

RESTAURANT/TAKEAWAY
Kosher
Neuilly Traiteur
3 rue de Chartres 92200
Telephone: 01 47 221 60 32
Supervision: Beth Din
delivers to Paris 8,16,17 and Neuilly, Boulogne Asnieres
and Levallois.

RESTAURANTS
Bassari-Kosher
Habiba
18 avenue Charles de Gaulle 92200
Telephone: 01 47 22 37 25
Supervision: Beth Din

Le Monde du Sandwich
203 avenue Charles de Galle 92200
Telephone: 01 46 24 60 01
Supervision: Beth Din

Meat
King David
14 rue Paul Chatrousse, Hauts de Seine 92200
Telephone: 01 47 45 18 19
Supervision: Beth Din of Paris
Deliver. Hours: 8 am to 10 pm.

Sushi-Kosher
Shishi Sushi
20 rue Paul Chatrousse 92200
Telephone: 01 40 88 31 39
Supervision: Beth Din
Delivers

SANDWICH BAR
Pizza-Kosher
Sandwiches and Traditions
19 rue Beffroy 92200
Telephone: 01 47 47 53 10
Supervision: Beth Din
Delivers

SYNAGOGUES
Orthodox
Neuilly Synagogue
12 rue Ancelle, Centre Communautaire, 44 rue
Jaques Dolud 92200
Telephone: 01 47 47 78 76
Fax: 01 47 47 54 79
Email: synaneuilly@club-internet.fr
Website: www.synaneuilly.com
Supervision: Beth Din de Paris
Central organisation: ACIP

PANTIN
BUTCHERS
Levy Baroukh
5/7 rue Antole France, Seine Saint Denis 93500
Telephone: 01 48 91 02 14

PATISSERIE
Kosher
Zazou
20 rue de la Paix 93500
Telephone: 01 41 83 11 40
Supervision: Beth Din

RESTAURANTS
Bassari-Kosher
Aux Delices de Yaffo
189 avenue Jean Iolive 93500
Telephone: 01 48 43 43 43

Sushi Azur
160 avenue du General Leclerc 93500
Telephone: 01 41 50 07 70
Supervision: Beth Din

Dairy
Chez Jacquy
24 rue Prè Saint Gervais, Seine Saint Denis 93500
Telephone: 01 48 10 94 24
Supervision: Beth Din of Paris

SYNAGOGUES
Orthodox
Pantin Synagogue
8 rue Gambetta, Seine Saint Denis 93500

PARIS
The city of Paris is divided into districts
(arrondissements) designated by the last two
digits of the post code. In the categories below,
establishments are listed in numerical order
according to the post code (that is, -01,-02,-03
and so on).
The historic centre of Paris Jewish life is found
in the Marais area (4th arrondissement),
although a synagogue stood on the Ile de Citè
before Notre Dame was built, Jews having lived
in the city since Roman times. Another more
central area is that around rue Richer (9th
arrondissement) which, although not as
historic as such, has many kosher restaurants
of varying styles and prices.
An important new site to be visited is the
Musee d'art et d'histoire du Judaisme which
opened in December 1998.

1eme arrondissment
Pah'ad David
11 rue du Plateau 75019
Telephone: 01 42 08 25 40
Fax: 01 42 08 50 85
Email: hevaatpinto@aol.com

RESTAURANTS
Chinese-Kosher
La Chine
83 avenue Paul Valery 95200
Telephone: 01 34 29 17 17
Supervision: Rabbinat Loubavitch de France

Thai-Kosher
Baan Hai
62 rue Jean-Jacques Rousseau 75001
Telephone: 01 40 28 99 04
Supervision: Beth Din of Paris

2eme arrondissment
Bassari-Kosher
Chez Jacky
24 rue du 4 septembre 75002
Telephone: 01 42 65 37 11
Supervision: Beth Din of Paris

Chez Kiki
9 rue de Mulhouse 75002
Telephone: 01 40 41 95 64
Supervision: Beth Din of Paris

Chez Papy
75002Telephone: 01 42 33 80 96
Supervision: Beth Din of Paris

Hoff Cafe
9 rue de Nil 75002
Telephone: 01 45 08 92 29
Supervision: Beth Din of Paris

Le Sable Blanc
6 passage du ponceau 75002
Telephone: 01 42 33 10 66
Supervision: Beth Din of Paris

Restaurant Henri
13/15 passage du ponceau 75002
Telephone: 01 40 13 91 72
Supervision: Beth Din of Paris

Sushi Ka
3 rue du ponceau 75002
Telephone: 01 40 41 99 62
Supervision: Beth Din of Paris

Burger-Kosher
Le Beverly
48 passage du Caire 75002
Telephone: 01 40 26 23 39
Supervision: Beth Din of Paris

Fast Food-Kosher
Panini Folie
11 rue du ponceau 75002
Telephone: 01 42 33 14 55
Supervision: Beth Din of Paris

3eme arrondissment
CAFE/PATISSERIE
Kosher
Ma Toque
76 rue Charlot 75003
Telephone: 01 48 04 76 76
Supervision: Beth Din of Paris

MIKVAOT
Mikvaot
176 rue du Temple 75003
Telephone: 01 42 71 89 28
16 21 rue Galvani 75017
Telephone: 01 45 74 52 80
The mikvah is located in the centre of Paris, near Place de la Rèpublique, at the rear of the building. The Staff is English speaking.

MUSEUMS
Musèe d'Art et d'Histoire du Judaisme
Hotel de Saint Aignan, 71 rue du Temple 75003
Telephone: 01 53 01 86 53
Fax: 01 42 72 97 47
Email: info@mahj.org
Website: www.mahj.org
Hours: Monday to Friday of 11am to 6pm and Sunday of

10am to 6pm. It is closed Saturdays, on January 1, on May 1, the 2 days of the Jewish New Year (Roch Hachana) and the day of Kippour The ticket office closes at 5.15pm for the museum and 5.30pm for the temporary exhibitions. For more information with following see the website www.mahj.org

RESTAURANTS
Bassari-Kosher
Bagel Store L.A.
31 rue de Turenne 75003
Telephone: 01 44 78 06 03
Supervision: Beth Din of Paris

Chez Isaac
52 rue Volta 75003
Telephone: 01 42 71 19 03
Supervision: Beth Din of Paris

Fast Food-Kosher
Corner
57 rue de Turenne 75003
Telephone: 01 40 29 07 07
Supervision: Beth Din of Paris

Japanese-Kosher
Sushi West
10 rue de Bretagne 75003
Telephone: 01 42 74 13 63
Supervision: Beth Din of Paris
Delivers

Kosher
Bagel's Club
24 rue Reaumur 75003
Telephone: 01 40 29 00 91
Supervision: Beth Din of Paris

Cafe D'Art Juif
71 Rue Du Temple 75003
Sited in the Museum of Jewish Art and History

Meat
La Petite Famille
32 rue des Rosiers 75003 75003
Telephone: 01 42 77 00 50
Supervision: Beth Din of Paris

SYNAGOGUES
Orthodox
Groupe Rabbi Yehiel de Paris
25 rue Michel Leconte 75003
Telephone: 01 42 78 89 17

Synagogue
15 rue Notre Dame de Nazareth 75003
Telephone: 01 42 78 00 30
Fax: 01 42 78 05 18
Central organisation: A.C.I.P.

4eme arrondissment

BAKERIES
Mezel
1 rue Ferdinand Duval 75004
Telephone: 01 42 78 25 01
Supervision: Beth Din of Paris

BAKERIES AND RESTAURANT
Korcarz
29 rue des Rosiers 75004
Telephone: 01 42 77 39 47
Fax: 01 48 58 28 44
Supervision: Beth Din of Paris/Chief Rabbi Mordechai Rottenberg

BUTCHERS
Saada
17 rue des Rosiers 75004
Telephone: 01 42 77 76 22

DELICATESSEN
Kosher
Micky's Deli
23 bis rue des Rosiers 75004
Telephone: 01 48 04 79 31
Supervision: Communautes orthodoxes de Paris

MONUMENT
Shoah Memorial
rue Geoffroy l'Asnier 17 75004
Telephone: 001 42 77 4472
Fax: 001 53 01 1744
The memorial is a tribute to the Jews who perished in the Holocaust. Erected in 1956 it contains the Archives of the Centre de Documentation Juive Contemporaine. At the centre is an 'eeternal flame'.

RELIGIOUS ORGANISATIONS
Communautè Israèlite Orthodox de Paris
10 rue Pavèe 75004
Telephone: 01 42 77 81 51
Fax: 01 48 87 26 29
Supervision: Rav Mordecai Rottenberg

RESTAURANTS
Dairy
Contini
42 rue des Rosiers 75004
Telephone: 01 48 04 78 32
Supervision: Beth Din of Paris

Glatt Kosher
La Verriere du Marais
23 Rue des Rosiers 75004
Telephone: 01 42 77 12 75

Israeli
L'as du Falafel
34 rue des Rosiers 75004
Telephone: 01 48 87 63 60
Supervision: Beth Din of Paris

Mivami
23 rue des Rosiers 75004
Telephone: 01 42 71 53 72
Supervision: Beth Din of Paris

Kosher
Hollywood Bagel
19 rue Ferdinand Duval 75004
Telephone: 01 42 77 19 80
Supervision: Beth Din of Paris

Murciano Benguigui
14 rue des Rosiers 75004
Telephone: 01 48 87 48 88
Supervision: Communautes orthodoxes de Paris
Patries, chocolates

Pitzman
8 rue Pavee 75004
Telephone: 01 42 71 17 17
Fax: 01 42 71 17 16
Supervision: Communautes orthodoxes de Paris

Pizza-Kosher
Kosher Pizza
11 rue des Rosiers 75004
Telephone: 01 48 87 17 83
Supervision: Communautes orthodoxes de Paris

SYNAGOGUES
Orthodox
Adath Yechouroun
25 rue des Rosiers 75004
Telephone: 01 44 59 82 36

Agoudas Hakehilos
10 rue Pavèe 75004
Telephone: 01 48 87 21 54
Fax: 01 48 87 26 29
A striking Art Nouveau synagogue designed by Hector Guimard, the creator of the world famous Metro entrances, in 1913

Fondation Roger Fleishmann
18 rue des Ecouffes 75004
Telephone: 01 48 87 97 86

Oratoire Mahzikè Adath Mouvement Loubavitch
17 rue de Rosiers 75004

Synagogue Charles Lichè
14 Place des Vosges 75004
Telephone: 1 48 87 79 45
Fax: 1 48 87 57 58
Email: synadesvosges@noos.fr
Website: www.synadesvosges.com
Shabbat meals ë Only Seouda Shlichit' the Third meal.

Synagogue des Tournelles
21 bis rue des Tourelles 75004
Telephone: 01 42 74 32 65; 01 42 74 32 80
Fax: 01 40 29 90 27

Synagogue Tephilat Israĺl Frank Forter
24 rue de Bourg Tibourg 75004
Telephone: 01 46 24 48 94

5eme arrondissment

LIBRARIES

Library Judica of the Seminaire Israelite de France
9 rue Vauquelin 75005
Telephone: 01 47 07 22 94
Email: sifbibli@free.fr
Website: www.rachelnet.net
Visit only by appointment

RESTAURANTS

Fast Food-Kosher
Centre Rachi
39 rue Broca 75005
Telephone: 01 47 70 91 25

Pizza-Kosher
Salade Cafe
10 rue Touillier 75005
Telephone: 01 40 51 74 55
Supervision: Rabbinat Loubavitch de France
Closed evenings and Sundays

SYNAGOGUES

Orthodox
Centre Rachi
30 boulevard du Port Royal 75005
Telephone: 01 43 31 98 20

Sèminaire Israèlite de France
9 rue Vauquelin 75005
Telephone: 01 47 07 21 22
Fax: 01 43 37 75 92

6eme arrondissment

RESTAURANTS

Japanese-Kosher
Sushi West
169 boulevard St. Germaine 75006
Telephone: 08 26 88 26 88
Supervision: Beth Din of Paris
Delivers

Kosher
Harry's Cafe
7 rue Clement Marche, St Germaine 75006
Telephone: 01 43 41 09 59
Supervision: Beth Din of Paris
Patisserie, Sunday brunch

Meat
Centre Edmond Fleg
8 bis, rue de l'Eperon 75006
Telephone: 01 46 33 43 31
Supervision: Beth Din of Paris

SYNAGOGUES

Orthodox
Centre Edmond Fleg
8 bis rue de l'Epèron 75006
Telephone: 01 46 33 43 31
Houses the Union des Centres Communautaires (UCC),
which can be contacted via the same telephone number.
Their fax number is 01 43 25 86 19. Tikvatènou, the Jewish
youth movenent of the Consistoire, is also located here, tel:
01 46 33 43 24; fax: 01 43 25 20 59.

7eme arrondissment

RESTAURANTS

Bassari-Kosher
La Telegraphe
41 rue de Lille 75007
Telephone: 01 42 92 03 04
Supervision: Beth Din of Paris
Sunday brunch, National monument

SYNAGOGUES

Orthodox
E.E.I.F.
27 avenue de Sègur 75007
Telephone: 01 47 83 60 33

8eme arrondissment

EMBASSY

Embassy of Israel
3 rue Rabelais 75008
Telephone: 01 40 76 55 00
Fax: 01 40 76 55 55

MUSEUMS

Musee Nissim de Camondo
63, rue de Monceau 75008
Telephone: 01 53 89 06 50
Fax: 01 53 89 06 42
Website: www.lesartsdecoratifs.fr
Reconstruction of an eighteenth century aristocratic home.
This home and its collection were bequeathed to France in
1935 by Comte Moise de Camondo in memory of his son
Nissim, who died in combat in 1917.

RESTAURANTS

Bassari-Kosher
Kavod
26 rue Jean Mermoz 75008
Telephone: 01 42 25 65 26
Supervision: Beth Din of Paris

Italian-Kosher
Art Up Kafee
17 rue Jean Mermoz 75008
Telephone: 01 42 25 00 55
Supervision: Beth Din of Paris

Cinecitta Cafè
7 rue d'Aguesseau 75008
Telephone: 01 42 68 05 03
Supervision: Beth Din of Paris

Deloren Cafe
45 avenue Friedland 75008

Franck Souffan
81 rue de mirosmenil 75008
Supervision: Beth Din of Paris
Patisserie

Inte Caffe
22 rue de cambaceres 75008
Telephone: 01 40 07 03 90
Supervision: Beth Din of Paris

Kosher

Beth habad des Champs Elysees
102 avenue des Champs Elysees 75008
Telephone: 01 53 75 36 01
Supervision: Beth Din of Paris
Sandwiches

Coffee World
36 rue de Berri 75008
Telephone: 01 49 53 07 34
Supervision: Communautes orthodoxes de Paris

Monteko Cafe
45 rue de Ponthieu 75008
Telephone: 01 45 63 14 10
Supervision: Beth Din of Paris
Sandwiches, delivers

Monteko Cafe
12 rue pasquier 75008
Telephone: 01 42 65 32 84
Supervision: Beth Din of Paris
Sandwishes, delivers

Pizza-Kosher

Il Conte
26 rue d'artois 75008
Telephone: 01 49 53 01 21
Supervision: Beth Din of Paris

Sushi-Kosher

Sushi Kom
7 rue Berryer 75008
Telephone: 01 42 56 01 76
Supervision: Beth Din of Paris

Time Sushi
2 rue Joseph Sanboeuf 75008
Telephone: 01 44 70 07 44
Supervision: Beth Din of Paris

SYNAGOGUES

Orthodox

Elie Dray
218-220 rue du Faubourg St Honorè 75008
Telephone: 01 45 61 20 25
Fax: 01 45 61 14 35
Website: www.aio-syna.org
Supervision: SEM
Located behind the Golden Tulip Hotel.

9eme arrondissment

BAKERIES

Douieb
11 bis rue Geoffroy Marie 75009
Telephone: 01 47 70 86 09
Fax: 01 42 46 38 10
Supervision: Beth Din of Paris

BUTCHERS

Berbeche
46 rue Richer 75009
Telephone: 01 47 70 50 58

Charlot
33 rue Richer 75009
Telephone: 01 45 23 10 34

La Rose Blanche
43 rue Richer 75009
Telephone: 01 48 24 84 65

CAFE/PATISSERIE

kosher

Ma Toque Golan
10 rue Geoffroy Marie 75009
Telephone: 01 48 00 94 71
Supervision: Beth Din of Paris
Salon de thè

GROCERIES

Doueib
11 bis rue Geoffroy Marie 75009
Telephone: 01 47 70 86 09

Chocolatier-Kosher

Damyel
35 rue Richer 75009
Telephone: 010 42 46 19 44
Supervision: Communautes orthodoxes de Paris

HOTELS

Hotel de la Havane
44 rue de Trevise 75009
Telephone: 01 47 70 79 12
Fax: 01 47 70 05 12

Pavillon De Paris
7 rue de Parme 75009
Telephone: 01 55 31 60 00
Fax: 01 55 31 60 01
Website: www.pavillondeparis.com

Kosher

Hotel Aida Opèra
17 rue du Conservatoire 75009
Telephone: 01 45 23 11 11
Fax: 01 47 70 38 73
Website: www.aida-opera.com
Supervision: Beth Din of Paris
Breakfast / Brunch is open to non residents.

Hotel Lebron
4 rue Lamartine 75009
Telephone: 01 48 78 75 52
Fax: 01 49 95 94 64
Supervision: Beth Din of Paris

Hotel Touring
21 rue Buffault 75009
Telephone: 01 48 78 09 16
Fax: 01 48 78 27 74
Website: www.hotel touring.fr
Shabbat meals no longer available

RESTAURANTS

Fast Food-Kosher

Joey's Cafe
34 rue de la Victoire 75009
Telephone: 01 40 82 97 39
Supervision: Beth Din of Paris

Mazal Cafe
31 rue St. Georges 75009
Telephone: 01 48 78 08 00
Supervision: Beth Din of Paris

Israeli

Chez Jonathan
24 rue du Faubourg-Montmartre 75009
Telephone: 01 48 24 03 83
Supervision: Rabbinat Loubavitch de France

Sova Chez nissim
10 rue de la Boule Rouge 75009
Telephone: 01 47 70 01 55
Supervision: Beth Din of Paris

Japanese-Kosher

Izaaki
35 rue Lafayette 75009
Telephone: 01 53 16 43 48
Supervision: Beth Din of Paris

Sushi West
26 rue Lamartine 75009
Telephone: 01 42 74 13 63

Supervision: Beth Din of Paris
Delivers

Kosher

Hotel Geoffroy Marie Opèra
12 rue Geoffroy Marie 75009
Telephone: 01 47 70 11 85
Supervision: Beth Din of Paris
Kosher breakfast

Meat

Chez David
11 rue Montyon 75009
Telephone: 01 44 83 01 24
Supervision: Beth Din of Paris

Synagogue Beth El
4 rue Saulnier 75009
Telephone: 01 45 23 34 89
Fax: 01 45 23 10 75
Supervision: Beth Din of Paris
Prepaid Shabbat meals by arrangement.

Oriental-Kosher

Chez Mimi
26 rue Richer 75009
Telephone: 01 48 24 42 77
Supervision: Beth Din of Paris

Les Ailes
34 rue Richer 75009
Telephone: 01 47 70 62 53
Supervision: Beth Din of Paris
Shabbat meals to take away; delivers. Patisserie

Zazou
2 rue du Faubourg Montmarte 75009
Telephone: 01 40 22 08 33
Supervision: Beth Din of Paris
Patisserie

Pizza-Kosher

Casa Rina
18 Faubourg Monmarte 75009
Telephone: 01 45 23 02 22
Supervision: Beth Din of Paris

Dizengoff Cafè
27 rue Richer 75009
Telephone: 01 47 70 81 97
Supervision: Beth Din of Paris
Open from 12pm to 10.30pm.

il Pazzo
17 rue Lafayette 75009
Telephone: 01 48 74 60 31
Fax: 01 92 81 57 32
Supervision: Beth Din of Paris

SYNAGOGUES

Orthodox
Adass Yereim
10 rue Cadet 75009
Telephone: 01 42 46 36 47; 01 48 74 51 78
Fax: 01 48 74 35 35

Beth El
3 bis rue Saulnier 75009
Telephone: 01 45 23 15 75

Beth Israĺl
4 rue Saulnier 75009
Telephone: 01 45 23 34 89

Grande Synagogue de Paris
44 rue de la Victoire 75009
Telephone: 01 40 82 26 26 ext. 2773, 01 45 26 95 36
Fax: 01 45 26 95 36
Email: infos@lavictoire.org
Website: www.lavictoire.org
Supervision: Chief Rabbi Gilles Bernheim

Rachi Chull
6 rue Ambroise Thomas 75009
Telephone: 01 48 24 86 94

Siège du Beth Loubavitch
8 rue Lamartine 75009
Telephone: 01 45 26 87 60
Fax: 01 45 26 24 37

Synagogue Berit Chalom
18 rue Saint Lazare 75009
Telephone: 01 48 78 45 32; 01 48 78 38 80

Tiferet Yaacob
71 rue de Dunkerque 75009
Telephonc: 01 42 812 32 17; 01 42 49 65 12
4 rue Martel 75010
Telephone: 01 42 85 12 74

10eme arrondissment

BUTCHERS
Chez Jacques
19 rue Bouchardon 75010
Telephone: 01 42 06 76 13

HOLIDAY VILLAGE
Kosher
Art Hotel
98 rue d'Hauteville 75010
Telephone: 01 45 23 85 00
Supervision: Beth Din of Paris
Kosher breakfast

RESTAURANTS
Bassari
Cash Food
63 rue des Vinaigriers 75010
Telephone: 01 42 03 95 75
Supervision: Beth Din of Paris

Fast Food-Kosher
Banana Republik
8 rue Beaupaire 75010
Telephone: 01 42 38 26 13
Supervision: Beth Din of Paris

Japanese-Kosher
Nina Sushi Bar
16 rue Beaupaire 75010
Telephone: 01 42 39 04 38
Supervision: Beth Din of Paris

Sushi West
10 rue de bretagne 75010
Telephone: 08 26 88 26 88
Supervision: Beth Din of Paris
Delivers

Kosher
Le Petit Kif
18 rue de Chateau d'Eau 75010
Telephone: 01 40 40 79 62
Supervision: Beth Din of Paris

Resto Flash
10 rue Lucien SamPaix 75010
Telephone: 01 42 45 03 30
Supervision: Beth Din of Paris

Meat
Dolly's Food
9 rue citè Riverain 75010
Telephone: 01 48 03 08 40
Supervision: Beth Din of Paris

Les Cantiques
16 rue Beaurepaire 75010
Telephone: 01 42 4064 21
Supervision: Beth Din of Paris

Pizza-Kosher
pizza au metre
260 rue du Faubourg Saint-martin 75010
Telephone: 01 42 09 15 15
Supervision: Rabbinat Loubavitch de France
Delivers

Pizza Tova
2 rue Lucien Sampaix 75010
Telephone: 01 40 40 99 90
Supervision: Rabbinat Loubavitch de France
order online, delivers all over Paris

Sushi-Kosher
Cine Sushi
3 rue Gabriel Laumain 75010
Telephone: 01 42 71 70 70
Supervision: Beth Din of Paris

Kmaro Sushi
270 rue de Faubourg Saint-Martin 75010
Telephone: 01 42 05 05 20
Supervision: Beth Din of Paris

Sushi Arts
48 rue rene Boulanger 75010
Telephone: 01 42 49 02 40
Supervision: Beth Din of Paris

SYNAGOGUES
Orthodox
Rav Pealim (Braslav)
49 boulevard de la Villette 75010
Telephone: 01 42 41 55 44

Synagogue Torath Hayim -Ohr Hanania
130 rue du Faubourg Saint Martin 75010
Telephone: 06 81 86 07 63
Fax: 09 55 88 58 96

11eme arrondissment

BAKERIES
Mendez
3 ter rue de la Prèsentation 75011
Telephone: 01 43 57 02 03
Supervision: Beth Din of Paris

Nathan de Belleville
67 boulevard de Belleville 75011
Telephone: 01 43 57 24 60
Supervision: Beth Din of Paris

BUTCHERS
Charly Halak B. Y.
51 rue Richard Lenoir 75011
Telephone: 01 43 4862 26

Chez Andre
69 boulevard de Belleville 75011
Telephone: 01 43 57 80 38

Chez Jojo
20 rue Louis Bonnet 75011
Telephone: 01 43 55 10 29

Maurice Zirah
91 rue de la Roquette 75011
Telephone: 01 43 79 62 53

CAFE/PATISSERIE
Kosher
Charles Traiteur
244 boulevard Voltaire 75011
Telephone: 01 43 73 70 00
Supervision: Beth Din of Paris
Take away for Shabbat

Franck Souffan
264 boulevard Voltaire 75011
Telephone: 01 43 67 49 64
Supervision: Beth Din of Paris
Outside tables

ivin
159 avenue Ledru Rollin 75011
Telephone: 01 43 67 73 30
Supervision: Beth Din of Paris

Les Jasmins de Tunis
3 ter rue de la presentation 75011
Telephone: 01 43 38 63 18
Supervision: Beth Din of Paris
Tunisian

Ma Toque
67 boulevard de Belleville 75011
Telephone: 01 43 57 24 60
Supervision: Beth Din of Paris

Ougaland
250 boulevard Voltaire 75011
Telephone: 01 40 09 92 00
Supervision: Beth Din of Paris

HOTELS
L'Hotel de Mericourt
50 rue de la Folie Mericourt 75011
Telephone: 01 43 38 73 63
Fax: 01 43 38 66 13
Email: hoteldemericourt@wanadoo.fr
Situated in an area with many kosher facilities

RESTAURANTS
Chinese-Kosher
China seven
231 boulevard Voltaire 75011
Telephone: 01 43 73 02 02
Supervision: Beth Din of Paris

Le Lotus de Nissan
39 rue Amelot 75011
Telephone: 01 43 55 80 42
Supervision: Beth Din of Paris

Dairy
Cocktail Cafè
82 avenue Parmetier 75011
Telephone: 01 43 57 19 94
Supervision: Beth Din of Paris

Fast Food-Kosher
Carmel Delice
144 boulevard Voltaire 75011
Telephone: 01 43 56 06 05
Supervision: Beth Din of Paris

King Delice
30 boulevard Voltaire 75011
Telephone: 01 43 38 26 42
Supervision: Beth Din of Paris
Israeli; oriental

La Delicieuse
234 boulevard Voltaire 75011
Telephone: 01 42 01 26 26
Fax: 01 40 24 26 28
Supervision: Beth Din of Paris
Patisserie, bread

French-Kosher
L'eden
247 rue du Faubourg St. Antoine 75011
Telephone: 01 43 72 88 99
Supervision: Rabbinat Loubavitch de France

Indochinese-Kosher
Yung Pana
115 boulevard Voltaire 75011
Telephone: 01 43 79 20 48
Supervision: Beth Din of Paris

Italian-Kosher
Ima Mia
44 boulevard Voltaire 75011
Telephone: 06 99 28 81 11
Supervision: Beth Din of Paris

Le New's
56 avenue de la Règublique 75011
Telephone: 01 43 38 63 18
Supervision: Beth Din of Paris

Kosher
Americano
54 rue basfroi 75011
Telephone: 01 43 72 96 06
Supervision: Beth Din of Paris

Beggel Off
246 boulevard Voltaire 75011
Telephone: 01 43 70 50 50
Supervision: Beth Din of Paris

Beggel Toast
248 boulevard Voltaire 75011
Telephone: 01 43 70 50 50
Supervision: Beth Din of Paris

Meat
Le Cabourg
102 boulevard Voltaire 75011
Telephone: 01 47 00 71 43
Supervision: Beth Din of Paris
Hours: 12pm to 2.30pm and 7pm to 11pm.

Le Manahattan
231 boulevardVoltaire 75011
Telephone: 01 43 56 03 30
Supervision: Beth Din of Paris

Mexican-Kosher
Tchapaï
53 rue Amelot 75011
Telephone: 01 43 38 88 40
Supervision: Beth Din of Paris

Pizza-Kosher
Pizza Gina
256 boulevard Voltaire 75011
Telephone: 01 43 56 02 72
Supervision: Beth Din of Paris

Tchic Rchac
96 rue de Clery 75011
Telephone: 01 42 33 13 70
Supervision: Rabbinat Loubavitch de France
Delivers

Sushi-Kosher
Yapany Sushi
56 rue Richard lenoir 75011
Telephone: 01 43 70 55 55
Supervision: Beth Din of Paris
Japanese and Chinese

Yapany Sushi
219 boulevard Voltaire 75011
Telephone: 01 43 70 66 66
Supervision: Beth Din of Paris

B.S.D., B.N
OHEL MENACHEM
**FREE assistance for the Jewish visitor to Paris.
Help with any questions, any need, for example:
Shiurim; other Torah learning oppotunities; places to eat;
places to stay, drivers, etc.**

There is no ERUV in Paris

**FREE Shabbat hospitality
Telephone: +33 6 72 96 58 95**

SYNAGOGUES

Orthodox

Adath Israîl
36 rue Basfroi 75011
Telephone: 01 43 67 89 20
Email: adathisrael@gmail.com
Website: www.picasaweb.google.com/adathIsrael
Rav Yermiyahu M. Kohen (av beth din of Paris)
Mikwe for men and kelim

Ets Haim
18 rue Basfroi 75011
Telephone: 01 43 48 82 42

Ora Vesimha
37 rue des Trois Bornes 75011
Telephone: 01 43 57 49 84

Synagogue Don Isaac Abravanel
84 86 rue de la Roquette 75011
Telephone: 01 47 00 75 95

12eme arrondissment

BUTCHERS
Boucherie Guy
266 rue de Charenton 75012
Telephone: 01 43 44 60 90

J V (Temim)
2 rue de Dr Goujon 75012
Telephone: 01 43 45 78 77

CAFE/PATISSERIE
Kosher
Haim et Gordon
55 avenue du general Michel Bizot 75012
Telephone: 01 43 45 55 55
Supervision: Beth Din of Paris
Sandwiches

Harry's cafe
85 avenue du general michel bizot 75012
Telephone: 01 43 41 09 59
Supervision: Beth Din of Paris
Sunday brunch

Le sully
203 avenue Daumesnil 75012
Telephone: 01 43 07 67 05
Supervision: Beth Din of Paris

RESTAURANTS
Fast Food-Kosher
Fresh
8 rue Parrot 75012
Telephone: 01 43 43 35 35
Supervision: Beth Din of Paris

French-Kosher
O You
164 avenue Daumesnil 75012
Telephone: 01 43 07 68 97
Supervision: Beth Din of Paris

Italian-Kosher
Eden's Coffee
75/79 boulevard Soult 75012
Telephone: 06 60 46 84 61
Supervision: Beth Din of Paris
Delivers

La Stella
158 avenue Daumesnil 75012
Telephone: 01 43 47 18 68
Supervision: Beth Din of Paris

Kosher
K'Rolls
266 rue de Charenton 75012
Telephone: 01 43 44 26 40
Supervision: Beth Din of Paris

Pizza-Kosher
La Tayelet
34 rue Louis Braille 75012
Telephone: 01 43 43 20 43
Supervision: Rabbinat Loubavitch de France

Tib's
177 avenue Daumesnil 75012
Telephone: 01 42 45 00 45
Supervision: Communautes orthodoxes de Paris
Crepes, sushi delivers

SYNAGOGUES
Orthodox
Chivtei Israel
12-14 Citè Moynet 75012
Telephone: 01 43 40 45 71
Fax: 01 40 19 97 24
Mobile Phone: 0661 252 525
Supervision: Rav Dov Lellouche

Nèvè Chalom
29 rue Sibuè 75012
Telephone: 01 43 42 07 70
Fax: 01 43 48 44 50

Religious Sephardic
Oratoire de la Fondation Rothschild (Maison de Retraite)
76 rue de Picpus 75012
Telephone: 01 4468 72 98

13eme arrondissment

BUTCHERS
Berbeche
5 rue Vandrezanne 75013
Telephone: 01 45 88 86 50
6 rue du Mouliet 75013
Telephone: 01 45 80 89 10

CAFE/PATISSERIE
Kosher
Mazaline
13 rue Henri Michaud 75013
Telephone: 01 53 80 04 05
Supervision: Beth Din of Paris

GROCERIES
Le Haim
6 rue Paulin Enfert 75013
Telephone: 01 44 24 53 34

RESTAURANTS
Kosher
David
123/125 boulevard Massena 75013
Telephone: 01 45 85 03 43
Supervision: Beth Din of Paris
Yav Ketring
6 rue Paulin Enfert 75013
Telephone: 01 44 34 01 98
Supervision: Beth Din of Paris

Pizza-Kosher
Antipasti Cafe
8 rue Jeanne d'Arc 75013
Telephone: 01 44 06 06 14
Supervision: Rabbinat Loubavitch de France
Bagels, panini, delivers

SYNAGOGUES
Orthodox
Avoth Ouvanim
59 avenue d'Ivry 75013
Telephone: 01 45 82 80 73
Fax: 01 45 85 94 39
223 rue Vercingètorix 75014
Telephone: 01 45 45 50 51
6 bis villa d'Alèsia 75014
Telephone: 01 45 40 82 35
Fax; 01 45 40 72 89

Merkaz Beth Myriam
19 rue Domrèmy 75013
Telephone: 01 45 86 83 99
Fax: 01 45 86 83 99

14eme arrondissment
Beith Chalom
25 villa d'Alèsia 75014
Telephone: 01 45 45 38 71
Fax: 01 43 37 58 49

15eme arrondissment

BUTCHERS
Boucherie Claude
174 rue Lecourbe 75015
Telephone: 01 48 28 02 00

RESTAURANTS
Japanese-Kosher
Sushi west
236 rue de la Croix Nivert 75015
Telephone: 08 26 88 26 88
Delivers

Pizza-Kosher
Mona Lisa
55 boulevard Lefebvre 75015
Supervision: Beth Din of Paris
Delivers and take away

SYNAGOGUES
Masorti
Communaute Juive Massorti de Paris
8 rue George Bernard Shaw (off rue Dupleix) 75015
Telephone: 01 45 67 97 96
Fax: 01 45 56 89 79
Website: ww.jtsa.edu/synagogues/adathsfr/
Services Friday night 6.30 pm. Shabbat morning 10 am
festivals and Rosh Chodesh.

Orthodox
Ohel Mordekhai
13 rue Fondary 75015
Telephone: 01 40 59 96 56

16eme arrondissment

BUTCHERS
Gm Levy
83 rue de Lonchamp 75016
Telephone: 01 45 53 04 24

Kassab
88 boulevard Murat 75016
Telephone: 01 40 71 0734

Ste Delicatess
209 avenue de Versailles 75016
Telephone: 01 44 40 07 59

CAFE/PATISSERIE
O de Rose/Chez Gary
209 avenue de Versailles 75016
Telephone: 01 40 71 06 00
Supervision: Beth Din of Paris

Kosher
Diamantine
28 boulevard Flandrin 75016
Telephone: 01 45 03 50 57
Supervision: Beth Din of Paris
Sandwiches, chocolates and pizzas

Nogaline Prestige
27 rue Claude Terrasse 75016
Telephone: 01 44 96 71 06
Supervision: Beth Din of Paris

DELICATESSEN
Micky's Deli
33 rue Greuze 75016
Telephone: 01 45 05 47 70
Supervision: Communautes orthodoxes de Paris

GROCERIES AND DELICATESSEN
Keter David
5 rue Benjamin Franklin 75016
Telephone: 01 42 24 04 42
Fax: 01 42 24 04 41

RESTAURANTS
Chinese-Kosher
L'asiatik
47 avenue Raymond poincarre 75016
Telephone: 01 44 05 05 44
Supervision: Beth Din of Paris

Italian-Kosher
Little trendy
7 bis rue des Boulainvilliers 75016
Telephone: 01 40 50 81 81
Supervision: Beth Din of Paris

Japanese-Kosher
Nina Sushi Bar
81 rue de longchamps 75016
Telephone: 01 44 96 71 06
Supervision: Beth Din of Paris

Sushi West
12 rue de Longchamps 75016
Telephone: 01 45 05 50 00
Supervision: V
Delivers

Kosher
Osmose
31 avenue de Versailles 75016
Telephone: 01 45 20 74 12
Supervision: Beth Din of Paris

Pizza-Kosher
Devarim
168 avenue Victor Hugo 75016
Telephone: 01 56 26 07 07
Supervision: Beth Din of Paris

Il Conte
47 avenue Raymond poincarre 75016
Telephone: 01 47 27 98 40
Supervision: Beth Din of Paris

Sushi-Kosher
Yapany Sushi
27 rue Copernic 75016
Telephone: 01 45 00 12 12
Supervision: Beth Din of Paris
Japanese and Chinese

Tunisian-Kosher
Le 138
138 rue de la pompe 75016
Telephone: 01 47 27 99 39
Supervision: Beth Din of Paris

Liny's by Gabin
23/27 rue Copernic 75016
Telephone: 01 45 00 12 12
Supervision: Beth Din of Paris

SYNAGOGUES
Liberal/Conservative
Union Liberale Israelite de France
24 rue Copernic, Ile de France 75116
Telephone: 01 47 04 37 27
Fax: 01 47 27 81 02
Email: communications@ulif.com
Website: www.ulif.com
Supervision: Patrick Altar
Orthodox
Ohel Avraham
31 rue Montevideo 75016
Telephone: 01 45 05 66 73
Fax: 01 40 72 83 76
23 bis rue Dufrènoy 75016
Telephone:01 45 04 94 00; 01 45 04 66 73
17eme arrondissment

BUTCHERS
Berbeche
39 rue Jouffroy 75017
Telephone: 01 44 40 07 59
Espaces Courses Elles
177 rue de Courcelles 75017
Telephone: 01 47 63 36 26
Krief
104 rue Legendre 75017
Telephone: 01 46 27 15 57

CAFE/PATISSERIE
Kosher
Aux Suprises
17 rue Galvani 75017
Telephone: 01 44 09 76 83
Supervision: Beth Din of Paris
L'arbre de vie
16 boulevard Gouvion St Cyr 75017
Telephone: 01 45 74 48 48
Supervision: Beth Din of Paris
Take away for Shabbat

GROCERIES
Chekel
14 avenue de Villiers 75017
Telephone: 01 48 88 94 97

Compt Pdts Alimentaires
111 avenue de Villiers 75017
Telephone: 01 42 27 16 91

PATISSERIE
Kosher
Charles Patissier
47 rue Jouffrey d'Abbans 75017
Telephone: 01 53 35 99 55
Supervision: Beth Din of Paris

RESTAURANT/TAKEAWAY
Pizza-Kosher
Mie and y, Chez David et Deborah
10 rue Leon Jost 75017
Telephone: 01 42 67 14 14
Supervision: Rabbinat Loubavitch de France
Delivery and take away ONLY

RESTAURANTS
Chinese-Kosher
Missada
45 rue Laugier 75017
Telephone: 01 46 22 11 77
Supervision: Beth Din of Paris

Fast Food-Kosher
C Wagram
81 avenue de Wagram 75017
Telephone: 01 48 88 98 16
Supervision: Beth Din of Paris

Kolnos
47 rue des Acacias 75017
Telephone: 01 45 74 75 96
Supervision: Beth Din of Paris

Les Jardins du belvedere
111 avenue de Villiers 75017
Telephone: 01 42 27 16 91
Supervision: Beth Din of Paris
Take away and groceries

Papy Youda Cafe
100 rue Saussure 75017
Telephone: 01 40 54 77 27
Supervision: Rabbinat Loubavitch de France

French-Kosher
Chez Vicky and Juliette
13 rue Rennequin 75017
Telephone: 01 40 53 03 32
Supervision: Beth Din of Paris

La Brasserie du belvedere
109 avenue de Villiers 75017
Telephone: 01 42 27 16 91
Supervision: Beth Din of Paris

Le Chateaubriand
125 rue de Tocqueville 75017 75017
Telephone: 01 47 63 96 90
Fax: 01 47 63 42 55

Website: www.le chateaubriand.com
Supervision: Beth Din of Paris
Le Cosy
88 rue Pierre Demours 75017
Telephone: 01 46 22 17 07
Supervision: Beth Din of Paris

Indian- Kosher
Darjeeling
rue des Colonels Renard 75017
Telephone: 01 45 72 09 32
Fax: 01 45 72 03 27
Website: www.darjeeling-ontable.com
Supervision: Chief Rabbi Mordechai Rottenberg.
Delivers all over Paris, take away
Darjeeling
1 rue des Colonels Renard 75017
Telephone: 01 45 72 09 32
Supervision: Communautes orthodoxes de Paris

Darjeeling, La Boutique
39 rue Davy 75017
Telephone: 01 42 26 35 35
Fax: 01 44 85 77 93
Website: www.darjeeling-ontable.com
Supervision: Communautes orthodoxes de Paris
Delivers all over Paris, take away

Italian-Kosher
Cocoon
3 rue Galvani 75017
Telephone: 01 45 72 59 12
Supervision: Rabbinat Loubavitch de France

Pasta et Dolci
1 rue Rennequin 75017
Telephone: 01 47 64 13 46
Supervision: Beth Din of Paris

Japanese-Kosher
Cine Sushi
57 boulevard Pereire 75017
Telephone: 01 40 53 00 00
Supervision: Beth Din of Paris
Sushi

Sushi West
1 rue Jooy d'Abbans 75017
Telephone: 01 42 27 50 00
Supervision: Beth Din of Paris
Delivers

Sushi West
39 avenue de Villiers 75017
Telephone: 08 26 88 26 88
Delivers

Kosher
Nathy's Bagel
12 rue Jouffroy d'Abbans 75017
Telephone: 01 40 53 08 97
Supervision: Beth Din of Paris
Take away for Shabbat

NOA
142 rue de Courcelles 75017
Telephone: 01 44 40 04 47
Supervision: Beth Din of Paris

Ventura Avenue
98 avenue des Ternes 75017
Telephone: 01 45 74 41 30
Supervision: Beth Din of Paris

North African-Kosher
Fio
73 bis avenue Niel 75017
Telephone: 01 42 27 42 20
Supervision: Beth Din of Paris
Salon de thè

Jeannot
110 bis rue Cardinet 75017
Telephone: 01 4763 71 02
Supervision: Beth Din of Paris

Michel Benittah
3 boulevard Pershing 75017
Telephone: 01 44 09 76 87
Supervision: Beth Din of Paris

Oriental-Kosher
Chez Miguel
rue Jouffrey d'Abbans 75017
Telephone: 01 40 53 88 88
Supervision: Beth Din of Paris
Take away for Shabbat

Dado's
39 rue Jouffroy d'Abbans 75017
Telephone: 01 47 63 06 06
Supervision: Beth Din of Paris
Lunch: weekdays only. Takeaway open 8am to 8pm

Fradji
42 rue Poncelet 75017
Telephone: 01 47 54 91 40
Supervision: Beth Din of Paris

Nini
24 rue Saussier Leroy 75017
Telephone: 01 46 22 28 93
Supervision: Beth Din of Paris

Pizza-Kosher
Daily's Cafe
19 rue Jouffroy d'Abbans 75017
Telephone: 01 47 66 40 82
Supervision: Rabbinat Loubavitch de France

Tib's
51 rue Bayen 75017
Telephone: 01 45 72 03 59
Fax: 01 45 72 13 25
Supervision: Communautes orthodoxes de Paris
Delivers

Sushi-Kosher
California Sushielivers
3 rue Galvani 75017
Telephone: 01 45 72 54 75
Supervision: Beth Din of Paris

SYNAGOGUES
Liberal
The American Synagogue of Paris
7 rue de Lèon Cogniet 75017
Telephone: 01 39 21 97 19
Fax: 01 39 21 97 19
Website: www.kehilatgesher.org
Alternative address: 10 rue de Pologne, St Germain en Laye 78100
A liberal, egalitarian congregation embracing both reform and Conservative tendencies. All services,which alternate between two locations, are in English, French and Hebrew.

Orthodox
Beth Hamidrach Lamed
67 rue Bayen 75017
Telephone: 01 45 74 52 80

Centre Rambam
19 21 rue Galvani 75017
Telephone: 01 45 74 52 80
Fax: 01 45 74 51 81

18eme arrondissment

MIKVAOT
Mayan Hai Source de Vie Haya Mouchka
2-4 rue Tristan Tzara 75018
Telephone: 01 40 38 18 29; 01 46 36 11 09
1 rue des Annelets 75019
Telephone: 01 42 45 57 87
For men and women. Telephone is an answer machine for women only.

PATISSERIE
Kosher
Zohar
12 rue Tristan Tzara 75018
Telephone: 01 44 72 06 62
Supervision: Rabbinat Loubavitch de France

RESTAURANTS
Messaadoun
31 boulevard Barbes 75018
Telephone: 01 42 51 83 16
Supervision: Beth Din of Paris

Pizza-Kosher
Pizza Hai
18 rue Tchaikowski 75018
Telephone: 01 44 65 95 63
Supervision: Rabbinat Loubavitch de France
Take away and delivers

SYNAGOGUES

Orthodox

Synagogue ACIP
42 rue des Saules 75018
Telephone: 01 46 06 71 39
Fax: 01 46 06 71 39

Synagogue de Montmartre
13 rue Saint Isaure 75018
Telephone: 01 42 64 48 34

BAKERIES

Charles Tr. Patissier
10 rue Corentin Cariou 75019
Telephone: 01 47 97 51 83
Supervision: Beth Din of Paris

Kadoche
2 avenue Corentin Cariou 75019
Telephone: 01 40 37 00 14
Supervision: Beth Din of Paris

Le Relais Sucre
135 rue Manin 75019
Telephone: 01 42 41 20 98
Supervision: Beth Din of Paris

Mat'amim
17 rue de Crimèe 75019
Telephone: 01 42 40 89 11
Supervision: Beth Din of Paris

Medayo
17 rue de Meaux 75019
Telephone: 01 40 03 04 20
Supervision: Beth Din of Paris

BUTCHERS

Andre Manin
135 rue Manin 75019
Telephone: 01 42 38 00 43

Aux Viandes Cacheres
6 av. Corentin Cariou 75019
Telephone: 01 40 36 02 41

Berbeche
15/17 rue Henri Ribiere 75019
Telephone: 01 42 08 06 06

Emsalem
17 quai de la Gironde 75019
Telephone: 01 40 36 56 64
18 rue Corentin Cariou 75019
Telephone: 01 40 36 56 64

CAFE/PATISSERIE

Kosher

Contini
116 avenue Simon Bolivar 75019
Telephone: 01 42 00 70 80
Supervision: Beth Din of Paris

Eden Sol
27 rue de Meaux 75019
Telephone: 01 40 03 85 18
Supervision: Communautes orthodoxes de Paris

Mardoch
11 rue de Dr Potain 75019
Telephone: 01 42 40 15 24
Supervision: Beth Din of Paris

CHOCOLATE SHOPS

Golden delice
1 rue sadi Lecomte 75019
Telephone: 01 42 40 74 22
Supervision: Communautes orthodoxes de Paris

GROCERIES

Chochana
54 avenue Secretan 75019

MIKVAOT

Mikve Haya Moucha
25 rue Riquet 75019
Telephone: 01 40 36 40 92
Fax: 01 40 36 88 90
75 rue Julien Lacroix 75020
Telephone: 01 46 36 39 20; 01 46 36 30 10
Supervision: Rav Azimov
Central organisation: Lubavitch
For men and women.

PATISSERIE

Kosher

Au paradis Gourmand
48 rue Curial 75019
Telephone: 01 40 37 42 37
Supervision: Beth Din of Paris

Aux Delices de Maxime
68 rue Petit 75019
Telephone: 01 42 00 27 66
Supervision: Beth Din of Paris

Aux Delices de Maxime
177 rue de Crimee 75019
Telephone: 01 40 36 44 076
Supervision: Beth Din of Paris

Charles patissier
10 rue Corentin Cariou 75019
Telephone: 01 47 97 51 83
Supervision: Beth Din of Paris

Fanny's Delis
7 rue Curial 75019
Telephone: 01 40 37 02 04
Supervision: Rabbinat Loubavitch de France

Jaffa Pita Hadar-Arc en ciel
5 rue Dampierre 75019
Telephone: 01 46 07 27 77
Supervision: Communautes orthodoxes de Paris

Kadoche
2 avenue Corentin Cariou 75019
Telephone: 01 40 37 00 14
Supervision: Beth Din of Paris

L'Ideal
95 bis rue Manin 75019
Telephone: 01 42 06 45 77
Supervision: Beth Din of Paris

La Delicieuse
159 rue de Belleville 75019
Telephone: 01 42 01 29 29
Supervision: Beth Din of Paris
Bakery

La Relais Sucre
135 rue Manin 75019
Telephone: 01 42 41 20 98
Supervision: Beth Din of Paris

Nat Cachere
10/12 rue Adolphe Mille porte de Pantin 75019
Telephone: 01 42 03 52 93
Supervision: Beth Din of Paris

Ougaland
143/145 rue Manin 75019
Telephone: 01 42 01 44 44
Supervision: Beth Din of Paris

Patistory
45 rue de Meaux 75019
Telephone: 01 42 03 38 31
Supervision: Beth Din of Paris

Sareden
54 rue Petit 75019
Telephone: 01 42 02 62 08
Supervision: Communautes orthodoxes de Paris

RESTAURANTS

Bassari-Kosher
Bouba Joe
1 rue Goubert 75019
Telephone: 01 42 02 04 62
Supervision: Beth Din of Paris

Dav and Jo
49 Quai de Seine 75019
Telephone: 01 40 05 99 00
Supervision: Beth Din of Paris

Divin
11 rue du dr Potain 75019
Telephone: 01 463 67 73 30
Supervision: Beth Din of Paris

La Chaumiere
46 avenue Secretan 75019
Telephone: 01 42 06 54 69
Supervision: Beth Din of Paris

Maxou
42 rue Riquet 75019
Telephone: 01 42 05 31 25
Supervision: Beth Din of Paris

Chinese-Kosher
La Ville de Chine
159/161 boulevard Serrurier 75019
Telephone: 01 42 01 36 26
Supervision: Rabbinat Loubavitch de France

Fast Food-Kosher
Chez Avi/Chez Chlomi
159/161 rue de Flandres 75019
Telephone: 01 46 07 54 76
Supervision: Beth Din of Paris
Israeli, Bassari

Chez Chmouel
44 rue Curial 75019
Telephone: 01 40 36 19 99
Supervision: Beth Din of Paris

Chochana
54 avenue Secretan 75019
Telephone: 02 42 41 01 16
Supervision: Beth Din of Paris
North African

Crown Heights
18 rue Meynadier 75019
Telephone: 01 42 40 44 96
Supervision: Rabbinat Loubavitch de France

Le Roi de la salade
9 rue dampierre 75019
Telephone: 01 4034 78 12
Supervision: Beth Din of Paris

papy Youda cafe
68 bis rue Manin 75019
Telephone: 01 42 00 10 35
Supervision: Rabbinat Loubavitch de France
Hamburgers, Hot dogs. take away for Shabbat

French-Kosher
La Petit Pelleport
52 rue de Hautpoul 75019
Telephone: 01 42 01 20 17
Supervision: Beth Din of Paris

Japanese-Kosher
Nina Sushi Bar
31 avenue Simon Bolivar 75019
Telephone: 01 42 06 31 30
Supervision: Beth Din of Paris

O'woks
2 rue David d'Angers 75019
Telephone: 01 58 64 14 14
Supervision: Rabbinat Loubavitch de France
Delivers

Sushi West
avenue de la porte Chaumont 75019
Telephone: 08 26 88 26 88
Supervision: Beth Din of Paris
Delivers

Kosher
Cacher Delight
15/17 rue henri Ribiere 75019
Telephone: 01 42 08 00 00
Supervision: Beth Din of Paris
Chinese Thai, Japanese delivers all over Paris and vicinity

Chez Akol, Hot Bagel
65 rue d'Hautpoul 75019
Telephone: 01 42 08 99 90
Supervision: Beth Din of Paris

Creperie Keruzzan
50 rue de Crimee 75019
Telephone: 01 42 40 04 72
Supervision: Rabbinat Loubavitch de France

Itsik
78 avenue Secretan 75019
Telephone: 06 11 08 93 41
Supervision: Beth Din of Paris

olfino Cafe
44 rue d'Hautpoul 75019
Telephone: 01 42 01 20 30
Supervision: Beth Din of Paris

Ward
42 rue Riquet 75019
Telephone: 01 42 05 59 54
Supervision: Beth Din of Paris

Meat
Mille Delices
52 avenue Secrètan 75019
Telephone: 01 40 18 32 32
Supervision: Beth Din of Paris
Fast food

North African-Kosher
Allo Sarina
38 rue Curial 75019
Telephone: 01 40 35 08 98
Supervision: Beth Din of Paris
Delivers

Cacher Delight-L'orientale
43 rue des alouettes 75019
Telephone: 01 42 08 00 00
Supervision: Beth Din of Paris
Delivers

Douieb D et D
20 rue Rouvet 75019
Telephone: 01 42 29 94 03
Supervision: Beth Din of Paris

Tsipora
3/5 rue de Plateau 75019
Telephone: 01 42 00 85 22
Supervision: Beth Din of Paris

North African-Kosher and Israelian
Mipi El
41 avenue Secretan 75019
Telephone: 01 40 18 16 16
Fax: 01 40 18 16 16
Supervision: Beth Din of Paris

Pizza-Kosher
260 Two Sixty
36 rue Archereau 75019
Telephone: 01 40 36 07 55
Supervision: Beth Din of Paris

Don Pepe Pizza
14 rue Manin 75019
Telephone: 01 42 03 16 96
Supervision: Beth Din of Paris

Family Pizza
59 rue petit 75019
Telephone: 01 45 72 59 12
Supervision: Rabbinat Loubavitch de France
Delivers

Gin Fizz
157 boulevard Serruier 75019
Telephone: 01 42 00 51 28
Supervision: Beth Din of Paris

La Marina
159 rue Manin 75019
Telephone: 01 42 01 36 26
Supervision: Beth Din of Paris
Sushi

Mie and You
1 rue de l'Encheval 75019
Telephone: 01 42 02 55 55
Supervision: Rabbinat Loubavitch de France

Nat Pizza
12 rue Adolphe Mille porte de Pantin 75019
Telephone: 01 42 03 52 93
Supervision: Beth Din of Paris

Papy Youda Cafe
68 rue Manin 75019
Telephone: 01 42 06 00 88
Supervision: Rabbinat Loubavitch de France
Delivers

Starlight
1 allee Darius Milhaud, angle rue Manin et rus
Crimee 75019
Telephone: 01 40 03 06 94
Supervision: Communautes orthodoxes de Paris

Tib's Manin
161 rue Manin 75019
Telephone: 01 42 45 00 45
Supervision: Communautes orthodoxes de Paris
Delivers, open all Saturday night

Todah L'akel
169 rue de Crimee 75019
Telephone: 01 40 38 47 08
Supervision: Rabbinat Loubavitch de France

Yad Pizza
50 boulevard Serrurier 75019
Telephone: 01 44 84 71 71
Supervision: Rabbinat Loubavitch de France
Delivers in Paris and suburbs

Sushi-Kosher
Sushi Azur
69 RUE PETIT 75019
Telephone: 01 42 00 07 07
Supervision: Beth Din of Paris

SANDWICH BAR
Kosher
O' Bagels
107 rue Manin 75019
Telephone: 01 42 40 50 50
Supervision: Rabbinat Loubavitch de France

SYNAGOGUES
Orthodox
Beth Chalom
11 13 rue Curial 75019
Telephone: 01 40 37 65 16; 01 40 37 12 54

Beth Loubavitch
53 rue Compans 75019
Telephone: 01 42 02 20 35

Beth Loubavitch
25 rue Riquet 75019
Telephone: 01 40 36 93 90
Fax: 01 40 36 60 15

Chaare Tora
1 rue Henri Turot 75019
Telephone: 01 42 06 41 12
Fax: 01 42 06 95 47

Kollel Ysmah Mochè
36 rue des Annelets 75019
Telephone: 01 43 63 73 94

Ohaley Yaacov
11 rue Henri Murger 75019
Telephone: 01 42 49 25 00

Ohr Tora   AJJ
15 Rur Riquet 75019
Telephone: 01 40 38 23 36
Fax: 01 40 36 42 23
Website: www.ajj.fr

Synagogue Michkan Yaacov
118 boulevard de Belleville 75019
Telephone: 01 43 49 39 59

Synagogue Michkenot Israel
6 rue Jean Nohain 75019
Telephone: 01 48 03 25 59
Fax: 01 42 00 26 87

20eme arrondissment

BAKERIES
Lilo
20 rue Desnoyer 75020
Telephone: 01 47 97 63 20
Supervision: Beth Din of Paris

BUTCHERS
Boucherie Smadja
90 boulevard Belleville 75020

Henrino
122 boulevard de Belleville 75020
Telephone: 01 47 97 24 52

PATISSERIE
Kosher
Zazou
20 rue Rouvet 75020
Telephone: 01 40 34 25 22
Supervision: Beth Din of Paris

RESTAURANTS
Meat
Elygel
116 boulevard de Belleville 75020
Telephone: 01 47 97 09 73
Supervision: Beth Din of Paris

Tunisian-Kosher
Chez Rene et Gabin
92 boulevard de Belleville 75020
Telephone: 01 43 58 78 14
Supervision: Beth Din of Paris

kifoli
112 boulevard de Belleville 75020
Telephone: 01 47 97 53 13
Supervision: Beth Din of Paris

La Relais
69 boulevard de Belleville 75020
Telephone: 01 43 57 83 91
Supervision: Beth Din of Paris

Lumieres de Belleville
102 boulevard de Belleville 75020
Telephone: 01 47 97 51 83
Supervision: Beth Din of Paris

SYNAGOGUES
Orthodox
Beth Loubavitch
93 rue des Orteaux 75020
Telephone: 01 40 24 10 60

Maor Athora
16 rue Ramponeau 75020
Telephone: 01 47 97 69 42

Ohr Chimchon Raphaîl
5 passage Dagorno 75020
Telephone: 01 46 59 39 02
Fax: 01 46 59 14 99

Synagogue Aschkenaze & Sephardi
49 rue Pali Kao 75020
Telephone: 01 46 36 30 10

Synagogue Bet Yaacov Yossef
5 square des Cardeurs, 43 rue Saint Blaise 75020
Telephone: 01 43 56 03 11

PATISSERIE
Kosher
Nani
104 boulevard de belleville 75029
Telephone: 01 47 97 38 05
Supervision: Beth Din of Paris

RIS ORANGIS
SYNAGOGUES
Orthodox
Ris Orangis Synagogue
1 rue Jean Moulin, Essone 91130
Telephone: 01 69 43 07 83

ROISSY EN BRIE
MIKVAOT
Mikvaot
Rue Paul Cèzanne, Centre Commercial Bois
Montmartre, Seine et Marne 77680
Telephone: 01 60 28 34 65; 01 60 29 09 44

ROSNY SOUS BOIS
SYNAGOGUES
Orthodox
Rosny Sous Bois Synagogue
62 64 rue Lavoisier, Seine Saint Denis 93110
Telephone: 01 48 54 04 11
Fax: 01 69 43 07 83

SAINT DENIS
RESTAURANTS
Kosher
Pizza Communautaire
1 rue Emile Connoy 93200
Supervision: BHaBaD
Lunch only

SAINT GERMAIN
SYNAGOGUES
Orthodox
Saint Germain Synagogue
6 Impasse Saint Leger 78103
Telephone: 01 34 51 26 60

SAINT LEU LA FORET
MIKVAOT
Mikvaot
2 rue Jules Vernes, Val d'Oise 95320
Telephone: 01 39 95 96 90; 01 34 14 24 15

SYNAGOGUES
Orthodox
Saint Leu La Foret Synagogue
2 rue Jules Verne, Val d'Oise 95320
Telephone: 01 39 95 96 90
Fax: 01 39 95 72 13

SAINT MANDE
RESTAURANTS
French-Kosher
Le cadre
87 avenue de Paris 94160
Telephone: 01 43 28 38 43
Supervision: Beth Din

Japanese-Kosher
Cine Sushi
37 avenue du General de galle 94160
Telephone: 01 43 28 20 00
Delivers

Nina Sushi Bar
49 avenue du General de Galle 94160
Telephone: 01 48 08 16 12
Supervision: Beth Din

SAINT OUEN L'AUMÔNE
SYNAGOGUES
Orthodox
Maison Communautaire
9 rue de Chenneviìres, Val d'Oise 95310
Telephone: 01 30 37 71 41

SARCELLES
BAKERIES
Zazou
C.C. les Flanades, Val d'Oise 95200
Telephone: 01 34 19 08 11
Supervision: Beth Din of Paris

BUTCHERS
Boucherie Du Coin
60 boulevard Albert Camus, Val d'Oise 95200
Telephone: 01 39 90 53 02

Hazout
5 avenue Paul Valèry, Val d'Oise 95200
Telephone: 01 39 90 72 95

CHOCOLATE SHOPS
Kosher
Damyel
65 avenue Paul Valery 95200
Telephone: 01 39 94 91 81
Supervision: Communautes orthodoxes de Paris

MIKVAOT
Mayanot Rachel
14 avenue Ch. Pèguy, Val d'Oise 95200
Telephone: 01 39 90 40 17
Postal address:c/o 1 AC 15 av. de l'Escouvrier 95200

PATISSERIE
Kosher
Friantel
5 place Jean Moulin 95200
Telephone: 01 34 19 10 74
Supervision: Beth Din

L'Ile aux Desserts
48 boulevard Albert Camus 95200
Telephone: 01 34 04 25 53
Supervision: Beth Din

Le Relais Sucre
1 place Navarre 95200
Telephone: 01 34 04 02 81
Supervision: Beth Din

Louis D'or
90 avenue Paul Valèy, Val d'Oise 95200
Telephone: 01 39 90 25 45
Supervision: Beth Din of Paris

Natania
34 boulevard Albert Camus, Val d'Oise 95200
Telephone: 01 39 90 11 78
Supervision: Beth Din of Paris

Oh Delices
71 avenue Paul Valèry, Val d'Oise 95200
Telephone: 01 39 92 41 12
Supervision: Beth Din of Paris

RESTAURANT/COFFEE SHOP
Pizza-Kosher
Erev
40 boulevard Albert Camus 95200
Telephone: 01 39 90 43 14
Supervision: Beth Din

RESTAURANTS
Japanese-Kosher
West Side Sushi
28 boulevard Albert Camus 95200
Telephone: 01 34 29 62 02
Supervision: Beth Din
Delivers, takeaway

Meat
Berbeche Burger
13 avenue Edouard Branly, Val d'Oise 95200
Telephone: 01 34 19 12 02
Supervision: Beth Din of Paris

Pizza-Kosher
Domijo
78 avenue Paul Valery 95200
Telephone: 01 39 33 60 60
Central organisation: HaBaD

Marina
103 avenue Paul Valèry, Val d'Oise 95200
Telephone: 01 34 19 23 51
Supervision: Beth Din of Paris
Halavi

SYNAGOGUES
Orthodox
Maison Communautaire
74 avenue Paul Valèry, Val d'Oise 95200
Telephone: 01 39 90 59 59
Mikva on premises

SARTROUVILLE
Synagogue Rabbi Shimon bar Yohai et Rabbi Meir Baal Hannes
1 rue de Stalingrad, Yvelines 78500
Telephone: 01 39 15 22 57

SAVIGNY SUR ORGE
MIKVAOT
Mikvaot
1 avenue de l'Armèe Leclerc, Essonne 91600
Telephone: 01 69 24 48 25, 01 69 96 30 90

SYNAGOGUES
Orthodox
Savigny Sur Orge Synagogue
1 avenue de l'Armèe Leclerc, Essonne 91600
Telephone: 01 69 96 30 90

SEVRAN
MIKVAOT
Mikvaot
25 bis du Dr Roux, Seine Saint Denis 93270
Telephone: 01 43 84 25 40
Mikva Kelim

SYNAGOGUES
Orthodox
Synagogue Mayan Thora
25 bis rue du Dr Roux, BP. 111, Seine Saint Denis 93270
Telephone: 01 43 84 25 40

STAINS
Stains†Synagogue
8 rue Lamartine (face n-2), Clos St Laxare, Seine
Saint Denis 93240
Telephone: 01 48 21 04 12
Provisional address: 8 avenue Louis Bordes (Ancient
Conservatoire Municipal)

THIAIS
COMMUNITY ORGANISATIONS
Community Centre Choisy Orly Thiais
Voie du Four, 128 avenue du Marechal de Lattre de
Tassigny, Val Marne 94320
Telephone: 01 48 92 68 68
Fax: 01 48 92 72 82

TRAPPES
SYNAGOGUES
Orthodox
Trappes Synagogue
7 rue du Port Royal, Yvelines 78190
Telephone: 01 30 62 40 43

VAL DE MARNE
BUTCHERS
Tiness
12 Etienne Dollet, Val de Marne 94140
Telephone: 01 49 77 95 79

SYNAGOGUES
Orthodox
Val de Marne Synagogue
1 rue Blanche 94140
Telephone: 01 43 78 86 43

VERSAILLES
Samuel Sandler
10 rue Albert Joly, Yvelines 78000
Telephone: 01 39 07 19 19
Fax: 01 39 50 96 34
Mikva on premises

VILLEJUIF
Orthodox
Villejuif Synagogue
106 avenue de Gournay, Val de Marne 94800
Telephone: 01 46 78 76 53

VILLENEUVE LA GARENNE
MIKVAOT
Mikvaot
42 44 rue du Fond de la Noue, Hauts de Seine
92390
Telephone: 01 47 94 89 98

SYNAGOGUES
Orthodox
Maison Communautaire
44 rue du Fond de la Noue, Hauts de Seine 92390
Telephone: 01 47 94 89 98

VILLIERS LE BEL GONESSE
MIKVAOT
Mikvaot
1 rue Lèon Blum, Val d'Oise 95400
Telephone: 01 39 94 45 51; 01 34 19 64 48

SYNAGOGUES
Orthodox
Villiers Le Bel Gonesse Synagogue
1 rue Lèon Blum, Val d'Oise 94500
Telephone: 01 39 94 30 49; 01 39 94 94 89

VILLIERS SUR MARNE
Villiers Sur Marne Synagogue
30 rue Lèon Douer, B.P. 15, Val de Marne 94350
Telephone: 01 49 30 01 47
Fax: 01 49 30 85 40

VINCENNES
BUTCHERS
Boucherie Des Levy
32 rue Raymond du Temple, Val de Marne 94300
Telephone: 01 43 74 94 18

Boucherie Hayache
146 avenue de Paris, Val de Marne 94300
Telephone: 01 43 28 16 04

RESTAURANTS
French/Moroccan-Kosher
La Taverne
56 rue Charles Silvestri 94300
Telephone: 01 48 08 52 13

Kosher Take-away
Le Petit Cadre
2/4 avenue du Chateau 94300
Telephone: 01 43 98 24 24
Supervision: Beth Din
Sandwiches patisserie, delivers take away for Shabbat

Pizza-Kosher
La Pizza
20 rue de la paix 94300
Telephone: 01 43 98 17 17
Supervision: Rabbinat Loubavitch de France
Halavi

SNACK BAR
Kosher
Les delices D'ornella
88 avenue de Paris 94300
Telephone: 01 58 64 30 00
Supervision: Beth Din

SYNAGOGUES
Orthodox
Synagogue Achkenaze
30 rue Cèline Robert, 94300
Telephone: 01 43 74 38 47
Email: bruno.blum@nexans.com
Supervision: affiliated to ACIP - Consistoire de Paris
The Ashkenazi synagogue in Vincennes holds service on
Friday evening, shabat sharahit, Minha and Maariv as well
as every Sunday morning. We also provide service on Rosh
Hodesh days and all festivals. We welcome travellers from
worldwide to attend our services.

Synagogue Sepharade
30 rue Cèline Robert, Val de Marne 94300
Telephone: 01 47 55 65 07

VITRY SUR SEINE
Vitry Sur Seine Synagogue
133-135 avenue Rouget de l'Isle, Val de Marne
94400
Telephone: 01 46 80 76 54; 01 45 73 06 58
Fax: 01 45 73 94 01

YERRES
MIKVAOT
Beth Rivkah
43/49 rue R. Poincare, Essone 91330
Telephone: 01 69 49 62 74; 01 69 49 62 62
Fax: 01 69 79 27 70

South East

AIX EN PROVENCE
BUTCHERS
Zouaghi
7 rue de Sevigne, Bouches du Rhône 13100
Telephone: 04 42 59 93 94
Supervision: Grand Rabbinate of Marseille

SYNAGOGUES
Aix En Provence Synagogue
5 rue de Jerusalem 13100
Telephone: 04 42 26 69 39

AIX LES BAINS
BUTCHERS
Berdah
29 avenue de Tresserve 73100
Telephone: 04 79 61 44 11

HOTELS
Kosher
Auberge de La Baye
Chemin du Tir Aux Pigeons, Savoie 73100
Telephone: 04 79 35 69 42
Fax: 04 79 88 49 54
Supervision: Vaad Aix les Bains
Strictly kosher.

MIKVAOT
Pavillon Salvador
Rue du President Roosevelt 73100
Telephone: 04 79 35 38 08

SYNAGOGUES
Aix Les Bains Synagogue
Rue Paul Bonne 73100
Telephone: 04 79 35 28 08
Mikva on premises

ANNECY
Association Cultuelle Israelite
18 rue de Narvik 74000
Telephone: 04 50 67 69 37

ANNEMASSE
BUTCHERS
Yarden
59 avenue de la Liberation, Gaillard 74100
Telephone: 04 50 92 64 05

SYNAGOGUES
Orthodox
Annemasse Synagogue
8 rue du Docteur Coquart 74100

ANTIBES JUAN LES PINS
BUTCHERS
Berreche
12 avenue Courbet 6160
Telephone: 04 93 67 16 77
Le Kineret
25 avenue D l'Esteral 6160
Telephone: 04 92 93 16 01
Fax: 04 93 88 14 76

RESTAURANTS
Maxime
6 boulevard de la Pinede 6160
Telephone: 04 92 93 99 40

SYNAGOGUES
Eliaou Hanabi
Villa la Monada, 30 Chemin des Sables, 9 Chemin
des Sabber (In Summer) 06160
Telephone: 04 93 61 59 34
Fax: 04 93 67 03 76

AVIGNON
The first archaeological evidence of a Jewish
presence dates from the fourth century. For years
the Avignon Jewish population flourished and
there were many Jewish scholars and writers
who were born and lived there. The first printing
venture in Hebrew was attempted in Avignon in
1446 before Gutenberg's success in 1450.

BUTCHERS
Cachere Royale
15 rue Chapeau Rouge 84000
Telephone: 04 90 82 47 50
Supervision: Grand Rabbinate of Marseille

HOTELS
Hotel Danieli
17 rue de Republique, 84000
Telephone: 04 90 86 46 82
Fax: 04 90 27 09 24
Website: www.hoteldanieliavignon.com

MIKVAOT
Mikvaot
Vaucluse
Telephone: 04 90 86 30 30
Mme Cohen Zardi

SYNAGOGUES
Orthodox
Avignon Synagogue
2 Place de Jerusalem 84000
Telephone: 04 90 85 21 24
Fax: 04 90 85 21 24
This circular synagogue was built in 1847 on the site of a 13th century synagogue

BEZIERS
MIKVAOT
A.C.I.B.
19 Place Pierre Semard 34500
Telephone: 04 67 28 75 98 - Dr Maurice Abitbol
Fax: 04 67 28 75 98
Mobile Phone: 06 62 38 76 45 - Dr Nicole Abitbol
Email: acibeziers@free.fr
Dr Nicole Abitbol Tel: 06 62 38 76 45

SYNAGOGUES
Beziers Synagogue
19 Place Pierre Semard 34500
Telephone: 04 67 28 75 98
Fax: 04 67 30 55 22
Central organisation: ACIB
Operates a kosher food store

TOURIST SITES
Ghetto
To visit the old Ghetto (Beziers was known as ëthe little Jerusalem'); contact Mr Benyacar (04 67 31 14 23)

CALUIRE ET CUIRE
SYNAGOGUES
Caluire Et Cuire Synagogue
107 A. Fleming 69300
Telephone: 04 78 23 12 37

CANNES
BUTCHERS
Cannes Casher
9 rue Marceau 6400
Telephone: 04 93 39 85 08

Chez Sylvie
15 rue Mal. Joffre 6400
Telephone: 04 93 39 57 92
Fax: 04 93 3957 92
Email: raziz.sylvie@neuf.fr
Caterers 21 rue Mal. Joffre

CATERER
Meat
Dany's Traiteur
2 avenue du petit juas 06400
Telephone: 04 92 59 35 50; 06 11 16 34 51
Fax: 04 93 39 74 40
Email: danystraiteur@yahoo.fr
Website: www.danystraiteur.com
Delivery of kosher meals for Shabbat. Weddings, bar mitzvan parties organised.

COMMUNITY ORGANISATIONS
Cannes Jewish Community Organizations
20 boulevard d'Alsace 6400
Telephone: 04 93 38 16 54
Fax: 04 93 68 92 81

GROCERIES
La Emounah
32 rue de Mimont 6400
Near the main synagogue

Monoprix
Rue Marechal Fox
Has a comprehensive kosher section

MIKVAOT
Mikvaot
20 boulevard d'Alsace
Telephone: 04 93 99 79 03
Contact: Mme Annie Rebibo

RESTAURANTS
Meat
Le Tovel
3 Rue Dr Gerard Monod 06400
Telephone: 04 93 39 36 25
Fax: 04 92 98 81 29
Supervision: Rabbanut and Lubavitch

Pizza Dick
7 bis rue de Mimont 6400
Telephone: 04 92 59 10 82

SYNAGOGUES
Chabad Lubavitch
22 rue Commandant Vidal 6400
Telephone: 04 92 98 67 51
Fax: 04 92 98 81 29
Email: canorhabad@aol.com
Website: www.jriviera.com

Sephardi
Cannes Synagogue
20 boulevard d'Alsace 6400
Telephone: 04 93 38 16 54
Fax: 04 93 68 92 81

CARPENTRAS
Jews first settled in Carpentras in the 12th century. In 1343 permission was granted for the erection of a synagogue which had two prayer rooms, one above the other, the lower level being reserved for women, with the men above. The only communication between them was via a small window, latticed with iron and open in front of the tabernacle, allowing the women to see the sacred books.

Carpentras Synagogue
Place de la Maire
Telephone: 04 90 63 39 97
The synagogue originally built in 1367 and the oldest in France was reconstructed in 1741-43 and again in 1959. The French government has declared it a historic site.

TOURIST SITES
Cathedral St Siffrein
The 15th century door on the south side is where Jews had to go on their way to conversion and is known as ëPorte des Juifs'.

CAVAILLON
The Jews originally lived in rue Hebraique. The present synagogue, classified as a historical monument, was built in 1772 and incorporates parts of the 16th-century former building.

MUSEUMS
Musee Judeo Comatdin
Telephone: 04 90 76 00 34
The museum, a part of the synagogue, contains items dating back to the 14th century

SYNAGOGUES
Cavaillon synagogue
Telephone: 04 90 76 00 34
Fax: 04 90 71 47 06

CLERMONT FERRAND
Clermont Ferrand Synagogue
6 rue Blatin 63000
Telephone: 04 73 93 36 59

EVIAN
Evian Synagogue
Adjacent to 1 avenue des Grottes, 74502
Telephone: 04 50 75 15 63

EZE VILLAGE
HOTELS
Hotel les Terrases d'Eze
Route de la Turbie 6360
Telephone: 04 92 41 55 55
Fax: 04 92 41 55 10
Supervision: Nice Beth Din

FREJUS
SYNAGOGUES
Orthodox
Frejus Synagogue
Rue de Progres, Frejus Plage 83600
Telephone: 04 94 52 06 87

GRENOBLE
BUTCHERS
C. Cohen
19 rue de Turenne 38000
Telephone: 04 76 46 48 14

GROCERIES
Aux Delices du Soleil
49 rue Thiers 38000
Telephone: 04 76 46 19 60

Ghnassia
15 place Gustave Rivet 38000
Telephone: 04 76 87 80 90

MEDIA
Radio
Radio Kol Hachalom 100 FM
BP 342 Grenoble (38 lsËre) 38013
Telephone: 04 76 87 21 22
Fax: 04 76 47 58 31
Website: www.rkhfm.com
24 hours a day broadcasting, news in French and Hebrew

SYNAGOGUES
Rachi
11 rue Maginot, lsËre 38000
Telephone: 04 76 87 02 80
Fax: 04 76 87 27 14
Mikva at same address

Synagogue and Community Centre
4 rue des Bains, lsËre 38000
Telephone: 04 76 46 15 14

HYERES
Hyeres Synagogue
Chemin de la Ritorte 83400
Telephone: 04 94 65 31 97

IZIEU

MUSEUMS

The Izieu Children's Home
Bouches du Rhône 1300
Telephone: 04 79 87 20 08
Fax: 04 79 87 25 01
Website: www.izieu.alma.fr

The Izieu Children's Memorial Museum is dedicated to the memory of forty four children and their guardians taken away on 6 April 1944 by the Gestapo under the command of Klaus Barbie. The Museum's mission is to defend dignity, justice and to contribute to the fight against all forms of intolerance. Two buildings may be visited: the House takes the visitors back to everyday life of the children's home, the Barn presents the historical background through permanent and temporary exhibitions. Meetings, conferences and discussions are organized throughout the year.

LA CIOTAT

SYNAGOGUES

La Ciotat Synagogue
1 Square de Verdun 13600
Telephone: 04 42 71 92 56
Email: mic-mad@wanadoo.fr

Services Friday 7 pm (Winter), 7.30 pm (Summer) Saturday 9 am

LA SEYNE SUR MER

BUTCHERS

Elie Benamou
17 rue Batistin Paul 83500
Telephone: 04 94 94 38 60

SYNAGOGUES

La Seyne Sur Mer Synagogue
5 rue Chevalier de la Barre 83501
Telephone: 04 94 94 40 28

LYON

BAKERIES

Jo Delice
44 rue Rachais
Telephone: 04 78 69 22 98

Nassy Gourmand
41 rue A Boutin, Villeurbanne 69100
Telephone: 04 78 85 72 88

BUTCHERS

Ittah David
267 avenue Berthelot 69008
Telephone: 04 78 00 82 35

William (Mr Dahan)
50 rue Tete d'Or 69006
Telephone: 04 78 24 10 10

COMMUNITY ORGANISATIONS

Consistoire Israelite de Lyon
13 Quai Tilsitt 69002

Telephone: 04 78 37 13 43
Fax: 04 78 38 26 57

Consistoire Israelite Sepharade de Lyon
Yaacov Molho Community Centre, 317 rue Duguesclin 69007
Telephone: 04 78 58 18 74
Fax: 04 78 58 17 49

MEDIA

CIV News
4 rue Malherbe, Villeurbanne 69100
Telephone: 04 78 84 04 32

Hachaar
18 rue St. Mathieu 69008
Telephone: 04 78 00 72 50
Fax: 04 78 75 89 74

La Voix Sepharade
317 rue Duguesclin 69007
Telephone: 04 78 58 18 74

MIKVAOT

Chaare Tsedek (Sepharades)
18 rue St. Mathieu 69008
Telephone: 04 78 00 72 50
Fax: 04 78 75 89 74

Orah Haim
17 rue Albert Thomas, St Fons 69190
Telephone: 04 78 67 39 78

Rav Hida (N. African)
La Sauvegarde, La Duchere 69009
Telephone: 04 78 35 14 44

RELIGIOUS ORGANISATIONS

Beth Din
34 rue d'Armenie, 3e
Telephone: 04 78 62 97 63
Fax: 04 78 95 09 47

RESTAURANTS

Dairy
Le Pinnocchio
5 rue A. Boutin, Villeurbanne 69100
Telephone: 04 78 68 62 95

Lippo
9 rue Michel Servet, Villeurbanne 69100
Telephone: 04 78 84 15 00

Pizza Cach
13 rue d'Inkerman, Villeurbanne 69100
Telephone: 04 72 74 44 98

Prestopizza
61 rue Greuze, Villeurbanne 69100
Telephone: 04 78 68 08 41

Meat
Croq Sandwiches
32 Crs Emile Zola, Villeurbanne 69100
Telephone: 04 78 84 16 07

La Palmeraie
27 rue des Charmettes, Villeurbanne 69100
Telephone: 04 78 24 37 03

La Petite Ma0ison
35 rue P. Corneille 69006
Telephone: 04 78 24 99 43

Le Belvedere
14 rue Jean Jaures, Villeurbanne 69100
Telephone: 04 78 54 72 312

Lippmann Henry
4 rue Tony Tolletf 69002
Telephone: 04 78 42 49 82
Fax: 04 78 42 93 52
Website: www.lippmann-traiteur.com
Supervision: Lyon Beth Din

Mac David
28 rue Michel Servet, Villeurbanne 69100
Telephone: 04 78 03 31 62

SYNAGOGUES
Orthodox
Chaare Tsedek
18 rue Saint Mathieu (8e) (T.T.)
Telephone: 04 78 00 72 50
Fax: 04 78 75 89 74

Grande Synagogue
13 quai Tilsitt 69002
Telephone: 04 78 37 13 43
Fax: 04 78 38 26 57
Email: acie@gonline.f2

Rav Hida
501 Sauvegarde La Duchere (9e) (T.T.)
Telephone: 04 78 35 14 44
Fax: 04 78 64 95 90

MACON
Macon Synagogue
32 rue des Minimes 71000

MARIGNANE
Marignane Synagogue
9 rue Pilote Larbonne 13700

MARSEILLES
BAKERIES
Atteia et Fils
19 place Guillardet, Bouches du Rhône 13013
Telephone: 04 91 66 33 28
Supervision: Grande Rabbinate of Marseille

Avyel Cash
28 rue St Suffren, Bouches du Rhône 13006
Telephone: 04 91 87 95 25
Supervision: Grande Rabbinate of Marseille

Cacher Food
31 boulevard Barry, Bouches du Rhône 13013
Telephone: 04 91 70 13 43
Supervision: Grande Rabbinate of Marseille

Erets
205 rue de Rome, Bouches du Rhône 13006
Telephone: 04 91 92 88 73
Supervision: Grande Rabbinate of Marseille

Le Parve
72 avenue Alphonse Daudet, Bouches du Rhône 13013
Telephone: 04 91 66 95 16
Supervision: Grande Rabbinate of Marseille

BUTCHERS
Chez David
9 boulevard G. Ganay, Bouches du Rhône 13009
Telephone: 04 91 75 04 56
Supervision: Grande Rabbinate of Marseille

Jamap
13 place Mignard Bouches du Rhône 13009
Telephone: 04 91 71 11 70
Supervision: Grande Rabbinate of Marseille

Sebane
59 rue Alphonse Daudet, Bouches du Rhône 13013
Telephone: 04 91 66 98 76
Supervision: Grande Rabbinate of Marseille

Zennou Raphael
20 marchè Capucin, Bouches du Rhône 13001
Telephone: 04 91 54 02 54
Supervision: Grande Rabbinate of Marseille

EMBASSY
Consul General of Israel
146 rue Paradis, Bouches du Rhône 13006
Telephone: 04 91 53 39 87
Fax: 04 91 53 39 94

GROCERIES
Av bon gout
28 rue St Suffren, Bouches du Rhône 13006
Telephone: 04 91 37 95 25

Delicash
94 boulevard Barry, Bouches du Rhône 13013
Telephone: 04 91 06 39 04

Emmanuel
93 avenue Clot Bey, Bouches du Rhône 13008
Telephone: 04 91 77 46 08

King Kasher
25 rue FranÁois Mauriac, Bouches du Rhône 13010
Telephone: 04 91 80 00 01

Raphael Cash
299 avenue de Mazargues, Bouches du Rhône 13009
Telephone: 04 91 76 44 13

MEDIA
Radio
Radio JM
4 impasse Dragon 13006
Telephone: 04 91 37 78 78

MEMORIAL
Memorial of the Death Camps
Quai de la Tourette 13002
Telephone: 04 91 90 73 15

MIKVAOT
Mikve Esther
47 rue St Suffren 13006
Telephone: 04 91 81 45 15
There are some eight mikvaot in Marseilles. This one is close to the main synagogue. The Consistoire will provide details of others.

RELIGIOUS ORGANISATIONS
Consistoire de Marseille
117 rue de Breteuil, Bouches du Rhône 13006
Telephone: 04 91 37 49 64; 04 91 81 13 57
Fax: 04 91 37 83 90
Website: consistoiremarseille.com

RESTAURANTS
Dairy
Pizzeria Gan Eden
225, Paul Claudel 13010
Telephone: 04 91 75 12 72

Meat
Erets
205 rue de Rome, Bouches du Rhône 13006
Telephone: 04 91 92 88 73
Supervision: Grande Rabbinate of Marseille

Nathania
17 rue du Village, Bouches du Rhône 13006
Telephone: 04 91 42 05 31
Supervision: Grande Rabbinate of Marseille

SYNAGOGUES
Merlan
La Cerisaie, Batiment G1 13014
Telephone: 04 91 98 53 92

Ohel Yaakov
20 chemin Ste Marthe 13014
Telephone: 04 91 62 70 42

Ashkenazi
Synagogue
8 Impasse Dragon 13006

Reform
Marseilles Reform Synagogue
337 rue Paradis Marseille 13008
Telephone: 04 91 37 54 31
Fax: 04 91 37 54 31

Sephardi
Bar Yohai
171 rue Abbe de l'Epee 13005
Telephone: 04 91 42 38 19

Beth Simha
13 avenue. Des Olives 13013
Telephone: 04 91 70 05 45

Main Synagogue
117 rue Breteuil 13006
Telephone: 04 91 37 49 64
Fax: 04 91 37 83 89
Website: consistoiremarseille.org

Merkaz Netivot Chalom
27 boulevard Bonifay 13004
Telephone: 04 91 89 40 62
There are over forty more synagogues in Marseilles. The Consistoire de Marseilles will supply details if required.

MENTON
Menton Synagogue
Centre Altyner, 106 cours du Centenaire 6500
Telephone: 04 93 35 28 29

MONTPELLIER
BUTCHERS
Eretz
41 rue de Lunaret 3400
Telephone: 04 67 72 67 94

COMMUNITY ORGANISATIONS
Centre Communautaire et Cultural Juif
500 boulevard d'Antigone 3400
Telephone: 04 67 15 08 76

GROCERIES
A.C.P.C.
45 rue Proudhon
Telephone: 04 67 02 10 99

SYNAGOGUES
Ben Zakai
7 rue General Laffon 34000
Telephone: 04 67 92 92 07

Mazal Tov
18 rue Ferdinand Fabre 34000
Telephone: 04 67 79 09 82

NICE
The first reference to Jews in Nice was in 1342. The first cemetery was established in 1408 and the synagogue in 1492.

The main synagogue, built in 1886,is worth a visit. Nice is home to the Chagall Museum which contains a permanent collection of his work, including a number of stained glass mosaics.

BOOKSELLERS
Librairie Tanya
25 rue Pertinax 6000
Telephone: 04 93 80 21 74
Fax: 04 93 13 87 90

BUTCHERS
K'Gel
18 rue Dante 6000
Telephone: 04 93 86 33 01

GROCERIES
Mickael
37 rue Dabray 6000
Telephone: 04 93 88 81 23
Riviera Cacher
11 avenue Villermont 6000
Telephone: 04 93 92 92 00

KASHRUT INFORMATION
Nice Kashrut
Telephone: 04 93 85 82 06
A list of kosher butchers and bakers can be obtained from
the Chief Rabbi

KOSHER FOODS
Galleries Lafayette
Has a kosher food section

MIKVAOT
Nice Mikvaot
22 rue Michelet 6100
Telephone: 04 93 51 89 80

MUSEUMS
Chagall Museum
Avenue Docteur Menard 6000
Telephone: 04 93 53 87 20
Fax: 04 93 53 87 39
Mobile Phone: 04 93 53 87 39
Website: www.musee-chagall.fr
The Museum has a permanet exhibition of the largest
existing collection of the works of Marc Chagall

RELIGIOUS ORGANISATIONS
Centre Consistorial
22 rue Michelet 6100
Telephone: 04 93 51 89 80
Publishes an annual calendar and guide to Nice and district

**Regional Chief Rabbinate of Nice, Côte
d'Azur and Corsica**
1 rue Voltaire 6000
Telephone: 04 93 85 82 06

RESTAURANTS
Dairy
Le Leviathan
1 avenue Georges Clemenceau
Telephone: 04 93 87 22 64

Meat
L'Alliance
13 rue Andrioli 6000
Telephone: 04 93 44 11 94

Le Dauphin Bleu
22 avenue Malaussena 6000
Telephone: 04 93 82 98 74

SYNAGOGUES
Main Synagogue
7 rue Gustave Deloye 6000

Telephone: 04 93 92 11 38
Ashkenazi
Synagogue Achkenaze
1 rue Blacas
Telephone: 04 93 62 38 68
Website: www.synablacas.org

NIMES
COMMUNITY ORGANISATIONS
Community Organisation
5 rue d'Angouleme 30000
Telephone: 04 66 26 19 51

SYNAGOGUES
Nimes Synagogue
40 rue Roussy 30000
Telephone: 04 66 29 51 81
Mikva on premises

PERPIGNAN
BUTCHERS
Gilbert Sabbah
3 rue P. Rameil 66000
Telephone: 04 68 35 41 23
Fax: 04 68 51 09 83

SYNAGOGUES
Perpignan Synagogue
54 rue FranÂois Arago 66000
Telephone: 04 68 34 75 81
Fax: 04 68 51 13 31

ROANNE
ACIR
9 rue Beaulieu 42300
Telephone: 04 77 71 51 56

SAINT ETIENNE
Saint Etienne Synagogue
34 rue d'Arcole 42000
Telephone: 04 77 33 56 31

SAINT FONS
Saint Fons Synagogue
17 avenue Albert Thomas 69190
Telephone: 04 78 67 39 78

SAINT LAURENT DU VAR
Saint Laurent Du Var Synagogue
Villa ëLe Petit Clos', 35 av. des Oliviers 06700
Telephone: 04 93 31 34 43

ST TROPEZ
SYNAGOGUE
Chabad Lubavitch of St Tropez
41 Avenue General Leclerc 83990
Telephone: 06 20 60 72 58
Email: canorhabad@aol.com
Website: www.jtropez.com

TOULON

BUTCHERS
Abecassis
8 rue Vincent Courdouan, Var 83000
Telephone: 04 94 97 39 86
Supervision: Grand Rabbinate of Marseille

Fennech
15 avenue Colbert, Var 83000
Telephone: 04 94 92 70 39
Supervision: Grand Rabbinate of Marseille

SYNAGOGUES
Toulon Synagogue
184 avenue Lazare Carnot 83050
Telephone: 04 94 92 61 05
Mikva on premises

VALENCE

Valence Synagogue
1 place du Colombier 26000
Telephone: 04 75 43 34 43

VENISSIEUX

Venissieux Synagogue
10 avenue de la Division Leclerc 69200
Telephone: 04 78 70 69 85

VICHY

Vichy Synagogue
2 bis rue du Marechal Foch 3200
Telephone: 04 70 59 82 83

South West

AGEN

Agen Synagogue
52 rue Montesquieu 47000
Telephone: 05 53 66 24 20

TOURIST SITES
Historic ghetto
rue des Juifs 47000
Site of old ghetto of the 15th century

ARCACHON

SYNAGOGUES
Orthodox
Arcachon Synagogue
36 avenue Gambetta
Telephone: 05 56 83 63 40
Fax: 05 56 83 63 40

BAYONNE

Bayonne Synagogue
35 rue Maubec 64100
Telephone: 05 59 55 03 95

BORDEAUX

BAKERIES
Boucherie Peres
64 rue Bouquiere
Telephone: 05 56 52 88 18

COMMUNITY ORGANISATIONS
Centre Yavneh
11 rue Poquelin Moliere 33000
Telephone: 05 56 52 62 69
Fax: 05 56 51 71 95
Meals are available on Shabbat and other occasions

MIKVAOT
Bordeaux Mikvaot
213 rue Ste. Catherine 33000
Telephone: 05 56 91 79 39

RESTAURANTS
Mazal Tov
137 cours Victor Hugo 33000
Telephone: 05 56 52 37 03

SYNAGOGUES
Bordeaux Synagogue
8 rue du Grand Rabbin Joseph Cohen 33000
Telephone: 05 56 91 79 39
Fax: 05 56 94 05 12

LA ROCHELLE

Orthodox
Centre Communautaire
M.C.I. 40 Cours des Dames 17000
Telephone: 05 56 46 41 17 66

LIBOURNE

Liborne Synagogue
33 rue Lamothe 33500

LIMOGES

Synagogue
25-27 rue Pierre Leroux 87000
Telephone: 05 55 77 47 26

MONTAUBAN

Montauban Synagogue
12 rue St Claire 82000
Telephone: 05 63 03 01 37

PAU

Pau Synagogue
8 rue des Trois Freres Bernadac 64000
Telephone: 05 59 62 37 85

PÈRIGVEUX

Pèrigveux Synagogue
13 rue Paul Louis Courrier 24000
Telephone: 05 53 53 22 52

POITIERS
Poitiers Synagogue
1 rue Guynemer 86000

TOULOUSE

BUTCHERS
Cacherout Diffusion
37 boulevard Carnot 31000
Telephone: 05 61 23 07 59

Lasry
8 rue Matabiau 31000
Telephone: 05 61 62 65 28

Maalem
7 rue des Chalets 31000
Telephone: 05 61 63 77 39

COMMUNITY ORGANISATIONS
Community Centre
2 place Riquet 31000
Telephone: 05 61 23 36 54

GROCERIES
Novogel
14 rue Edmund Guyaux 31200
Telephone: 05 61 57 03 19

MIKVAOT
Toulouse Mikvaot
13 rue Francisque Sarcey 31000
Telephone: 05 61 48 89 84

RELIGIOUS ORGANISATIONS
Grand Rabbinat du Toulouse et des Pays de la Garonne A.C.I.T
2 Place Riquet 31000
Telephone: 05 62 73 46 46
Fax: 05 62 73 46 47

RESTAURANTS
Community Centre
2 place Riquet 31000
Telephone: 05 62 73 56 56

SYNAGOGUES
Chaare Emeth
35 rue Rembrandt 31000
Telephone: 05 61 40 03 88

Ashkenazi Habad
Adat Yechouroun
3 rue Jules Chalande 31000
Telephone: 05 61 62 30 19
Fax: 05 61 62 86 79

Orthodox
Hekhal David
2 place Riquet 31000
Telephone: 05 62 76 46 46

Sephardi
Palaprat
2 rue Palaprat 31000
Telephone: 05 61 21 69 56

NOISY LE SEC
Orthodox
Beth Gabriel
2 rue de la Pierre FeuillÈre, Seine Saint Denis 93
Telephone: 01 48 46 71 79

ROISSY EN BRIE
Maison Communautaire
1 rue Paul Cèzanne, Centre Commercial Bois, Montmartre, Seine et Marne 77680
Telephone: 01 60 28 36 38

CORSICA

AJACCIO
CONTACT INFORMATION
Jean-Claud Sillamy
Le Sicile E - Résidence des Iles 20000
Telephone: 04 95 21 67 88
Mobile Phone: 06 13 96 19 26
There are between ten and fifteen families in the town

BASTIA
SYNAGOGUES
Bastia Synagogue
3 rue du Castagno Bastia, 20200
Services Shabbat morning and festivals.

GEORGIA

Georgia has had a very long history of Jewish settlement, dating back to two centuries before the destruction of the Second Temple if the archaeological findings are correct. These earliest Jewish communities may have descended from the Babylonian exiles. Like the Jews in the other Caucasus regions (Armenia and Azerbaijan) they are known as 'mountain Jews'.

Synagogues are found in major towns, there is a school in the capital Tbilisi and there are some newsletters. It is worth noting that the non-Jewish population has traditionally been far less anti-semitic than the populations of some other ex-Soviet republics.

GMT +4 hours
Country calling code: (**+995**)
Total population: **5,434,000**
Jewish population: **9,000**
Emergency telephone: (**police–02**) (**fire–01**)
(**ambulance–03**)
Electricity voltage: **220**

AKHALTISIKHE
SYNAGOGUES
Akhaltisikhe Synagogue
109 Guramishvili Street

BATUMI
Batumi Synagogue
6 9th March Street

GORI
Gori Synagogue
Chelyuskin Street

KUTAISI
Kutaisi Synagogue
12 Gapanove Street
Near main square

ONNI
Onni Synagogue
Baazova Street

POTI
Poti Synagogue
23 Ninoshivili Tskhakaya Street

SUKHUMI
Sukhumi Synagogue
56 Karl Marx Street

SURAMI
Surami Synagogue
Internatsionalaya Street

TBILISI
COMMUNITY ORGANISATIONS
Chabad Lubavith & Jewish Community of Georgia
10 Shevchenko Street 0108
Telephone: (32) 933 999
Fax: (32) 999 040
Website: www.fjc.ru/tbilisi

Jews of Georgia Assoc.
Tsarity Tamari Street 8 380012
Telephone: (32) 234 1057

SYNAGOGUES
Synagogue
10 Shevchenko Street
Telephone: (32) 933 999
Fax: (32) 994 040

The Ashkenazi Synagogue
13 Kozeveny St
Ashkenazi

Synagogue
65 Kozhevenny Lane
Sephardi

The Georgian Synagogue
45–47 Leselidze Street

TSHKINVALI
Synagogue
Isapov Street

TSKHAKAYA
Synagogue
Mir Strret

VANI
Vani Synagogue
4 Kaikavadze Street

GERMANY

It may be a surprise to many that Germany comes immediately after France and the UK in the population table of Western European Jews. German Jews have contributed much to the culture of European Jews in general since their arrival in what is now Germany in the fourth century. The massive Jewish presence in Poland and other east European states stemmed from German Jews escaping persecution in the late Middle Ages. They took the early Medieval German language with them, which formed Yiddish, the old *lingua franca* of European Jews.

The Jews who stayed behind in Germany contributed much towards Jewish and German culture, with the Reform movement starting in nineteenth-century Germany, and Heine and Mendelssohn contributing to German poetry and music respectively. The Enlightenment and modern Orthodoxy also began in Germany.

The rise of Nazism destroyed the belief that the German Jews were more German than Jewish. Many managed to escape before 1939, but 180,000 were killed in the Holocaust (of the 503,000 who lived in Germany when Hitler came to power). Following the events of 1933–45, it seems incredible that any Jew should want to live in Germany again. However, the community began to re-form, mainly with immigrants from eastern Europe, especially Russia. Now there are again Jewish shops in Berlin, and kosher food is once more available. There are many old synagogues which have been restored, and several concentration camps have been kept as monuments. There is also a great interest in Jewish matters among some of the non-Jewish younger generation.

Visitors to Berlin should try to visit the new Jewish Museum (officially opened in September 2001). It covers the history of German Jewry through the Middle Ages and up to the present. It revives the tradition of an earlier museum opened in 1933 before the Nazis came to power.

GMT +1 hours
Country calling code: (+49)
Total population: 82,071,000
Jewish population: 100,000
Emergency telephone: (police–110) (fire–112) (ambulance–112)
Electricity voltage: 220

AACHEN
COMMUNITY ORGANISATIONS
Bundesverband Jüdischer Studenten in Deutschland
Oppenhoffallee 50 52066
Telephone: (241) 75998

ALSENZ
SITE
Historic synagogue
Kirchberg 1 67821
Telephone: (636) 23149
Fax: (636) 23149
Restrored eighteenth century synagogue

ANDERNACH
TOURIST SITES
Historic Mikva
Rhine Valley
This Rhine Valley town cotains an early fourteenth century mikva. Key obtainable from the Town Hall.

ANNWEILER
Cemetery
Telephone: (623) 53333
The oldest cemetery in the Palatinate dating from the 16th century

AUGSBURG
SYNAGOGUES
Augsburg Synagogue
Halderstrasse 8 86150
Telephone: (821) 517 985
Museum of Jewish Culture is housed in this building.

BAD NAUHEIM
Judische Gemeinde
Karlstrasse 34, Postfach 1651 61231
Telephone: (6032) 5605; 0171 432 7519
Fax: (6032) 938 956
Email: juedischegemeinde-badnauheim@gmx.de
In the Jewish Community Centre.

BADEN BADEN
Conservative
Baden Baden Synagogue
Werderstr. 2 76530
Telephone: (72) 2139 1021
Fax: (72) 2139 1024

BAMBERG
COMMUNITY ORGANISATIONS
Community Centre
Willy Lessing Str. 7a 96047
Telephone: (951) 297870

BAYREUTH
Bayreuth Synagogue
Munzgasse 2 95444
Telephone: (921) 65404

BERLIN
Jewish life is beginning to grow again in Berlin, formerly an important centre for German Jewry. There are many sites which testify to the tragedy that befell the community before and during the war, such as the ruined Oranienburgerstrasse Synagogue, which has been turned into a Jewish centre. The site of the Wannsee Conference, to the south west of the city, (where the Holocaust was officially planned), has been turned into a museum.

BAKERIES
Backerei Kadtler
Danzigerstrasse 135 10407
Telephone: (30) 030 423 3233
Kasanien Allee 88 10349
Telephone: (30) 281 31222
Supervision: Rabbi Ehrenberg

BOOKSELLERS
Judaica and Jewellery
Literaturhandlung
Joachimstalerstrasse 13 10719
Telephone: (30) 882 4250
Fax: (30) 885 4713
Email: literaturhandlung-berlin@t-online.de
Website: www.literaturhandlung.com
Klezmer Israel pop Jiddisch

BUTCHERS
Kosher Butcher
Goethestr. 61 10625
The butcher sells certain groceries. Opening hours: 10 am
to 5 pm (Friday until 2 pm only).

CATERING AND GUESTROOMS
Bleibergs Cafe
Nuernberger Str. 45a 10789
Telephone: (30) 2191 3624
Fax: (30) 2191 3624
Mobile Phone: 17231 15277
Email: coffeeandtour@bleibergs.de
Website: www.bleibergs.de
Supervision: Rabbi Yitshak Ehrenberg
Central organisation: Jewish Community of Berlin
dairy(chalav israel),vegetarian,fish

CEMETERIES
Adass Jisroel
Wittlicherstrasse 2 Weissensee 13088
Telephone: (30) 925 1724
Established in 1880, this historic cemetery is still in use.
Rabbi Esriel Hildesheimer, Rabbi Prof. David Zvi Hoffmann,
Rabbi Eliahu Kaplan and many other wise and pious Jews
are buried here.

Friedhof Heerstaße
Heerstaße 141 Berlin 14055
Telephone: (30) 304 3234
This cemetery of the Jewish Community was opened in
1956. Some 6,000 souls are resting here. The cemetery is
still in use.

Friedhof Schönhauser
Allee 23 25 10435
Telephone: (30) 441 9824
This cemetery of the Jewish Community was opened in
1827. It has some 25,000 graves.

Friedhof Weissensee
Herbert Baum Strasse 45
Telephone: (30) 925 3330
This cemetery of the Jewish Community was opened in
1882. After the liberation in 1945 a memorial for the
murdered Jews was mounted near the entrance. More than
107,000 souls rest here. The cemetery is still in use.

COMMUNITY ORGANISATIONS
Judische Gemeinde zu Berlin
Joachimstaler Str 13 10719
Telephone: (30) 88020 0
Fax: (30) 88028 150

Judischer Kulturverein Berlin (Jewish Cultural Association Berlin)
Oranienburgerstr. 31 Berlin Mitte 10117
Telephone: (30) 282 6669; 880 28450
Fax: (30) 285 98053
Email: jkv.berlin@t-online.de
Hours: Mon, Tue, Wed 11am to 4pm

Leo Baeck Haus
Tucholskystrasse 40 Mitte 10117
Telephone: (30) 284 4560
Fax: (30) 284 45613
Here the Zeutralrat der Juden in Deutschland has its
administration

Noah's Arche Community Centre
Fasanenstr. 79 80 off the Kurfurstendamm 10623
Telephone: (30) 88028 250
Fax: (30) 88028 250
Website: www.jgberlin.org
This has been built on the site of a famous synagogue
destroyed by the Nazis.

Zentralrat der Juden in Deutschland
Tucholskystr. 9 10117
Telephone: (30) 28 44 56 0
Fax: (30) 28 44 56 13
Website: www.zentralratdjuden.de

EMBASSY
Embassy of Israel
Auguste Viktoria Strasse 74-76 14193
Telephone: (30) 89045 500
Fax: (30) 89045 555
Website: www.israel.de

GROCERIES
Kolbo
Auguststrasse 77 78 Mitte 10117
Telephone: (30) 281 3135
In addition to kosher food and wines, sifrei kodesh as well
as general literature about Jewish subjects can be obtained
here

Platzl
Passauer Str. 4 10789
Telephone: (30) 217 7506

Schalom
Wielandstr. 43 10625
Telephone: (30) 312 1131
Fax: (30) 318 09905
Opening hours: 11am to 5pm (Friday until 3.30pm)

LIBRARIES
Jewish Community
Fassensstrasse 79 10623

Jewish Library
Oranienburger Str. 28 10117
Telephone: (30) 880 28 427/429

MEDIA
Allgemeine Judische Wochenzeitung
Hausrogteiplatz 12 10117
Telephone: (30) 4998 8880
Fax: (30) 4998 8899
Email: verlag@juedische-allgemeine.de
Website: www.juedische-allgemeine.de
Weekly

Newspapers
Allgemeine Judische Wochenzeitung
Postfach 04 03 69, Haus jur Berlina Haus
Vogleiplatz 12, Berlin 10117
Telephone: (30) 2844 5650
Fax: (30) 2844 5699
Fortnightly

Hadshot Adass Jisroel
Tucholsky str. 40 10117
Telephone: (30) 281 3135
Published by Adass Jisroel

Periodical
Judisches Berlin
Oranienburger Str. 29 10117
Telephone: (30) 88028 260; 88028 269
Fax: (30) 88028 266
Email: jb@jg-berlin.org
Monthly

MUSEUMS
Jewish Museum
Lindenstrasse 9 14 10969
Telephone: (30) 2599 3305
Fax: (30) 2599 3409
Website: www.jmberlin.de
The permanent exhibition is a journey through German Jewish history and culture. In addition there are relevant changing exhibitions. There is a restaurant on the premises. Opening hours: Monday 10am to 10pm Tuesday to Sunday 10am to 8pm.

Topographie des Terrors
Niederkirchnestr 8 U & S bahn Potsdamer Platz,
Former site of Gestapo headquarters
Telephone: (30) 2548 6703
Fax: (30) 262 7156

RESTAURANTS
Dairy Vegetarian
Bleiberg's
Nürnberger st 45a 10789
Telephone: (30) 2191 3624
Fax: (30) 2191 3625
Email: coffeeandtour@bleibergs.de
Website: www.bleibergs.de
Supervision: Rabbi Yitshak Ehrenberg
Central organisation: Jewish Community of Berlin
Rooms to let
Dairy (Chalav Israel) Vegetarian Fish
Meat

Bäckerei Taitles
Dahlmannst 22
Restaurant Gabriel
Fasanstr 79/80 10623
Telephone: (30) 882 6138
Website: www.itsgabriel.de
Shabbat reservations and payment have to be arranged before the beginning of Shabbat. The restaurant is located on the first floor of the community building. Opening hours: daily 12 noon to 3.30pm and 6.30pm to 10.30pm.

SYNAGOGUES
Conservative
Synagogue
Fraenkelufer 10 16

Liberal
Synagogue
Pestalozzistr. 14 1000 10625
Telephone: (30) 313 8411

Orthodox
Adass Jisroel
Tucholskystrasse 40 Mitte 10117
Telephone: (30) 281 3135
Fax: (30) 281 3122
Email: adassjisroelberlin@web.de
Website: www.adassjisroel.de
Supervision: Rabbinate of the Congregation
Established 1869. Rabbinate, kashrut supervision and mohel can all be reached at this number. In the community centre, there is a kosher restaurant ("Beth Cafe") and around the corner a shop ("Kolbo") which sells kosher products. Daily minian at 8.30am, Shabbat at 9.30am. Kosher meals can be booked in advance for Friday evening and Shabbat.
Synagogue
Joachimstaler Strasse 13 Mitte 16719
Daily minyan, Jewish bookshop on site

Reform
Synagogue
Synagogue Hüttenweg 46, Berlin 14195
Telephone: (30) 327 9666
Website: www.huettenweg.de

TOURS
Tours of Berlin
Contact: Iris Weiss
Telephone: (30) 453 5304
Email: iris.weiss@snafu.de
Website: www.berlin-juedisch.de
22 tours about Jewish history and Jewish life

BONN
SYNAGOGUES
Bonn Synagogue
Templestrasse 2 4, cnr. Adenauer Allee 53113
Telephone: 213560
Fax: 2618366

BRAUNSCHWEIG

COMMUNITY ORGANISATIONS
Community Centre
Steinstr. 4 38100
Telephone: (531) 45536

MUSEUMS
Braunschweigisches Landesmuseum
Abt. Judisches Museum, Burgplatz 1 D 38100
Telephone: (531) 1215 0
Fax: (531) 1215 2607
Website: www.landesmuseum bs.de
Founded in 1746, this museum was formerly the oldest Jewish museum in the world. It was re-opened in 1987 under the auspices of the Braunschweigisches Landesmuseum. Hours Tuesday to Sunday: 10am to 5pm.

BREMEN

SYNAGOGUES
Bremen Synagogue
Schwachauser Heerst. 117 28211
Telephone: (421) 498 5104
Fax: (421) 498 4944

CELLE

MUSEUMS
Jewish Museum
Im Kreise 24 29221
Formerly a beautiful synagogue, it now houses travelling exhibits on various themes of Jewish history and Jewish life in Celle, where a community started between 1671 and 1691. There are now enough Jews in the town to form a minyan. Opening hours: Tuesday to Thursday 3pm to 5pm, Friday 9am to 11am and Sunday 11am to 1pm. Conducted tours of the synagogue and tours on the history of the Jews of Celle are also available by arrangement. Inquire at the Tourist Office, Celle, telephone (421) 5141 1212.

CHEMNITZ

COMMUNITY ORGANISATIONS
Community Centre
Stollberger Str. 28 Chemnitz 9119
Telephone: (371) 354 970
Fax: (371) 345 9719

COBLENZ (KOBLENZ)

Community Centre
Schlachtof Str. 5
Telephone: (261) 42223

COLOGNE

HOTELS
Leonet
Rubensstr. 33
Telephone: (221) 272 300
Fax: (221) 210 893
Website: www.leonet koeln.de

RESTAURANTS
Meat
Community Centre
Roonstr. 50 50674
Telephone: (221) 240 4440
Fax: (221) 240 4440
Phone in advance. Glatt kosher.

SYNAGOGUES
Liberal
Juedische Liberale Gemeinde
Stammheimer Strasse 22 50735
Telephone: (221) 287 0424
Fax: (221) 719 5024
Website: www.gescherlamassoret.de

Orthodox
Synagogue
Roonstrasse 50 50674
Telephone: (221) 921 5600
Fax: (221) 921 5609
Website: www.sgk.de
Daily services. There is a youth centre, mikva, glatt kosher restaurant (meat), Jewish museum and library at the same address. Old age home (Elternheim), kindergarten, primary school, social department and administration are located in: Jüdisches Wohlfahrtzentrum Köln–Ehrenfeld Ottstr. 85 / Eingang Nussbaumer Str. 50923 Köln
Telephone: 49 (221) 716 620 Fax: 49 (221) 7166 2599

DORTMUND

COMMUNITY ORGANISATIONS
Landesverband der Judischen Gemeinden von Westfalen
Prinz Friedrich Karl Str. 12 44135
Telephone: (231) 528495
Fax: (231) 5860372
Email: lvjuedwest@aol.com

SYNAGOGUES
Dortmund Synagogue
Prinz Friedrich Karl Str. 9 44135
Telephone: (231) 527 4720
Fax: (231) 5274 7220
Email: verwaltung@jkgd.de
Website: www.JG-Dortmund.de

DRESDEN

In November 2001 the first new synagogue in what was East Germany was consecrated. It is on the site of the Semper synagogue originally built in 1838 and destroyed one hundred years later on Kristallnacht.

A three foot high Star of David, one of the two that was on the top of the synagogue, was all that remained. It will stand above the new synagogue's gate.

Up to date information may be found on www.Synagogue-dresden.de

COMMUNITY ORGANISATIONS
Landesverband Sachsen der Judischen Gemeinden K.d.o.R.
Bautzner Strasse 20 1099
Telephone: (351) 804 5491; 802 2739
Fax: (351) 804 1445
A memorial to the six million Jews killed in the Holocaust stands on the site of the Dresden Synagogue, burnt down by the Nazis in November 1938

SYNAGOGUES
Dresden Synagogue
Fiedlerstrasse 3 1307
Telephone: (351) 693317

DUSSELDORF
JCC
Dusseldorf Synagogue
Paul-Spiegel-Platz 1 40476
Telephone: (211) 469120
Fax: (211) 485156
Email: info@jgdus.de
Website: www.jgdus.de

EMMENDINGEN
Orthodox
Juedische Gemeinde Emmendingen
Synagogue and Youth Centre, Landvogtei 11, Office and Community Centre Kirchstrasse 11, POB 1423 D 79312
Telephone: (7641) 571 989
Fax: (7641) 571 980
Email: juedgemem@aol.com
Website: www.juedgemen.de

ERFURT
COMMUNITY ORGANISATIONS
Community Centre
Juri Gagarin Ring 16 99084
Telephone: (361) 24964

ESSEN
Essen Community Organizations
Sedanstrasse 46 45138
Telephone: (201) 273413
Fax: (201) 287112

ESSINGEN
TOURIST SITES
Cemetery
Largest cemetery in the Palatinate dating from the sixteenth century, where Anne Frank's ancestors are buried. Key at the Mayor's Office.

FRANKFURT AM MAIN
BUTCHERS
Aviv Butchery & Deli
Hanauer Landstrasse 50 60314

Telephone: (69) 433013
Fax: (69) 448064
Website: www.aviv.de
Supervision: Frankfurt Rabbinate
Fresh Challa for shabbat is available as well as kosher bread, buns and cakes. These items are the best to be ordered in advance in order to get as fresh as possible. Beside this we also have a variety of dishes for shabbat which are prepared every week fresh from Wednesday through Friday.

COMMUNITY ORGANISATIONS
Community Centre (Ignatz Bubis Gemeindezentrum)
Westendstrasse 43 60325
Telephone: (69) 768 0360
Fax: (69) 746874
Website: www.jg-ffm.de
This community produces a magazine, 'Judische Gemeinde Zeitung Frankfurt'

Zentralwohlfahrtsstelle de Juden in Deutschland
Hebelstrasse 6 60318
Telephone: (69) 94 43 71 15
Fax: (69) 49 48 17
Website: www.zwst.org

GROCERIES
Koschermarket
36 Bornheimer Landwehr 60385
Telephone: (69) 9441 1238
Fax: (69) 9441 2174

MIKVAOT
Judische Gemeinde
Freiherr-von-Stein 30 D-60323
Telephone: (69) 768 0360
Fax: (69) 746 874
Website: www.jg-ffm.de

MUSEUMS
Jewish Museum
Untermainkai 14–15 60311
Telephone: (69) 2123 5000
Fax: (69) 2123 0705
Website: www.juedischesmuseum.de
Central organisation: Stadt Frankfurt am Main Der
Sunday, Tuesday to Saturday 10am to 5pm, Wednesday 10am to 8pm. Closed Monday.

Museum Judengasse
Kurt Schumacher Strasse 10 60311
Telephone: (69) 297 7419
Fax: (69) 212 30705
Website: www.jewishmuseum.de

RESTAURANTS
Sohar's Kosher Restaurant
Savignystrasse 66 60325
Telephone: (69) 752 341
Fax: (69) 741 0116
Website: www.sohars restaurant.com

Supervision: Rabbi Menachem Halevi Klein, Frankfurt Rabbinate

Hours: Tuesday to Thursday and Sunday, 12pm to 8pm; Friday 12pm to Shabbat; Shabbat, 1.30pm to 4pm; Monday closed. Special arrangements can be made by phone. Friday and Shabbat meals must be ordered in advance. Provides part services, airline catering and delivery to hotels. Fifteen minute walk from synagogue, fair centre and main train station.

SYNAGOGUES
Synagogue
Baumweg 5 7 60316
Telephone: (69) 439 381

Westend Synagogue
Freiherr vom Stein Strasse 30 60323
Telephone: (69) 723 263
This is the city's main synagogue

FREIBURG
COMMUNITY ORGANISATIONS
Community Centre
Engels Strasse
Telephone: (761) 383 096
Fax: (761) 382 332
Services: Erev Shabbat in Summer 7.30pm. in Winter 6.30pm. Shabbat morning 9.30am. Kosher Kiddush after services.

FRIEDBERG
TOURIST SITES
Historic Mikva
Judengasse 20 61169
Telephone: (06031) 88215
Fax: (06031) 18396
Email: wetteraumuseum@friedberg-hessen.de
A Gothic style mikva built in 1260. The town council has issued a special explanatory leaflet about it. It has been restored and it is now scheduled as a historical monument of medieval architecture.

FURTH
COMMUNITY ORGANISATIONS
Synagogue
Community Centre
Blumenstrasse 31, Hallemannstr 2 90762
Telephone: (911) 770 879
Fax: (911) 770 853

TOURIST SITES
Synagogue and Mikva
Julienstrasse 2
There is a beautifully restored synagogue as well as a historic mikva

GELSENKIRCHEN
COMMUNITY ORGANISATIONS
Community Centre
GeorgStrasse 2 45879

Telephone: (20) 155231-0
Fax: (20) 155231-23

HAGEN
Hagen Community Organisation
Pottofstrasse 16 58095
Telephone: (2331) 711 3289

HALLE
Halle Community Organisation
Grosse Markerstrasse 13 06108
Telephone: (345) 233 110
Fax: (345) 233 1122
Website: www.jghalle.de

HAMBURG
Hamburg Community Organisation
Schaferkampsalle 27 20357
Telephone: (40) 440 9440
Fax: (40) 410 8430
Mikvah on premises

SYNAGOGUES
Orthodox
Hamburg Synagogue
Hohe Weide 34 20253
Telephone: (40) 4409 4429
Fax: (40) 410 8430
Email: info@jghh.org
Website: www.jghh.org
Central organisation: Jüdische Gemeinde in Hamburg Administration, Grindelhof 30, 20146 Hamburg (formerly Talmud
Tora Schule)

HANOVER
COMMUNITY ORGANISATIONS
Community Centre
Haeckelstrasse 10 30173
Telephone: (311) 810 472

SYNAGOGUES
Hanover Synagogue
Haeckelstrasse 10 30173
Telephone: (311) 810 472

HEIDELBERG
RESTAURANTS
College Restaurant
Theaterstrasse 9 69117
Telephone: (6221) 168 767
Kosher meals are available (by arrangement it is open all year round) Monday to Friday at the college restaurant, 100 yards from the College of Jewish Studies, situated at Friederichstrasse 9

HERFORD
COMMUNITY ORGANISATIONS
Community Centre
Komturstraße 21 32052
Telephone: (52) 21924702
Fax: (52) 21924704

HILDESHEIM
SYNAGOGUES
Jewish Community in Hildesheim
Postfach 10 07 07, 31107 Hildesheim, Einumer
Strasse 37 D31135
Telephone: (512) 170 4962
Fax: (512) 170 4964
Website: www.jg-hildesheim.de
Supervision: Rabbi Jonah Sievers
Central organisation: Landesverband der Jüdischen
Gemeinden in Niedersachsen

HOF
COMMUNITY ORGANISATIONS
Community Centre
Am Wiesengrund 20 95032
Telephone: (92) 815 3249

ICHENHAUSEN
MUSEUMS
Museum of Jewish History
Ehemalige Synagoge
Vordere Obergasse 22 89355
Telephone: 8221 95272
Located in the fine baroque synagogue, not far from Ulm

INGENHEIM
TOURIST SITES
Cemetery
Klingenerstrasse 20 76831
Sixteenth century cemetery can be visited. Key obtained
from Klingenerstrasse 20.

KAISERSLAUTERN
COMMUNITY ORGANISATIONS
Community Centre
Basteigasse 4 67655
Telephone: (63) 169720

KARLSRUHE
Karlsruhe Community Organizations
Knielinger Alle 11 76133
Telephone: (72) 172035
Website: www.jg-karlsruhe.de

KIEL
SYNAGOGUES
Orthodox
Kiel Synagogue
Wikingerstrasse 6 24143

Telephone: (431) 739 9096
Fax: (431) 739 9095

KONSTANZ
COMMUNITY ORGANISATIONS
Community Centre
Sigismundstr. 19 78462
Telephone: (75) 312 3077

KREFELD
Krefeld Community Organisations
Wiedstrasse 17b 47799
Telephone: (21) 512 0648

LANDAU
SYNAGOGUES
Landau Synagogue
Frank Loebsches Haus, Kaufhausgasse 9 76829
Telephone: (6341) 86472
Fax: (6341) 13294

LUBECK
Orthodox
Synagogue & Community Centre
St. Annen Strasse 13 23552
Telephone: (451) 798 2182
Fax: (451) 7074 9207

MAGDEBURG
COMMUNITY ORGANISATIONS
Community Centre
Groperstrasse 1a 39106
Telephone: (391) 52665

MAINZ
Mainz Community Organisations
Forsterstrasse 2 55118
Telephone: (6131) 613 990
Fax: (6131) 611 767
Website: www.magenza.org

TOURIST SITES
Jewish Cemetery
Untere Zahlbacherstr. 11
The key to the twelfth century Jewish cemetery can be
obtained at the 'new' Jewish cemetery

MARBURG AN DER LAHN
COMMUNITY ORGANISATIONS
Community Centre
Unterer Eichweg 17 35041
Telephone: (642) 132 881

MICHELSTADT
SYNAGOGUES
DR I. E. Lichtigfeld Museum
Mauerstrasse 19
Telephone: (6061) 706 145; 922 102; 12496

Fax: (6061) 706 145
Hours: Sunday to Thursday from 2.30pm to 5.30pm. On Sabbath and the Jewish Holydays it is closed to visitors, from November to March it is only partly opened.

Dr. I.E. Lichtigfeld Museum
Mauerstraße19 64720
Telephone: (6061) 14146; 706 145; 922 102
Fax: (6061) 706 145
Email: stadtarchiv@michelstadt.de
Website: www.michelstadt.de/synagoge
This museum of both Judaism and Jewish history has re-opened as a synagogue. Hours: Sunday to Thursday from 2.30pm to 5.30pm. On Sabbath and the Jewish Holydays it is closed to visitors, from November to March it is only partly opened.

MINDEN
COMMUNITY ORGANISATIONS
Community Centre
Kampstrasse 6 32423
Telephone: (57) 123437

MONCHENGLADBACH
SYNAGOGUES
Monchengladbach Synagogue
Albertusstrasse 54 41363
Telephone: (216) 23879
Fax: (216) 14639

MULHEIM
COMMUNITY ORGANISATIONS
Mulheim Community Organisations
Kampstr. 7 45468
Telephone: 835191

MUNICH
Literaturhandlung, Literatur Zum Judentum
Im Jüdischen Museum literatur zum Judentum, St. Jakobs-Platz

BOOKSELLERS
Judaica and Jewellery
Literaturhandlung, Literatur Zum Judentum
Fürstenstr. 11 80333
Telephone: (89) 2800135
Fax: (89) 281601
Email: literaturhandlungim@googlemail.com
Website: www.literatuhandlung.com
Programs on Jewish subjects

Literaturhandlung, Literatur Zum Judentum
Im Jüdischen Museum, St Jakobs-Platz 16 80331
Telephone: (89) 2323 0760
Fax: (89) 2323 0715
Email: Literaturhandlungim@googlemail.com
Website: www.Literaturhandlung.com
Programs on Jewish subjects

COMMUNITY ORGANISATIONS
Israelitische Kultusgemeinde München und Oberbayern (Community Centre)
St Jakobs-Platz 18 80337
Telephone: (89) 2024 00100
Fax: (89) 2024 00170
Email: info@ikg-m.de
Website: www.ikg muenchen.de

GROCERIES
Danel Feinkost
Pilgersheimerstrabe 44 81543
Telephone: (89) 669 888
Fax: (89) 669 820
Website: www.koscher.net/danel/
Will deliver to hotels or other addresses, throughout Germany.

MUSEUMS
Jewish Museum Munich
St.-Jakobs-Platz 16 80331
Telephone: (89) 233 96096
Fax: (89) 233 989 96096
Email: juedisches.museum@muenchen.de
Website: www.juedisches-museum-muenchen.de
On our three exhibition floors, visitors gain a world of insights into Jewish life and culture in Munich. A special section geared towards young as well as adults audiences provides in-depth information on Jewish history and religion. On each gallery floor is a study area, either a learning center or library, where visitors will be able to explore issues of interest and find answers to their questions.

RESTAURANTS
Einstein
St Jacobs Platz 2 18 80331
Telephone: (89) 202 400332
Fax: (89) 202 400334
Website: www.carmel prestige.de
Hours: 11.30am to 10.30pm. Shabbat meals must be ordered by Thursday noon.

Kosher
Fleming's Kosher Restaurant
St.-Jakobs-Platz 18 80311
Telephone: (89) 2024 00333
Fax: (89) 2024 00334
Website: www.flemings-hotels.com/de/flemings_kosher_muenchen
The only kosher restaurant in Bavaria.
Menu ranging from Israeli specialities to traditional Bavarian dishes.
Prepared following glatt kosher guidelines.
The conference and event area of 1.000 sqm offers 3 air-conditioned banquet rooms from 2 up to 700 people.

SYNAGOGUES
Schwabing Synagogue (Schaarei Zion)
Georgenstr. 71 80798
Telephone: (89) 202 4000
Friday evenings and Sabbath mornings only

Synagogue
Possartstrasse15 81679
Telephone: (89) 474 440
Reichenbachstrasse 27 80469
Telephone: (89) 202 4000
Fax: (89) 201 4604
Mikva on premises.

Progressive
Beth Shalom
Telephone: (89) 20330385
Fax: (89) 8980 9374
Website: www.beth shalom.de
Central organisation: World Union for Progressive Judaism
Please ask for address and timetable

NEUSTADT
COMMUNITY ORGANISATIONS
Community Centre
Ludwigstrasse 20 67433
Telephone: (0) 6321 2652
Fax: (0) 6321 397492

ODENBACH
TOURIST SITES
Synagogue
Kirchhofstrasse 9 67748
Telephone: (67) 6382 993299
Fax: (67) 6382 993299
Email: fv-synagogeodenbach@t-online.de
Website: www.ehemalige-synagoge-odenbach.de
There is a unusually shaped historic synagogue built in 1752 with baroque paintings in this small village. Arrangements to visit need to be made in advance.

OFFENBACH
COMMUNITY ORGANISATIONS
Community Centre
Kaiserstrasse 109 63065
Telephone: (69) 820036
Fax: (69) 820026

OSNABRÜCK 2
Osnabrück Community Organization
In der Barlage 41 49078
Telephone: (541) 148420
Fax: (541) 143 4701
Kashrut information for visitors who wish to eat kosher on Shabbat, please contact Rabbi Marc Sterm at Tel: (541) 48553

SYNAGOGUES
Orthodox
Jewish Congregation Synagogue
In der Barlage 41 49078
Telephone: (541) 48420
Fax: (541) 434701
Website: juden-in-osna.de

TOURIST SITES
The Felix Nussbaum House
Lotter Strasse 49078
Telephone: (541) 323 2207
Fax: (541) 323 2739
Email: jaehner@osnabrueck.de
Website: www.osnabrueck.de/fmh
About 20 minutes walk from the synagogue

PADERBORN
COMMUNITY ORGANISATIONS
Community Centre
Pipinstrasse 32 33098
Telephone: (52) 512 2596

REGENSBURG
Regensburg Community Organizations
Am Brixener Hof 2 93047
Telephone: (94) 157093; 21819

SAARBRUCKEN
SYNAGOGUES
Synagogengemeinde Saar
Lortzingstrasse 8 66111
Telephone: (681) 910 380
Fax: (681) 910 3813
Website: www.synagogengemeinde.de

SCHWERIN
COMMUNITY ORGANISATIONS
Judische Gemeinde Schwerin
Schlachtermarkt 7 19055
Telephone: (38) 5550 7345
Fax: (38) 5593 60989

SPEYER
TOURIST SITES
11th Century Mikva
Telephone: (62) 353332
This town contains the oldest (eleventh century) mikva in Germany, Judenbadgasse. To visit it, obtain the key by contacting the Tourist Office (Maximilianstrasse 11). Guided tours are available.

STRAUBING
COMMUNITY ORGANISATIONS
Community Centre
Wittelbacherstrasse 2 94315
Telephone: (94) 211387

STUTTGART
RELIGIOUS ORGANISATIONS
Israelitische Religionsgemeinschaft
Hospitalstrasse 36 70174
Telephone: (711) 228360
Fax: (711) 2283636

RESTAURANTS

Meat
Schalom Kosher Restaurant
Hospitalstrasse 36 70174
Telephone: (711) 294752
Supervision: Orthodox Rav of the Stuttgart community
Open during morning hours through to about 7pm except
Mondays (when closed). Located on the premises of the
Stuttgart Jewish community centre.

TRIER
COMMUNITY ORGANISATIONS
Judische Kultugemeinde Trier
Kaiserstrasse 25 D 54290
Telephone: (0) 651 994 5575
Fax: (0) 651 994 5577

VEITSHOECHHEIM
Located a few miles from Wurzburg is the town
of Veitshoechheim, which reconsecrated a pre-
First World War Synagogue and opened as a
Jewish Museum in March 1994. Originally built
in 1730 the synagogue was the community
centre for local Jews who had lived in the area
for nearly three hundred years, from 1644 to
1942, when the last Jews were deported from
Veitshoechheim to the Nazi concentration
camps.

In 1986 the stone fragments of the original
interior, including the Bima and the Ahron
Hakodesch, were discovered beneath the floor,
where they had been buried in 1940. This find
prompted local officials to transform the
Synagogue back to its original function and
splendour, using photographs from the 1920s as
a guide.

MUSEUMS
Judisches Kulturmuseum Veitshoechheim
Thuengersheimer Strasse 17 97209
Telephone: (931) 9802 764/754
Fax: (931) 9802 876
Email: museum@veitshoechheim.de
Website: www.veitshoechheim.de

WIESBADEN
COMMUNITY ORGANISATIONS
Judische Gemeinde Wiesbaden
Friedrichstrasse 31 33 65185
Telephone: (611) 933 3030
Fax: (611) 933 30319
Email: info@jg-wi.de
Services every Friday evening and Saturday morning with
kiddush and Jewish holidays

SYNAGOGUES
Community Centre
Wiesbaden Synagogue
Friedrichstrasse 31 65085
Telephone: (611) 301 870

WUPPERTAL
COMMUNITY ORGANISATIONS
Community Centre
Friedrich Ebert Strasse 73 42103
Telephone: (202) 300233

WURZBURG
Wurzburg Community Organisations
Valentin Becker Strasse 11 97072
Telephone: (931) 404 140
Fax: (931) 465 5249
Email: shalomeuropa@gmx.de
Also guest rooms for tourists; kosher meals available.
Newly opened Lauder CHerev Centre (Seminar Centre for
Young People) and a Jewish Museum.

MIKVAOT
Wurzburg Mikvaot
Valentin Becker Strasse 11 97072
Telephone: (931) 404140
Fax: (931) 465 5249
Email: shalomeuropa@gmx.de
Appointments must be made

SYNAGOGUES
Community & Culture Centre
Wurzburg Synagogue
Valentin Becker Strasse 11 97072
Telephone: (931) 404 140
Fax: (931) 465 5249
Email: shalomeuropa@gmx.de
Website: www.juedischegemeindewuerzburg.de
Jewish Museum Shalom Europa

TOURIST SITES
Cemeteries
There are old Jewish cemeteries in Wurzburg, Heidingsfeld
and Hochberg

GIBRALTAR

The first Jewish people in Gibraltar were
Sephardi, who had crossed over the border
from Spain before the Inquisition began in
the fourteenth century. Many more followed in the ensuing centuries. When
Britain took possession Jews were banned,
but later they were allowed in as traders
and finally, in 1749, they were granted full
permission to live there. The community
began to flourish and the Jewish population, which now also included many North
African Jews rose to 2,000.

At the end of the Second World War some
of the community returned after being
evacuated to Britain. There are now fairly

good Jewish facilities, namely four synagogues, and newsletters. There are no
kosher hotels in Gibraltar.

Gibraltar has an Eruv. Gibraltar has had a
Jewish prime minister and a Jewish mayor,
Gibraltar's highest offices.

GMT +1 hours
Country calling code: (**+350**)
Total population: **28,000**
Jewish population: **650**
Emergency telephone: (**police–199**) (**fire–190**)
(**ambulance–190**)
Electricity voltage: **220/240**

BAKERIES
J. Amar
47 Line Wall Road
Telephone: (200) 73516
Fax: (200) 76914
Hours: Monday to Friday 6.30am to 5pm, Sunday 6.30am
to 1.30pm

BREAD & CONFECTIONERY
Cafeteria
J.J.B. Amar Limited
1/A Convent Place, PO Box 86
Telephone: (200) 73516
Fax: (200) 76914
Email: sofergib@gibtelecom.net
Bread, cakes, fast food, sitting area for coffee

BUTCHERS AND DELICATESSEN
A. Edery International Ltd
26 John Mackintosh Square
Telephone: (200) 75168
Fax: (200) 42529
Website: www.ederykosher.com
Supervision: Dayan Ch. Ehrentreu Head of London Beth Din
and Rabbi R Hassid Chief Rabbi of Gibraltar
Glatt Kosher meat, delicatessen lamb and poultry
Specialise in orders to hotels and caterers

COMMUNITY ORGANISATIONS
Managing Board of Jewish Community
10 Bomb House Lane
Telephone: (200) 72606
Fax: (200) 40487
Email: mbjc@gibtelecom.net

CONTACT INFORMATION
Solomon Levy M.B.E. J.P
3 Convent Place, PO Box 190
Telephone: (200) 77789; 428128; 78047 (home)
Fax: (200) 42527
Mr Levy is happy to provide information for Jewish
travellers.
As from 1st August 2008 to 31st July 2009 Mr Levy will be
Mayor of Gibraltar.

CULTURAL ORGANISATIONS
Jewish Social & Cultural Club
7 Bomb House Lane
Telephone: (200) 50611
Fax: (200) 51415
Mailing address: Abner Suissa, 20 Lime Tree Lodge,
Montagu Gardens, Gibraltar

DELICATESSEN/TAKEAWAY
Uncle Sam's Deli
62 Irish Town, 17 Cornwall Lane
Telephone: (200) 51236; 51226
Fax: (200) 42516
Provides kosher groceries and wine. Catering and takeaway
service. Full glatt kosher service. Fully licensed. Delivery of
kosher food in Spain.

EMBASSY
Consul General of Israel
Marina View, Glacis Road, Po Box 141
Telephone: (200) 77244

GROCERIES
I&D Abudarham
32 Cornwall's Lane, PO Box 216
Telephone: (200) 78506
Fax: (200) 73249
Kosher wines, meats & poultry

HOTELS
The Rock Hotel Ltd
3 Europa Road
Telephone: (200) 73000
Fax: (200) 73513
The hotel has kosher facilities (meat and dairy) and can
cater for pre booked groups of 10 or more. Kosher
takeaway food can also be delivered to a room.

JUDAICA
A. Cohen
3 Convent Place, PO Box 86
Telephone: (200) 52734
Fax: (200) 42527
Mobile Phone: 20054016058
Email: sofergib@gibtelecom.net
Supplier of Mezutot, Tephilim, Sifre Tora, Shaatnez

MIKVAOT
Gibraltar Mikvaot
12 Bomb House Lane, Office 91, Irish Town
Telephone: (200) 77658 / 73090

RESTAURANTS
The Leanse
7 Bomb House Lane
Telephone: (200) 41751
Fax: (200) 41751
Open daily from 10am to 11pm, except Shabbat, but
arrangements can be made with the restaurant owner for
Shabbat meals

SYNAGOGUES
Orthodox
Abudarham
22 Parliament Lane 78506
Telephone: (200) 78047
Fax: (200) 42527
Anyone visiting Gibraltar over the weekend and needing hospitality kindly contact
Solomon Levy MBE 3 Convent Place Tel (00 350) 77789
Etz Hayim
91 Irishtown; P.O. Box 31
75955
Telephone: (200) 75563
Fax: (200) 42939
Mobile Phone: 00346 19957 141

Nefusot Yehudah
65 Line Wall Road G1
Telephone: (200) 76477
Fax: (200) 73201
Central organisation: Managing Board Jewish Community
Shaar Hashamayim
47 Engineer Lane, Box 174 78069
Telephone: (200) 74030
Contact Gabriel Belilo tel: 5400 8185

TOURS
Holyland Travel ltd
21 Bell Lane
Telephone: (200) 75965
Jewish related tours

GREECE

After the Hellenistic occupation of Israel (the Jewish revolt during this occupation is commemorated in the festival of Hanukah), some Jews were led into slavery in Greece, beginning the first recorded Jewish presence in the country. The next significant Jewish immigration occurred after the Inquisition, when many Spanish Jews moved to Salonika, which was a flourishing Jewish centre until the German occupation in the Second World War. In 1832 Jews were granted equal civil rights to all other Greek citizens.

By the early 1940s, the Jewish population had grown to over 70,000, with 45,000 living in Salonika. The country was occupied in July 1941 and split among the Axis (German, Italian and Bulgarian) forces. During the occupation a relatively large

number of Jews joined the partisans. Many local Christians did protect their Jewish neighbours in Athens. After the war many of the survivors emigrated to Israel.

Today there are Sephardi synagogues in Greece and, in Athens, a community centre and a Jewish museum. There are Jewish publications and a library in the community centre. In Aegina, Corfu and other Greek islands, ancient synagogues may be visited.

GMT +2 hours
Country calling code: (+30)
Total population: **10,552,000**
Jewish population: **4,500**
Emergency telephone: (**police–100**) (**fire–199**) (**ambulance–166**)
Electricity voltage: **220**

ATHENS
Almost 3,000 Jews live in Athens. The community has access to a centre containing a library, and the opportunity to have a kosher meal. The Jewish museum in the centre of the city details the rise and tragic fall of Greek Jewry.

Kosher meals are served at the Athens Jewish Cultural Centre upon request (contact Mrs Rachel Sasson, Tel. (1) 213 3371. – Delivery to hotels in Athens can also be arranged).

COMMUNITY ORGANISATIONS
Central Board of the Jewish Communities of Greece
36 Voulis Street 10557
Telephone: (210) 324 4315 18
Fax: (210) 331 3852
Email: hhkis@oth.forthnet.gr
Website: www.kis.gr
EMBASSY
Embassy of Israel
Marathonodromou Street 1, Paleo Psychico, 15452
Telephone: (210) 671 9530
Fax: (210) 674 9510
Website: www.athens.mfa.gov.il

MUSEUMS
Jewish Museum of Greece
39 Nikis Str. 10557
Telephone: (210) 322 5582
Fax: (210) 3231 1577
Email: info@jewishmuseum.gr
Website: www.jewishmuseum.gr
Open: Monday to Friday 9am to 2.30pm, Sunday 10am to 2pm, Saturday closed.

RESTAURANTS
Meat
Kosher restaurant
5 Averof St. 10433
Telephone: (210) 520 2880
Fax: (210) 520 2881
Email: chabad@otenet.gr
Telephone for orders

Vegetarian
Eden
Odos Flessa 3, Plaka

SYNAGOGUES
Sephardi
Beth Shalom
5 Melidoni Street 10553
Telephone: (210) 325 2773; 2823; 2875
Fax: (210) 322 0761

TOURIST INFORMATION
Community Office
8 Melidoni Street 10553
Telephone: (210) 325 2875
Fax: (210) 322 0761

Meals on Wheels
Glatt Kosher Meals delivered
Telephone: (210) 520 2880

CHALKIS
COMMUNITY ORGANISATIONS
Community Centre
35 Kotsou Street 34100
Telephone: (2221) 80690

KASHRUT INFORMATION
Community Centre
Telephone: (2221) 27297

SYNAGOGUES
Chalkis Synagogue
36 Kotsou Street
This synagogue has been rebuilt and renewed many times on its original foundations. Tombstone inscriptions in the cementery go back more then fifteen centuries. Only open on High Holy Days.

CORFU
COMMUNITY ORGANISATIONS
Community Centre
5 Riz. Voulephton St. 49100
Telephone: (2661) 45650
Fax: (2661) 43791

SYNAGOGOUE
Scuola Greca
4 Velissariou St.
Telephone: (2661) 38802
Services on High Holydays only

CRETE
SYNAGOGUES
Etz Hayyim Synagogue
Parados Kondyllaki 730 11, Hania
Telephone: (2821) 086 286
Fax: (2821) 086 286
Website: www.etz hayyim hania.org

IOANNINA
COMMUNITY ORGANISATIONS
Ioannina Community Organisations
18 Josef Eliyia St. 45221
Telephone: (2651) 25195
Contact: John Kalef Ezra on 32390

LARISSA
SYNAGOGUES
Community Centre
Platia Evreon Martiron, 29 Kentavron St. 412 22
Telephone: (241) 532 965

RHODES
Jewish Museum Of Rhodes
Kahal Shalom Kadosh
Simmiou and Dossiadou Street, Old City 85100
Telephone: (22410) 22364 70964
Fax: (22410) 73039
Email: jcrhodes@otenet.gr
Website: www.jewishrhodes.org
www.RhodesJewishMuseum.org
Central organisation: Central Jewish Board of Greece (KIS)
The synagogue belongs to the Jewish Community of Rhodes which has 38 members. It was built around 1577 in the old Jewish Quarter. The synagogue is on the World Monuments Fund list of 100 most endangered sites. Adjoining the Synagogue is the Jewish Museum which has been restructured and extended. Tourists wishing to visit these sites should contact: Mrs Carmen Cohen
Jewish Community of Rhodes, No. 5 Polydorou St. Old City. Rhodes. Tel: 22410 22364 /70964 or Fax: 22410 73039

THESSALONIKI
For many years around the turn of the 20th century Jews formed the majority of Salonika's inhabitants. It was known as the 'Jerusalem of the Balkans'. The official day off was Saturday.

CULTURAL ORGANISATIONS
The Israelite Fraternity House
24 Vassileos Irakliou St.
Telephone: (231) 221030

Yad le Zikaron
26 Vassileos Irakliou St. 546 24
Telephone: (231) 275 701
Fax: (231) 229 063

MUSEUMS
Jewish Museum of Thessaloniki
13 Agiou Mina Street 54624
Telephone: (231) 0025 0406
Fax: (231) 0025 0407
Email: jctmuseo@otenet.gr
Website: www.jmth.gr
Tuesday, Friday & Sunday: 11am to 2pm, Wednesday &
Thursday: 11am to 2pm and 5pm to 8pm. Guided tours for
groups, educational programmes for youngsters.
SYNAGOGUES

Monastirioton
35 Sygrou Street 54630
Telephone: (231) 524968

TRIKKALA
Synagogue
15 Athanassiou Diakou Street

Yad Lezicaron
24 Vassileos Irakliou Street
Telephone: (231) 223231

VOLOS
COMMUNITY ORGANISATIONS
Volos Community Organisations
Xenophontos & Moisseos Streets 38333
Telephone: (2421) 25302
Fax: (2421) 25302

KASHRUT INFORMATION
Volos Kashrut Information
20 Parodos Kondulaki

SYNAGOGUES
Volos Synagogue
Xenophontos & Moisseos Streets
Open primarily on High Holy Days

TOURIST SITES
Holocaust Monument
Riga Ferreou Square

GUADELOUPE
GMT -4 hour
Country calling code: **(+590)**
Emergency telephone: **(police–17) (fire–18)
(ambulance–15)**
**Emergency services: 112 (which can be called
from any mobile phone, even if not connected
to a GSM network);**

GOSIER
SYNAGOGUES
Gosier Synagogue
Bas du Fort, Lot 1
Telephone: (0590) 909 909
The Synagogue, community centre and restaurant/kosher
store are all located here.

GUATEMALA

Conversos were the first recorded Jews in the country, but a few centuries later, the next Jewish immigration occurred with the arrival of German Jews in 1848. Later, some east European Jews arrived but Guatemala was not keen to accept refugees from Nazism, and, as a result, passed some laws which, although not mentioning Jews directly, were aimed against Jewish refugees.

Even though these laws were in place, in 1939 there were 800 Jews in Guatemala. An Ashkenazi community centre was built in 1965, but despite accepting some Jewish Cuban refugees, the community is shrinking owing to assimilation and intermarriage.

Most Jews live in Guatemala City, and others in Quetzaltenango and San Marcos. There is a Jewish school and kindergarten.

GMT -6 hours
Country calling code: **(+502)**
Total population: **10,517,000**
Jewish population: **1,000**
Emergency telephone: **(police–110) (fire–110)
(ambulance–125)**
Electricity voltage: **110**

GUATEMALA CITY
COMMUNITY ORGANISATIONS
Comunidad Judia Guatemalteca
Apartado Postal 502
Telephone: (2) 360 1509
Fax: (2) 360 1589
Website: www.comunidadjudia.com
Has a kosher grocery

EMBASSY
Embassy of Israel
13 Avenida 14-07, Zona 10
Telephone: (2) 371305

SYNAGOGUES
Ashenkenazi
Centro Hebreo, 7a Avenida 13-51, Zona 9
Telephone: (2) 331 1975

Sephardi
Maguen David
7a Avenida 3-80, Zona 2
Telephone: (2) 232 0932

HAITI

Christopher Columbus brought the first Jew to Haiti–his interpreter, Luis de Torres, a *Converso* who had been baptised before the voyage. Thereafter more Jews settled but the community was destroyed in an anti-European revolt by Toussaint L'Ouverture in 1804. A hundred or so years later, Jews from the Middle East and some refugees from the Nazis settled in Haiti, but many subsequently emigrated to Israel.

The remaining community has benefited from the help of the Israeli embassy, and services are held in the embassy or in private homes. There is no central Jewish organisation, and the community is too small to support other Jewish facilities.

GMT -5 hours
Country calling code: (+509)
Total population: 7,492,000
Jewish population: Under 100
Emergency telephone: (police–114)
(ambulance–118)
Electricity voltage: 110

PORT AU PRINCE
COMMUNITY ORGANISATIONS
The Jewish Community in Haiti
P.O. Box 687
Telephone: 1 20 638

CONTACT INFORMATION
Tourist Information
Religious services are held at the home of the Honorary Israeli Consul, Mr Gilbert Bigio

HONDURAS

During the Spanish colonial period, some *Conversos* did live in Honduras, but it was only in the nineteenth century that any significant Jewish immigration occurred. In the early twentieth century refugees from Nazism followed a handful of immigrants from eastern Europe. Honduras was one of the small number of countries to aid refugees from Nazism, and many Jews owe their lives to the help of Honduran consulates which issued visas in wartime Europe.

The capital Tegucigalpa contains the largest Jewish population, but the only

synagogue in the country is in San Pedro Sula (services are held in private homes in Tegucigalpa). There is also a Sunday school and WIZO branch.

GMT -6 hours
Country calling code: (+504)
Total population: 76,338,000
Jewish population: Under 100
Emergency telephone: (police–119) (fire–198)
(ambulance–37 8654)
Electricity voltage: 110/220

BALATONFURED
GUEST HOUSE
Balatonfured Guest House
Holiday Center Udulo, Liszt Ferecc utca 6
Telephone: 8734 3404
Open May to September. It is also a restaurant and there is a synagogue on the premises.

SAN PEDRO SULA
CONTACT INFORMATION
Tourist Information
Telephone: 530157
Services Friday and Shabbat at synagogue and community centre

TEGUCIGALPA
Tourist Information
Telephone: 315908
Services usually held in private homes. Contact secretary at the above number.

EMBASSY
Embassy of Israel
Palmira Building, 5th Floor
Telephone: 324232; 325176

HUNGARY

There were Jews living in Hungary in Roman times, even before the arrival of the Magyars (ancestors of the present-day Hungarians). The Jews suffered during the

Middle Ages when there was some anti-semitism, but conditions improved under Austro-Hungarian rule, and Judaism was recognised as being on a legal par with Christianity in 1896.

Hungary lost a considerable amount of territory after the First World War, and as a result many of its original Jewish communities (such as Szatmar) found themselves within other countries. Anti-semitism reached a peak in March 1944, when, during the German occupation, most Jewish communities began to be transported to Auschwitz. A number of those who were deported survived when Auschwitz was liberated by the Red Army in January 1945.

After the war Hungary had the largest Jewish community in central Europe. Inevitably the community dwindled through emigration (especially after the 1956 uprising) and assimilation. Communism in Hungary was far more lenient than in other Warsaw Pact countries, and synagogues were allowed to operate. Since 1989, religious interest has increased, and the government has recently renovated the Dohany Synagogue, the second biggest synagogue in the world and the largest in Europe. The Jewish population is still the largest in the region, although most are not religious. The Hungarian national tourist office had published 'Shalom', an excellent guide to Jewish Hungary.

GMT +1 hours
Country calling code: (+36)
Total population: **10,153,000**
Jewish population: **60,000**
Emergency telephone: (**police–107**) (**fire–105**) (**ambulance–104**)
Electricity voltage: **220**

APOSTAG
TOURIST SITES
Synagogue of Apostag
Iskola Street 5
Telephone: (78) 427 227
Built in 1768 The Late Baroque building and classicist facade along with the interior has been faithfully preserved.

BAJA
Synagogue of Baja
Munkácsy Mihály Street 9
Telephone: (79) 322 741
Website: www.c3.hu/~aevk/
Dedicated in1845. In 1985 the local library was relocated to the renovated and transformed building. Memorial to the victims of the Holocaust on one side.

BÉKÉSCSABA
SYNAGOGUES
Békéscsaba Synagogue
Széchenyi liget

BUDAPEST
Budapest contains the majority of Hungarian Jews and there are many Jewish sights to visit, primarily in the area of "Terézváros and Erzsébetváros" – the old Jewish Quarter founded in the 18th Century. The community has kosher shops and restaurants, a Jewish museum and the offices of the Hungarian and Budapest Jewry and the World Jewish Congress can be found here. Budapest is also home to Europe's largest synagogue on Dohany Street, which contains manuscripts from the 11th and 12th centuries and the third largest Jewish library in the world.

BOOKSELLERS
Biblical World Judaica Gallery
Wesselényi utca. 13 H 1077
Telephone: (1) 354 1561
Fax: (1) 354 1561
Website: www.judaica.hu
Klezmer-Hois Agencia Artystyczna
Nagydiofa st.30- 32
Jewish books and publications

COMMUNITY CENTRE
Bálintház
VI. Révay Street 16
Telephone: (1) 311 9214
Email: info@balinthaz.hu
Website: www.balinthaz.hu
Computer room, modern fitness centre and different clubs
COMMUNITY ORGANISATIONS
Autonomous Orthodox Israelite Community in Hungary
VII. Dob Street 35
Telephone: (1) 351 0525
Fax: (1) 322 7200
Federation of Jewish Communities in Hungary(MAZSIHISZ)
Sip Street 12, Pf. 33 1075
Telephone: (1) 413 5564
Fax: (1) 413 5504
Website: www.mazsihisz.com

CULTURAL ORGANISATIONS

Tourism and Cultural Center of the Budapest Jewish Community
Sip u. 12 H 1075
Telephone: (1) 343 0420
Fax: (1) 462 0478
Website: www.jewishfesival.hu

EMBASSY

Embassy of Israel
Fullank utca 8 1026
Telephone: (1) 392-6200
Email: ambassador-sec@budapest.mfa.gov.il
Website: www.budapest.mfa.gov.il
Telephone: (1) 392-6200
Email: ambassador-sec
Website: http://budapest.mfa.gov.il

GROCERIES

Rothschild Kosher Food Store
Dob Street 12 1072
Telephone: (1) 267 5691

HOTELS

Kosher

King's Hotel
Nagydiófa u. 25-27, 1075 1075
Telephone: (1) 352 7675
Strictly kosher hotel with a restaurant

LIBRARIES

Jewish Theological Seminar - University of Jewish Studies
Bérkocsis Street2
Telephone: (1) 317 2396

MEDIA

Múlt és Jövõ
II. Keleti Káro;y Street 27
Telephone: (1) 316 7019
Website: www.multesjovo.hu

Remény
VII. Sip Street 12
Telephone: (1) 342 2355
Jewish social, public life and cultural periodical

Szombat
VI. Révay Street 16
Telephone: (1) 311 6665
Website: www.szombat.org
Hungarian Jewish periodical of the 21st century

Newspapers

Új Élet (New Life)
Sip Street 12
Telephone: (1) 413 5537
Email: ujelet@bzsh.axelero.net

MIKVAOT

Budapest Mikvaot
VII Kazinczy utca 16 1074

Telephone: (1) 321 7332 (evenings)
Fax: (1) 322 7200
Supervision: Moise Tovia Weiszberger
Contact for women (20) 317 1351

MUSEUMS

Holocaust Document Centre
IX. Páva Street 39
Telephone: (1) 455 3333
Fax: (1) 455 3399
Email: info@hdke.hu
Website: www.hdke.hu
The proper elaboration of the Holocaust era in Hungary began only recently after decades of delay in comparison with other European countries.

The main goal is to examine the overall history of the Holocaust with special emphasis on its socio-historical impact.

Hungarian Jewish Museum and Archives
VII. Dohany Street 2 1077
Telephone: (1) 343 6756
Fax: (1) 343 6756
Email: museum@bpjewsmus.hu
Website: www.bpjewmus.hu

RELIGIOUS ORGANISATIONS

Chabad Lubavits
VII. Károly Boulevard 18
Telephone: (1) 267 5746
Website: www.hitkozseg.hu

The Central Rabbinical Council
VII, Sip Street 12
Telephone: (1) 142 1180
Rabbi Schweitzer is Chief rabbi of Hungary and Director of the Rabbinical Seminary

RESTAURANTS

Hanna Kosher Restaurant
VII. Dob Street 35 1074
Telephone: (1) 342 1072
Fax: (1) 322 7200
Opening Hours: 11.30am to 4pm

Glatt Kosher

Carmel Pince – Carmel Cellar
VII. Kazinczy Street 3l 1074
Telephone: (1) 322 1834
Fax: (1) 461 0024
Mobile Phone: 36306 873997
Email: carmel@carmel.hu
Website: www.carmel.hu

Salamon glatt-kosher Restaurant
VII. Nagydiófa Street 27-29 – 1074
Telephone: (1) 413-6969

Meat

Kinor David Restaurant
Nagydio fa street 25-27, near Kings Hotel H 1075
Telephone: (1) 413 7304 / 5
Fax: (1) 413 7304 / 5

Mobile Phone: 06305128783
Email: kinordavid@hotmail.com
Website: www.zsido.com/kinor
Supervision: Chug Hatam Szofer Bne Brak
Opening hours: 12.30pm to 9.30pm.
Israeli-Hungarian kitchen
Payment is cash only Ft\Dollar\Euro
SYNAGOGUES
Bérkocsis Synagogue (Jewish Theological Seminary)
VIII. Bérkocsis Street 2
Telephone: (1) 317 2396
Built in 1877
Bethlen Synagogoue
VII. István Street 17
Telephone: (1) 342 6170

Buda Synagogue
II. Frankel Leó Way 49 1023
Telephone: (1) 326 1445
Fax: (1) 326 1445
Mobile Phone: 36309 606990
Email: info@frankel.hu
Website: www.frankel.hu
Central organisation: Mazsihisz
Built 1888 in French-Gothic style
Dohány Street Synagogue
VII, Dohany Street 4-6
Telephone: (1) 342 2353
Built in 1859, it is the largest in Europe and the second largest in the world. In its grounds lie buried Hungarian Jewish victims of the Nazis. There is also a commemorative plaque to Hanna Senesh, the Jewish parachutist who was captured and tortured before being shot by the Nazis. A plaque commemorating Theodor Herzl, the founder of Zionism is in the Jewish Museum. The congregation practises Neolog Judaism.
Hegedûs Synagogue
XIII. Hegedûs Gyula Street 3
Telephone: (1) 349 3120
Email: bzstitk@mazsihisz.com
First house in a tenement in 1911, remodelled in 1927
Heroes Synagogue
VII Wesselenyi utca 5
Telephone: (1) 3432 2353
Heroes' Synagogue
VII. Wesselényi Street 5
Telephone: (1) 342 2353
Built in 1929-31 in remembrance of the heroes of WW1. Traditionally in winter the congregation of the Dóhany synagogue prays here.
Hunyadi Synagogue
VI. Hunyadi Square 3
Telephone: (1) 342 5322
Founded 1896 at present on the mezzanine floor of a tenement.

Lágymányos Synagogue
XI. Károlyi Gáspár Square 5 1114
Telephone: (1) 361 1965
Email: rabbi@chello.hu
Website: www.zsinagoga.net
Smaller prayer house of the Buda community
Nagyfuvaros Synagogue
VIII. Nagyfuvaros Street
Telephone: (1) 334 2731
Email: nagyfuvaros@freemail.hu
Very active community life, stages cultural events
Páva Synagogue
IX. Páva Street 39
Telephone: (1) 215 8796
Within the premises of the Holocaust Museum and Document Centre.

Újpest Synagogue
IV. Berzeviczy G. Street 8
Telephone: (1) 369 0827
Built 1886
Vasvári Synagogue
VI. Vasvári Pál Street 5
Telephone: (1) 268 0183
Website: www.zsido.com/szoveg/English/42
Supervision: Chabad Lubavits
Yeshiva
Zugló Synagogue
XIV. Thököly Road 83
Telephone: (1) 251 3970
Situated in a mansion which was turned into a synagogue in 1930 by Colonel Aron Aronffy a WW1 doctor.

Orthodox
Carimama
VII, Kazinczy Street 28
Telephone: (1) 342 0231
Website: www.carimama.hu
Bakery, Pizza Store and dairy
The Orthodox Central Synagogue
VII. Kazinczy Street 27
Telephone: (1) 351 0526
Fax: (1) 322 7200

Progressive
Sim Shalom Progressive Congregation
Gyorgy A. u. 19/A 1125
Telephone: (1) 326 5113
Website: www.sim-shalom.org
Sephardi
Teleki Squere Synagogue
Teleki Squere 22
Telephone: (1) 351 0524
Chortkow Synagogue (with musach Sephardic)

TOURIST SITES
Rumbach Synagogue
VII. Rumbach Sebestyén Street 11-13
Open:10am to 4pm

TOURS
Heritage Tour
Mazsike (Hungarian Jewish Cultural Association, VI. Révay Street 16
Telephone: (1) 311 6665
Email: mazsike@gmail.com
Website: www.mazsike.hu
Jewish Heritage in Budapest - AVIV Travel
VII. Sip Street 12 H 1075
Telephone: (1) 317 2754
Email: aviv@aviv.hu
Website: www.aviv.hu
A walking tour of Jewish Budapest, arranged by the Municipality. Dohany Synagogue Tour.

DEBRECEN
SYNAGOGUES
Debrecen Synagogue
Bajcsi Zs. Street 26
Telephone: (52) 415 861
Hours 8am to 4pm

DESSEWFFY
Orthodox
Dessewffy Synagogue
Dessewffy Street 23
Contact through the orthodox community

GYOR
MUSEUM
Art
Synagogue of Gyor
Kossuth Lajos Street 5 9025
Telephone: (96) 322 695
Fax: (96) 311 245
Email: artmuz@t-online.hu
Website: www.artmuz.hu
Central organisation: Municipal Museum of Art
Built between 1868 and 1870 in neo-Romanesque style with octagonal plan, circular balconies and dome. Houses János Vasilescu's Hungarian fine arts collection as well as paintings and statues by Lili Országh and her contemporaries.
Wed to Thu 10am to 6pm

HÓDMEZÕVÁSÁRHELY
SYNAGOGUES
Hódmezõvásárhely Synagogue
Szeremlei Street 3
Telephone: (62) 249 689
Hours: 1pm to 5pm

JÁNOSHALMA
Jánoshalma Synagogue
Petõfi Sándor Street 3
Telephone: (70) 361 9157

KAPOSVÁR
Kaposvár Synagogue
Berzsenyi Street 14
Telephone: (30) 936 1582

KARCAG
Karcag Synagogue
Kertész József Street 7
Telephone: (30) 925 9594

KECSKEMÉT
SYNAGOGUE
Synagogue
Nagykõr̃si Street 5
Telephone: (76) 504 727
Email: grosza@rpulok.aeromed.hu
Open Friday evening. Schul with active Rabbi, please contact before visiting.

KESZTHELY
SYNAGOGUES
Keszthely Synagogue
Kossuth Lajos Street 20
Telephone: (83) 312 188

KISLUNHALAS
Kislunhalas Synagogue
Petõfi Street 1
Telephone: (30) 347 3333

MÁD
TOURIST SITES
Synagogue of Mád
Rákoczi Way 25
Telephone: (47) 348 043
The late-Baroque style of Mád is one of the oldest in Hungary. The synagogue was restored in compliance with orthodox jewish traditions and is suitable for religious services.

MAKÓ
Synagogue of Makó
Eötvös Street 15
Telephone: (30) 389 0613
Built as an Orthodox synagogue in the 1870's it fell into disrepair after the Holocaust but was reconstructed in 2002.

MISKOLC
Synagogue of Miskolc
Kazinczy Street 7
Telephone: (46) 505 044
Built in the 1860's it is one of the most famous monuments of Hungarian Romantic architecture. Visiting on Sunday should be arranged in advance.
Hours: Sun to Fri 9am to 3pm

NAGYKANIZSA
SYNAGOGUES
Nagykanizsa
Fõ Street 6
Telephone: (30) 385 2503

NAGYKÕRÖS
Nagykõrös Synagogue
Rákóczi Way 21
Telephone: (53) 552 423
Schul with active Rabbi, please contact before visiting

NYIREGHÁZA
Ny'regháza Synagogue
Mártirok Square 6
Telephone: (42) 417 939
Hours:Mon to Thu 8am to 2pm

PÉCS
Fürdõ Street 1
Schul with active Rabbi, please contact before visiting.
Hours: May to Sept 10am to 5pm

SALGÓTARJAN
Salgótarjan Synagogue
Füleki Way 55
Telephone: (30) 370 3265

SIÓFOK
Siófok Synagogue
Széchenyi Street 4
Telephone: (84) 10754

SOPRON
Sopron was a Jewish quarter, which dates back to the 14th century. It has been excavated with meticulous attention to detail and includes the oldest mikvah in Hungary and a 13th century prayer house.

GROCERIES
Rothschild Retail Kosher Food
Szt. Istvdn krt. 4 1137
Telephone: (99) 320 4147

MUSEUMS
The Old Synagogue
Új Street 22 9400
Telephone: (99) 311 327
Fax: (99) 311 347
Email: soproni@gymsmuzeum.hu
Website: www.museum.sopron.hu
In the 13th century the program of King Béla IV welcomed the Jews in Sopron. A street was allocated to them (today it is called Új street). The old synagogue was erected around 1300. Under a high pyramid roof the Old Synagogue consists of a large two-storied prayer hall and a prayer for woman. It belongs to the protected monuments of the town.
The museum is only open when the synagogue opens.

SYNAGOGUES
Orthodox
Jewish Orthodox
Kiss Janos u. 3 H 9400
Telephone: (99) 313 508

TOURIST SITES
The Neologue Cemetery
Dating from the nineteenth century. There is a memorial wall dedicated to the 1,600 local victims of the Holocaust.

SZEGED
SYNAGOGUES
Szeged Synagogue
Guttenberg Street 20
Telephone: (62) 423 849
Website: www.zsingoga.szeged.hu
Schul with active Rabbi, please contact before visiting.
Hours: April Till Sept 10am t0 12pm and 1pm to 5pm, Oct to Mar 9am to 2pm

SZÉKESFEHÉRVÁR
Székesfehérvár Synagogue
Várkõrút 19
Telephone: (20) 955 3580
Hours: Weekdays 5pm to 6pm

SZEKSZÁRD
Bokharan
Szekszárd Synagogue
Szent István Square
Telephone: (74) 511 247

SZENTENDRE
MUSEUM
Tiny Shul of Szentendre
Telephone: (30) 932 2900
Small Jewish museum which occasionally serves as a synagogue.

SZOLNOK
SYNAGOGUES
Szolnok Synagogue
Templom Street 2
Hours: 9am to 5pm except Mondays.

SZOMBATHELY
Szombathely Synagogues
Batthyanyi Square 9
Telephone: (94) 505 033
Hours: Tue 3pm to 5pm, Fri 3pm to 7pm

TOKAJ
TOURIST SITES
Synagogue of Tokaj
Serház Street 55
Telephone: (20) 969 4493
Website: http://konferencia.tokaj.hu

VÁC
SYNAGOGUES
Vác Synagogue
Eötvös Street
Telephone: (30) 945 7276
Schul with active Rabbi, please contact before visiting

VISEGRÁDI
Orthodox
Visegrádi Synagogue
XIII. Visegrádi Street 3
Contact through orthodox community

INDIA

The Jewish population of India can be divided into three components: the Cochin Jews, the Bene Israel and the Baghdadi Jews. The Cochin Jews are based in the south of India in Kerala. This community can be further divided into Black (believing themselves to be the original settlers) and White (of European or Middle Eastern origin), and the Paradesi. Most of the community has emigrated, but there is still a synagogue in Cochin that is a major tourist attraction.

The Bene Israel believe they are descended from Jewish survivors of a ship wrecked on its voyage from ancient Israel during the period of King Solomon. No reliable documentary evidence, however, exists to support this claim. More reliable evidence dates settlement to around the tenth century. The Bene Israel follow only certain Jewish practices, such as kosher food and Shabbat, and also adhere to certain Muslim and Hindu beliefs; for example, they abstain from eating beef. In the eighteenth century, they settled in Bombay and now form the largest group of Indian Jews.

Baghdadi Jews, immigrants from Iraq and the other Middle Eastern countries, arrived in India in the late eighteenth century, and followed British Colonial rather than local custom. Many emigrated to Israel in the 1950s and 1960s.

During the Indo-Pakistan war of 1972, the leading Indian military figure was General Samuels. In 1999 Lt-Gen J.F.R. Jacob was appointed Governor of Punjab State.

There is a central Council of Indian Jewry, based in Mumbai, where most of the Indian Jews live. Kosher food is available, and there are three Jewish schools in the city. Relations with Israel have recently improved and it is now a major trade partner.

GMT +5 1/2 hours
Country calling code: (+91)
Total population: **1,013,662,000**
Jewish population: **5,000**
Emergency telephone:
Electricity voltage: **220**

ALIBAG
Magen Aboth Synagogue
"Israil" Alley
Established in 1848 the synagogue is in what is known as 'Israel' alley to the south east of the town

COCHIN
COMMUNITY ORGANISATIONS
Association of Kerala Jews
Thekkumbhagom Synagogue Jews Street
Telephone: 366 247; 362 454
Fax: 363 747

CONTACT INFORMATION
Inquiries
Princess Street, Fort
Telephone: 24228; 24988

SYNAGOGUES
Chennamangalam
Jews Street
Built in 1614 and restored in 1916, this synagogue has been declared a historical monument by the Government of India. A few yards away is a small concrete pillar into which is inset the tombstone of Sara Bat Israel, dated 5336 (1576)

Paradesi
Jew Town, Mattancherry 2
The only Cochin synagogue that is still functioning. Built in 1568. Closed Friday & Saturday.

ERNAKULAM
TOURIST SITES
Kadavumbagom Synagogue
Built in 1200 and rebuilt in 1690
Thekkumbagon Syngogue
Telephone: (484) 390 187
Built in 1580 and rebuilt in 1939

KHAMASA
SYNAGOGUES
Magen Abraham
Bukhara Mohalla, opp. Parsi Agiari 380001
Telephone: (79) 535 5224

KOLKATA

COMMUNITY ORGANISATIONS

Jewish Association of Kolkata
1 & 2 Old Court House Corner
Telephone: (33) 224861
General inquiries to this telephone number

SYNAGOGUES

Bethel Synagogue
26/1 Pollack Street

Magen David Synagogue
109a Peplabi Rash, Bihari Bose Road, 1, (formerly
Canning Steet)

Neveh Shalome Synagogue
9 Jackson Lane, 1

MUMBAI

EMBASSY

Consul General of Israel
50 Kailash, G. Deshmukh Marg, 26
Telephone: (22) 386 2793

GROCERIES

ORT India
68 Worli Hill Estate, PO Box 6571 400018
Telephone: (22) 496 2350; 8423; 8457
Fax: (22) 496 2350; 491 3203
Website: www.ortindia.com
The Jewish Education Resource Centre provides kosher
food from its bakery and kitchen to all travellers. ORT India
also arranges conducted tours to places of Jewish interest
in Mumbai and to ancient synagogues in the Konkan
region of Maharashtra State.

SYNAGOGUES

Beth El Synagogue
Mirchi Galli, Mahatma Gandhi Road, Panvel
410206
Telephone: (22) 2745 8126

Etz Haeem Prayer Hall
2nd Lane, Umerkhadi 400009
Telephone: (22) 377 0193

Gate of Mercy (Shaar Harahamim)
254 Samuel Street, Nr Masjid Railway Station
400003
Telephone: (22) 345 2991
This is the oldest Bene Israel synagogue in use in India,
established in 1796 and known as the Samaji Hasaji
Synagogue or Juni Masjid until 1896 when its name was
changed to Shaar Harahamim

Magen David Synagogue
340 Sir J.J. Road, Byculla 400008
Telephone: (22) 300 6675
The synagogue, built in 1861 with the assistance of the
Sasoon family, has a gothic character

Magen Hassidim Synagogue
8 Mohammaed Shahid Marg, (formerly Moreland
Road), Agripada 400011
Telephone: (22) 309 2493
Most marriages and bar mitzvahs are held here, it can seat

1000. Only Bene Israel carpenters were used, and they
gave their services free.

Rodef Shalom Synagogue
Sussex Road, Byculla 400027

Shaar HaRahamim Synagogue
Tembi Naka, opp. Civil Hospital, Thane 400601
Telephone: (22) 853 4817
Established in 1796, it is the oldest Bene Israel synagogue
in India

Shaare Rason Synagogue
90 Tantanpura Street, 3rd Road , Don Tad, Israel
Mohalla, Khadak 400009

Tifereth Israel Synagogue
92 K.K. Marg, Jacob Circle 400011
Telephone: (22) 305 3713

Orthodox

Knesseth Eliahu Synagogue
55 V.B. Gandhi Road (Forbes Street) 400023
Telephone: (22) 283 1502/2368 2296
Fax: (22) 2363 2445
Website: www.jacobsassoon.org
The synagogue was constructed in 1884. Kiddus is held
with a lunch after Shabbath services at the synagogue

Kurla Bene Israel Prayer Hall
275 S.G. Barve Road (c.S.T. Road), Kurla 400070
Telephone: (22) 511 8795

TOURS

ORT India
68 Worli Hill Estate, PO Box 6571 400018
Telephone: (22) 496 2350; 8423
Fax: (22) 364 7308
The Travel and Tourism Department arranges tours in
Mumbai and Raighad District

TOV Jewish India Tours
96 Penso Villa, 1st Floor, Mbraut Rd., Shivaji Park
400028
Telephone: (22) 244 50134
Mobile Phone: 09867 430775
Email: indoisr@hotmail.com
Supervision: Clement Aaron

NEW DELHI

SYNAGOGUES

Judah Hyam Synagogue
2 Humayun Road (opposite Taj Mahal Hotel)
110003
Telephone: (11) 2463 5500; 2464 1058
Email: eze_malekar@yahoo.co.in
Supervision: Ezekiel Isaac Malekar, Honorary Secretary and
Cantor

The Judah Hyam Annexe houses a library, Hebrew classes
and centre for Jewish and inter faith studies and conducts
services on Friday evening starting at 7 P.M. during summer
and 6.30 P.M. during winter as well as services during
festivals and high holidays.

Honorary Secretary and Hazzan of the Judah Hyam
Synagogue. Tel: 9818317674.

PARAVUR
Paravur Synagogue
Built in 1165, the synagogue was rebuilt in 1616 by the local Jewish communiy with the help of David Kastiel, who was not a Paradesi Jew but a man of local origin. Paradesi Jews were associated with Mattancherry and their synagogue was built in 1568.

PUNE
Succath Shelomo
93 Rasta Peth 411011
Inquiries to Hon. Sec. 24/1 Rasta Peth, Trupti Apt., Pune 411011 or Dr S.B. David 9, Bund Garden Road, Pune 411001

Orthodox
Ohel David Synagogue
9 Dr Ambedkar Road 411001
Telephone: (20) 613 2048
The synagogue was built by David Sasoon in 1867. His grave is in the synagogue grounds.

TOURS
Tov Jewish India Tours
118 Citadel Palace Orchard, Rdindhari, Green Forest
Telephone: (20) 693 1488

THANE
KASHRUT INFORMATION
Pearl Farm
A/1 Dhobi Alley, Sulabha, Maharashtra 400601
Telephone: (22) 536 0539
Kosher goat meat and fish

IRAN

Iran, formerly known as Persia, has an ancient connection with Jews. The first Jewish communities in Persia date from the time of the First Temple. King Cyrus, the Persian king who conquered Babylon, allowed the Jews to return to Israel from their exile. Not all returned, however, and some settled in Persia. The Persian community grew over time, suffering oppression after the Islamic conversion in 642. Certain segments of the Jewish community also grew in wealth in early medieval times.

In the twentieth century there was a brief period of hope for the Jews in Iran when the country became more western-oriented after 1925. However, the 1979 revolution quashed the hope for a more tolerant Iran, and many thousands of Jews decided to

emigrate. Association with Zionism became a capital offence and a number of Jews have been executed since 1979. The Jews are seen as 'dhimmi', (subordinates), to Islam, and as such are allowed some religious practices, but are so closely watched that maintaining a Jewish life is difficult. The tombs of Esther and Mordecai (from the Purim story) are in Hamadan, south-west of the capital Tehran. Iran currently has the largest Jewish community in the Middle East outside Israel.

Kosher food has become expensive and is difficult to obtain.

GMT +3 1/2 hours
Country calling code: (+98)
Total population: **60,694,000**
Jewish population: **18,000**
Emergency telephone:
Electricity voltage: **220**

ISFAHAN
SYNAGOGUES
Isfahan Synagogue
Shah Abass Street

TEHRAN
Haim
Gavamossaltaneh Street

TOURIST SITES
Jewish Quarter of Tehran
Mahalleh, off Sirus Avenue

IRISH REPUBLIC

The first report of Jews in Ireland records that in 1079 'five Jews came over the sea'. The small community was expelled in 1290, along with the Jews from the rest of the British Isles. The community slowly grew again after Jews were allowed to return and a few *conversos* settled in Dublin. There was never a strong community, however, and only in 1822 did a significant influx of Jews occur when immigrants came from England and eastern Europe.

Immigration continued and large numbers arrived from the Russian Empire after 1881. Some settled in Ireland intentionally, but others believed that they had landed in

America, deceived by the ships' captains. In 1901, the community was 3,800 strong. The highest figure for the Jewish population of Ireland has been estimated at 8,000.

Robert Briscoe (1894–1969) who played an important role in the struggle for Irish independenc, was twice Lord Mayor of Dublin.

Currently most Jews live in Dublin although the community is now shrinking.

GMT +0 hours
Country calling code: **(+353)**
Total population: **3,626,000**
Jewish population: **1,200**
Emergency telephone: **(police–999) (fire–999) (ambulance–999)**
Electricity voltage: **220**

CORK

RESTAURANTS
Café Paradiso
16 Lancaster Quay
Telephone: (21) 427 7939

SYNAGOGUES
Orthodox
Cork Synagogue
10 South Terrace
Telephone: (21) 487 0413
Fax: (21) 487 6537
Email: rosehill@iol.ie
Erev Shabbat Services at 7.30pm 1st Friday of the month,

DUBLIN

The centre of Irish Jewry, Dublin's position on the east coast meant that many Jews settled there in the flight from Eastern Europe in the nineteenth century. The Jewish Museum in Dublin, opened by the then President of Israel, Irish-born Chaim Herzog, in 1985 during a state visit to Ireland, gives much information on the town's Jewish history.

Dublin was also the home of possibly the world's most famous fictional Jew, Leopold Bloom of James Joyce's 'Ulysses'.

The Bretzel
1 Lennox Street, Near Kelly's Corner S.C. Road 8
Telephone: (1) 475 2724

BAKERIES
Connolly's Bakery
Super Valu 13 Braemore Road, Churchtown 14
Supervision: The Chief rabbi
Challaha and baked goods with Kosher symbol only.

Hemmingway's Deli
Ballsbridge Terrace 4

Rowan's Deli
Main Street, Rathfarnham 14

CONTACT INFORMATION
Vegetarian Society of Ireland
PO Box 3010, Ballsbridge 4
Website: www.vegetarian.ie
The society will provide details of establishments which cater for vegetarians

DELICATESSEN
The Big Cheese
St Andrew's Lane 2
Telephone: (1) 671 1399
Fax: (1) 490 9917
Has a kosher section and is open on Sunday morning

EMBASSY
Embassy of Israel
Carrisbrook House, 122 Pembroke Road, Ballsbridge 4
Telephone: (1) 668 0303
Fax: (1) 668 0418

MIKVAOT
Dublin Hebrew Congregation
Rathfarnham Road, Terenure 6
Telephone: (1) 490 5348
Mobile Phone: 087 798 7627
Email: dhebc@eivcom.net
Shul: (1) 490 5969

MUSEUMS
Irish Jewish Museum
3 Walworth Road, South Circular Road, Portobello 8
Telephone: (1) 490 1857
Fax: (1) 490 1857
Holocaust Educational Centre
Open Tuesday, Thursday and Sunday May to September 11am to 3.30pm; October to April 10.30am to 2.30pm. Group visits by arrangement. Closed on Jewish Holy Days.

RELIGIOUS ORGANISATIONS
Jewish Representative Council of Ireland and Kashrut Commission
1 Zion Road, Rathgar
Telephone: (1) 492 3751
Fax: (1) 492 4680
Email: irishcom@iol.ie
Website: www.jewishireland.org

The Chief Rabbinate of Ireland
Herzog House, 1 Zion Road Rathgar, 6
Telephone: (1) 492 3751
Fax: (1) 492 4680
Email: irishcom@iol.ie
Website: www.jewishireland.org
Supervision: Chief Rabbi of Ireland
A list of Kosher foods in Ireland may be obtained from our website or on request. Shul restaurant open on Sundays only. Contact Ms Hinda Bloom on (1) 456 2464 or 086 278 8326 for kosher meals under supervision.

RESTAURANTS

Cornucopia
19 Wicklow St. 2
Telephone: (1) 677 7583

Juice
South Great Georges St. 2
Telephone: (1) 475 7856

Vegetarian
Blazing Salads
25c Powerscourt Town House 2
Telephone: (1) 672 9552

SYNAGOGUES

Orthodox
Dublin Hebrew Congregation
"Leoville", Rathfarnham Road, Terenure 6
Telephone: (1) 490 5969
Mobile Phone: 08673 59558
Email: dhebc@eircom.net

Machzekei Hadass
Rathmore Villas, Rear of 77 Terenure Road North 6W
Email: machzekeihadass@eircom.net

The Jewish Home of Ireland
Denmark Hill, Leinster Road West, Rathmines 6
Telephone: (1) 497 6258
Fax: (1) 497 2018
Website: www.jewishireland.org
Supervision: The Chief Rabbi
Services are held Friday evening at start of Sabbath and
Sabbath morning. The cafeteria is open to the public for
lunch and dinner but reservations for a Kosher meal in the
Kosher section of the cafeteria must be made in advance.
Tel: 495 0021

Progressive
Dublin Jewish Progressive Congregation
7 Leicester Avenue, Rathgar, PO Box 3059 6
Email: djpc@liberaljudaism.org
Friday evening at 8.15 pm.

ISRAEL

General Information

Israel, the Promised Land of the Bible, is today a modern, thriving, bustling and vibrant country. For centuries the sites of many of the most stirring events in the history of mankind lay dormant beneath shifting sands and crumbling terraces, until the land was reclaimed by the People of Israel returning from exile. In today's Israel, cities, towns and villages, fertile farms and green forests, sophisticated industries and well-developed commercial enterprises have replaced barren hillsides, swamps and desert wilderness.

Climate

Israel enjoys long, warm, dry summers (April–October) and generally mild winters (November–March), with somewhat drier, cooler weather in hilly regions such as Jerusalem and Safed. Rainfall is relatively heavy in the north and centre of the country with much less in the northern Negev and almost negligible amounts in the southern areas. Regional conditions vary considerably, with humid summers and mild winters on the coast; dry summers and moderately cold winters in the hill regions; hot, dry summers and pleasant winters in the Jordan Valley; and year-round semi-desert conditions in the Negev.

Languages

Hebrew, the language of the Bible, and Arabic, are the official languages of Israel. Hebrew, Arabic and English are compulsory subjects at school. French, Spanish, German, Yiddish, Russian, Polish and Hungarian are widely spoken. Local and international newspapers and periodicals in a number of languages are readily available. All street and most commercial signs are in Hebrew and English, and often in Arabic.

Passports and Visas

Every visitor to Israel must hold a valid passport; valid for a minimum of six months beyond the intended date of arrival, stateless persons require a valid travel document with a return visa to the country of issue. Visitors may remain in Israel for up to three months from the date of arrival, subject to the terms of the visa issued. Visitors who intend to work in Israel must apply to the Ministry of the Interior for a special visa (B/1).

Electrical Appliances

The electric current in Israel is 220 volts AC, single phase, 50 Hertz. Most Israeli sockets are of the three-pronged variety but many can accept some European two-pronged plugs as well. Electric shavers, travelling irons and other small appliances may require adapters and/or transformers which can be purchased in Israel.

Health Regulations

There are no vaccination requirements for visitors entering Israel.

Pets

Dogs or cats accompanying visitors must be over four months old, inoculated against rabies and bear a valid official veterinary health certificate from the country of origin.

Accommodation

Kashrut

In Israel, kosher means under official rabbinical supervision. Most hotels (but not all) do adhere. Kosher restaurants, hotels and youth hostels are by law required to display a kashrut certificate.

Hotels

Israel has over 300 hotels offering a wide choice of accommodation to suit all tastes, purposes and budgets, ranging from small, simple facilities to five-star luxury establishments, with prices varying according to grade and season. Hotel rates are generally quoted in US dollars and do not include the 15 per cent service charge.

Kibbutz Hotels

The kibbutz (collective settlement) is an Israeli social experience in which all property is collectively owned and members receive no salaries but are provided with housing, education for their children, medical services, social amenities and all other necessities. Most of the 280 kibbutzim throughout Israel are essentially agricultural settlements but many are moving to a more industrially orientated economy.

Several kibbutzim, mostly in northern and central Israel, have established hotels on their premises, providing visitors with a close view of this world-renowned lifestyle. They offer guests the opportunity of a relaxed, informal holiday in delightful rural surroundings. Some present special evening programmes about the kibbutz experience.

For further information and a special tour of Israel's kibbutzim and kibbutz hotels, contact any Israel Government Tourist Office (IGTO), or the tourist information offices (TIO) in Israel, or Kibbutz Hotels, 1 Smolinskin St., Tel Aviv. Tel: 03-527 8085. Fax: 03-523 0527.

Youth Hostels

The Israel Youth Hostels Association (IYHA), affiliated with the International Youth Hostels Association, operates some 32 youth hostels throughout the country for guests of all ages. All offer dormitory, usually single sex, accommodation and most also provide meals and self-service kitchen facilities. Some hostels also provide family accommodation for parents accompanied by at least one child. Individual reservations should be booked directly at specific hostels and group reservations with the IYHA.

The IYHA also arranges individual 14, 21 or 28 day package tours, called 'Israel on the Youth Hostel Trail'. These include nights in any of 25 hostels with breakfast and dinner, unlimited bus travel, a half-day guided tour, free admission to National Parks, a map and other informative material.

For further information, contact the Israel Youth Hostels Association, 1 Sazar Street, 91060 Jerusalem, Tel: 02 655 8400, Fax: 02 655 8401.

Currency and Bank Information

The currency of Israel is the New Israeli Sheqel (NIS) (plural sheqalim). Each sheqel is divided into 100 agorot (singular agora). Bank notes circulate in denominations of NIS 20, 50, 100 and 200 sheqels and coins in denominations of 1 sheqel 5 sheqels, 10 sheqels, and 10 and 50 agorot. One may bring an unlimited amount of local and foreign currency into Israel in cash, travellers' cheques, letters of credit, or State of Israel Bonds. Foreign currency may be exchanged at any bank and at many hotels.

Most banks are open from Sunday to Thursday from 8.30am to 12midday, and from 4pm to 6pm on Sunday, Tuesday and Thursday. On the eve of major Jewish holidays, banks are open from 8.30am to 12midday. Bank branches in major hotels usually offer convenient additional banking hours.

Shopping

Colourful oriental markets and bazaars may be found in the old city of Jerusalem and in several other towns and villages. Bargaining is often expected. The unique variety of goods available includes handmade items of olive wood, mother-of-pearl, leather and straw, as well as hand-blown glass and exotic clothing. In all cities and towns there are shopping malls which are open from 08am to 10pm. There are duty-free shops at Ben Gurion, Eilat and Ovda International Airports.

Opening Hours:

Most shops are open daily, Sunday to Thursday, from 9am to 7pm, although some close for a mid-day break between 1pm and 4pm. On Fridays and the eve of major Jewish holidays, shops close early in the afternoon. Some Muslim-owned establishments are closed on Fridays and some Christian shops on Sundays

Radio and Television

Radio programmes are broadcast daily in English, Arabic, French, Yiddish, Russian and other languages. There are three daily news programmes in English and French. Many programmes shown on Israeli TV are in English with Hebrew, Arabic and Russian subtitles.

The Israel Broadcasting Authority news in English is screened nightly on Channel 1 at 6pm.

Facilities for the Handicapped

Many hotels and public institutions in Israel (including Ben Gurion International Airport) provide ramps, specially equipped lavatories, telephones and other conveniences for the handicapped.

Milbat, the Advisory Centre for the Disabled at Sheba Medical Center in Tel

Aviv (Tel: 03 5303 739), will be pleased to answer visitors' questions.

The Yad Sarah Organisation with branches located throughout Israel provides wheelchairs, crutches and other medical equipment on loan, free of charge (a small deposit is requested). For more specific information, contact the organisation's main office in Jerusalem, Tel: 02 624 4242.

Travellers to Israel, especially those with specific medical/paramedical needs, can turn to Traveller Hotline operated by Ezer Mizion, the Israel Health Support Fund. This volunteer organisation provides all paramedical information and needs free of charge to the traveller, via the International Office (02 537 8070) and Travellers Hotline (02 500 211). Transport and other arrangements can be organised prior to arrival and special inquiries/needs can be seen to while in Israel.

Organised Tours

Numerous organised tours, mostly in air-conditioned buses or minibuses, are conducted by licensed tour operators. Itineraries and prices are determined in accordance with the Ministry of Tourism guidelines to ensure a full sightseeing programme in maximum comfort. Half-day, full-day and longer tours are available, some combining air with road travel. Tours depart regularly from major cities as well as from popular resort areas during the peak season. All organised tours are accompanied by experienced, licensed multilingual guides identified by an official emblem bearing the words Licensed Tourist Guide.

Smaller groups may hire a licensed driver-guide and a special touring limousine or minibus, identified by the red Ministry of Tourism emblem.

Full details of itineraries, prices and schedules are available at travel agencies, tour companies, IGTOs and TIOs.

Major public institutions and organisations such as WIZO, Hadassah, universities and the Knesset (Parliament) conduct guided tours of their facilities. Walking tours of the larger cities are arranged by the municipalities.

Visitors should be aware that certain tourist sites such as the Tomb of the Patriachs and Jericho are now within the boundaries of the Palestinian Authority. They should consult the local tourist offices in Israel concerning travel to those areas.

When visiting religious sites always take care to be modestly dressed. You may be refused entry.

Buses

Buses are the most popular means of urban and inter-city transport throughout Israel. The Egged Bus Cooperative operates nearly all inter-city bus lines and also provides urban services in most cities and towns. (The greater Tel Aviv area is serviced by the Dan Cooperative and independent bus companies operate in Beer Sheva and Nazareth.) Fares are reasonably priced and service is regular. Most bus lines do not operate on the Sabbath (Friday evening to Saturday evening) and on Jewish holidays. Students are eligible for discount fares on inter-urban bus routes on presentation of an International Student Card. Special monthly tickets are available for Dan and Egged urban bus lines. Overseas visitors can purchase Israbus passes valid on all Egged bus lines for periods of 7,14, 21 and 30 days. Tickets can be obtained at any Egged bus station.

Taxis

These are both shared taxis (sheruts) and normal taxis. Taxis are required to operate a meter.

Traffic Regulations

A valid International Driving Licence is recognised and preferred, although a valid national driving licence is also accepted, provided it has been issued by a country maintaining diplomatic relations with Israel and recognising an Israeli driving licence.

An excellent system of roads connects all towns. Traffic travels on the right and over-

takes on the left. It is compulsory for the driver and all passengers to wear seat belts. Drivers coming from the right have priority, unless indicated otherwise on the road signs, which are international. Distances on road signs are always given in kilometres (1 km is equal to 0.621 miles).

The speed limit is 50 km (approx. 31 miles) per hour in built-up areas; 80-90 km (approx. 50-56 miles) per hour on open roads.

Special Programmes For Tourists Plant a Tree With Your Own Hands

Tree-planting centres have been established by the Jewish National Fund at several locations throughout Israel. For a nominal contribution, visitors may plant trees and receive a certificate and pin to mark the event. For further information, contact the Jewish National Fund, PO Box 283, 91002 Jerusalem, Tel: 02 670 7402, or 96 Hayarkon Street, 63432 Tel Aviv, Tel: 03 523 4367, Fax: 03 5246084.

GMT +2 hours
Country calling code: (**+972**)
Total population: **6,100,000**
Jewish population: **5,000,000**
Emergency telephone: (**police–100**) (**fire–102**) (**ambulance–101**)
Electricity voltage: **220**

AFULA
RESTAURANTS
La Cabania
Ha'atzmaut Square
Telephone: (4) 659 1638

San Remo
4Ha'atzmaut Square
Telephone: (4) 640 5705
Fax: (4) 640 5705
Email: san_remo2@walla.com

AKKO
HOTELS
Palm Beach Sport E Spa Hotel
Acre Sea Shore, PO Box 2192 24101
Telephone: (4) 987 7777
Fax: (4) 991 0434
Website: www.palmbeach.co.il
Hotel, restaurant and convention centre, spa and sports centre

MUSEUMS
Akko Municipal Museum
Old City
Telephone: (4) 991 8251
Fax: (4) 981 6686

RESTAURANTS
Vegetarian
Amirei Hagalil
Akko Safed Road, nr. Moshav Amirim 20115
Telephone: (4) 698 9815/6

YOUTH HOSTELS
Acre Youth Hostel
Telephone: (4) 991 1982
Fax: (4) 991 1982

ARAD
HOTELS
Arad
6 Hapalmach Street
Telephone: (8) 995 7040
Fax: (8) 995 7272

Maragoa
Mo'av Street, POB 20 89100
Telephone: (8) 995 1222
Fax: (8) 995 7778

Nof Arad
Mo'av Street
Telephone: (8) 995 7056
Fax: (8) 995 4053

YOUTH HOSTELS
Blau Weis
Telephone: (8) 995 7150
This organisation is located in the centre of town

ASHKELON
HOTELS
Dan Gardens Ashkelon
56 Hatayassim Street
Telephone: (8) 677 1777
Email: dangardensashkelon@danhotels.com
Website: www.danhotels.com
Supervision: Chief Rabbinate of Israel
Central organisation: Dan Hotels Corporation Ltd.
4 Star Hotel
Located right on the Mediterranean, and the only Israeli
hotel dedicated to family fun vacation. 'Magic Land' – a
self-contained world created for children. With the new
marina and ancient sites within easy reach.

AVIHAIL
MUSEUMS
Beit Hagedudim (History of Jewish Brigade WWI)
Telephone: (9) 882 2212
Fax: (9) 862 1619

B'NEI BERAK
HOTELS
Wiznitz Ziperi Class
16 Damesek Elizier Street 51610
Telephone: (3) 777 1413
Fax: (3) 677 7141
Email: info@vzchotel.net
Website: www.vzchotel.net

ORGANISATIONS
Ezer Mizion
5 Rabinov Street 51561
Telephone: (3) 614 4572
Fax: (3) 614 4571
Email: information@ezermizion.org
Website: www.ezermizion.org
Israel's Health Support Organisation

RESTAURANTS
Dairy
Dairy Capit
34 Rabbi Akiva St
Telephone: (3) 579 6927

TOURS
Tour Olam
79A Kahaneman St. Bene Berak 51544
Telephone: (3) 579 17190
Fax: (3) 579 1710
Website: www.tour olam.com

BEERSHEBA
HOTELS
Desert Inn
Tuviyahu Av.
Telephone: (8) 642 4922
Fax: (8) 641 2722

MUSEUMS
The Negev Museum of Art
60 Haátemaut Street 84100
Telephone: (8) 620 6570
Fax: (8) 620 6536
In the heart of the old city

TOURS
Bedouin Market
The market is held every Thursday but it has been affected
negatively by tourism and modernization. Permanent
Bedouin encampments can be seen south of town.

CAESAREA
HOTELS
Dan Caesarea Hotel
PO Box 1120 30600
Telephone: (4) 626 9111
Fax: (4) 626 9122
Email: caesarea@danhotels.com
Website: www.danhotels.com

Supervision: Chief Rabbinate of Israel
Central organisation: Dan Hotels
5 Star Deluxe Hotel
A garden enclosed hotel with an 18-hole golf course right next door and Roman antiquities underfoot.

RESTAURANTS
Caesarean Self Service
Paz Petrol Station
Telephone: (4) 633 4609

DAN
MUSEUMS
Natural History and Archeaology
Beit Ussishkin, Kibutz Dan, 12245
Telephone: (4) 694 1704
Fax: (4) 690 2755

DEAD SEA
HOTELS
Crown Plaza
Telephone: (8) 659 1919

Grand Nirvana
Telephone: (8) 668 9444
Fax: (8) 668 9400

Hod
Telephone: (8) 658 4644

Hyatt Regency
Telephone: (8) 659 1234

Moriah Gardens
Telephone: (8) 659 1591
Fax: (8) 658 4238

Radisson Moriah Plaza
Telephone: (8) 659 1591

Spa
Caesar Premier
Telephone: (8) 668 9666
Fax: (8) 652 0303
Website: www.caesarhotels.co.il
Contact the Caesar Group sales office in Tel Aviv for information, Tel: (03) 693 0000

DEGANIA ALEF
MUSEUMS
Beit Gordon
Telephone: (4) 675 0040
Fax: (4) 670 9514

EILAT
HOTELS
Ambassador
Coral Beach, PO Box 390 88103
Telephone: (8) 638 2222
Fax: (8) 638 2200
Website: www.ambassador.co.il

Americana Eilat
PO Box 27, North Beach 88000
Telephone: (8) 633 3777
Fax: (8) 633 4174
Website: www.americanahotel.co.il

Caesar
North Beach
Telephone: (8) 680 5555
Fax: (8) 633 3497

Club In Villa Resort
Rte. 90 (Eilat Taba Road), Box 1505 Coral Beach 88000
Telephone: (8) 633 4555
Fax: (8) 633 4519

Dalia
North Beach
Telephone: (8) 633 4004
Fax: (8) 633 4072

Dan Eilat
Promenade, North Beach
Telephone: (8) 636 2222
Fax: (8) 636 2333
Email: daneilat@danhotels.com
Website: www.danhotels.com
Supervision: Chief Rabbinate of Israel
Central organisation: Dan Hotels Corporation Ltd.
daneilat
Website: www.danhotels.com
Supervision: Kosher, Chief Rabbinate of Israel
5 Star Deluxe Hotel
Situated right on the beachfront, in a vacation resort acclaimed for its resort facilities.

Dan Panorama Eilat
North Beach
Telephone: (8) 638 9999
Fax: (8) 638 9990
Email: panoramaeilat@danhotels.com
Website: www.danhotels.com
Supervision: Chief Rabbinate of Israel
Central organisation: Dan Hotels Corporation Ltd.
5 Star Hotel

Edomit
New Tourist Center
Telephone: (8) 637 9511
Fax: (8) 637 9738

King Solomon's Palace
Promenade, North Beach
Telephone: (8) 633 3444
Fax: (8) 633 4189
Website: www.isrotel.co.il

Marina Club
North Beach
Telephone: (8) 633 4191
Fax: (8) 633 4206

Orchid
Rte. 90 (Eilat Taba Road), Box 994 88000
Telephone: (8) 636 0360
Fax: (8) 637 5323

Princess
Rte. 90 (Eilat Taba Road), Box 2323 88000
Telephone: (8) 636 5555
Fax: (8) 637 6333

Red Rock
North Beach
Telephone: (8) 637 3171
Fax: (8) 637 1705

Royal Beach
North Beach
Telephone: (8) 636 8888
Fax: (8) 636 8811
Website: www.isrotel.co.il

Sheraton Eilat
Promenade, North Beach
Telephone: (8) 636 1111
Fax: (8) 633 4158

The Neptune Hotel
North Beach
Telephone: (8) 636 9369
Fax: (8) 633 4389

RESTAURANTS
Café Royal
King Solomon's Palace Hotel, North Beach
Telephone: (8) 667 6111

Chinese Restaurant
Shulamit Gardens Hotel, North Beach
Telephone: (8) 667 7515

Dolphin Baguette
Tourist Centre

Egged
Central Bus Station
Telephone: (8) 667 5161

El Morocco
Tourist Centre

Golden Lagoon
New Lagoona Hotel, North Beach
Telephone: (8) 667 2176

Halleluyah
Building 9, Tourist Centre
Telephone: (8) 667 5752

Dairy
La Trattoria
Radisson Moriah Plaza Hotel, North Beach
Telephone: (8) 636 1111

Meat
El Gaucho
Arrava Road (Rte. 90)
Telephone: (8) 633 1549

Shipudei Habustan
The Dan Eilat Promenade
Telephone: (8) 636 2294

GALILEE
HOTELS
Ayelet Hashahar
Upper Galilee, Katzrin 12200
Telephone: (4) 693 2611
Fax: (4) 693 4777

Hacienda
Ma'alot
Telephone: (4) 957 9000
Fax: (4) 997 4404

Rakefet
Mishgav, Western Galilee
Telephone: (4) 980 0403
Fax: (4) 980 0317

MUSEUMS
Bar David Museum of Jewish Art
Kibbutz Bar'am, off Route 899
Telephone: (4) 698 8295
Fax: (4) 698 7505
Website: www.galil elion.org.il

Ghetto Fighters' House, Holocaust & Resistance Museum
M.P. Western Galilee 25220
Telephone: (4) 995 8080
Fax: (4) 995 8007
Website: www.gfh.org.il

Sculpture Gallery for Peace and Coexistence
Kawkab Abu Elhija, Gush Segev, Lower Galilee
Telephone: (4) 852 5251
Fax: (4) 852 9166
Website: www.haifa.gov.il/beit hagefen/index

Tel Hai Sculpture Garden
Tel Hai, Upper Galilee Region
Telephone: (4) 694 3731
Fax: (4) 695 0697

The Museum of Photography
Tel Hai Industrial Park
Telephone: (4) 695 0769
Fax: (4) 695 0771
Website: www.iscar.com

The Open Museum
Tefen Industrial Park, Migdal Tefen
Telephone: (4) 987 2977
Fax: (4) 987 2861
Website: www.iscar.com

RESTAURANTS
Lev Hagolan
30 Dror. Street, Katzin
Telephone: (4) 961 6643

Orcha
Commercial Centre, Katzin
Telephone: (4) 696 1440

YOUTH HOSTELS
Karei Deshe (Tabgha)
Yoram
Telephone: (4) 672 0601
Fax: (4) 672 4818
Eleven miles north of Tiberias

GOLAN HEIGHTS
LEISURE
Hamat Gader

The Golan Heights rise steeply from the Sea of Galilee to the Mount Avital plateau. The Hamat Gader were thought to be the nicest spa baths in the whole Roman world, according to the Byzantine empress Eudocia. There are impressive ruins including the extensive Roman and Byzantine spa, which served as a grand bathing resort for six centuries, and an ancient synagogue. Four mineral springs and freshwater spring emerge at Hamat Gader and so it is used today as a modern bathhouse. There is also an alligator farm where alligators and crocodiles can be seen.

MUSEUMS
The Golan Archeological Museum
Katzrin
Telephone: (4) 696 9636
Fax: (4) 696 9637

NATURE RESERVE
Gamla Nature Reserve
Telephone: (4) 682 2282
Fax: (4) 682 2285
Fifteen kilometres southeast of Katzrin

RESTAURANTS
Hamat Gader Restaurant
Telephone: (4) 675 1039

GUSH ETZION
Pizzeria Efrat
Te'ena Shopping Center, Efrat
Telephone: (2) 993 1630

RESTAURANTS/SHOP
Judaica Center, Gift Shop, Gallery and Restaurant
Judaica Center, Gush Etzion Junction 90433
Telephone: (2) 993 4370
Fax: (2) 993 4949
Website: www.judaica.org.il
Available for groups and events

TOURS
Gush Etzion Judaica Center
Gush Etzion Junction, 90433
Telephone: (2) 993 4040; Tourism Dept: 993 8388
Fax: (2) 993 4949
Website: www.judaica.org.il
Display and sales hall that features the items of over 200 items of Israeli Judaica. Can be combined with a visit to Kibbutz Kfar Etzion to see an audio visual show that movingly describes the history of Gush Etzion. Available for groups and events.

HADERA
MUSEUMS
The Khan Museum
74 Hagiborim Street. POB 3232 38131
Telephone: (4) 632 2330; 632 4562
Fax: (4) 534 5776
Email: khanhadera@013.net.ll
Website: www.khan-hadera.org.il
Hours: Sunday to Thursday, 8am to 1pm; Friday, 9am to 12pm; Sunday and Tuesday, 4pm to 6pm

HAIFA
HOTELS
Dan Carmel
85-87 Hanassi Avenue 34642
Telephone: (4) 830 3030
Fax: (4) 838 7504
Email: dancarmel@danhotels.com
Website: www.danhotels.com
Supervision: Chief Rabbinate of Israel
Central organisation: Dan Hotels Corporation Ltd.
5 Star Deluxe Hotel
This luxury hotel is situated on the slopes of Mount Carmel overlooking Haifa bay. Just 50 metres from the magnificent Bahai Hanging Gardens.
Dan Gardens Haifa
124 Yefe-Nof Street
Telephone: (4) 830 2020
Fax: (4) 830 2021
Email: dangardenshaifa@danhotels.com
Website: www.danhotels.com
Supervision: Chief Rabbinate of Israel
4 Star Hotel
Set on Mt. Carmel overlooking Haifa Bay and Bahai Gardens, in an exclusive neighborhood. 31 modern guestrooms.
Dan Panorama
107 Hanassi avenue
Telephone: (4) 835 2222
Fax: (4) 835 2235
Email: panoramahaifa@danhotels.com
Website: www.danhotels.com
Supervision: Chief Rabbinate of Israel
Central organisation: Dan Hotels Corporation Ltd.
5 Star Hotel
A hotel with a chic, contemporary ambiance, the Dan Panorama rises 21 stories above Mt. Carmel, affording inspiring views of Haifa bay and long stretches of coastline. New public areas.
Dvir
124 Yafe Nof Street
Telephone: (4) 838 9131
Fax: (4) 838 1068
Nof Haifa
101 Hanasi Avenue
Telephone: (4) 835 4311
Fax: (4) 838 8810
Website: nof hotels.co.il

Shulamit
15 Kiryat Sefer Street 34676
Telephone: (4) 834 2811
Fax: (4) 825 5206
Website: www.shulamit.biz

MUSEUMS

Haifa Museum of Art
26 Shabbtai Levi Street 33043
Telephone: (4) 852 3255
Fax: (4) 855 2714
Website: www.hms.org.il
This museum presents the living pulse of contemporary
international and local art Hours: Monday, Tuesday,
Wednesday, 10am to 4pm; Thursday, 4pm to 7pm; Friday
and holidays, 10am to 1pm; Saturday, 10am to 3pm.

Israel Edible Oil Industry Museum
Shemen Factory, 2 Tovim Street, POB 136 31000
Telephone: (4) 860 4600
Fax: (4) 862 2555

Israel Railways Museum
Haifa East Railway Station
Telephone: (4) 856 4293
Fax: (4) 856 4310
Website: www.israrail.org.il/general information
Museum is open Sunday to Thursday (Holidays excepted),
8.30am to 2pm.

MADATECH- The Israel National Museum of Science, Technology & Space
The Historic Technion Building, Balfour Street,
Hadar Ha Carmel
Telephone: (4) 861 4444
Fax: (4) 867 9103
Website: Madatch.org.il

Mane Katz Museum
89 Yafe Nof Street 34641
Telephone: (4) 838 3482
Fax: (4) 836 2985
Website: www
Opening hours
Sun, Mon, Wed & Thu 10am to 4pm;
Tue 2pm to 6pm, Fri10am to1pm
Sat & holidays 10:00-14:00
holidays 10am to 2pm

Museum of Clandestine Immigration & Navy Museum
204 Allenby Street 35472
Telephone: (4) 853 6249
Fax: (4) 851 2958
Open: Sunday to Thursday 8.30am to 4pm

Museum of Pre History
124 Hatishbi Street, Entrance from Gan Ha'em
Telephone: (4) 837 1833
Fax: (4) 855 2714

Reuben & Edith Hecht Museum
Haifa University 31905
Telephone: (4) 825 7773

Fax: (4) 824 0724
Email: mushecht@research.haifa.ac.il
Website: www.mushecht.haifa.ac.il
Archaeology & Art
Hours: Sunday, Monday, Wednesday, Thursday, 10am to
4pm; Tuesday, 10am to 7pm; Friday, 10am to 1pm;
Saturday, 10am to 2pm. Admission free. All restaurants at
the University are kosher.

The Haifa City Museum
11 Ben Gurion Avenue
Telephone: (4) 851 2030

The National Maritime Museum
198 Allenby Road
Telephone: (4) 853 6622
Fax: (4) 853 9286
Hours: Sunday, Monday, Wednesday, Thursday, 10am to
4pm; Tuesday, 4pm to 7pm; Friday and holidays, 10am to
1pm; Saturday 10am to 2pm.

Tikotin Museum of Japanese Art
89 Hanassi Avenue, Mount Carmel 34642
Telephone: (4) 838 3554
Fax: (4) 837 9824
Email: curator@tmja.org.il
Website: www.hms.org.il
Hours: Monday, Tuesday, Wednesday, 10:30am to 4pm;
Thursday 6pm to 7pm; Friday and holiday eves, 10:30am to
1pm; Saturday, 10:30am to 3pm.

University of Haifa The Art Gallery
University of Haifa, Mount Carmel 31905
Telephone: (4) 824 0660
Fax: (4) 824 9298
Email: gallery@research.haifa.ac.il
Website: www.art-gallery.haifa.ac.il

Zoo

Beit Pinchas Biological Insititute and Haifa Educational Zoo
124 Hatishbi Street
Telephone: (4) 810 0476
Fax: (4) 810 3599
Mobile Phone: 0507 482400
Supervision: Dr Etty Arafat
Includes nature museum, zoo and botanical garden.
Entrance via Gan Ha'em. Hours: Sunday to Friday, Winter,
8am to 5pm, July to August, 9am to 7pm; Friday and
holiday eves, 9am to 2pm.

RESTAURANTS

Egged
Central Bus Station
Telephone: (4) 851 5221
Self service

Hamber Burger
61 Herzl Street
Telephone: (4) 866 6739

Rondo
Dan Carmel Hotel, 87 Hanassi Boulevard
Telephone: (4) 838 6211

Techion
Neve Shaanan
Telephone: (4) 823 3011
Self service lunch only.

The Chinese Restaurant of Nof
Nof Hotel, 101 Hanassi Boulevard
Telephone: (4) 838 8731

Dairy
Milky Pinky (Milk Bar)
29 Haneviim Street
Telephone: (4) 866 4166

Meat
Mac David
131 Hanassi Boulevard
Telephone: (4) 838 3684

TOURIST INFORMATION
Tourist Office
48 Ben Gurion Street
Telephone: (4) 853 5606
Fax: (4) 853 5610

What's on in Haifa
Telephone: (4) 864 0840

TOURS
Tour Company
Telephone: (4) 867 4342
Bahai shrine and gardens, Druse villages, Muchraka, the
Moslem village of Kabair, the Carmelite monastery and
Elijah's cave, Wednesday, 9.30am. Mt Carmel, Druse
villages, Kibbutz Ben Oren and Ein Hod artists' colony:
Sundays, Mondays, Tuesdays, Thursdays, Saturdays,
9.30am.

HANITA
MUSEUMS
Tower & Stockade Museum
Route 8990
Telephone: (4) 985 9677
Fax: (4) 985 9677

HAON
HOLIDAY VILLAGE
Kibbutz Haon
Jordan Valley
Telephone: (4) 675 7555/6

HAZOREA
MUSEUMS
Wilfrid Israel House of Oriental Art
Telephone: (4) 989 9566
Fax: (4) 989 0942

HERZLIYA
HOTELS
Dan Accadia

Herzliya on Sea
Telephone: (09) 959 7070
Fax: (09) 959 7090
Email: accadia@danhotels.com
Website: www.danhotels.com
Supervision: Chief Rabbinate of Israel
Central organisation: Dan Hotels Corporation Ltd.
5 Star Deluxe Hotel
Carved into the coastline overlooking the Mediterranean,
the Dan Accadia is a resort hotel in a dream setting.

Tadmor
38 Basel Street
Telephone: (09) 952 5000
Fax: (09) 957 5124

The Sharon
4 Ramot Yam Street, Herzlia on Sea 46748
Telephone: (09) 952 5777
Fax: (09) 927 2448
Website: www.sharon.co.il

MUSEUMS
Herzliya Museum of Contemporary Art
4 Habanim Street 46379
Telephone: (09) 950 2301
Fax: (09) 950 0043
Email: info@herzliyamuseum.co.il
Website: www.herzliyamuseum.co.il

RESTAURANTS
Tadmor Hotel School
38 Basel Street 46660
Telephone: (09) 952 5050
Fax: (09) 957 5124

Dairy-Kosher
Lobbystro
Daniel Hotel, 60 Ramot Yam Street
Telephone: (09) 952 8210

Meat
Steak.com
27 Rehov Maskit, Herzliya Pituah
Telephone: (09) 956 1145

TOURIST INFORMATION
English Speaking Residents Association
PO Box 3132 46104
Telephone: (09) 950 8371
Fax: (09) 954 3781
Email: esra@trendline.co.il
Website: www.esra.org.il

JAFFA
CAFETERIA
Kosher
Puah
3 Yochanan Street, Jaffa Flea Market
Telephone: (03) 682 3821

MUSEUMS
The Antiquities Museum of Tel Aviv Yafo (Jaffa Museum)
10 Mifratz Shlomo Street, Old Jaffa 68038
Telephone: (03) 682 5375
Fax: (03) 681 3624
Part of Eretz Israel Museum Tel Aviv, Opening hours: Sunday to Thursday 9am to 1pm

JERUSALEM
ACCOMMODATION INFORMATION
Good Morning Jerusalem
17 Ezrat Israel Street
Telephone: (02) 623 3459
Fax: (02) 625 9330
Email: gmjer@netvision.net.il
Website: www.accommodation.co.il
Lists rooms and apartments available for touristsBED
AND BREAKFAST

Le Sixteen
16 Midbar Sinai Street, Givat Hamivtar 97805
Telephone: (02) 532 8008
Fax: (02) 581 9159
Website: www.le16-bnb.co.il
Member of the Jerusalem Home Accomodation Association. Can provide guest studios with kosher dairy kichenettes.

CAFETERIA
Kosher
Cafe Hillel
8 Hillel Street
Telephone: (02) 624 7775
More branches around town

Coffee Shop
2 Rachel Imenu Street
Telephone: (02) 563 2529
Also at 24 Hillel Street Tel (02) 624 8528

Faza
51 HaPalmach Street
Telephone: (02) 567 1791

HaKol LaOfe VeGam HaCafe
Machane Yehuda Market
Telephone: (02) 624 2105

Vegetarian -Kosher
BAu House
16 Ein Kerem Street
Telephone: (02) 643 7171

CONTACT INFORMATION
Jeff Seidel's Jewish Student Information Centre
5 Bet El, Jewish Quarter, Old City
Telephone: (02) 628 2634
Fax: (02) 628 8338
Email: jseidel@jeffseidel.com
Website: www.jeffseidel.com

Jeff Seidel's Jewish Student Information Centre
14 Lechi
Telephone: (02) 581 2240
Fax: (02) 628 8338
Website: www.jeffseidel.com

GUEST HOUSE
Bet Shumuel
6 Shamma Street 94101
Telephone: (02) 620 3473; 620 3465
Fax: (02) 620 3467
Single and family guest rooms with capacity of 240 beds; conference facilities and banquet services; restaurant and coffee shop; international culture and education centre with a central location

HOTELS
Caesar
208 Jaffa Road
Telephone: (02) 538 4111
Fax: (02) 538 1480

Dan Boutique Jerusalem
31 Hebron Road
Telephone: (02) 568 9999
Fax: (02) 673 4066
Email: danboutiquejlm@danhotels.com
Website: www.danhotels.com
Supervision: Chief Rabbinate of Israel
Central organisation: Dan Hotels Corporation Ltd.
4 Star Gallery Hotel
Located opposite Mt. Zion and the Old City Walls.

Dan Panorama Jerusalem
39 Keren Hayesod Street
Telephone: (02) 569 5695

Fax: (02) 625 0120
Email: panoramajlm@danhotels.com
Website: www.danhotels.com
Supervision: Chief Rabbinate of Israel
Central organisation: Dan Hotels Corporation Ltd.
5 Star Hotel
Dignified and limestone-faced, located in the heart of the eternal city, a short stroll past historic landmarks to the ancient walls, holy sites and exotic markets of the Old City.

Four Points
4 Vilnai Street 96110
Telephone: (02) 655 8888
Fax: (02) 651 2266
The hotel is located in the hotel area at the enterance to the city and within walking distance of the Israel Museum and the Knesset.

Hotel Jerusalem
4 Agripas Street 94301
Telephone: (02) 623 1141
Fax: (02) 625 9323
Website: www.hotel-palatin.co.il

Hyatt Regency Jerusalem
32 Lehi Street
Telephone: (02) 533 1234
Fax: (02) 581 5947
Website: www.hyattjer.co.il

Inbal
Liberty Bell Park, 3 Jabotinsky Street 92145
Telephone: (02) 675 6666
Fax: (02) 675 6777
Website: www.inbal hotel.co.il

Jerusalem Tower
23 Hillel Street 94581
Telephone: (02) 620 9209
Fax: (02) 625 2167
Website: www.jthotels.com

King David
23 King David Street 94101
Telephone: (02) 620 8888
Fax: (02) 620 8882
Email: kingdavid@danhotels.com
Website: www.danhotels.com
Supervision: Chief Rabbinate of Israel
Central organisation: Dan Hotels Corporation Ltd.
5 Star Deluxe Hotel and a member of 'The Leading Hotels of the World'

King Solomon
32 King David Street
Telephone: (02) 569 5555
Fax: (02) 624 1174

Lev Yerushalayim
18 King George Street
Telephone: (02) 530 0333
Fax: (02) 623 2432
Website: www.levjerusalem.co.il

Mount Zion Hotel
17 Hebron Road 93546
Telephone: (02) 568 9555
Fax: (02) 673 1425
Email: hotel@mountzion.co.il
Website: www.mountzion.co.il

Radisson Moriah Plaza Jerusalem
39 Keren Hayessod Street 94188
Telephone: (02) 569 5695
Fax: (02) 623 2411

Reich
1 Hagai Street, Bet Hakerem
Telephone: (02) 652 3121
Fax: (02) 652 3120

Renaissance Jerusalem Hotel
Ruppin Bridge, at Herz Blvd 91033
Telephone: (02) 659 9999
Fax: (02) 651 1824
Contact: Gerry Budwig

Sheraton Jerusalem Plaza
47 King George Street
Telephone: (02) 629 8666
Fax: (02) 623 1667

The David Citadel
7 King David Street 94101
Telephone: (02) 621 1111
Fax: (02) 621 1000
Website: www.thedavidcitadel.com

The Jerusalem Hostel & Guest House
44 Jaffa Road
Telephone: (02) 613 0102
Fax: (02) 613 6092
Website: www.jerusalem hostel
Very centrally located (Zion Square). All rooms have attached shower and W.C. No meals served but a modern clean kitchen is available for use of the guests.

Windmill
3 Mendele Street
Telephone: (02) 566 3111
Fax: (02) 561 0964

MUSEUM
The Burnt House Museum
2 Tiferet Street, The Jewish Quarter
Telephone: (02) 628 8141 ext. 102
Sun to Thu 9am to 5pm, Fri 9am to 1pm. An audio-visual and archeogological display that depicts the priestly Kathrus family's life and the 70AD battle in which the Romans burned down their house.

Wohl Museum
1 HaKara'im Street, The Jewish Quarter
Telephone: (02) 628 8141
Sun to Thu 9am to 5pm, Fri 9am to 1pm

World Centre for North African Jewry's Heritage
13 HaMa'aravim Street
Telephone: (02) 623 5811

MUSEUMS
Ammunition Hill Memorial & Museum, Ramat Eshkol
Shrazai 5 Street 91181
Telephone: (02) 582 8442
Fax: (02) 582 9132
Email: admin@givathatachmoshet.org.il
Website: www.givathatachmoshet.org.il
National Memorial site

Bible Lands Museum Jerusalem
25 Granot Street, Museum Row, POB 4670 91046
Telephone: (02) 561 1066
Fax: (02) 563 8228
Email: contact@blmj.org
Website: www.blmj.org
The home of one of the most important collections of ancient artifacts displaying rare works of art from the dawn of civilisation to the Byzantine period. Gift shop, special exhibitions, weekly lectures and concerts. Daily guided touts in English. Groups by advance reservation. Open daily except Shabbat and Holidays. Call or email the museum for hours and program details. 'Kosher Cafeteria'.

JEWISH TRAVEL GUIDE 2009

Herzl Museum
Herzl Blvd, Mount Herzl
Telephone: (02) 651 1108

L.A. Mayer Museum for Islamic Art
2 Hapalmach Street 91040
Telephone: (02) 566 1291/2
Fax: (02) 561 9802
Email: islamart@netvision.net.il
Website: www.islamicart.co.il
Display of art of Islamic countries from the 7th-20th centuries including jewelery, ceramics, metal ware, glass, manuscripts, miniature paintings, arms and armour and the famed David Salomons collection of antique European watches and clocks.

Museum of Natural History
6 Mohilever Street
Telephone: (02) 563 1116
Fax: (02) 566 0666

Nahon Museum of Italian Jewish Art
27 Hillel Street 94581
Telephone: (02) 624 1610
Fax: (02) 625 3480
Email: jija@netvision.net.il
Website: www.jija.org
Collects and preserves objects pertaining to the life of the Jews in Italy from the Middle Ages to the present day. The main attraction is the ancient synagogue of Conegliano Veneto, a township some 60 km from Venice relocated entirely to Israel. Hours: Sunday, Tuesday, Wednesday, 9am to 5pm, Monday, 9am to 2pm, Thursday, Friday, 9am to 1pm. For guided tours contact the number above.

Old Yishuv Court Museum
6 Or Hayim Street 91016t
Telephone: (02) 628 4636
Fax: (02) 628 4636
The museum is located in the heart of the Jewish Quarter in the old City of Jerusalem in a sixteenth century building. It displays the story of the Jewish community from the period under Ottoman rule, through the final days of the British Mandate. Hours Sunday to Thursday, 9am to 2pm.

S.Y. Agnon's House
16 Joseph Klausner Street, Talpiot 93388
Telephone: (02) 671 6498
Fax: (02) 673 8285
Email: agnon-h@zahav.net.il
Supervision: www.agnonhouse.org.il
Hours: Sunday to Thursday, 9am to 1pm

Siebenberg House of Archaeological Museum
7 Hagittit Street, Jewish Quarter
Telephone: (02) 628 2341

The Chagall Windows at the Hadassah University Hospital
Ein Kerem 91120
Telephone: (02) 677 6271
Fax: (02) 643 9203
Closed on Fridays and Saturdays. There is an entrance fee.

The Israel Museum, Jerusalem
Ruppin Blvd
Telephone: (02) 670 8811
Fax: (02) 677 1332

Website: www.imj.org.il
Includes Bezalel Art wing, Bronfman Biblical & Archaeology wing Judaica and jewish Ethnography wing Ruth Youth wing, Shrine of the Book, Ticho House in the centre of Jerusalem & Rockefeller Museum in East Jerusalem.

Tourjeman Post Museum
4 Hail Hahandasa Street
Telephone: (02) 628 1278
Fax: (02) 627 7061

Tower of David Museum of the History of Jerusalem
Jaffa Gate
Telephone: (02) 626 5333
Fax: (02) 628 3418
24 hour information line: (2) 626 5310

Yad Vashem, The Holocaust Martyrs' and Heroes' Remembrance Authority
Har Hazikaron, PO Box 3477 91034
Telephone: (02) 644 3400
Fax: (02) 644 3443
Website: www.yadvashem.org
Open 9am to 5pm Sunday to Wednesday, 9am to 8pm Thursday, 9 am to 2 pm Friday and eves of holidays, closed on Saturday and all Jewish holidays.

Jewish Art

The Sir Isaac & Lady Edith Wolfson Museum, Hechal Shlomo
3rd Floor, 58 King George Street 91073
Telephone: (02) 624 7908
Fax: (02) 623 1810
Email: hechalshlomo@gmail.com
Website: www.hechalshlomo.org.il
Opening hours Sunday to Thursday 10am to 3pm

ORGANISATIONS
Travelers Aid of Israel
PO Box 2828
Telephone: (02) 582 0126
Fax: (02) 623 2742
Legal counselling, social and human services, accident victims legal assistance, immigrant assistance, interest free loans, stranded travellers, medical assistance, crime victim assistance, homelessness, emergency assistance

Yad Sarah's Service for Tourists with Special Needs
Yad Sarah House, 124 Herzl Boulevard 96187
Telephone: (02) 644 4633
Fax: (02) 644 4628
Website: www.yadsarah.org
Supervision:
email: tourism
Yad Sarah is a voluntary organization that lends, free against a returnable deposit medical rehab. equipment. Visitors with mobility limitations can use the Yad Sarah special transportation vans at a low fee. By pre-arrangement you can have the van and driver waiting at Ben Gurion airport. Two weeks notice for this service. Yad Sarah has over 100 branches in Israel. More information for visitors with special needs on the website

RELIGIOUS ORGANISATIONS
Israel Council of Young Israel
Heichal Shlomo Building, 58 King George Street
Telephone: (02) 623 1631
Fax: (02) 623 1363
Mailing address: POB 7306 91072 Jerusalem, Israel. Office hours: Sunday through to Thursday 9am to 3pm.

RESTAURANTS
Nona
Givat Shaul atPaz Gas Station
Telephone: (02) 651 2922

Dairy
Belinda Cafe
9a Diskin Street
Telephone: (02) 563 3995
Fax: (02) 561 1176
Supervision: Mehadrin Yerushalim

Dairy Italian-Kosher
Primavera
Sheraton Plaze Hotel, 47 King George Street
Telephone: (02) 629 8691

Dairy-Kosher
Azura
8 Machane Street
Telephone: (02) 623 5204
Flavours, scents and customs of days past all foodc ooked on paraffin stoves.

Shmil BaMaabada
28 Hebron Road
Telephone: (02) 673 1629

Fish-Kosher
Taverna
2 Naomi Street
Telephone: (02) 671 9796
Pasta

Fish/Dairy-Kosher
Seven Species
Botannical Gardens, Burila Street
Telephone: (02) 622 7577

Fish/Meat-Kosher
Olive and Fish
2 Jabotinsky Street
Telephone: (02) 566 5020
Fax: (02) 563 5937
Email: oliveandfish@gmail.com
Supervision: Jerusalem Rabbanute

French-Kosher
Canela
8 Shlomzion Ha Malka Street
Telephone: (02) 622 2293

Eldad VeZehoo
31 Jaffa Street, Feingold Courtyard
Telephone: (02) 625 4007; 624 7033

La Guta
18 Rivlin Street 92149
Telephone: (02) 623 2322
Middle Eastern influences

Tzachku
Machane Yehuda Market
Telephone: (02) 623 4916
Middle Eastern versions of French classics.Must reserve in advance

French/Italian-Kosher
1868
10 King David Street
Telephone: (02) 622 2312

Fusion Asian-kosher
Sheyan
8 Rambam Street at the Windmill
Telephone: (02) 561 2007
Sushi, noodles

Indian- Kosher
Kohinor
Crown Plaza Hotel, HaAliya Street
Telephone: (02) 658 8867

Italian-Kosher
Agas VeTapauch
7 HaMa'alot Street
Telephone: (02) 623 0280

Al Dente
55 Osishkin Street
Telephone: (02) 625 1479

Kosher
9 Horkenos Street
Telephone: (02) 623 6095

Ragu
41 Beit Lechen Road
Telephone: (02) 673 0760

Kurdish-Kosher
Misedet Ima
189 Agrippas Street
Telephone: (02) 624 6860

Meat
Vaqueiro
54 HaNevi'im Street
Telephone: (02) 624 7432

Meat Argentinian Grill
El Gaucho
22 Rivilin Street 91313
Telephone: (02) 624 2227
Fax: (02) 623 2660
Email: gaucho@netvision.net.il
Website: www.el-gaucho.co.il

Mid-Eastern-Kosher
Pinati
13 King George Street
Telephone: (02) 6254540

Pizzerias
Pizzeria Trevi
8 Leib Yaffe Street
Telephone: (02) 672 4136

Thai/mediterranean-Kosher
Olive
36 Emek Refa'im Street
Telephone: (02) 561 1102

Turkish-Kosher
Pasha
28 Pier Koenig Street
Telephone: (02) 648 2220

Vegetarian-Kosher
Te'enim
12 Eme=ile Botta Street
Telephone: (02) 625 1967

Yemenite-Kosher
Marvad Haksamim
42 Emek Refa'im Street
Telephone: (02) 623 4916

SYNAGOGUES
The Jerusalem Great Synagogue
56 King George Street
Telephone: (02) 623 0628
Fax: (02) 625 5361
Email: jgs@zahav.net.il

Yeshurun
44 King George Street
Telephone: (02) 624 3942
Fax: (02) 622 4528

TOURIST INFORMATION
Ministry of Tourism
24 King George Street
Telephone: (02) 675 4811

Tourism Coordinator with the Palestinian Authority
Israel Ministry of Tourism, PO Box 1018, Jerusalem 91009
Telephone: (02) 675 4903
Fax: (02) 624 0571

TOURS
American P'eylim Student Union
10 Shoarim Street
Telephone: (02) 653 2131
Free tours of Jewish Quarter and free accommodation in the hostel quarters

Knesset (Parliament)
Telephone: (02) 675 3416
Fax: (02) 561 1201
Website: www.knesset/gov.il
Sunday & Thursday 8.30am to 2.30pm

Old City Guesthouse and Youth Centre
9 Shoney Halachot Street, Old City of Jerusalem 97501
Telephone: (02) 628 9313
Fax: (02) 628 9314
Free accommodation

Society for the Protection of Nature in Israel: Israeli Nature Trails
13 Heleni Hamalka Street 950 101
Telephone: (02) 625 7682
Fax: (02) 623 4155
Email: spnijeru@015.net.il
Website: www.teva.org.il www.sustainable-jerusalem.org
YOUTH HOSTELS
Bet Bernstein
1 Keren Hayesod Street
Telephone: (02) 625 8286
80 rooms

Davidka
67 Ha Nevi'im Street, PO Box 37110
Telephone: (02) 538 4555
Fax: (02) 538 8790
Seventy five rooms; 4-6 bed

Ein Karem
Telephone: (02) 641 6282
Ninety seven rooms

Israel Youth Hostels Association
Youth Travel Bureau, Jerusalem International Convention Center, POB 6001 91060
Telephone: (02) 655 8442
Fax: (02) 655 8431
Email: iyha@iyha.org.il
Website: www.iyha.org.il
There are 22 youth hostels in Israel for students, youth groups and adults, which are supervised by the Israel Youth Hostels Association (a member of the International Youth Hostels Federation). All hostels offer the standard facilities of dormitories, kosher dining rooms etc. All are air conditioned.

KFAR GILADI
MUSEUMS
Beit Hashomer
Telephone: (4) 694 1565
Fax: (4) 695 1505

KIBBUTZ HARDUF
RESTAURANTS
Vegetarian
Jutka's Restaurant
Telephone: (4) 905 9229
Fax: (4) 986 1106
Email: rest@harduf.org.il
Website: www.harduf.org.il/rest

ISRAEL

KIBBUTZ YOTVATA
LEISURE
Biblical Wildlife Reserve Hai Bar Arava

The reserve is situated thirty seven miles north of Eilat. Biologists have settled every breed of animal that is mentioned in the Bible. Animals include herd of Somalian wid asses, oryx antelope, ibex, ostriches, desert foxes, lynx, hyenas and the last desert leopard in the Negev, living out her days on the reserve. Guided tours start at 9am and 10.30am, noon and 1.30pm.

RESTAURANTS
Dairy
Dairy Restaurant
Telephone: (8) 635 7449

KORAZIM
HOLIDAY VILLAGE
Amnon Bay Recreation Centre
Telephone: (4) 693 4431

Vered Hagalil Guest Farm
Telephone: (4) 693 5785
Fax: (4) 693 4964
Email: vered@veredhagalil.co.il

LOD
MUSEUMS
Museum of Jewish Ethnic Heritage
20 David Ha'melech Boulevard, Lod
Telephone: (8) 924 1160
Fax: (8) 924 9466
Mobile Phone: 0544 464 803
Email: zmalachi@post.tau.ac.il
P.O.B 383 Lod, 71101

The Museum presents the tradition, culture and art of the Jews of North Africa, Bulgaria, Ethiopia, Bochara, India, The European Shtetle etc.

TOURIST INFORMATION
Ministry of Tourism
Ben Gurion International Airport
Telephone: (8) 971 1485

LOHAMEI HAGETAOT
MUSEUMS
Ghetto Fighters' House, Holocast & Resistance Museum
M.P. (Mobile Post) 25220
Telephone: (4) 995 8080
Fax: (4) 995 8007
Website: www.gfh.org.il
Hours: Sunday to Thursday 9am to 4pm

MAAGAN
HOLIDAY VILLAGE
Maagan Holiday village
Sea of Galilee, Jordan Valley 15160

Telephone: (4) 665 4400
Fax: (4) 665 4455
Website: www.maagan.com

MAAYAN HAROD
YOUTH HOSTELS
Hankin
Telephone: (4) 658 1660
Seven miles east of Afula

MAHANAYIM
TOURIST INFORMATION
Information Office
Zomet Mahanayim
Telephone: (4) 693 5016

MOSHAV SHORESH
BED AND BREAKFAST
Green Hills Suites
Harey Yehuda 90860
Telephone: (2) 533 8338
Fax: (2) 534 0262
Website: www.shoresh.co.il
Situated on a mountain top in the Judean Hills with an amazing view of almost all of Israel. Each suite has air-conditioned bedroom + lounge.

NAHARIYA
HOTELS
Carlton
23 Ha'agaaton Blvd
Telephone: (4) 900 5555
Fax: (4) 982 3771
Website: www.carlton hotel.co.il

Rosenblatt
59 Weizmann Street
Telephone: (4) 992 0069
Fax: (4) 992 8121

LEISURE
Rosh Hanikra
 22825 Telephone: (4) 985 7109
Fax: (4) 985 7107
Website: www.rosh hanikra.com
Rosh Hanikra is situated four miles north of Nahariya, on the Lebanese border. Rosh Ha Nikra grottos–one of the wonders of creation. The site offers a variety of attractions: ride from the top of the mountain down to sea level via state–of–the–art cable cars, explore the grottos formed over millennia by the contact of rock and sea.

MUSEUMS
Nahariya Municipal Museum
19 Hagaaton Boulevard
Telephone: (4) 987 9863
Fax: (4) 992 2303

NAZARETH

RESTAURANTS
Iberia
Rassco Centre, Nazareth Elite
Telephone: (4) 655 6314

NEGEV

Bulgarian
112 Keren Kayemet Street, Beersheba
Telephone: (8) 623 8504

YOUTH HOSTELS
Bet Noam
Mitzpeh Ramon
Telephone: (8) 658 8433
Fax: (8) 658 8074
Supervision: Israel YHA

Bet Sara
Ein Gedi
Telephone: (8) 658 4165
1.5 miles north of Kibbutz Ein Gedi on Dead Sea

Hevel Katif: Hadarom
Telephone: (8) 684 7597
Fax: (8) 684 7680

NETANYA

CULTURE CENTRE/THEATRE
Netanya Cultural Center
4 Raziel Street
Telephone: (9) 830 8800
Fax: (9) 861 7555

FOOD DELIVERY
Kosher Services Worldwide
Hashaked 16 42214
Telephone: (9) 98 626 422
Email: kosherisrael@013.net
Website: www.kosherservicesworldwide.com
Destination Wedding specialists
Designer Glatt kosher holidays.

HOLIDAY VILLAGE
Green Beach Holiday Village
Telephone: (9) 865 6166
Fax: (9) 835 0075

HOTELS
Arches
4 Remez Street 42271
Telephone: (9) 860 9860
Fax: (9) 860 9866

Galei Hasharon
42 Ussishkin Street 42273
Telephone: (9) 834 1946
Fax: (9) 833 8128

Galil
26 Nice Boulevard
Telephone: (9) 862 4455
Fax: (9) 862 4456

Ginot Yam
9 David Hamelech Street
Telephone: (9) 834 1007
Fax: (9) 861 5722

Goldar
1 Ussishkin Street
Telephone: (9) 833 8188
Fax: (9) 862 0680

Grand Yahalom
15 Gad Machnes Street
Telephone: (9) 862 4888
Fax: (9) 862 4890

Green Beach
PO Box 230
Telephone: (9) 865 6166
Fax: (9) 835 0075

Jeremy
11 Gad Machnes Street
Telephone: (9) 862 2651
Fax: (9) 862 2651

King Koresh
6 Harav Kook Street
Telephone: (9) 861 3555
Fax: (9) 861 3444

King Solomon
18 Hamaapilim Street
Telephone: (9) 833 8444
Fax: (9) 861 1397
Website: www.inisrael.com/kingsolomon.com

Margoa
9 Gad Machnes Street
Telephone: (9) 862 4434
Fax: (9) 861 1397

Maxim
8 King David Street
Telephone: (9) 862 1062
Fax: (9) 862 0190

Metropol Grand
17 Gad Machnes Street
Telephone: (9) 862 4777
Fax: (9) 861 1556

Orly
20 Hamaapilim Street
Telephone: (9) 833 3091
Fax: (9) 862 5453

Palace
33 Gad Machnes Street
Telephone: (9) 862 0222
Fax: (9) 862 0224

Park
7 David Hamelech Street
Telephone: (9) 862 3344
Fax: (9) 862 4029

Residence
18 Gad Machnes Street
Telephone: (9) 862 3777
Fax: (9) 862 3711

The Seasons
1 Nice Boulevard
Telephone: (9) 860 1555
Fax: (9) 862 3022

SYNAGOGUES
Orthodox
New Synagogue of Netanya
7 MacDonald Street, P.O.Box 1115 42110
Telephone: (9) 861 4591
Fax: (9) 887 5079
Email: macshul@netvision.net.il
Website: www.macshul.org
Synagogue and Community Centre. Rabbi: Rabbi Raphael Katz.
Young Israel Congregation of North Netanya
39 Shlomo Hamelech Street
Telephone: (9) 862 8737
Website: www.yinn.org

TOURIST INFORMATION
Information Office
Ha Atzma'ut Square
Telephone: (9) 882 7286

NEVE TZEDEK
CAFETERIA
Kosher
Suzanna
9 Shabazi Street
Telephone: (03) 517 7580

KOSHER GRILL BAR
La Terrasse
14 Ahad Ha'am Street
Telephone: (03) 510 5555
Email: mm18@bezeqint.net
Website: www.rol.co.il/mm

PETACH TIKVA
MUSEUMS
Beit Yad Labanim
30 Arlozorov Street
Telephone: (3) 922 3450
Fax: (3) 922 3450

QATZRIN
Golan Archaeological Museum
Telephone: (4) 696 9636
Fax: (4) 696 2412

RA'ANANA
RESTAURANTS
Ady D
158 Achuza
Telephone: (9) 791 6517

Limosa
5 Eliazar Jaffe
Telephone: (9) 790 3407

Pica Aduma
87 Achuza
Telephone: (9) 791 0508

RAMAT GAN
MUSEUMS
Museum of Israeli Art
146 Abba Hillel Street 52572
Telephone: (03) 752 1876
Fax: (03) 752 7377
Website: www.m-i-a.co.il
Pierre Gildesgame Maccabi Sports Museum
Kfar Hamaccabiah
Telephone: (03) 671 5729
Fax: (03) 574 6565
Yechiel Nahari Museum of Far Eastern Art
18 Hibat Zion Street
Telephone: (03) 578 1216
Fax: (03) 619 5837

RESTAURANTS
French-Kosher
Arugola
Sheraton City Tower, 14 Zisman Street
Telephone: (03) 754 4482

RAMAT HANEGEV
TOURIST INFORMATION
Information Office
Zomet Mashabay Sadeh
Telephone: (8) 655 7314

RAMAT HASHARON
CAFETERIA
Kosher
Reviva and Celia
1 HaMeyasdim
Telephone: (03) 540 0179

RAMAT YOHANAN
YOUTH HOSTELS
Yehuda Hatzair
Telephone: (4) 844 2976
Fax: (4) 844 2976
Eleven miles north east of Haifa

REHOVOT
MUSEUMS
Havayeda–Science Through Fun Science Park
5 Yechezkai Habibi Street 76000
Telephone: (8) 945 2949
Fax: (8) 945 2949
Website: www.weizmann.ac.il
Weizmann House
Yad Haim Weizmann 76100
Telephone: (8) 934 4499
Fax: (8) 934 4180
Website: www.weizmann.ac.il

ROSH HANIKRA
YOUTH HOSTELS
Rosh Hanikra
Telephone: (4) 998 2516

ROSH PINA
Hovevei Hateva
Telephone: (4) 693 7086
Sixteen miles north of Tiberias

SAFED
HOTELS
David
Mount Canaan
Telephone: (4) 692 0062

Nof Hagalil
Mount Canaan
Telephone: (4) 692 1595

Rimon Inn
Artist Colony
Telephone: (4) 692 0665/6

Ron
Hativat Yiftah Street
Telephone: (4) 697 2590

MUSEUMS
Beit Hameiri Institute (History & Heritage of safed)
Keren Hayesod Street 13110
Telephone: (4) 697 1307
Fax: (4) 692 1902

Israel Bible Museum
Citadel Hill
Telephone: (4) 699 9972
Fax: (4) 699 9972

Museum of Printing History
Artists' Colony
Telephone: (4) 692 3022

TOURIST INFORMATION
Information Office
50 Jerusalem Street
Telephone: (4) 692 0961/633

YOUTH HOSTELS
Bet Benyamin
Telephone: (4) 692 1086
Fax: (4) 697 3514

TEL AVIV
CONTACT INFORMATION
Jeff Seidel's Jewish Student Information Centre
Tel Aviv University, 43 Brodetsky Street
Telephone: (03) 642 5748

Jewish Student Information Centre
Tel Aviv University Off Campus Center, 82/10
Levanon Street, Ramat Aviv

HOTELS
Adiv
5 Mendele Street
Telephone: (03) 522 9141
Fax: (03) 522 9144
Website: www.adivhotel.com

Ambassador
56 Herbert Samuel Street
Telephone: (03) 510 3993
Fax: (03) 517 6308

Armon Hayarkon
268 Hayarkon Street
Telephone: (03) 605 5271
Fax: (03) 605 8485

Avia
Ben Gurion Intl Airport area
Telephone: (03) 539 3333
Fax: (03) 539 3319

Basel
156 Hayarkon Street
Telephone: (03) 520 7711
Fax: (03) 527 0005

Bell
12 Allenby Street
Telephone: (03) 517 7011
Fax: (03) 517 4352

Carlton Tel Aviv
10 Eliezer Peri Street 63543
Telephone: (03) 520 1818
Fax: (03) 520 1886
Email: request@carlton.co.il
Website: www.carlton.co.il
268 guest rooms and suites

City
9 Mapu Street
Telephone: (03) 524 6253
Fax: (03) 524 6250

Dan Panorama
Charles Clore Park
Telephone: (03) 519 0190
Fax: (03) 517 1777
Email: panoramatelaviv@danhotels.com
Website: www.danhotels.com
Supervision: Chief Rabbinate of Israel
Central organisation: Dan Hotels Corporation Ltd.
A 5 star city hotel in a resort setting.
Located on the Mediterranean overlooking the Old City of Jaffa, comprehensive convention and conference facilities.

Dan Tel Aviv
99 Hayarkon Street
Telephone: (03) 520 2525
Fax: (03) 524 9755
Email: dantelaviv@danhotels.com
Website: www.danhotels.com
Supervision: Chief Rabbinate of Israel
Central organisation: Dan Hotels Corporation Ltd.
www.danhotels.com
Supervision: Kosher, Chief Rabbinate of Israel
5 Star Deluxe Hotel and a member of 'The Leading Hotels of the World.l

Grand Beach
250 Hayarkon Street
Telephone: (03) 543 3333
Fax: (03) 546 6589
Website: www.grandbeach.co.il
Synagogue on premises

Howard Johnson–Shalom
216 Hayarkon Street
Telephone: (03) 524 3277
Fax: (03) 523 5895

Maxim
86 Hayarkon Street, P.O.B. 3442 63903
Telephone: (03) 517 3721/5
Fax: (03) 517 3726

Metropolitan
11 15 Trumpeldor Street 63803
Telephone: (03) 519 2727
Fax: (03) 517 2626
Website: www.hotelmetropolitan.co.il

Ramat Aviv
151 Namir Road
Telephone: (03) 699 0777
Fax: (03) 699 0997

Renaissance Tel Aviv
121 Hayarkon Street 63453
Telephone: (03) 521 5555
Fax: (03) 521 5588
Email: resrv@renaissance-tlv.co.il
Website: www.renaissancehotels.com/TLVBR
Central organisation: Marriott International
All rooms with private balcony and sea view. Direct access to the beach.

Sheraton Moriah
155 Hayarkon Street
Telephone: (03) 521 6666
Fax: (03) 527 1065

Sheraton Tel Aviv Hotel & Towers
115 Hayarkon Street
Telephone: (03) 521 1111
Fax: (03) 523 3322

Tal
287 Hayarkon Street
Telephone: (03) 542 5500
Fax: (03) 542 5501

Tel Aviv Hilton
Independence Park 63405
Telephone: (03) 520 2222
Fax: (03) 527 2711

Yamit Park Plaza
79 Hayarkon Street
Telephone: (03) 517 7111
Fax: (03) 517 4719

MUSEUMS
Beit Bialik
22 Bialik Street
Telephone: (03) 525 3403
Fax: (03) 525 4530

Ben Gurion House
17 Ben Gurion Bulevard 63454
Telephone: (03) 522 1010
Fax: (03) 524 7293
Email: bghouse@bezegint.net
Website: www.ben-gurion-house.org.il
Home of Israel's first Prime Minister., contains his private library.

Eretz Israel Museum
2 Haim Levanon Street 69975
Telephone: (03) 641 5244
Fax: (03) 641 2408

Haganah Museum
23 Rothschild Boulevard 65122
Telephone: (03) 560 8624
Fax: (03) 566 1208

Helena Rubenstein Pavilion for Contemporary Art
6 Tarsat Street
Telephone: (03) 528 7196

Independece Hall
16 Rothschild Avenue 66085
Telephone: (03) 517 3942
Reconstruction of the hall in which the declaration of the establishment of the State of Israel was pronounced. rare recordings and a duplicate of the declaration.

Jabotinsky Museum
38 King George Street, P.O.B 23110 61230
Telephone: (03) 621 0806
Fax: (03) 528 5587
Website: www.jabotnsky.org
Hours: Sunday to Thursday, 8am to 4pm. Friday 9am to 1pm

Museum of the Jewish Diaspora (Beth Hatefutsoth)
Klausner Street, Ramat Aviv
Telephone: (03) 640 8000
Fax: (03) 640 5767
Website: www.bh.org.il

Tel Aviv Museum of Art
27 Shaul Hamelech Boulevard 61332
Telephone: (03) 607 7000
Fax: (03) 695 8099
Website: www.tamuseum.com
Hours: Monday to Wednesday 10am to 4pm, Tuesday and Thursday 10am to 10pm, Friday 10am to 2pm and Saturday, 10am to 4pm. Public transport: buses 9, 11, 18, 28, 70, 82, 90, 91, 111. Parking facilities.

RESTAURANTS
Chinese-Kosher
China Lee
7 Montifiore Street
Telephone: (03) 510 3140
Fax: (03) 516 4628
Website: www.rol.co.il/china-lee
Chinese food

Meat
Olive Leaf
Sheraton Tel Aviv Hotel and Towers, 115 Hayarkon
Street
Telephone: (03) 521 9300
Fax: (03) 521 9301
Website: www.sheraton.com/telaviv
Innovative cuisine with Mediterranean flavours.

Turkish-Kosher
Pasha
8 HaArba Street
Telephone: (03) 561 7778

Vegetarian-Kosher
Idelson
57 Weitzman Street
Telephone: (03) 691 1446
Also at117 Dizengogff Street (03) 529 9295 and 252 Ben
Yehuda Street (03) 544 4145

SYNAGOGUES
Bilu
122 Rothchild Blvd.
Central European rite

Ihud Shivat Zion
86 Ben Yehuda Street
Telephone: (03) 522 4047
Fax: (03) 524 0014
Central European rite.

Ashkenazi
Main Synagogue
110 Allenby Road

TOURIST INFORMATION
ISSTA
109 Ben Yehuda Street
The Ministry of Tourism
6 Wilson Street
Telephone: (03) 556 2339
The Ministry of Tourism publishes a guide called 'The Best
of Israel'. detailing shops participating in the VAT refund
scheme and recommended restaurants.

TIBERIAS
HOTELS
Ariston
19 Herzl Boulevard
Telephone: (4) 679 0244
Fax: (4) 672 2002

Astoria
13 Ohel Ya'akov Street
Telephone: (4) 672 2351
Fax: (4) 672 5108

Caesar
103 Promenade
Telephone: (4) 672 7272
Fax: (4) 679 1013

Carmel Jordan River
Habanim Street
Telephone: (4) 671 4444
Fax: (4) 679 2111

Gai Beach
Derech Hamerchatzaot
Telephone: (4) 670 0700
Fax: (4) 679 2766
Website: www.gaibeachhotel.com

Galei Kinnereth
1 Kaplan Street
Telephone: (4) 672 8888
Fax: (4) 679 0260

Golan
14 Achad Ha'am Street
Telephone: (4) 671 1555
Fax: (4) 672 1905
Email: golanhotel@hotmail.com
Website: www.golanhotel.com
Tourist hotel with restaurant

Kinar
N.E. Sea of Galilee
Telephone: (4) 673 8888
Fax: (4) 673 8811

Pagoda
Lido Beach, PO Box 253 14102
Telephone: (4) 672 5513
Fax: (4) 672 5518
Email: pagoda@lido-galilee.com
Website: www.lido-galilee.com
Open Sunday to Thursday 12.30pm to 11.30pm. Saturday
opens for dinner only.

Quiet Beach
Gedud Barak Street
Telephone: (4) 679 0125
Fax: (4) 679 0261

Restaurant/Caterer
Lavi Kibbutz Hotel
Lower Galilee 15267
Telephone: (4) 679 9450/9061
Fax: (4) 679 9399
Mobile Phone: 05032 31582
Email: hotel@lavi.co.il
Website: www.lavi.co.il
Supervision: Glatt Kosher Mehadrin
Mikvas: One each for men and women Luxury hotel with
ambiance of religious kibbutz, pastoral and secluded.
Many sights and attractions nearby and on Lavi itself.
TOURIST INFORMATION
Tourist Office
Ha banim Street, in the Archaeological Park
Telephone: (4) 672 5666

ZICHRON YA'ACHOV
MUSEUMS
Nili Museum & Aaronson House
40 Hameyasdim Street 30950
Telephone: (2) 639 0120
Fax: (2) 639 0119

RESTAURANTS
Dairy
Habayit Bayekev
Carmel Mizachi Winery, Rehov Hayayin
Telephone: (2) 629 0977
Fax: (2) 629 0957

ITALY

Italy has an ancient connection with the Jews, and was home to one of the earliest Diaspora communities. Before the Roman invasion of ancient Israel, Judah Maccabee had a representative in Rome, and one of the reasons for the invasion was the Romans' desire to access the salt supply from the Dead Sea. There were Jewish communities in Italy after the destruction of the Second Temple, as Italy was the trading hub of the Roman empire. After Christianity became the official religion in 313CE, restrictions began to be placed on the Jewish population, forcing the community to migrate from town to town across the country.

In the medieval period there was a brief flourishing of learning, but the Spanish conquered southern Italy in the fifteenth century, expelling the Jews from Sicily, Sardinia and, eventually, Naples. The first ever ghetto was established in Venice in 1516. Later in the century descendants of those expelled from Spain and Portugal arrived. Conquest by Napoleon led to the emancipation of Italian Jewry, and full equal rights were granted in 1870.

Ironically, the Italian Fascist party contained some Jewish members, as Mussolini was not anti-semitic and, even under pressure from Hitler, did not instigate any major anti-semitic policy. The situation changed after Germany's occupation of the north in 1943. Eventually almost 8,000 Italian Jews were killed in Auschwitz,

although the local population hid many of those who survived.

Today there is a central organisation which provides services for Italian Jews. There are kosher restaurants in Rome, Milan and other towns. There are also Jewish schools.

GMT +1 hours
Country calling code: (+39)
Total population: 57,523,000
Jewish population: 30,000
Emergency telephone: (police–112) (fire–115) (ambulance–116)
Electricity voltage: 220

ANCONA
COMMUNITY ORGANISATIONS
Community Offices
Via Fanti 2 bis
Telephone: (071) 202 638

MIKVAOT
Ancona Mikvaot
Via Astagno

ASTI
MUSEUMS
Asti Jewish Museum
Via Ottolenghi 8, Torino
Telephone: (0141) 539 281

SYNAGOGUES
Asti Synagogue
Via Ottolenghi 8, Torino

BOLOGNA
CAFETERIA
Comunita Ebraica Bologna
Via Gombruti 9 40123
Telephone: (051) 232 066
Fax: (051) 229 474
Supervision: Rabbi Alberto Sermoneta
Lunch Sunday to Friday; dinner Friday; closed mid July and August

COMMUNITY ORGANISATIONS
Bolgona Community Organization
Via Gombruti 9 40123
Telephone: (051) 232 066 & 227 931 (office of Rabbi)
Fax: (051) 229 474
Website: wwww.menorah.it/ceb/indice.htm

MIKVAOT
Mikveh Chaya Mushkah
Via Oreste Regnoli 17/1
Telephone: (051) 623 0316

MUSEUMS
Museo Ebraico di Bologna
Via Valdonica, 1/5 40126
Telephone: (051) 291 1280
Fax: (051) 235 430
Website: www.museoebraicobo.it
The Jewish Museum of Bologna is located in the area of the former ghetto. It was established as a means of conserving the Jewish cultural heritage that for centuries has been deeply rooted in Bologna and in the Emila Romagna region. It has a bookshop specialising in Jewish matters. Jewish itineraries.

ORGANISATIONS
Jewish Community
Via Etrurian n 6 40139
Telephone: (051) 533 699
Kosher food by arrangement

SYNAGOGUES
Bologna Synagogue
Via Mario Finzi

CASALE MONFERRATO
Community Offices
Vicolo Salomone Olper 44
Telephone: (0142) 71807
Fax: (0142) 76444
Website: www.menorah.it/qqcasale/indice.htm
The synagogue was built in 1595 is one of the most interesting in North Italy. It also contains a Jewish museum. Casale Monferrato is on the Turin–Milan road. It is advisable to make advance appointments for visiting either the synagogue or museum. Closed in the months of January, February and August.

CUNEO
TOURIST SITES
Cuneo Synagogue
Via Mondovi
Telephone: (0171) 692 007
A beautiful synagogue; parts dating from the fifteenth century. Services are now held on Yom Kippur. In 1799 a special Purim was established after the synagogue was saved from destruction by a shell.

FERRARA
COMMUNITY ORGANISATIONS
Community of Ferrara
Via Mazzini 95 44100
Telephone: (0532) 247 004
Fax: (0532) 247 004

MIKVAOT
Ferrara Mikvaot
Via Mazzini 95
Telephone: (0532) 247 004

MUSEUMS
Jewish Museum of Ferrara
Via Mazzini 95 44100 44100

Telephone: (0532) 210 228
Fax: (0532) 210 228
Website: www.comune.fe.it/museoebraico
Guided tour in English on Sunday to Thursday 10am, 11am, 12pm. Closed on Fridays and Saturdays.

SYNAGOGUES
Ferrara Synagogue
Via Mazzini 95
Telephone: (0532) 247 033

FLORENCE
Although there is a belief that Jewish merchants lived in the city during Roman times there is no real evidence to substantiate this.

The known community was established in 1437 when Jewish financiers were invited to the city. The Medici family protected the community. Following the Medici leaving in 1494 the Jews were expelled. In due course they returned and a ghetto was established in 1571. Emancipation was only achieved with the entry of Napoleon in 1799.

BAKERIES
Forno dei Ciompi
Piazza dei Ciompi
Telephone: (055) 241 256

BUTCHERS
Bruno Falsettini
Mercato Coperto di S., Ambrogio
Telephone: (055) 248 0740
8am to 10am. Order in advance specifying kosher.

Delicatessen
Gionvannino
Via dei Macci 106
Telephone: (055) 248 0734
7.30am to 1pm. Order in advance specifying kosher.

COMMUNITY ORGANISATIONS
Community Offices
Via L.C. Farini 4, Firenze 50121
Telephone: (055) 245 252
Fax: (055) 241 811
Email: comebrfi@tin.it
Website: www.firenzebraica.net
Open from Sunday to Friday from 9.30am to 12.30pm (Sunday closed in July and August).

HOTELS
Hotel Regency
Piazza Massimo D'Azeglio 3 50121
Telephone: (055) 245 247
Fax: (055) 234 6735
Email: info@regency-hotel.com
Website: www.regency-hotel.com
The Hotel overlooks the Piazza D'azeglio and is close to the city's main tourist attractions and the Synagogue

MARKET
Kosher Market and Fast Food
Via dei Pilastri 7r 50121
Telephone: (055) 240 508

MIKVAOT
Florence Mikvaot
Via L.C. Farini 4, firenze 50121
Telephone: (055) 245 252
Fax: (055) 241 811
Website: www.firenzebraica.net
To reserve phone at least 24 hours in advance

MUSEUMS
Florence Jewish Museum
Via L.C. Farini 4, Firenze 50121
Telephone: (055) 245 252
Fax: (055) 241 811
Website: www.firenzebraica.net
There is also a religious and artistic souvenir shop. Open
Sunday to Thursday. Groups are kindly requested to book in
advance. For further information and booking, please
contact the Administration Office. (55) 234 6054.

RESTAURANTS
Chabad House
6 Via dei Banchi
Traditional Jewish Meat

Vegetarian Kosher
Ruth's
Via Farini, 2/a 50121
Telephone: (055) 2480888
Fax: (055) 2480888
Email: info@kosheruth.com
Website: www.kosheruth.com
Supervision: Chief Rabbi of Jewish Community of Florence
Opening hours: from Sunday to Thursday Lunch: 12.30 to
2.30pm. Dinner: 7.30 to 10pm - Friday: open only for lunch-
Saturday: open only for dinner
For Shabbat meals and Jewish holidays: open only on
reservation.

SYNAGOGUES
Orthodox
Florence Orthodox Synagogue
Via De Banchi
Telephone: (055) 212 474
For the timetable of service ask in the Community Office.

Florence Syngagogue
Via L.C. Farini 4 Firenze 50121
Telephone: (055) 245 252
Fax: (055) 241 811
Email: comebrfi@tin.it
Website: www.firenzebraica.net
Services on Shabbat and holidays, also on Mondays and
Thursdays. After service there is a public Kiddush. The
synagogue is open for tourists from Sunday to Thursday
(hours vary). Groups should book in advance.

GENOA
Synagogue and Community Offices
Via Bertora 6 16122
Telephone: (010) 839 1513
Fax: (010) 846 1006
Email: info@cegenova.it
Service every Friday evening and Shabbat morning

GORIZIA
Gorizia Synagogue
Via Ascoli 19, Gradicia
Telephone: (03831) 532 115

LIVORNO
BUTCHERS
Corucci
Banco 25, Mercato Centrale
Telephone: (0586) 884 596

MIKVAOT
Community Offices
Piazza Benamozegh 1
Telephone: (0586) 896 290
Fax: (0586) 896 290

MUSEUMS
Jewish Museum
Via Micali 21 57123
Telephone: (0586) 896 290
Fax: (0586) 896 290
Email: comunitaebraica.livorno@gmail.com
Visits only by appointment

SYNAGOGUES
Community Offices
Piazza Benamozegh 1
Telephone: (0586) 896 290
Fax: (0586) 896 290

MANTUA
Mantua Synagogue
Via G. Govi 11, Mantova
Telephone: (0379) 321 490

MERANO
MUSEUMS
Jewish Museum
Via Schiller 14
Telephone: (0473) 236 127
Fax: (0473) 206 210
Hours: Tuesday and Wednesday 3pm to 6pm. Thursday 9am
to 12pm. Friday 3pm to 5pm.

SYNAGOGUES
Community Offices
Via Schiller 14
Telephone: (0473) 236 127
Fax: (0473) 206 210

MILAN
Home to the second largest community in Italy, (10,000). The Ambrosiana Museum (Piazza Pio XI) contains a number of Hebrew books, manuscripts and other Judaica.

BOOKSELLERS
Claudiana s.r.l. - Libreria di Milano
Via Francesco Sforza, 12/A 20122
Telephone: (02) 7602 1518
Fax: (02) 7602 1518
Email: libreria.milano@claudiana.it
Website: www.libreriecludiana.it

CULTURAL ORGANISATIONS
Milan Cultural Organization
Sally Mayer 2
Telephone: (02) 483 02806
Fax: (02) 483 04660

DOCUMENTATION CENTRE
Contemporary Jewish Documentation Centre
Via Eupili 8
Telephone: (02) 316 338
Fax: (02) 336 02728
Website: www.cdec.it
The Institute promotes the study of the history, culture and life of Jews, particularly with regard to Italy and the present age. Through its activities, the Foundation aims to preserve remembrance of Fascist and Nazi persecutions aginst Jews. It includes: the library with volumes, collections of periodicals, university theses and posters; the historical archives that house a variety of documents dating from 1850, focusing particularly on the period of 1938–1945; the video library containing videos of feature films, historical documentaries, inquiries and eyewitness accounts of events; the observatory on prejudice and anti semitism in Italy today collects testimonies and documentation, undertakes research, and supports independent studies on the subject.

MIKVAOT
Central Synagogue
Via Guastalla 19
Telephone: (02) 551 2101
Fax: (02) 5519 2699

Chaya Mushka
35 Carlo Poerio

Persian
Angelo Donati Beth Hamidrash
Via Sally Mayer 4–6

RESTAURANTS
Eschel Israel
Via Benvenuto Cellini 2/A First Floor
Telephone: (02) 545 5076
Supervision: Rav G.H. Garelik
Open weekdays. Situated on 1st floor of synagogue.

Mifgash Jewish Center
Via Montecuccoli 35 20146

Telephone: (02) 415 6199
Fax: (02) 412 91105

Dairy
Carmel
Via le San Gimignano 10 20146
Telephone: (02) 416 368
Fax: (02) 416 368
Website: www.carmelbylolita.com
Supervision: Kasrut : Rav M. Malki
Hours 12pm to 2.30pm and 6pm to 11.30pm

Meat
Glat Kosher Beit Yosf
Via Montecuccoli 35 20146
Telephone: (02) 415 6199
Fax: (02) 415 91105

Re Salomone
Via Washington 9
Telephone: (02) 469 4643
Fax: (02) 433 18049
Website: www.resalomone.it
International Meat restaurant with Mediterranean, Italian and Oriental food and takeaway.

SYNAGOGUES
Central Synagogue
Via Guastalla 19
Telephone: (02) 551 2101
Fax: (02) 5519 2699

Merkos L'Inyonei Chinuch
Via Carlo Poerio 35 20129
Telephone: (02) 295 31213

New Home for Aged
Via Leone XIII
Telephone: (02) 498 2604
Services on Sabbaths and festivals. Kosher food available upon reservation.

Oratorio Beit Yoseph ve Eliahu
Via Eupili 8
Email: eupili@gimail.com
Central organisation: Jewish Comunity of Milan

Orthodox
Ohel Yacob
Via Benvenuto Cellini 2
Telephone: (02) 545 5076

Orthodox Ashkenazi
Beth Shlomo
Galleria Vittorio Emanuele, (Via Ugo Foscolo 3 Scala 8) 20121
Telephone: (02) 8646 6118
Fax: (02) 8646 6118
Email: info@bethshlomo.it
Website: www.bethshlomo.it
Services are held on Friday evening, Shabbat, Rosh Hodesh and Holy Days

Orthodox Sephardi
Milan Sephardi Orthodox Synagogue
Via Guastalla 19
Telephone: (02) 551 2029
Fax: (02) 551 92699
Rabbi Dr Laras is the Chief Rabbi

MODENA
BUTCHERS
Macelleria Duomo
Mercato Coperto (Covered Market), Stand 25
Telephone: (059) 217 269

SYNAGOGUES
Community Offices
Piazza Mazzini 26
Telephone: (059) 223 978

NAPLES
Naples Synagogue
Via Cappella Vecchia 31, Napoli
Telephone: (081) 764 3480

PADUA
MIKVAOT
Padua Mikvaot
Via S. Martino e Solferino 9, Padova
Telephone: (049) 871 9501

SYNAGOGUES
Community Offices
Via S. Martino e Solferino 9, Padova
Telephone: (049) 875 1106

PARMA
Parma Synagogue
Vicolo Cervi 4

TOURIST SITES
Biblioteca Palatina
Palazzo della Pioltta 1 43100
Telephone: (0521) 282 217
Fax: (0521) 235 662
The collection of 1,700 Hebrew manuscripts, derived from the collection of Giovanni Bernardo Rossi (1742–1831) the first bibliographer of Hebrew incunabula Is said to be the greatest collection of Judaica put together by a Christian scholar.

PERUGIA
SYNAGOGUES
Perugia Synagogue
P. della Republica 77
Telephone: (075) 21250

PISA
Community Offices
Via Palestro 24
Telephone: (050) 542 580
Fax: (050) 542 580

Website: www.pisaebraica.it
Services are held on festivals and Holy Days. During the week the resident beadle will be glad to show visitors round the synagogue, which is famed for its beauty.

RICCIONE
HOTELS
Vienna Touring Hotel
Telephone: (054) 160 1245
In the summer kosher food is obtainable. Provides vegetarian food and particularly welcomes Jewish guests.

ROME
About half of Italian Jewry (some 15,000) live in Rome. As there has been such a long period of Jewish settlement, a Nusach Italki (Italian prayer ritual) has developed, which is practised in some synagogues in the city Kosher restuarants and kosher food are available. Titus' Arch, depicting the destruction of Jerusalem by the Romans, is in the city, and Jews were forbidden to walk under it. The ghetto of Rome is behind the Great Synagogue. A visit worth considering is to the ancient Jewish burial sites along the Appian Way. Check about tour arrangements with the Jewish Community offices, Tel: (06) 580 3667.

BAKERIES
Limentani Settimio
Via Portic0 d'Ottavia 1 186
Telephone: (06) 687 8637

Pasticceria Bernassconi
Piazza Benedetto Cairoli 16 00186
Telephone: (06) 6880 6264

BED AND BREAKFAST
Italian Kosher Bed & Breakfast
Via Nazionale 00184
Telephone: (06) 627 6995
Fax: (06) 4893 0253
Situated in the heart of the historic center.

Soggiorno il Boschetto
Via del Boschetto 13 00184
Telephone: (06) 349 182 0287
Fax: (06) 4890 7215
Website: www.soggiornoilgirasole.com
Kosher pension situated in the old town center. Kosher breakfast. Accommodation for Shabbat dinner and lunch.

Kosher
Simcha Labi
Via Imperia 2, CAP 00161
Telephone: (06) 4423 0332
Supervision: Chabad Rabbi

BOOKSELLERS
Menorah
Via del Tempio 2 00186
Telephone: (06) 687 9297
Website: www.menorah.it

BUTCHERS

Babani Ben David
Via Lorenzo il Magnifico 70 00161
Telephone: (06) 4424 3959
Supervision: Chief Rabbinate of Rome

Di Porto
Via Damaso Cerquetti 2 00152
Telephone: (06) 534 6992
Supervision: Chief Rabbinate of Rome

Di Veroli
Via Galla e Sidama 51 00199
Telephone: (06) 8620 7971
Supervision: Chief Rabbinate of Rome

Gepe Gean
Via Stamira 2/B 00162
Telephone: (06) 4424 4055
Supervision: Chief Rabbinate of Rome

Ouazana
Via S. Gherardi 16 18 00146
Telephone: (06) 556 5231
Via Giacomo Boni 18 00162
Telephone: (6) 4420 2626
Supervision: Chief Rabbinate of Rome

Pascarella
Via Cesare Pascarella 36 00153
Telephone: (06) 588 1698
Supervision: Chief Rabbinate of Rome

Sciunnach Umberto
Via F. Maurolico 28–30 00146
Telephone: (06) 559 4681; 5530 7780
Fax: (06) 4549 1747
Supervision: Chief Rabbinate of Rome
Meat and prepared food

Spizzichino
Via del Forte Bravetta 148 00164
Telephone: (06) 6615 7796
Supervision: Chief Rabbinate of Rome

Terracina
Via S. Maria del Pianto 62 00186
Telephone: (06) 6880 1364
Supervision: Chief Rabbinate of Rome

COMMUNITY ORGANISATIONS

**Unione delle Comunia Ebraiche Italiane
(Union of Italian Jewish Communities)**
Lungotevere R. Sanzio 9
Telephone: (06) 580 3667
Fax: (06) 589 9569
Website: www.ucei.it
Information on Italian Jewry, its monuments and history
may be obtained here.

DELICATESSEN

Kosher Bistrot
Terracina Angelo, via Santa Maria del Pianto 68 69
Telephone: (06) 686 4398
Supervision: Chief Rabbinate of Rome

Kosher Point Minimarket
Via Orso Maria Corbino 17 00146
Telephone: (06) 556 5760

EMBASSY

Embassy of Israel
Via Michele Mercati 14 00197
Telephone: (06) 322 1541
Fax: (06) 3619 8555
Website: www.israel amb.it

Embassy of Israel to The Holy See
Via Michele Mercati 12 00197
Telephone: (06) 3619 8690
Fax: (06) 3619 8626

GUEST HOUSE

Locanda Carmel
Via Goffredo Mameli 11 00153
Telephone: (06) 580 9921
Fax: (06) 581 8853
Email: reservation@hotelcarmel.it
Website: www.hotelcarmel.it
Supervision: Rav Shalom Bahbout
Pension situated in the old district of Trastevere. Kosher
breakfast only.

KOSHER STORES

Kosher Delight
Via Giacomo Boni 18a
Telephone: (06) 4420 2626
Also at:
Via S Gherardi 16/18 Tel: 5565 5231 and
Via S Gherardi 44/a Tel: 5565 5231

MEDIA

Newspapers

Shalom
Lungotevere Cenci 1
Telephone: (06) 687 6816
Fax: (06) 686 8324
Website: www.shalom.it
Monthly

MIKVAOT

Rome Mikvaot
Lungotevere Cenci (Tempio) 9
Telephone: (06) 6840 0651
Ask for Mrs Elena Di Capua

Rome Mikvaot
Via Balbo 33
Telephone: (06) 721 4210

MUSEUMS

The Jewish Museum of Rome
Lungotevere Cenci (tempio) 00186
Telephone: (06) 6840 0661
Fax: (06) 6840 0639
Email: info@museoebraico.roma.it
Website: www.museoebraico.roma.it
Renovated in November 2005

Hours: Sunday-Thursday 10-4.15pm, Friday 9-1.15pm (16th June-15th September Sunday-Thursday 10-6.15pm, Friday 10-3.15pm). Closed 1st January, 15th August and Jewish holidays.Guided tours of the synagogue in Italian and English every hour. Guided tours of the synagogue in Italian, English, French, German, Hebrew for groups (reservation required)

Library
Museo Storico della Liberazione
Via Tasso 145 00185
Telephone: (06) 700 3866
Fax: (06) 7720 3514
Email: viatasso@viatasso.it
Website: www.viatasso.eu
The Museum is placed in the same building used as a prison by the German Security Police during the Nazi occupation of Rome, from 11 September 1943 to 4 June 1944. It still keeps unchanged the main aspects of that period and the cells are still as they were during the German occupation. The Museum displays original documents, newspapers,posters, war letters from the fronts as well as objects belonging to the men jailed here and their moving memories recorded on the walls of the isolation cell. The museum was extended in 2001 with new displays dedicated to the fate of Roman Jews between 1938 and 1944
Information on the specialist library (Nazi occupation and resistance), the papers and audiovisual archives is on the website www.viatasso.eu

RELIGIOUS ORGANISATIONS
The Italian Rabbinical Council
Headquarters, Lungotevere Sanzio 9
Telephone: (06) 580 3667; 580 3670

RESTAURANTS
Yesh
Via Silvestro Gherardi, 51 (zona Marconi) 00146
Telephone: (06) 556 1697
Email: info@yesh.it
Website: www.yesh.it
Via Silvestro Gherardi, 51 (zona Marconi)
00146 Roma - Italy
Tel, 065561697
Email info
Dairy
Ristorante Yotvatc
Piazza Cenci 70 186
Telephone: (06) 6813 4481
Supervision: Chief Rabbinate of Rome
Open at noon

Meat
Gan Eden
Via Eleonora d'Arborea
Telephone: (06) 4423 1457
Kasher Pizza
Via Luigi Magrini 12 146
Telephone: (06) 559 0790

Kosher Bistrot
Via S. Maria del Pianto, 6869 186
Telephone: (06) 686 4398
Fax: (06) 6880 1364
La Taverna Del Ghetto
Via Portico D'Ottavia 8
Telephone: (06) 68809771
Website: www.latavernadelghetto.com
Oriental Foods Kosher
Via Livorno, 8 10
Telephone: (06) 440 4840
Fax: (06) 440 4840
Yesh
Via Sivestro Gherardi, 51
Telephone: (06) 556 1697

SYNAGOGUES
Orthodox Ashkenazi
Beth Habad Synagogue
Via Ruggero Fauro 94 00197
Telephone: (06) 8069 227

Orthodox Nussah Italk
Oratorio Di Castro
Via Ceszie Balbo 33
Daily services
The Great Synagogue
Lungotevere Cenci (Tempio)
Telephone: (06) 6840 0061
Fax: (06) 6840 0655
Daily services

Orthodox Sephardi
Tempio Beth El
Via Padova 92, Piazza Bologna 00161
Telephone: (06) 4424 2857; 440 3027
Fax: (06) 4429 1093
Supervision: Shalom Teshuba & Bondi Nahum
Open every day of the year.
Tempio Spagnolo
Via Catalana, (behind the great synagogue)
Daily services.

Orthodox–Ashkenazi
Agudat Ashkenazlm
Via Cesare Balbo 33 00184
Daily services in basement

TOURS
G. Palombo
Via Maggia 7
Telephone: (06) 810 3716; 993 2074
Guides can be contacted also through the Jewish Museum, Tel: (06) 6840 0661
Ruben E. Popper
12 Via dei Levii
Telephone: (06) 761 0901
Telephone number is afternoons only

SENIGALLIA
SYNAGOGUES
Senigallia Synagogue
Via dei Commercianti

SIENA
Siena Synagogue
Vicolo delle Scotte 14
Telephone: (0577) 284 647
The committee has issued a brochure in English giving the
history of the community which dates back to medieval
times. The synagogue dates from 1750. Services are held on
the Sabbath and High HolyDays. Further information from
Burroni Bernardi, Via del Porrione. M. Savini, via Salicotta
23. Tel: 283 140 (close to the synagogue)

SPEZIA
Spezia Synagogue
Via 20 Settembre 165

TRIESTE
Trieste Synagogue
Via Donizetti 2
Telephone: (040) 631 898

TOURS
Smile Tech Srl - Smileservice
Via Valdirivo 19 34132
Telephone: (040) 348 1631
Fax: (040) 348 7023
Website: www.smileservice.it
Smile Tech Srl organises tours around the Jewish sites of
the region Friuli Venezia Giulia.

TURIN
BOOKSELLERS
Biblioteca 'E. Artom'
P.tta Primo Levi 12, Torino 10125
Telephone: (011) 658 585
Website: www.torinoebraica.it

Libreria Claudiana
Via Principe Tommaso 1, Torino 10125
Telephone: (011) 669 2458
Fax: (011) 669 2458
Email: libreria.torin@claudiana.it

Judaica
Libreria Internazionale Luxemburg
via Cesare Battisti 10123
Telephone: (011) 561 3896
Fax: (011) 540 370
Email: luxbooks@libero.it
Website: www.librerialuxemburg.com
Specializing in Hebrew and Israeli subjects. Open 7 days a
week 8am to 7.30pm.

COMMUNITY ORGANISATIONS
Community Centre
P.tta Primo Levi 12, Torino 10125

Telephone: (011) 658 585
Fax: (011) 669 1173

GROCERIES
Panetteria Bertino
Via B. Galliari 14, Torino 10125
Telephone: (011) 669 9527

MIKVAOT
Turin Synagogue
P.tta Primo Levi 12 Torino 10125
Telephone: (011) 658 585
Fax: (011) 669 1173
Email: comebrato@libero.it

RESTAURANTS
Salomon e Augusto Segre–Jewish Rest Home
Via B. Galliari 13, Torino 10125
Telephone: (011) 658 585
Only by reservation

SYNAGOGUES
Turin Synagogue
P.tta Primo Levi 12 10125
Telephone: (011) 658 585
Fax: (011) 669 1173
Email: comebrato@libero.it
Mon.&Thur. 7am and sunset; Shabbat 9am and half an
hour before sunset (winter) or 6.30pm (summer).
TOURIST SITES
Mole Atonellianta
Now the National Cinema Museum, it was originally built
in the nineteenth century and was meant to be the
grandest synagogue in Europe but was never completed.

URBINO
SYNAGOGUES
Urbino Synagogue
Via Stretta

VENICE
Jews settled in Venice early in the tenth century
and became an important factor in the
economic life of the city. In 1516 however, the
authorities banished the Jews to the Ghetto
Nuovo (new foundry) district so establishing
the first ghetto. The high walls surrounding the
area still exist.

The 14th century Jewish cemetery (the second
oldest in Europe) has recently been restored
and was reopened in 1999 for guided tours (for
details call the Jewish Museum).

GIFT SHOP
Arte Ebraica Shalom
Ghetto Nuovo 1219
Telephone: (041) 720 092
Jewish articles & religious appurtenances are available

David's Shop di David Curiel
Campo del Ghetto Nuovo 2895 30121
Telephone: (041) 275 0418
Fax: (041) 275 0418
Email: davidshop@yahoo.com
Website: www.davidshop.com
Jewish articles & religious appurtenances are available
HOTELS

Kosher
Locanda del Ghetto
Campo del Ghetto Novo, Cannaregio 2893 30121
Telephone: (041) 275 9292
Fax: (041) 275 7987
Website: www.locandadelghetto.com

JEWISH COMMUNITY OF VENICE
Bakery/Pizzareia
Jewish Rest Home
2874 Cannaregio, Ghetto Nuovo
Telephone: (041) 716 002
It is necessary to book in the morning.
Kosher ice cream
Community Offices
Community Offices
1146 Cannaregio, Ghetto Vecchio 30121
Telephone: (041) 715 012
Fax: (041) 524 1862
Supervision: Elia Richetti
Central organisation: Union Of italian Jewish Communities

Guset House
Jewish Rest Home
2874 Cannaregio, Ghetto Nuovo 30121
Telephone: (041) 716 002
Fax: (041) 714 394
Kosher meals and accommodation available. Early booking
is advised.

Libraries
Jewish Library and Archives 'Renato Maestro'
2899 Cannaregio, Ghetto Nuovo / 30121
Telephone: (041) 718 833

Mikvaot
Jewish Rest Home
2874 Cannaregio Ghetto Nuovo
Telephone: (041) 722 036
Booking 24 hours in advance

Museums
Jewish Museum
Canneregio, Ghetto Nuovo 2902/B
Telephone: (041) 715 359
Fax: (041) 723 007
Jewish Museum (Open Sunday through Friday from 10am
to 4.30pm from October to May and from 10am to 7pm
from June to September). Closed on Saturdays and Jewish
holidays. Guided visits to the synagogue in English start
every hour from the Jewish Museum. Sandwiches and
drinks are available.

Synagogues
Schola Levantina
1228 Cannaregio, Ghetto Vecchio
Telephone: (041) 715 012
Fax: (041) 524 1862
Shabbath services are held during winter, Friday about one hour before sunset and Saturday at 9am; on Saturday at 4pm (later in spring and summer). Tefillah Mincha and Seuda Shelishit.

Schola Spagnola
1149 Cannaregio, Ghetto Vecchio
Telephone: (041) 715 012
Fax: (041) 524 1862
Shabbath services are held during winter, Friday about one hour before sunset and Saturday at 9am; on Saturday at 4pm (later in spring and summer). Tefillah Mincha and Seuda Shelishit.

RESTAURANTS
Dairy and Parve
Teva
2659 Telephone: (041) 524 4486

Meat
Gam Gam
1122 Cannaregio, Sottoportico di Ghetto Vecchio
Telephone: (041) 715 284
Fax: (041) 715 284
Shabbat arrangements available. Open lunch and dinner. Glatt kosher.

SYNAGOGUES
Orthodox
Chabad of Venice
Cannaregio, Ghetto Nuovo 2915
Telephone: (041) 715 284
Fax: (041) 715 284
Website: www.jewishvenice.org
Shabbat and Holiday hospitality available

VERCELLI
COMMUNITY ORGANISATIONS
Community Offices
Via Oldoni 20

SYNAGOGUES
Vercelli Synagogue
Via Foa 70 c.p. 91 13100
Fax: (03)2198 7412
Mobile Phone: 3392579283
Email: didattica.comebravc@libero.it
Built in 1878

VERONA
COMMUNITY ORGANISATIONS
Community Centre
Via Portici 3
Telephone: (045) 800 7112
Fax: (045) 804 8295

SYNAGOGUES
Verona Synagogue
Via Portici 3

VIAREGGIO
CONTACT INFORMATION
Mr Joseph Sananes
Via Pacinotti 172/B 55049
Telephone: (0584) 961 025
Fax: (0584) 49871
Email: joseph.sananes@tirrenotour.it
Private office: Tirreno Tour, 26 Viale Carducci, Tel: (0584) 30777, during daytime

SICILY

Although there are very few Jews in Sicily today, there is a long and varied history of Jewish Settlement on the island stretching back to at least the sixth century and possibly according to some scholars to the first or second centuries.

By the late Middle Ages, the community numbered 40,000. In 1282, Sicily came under Spanish rule. A century or so later, there was a wave of massacres of Jews, and another in 1474. These culminated in the introduction of the inquisition in 1479 and the expulsion of the Jews in 1492.

There are no other specific locations of interest to travellers.

JAMAICA
Spanish During the time of Spanish colonisation, Jamaica witnessed many *Conversos* arriving from Portugal. After the British took over in 1655 many of these could again practise Judaism openly. Soon other Jews, mainly Sephardim, followed from Brazil and other nearby countries. The community received full equality in 1831 (before a similar step was taken in England).

The Jews played an important role in Jamaican life, and in 1849 the House of Asembly did not meet on Yom Kippur! However, assimilation and intermarriage took their toll and in 1921 the Ashkenazi and Sephardi synagogues combined. There is now only one synagogue on the island, but there are remains of old synagogues in Kingston, Port Royal and other towns.

Community life includes WIZO, B'nai B'rith and a school (the Hillel Academy). The community lost members after the Cuban revolution, because many feared a similar revolution in Jamaica.

GMT -5 hours
Country calling code: **(+1 809)**
Total population: **2,590,000**
Jewish population: **300**
Emergency telephone: **(police–119) (fire–110) (ambulance–110)**
Electricity voltage: **110**

KINGSTON
SYNAGOGUES
Shaare Shalom
Duke Street & Charles Street
Telephone: (9) 927 7948
Fax: (9) 978 6240
Services, Friday, 5.30pm (all year), Shabbat, 10am; festivals, 9am all year round

JAPAN

After Japan became open to Western ideas and Westerners in the mid-nineteenth century, a trickle of Jewish immigrants from the Russian Empire, the UK and the USA began to make their homes there. The first Jewish community at Yokohama was founded in 1860. Many were escaping anti-semitism and by 1918 there were several thousand in the country.

Individual Japanese, despite being allied to Nazi Germany, did not adopt the anti-Semitic attitude of the Nazis, and the Japanese consul in Kovno Lithuania even helped the Mir Yeshivah escape from occupied Europe in 1940.

The post-war American occupation of the country brought many Jewish servicemen, and the community was also augmented by Jews escaping unrest in China. In recent years, there have been some Jewish 'gaijin', or (foreign workers).

In Tokyo there is a synagogue which provides meals on Shabbat, a Sunday school, and offices for the Executive Board of the Jewish Community of Japan, which is the central body.

GMT +9 hours
Country calling code: **(+81)**
Total population: **125,638,000**
Jewish population: **1,500**
Emergency telephone: **(police–110) (fire–119) (ambulance–119)**
Electricity voltage: **110**

HIROSHIMA
TOURIST SITES
Holocaust Education Centre
866 Nakatsuhara, Miyuki, Fukuyama 720
Telephone: (849) 558 001
Fax: (849) 558 001
Website: www.urba.ne.jp/home/hecjpn/
Open Tuesday, Wednesday, Friday and Saturday, 10.30 am to 4.30 pm

KOBE
SYNAGOGUES
Orthodox Sephardi
Ohel Shelomoh (Jewish Community of Kansai)
4–12–12 Kitano cho, Cho ku 650-0002
Telephone: (78) 221 7236
Fax: (78) 242 7254
Mobile Phone: 08061 440652
Website: www.jckkobe.com
Kabalat Shabbat sunset Friday, Shacharit 10.Saturday, each followed by kiddush meal (groups please enquire in advance), Mincha 2.30pm. Mikveh by prior appointment.

TOKYO
COMMUNITY ORGANISATIONS
Japan Jewish Community Centre
8–8 Hiroo, 3 chome, Shibuya ku 150 150-0012
Telephone: (3) 3400 2559
Fax: (3) 3400 1827
Website: www.jccjapan.co.jp

EMBASSY
Embassy of Israel
3 Niban cho, Chiyodaku
Telephone: (3) 3264 0911
Website: www.tokyo.mfa.gov.it

MIKVAOT
Tokyo Mikvaot
Telephone: (3) 3409 9443
Fax: (3) 3409 9443

RESTAURANTS
Jewish Community of Japan
8–8 Hiroo, 3 chome, Shibuya ku 150-0012
Telephone: (3) 3400 2559
Fax: (3) 3400 1827
Website: www.jccjapan.or.jp
They sell prepared foods and kosher wine, as well as serve meals on Friday evening and Shabbat. Reservation strongly recommended.

Kosher
Chabad Tokyo Japan
1-25-18 Sanno, Ota-ku 143-0023
Telephone: (3) 3772 7707
Website: www.chabadjapan.org
Mini Market

Kosher Food
Kosher Delica
2-7-31 Minami Azubu, Minato-ku
Telephone: (3) 5441 4770
Mobile Phone: 09036 837707
Email: info@chabadjapan.org
Website: www.chabadjapan.org; www
kosherdelicia.com
Supervision: Central Vaad Hakashrus of Japan
Central organisation: Chabad House of Japan
Hours: Sun to Fri 10am to 4pm
Mini market

SUPERMARKET
National Azabu
4–5–2 Monami Azabu
Telephone: (3) 3442 3186
Some kosher items stocked. Telephone for details.

Nissin
2–34–2 Higashi Azubu
Telephone: (3) 3583 4586
Some kosher items stocked. Telephone for details.

SYNAGOGUES
Beth David Synagogue
8–8 Hiroo, 3 chome, Shibuya-ku 150-0015
Telephone: (3) 3400 2559
Fax: (3) 3400 1827
Website: www.jccjapan.or.jp
Services are held Friday evening at 6.30pm (7pm during
summer); Shabbat morning, 10am; and on Holy days and
festivals. Advance notification requested. Mikvah on
premises.

Chabad Japan
2–27–23 Ebisu Shibuya ku 150 0013
Telephone: (3) 5789 2846
Fax: (3) 5789 2847
Website: www.chabadjapan.com
Contact them for details of services and meal reservations

KAZAKHSTAN

Essentially this community began when
the Soviets rescued several thousand Jews
at the time of the Nazi invasion of the
Soviet Union in 1941. Others joined after
the war. The community is mainly based
in Almaty, the former capital, and also in
Chimkent. Some 2,000 Bukharan and Tat
Jews also live in the country.

The central organisation is the Mitzvah
Association, which heads various Jewish
groups. It even has a chair on the All-
Peoples Assembly of Kazakhstan. There is
a high rate of emigration to Israel.

GMT +6 hours
Country calling code: (+7)
Total population: **16,223,000**
Jewish population: **10,000**
Emergency telephone: **(police–03)** **(fire–03)**
(ambulance–03)
Electricity voltage: **220**

ALMATY
COMMUNITY ORGANISATIONS
Almaty Community Organization
206 e Raimbek St.
Telephone: (3272) 539 358
Fax: (3272) 507 770
Website: www.chabad.kz
Also has a store, kosher butcher, library and mikvah
**The Association of Jewish Communities in
Kazakhstan**
66/120 Buhar Zhirau Street 480057
Telephone: (3272) 450 043
Fax: (3272) 450 043

RESTAURANTS
Kosher
Kosher
Suyuybaya 2
Telephone: (3272) 259 7074

SYNAGOGUES
Orthodox
Almaty Synagogue
206e Raimbek St.
Telephone: (3272) 439 358
Fax: (3272) 507 770

ASTANA
Jewish Center of Astana
11 Respublki Street, #3 473000
Telephone: (3172) 216 913

CHIMKENT
COMMUNITY ORGANISATIONS
Jewish Community in Chimkent
President, Grigory Tzeytlin, 76 Makarova St.
486012Gp JP 500

SYNAGOGUES
Sephardi
Chimkent Synagogue
Svobody Street, 47th Lane

KENYA

GMT +3 hours
Country calling code: **(254)**
Total population: **33,144,000**
Jewish population: **400**
Emergency telephone: **(police–999) (fire–999)**
(ambulance–999)
Electricity voltage: **220/24**

NAIROBI

COMMUNITY ORGANISATIONS
Community Centre
Vermont Memorial Hall
Open Monday, Tues

CULTURAL ORGANISATIONS
Community Centre
Vermont Memorial Hall
Open Monday, Tuesday, Friday 9am to 1pm; Wednesday
2.3pm to 5.30 pm; services Friday evening at 6.30 pm;
Saturday morning at 8am. All festivals. Kosher chickens
available.

SYNAGOGUES
Nairobi Hebrew Congregation
cnr. University Way & Uhuru Highway. PO Box
40990 00100
Telephone: (20) 2222 770; 2219 703
Fax: (20) 2571 655
Email: info@nhc.co.ke
Website: www.nhc.co.ke

KYRGYZSTAN

This central Asian ex-Soviet republic has
only a short history of Jewish settlement.
The community originated from migrants
after the Russian Revolution and evacuees
from the German advance into the Soviet
Union in the Second World War. As a result,
community members are almost all Russian
speakers and are assimilated into the
Russian minority of the country.

Before the collapse of the Soviet Union there
was no organised community.There has
been a synagogue in the capital Bishkek
since 1991, where there is also a Jewish
library and an Aish Ha Torah centre. The
main umbrella group is the Menorah Society
of Jewish Culture.

GMT +5 hours
Country calling code: **(+996)**
Total population: **4,856,000**
Jewish population: **2,500**

Emergency telephone: **(police–03) (fire–03)**
(ambulance–03)
Electricity voltage: **220**

BISHKEK

Bishkek Synagogue
193 Suymbaeva (Karpinsky) Street
Telephone: (3312) 681 966
Fax: (3312) 681 966

LATVIA

The Jews in the medieval principalities of
Courland and Livonia represent the earliest
Jewish settlement in Latvia. Tombstones
from the fourteenth century have been
found. After the Russian take-over Jews
were only allowed to live in the area if they
were considered 'useful', or had lived there
before the Russians took control, because
the area was outside the 'Pale of Settlement'
that the Russian Empire had designated for
the Jews.

The Jews contributed much to Latvia's
development, but this was never recognised
by the government, which tried to restrict
their influence in business matters. Religious
Jewish life, however, was strong. When the
Nazis invaded Latvia, 90 per cent of the
85,000 Jews were systematically murdered
by them and their Latvian collaborators.

The bulk of today's community originates
from immigration into Latvia after the war,
although 3,000 Holocaust survivors did
return to Latvia. Before the collapse of
communism there was much Jewish dissi-
dent activity. There is a Jewish school and
a Jewish hospital. There are some
Holocaust memorial sites in the capital
Riga, and also in the Bierkernieki Forest,
where 46,000 Holocaust victims were shot.

GMT +2 hours
Country calling code: (+371)
Total population: **2,474,000**
Jewish population: **10,000**
Emergency telephone: **(police–02)** **(fire–01)**
(ambulance–03)
Electricity voltage: **220**

DAUGAVPILS
COMMUNITY ORGANISATIONS
Jewish Community Organization
Saules Street 47
Fax: (54) 8254 24658

SYNAGOGUES
Daugavpils Synagogue
Cietoksna 38 LV5400
Mobile Phone: 25902071

LIEPAJA
COMMUNITY ORGANISATIONS
Jewish Community
Kungu Street 21
Telephone: (34) 25336

REZHITSA
SYNAGOGUES
Rezhitsa Synagogue
Kaleyu Street

RIGA
CULTURAL ORGANISATIONS
Latvian Society for Jewish Culture
Skolas 6 LV1322
Telephone: (2) 289 580
Fax: (2) 821 494

EMBASSY
Embassy of Israel
Elizabetes Street 2a LV1340
Telephone: (2) 732 0980
Fax: (2) 783 0170

JEWISH CENTER
Chabad Lubavitch Latvia
141 Lacplesa St., LV1003
Telephone: (2) 6720 4022
Fax: (2) 6783 0444
Mobile Phone: 371 2951 8700
Website: www.jewish.lv/www.chbad.lv
Visitors welcomed for Shabbat and holiday meals. Kosher
Cafe L'Chaim at Skolas 6 (entrance from Dzirnavu) open
10am to 10pm, takeout available.

MUSEUMS
The Jewish Museum of Riga
6 Skolas Street LV1322
The museum is small but has many moving exhibits and
photos. A short video is shown depicting the tragedy of the
Holocaust in Latvia.

SYNAGOGUES
Orthodox
Riga Central Synagogue
6/8 Peitavas Street, Riga 1050
Telephone: (2) 721 4507
Fax: (2) 721 4507
Website: www.jrcr.co
Services 3 times daily. Call or write for schedule.

LITHUANIA

The history of Lithuanian Jewry is as old
as the state of Lithuania itself. There were
Jews in the country in the fourteenth century, when Grand Duke Gedeyminus
founded the state. The community eventually grew, and produced many famous
yeshivas and great commentators, such as
the Vilna Gaon. The community began to
emigrate (particularly to South Africa) at
the beginning of the nineteenth century;
even so, in 1941 there were still 160,000
Jews in the country. Ninety-five per cent of
these were murdered in the Holocaust by
the local population as well as the Nazis.

The remaining post-war community
included some who had hidden or had
managed to survive by other means, and
some Jews from other parts of the Soviet
Union. Interestingly, the Lithuanian Soviet
Socialist Republic was more tolerant of
Jewish activity than some of the neighbouring republics, such as Latvia. Now
that Lithuania is independent, Jewish life
is free once again.

The Lubavitch movement is present, and
there are synagogues in the capital Vilnius
(known to many as Vilna) and Kaunas.

There is also a school and it is possible to study Yiddish. There are tours available to show the old Jewish life in Lithuania. The grave of the Vilna Gaon can be visited, as well as Paneriai, otherwise known as Ponary, where thousands of Jews were shot during the Holocaust.

GMT +2 hours
Country calling code: **(+370)**
Total population: **3,701,000**
Jewish population: **5,000**
Emergency telephone: **(police–02) (fire–01) (ambulance–03)**
Electricity voltage: **220**

DRUSKININKAI
COMMUNITY ORGANISATIONS
Jewish Community
9/15 Sporto Street
Telephone: 54590

KAUNAS
Kaunas Community Organization
26 B Gedimino Street
Telephone: (7) 203 717
Fax: (7) 201 135
Hours of opening Sunday to Thursday 3pm to 6pm

SYNAGOGUES
Kaunas Synagogue
11 Ozheshkienes Street

KLAIPEDA
COMMUNITY ORGANISATIONS
Jewish Community
Ziedu Skersqatvis 3
Telephone: (46) 493 758
Email: lavan@takas.lt

PANEVEZYS
Panevezys Community Organization
6/22 Sodu Street 5300
Telephone: (54) 68848

SHIAULIAI
Shiauliai Community Organization
24 Vyshinskio
Telephone: (1) 26795

VILNIUS
Otherwise known as Vilna, this city used to be known as the 'Jerusalem of the North'. Jews started to live in Vilnius during the middle of the sixteenth century. In due course it became a pre-eminent centre for rabbinical studies. The town still has the largest community of Lithuanian Jews, and there are many sites of

historical interest, including the Vilna Gaon's grave and the State Jewish Museum.

BAKERIES
Matzah Bakery
39 Pylimo Street
Telephone: (5) 61 2523

COMMUNITY ORGANISATIONS
Jewish Community of Lithuania
Pylimo Street4 2nd Floor 01117
Telephone: (5) 61 1736, 65 2139
Website: www.litjews.org
Opening hours: Monday to Thursday 10am to 6pm, Friday 10am to 4pm

CULTURAL ORGANISATIONS
The Israel Centre of Cultures and Art in Lithuania
4 Pylimo, 2nd Floor 2001
Telephone: (5) 61 1736 or 65 2139

MUSEUMS
The Vilna Gaon Jewish State Museum
Naugarduko str. 10/2 LT 01117
Telephone: (5) 231 2357
Fax: (5) 212 7083
Email: jewishmuseum@jmuseum.lt
Website: www.jmuseum.lt
Supervision: Markas Zingeris/Rachel Kostanian
The Tarbut School, Exhibition and seat of Jewish Community.
Opening hours: Tolerance Center (Naugarduko str.): Monday to Thursday 10am to 6pm and Sunday 10am to 2pm.
Holocaust(Katastrophe) branch, Pamenkalnio 12, open from 10am to 5pm Monday to Thursday, Sunday 10am to 4pm. tel: 2620730

The Vilna Gaon Jewish State Museum - The Holocaust Exhibition
The Green House, Pamenkalnio 12
Opening hours: Mon to Thu 9am to 5pm and Sun 10am to 4pm.

The Vilna Gaon Jewish State Museum - Tolerance Centre
Naugarduko10/2, LT 01141
Telephone: (5) 262 4590
Fax: (5) 212 7083
Email: jewishmuseum@jmuseum.lt
Website: www.jmuseum.lt
Opening hours: Mon to Thu 10am to 6pm and Sun 10am to 4pm.

SYNAGOGUES
Central synagogue of Vilnius Chabad
12 Saltiniu g. St. 2006
Telephone: (5) 250 387

Main Synagogue (Choral Synagogue)
39 Pylimo Street
Telephone: (5) 61 2523

LUXEMBOURG

The small community in Luxembourg faced massacres and expulsions during medieval times, and Jews only began to resettle here several hundred years later. Napoleon heralded the rebirth of the community when he annexed Luxembourg, and by 1823 a synagogue had been built but the community remained small, although in 1899 another synagogue was built.

Later many refugees from the Nazis arrived in the country, bringing the number of Jews to nearly 4,000. After the Nazi takeover 750 Luxembourg Jews were killed, but many others were saved by the local population.

The present community is generally prosperous and assimilated. The Consistoire Israelite, established by Napoleon, is recognised by the government as the representative of the community, and is also financed by the government. The Orthodox synagogue is situated fairly centrally in Luxembourg City.

GMT +1 hours
Country calling code: **(+352)**
Total population: **417,000**
Jewish population: **600**
Emergency telephone: **(police–133) (fire–112)**
(ambulance–112)
Electricity voltage: **220**

ESH SUR ALZETTE
Esh Sur Alzette Synagogue
52 rue de Canal
Services held on Friday evenings

LUXEMBOURG CITY
COMMUNITY ORGANISATIONS
Consistoire Israelite de Luxembourg
45 avenue Monterey 2018
Telephone: 452914
Fax: 473772

GROCERIES
Calon
rue de Reins 3

North East

HONORARY CONSULATE
Honorary Consul General of Israel

KASHRUT INFORMATION
Luxembourg City Kashrut
34 rue Alphonse munchen 2172
Telephone: 452366

SYNAGOGUES
Luxembourg City Synagogue
45 avenue Monterey
Telephone: 452914
Fax: 250430

MACEDONIA

At the southern end of the former Yugoslavia, this new country has an ancient Jewish heritage dating back to Roman times. The Jews took advantage of the area's favourable commercial position, lying between Turkey and Western Europe, and the remains of a synagogue at Stobei dating back to the second and third centuries is evidence of a once thriving Jewish community.

Iberian Jews escaping the Inquisition settled in the area, and brought with them Sephardi customs and the Ladino language (based on Spanish). The fate of the 8,000 Macedonian Jews under Bulgarian occupation during the Second World War is in stark contrast to the fate of the Bulgarian Jews. The Macedonian Jews were deported to their deaths, yet the Bulgarian Jews were saved by the defiance of the king and the people. Only ten per cent of the Macedonian community survived, of whom many have emigrated to Israel.

Today's community is mainly based in the capital Skopje, but there are no synagogues and there is little access to Jewish life. However, the community does have contact with Jews in Serbia and Greece.

GMT +1 hours
Country calling code: **(+389)**
Total population: **2,190,000**
Jewish population: **Under 100**
Emergency telephone: **(police–92) (fire–93)**
(ambulance–94)
Electricity voltage: **220**

SKOPJE
Community Offices / Beth Yaakov
Borka Talevski Street 24 1000
Telephone: (2) 3237 543
Fax: (2) 3214 880

MALTA

There is evidence of an ancient Jewish community on Malta, as archaeologists have discovered remains from 2,000 years ago. Malta fell into Arab hands in the early Middle Ages when there were still a few Jews on the island. The island then changed to Sicilian hands and, in 1492, the Jews were expelled.

Between the sixteenth and eighteenth centuries the island was used as a prison for Jewish captives of the Knights of St John. They were held for ransom, but managed to find time to build a synagogue. A synagogue in Spur Street, Valetta, opened in 1912, but was demolished in 1995 as part of a redevelopment scheme.

GMT +1 hours
Country calling code: **(+356)**
Total population: **378,000**
Jewish population: **100**
Emergency telephone: **(police–191) (fire–199) (ambulance–196)**
Electricity voltage: **24**

BIRKIRKARA
COMMUNITY ORGANISATIONS
Birkirkara Community Organization
P.O. Box 4
Telephone: 445924

TA XBIEX
SYNAGOGUES
Conservative
Jewish Community of Malta
Flat 1, Florida Mansions, Enrico Mizzi St., MSD 02 XBX 1452
Telephone: 2123 7309; 2131 2666
Spokesperson: 2138 6266
Fax: 2124 9410
Website: www.jewsofmalta.org
Spokesperson: 2138 6266
Synagogue services on the 1st & 3rd Sabbath of the month, and on all High Holidays

MARTINIQUE

GMT -4 hours
Country calling code: **(+596)**
Emergency telephone: **(police–17) (fire–18) (ambulance–633 333)**
SAMU (Urban Ambulatory Medical Service) 751 575/15 Sea Rescue 709 292

SCHOELCHER
Kenafe Haarets A.C.I.M.
12 rue de l'Ecole Hoteliere 97233
Telephone: 616 672
A community centre is also located here, which supplies kosher food, plus a kosher meat restaurant.

MELILLA

Jewish Community
Akda Duguese de la Victoria 52004
Telephone: (3495) 267 4057
Fax: (3495) 267 4057

SYNAGOGUES
Isaac Benarroch
Calle Marina 7
Jacob Almonznino
Calle Luis de Sotomayor 4
Salama
Calle Alfonso XII 6
Solinquinos
Calle O'Donnell
Yamin Benarroch
Calle Lopez Moreno 8

MEXICO

Conversos were the first Jews in the country, and some achieved high positions in early Spanish colonial Mexico. As the Inquisition was still functioning there some 200 years after the sixteenth century, the number of Jewish immigrants was small. When Mexico became independent Jews gradually began to enter the country, coming from German and other European communities.

It was during the twentieth century that most Jewish immigrants entered Mexico. There were both Ashkenazis and Sephardis, and they settled throughout the country. The communities grew parallel, rather than together, with two languages, Yiddish and Ladino.

The current community is largely middle class, and all the various factions come under the Comite Central Israelita. There are numerous synagogues and there are also kosher restaurants. The community is well equipped with Jewish schools and yeshivas.

GMT -6 to 8 hours
Country calling code: (+52)
Total population: **96,400,000**
Jewish population: **41,000**
Emergency telephone: (**police–080**) (**fire–080**)
(**ambulance–080**)
Electricity voltage: **110**

ACAPULCO
HOTELS
The Hyatt Regency
Costera Miguel Aleman 1 39869
Telephone: (744) 69 1234
Fax: (744) 84 3087
Website: www.acapulco.regency hyatt.com
Supervision: Rabbinical
The hotel has a synagogue and a mikva. Kosher restaurant
is open from December 15th–February 28th.

RESTAURANTS
Kosher Restaurant
Costera Miguel Aleman 1 39869
Telephone: (744) 69 1234
Fax: (744) 84 3087
Open only during the high season (generally Nov/Dec to
March/April).

CUERNAVACA
SYNAGOGUES
Cuernavaca Synagogue
Madero 404
Telephone: (777) 186 846
At the old peoples' home.

GUADALAJARA
COMMUNITY ORGANISATIONS
Comunidad Israelita de Guadalajara
Juan Palomar y Arias 651
Telephone: (33) 416 463
Fax: (33) 427 168
Includes kosher restaurant, mikva and two synagogues.
Phone in advance.

MEXICO CITY
Despite the fact that the first *auto-da-fe* at
which *conversos* were burnt at the stake took
place in Mexico City, it has been said that in
1550 there were more crypto-Jews in Mexico
City than Roman Catholics. The vast majority of
Mexican Jewry now live in Mexico City. With
twenty-three synagogues, kosher restuarants
and Jewish schools, the city is well equipped
with Jewish facilities. Polanco is a Jewish area
in the city with some synagogues. The first
synagogue, dating from 1912, is in the
downtown area.

BUTCHERS
Carniceria Sary
Tecamachalco
Mehadrin.

Pollos Mugrabi
Platon 133, Polanco
Mehadrin

Kosher Restaurant
Shuky Kosher
Fuente de Templanza 17, Tecamachalco 11560
Telephone: (55) 5293 1912
Fax: (55) 5202 4569
Mobile Phone: (155) 5102 7825
Supervision: Maguen David
Mehadrin

COMMUNITY ORGANISATIONS
Comunidad Monte Sinai
Tennyson 134, Polanco
Telephone: (55) 280 6369

EMBASSY
Embassy of Israel
Sierra Madre 215 11000
Telephone: (55) 201 1500

GROCERIES
Casa Amiga
Horacio 1719, Col. Polanco
Telephone: (55) 5280 8587/8460

Kurson Kosher
Acuezunco 15, San Miguel
Telephone: (55) 899 823/860;893 225;894 526
Fax: (55) 899 823
Email: kkurson@aol.com
Website: www.kursonkosher.com
Supervision: Rabbi Machpud Badatz Yoreh Deah Bnei Berak
Central organisation: Comunidad Monte Sinai
Meat, deli, dairy departments, bakery and groceries, Will
also deliver and ship to any resort in Mexico.

Kurson Kosher
emilio castelar 204, Polanco 11560
Telephone: (55) 280 3500
Fax: (55) 280 3361
Email: kkurson@aol.com
Website: www.kursonkosher.com
Supervision: Rabbi Machpud Badatz Yoreh Deah Bnei Berak
Central organisation: Comunidad Monte Sinai
Meat , dairy department, deli, bakery and groceries. Will
also deliver and ship to any resort in Mexico.
Kurson Kosher
Avenida Palo Solo 17, Interlomas 52760
Telephone: (55) 473 592/93/94/95
Fax: (55) 473 592/93/94/95
Email: kkurson@aol.com
Website: www.kursonkosher.com
Supervision: Rabbi Machpud Badatz Yoreh Deah Bnei Berak

Central organisation: Comunidad Monte Sinai
Meat , dairy departmenst, deli, bakery and groceries. Will
also deliver and ship to any resort in Mexico

MEDIA
Newspapers
Foro de Vida Judia en el Mundo
Aviacion Commercial 16, Col. Polanco 15700
Telephone: (55) 571 1114
Spanish monthly

Kesher
Leibnitz 13 10, Colonia Anzures CP 11590
Telephone: (55) 202 0446
Spanish bi weekly

MIKVAOT
Mexico City Mikvaot
Platon 413
Telephone: (55) 520 9569
Avenida de los Bosques 53, Tecamachalco
Telephone: (55) 589 5530
Bernard Shaw 110, Polanco
Telephone: (55) 203 9964

Tevila Cuernavaca
Priv. de Antinea 4, Col. Delicias
Telephone: (55) 150 841, 181 655

MUSEUMS
The Holocaust Museum
Acapulco 70, Col Condesa
Telephone: (55) 211 051

RELIGIOUS ORGANISATIONS
Comite Central
Telephone: (55) 520 9393, 540 7376

Comunidad Maguen David
Contact for any religious questions

Jerusalem de Mexico
Anatore France 359, Local C. Polanco
Telephone: (55) 531 2269

RESTAURANTS
Meat
Aladinos
Ingenieros Militares 255
Telephone: (55) 395 2959
Fax: (55) 395 9219

O Grill/Kosher House
37 Polanco, Mexico City
Telephone: (55) 280 1638

Restuarant Pini
Ejercito Nacional 458d
Supervision: Maguen David

SYNAGOGUES
Agudas Achim
Montes de Oca 32, Condesa 6140
Telephone: (55) 553 6430

Bet Midrash Tecamachalco
Fuente de Marcela 23, Col. Tecamachalco
Telephone: (55) 251 8454

Beth Moshe
Tennyson No 134, Col. Polanco 11560
Telephone: (55) 280 6369; 6375

Beth Yehoshua
Fuente de San Sulpicio No. 16, Col Tecamachalco
53950
Telephone: (55) 294 8617

Bircas Shumel
Plinio 311, Polanco
Telephone: (55) 5280 2769/ 2392

Jajam Elfasi
Fuente del Pescador 168, Col. Tecamachalco
Shabbat services only

Kolel Aram Zoba
Sofocles 346, Col. Polanco
Telephone: (55) 280 2669/4886

Kolel Maor Abraham
Lafontaine 344, Col. Polanco
Telephone: (55) 5545 2482
Fax: (55) 5250 0376
kollel abrechim Night classes for public in general

Nidche Israel
Acapulco 70, Condesa
Telephone: (55) 211 0575

Or Damesek
Seneca 343
Telephone: (55) 280 6281

Ramat Shalom
Fuente de Prescador 35, Tecamachalco
Telephone: (55) 251 3854
Website: www.ramat.org

Shaare Shalom
Avenida de Los Bosques 53, Tecamachalco
Telephone: (55) 251 0973

Shuba Israel
Edgar Alan Poe 43, Col. Polanco
Telephone: (55) 280 0136

Conservative
Bet El
Horacio 1722, Polanco los Morales
Telephone: (55) 281 2592

Beth Israel
Virreyes 114, Lomas
Telephone: (55) 520 8515

Orthodox
Beth Itzjak de Polanco
Eujenio Sue 20, Polanco
Telephone: (55) 280 9296

Eliahu Fasja
Fuente de Templanza 13, Col. Tecamachalco
Telephone: (55) 294 9388
Supervision: Kehila magven David

Midrash Latorah
Cerrada de Los Morales 8, Col. Polanco 11510
Telephone: (55) 5280 0875
Fax: (55) 5281 6801
Rabbi Asher Zrihen, formerly of London, will be happy to welcome and assist visitors

Sephardi
Maguen David
Bernard Shaw 110, Polanco
Telephone: (55) 203 9964

Sephardi Synagogue
Monterey 359
Telephone: (55) 564 1197, 1367

MONTERREY
COMMUNITY ORGANISATIONS
Centro Israelita de Monterrey
Canada 207, Nuevo León
Telephone: (81) 461 128
Includes a synagogue and mikva

PUERTA VALLARTA
PVJC - Mel and Barb Bornstein
Quinta Esmeralda Condos #1, 6.5m carr. a
Mismaloya, Playa Punta Negra, Jalisco, 48300
Telephone: (322) 221 5659
Fax: (322) 221 5643
Mobile Phone: 847 209 1448
Email: melbornstein@hotmail.com
Central organisation: Jewish community of Puerto Vallarta
International Friendship Club, a charitable group...

TIJUANA
CONTACT INFORMATION
JCC Chabad House
Centro Social Israelita de Baja California, Avenida
16 Septiembre, Baja California 3000
Telephone: (664) 862 692; 862 693
Synagogue and mikva on premises

SYNAGOGUES
Tijuanua Hebrew Congregation
Amado Nervo 207, Baja California

MOLDOVA

Moldova used to be a Soviet Republic bordering Romania to the west and the Ukraine to the east. When Jews first entered what is now Moldova the area was known as Bessarabia, and was on an important trade route between Turkey and Poland. By the time of Russian rule in 1812 there was a permanent Jewish community. The Russians included the area in the 'Pale of Settlement', which held the majority of the Jews of their empire. By the end of the nineteenth century there were over 200,000 Jews in the region. However, the twentieth century started with the infamous progrom in the capital Chisinev where 49 Jews were killed, and much damage was done to Jewish property. Emigration began to increase. The area fell under Romanian control between 1918 and 1940, but the community continued to lead a normal life until the Second World War, when many thousands of the pre-war community of over 250,000 were killed during the German occupation.

After the war some survivors continued to live in Moldova, and Jews from other parts of the Soviet Union joined them. There is an umbrella society for Moldovan Jews, and there are synagogues and schools. The Lubavitch movement is active in building up religious life

GMT +2 hours
Country calling code: **(+373)**
Total population: **4,335,000**
Jewish population: **15,000**
Emergency telephone:
Electricity voltage: **220**

CHISINAU
Most of Moldova's Jews live in Chisinau (formerly Kishinev). This city was the scene for two notorious progroms in 1903 and 1905.

RELIGIOUS ORGANISATIONS
Yeshiva of Chisinau
Sciusev 5 277001
Telephone: (2) 274 362
In addition to Jewish studies, a mikva and kosher food supplies are on premises

SYNAGOGUES
Chisinau Synagogue
Chabad Lubavitch Street 8 27005
Telephone: (2) 541 023
A mikvah is on the premises and kosher food may be obtained

TELENESHTY
Teleneshty Synagogue
4 28th June Street

TIRASPOL

Tiraspol is in the region known as
Transdniestra, which is not under the effective
control of the Moldovan government and
considers itself independent. To avoid
problems, those visiting Transdniestra shoud
ensure they obtain the correct papers on
crossing from Moldova proper into the disputed
territory

CONTACT INFORMATION
Tourist Information
Telephone: 336 495
Fax: 332 208
Details of the Jewish Community from Dr Vaisman

MONACO

Some French Jews lived in Monaco before
1939, and the government issued them
with false papers during the war, thus
saving them from the Nazis. This tiny
country has also attracted retired people
from France, North Africa and the UK.

There is an official Jewish body, the
Association Culturelle Israelite de Monaco,
and there is a synagogue, a school and a
kosher food shop. Half of the total Jewish
population are Ashkenazi and the other
half are Sephardi, and 60 per cent of the
community is retired.

GMT +1 hours
Country calling code: (+377)
Total population: **32,000**
Jewish population: **800**
Emergency telephone: (**police–17**) (**fire–18**)
(**ambulance–18**)
Electricity voltage: **220**

MONTE CARLO
BUTCHERS
Kosher
M Sam Amar's Boucherie
2 avenue Saint-Laurent
Telephone: (4) 9330 1173

COMMUNITY ORGANISATIONS
Association Culturelle Israelite de Monaco
15 avenue. de la Costa
Telephone: (4) 330 1646

GROCERIES
Carrefour
SYNAGOGUES

Monte Carlo Synagogue
15 avenue. de la Costa
Telephone: (4) 330 1646
Services Friday evening at 6.30pm and Saturday morning at
8.45am and Saturday afternoon at 5.30pm

MOROCCO

There were Jews in Morocco before it
became a Roman province (they first
arrived after the destruction of the Temple
in 587 BCE). Since the first century, the
Jewish population settled in Morocco has
increased steadily owing to several waves
of immigration from Spain and Portugal
following the expulsion of Jews by the
Inquisition in 1492.

Under Moslem rule the Jews experienced
a general climate of tolerance, although
they did suffer some persecution. During
the Vichy period in the Second World War,
Sultan Mohammed V protected the community. Almost 250,000 Jews have emigrated to Israel, Canada, France, Spain and
Latin America, but they maintain strong
links with the Kingdom.

Since ancient times the Jewish community
has succeeded in cohabiting harmoniously
with the Berber and then with the Arab
community. Today the present Jewish population is an active community, playing a
significant role in Moroccan society
although they have declined in number.

Country calling code: (+212)
Total population: **27,310,000**
Jewish population: **6,000**
Emergency telephone: (**police–19**) (**fire–15**)
(**ambulance–19**)
Electricity voltage: **110/170**

AGADIR
COMMUNITY ORGANISATIONS
Community Offices
Imm. Arsalane Avenue Hassan II
Telephone: (8) 840 091

MIKVAOT
Agadir Mikvaot
Avenue Moulay Abdallah, cnr. rue de la Foire
Telephone: (8) 842 339

SYNAGOGUES
Agadir Synagogue
Avenue Moulay Abdallah, cnr. rue de la Foire
Telephone: (8) 842 339

CASABLANCA

At the beginning of the 19th century around one quarter of the city's population was Jewish. The community thrived until restrictions were imposed by the Vichy government during the Second World War.

In 1948 the Jewish population was 74,000. Since then it has declined and is now considered to be around 5,000.

COMMUNITY ORGANISATIONS
Community Offices
Rue Abbou Abdallah al Mahassibi
Telephone: (2) 270 976; 222 861

MIKVAOT
Casablanca Synagogue
32 rue Officier de Paix Thomas
Telephone: (2) 276 688

RESTAURANTS
Americano
7 place d'Aknoul

Aux Bon Delices
261 boulevard Ziraoui, opp. Lycee Lyautey

SYNAGOGUES
Benisty
13 rue Ferhat Achad

Bennaroche
24 rue Lusitania

Em Habanim
14 rue Lusitania

Hazan Synagogue
rue Roger Farache

Ne'im Zemiroth
29 rue Jean–Jacques Rousseau

Temple Beth El
61 rue Jaber ben Hayane
Telephone: (2) 267 192

ESSAOUIRA (FORMERLY MOGADOR)

COMMUNITY ORGANISATIONS
Community Offices
2 rue Ziri Ben Atyah

SYNAGOGUES
Essaouira Synagogue
2 rue Ziri Ben Atyah

FEZ

Curiosites Marocaines
12 Boulevard Chefchaaouni
Telephone: (35) 622 394
Fax: (35) 942 251
Email: curiosites.maroc@iam.net.ma

COMMUNITY ORGANISATIONS
Community Offices
Rue Dominique Bouchery

CONTACT INFORMATION
Mrs Danielle Mamane
La Boutique, In the gardens of Hotel Palais Jamai 30.000
Telephone: (35) 622 353
Fax: (35) 942 251
Mobile Phone: 21261 353086
Email: boutique.palaisjamai@menara.ma
Mrs Mamane will be pleased to assist all Jewish vistitors

MIKVAOT
Talmud Torah
Rue Dominique Bouchery

SYNAGOGUES
Fez Synagogue
Rue de Beyrouth

Sadoun Synagogue
Boulevard Mohammed V.

Talmud Torah
Rue Dominique Bouchery

KENITRA

COMMUNITY ORGANISATIONS
Community Offices
58 rue Sallah Eddine

MIKVAOT
Kenitra Mikvaot
58 rue Sallah Eddine

SYNAGOGUES
Kenitra Synagogue
Rue de Lyon

MARRAKECH

COMMUNITY ORGANISATIONS
Community Offices
PO Box 515
Telephone: (4) 448 754

MIKVAOT
Marrakech Mikvaot
Boulevard Zerktouni (Gueliz)
Telephone: (4) 448 754
Contact: Mme Kadoch

RESTAURANTS
Le Sepharade
31 Lotissement Hassania, Gueliz
Telephone: (4) 439 809

Le Viennois Hotel Pulman Mansour Eddahbi
Avenue de France, Marrakech
Telephone: (4) 339 100

SYNAGOGUES
Bittoun
Medina, rue Arset Laamach, Touareg
In course of renovation

Rabbi Pinhas Ha Cohen
Medina rue Arset, Laamach
Telephone: (4) 389 798

Salat Laazama
Rue Talmud Torah, Mellah, Hay Essalam
Telephone: (4) 403 798

MEKNES
MIKVAOT
Meknes Mikvaot
5 rue de Ghana
Telephone: (5) 21968 or 22549
Tourists

SYNAGOGUES
Meknes Synagogue
5 rue de Ghana
Telephone: (5) 21968; 22549

OUJDA
COMMUNITY ORGANISATIONS
Community Offices
Texaco Maroc, 36 boulevard Hassan Loukili

RABAT
Rabat Community Organization
1 rue Boussouni

MIKVAOT
Rabat Mikvaot
3 rue Moulay Ismail

RESTAURANTS
Cerle de l'Alliance
3 rue Mellila
Telephone: (7) 727 679

The Menora
Villa 5, rue Er Riyad
Telephone: (7) 260 103

SYNAGOGUES
Rabat Synagogue
3 rue Moulay Ismail

SAFI
Mursiand Synagogue
Rue de R'bat

Synagogue Beth El
Rue de R'bat

TANGIER
COMMUNITY ORGANISATIONS
Community Centre
1 rue de la Liberte

Telephone: (039) 931 633
Fax: (039) 937 609

MIKVAOT
Shaar Raphael
27 boulevard Pasteur
Telephone: (039) 231 304

SYNAGOGUES
Tangier Synagogue
27 boulevard Pasteur
Telephone: (039) 231 304

TOURIST SITES
Historic Synagogues
Rue des Synagogues, off rue Siaghines
There are a number of synagogues in this street which is in the old part of the town

TETUAN
COMMUNITY ORGANISATIONS
Community Offices
16 rue Moulay Abbas

SYNAGOGUES
Benoualid Synagogue
The Old Mellah

MOZAMBIQUE

The small community in Mozambique originally consisted of South African Jews who were forced out of South Africa by President Kruger for supporting the British at the beginning of the twentieth century. The synagogue was opened in 1926, and there is a cemetery in Alto Maha. The biggest Jewish community is in Maputo.

GMT +2 hours
Country calling code: (+258)
Total population: **16,917,000**
Jewish population: **Under 100**
Emergency telephone: **(police–119) (fire–198) (ambulance–117)**
Electricity voltage: **220**

MAPUTO
COMMUNITY ORGANISATIONS
Jewish Community of Mozambique
Avenue Tomas Nduda 235, PO Box 235
Telephone: (1) 2132 1808
Mobile Phone: 82752 0880
Email: larryjerusalem@yahoo.com
The Jewish Community of Mozambique is small community made up of Mozambican and expatriate residents of Maputo and Mozambique. The community has weekly services at the Maputo Synagogue (built in 1926) on Fridays at 6:30 p.m. and also meets for holidays. The official

leader of the community is Rogerio Fonseca Levy and the lay leader is Larry Herman. Visitors are most welcome to join us and can get details of our activities through the email listed above

MYANMAR

The first Jews came to Myanmar in the early eighteenth century from Iraq and other Middle Eastern countries. A synagogue was built in 1896. In the first years of the twentieth century Rangoon and Bassein both had Jewish mayors. The Jewish population swelled to 2,000 before 1939, but most of these fled to Britain and India before the Japanese invasion in the Second World War. Only a few hundred more returned after the war, and the community began to decline through intermarriage and conversion. The handful of remaining Jews are elderly and services are held only on the High Holy Days when a minyan is made up with help from the Israeli embassy.

There is also a tribe of Jews in the north of the country (the Karens), who have their own prayer houses and who believe that they are descended from the tribe of Menashe.

GMT +6 1/2 hours
Country calling code: (+95)
Total population: 46,402,000
Jewish population: Under 100
Emergency telephone: (police–199) (fire–191) (ambulance–192)
Ambulance in Yangon [Rangoon] only
Electricity voltage: 220/230

YANGON (FORMERLY RANGOON)
EMBASSY
Embassy of Israel
No. 15, Khabaung Street, Hlaing Township
Telephone: (951) 515115
Fax: (951) 515116
Email: info@yangon.mfa.gov.il
Website: www.yangon.mfa.gov.il

SYNAGOGUES
Musmeah Yeshua
85 26th Street
Telephone: (951) 252814

NAMIBIA

Namibian Jewry began at the time when the country was a German colony before the

First World War. The cemetery at Swakopmund dates from that settlement. Keetmanschoop also had a congregation, but this no longer exists. The Windhoek synagogue is still in use, and was founded in 1924. Services are held on Shabbat and festivals.

South Africa provides some help for the community, such as a cantor on festivals, and the Cape Board of Jewish Education assists with Hebrew education. From approximately 100 Jewish families in the 1920s and 1930s, the number has dwindled.

GMT +2 hours
Country calling code: (+264)
Total population: 1,613,000
Jewish population: Under 100
Emergency telephone: (police–1011) (fire–2032270) (ambulance–2032276)
Electricity voltage: 220/240

WINDHOEK
Windhoek Synagogue
corner. Tal & Post Streets, PO Box 563
Telephone: (61) 127 0800

NEPAL

Nepal has no Jewish history. It is however well visited by Israeli and other young Jewish tourists. Each year a large Seder is organised by the Lubavitch movement. In 2000 approximately 1,000 attended at the Radisson Hotel.

GMT +5.45 hours
Country calling code: (+977)
Total population: 22,591,000
Jewish population: Under 100
Emergency telephone:

KATHMANDU
EMBASSY
Embassy of Israel
Bishramalaya House, Lazimpat Street, G.P.O. Box 371
Telephone: (1) 411 811

SYNAGOGUES
Chabad House
GHA 2-516-4 Thamel 3
Telephone: (1) 470 0492

NETHERLANDS

Although some historians believe that the first Jews in Holland lived there during

Roman times, documentary evidence goes back only to the twelfth century. The contemporary settlement occurred when Portuguese *Marranos* found refuge from the Inquisition in Holland. Religious freedom was advocated in the early seventeenth century and Jews contributed much to the Netherlands' 'golden age' of prosperity and power.

By the time of Napoleon, the community had grown to 10,000 (the largest in Western Europe), mainly by incoming Jewish traders from eastern Europe. The Jews were emancipated in 1796, but the community began to decline slowly during the nineteenth century. Of the 140,000 Jews (including 30,000 German Jewish refugees) in Holland in 1939, the Germans transported 100,000 to various death camps in Poland, but the local Dutch population tended to behave sympathetically towards their Jewish neighbours, hiding many. Anne Frank and her family are the most famous of the hidden Jews from Holland. Amsterdam witnessed a strike in February 1941, called as a protest against the Jewish deportations.

Today there are three Jewish councils in the Netherlands representing the Ashkenazi, Reform and Orthodox communities. There are many synagogues in Amsterdam, as well as synagogues in other towns. There are kosher restaurants in Amsterdam, which also has many historical sites: Anne Frank House, the Portuguese Synagogue, still lit by candlelight, and the Resistance Museum.

GMT +1 hours
Country calling code: (+31)
Total population: **15,604.00**
Jewish population: **28,000**
Emergency telephone: (**police–112**) (**fire–112**) (**ambulance–112**)
Electricity voltage: **220**

AMERSFOORT
Amersfoort Synagogue
PO Box 1039 3800 AB 3800 AB
Telephone: (33) 475 6722
Email: info@joodsegemeenteamersfoort.nl

AMSTERDAM
BAKERIES
Thee Boom
Bolestein 45 47
Telephone: (20) 642 7003
Maastraat 16
Telephone: (20) 662 4827
Supervision: Amsterdam Jewish Community
Hours: Sunday to Friday 9am to 5pm, closed on Tuesday.

BOOKSELLERS
Samech Books
Gunterstein 69 1081 ch
Telephone: (20) 642 1424
Fax: (20) 642 1424
Email: samech@dds.nl
Website: www.joodseboeken.nl

DELICATESSEN/SUPERMARKET
Mouwes Koshere Delicatessan
Kastelenstraat 261 1082 1082EG
Telephone: (20) 661 0180
Fax: (20) 641 8345
Email: info@mouwes.nl
Website: www.mouwes.nl

HOTELS
Golden Tulip Amsterdam Centre
Stadhouderskade 7 1054 ES
Telephone: (20) 685 1351
Fax: (20) 685 1611

Hotel Doria
Damstraat 3 1012 JL
Telephone: (20) 638 8826
Fax: (20) 638 8726
Website: www.intris.nl/hoteldoria
Kosher breakfast reception open 24 hours

Hotel la Richelle
Holbeinstr 41
Telephone: (20) 671 7971
Kosher breakfast on request

JEWISH LIBRARY
Ets Haim Library–Livraria Montezinos
Mr. Visserplein 3 1011 RD
Telephone: (20) 428 2596
Fax: (20) 420 2597
Email: biblio@etshaim.org
Website: www.etshaim.org
Open for research only Monday to Thursday 10am to 4pm,
Friday 10am to 12.30pm

LIBRARIES
Bibliotheca Rosenthaliana
Singel 425 1012 WP
Telephone: (20) 525 2366
Fax: (20) 525 2311
Website: www.uba.uva.nl/rosenthaliana
The Amsterdam University Library contains an extraordinary
collection of Judaic and Hebrew writings given to the city in
1880 by the heirs of Lesser Rosenthal (1794–1868). The
German occupation in the Second World War had severe
repercussions for the Bibliotheca Rosenthaliana. The books
were sent to Germany, where they were found by the
Americans, and returned to Amsterdam in 1946. The
collection now contains over 100,000 volumes, some dating
back to the fifteenth century.

MEDIA
Newspapers
Nieuw Israelietisch Weekblad
Burg. Haspelslaan 23 1181 NB Amstelveen
Telephone: (20) 627 6275
Fax: (20) 624 2519
Website: www.niw.nl

MIKVAOT
Mikwe Amsterdam
Heinzstraat 3
Telephone: (20) 662 0178; 671 9383

MUSEUMS
Anne Frank House
Prinsengracht 267, PO Box 730 1000 AS
Telephone: (20) 556 7105
Fax: (20) 620 7999
Website: www.annefrank.org
The original hiding place of Anne Frank where she wrote
her diary. Original objects including Anne's diary are on
display. Visitors can go on a 'virtual journey' through the
house, obtaining background information about those in
hiding and WWII. A contemporary exhibition is in the
exhibition hall.
Facilities: Museum cafe and museum bookstore are on the

premises. No cloakroom is present. Big rucksacks are not
allowed. Not easily accessible for the physically disabled
and only partly accessible for wheelchairs.
Please see website for details of opening hours and
admission fees.

Dutch Resistance Museum
Plantage Kerklaan 61 1018 CX
Telephone: (20) 620 2535
Fax: (20) 620 2960
Email: info@verzetsmuseum.org
Website: www.dutchresistancemuseum.org
Open all year, except January 1st, April 30th and December
25th. Hours: 10am to 5pm, Tuesday to Friday, 11am to 5
pm, Saturday to Monday.
Permanent Exhibition.
From 10th May 1940 to May 1945, the Netherlands were
occupied by Nazi Germany. Almost every Dutch person was
affected by the consequences of the occupation. In the
museum you can see, hear and read fascinating stories about
the exceptional as well as about everyday life during WWII.
A separate section tells the story of the former colony, The
Dutch East Indies, where the population suffered badly
under the Japanese reign of terror.
The Plancius Building, in which the museum is located, was
built in 1876 as the social club for a Jewish choir.

Jewish Historical Museum
Nieuwe Amstelstraat 1 1011 PL
Telephone: (20) 531 0310
Fax: (20) 531 0311
Email: info@jhm.nl
Website: www.jhm.nl
The Jewish Historical Museum is the only Jewish museum
in the Netherlands. It is located in four historical ,
monumental synagogues in the heart of Amsterdam's old
Jewish quarter.
A recently added Children's Museum.
Open daily from 11am to 5pm. Also open on 25th , 26th
December and 1st January. Closed for Jewish New Year and
Yom Kippur.

RELIGIOUS ORGANISATIONS
Ashkenazi Community Offices/Community Center
Van der Boechorststr. 26, PO Box 7967 1008 AD
Telephone: (20) 646 0046
Fax: (20) 646 4357
Website: www.nihs.nl

RESTAURANTS
Nasj Viel Restaurant
Jewish Youth Center, De Lairessestraat 13, (near
Concertgebouw) 1071
Telephone: (20) 676 7622
Fax: (20) 673 5215
Supervision: Amsterdam Rabbinate
Open: Sunday to Thursday, 6pm to 10pm (kitchen closes at
9pm). Groups can be accommodated, reserve in advance.

Pinto
Jodenbreestraat 144 1011 NS
Telephone: (20) 625 0923
Website: www.pinto-restaurant.com
Supervision: Amsterdam Ashkenazi & Sephardi rabbinate

Pizza & Co
Kastelenstr 105a 1082 EB
Telephone: (20) 404 4453
Supervision: Amsterdam Ashkenazi & Sephardi rabbinates

Sandwichshop Sal. Meijer
Scheldestraat 45 1078 GG
Telephone: (20) 673 1313
Supervision: Amsterdam Jewish Community

Dairy
Museum Café
Jewish Historical Museum, Nieuwe Amstelstraat 1
1011 PL
Telephone: (20) 531 0310
Fax: (20) 531 0311
Email: info@jhm.nl
Website: www.jhm.nl
Hours 11.00 am to 5.00 pm daily.

Meat
Carmel
Amstelveenseweg 2234 1075 XT
Telephone: (20) 675 7636
Fax: (20) 773 5960
Supervision: Amsterdam Jewish Community
Hours: 12pm to 11.30pm, Sunday to Thursday. Caters for Shabbat meals for groups if ordered in advance.

Vegetarian
Bolhoed
Prinsengacht 60 62
Telephone: (20) 626 1803
Hours: 12pm to 10pm daily. Serves organic vegetarian and vegan food.

Restaurant Betty's
Rijnstraat 75 1079 GX
Telephone: (20) 644 5896

SYNAGOGUES
Liberal
Liberaal Joodse Gemeente
Stadionweg 269 1076 NZ
Telephone: (20) 540 0122
Fax: (20) 442 0337
Email: ljgadam@ljg.nl
Website: www.ljg.nl
Also houses the Judith Druk Library and the Centre for Jewish studies

Orthodox
Gerard Doustraat Synagogue
Gerard Doustr. 238
Telephone: (20) 675 0932
Website: www.joods.nl/gd_sjoel
Services: Saturday and Festival mornings

Inter Provincial Chief Rabbinate
Van der Boechorstraat 26 1081 BT
Telephone: (20) 301 8495
Postal Address: PO Box 7967
1008 AD Amsterdam

Kehilas Ja'Akow (E. Europe)
Gerrit van der Veenstraat 26 1077 XG
Telephone: (20) 676 3602

Sephardi
Portuguese Jews' Congregation
Mr. Visserplein 3 1011 RD
Telephone: (20) 624 5351
Website: www.esnoga.com
The magnificent Portuguese Synagogue (the "Esnoga") in Amsterdam was inaugurated in 1675. It was built by Jews whose forebears had been expelled from Spain in 1492 and had settled in the Netherlands.
In the course of the ages, renovations have taken place, but the building's character has always been maintained - it still has no electricity. Services are being held on Shabbat and Jewish festivals. During the winter, services are held in an adjacent, smaller synagogue.
Open for visitors: Sunday to Friday from 10am to 4 pm.

Portuguese Synagogue & Community Centre
Texlstr. 82
Telephone: (20) 624 5351

TOURIST SITES
Portuguese Jewish Cemetery Beth Haim
Kerkstraat 10, Ouderkerk aan de Amstel 1191 JB
Telephone: (20) 496 3498
Website: www.bethaim.com
Established 1614. One of the oldest Sephardi cemeteries still in use in Europe. Menasseh ben Israel is buried here, as are the parents of the philosopher Spinoza. Ten kilometres south east of Amsterdam.

TOURS
Easy Rider Excursions
Kaag 10, 1423 CZ Uithoorn
Telephone: (20) 297 527 444
Mobile Phone: 06112 92616
Email: maxmeron@hotmail.com
Website: www.easyrider-excursions.nl
Drive or walk through the Jewish history of Amsterdam. Licensed tour guides. Tours of the Netherlands and Belgium in 9-seater a/c coach. .

Jeanette Loeb
Buitenzagerij 37 1021 NP
Telephone: (20) 636 0437
Email: info@jewishhistoryamsterdam.com
Jeanette Loeb has studied Jewish history and culture at the University of Amsterdam (UvA). She organises guided tours and lectures in the Jewish field.
In a personal consult you can develop your own programme

ARNHEM
SYNAGOGUES
Arnhem Synagogue
Pastoorstr. 17a
Telephone: (26) 4442 5154

Liberal
Liberaal Joodese Gemeente Arnhem
Veluws Hof 24, Ermelo 3852
Telephone: (26) 557 860

BUSSUM
Orthodox
Bussum Synagogue
Kromme Englaan 1a
Telephone: (35) 691 4882

DELFT
CULTURAL ORGANISATIONS
Beth Studentiem
Hillel House, Jewish Students Centre, Technical
University, Koornmarkt 9 2611EA
Telephone: (15) 212 0300
"Kosher Mensa" Mondays to Thursdays, in order to join for
dinner please call before 12.30pm on that day

EDAM
The first Jews were said to have come to the city
in 1598 following the Union of Utrecht when the
northern provinces proclaimed their
independence from Catholic Spain and abolished
religious discrimination. It soon became the
centre of the Converso Diaspora. The Jewish
Historical Museum and the Anne Frank house
are essential visits. The Rijksmuseum contains a
number of paintings of Jewish interest including
'The Jewish Bride' by Rembrandt.

TOURS
Footstep Tours
Twiskepolderstraat 8 1135 JV
Telephone: (20) 612 5252
Fax: (20) 689 3276
Mobile Phone: 6 1443 4530
Email: info@footsteptours.nl
Website: www.footsteptours.nl
Dutch and Jewish destinations from Amsterdam
throughout the Netherlands, licensed tour guides relate
history on site, walking & museum tours, city & country
tours all year round, by reservation only. 6 1443 4530. (on
request we make reservations for hotel, transport/driver
etc.) During tours, we also sell the "I AMSTERDAM CARD"
which offers many discounts for visitors to Amsterdam.

EINDHOVEN
SYNAGOGUES
Eindhoven Synagogue
H. Casimirstr. 23
Telephone: (40) 751 1253

ENSCHEDE
Enschede Synagogue
Prinsestr. 16
Telephone: (53) 432 3479
Fax: (53) 430 9725

Liberal
Liberal Congregation Inquiries
Haaksbergen
Telephone: (53) 435 1330

GRONINGEN
Groningen Synagogue
Postbus 550 9700 AN
Telephone: (50) 527 2573
Email: info@nig-groningen.nl
Website: www.nig-groningen.nl

HAARLEM
Haarlem Synagogue
Kenaupark 7
Telephone: (23) 332 6899;324 2051

HILVERSUM
CENTRAL ORGANISATIONS
Nederlandse Vegetariersbond
Larenseweg 26 1221 CM
Telephone: (31) 683 4796
Website: www.vegetariers.nl
Provides information on vegetarianism in the Netherlands,
including restaurants

LEIDEN
ORGANISATIONS
Jewish Students Centre
Levendaal 8
Telephone: (71) 513 0382

SYNAGOGUES
Jewish Congregation Leiden
Levendaal 14 16 2311 JL
Telephone: (71) 512 5793
Fax: (71) 513 6879
Email: nigleiden@hetnet.nl

MAASTRICHT
Maastricht Synagogue
Capucijnengang 2
Website: www.synagoguemaastricht.com
The present synagogue was built in 1841. It is believed that
there was one in the town in the 14th century.

ROTTERDAM
Liberal
**Liberaal Joodse Gemeente Rotterdam
(Liberal Jewish Community of Rotterdam)**
Mozartlaan 99 Rotterdam–Hillegersberg 3007
Telephone: (010) 461 2606
Email: info@ljgrotterdam.nl
Central organisation: Nederlands Verbond voor Progressief
Jodendom
Mailing Address: (Secretary) Rietvink 5, 2986 XD
Ridderkerk

Orthodox
Joodse Gemeente Rotterdam
A B N Davidsplein 2
Telephone: (180) 466 9765
Mikva on premises

THE HAGUE
DELICATESSEN
Jacobs
Haverkamp 220
Telephone: (70) 347 4980

EMBASSY
Embassy of Israel
Buitenhof 47 2513AH
Telephone: (70) 376 0500
Fax: (70) 376 0555
Website: www.thehague.mfa.gov.il or
www.israel.nl

RESTAURANTS
Vegetarian
Restaurant De Wankele Tafel
Mauritskade 79 2514
Telephone: (70) 364 3267

SYNAGOGUES
Liberal
Liberal Synagogue
Prinsessegracht 26
Telephone: (70) 750 4680
Fax: (70) 750 4681
Website: www.ljgdenhaag.nl

Orthodox
Beis Jisroel
Doorniksestraat 152 2587 2587
Telephone: (70) 358 6363

The Hague Synagogue
Corn. Houtmanstraat 11, Bezuidenhout 2593
Telephone: (70) 347 0222
Fax: (70) 347 9002
Mikva on premises, appointments should be made twenty four hours in advance by telephoning 350 7621

TOURIST SITES
Spinoza House
Paviljoensgracht
Spinoza House is of special interest, as is the eighteenth century Portuguese synagogue in the Prinsessegracht, which is now used by the Liberal congregation.

UTRECHT
RESTAURANTS
Eetkafee De Baas
Lijnmarkt 8 3511
Telephone: (30) 231 5185

SYNAGOGUES
Liberal
Synagogue LJG Utrecht
Magdalenastraat 1A 3512 NH
Fax: (30) 84710 5797
Email: ljg@vershtel.nl
Website: www.ljg.com

Orthodox
Utrecht Synagogue
Springweg 164 3511 VZ
Telephone: (30) 231 4742

Progressive Judaism
Liberaal Joodse Gemeente Utrechtaddress1
Telephone: (30) 251 5970
Website:
www.home.zonnet.nl/paul_smid/LJGU/LJGU.html
Central organisation: World Union for progressive Judaism
Inquiries to (30) 603 9343

ZWOLLE
Zwolle Synagogue
Samuel Hirschstr. 8 PO Box 1468 8001
Telephone: (38) 211 412

CURAÇAO

DAMACOR
CONSULATE
Consul of Israel
Blauwduifweg 5
Telephone: 736 5068
Fax: 737 0707
Mobile Phone: 560 0777
Email: midalya@onenet.an

WILLEMSTAD
KASHRUT INFORMATION
Telephone: (9)
There is no kosher restaurant in Curaçao. However many kosher items may be purchsed at the 'food store' of the Congregation Shaarei Tsedek.

MUSEUMS
Jewish Cultural Historical Museum
Hanchi di Snoa 29, PO Box 322
Telephone: (9) 461 1633
Fax: (9) 465 4141
Opening hours: Monday to Friday 9am to 11.45am and 2.30pm to 4.45pm. If there is a cruise ship in port, then also on Sundays from 9am to noon. Closed on Shabbats and Hply Days. On permanent displays are many of which date back to the seventeenth and eighteenth centuries and are still in use by the adjacent congregation Mikve Israel–Emanuel (founded 1651, oldest in hemisphere).

SYNAGOGUES

Ashkenazi
Congregation Shaarei Tsedek
Leliweg 1a, PO Box 498
Telephone: (9) 737 5738

Sephardi Reconstructionist
United Congregation Mikve'Israel Emanuel
Hanchi di Snoa 29, PO Box 322
Telephone: (9) 461 1067
Sabbath services are Friday at 6.30pm (second Friday in the
month is a family service), Saturday at 10am. Holy Day
services at the same time.

NEW ZEALAND

New Zealand Jewry is almost as old as the
European presence in the country. The
year 1829 marks the beginning of Jewish
settlement, and Jews played a prominent
role in the development of the country in
the nineteenth century, especially in trading with Australia and Britain. The
Auckland Jewish community was founded
in 1841, followed by one in Wellington in
1843. There was also a Jewish Prime
Minister, Sir Julius Vogel, in the nineteenth
century.

British Jews emigrated to New Zealand in
the twentieth century, but New Zealand
restricted immigration from Nazi Europe.

Today the community has six synagogues,
four on the North Island and two on the
South Island. Auckland and Wellington
have Jewish day schools, and the 'Kosher
Kiwi Guide' is published in Auckland.
There has been recent Jewish immigration
from South Africa.

GMT +12 hours
Country calling code: (**+64**)
Total population: **3,811,000**
Jewish population: **5,000**
Emergency telephone: (**police–111**) (**fire–111**)
(**ambulance–111**)
Electricity voltage: **230**

AUCKLAND
COMMUNITY ORGANISATIONS
Auckland Jewish Council
80 Webb Street Wellington
Telephone: (9) 384 4229
Has a small shop selling kosher food

SYNAGOGUES
Orthodox
Auckland Hebrew Congregation
108 Greys Avenue
Telephone: (9) 373 2908
Fax: (9) 303 2147
Email: office@ahc.org.nz
Website: www.ahc.org.nz
New Zealands largest selection of kosher goods. Open
Tuesday to Friday 8.30am to 3.30pm. Sundays 9am to
11am. Mailing address: PO Box 68224 Newton Auckland.
Kosher info: www.kosherkiwidirectory.co.nz
Shop info: www.ahc.org.nz/pshop.php
Kosher licensing: www.kosher.co.nz

Progressive
Beth Shalom Progressive Synagogue
180 Manukau Road, Epsom 1023, PO Box 26052
1344
Telephone: (9) 524 4139
Fax: (9) 524 7075
Email: bshalom@ihug.co.nz
Website: www.bethshalom.org.nz

CHRISTCHURCH
COMMUNITY ORGANISATIONS
Christchurch Jewish Council
Telephone: (3) 358 8769

WELLINGTON
Wellington Jewish Community Centre
80 Webb Street
Telephone: (4) 384 5081
There are no kosher restaurants in Wellington. Visitors who
want kosher meals & kosher food should contact the office
of the Community Centre or the Kosher Co-Op.

Wellington Regional Jewish Council
54 Central Terrace, Kelburn 6012
Telephone: (4) 475 7622
Email: zwartz@actrix.co.nz
Central organisation: New Zealand Jewish Council,
Auckland
DELICATESSEN
Dixon Street Delicatessen
Telephone: (4) 384 2436
Not fully kosher but provides kosher challahs and various
American & Israeli foods

EMBASSY
Embassy of Israel
Level 13, 111 The Terrace, Equinox House, PO Box
2171
Telephone: (4) 472 2368
Website: www.webnz.co.nz/israel

GROCERIES
Kosher Deli
80 Webb Street
Telephone: (4) 384 3136
Fax: (4) 384 5081
Email: kdeli@ihug.co.nz
Website: www.beth-el.org.nz
Open on Wednesday 9am to 1pm, Thursday 3pm to 7pm,
Friday 8.30am to 3.30pm and Sunday 11am to 3pm for
kosher meats, cheese, wine, ready made meals and
imported products. Goods can be sent anywhere in New
Zealand.

MEDIA
Newspapers
New Zealand Jewish Chronicle
PO Box 27 156 6011
Telephone: (4) 934 6077
Fax: (4) 934 6079
Email: mike@rifkov.co.nz
Monthly newspaper of local, Israeli and Jewish News

MIKVAOT
Wellington Jewish Community Centre
80 Webb Street
Telephone: (4) 384 5081
Website: www.beth-el.org.nz

SYNAGOGUES
Orthodox
Beth El Synagogue
80 Webb Street
Telephone: (4) 384 5081
Fax: (4) 384 5081
Email: bethel@ihug.co.nz
Website: www.beth-elWWW.BETH-EL*Progressive*
Temple Sinai, The Wellington Progressive Jewish Congregation
147 Ghuznee Street 6011
Telephone: (4) 385 0720
Fax: (4) 385 0971
Email: office@sinai.org.nz
Website: www.sinai.org.nz

NORWAY

The only way Jews could enter Norway before the nineteenth century was with a 'Letter of Protection', as Danish control limited the amount of Jewish entry. The situation changed in 1851 when a Norwegian liberal poet, Henrik Wergeland, argued for the admission of Jews into the country, and the parliament eventually agreed. There were only some 650 Jews in the country after emancipation in 1891, mainly in Oslo and Trondheim. By 1920

the community numbered 1,457, and by the time of the Nazi invasion there were 1,800. Despite attempts by the Norwegian resistance to smuggle Jews to Sweden, 767 Jews were transported to Auschwitz, although 930 were able to reach Sweden. The Jewish survivors were joined after the war by Displaced Persons, especially invited by the Norwegian government.

The current situation forbids shechita, but there are no other restrictions on Jewish life. There is a synagogue in Oslo, and a kosher food shop. There is also a Jewish magazine. An old-age home was built in 1988. Trondheim, in the north of the country, has the northernmost synagogue in the world.

GMT +1 hours
Country calling code: **(+47)**
Total population: **4,445,000**
Jewish population: **1,500**
Emergency telephone: **(police–112)** **(fire–110)** **(ambulance–113)**
Electricity voltage: **220**

OSLO
Oslo is the major centre of Norwegian Jewry, with 900 Jews living there. The Resistance Museum is of interest, as is the Wergerland Monument in the Var Frisler Cemetery. A monument consisting of 8 empty chairs in remembrance of the Norwegian Jews who were killed during the War is located near the Akershus fortification.

COMMUNITY CENTRE
Oslo Community Centre
Bergstien 13, 0172 131
Telephone: (2) 320 5750
Website: www.dmt.oslo.no
Kosher catering, Tone Rubin, Telephone: 9133 2575

EMBASSY
Embassy of Israel
Parkveien 35, P.O.Box 534 Skoyen N-0214
Telephone: (2) 101 9500
Fax: (2) 101 9530
Website: www.oslo.mfa.gov.il

RESTAURANTS
Kosher Food Centre
Corner Bergstien/Waldemar Thranes Gate 171
Telephone: (2) 260 9166
Supervision: Rabbi Michael Melchior
There are no kosher hotels or restaurants in Oslo but there
is the Kosher Food Centre. Open 4pm to 6pm Tuesday and
Thursday, and 12noon to 2pm on Friday. Closed Shabbat.

SYNAGOGUES
Orthodox
Mosaiske Trossamfund (The Jewish Community)
Bergsien 13 172
Telephone: (2) 320 5750
Fax: (2) 320 5781
Website: www.dmt.oslo.no
Postal address: Postboks 2722 St. Hanshaugen, 0131 Oslo, Norway

TOURIST SITES
Ostre Gravlund Cemetery
There is a Jewish war memorial here

TRONDHEIM
SYNAGOGUES
Synagogue
Ark. Christiesgt. 1
Telephone: 7362 6568, 4752 2030
Fax: 7353 1108
The world's northernmost synagogue. The synagogue also has a museum. Postal address Postboks 2722 St. Hanshaugen, 0131 Oslo, Norway.

PANAMA

Some Jews, most of them pretending to be Christians, came to Panama during colonial times. Panama was an important crossroads for trade and, as a result, many Jews passed through the country on their journeys in the region.

In 1849 immigrant Sephardic Jews in Panama founded the Hebrew Benevolent Society, the first Jewish congregation in the Isthmus. They came from the pious congregation of the Netherlands Antilles (Curaçao) to settle in Panama.

Jews from Saint-Thomas (Virgin Islands) and Curaçao founded 1876 the Kol Shearith Israel Synagogue in Panama City, and in 1890 the Kahal Hakadosh Yangacob in Colon.

By the end of the First World War a number of Middle Eastern Jews had settled in the country and founded the Israelite Benevolent Society Shevet Ahim. During the Second World War immigrants from Europe arrived in Panama, establishing Beth-El, the only Ashkenazi community in the country. The majority of Jewish community is Sephardi (around 80 per cent).

There have been two Jewish presidents in Panama, the only country – apart from Israel – where this has happened.

GMT -5 hours
Country calling code: (**+507**)
Total population: **2,719,000**
Jewish population: **7,000**
Emergency telephone: (**police–104**) (**fire–103**)
Electricity voltage: **120**

PANAMA CITY
BAKERIES
Pita Pan
Plaza Bal Harbour, Paitilla
Telephone: (2) 642 786

BUTCHERS
Shalom Kosher
Plaza Bal Harbour, Paitilla
Telephone: (2) 644 411

Super Kosher
Calle San Sebastian, Paitilla
Telephone: (2) 635 254
Fax: (2) 632 067
Email: mzakay@skosher.com
Supervision: Shevet Ahim Rabbinate
Mailing address Apartado 0823 05660 Panama. Also Kosher supermarket, bakery and restaurant. Open from 8.30am to 8.30pm Sunday to Thursday, Friday until 4.30pm.

CHOCOLATE SHOPS
Candies Bazaar
Via Argentina, 155 L 2
Telephone: (2) 694 857

La Bonbonniere
Calle Juan XXII, Paitilla
Telephone: (2) 645 704

COMMUNITY ORGANISATIONS
Jewish Centre: Centro Cultural Hebreo de Panama
Calle 50 Final, PO Box 7166 55
Telephone: (2) 260 455
Fax: (2) 260 869
Restaurant open daily for lunch and supper. Closed Saturday.

CULTURAL ORGANISATIONS
Consejo Central Comunitario Hebreo de Panama
PO Box 3309 4
Telephone: (2) 638 411

EMBASSY
Embassy of Israel
Edificio Grobman, Calle Manuel Maria Icaza, 5th Floor
Telephone: (2) 648 257

MIKVAOT
Beneficiencia Israelita Beth El
Calle 58E., Urb. Obarrio
Telephone: (2) 233 383

Sociedad Israelita Shevet Ahim
Calle 44 27
Telephone: (2) 255 990
Fax: (2) 271 268

RESTAURANTS
Dairy
Pita Pan
Plaza Bal Harbour, Paitilla
Telephone: (2) 642 786

Meat
Shalom Kosher
Plaza Bal Harbour, Paitilla
Telephone: (2) 644 411

Pizzeria
Pizzeria Italiana
Centro Cultural Hebreo de Beneficiencia, Calle 50 Final
Telephone: (2) 260 455
Fax: (2) 260 869

SYNAGOGUES
Ashkenazi
Beneficiencia Israelita Beth El
Calle 58E, Urb. Obarrio
Telephone: (2) 640 058
Fax: (2) 640 058
Mikva on premises

Singoge Beth El
Calle 58 Obarrio
Telephone: (2) 233 383
Fax: (2) 640 058

Orthodox Sephardi
Ahavat Sion
Calle XXIII, Paitilla
Telephone: (2) 651 891
Daily Services. Mikva for women on premises.

Sociedad Israelia Shevet Ahim
Calle 44 27
Telephone: (2) 255 990
Fax: (2) 271 268
Daily services.

Reform
Kol Shearith Israel
Av. Cuba 34 16 5
Telephone: (2) 254 100

PARAGUAY

Jewish settlement in this land-locked country came late for this area of South America.

The few who came over from Western Europe at the end of the nineteenth century rapidly assimilated into the general population. The first synagogue was founded early in the twentieth century by Sephardis from Palestine, Turkey and Greece. Ashkenazis arrived in the 1920s and 1930s from eastern Europe, and some 15,000 came to the country to escape Nazism, intending to move on into Argentina. Some of these settled in Paraguay.

Paraguay, in more recent times, has accepted Jews from Argentina who were fleeing from the military regime.

Today there are three synagogues, a Jewish school and a Jewish museum in Asuncion. There is a high rate of intermarriage, but children of mixed marriages may receive a Jewish education.

GMT -5 hours
Country calling code: (**+595**)
Total population: **5,085,000**
Jewish population: **900**
Emergency telephone: (**police–00**) (**fire–00**) (**ambulance–00**)
Electricity voltage: **220**

ASUNCION

COMMUNITY ORGANISATIONS
Chad Lubavitch Center
Paraguari 771, Asuncion
Telephone: (21) 228 669
Fax: (21) 440 598

Consejo Representativo Israelita de Paraguay
General Diaz 657, PO Box 756
Telephone: (21) 441 744
Fax: (21) 448 289

EMBASSY
Embassy of Israel
Calle Yegros No. 437 C/25 de Mayo, Edificio San Rafael, Piso 8, PO Box 1212
Telephone: (21) 495 097;496 043/044
Fax: (21) 496 355

SYNAGOGUES
Asuncion Synagogue
General Diaz, 657

PERU

The first Jews in Peru arrived with the first Europeans, as many *Conversos* were officers in the Spanish army which invaded the country in 1532. After the Inquisition was set up in 1570 the Jews were persecuted, and many were burned alive. From 1870 groups of Jews came over from Europe, but tended to disappear into the general population. In 1880 a group of North African Jews settled in Iquitos and worked in the rubber industry. More Jewish immigration occurred after the First World War, and later, Nazi refugees entered the country. By the end of the Second World War the Jewish population had reached 6,000, but this subsequently declined.

Almost all of the present Jewish population are Ashkenazi. There are two Jewish newspapers and most Jewish children go to the Colegio Leon Pinelo school, which is well known for its high standards. There is a cemetery at Iquitos built by the nineteenth-century community. The community is shrinking owing to intermarriage and assimilation.

GMT -5 hours
Country calling code: **(+51)**
Total population: **25,015,000**
Jewish population: **3,000**
Emergency telephone: **(police–105) (fire–116)**
(ambulance–470 5000)
Electricity voltage: **220**

CUSCO
Beit Jabad Peru
Avenida Nueva Baja 545
Mobile Phone: 84978 7007

Orthodox
Beit Jabad Cusco
Calle Granada 291, Cusco - Cusco
Telephone: (84) 9787007
Email: chabadcusco@gmail.com
Website: www.jabadperu.com
Synagogue, kosher restaurant, festive meals served Shabbat and holidays after tefilah.

LIMA
COMMUNITY ORGANISATIONS
Asociacion Judia de Beneficencia y Culto de 1870
Libertad 375, Miraflores 18
Telephone: (1) 445 1089
Fax: (1) 445 1089

EMBASSY
Embassy of Israel
Natalio Sanchez 125 Sexto Piso, Santa Beatriz 1
Telephone: (1) 433 4431
Fax: (1) 433 8925

GROCERIES
Minimarket Kasher
Av. Gral. Juan A. Pezet 1472, San Isidro 27
Telephone: (1) 264 2187
Fax: (1) 264 2187
Supervision: Rabbinate of the Union Israelita del Peru
Hours of opening: Monday to Thursday 9am to 6pm, Friday 9am to 3pm.

HOTELS
Hotel Libertador
Los Eucaliptos 550, San Isidro, 27
Telephone: (1) 421 6680
Fax: (1) 442 3011
Website: www.libertador.com.pe
A short walk away from the Union Israelita Synagogue

KASHRUT INFORMATION
Chief Rabbi Abraham Benhamu
Telephone: (1) 442 4505
Fax: (1) 442 8147
Rabbi Benhamu is the Chief Rabbi of Peru

KOSHER FOODS
Salon Majestic
Av. Bolivar 965, Pueblo Libre, 21
Telephone: (1) 463 0031
Fax: (1) 461 8912
Supervision: Chief Rabbi Abraham Benhamu
Catering for special groups and parties by prior arrangement only

MEDIA
Newspapers
Menora
Jose Quinones 290, Miraflores 18
Telephone: (1) 441 3461
Fax: (1) 422 5796
Daily

Shofar
Jose Bielovucic 1350, Lince 14
Telephone: (1) 440 0853
Fax: (1) 440 0853
Bimonthly

MIKVAOT
Beit Jabad Peru
Av. Salaverry 3075, San Isidro 27
Telephone: (1) 264 6060
Fax: (1) 264 5499
Email: chabadperu@telefonica.net.pe
Website: www.jabadperu.com
Mikveh for men and for women, daily minyan, kosher meals, including delivery to any city in Peru

Schedule of Prayers Shacharit Weekdays 7am, Shabbat and holidays 10am, followed by festive meal
Sunday 9am. Mincha and Arvit Weekdays 2.15pm to 8pm. Shabbat and holidays 5.30pm (winter) 6pm (summer)
Friday (followed by festive meal) and Sunday 5.40pm. (winter) 6.05pm (summer).
Union Israelita
Ave. Gral. Juan A. Pezet 1472, San Isidro, 27
Telephone: (1) 264 2187
Sociedad Israelita Sefardi, Beit Jabad

MUSEUMS
Inquisition and Congress Museum
Juin 548 1
Telephone: (1) 311 7801 / 311 7777 anexo 2910
Fax: (1) 311 7801
Website: www.congreso.gob.pe/museo.htm
The museum is open from Monday to Sunday, from 9am to 5pm. The services are free and the tour is given in Spanish, French, Italian, German and Portuguese.

Museum of the Inquistion
Junin 548 1
Telephone: (1) 427 0365
Dungeon and torture chamber of the headquarters of the Inquisition for all Spanish South America from 1570 to 1820

SYNAGOGUES
Conservative
Asociacion Judia de Beneficiencia y Culto de 1870
Jose Galvez 282, Miraflores 18
Telephone: (1) 445 1089, 445 5148
Fax: (1) 445 1089

Orthodox
Beit Jabad Peru
Av. Salaverry 3075, San Isidro, 27
Telephone: (1) 264 6060
Fax: (1) 274 5499
Email: chabadperu@telefonica.net.pe
Website: www.jabadperu.com
Synagogues (services daily), mikveh for men and women, kosher meals, including delivery to any city in Peru. Festive meals served Shabbat and holidays after tefilah.

Schedule of Prayers
Shacharit Weekdays 7am
Shabbat and holidays 10am., followed by festive meal, Sunday 9am.
Mincha and Arvit
Weekdays 2.15 p.m. to 8pm
Shabbat and holidays 5.30pm. (winter) 6pm(summer)
Friday (followed by festive meal) and Sunday 5.40pm. (winter) 6.05pm. (summer)

Sciedad de Beneficencia Israelita Sefardi
Enrique Villar 581, Santa Beatriz, 1
Telephone: (1) 471 7230
Fax: (1) 422 8147

Union Israelita del Peru
Carlos Porras osores 210, San Isidro, Esq. Cdra 18
Ave. Dos de mayo 27
Telephone: (1) 421 3684
Fax: (1) 421 3684
Email: unionisraelita@terra.com.pe
Website: www.kosherperu.com
Supervision: Rabbi Efraim Zik
Services are held at the Centro Sharon

TOURIST SITES
Pilatos House
Ancash 390, Lima 1
Telephone: (1) 427 5814
Seventeenth century private mansion, now used by the Constitutional Court. On the 2nd floor was the synagogue of the Converso Jews. Located in front of the San Francisco Monastery.

PHILIPPINES REPUBLIC

Conversos who came with the Spanish in the sixteenth century were the first Jewish presence in the region. In the late nineteenth century, western European Jews came to trade in the area, and after the Americans occupied the country in 1898 more Jews arrived from a variety of places, including the USA and the Middle East. The first synagogue was built in 1924. The Philippines accepted refugees from Nazism, but the Japanese occupied the islands during the war and the Jewish population was interned. After the war many of the community emigrated. However, a new synagogue opened in 1983, and services are also held in the US Air Force bases around the country.

GMT +8 hours
Country calling code: (+63)
Total population: **73,527,000**
Jewish population: **100**
Emergency telephone:
Electricity voltage: **220**

MANILA
EMBASSY
Embassy of Israel
Trafalgar Plaza 23rd Foor, 105 H.V. de la Costa Street, Salalcedo Village, Makkati City 1200
Telephone: (2) 891 5329/30/31/34
Fax: (2) 894 1027
Postal address: POB 1697 MCPO, Makati Metro, Manilla 1299

MIKVAOT
Jewish Association of the Philipines (Beth Yaacov Synagogue)
110 H.V. de la Costa corner Tordesillas West,
Salcedo Village, Makati City, Metro Manila 1227
Telephone: (2) 815 0265
Fax: (2) 840 2566
Email: jap.manila@gmail.com
By arrangement

SYNAGOGUES
Orthodox Sephardi
Beth Yaacov Synagogue
110 H.V. de la Costa corner Tordesillas West,
Salcedo Village, Makati City, Metro Manila 1227
Telephone: (2) 815 0265
Fax: (2) 840 2566
Email: rpjewish@gmail.com
Website: www.jewishphilippines.org
Services; Monday -Thursday 7.15am Friday at 6.30 pm, Saturday at 9.30 am

POLAND

After just five years of German occupation in the Second World War the thousand-year-old Jewish settlement in Poland, one of the largest Jewish communities in the world, had been almost totally eradicated. Jews came to Poland in order to escape anti-semitism in Germany in the early Middle Ages. They were initially welcomed by the rulers, and Jews became greatly involved in the economy of the country.

Until 1918 most Jews lived in the east and south of the country, under Russian and Austrian domination, respectively. After 1918 Poland became an independent country once more, with over 3,000,000 Jews

(300,000 in Warsaw.) The community continued to flourish before 1939, with Yiddish being the main language of the Jews. The community was destroyed in stages during the war, as Poland became the centre for the Nazi's destruction of European Jewry. After the war, the borders shifted again, and the 100,000 or so survivors mostly tried to emigrate. The few who remained endured several progroms even after the events of the Holocaust.

Today the community is comparatively small and most of the members are elderly, but there is a functioning synagogue in Warsaw and many Jewish historical sites are scattered throughout the country. The Polish Tourist Board publishes information about the Jewish heritage in Poland.

GMT +1 hours
Country calling code: **(+48)**
Total population: **38,650,000**
Jewish population: **5,000**
Emergency telephone: **(police–997) (fire–998) (ambulance–999)**
Electricity voltage: **220**

BIELSKO BIALA
ORGANISATIONS
Elzbieta Wajs
ul. Mickiewicza 26 43 300
Telephone: (2) 22438

CRACOW
Kazimierz District
The streets of the old Jewish city still evoke a sense of the past. Be sure to visit ul Szeroka, the old town square, which was the center of Jewish life in Kazimierz.
 Seven synagogues can be found in Kazimierz, but only one is still in use.
The Ghetto
The ghetto was built in March 1941, on the opposite side of the Vistula River from Kazimierz. In Bohaterow Ghetta (Ghetto Heroes) Square, the Jews were deported to Nazi death camps, mainly Belzec and Auschwitz-Birkenau. At No. 18, one can find the Museum of National Commemoration that was built in 1983. It contains exhibits on the ghetto and the Nazi occupation. Fragments of the ghetto walls are still visible.
Plaszow
Close to the former ghetto is the site of the Plaszow concentration camp. At this camp,

Oscar Schindler saved almost 1,100 Jews by putting them to work in his factory. A monument was built in commemoration of the 10,000 who did not survive. Nearby on ul Lipowa 4 is Schindler's pot and pan factory, which is in use today for making electronic parts. In the courtyard of the factory, there is a monument.

High or (Tall) Synagogue
ul Jozefa 38

Originally built in 1553-56 as a prayer room on the second floor above ground floor shops, it was destroyed during the Holocaust. Today its is used for a monument restoration workshop.

BOOKSELLERS
Jarden
2 Szeroka Street, 41 Miodowa Street
Telephone: (12) 429 1374
Fax: (12) 421 7166
Email: jarden@jarden.pl
Website: www.jarden

Klezmer-Hois Agencia Artystyczna
Józefa st.38,
Jewish books and publications

Cafe
Massolit Books
ul. Felicjanek 4 31-104
Telephone: (12) 432 4150
Fax: (12) 432 4150
Email: info@massolit.com
Website: www www.massolit.com
orders

COMMUNITY ORGANISATIONS
The Jewish Religion Congregation
2 Skawinska Street
Telephone: (12) 429 5735
Mondays to Thursdays 9am to 2pm, Friday 9am to 12pm.

CULTURAL FESTIVAL
Jewish Culture Festival
ul. Józeefa 36 31 056
Telephone: (12) 431 1517, 431 1535
Fax: (12) 431 2427
Website: www.jewishfestival.pl

HOTELS
Kosher
Hotel Eden
ul. Ciemna 15, PO Box 407 31-053
Telephone: (12) 430 6565
Fax: (12) 430 6767
Email: eden@hoteleden.pl
Website: www.hoteleden.pl

This hotel includes a kosher restaurant and Mikvah. Also WiFi, Salt grotto. Organised guided tours to all sites including Tzaddikim.

MUSEUM
The Galicia Jewish Museum
ul. Dajwór, Kazimierz,
Email: natalia@galiciajewishmuseum.org

The Galicia Jewish Museum exists to commemorate the victims of the Holocaust and to celebrate the Jewish culture of Polish Galicia, presenting Jewish history from a new perspective. Open daily from 9am till 7pm in the summer and from 10.am till 6pm in the winter, closed only for Yom Kippur and Christmas Day.

For group bookings or to arrange a private tour, contact natalia

MUSEUMS
Museum of the History and Culture of the Cracow Jews
The Old Syngogue, 24 Szeroka Street 31 053
Telephone: (12) 422 0962
Email: starasynagoga@mhk.pl
Website: www.mhk.pl

The synagogue was established in the 15th century and was remodeled many times. It is the oldest synagogue left standing in Poland. Most of its artwork and Jewish relics were looted during World War II. Afterward, the synagogue was remodeled and today it houses the Museum of Jewish History, containing collections of liturgical items, ancient Torah scrolls, textiles, dishes, utensils and shofars, as well as photographs, documents and artwork showing the history of the Jews of Cracow. In the plaza in front of the synagogue, there is a monument to 30 Poles shot by the Nazis.

PHARMACY UNDER THE EAGLE (Museum on site of Kraków Ghetto)
Apteka Pod Orlem (Ksiegarnia), Plac Bohaterów Getta 18 30-547
Telephone: (12) 656 5625
Email: apteka@mhk.pl

ORGANISATIONS
Judaica Foundation
ul. Rabina Meiselsa 17
Telephone: (12) 423 5595

RESTAURANTS
Klezmer-Hois Agencia Artystyczna
Ul Szeroka 6 21-053
Telephone: (12) 411 1245
Fax: (12) 411 1622
Email: Klezmer-hois@klezmer-hois.cracow.pl

This restaurant does not have rabbinical supervision or a certificate of kashrut but abides by the obligatory rules of kashrut.

SYNAGOGUES
Bociana or Popper's Synagogue
ul Szeroka 16

Built in 1620 by a wealthy merchant, this synagogue is no longer used for ritual purposes. All of its interior decorations were destroyed during the Holocaust. Today it hosts the cultural center.

High Synagogue -Ksiegarnie Austerii
ul. Józefa 38 31-053
Isaac Synagogue
18 Kupa Street
Contact Dominik Dybek
Kupa Synagogue
ul Warszawera 8
This synagogue was built in the late 17th century. After
WWII, it was turned into a matzah factory. Little remains of
the original interior beyond a few 20th century frescoes.
Remuh
ul Szeroka 40
Built in 1557 the synagogue is named after Rabbi Moses
Isserles the son of its founder, who is buried in the adjacent
cemetery. For information; contact 603 860 373 (mobile).
The synagogue has been remodeled and is in use today.
A beautiful mosaic wall of tombstone fragments was also
built.

TOURIST SITES
Temple Synagogue
24 Miodowwa Street
Built in 1862 it was used by the Germans during the war as
a stable, and is currently being restored

GLIWICE
CONTACT INFORMATION
Gliwice Synagogue
ul Dolnych Walow 9 44100
Telephone: (32) 314 797

KATOWICE
Tourist Information
ul. Mlynska 13 40098
Telephone: (32) 537 742

LEGNICA
Tourist Information
ul. Chojnowska 37 59220
Telephone: (76) 22730

LODZ
COMMUNITY ORGANISATIONS
Jewish Congregation
Zachodinia 78
Telephone: (42) 335 156

RELIGIOUS ORGANISATIONS
Jewish Chabad
Telephone: (42) 331 221, 336 825

LUBLIN
Once a major Jewish town in eastern Europe,
Lublin today has fewer than a hundred Jews.
Pre-war Lublin was a centre for Torah study,
and a large yeshivah was built only a few years
before the Second World War, now used as a
dental college. Majdanek Concentration Camp
lies within the city's boundary. There is a
particularly moving memorial in the camp
consisting of the ashes from the camp's
crematoria.

CONTACT INFORMATION
The memorial Chamber of the Lublin Jews
ul. Lubartowska 10 20-084
Telephone: (81) 524 1277
Email: pawel-nuatroshek@wr.pl
Central organisation: The Jewish Social and Cultural Society
in Poland

OSWIECIM
MUSEUMS
**Auschwitz Jewish Centre and Chevra Lomdei
Mishnayot Synagogue Jewish Museum**
Pl. Skarbka 5 32 600
Telephone: (33) 844 7002
Fax: (33) 844 7003
Email: info@ajcf.pl
Website: www.ajcf.pl
Hours of opening: April September: 8.30am to 8pm;
October to March:8.30am to 6pm; The centre is closed on
Saturday and Jewish holidays
Auschwitz–Birkenau State Museum
al. Wiezniow Oswiecimie 20 32 620
Telephone: (33) 844 8102
Website: www.auschwitz.org.pl

RZESZOW
SYNAGOGUES
Rzeszow Synagogue
ul Bonicza, edge of Pl. Ofiara Getta

SZCZECIN
CONTACT INFORMATION
Tourist Information
ul. Niemcewicza 2 71553
Telephone: (91) 221 674

WARSAW
Before the war Warsaw had approximately
300,000 Jews. Now there are only a couple of
thousand, mostly elderly. There are many sites
which can be visited, such as surving fragments
of the Ghetto walls and "A memorial Route to
the struggle and Martyrdom of the Jews
1940–1943" known as "Memory Lane". The old
Jewish cemetery, untouched by the Nazis, is
very imposing and is still in use. The Warsaw
Ghetto fighters are included in the inscription to
Tomb of the Unknown Soldier in the centre of
the city. In 2002 the Nozyk synagogue
celebrated its centenary.

EMBASSY
Embassy of Israel
ul. Krzywickiego 24 02 078

Telephone: (22) 825 0028
Website: www.warsaw.mfa.gov.il

MIKVAOT
Nozyk Synagogue
6 Twarda Street
Telephone: (22) 652 2805, 620 4324
Fax: (22) 652 2805, 620 1037
Website: www.jewish.org.pl;
www.warsaw.jewish.org.pl
Central organisation: Jewish Community of Warsaw
Contact: Sharona Kanofsky tel: 652 2150.

MONUMENT
Monument to the Ghetto Heroes
Zamenhofa
Erected in 1948 this monument symbolises the heroic
Ghetto defiance of the 1943 uprising

ORGANISATIONS
The Jewish Historical Institute
3/5 Tlomackie Street 00-090
Telephone: (22) 827 9221
Fax: (22) 827 8372
Email: secretary@jhi.pl
Website: www.jhi.pl
This establishment has a remarkable collection of Judaica.
It includes a library of documents on the manuscripts
stolen by the Germans from all over Europe.

RESTAURANTS
Jerozolima
Ul. Smocza 27
Telephone: (22) 838 3217
Fax: (22) 636 3371

Menora
Plac Grzybowski 2
Telephone: (22) 203 754

Nove Miasto Ecological Restaurant
Rynek Nowego Miasta 13/15
Telephone: (22) 831 4379
Website: www.novemiasto.waw.pl

Panorama
Al Witsoa 31
Telephone: (22) 642 0666

Pod Samsonem Restaurant
Ul. Freta 3/5
Telephone: (22) 831 1788
Opening Hours: 10am to 11pm

Salad Bar
ul. Tamka 37
Telephone: (22) 635 8463

Singing Waiters Restaurant Galeria Mokotow
Galeria Mokotow, 12 Woloska Street
Telephone: (22) 541 3767

SYNAGOGUES
**Nozyk Synagogue, Jewish Community of
Warsaw, Union of Jewish Communities in**

Poland.
6 Twarda Street 00 950
Telephone: (22) 620 4324
Fax: (22) 620 1037
Website: http://warszawa.jewish.org.pl/
The synagogue was renovated 1977–83 and is well worth a
visit. It is the only pre–war synagogue still standing in
Warsaw. Visitors welcomed. Friday night dinner available.
Kosher store in the synagogue.
Liberal

Beit Warszawa
ul. Wiertnicza 113 02-952
Telephone: (22) 885 2638
Fax: (22) 885 8982
Website: www.beit.org.pl
Bejt Simcha meets every Friday to celebrate Kabalat
Shabbat; it is usually combined with a lecture, a discussion
or a cultural program. We use our own Hebrew-Czech
siddur for the service. At least once a month there is a
Saturday morning service as well.
There is a small synagogue, library, room for social and
cultural events and bar.
Bejt Simcha is a member of the European Section – World
Union for Progressive Judaism (WUPJ)

THEATRE
Jewish National Theatre
Plac Grybowski 12/16
Performances are given in Yiddish

TOURS
Shalom Travel Service
Twarda Street 6 00 105
Telephone: (22) 652 2802
Fax: (22) 652 2803

WROCKLAW
MUSEUMS
Historical Museum
Slezna Street 37
Telephone: (71) 678 236

PORTUGAL

Portuguese Jewry had a parallel history to
Spanish Jewry until the twelfth century,
when the country emerged from Spain's
shadow Jews worked with the Portuguese
kings in developing the country. However,
they were heavily taxed and had to live in
special areas, although they were free to
practise their religion as they pleased. As
a result the community flourished.

Persecution began during the period of the
Black Death, and the Church was a key
instigator of the riots which broke out

against the Jews. After the Inquisition in neighbouring Spain many Jews fled to Portugal, but were expelled in 1496. Many Jews converted in order to remain in the country and help with the economy. These became the Portuguese 'Conversos' and some of their descendants are converting back to Judaism today.

Over the last century and a half Jews have begun to re-enter the country, and many others used it as an escape route to America during the last war. Most of the community are Sephardi, and there is a Sephardi synagogue in Lisbon. There is also a central Jewish organisation which is a unifying force for Jews in the country.

GMT +0 hours
Country calling code: **(+351)**
Total population: **9,921,00**
Jewish population: **800**
Emergency telephone: **(police–115) (fire–115)**
(ambulance–115)
Electricity voltage: **220**

ALGARVE
COMMUNITY ORGANISATIONS
Jewish Community of Algarve
Rua Judice Biker 11 5°.; Portimão 8500 -701
Telephone: 2824 16710
Fax: 2824 16710
Mobile Phone: 968440414
Email: Ralf.Pinto@sapo.pt
Website: www.farojewishheritagecentre.org/
MUSEUMS

Faro Jewish Heritage Centre
Telephone: 2898 92515
Fax: 2824 16515
Website: www.mibdevelopment.com/faro
Home to the New Isaac Bitton Synagogue Museum (inside the Faro Jewish Cemetery - the only remaining vestige of the 1st post inquistion Jewish presence in Portugal).
Weekdays 9.30 to 12.30 - situated opp entrance to Faro Hospital.
Contact João mobile 936394488
or Ralf Pinto Jewish Community of Algarve
www.farojewishheritagecentre.org/

BELMONTE
COMMUNITY ORGANISATIONS
Jewish Community of Belmonte
Apt. 18, Bairo de Santa Maina 6250
Telephone: (275) 912 465

LISBON
Jews settled in Lisbon in the 12th century. Many Jews were prominent in court circles. In 1496 when the Jews were expelled Lisbon was chosen as a point of embarkation.
In the Alfama district, Lisbon's oldest, is the Rua de Judiara and at 8 Beco dos Barretas is the site of what is believed to be an ancient synagogue.
The first official synagogue dates from 1813. The Shaar-7 kuah synagogue, opened in 1904, was constructed inside a garden because legislation at that time did not permit non-Catholic places of worship to be directly on a public highway. It was classified as a 'Building of Public Interest' in 1997.

Communal Offices
Rua do Monte Olivete 16 r/c 1200 280
Telephone: (21) 393 1130
Fax: (21) 393 1139
Website: www.cilisboa.org

Maccabi Country Clube
Rua Gonçalves Correia, 8 – Albarraque, Rio de Mouro 2637-037
Telephone: (21) 911 1188

EMBASSY
Embassy of Israel
Rua Antonio Enes 16 4 1020 025
Telephone: (21) 355 3640
Fax: (21) 355 3658

JEWISH TOURS
Jewish Heritage Tours
Avenida 5 de Outubro, 321 1649 015
Telephone: (21) 791 9954
Website: www.jewishheritage.pt
Tours to explore Jewish ancestral roots in Portugal and to meet the descendants of the *Conversos*, the 'secret' Jews.

KOSHER FOODS
Mrs R. Assor
Rua Rodrigo da Fonseca 38.1´D
Telephone: (21) 386 0396
Kosher meals and delicatessen are obtainable if prior notice is given. For kosher meals, contact the communal offices.

SYNAGOGUES
Shararé Tikvá
Rua Alexandre Herculano, 59 1250-010

OPORTO
Mekor Haim
Rua Guerra Junqueiro 340

TOMAR

TOURIST SITES

Sephardi Museum
between Rua Direita dos Açougues and Rua dos
Moinhos
There is an interesting Sephardi museum in the old
synagogue

PUERTO RICO

The Jewish community in Puerto Rico is
just over 100 years old, with the first Jews
arriving from Cuba in 1898 after the beginning of American rule. During the Second
World War, many Jewish American servicemen went to the island, along with refugees
from Nazism. The Jewish Community
Centre dates from the early war years. After
the war the community grew with an influx
of Cuban and American Jews.

The capital San Juan, has the largest Jewish
population, and there are two synagogues.
There is also a Hebrew school held in the
Community Centre. The first Chief Justice
of Puerto Rico was Jewish.

GMT -4 hours
Country calling code: (+1 787)
Total population: **3,771,000**
Jewish population: **2,500**
Emergency telephone: (police–343-2020)
(fire–343-2330)
Electricity voltage: 120

ISLA VERDE

SYNAGOGUES

Orthodox
Chabad of Puerto Rico
18 Rosa Street 00979
Telephone: (787) 253 0894
Fax: (787) 791 9255
Email: rabbi@chabadpr.com
Website: www.chabadpr.com
Supervision: Chabad Rabbi
Notes: Kosher takeout available, for menu please call (787)
253 0894
Postal Address: PMB 122 5900 Isla Verde Ave L 2 Carolina,
PR 00979

SAN JUAN SANTURCE

Shaare Zedeck
903 Ponce de Leon Av., Santurce 00907
Telephone: (787) 724 4157
Services: Monday 7am, Thursday 7am, Kabalat Shabbat
Friday 6.30pm, Shabbat 9am, Sunday 9am

ROMANIA

Romanian Jewish life began when the
Romans gave the country its name and language. Community life increased and
evolved in the 15th Century as Jews came
from Poland and other East European countries despite opposition from the Church.

After the Treaty of Berlin (which demanded
equal rights for Jews) in 1878 was not imple-
mented in Romania, Jews began to emigrate,
but by 1918 the Jews were emancipated and
the population increased once more.

Romania's alliance with Germany during the
Second World War however, led to 385,000
of the 800,000 Romanian Jews being killed
in the Holocaust.

In the post war decade's Jewish practices
were allowed to continue, and in 1967 the
then Chief Rabbi Dr Moses Rosen was even
allocated a seat in Parliament.

Today Romania has a central Jewish body –
the Federation of Jewish Communities- and
there is a good deal to entice the Jewish
tourist; it is home to more than 800 synagogues including the Choral synagogue in
Bucharest, built in 1857 and the Great
Synagogue dating from 1850, which now
houses the Jewish History Museum.

Of particular interest are Elie Wiesel's childhood home in Maramures, restored and is
open to visitors; Satu Mare – the birthplace
of Satmar Hasidim – whose community
keep up the magnificent Synagogue with an
interior covered in biblical frescoes; and Isai,
one of the major European centres of Jewish
learning during the 19th century

GMT +2 hours
Country calling code: (+40)
Total population: 22,520,000
Jewish population: 12,000
Emergency telephone: (police–995) (fire–981)
(ambulance–961)
Electricity voltage: 220

ARAD
COMMUNITY ORGANISATIONS
Community Offices
10 Tribunal Dobra Street 310101
Telephone: (257) 281 310
Fax: (257) 281 310
Email: cea@rdslink.ro

RESTAURANTS
Ritual
22, 7 Episcopei Street
Telephone: (257) 280 731

SYNAGOGUES
Muzeul Judetean
Piata George Enescu 1
Telephone: (257) 280 114

Orthodox
Arad Synagogue
12 Cozia Street

Reform
Neolog Synagogue
10 Tribunal Dobra Street

BACAU
COMMUNITY ORGANISATIONS
Community Offices
11 Alexandru cel Bun Street
Telephone: (234) 134 714

RESTAURANTS
Kosher Restaurant
11 Alexandru cel Bun Street

SYNAGOGUES
Avram A. Rosen Synagogue
31 V. Alecsandri Street

Cerealistilor
29 Stefan cel Mare Street

BOTOSANI
COMMUNITY ORGANISATIONS
Community Offices
220 Calea Nationala
Telephone: (231) 0315 14659

MIKVAOT
Botosani Mikvaot
67 7 Aprilie Street

RESTAURANTS
Kosher Restaurant
69 7 Aprilie Street
Telephone: (231) 0315 15917

SYNAGOGUES
Botosani Synagogue
1a Marchian Street

Mare
18 Muzicantilor Street

Yiddish
10 Gh. Dimitrov Street

BRASOV
COMMUNITY ORGANISATIONS
Community Offices
27 Poarta Schei Street ro   500020
Telephone: (268) 511 867
Mobile Phone: 0040744327105
Central organisation: Federation of Jewish Communities

RESTAURANTS
Kosher Restaurant
27 Poarta Schei Street 500020
Telephone: (268) 511 864
Fax: (268) 511 867
Website: www.jewish.brasov.googlepages.com

SYNAGOGUES
Brasov Synagogue
27 Poarta Schei Street

BUCHAREST
COMMUNITY ORGANISATIONS
Chabad Lubavitch of Romania
Stelea Spataru St. nr 10 #6
Telephone: (21) 312 3667
Federation of Jewish Communities of Romania
Str. Sf. Vineri 9 11, Sector 3 030202
Telephone: (21) 313 2538
Fax: (21) 312 0869
Website: www.romanianjewish.org /
www.jewish.ro
Kosher supervision on 9 restaurants in the main Jewish
communities of Romania, (Arad, Bacau, Brasov, Bucharest,
Clu, Galati, Ilasi, Oradea, Timisoara)

EMBASSY
Embassy of Israel
1 Dimitrie Cantemir Bd.
Telephone: (21) 613 2634/5/6

MIKVAOT
Bucharest Mikvaot
5 Negustori Street

MUSEUMS
The History Museum of the Romanian Jews "Chief Rabbi Dr. Moses Rosen"
3 Mamoulari Street
Telephone: (21) 3110870
Fax: (21) 3151045
Email: bucharestjewmuseum@gmail.com
Hours: Sunday to Thursday 9am to 1pm
Free entry but only with passport or ID

RELIGIOUS ORGANISATIONS
Chief Rabbi of Romania
Strada St. Vineri 9 020481
Telephone: (21) 312 2196
Fax: (21) 312 0869
Mobile Phone: 740540542

RESTAURANTS
Jewish Community
18 Popa Soare Street
Telephone: (21) 322 4067
Fax: (21) 322 4067
This restaurant is operated by the Jewish Community

SYNAGOGUES
Choral Temple
Strada Sf. Vineri 9, Sector 3
Telephone: (21) 312 2196
Fax: (21) 312 0869

Credinta
48 Vasile Toneanu Street

Orthodox
Chabad Lubavitch of Romania
Aleea Negru Voda 6
Telephone: (21) 312 3668

Sephardi
Great Synagogue
9 11 Vasile Adamache Street
Telephone: (21) 615 0846

THEATRE
Jewish State Theatre
15 Juliu Barash Str., Sector 3 74212
Telephone: (21) 323 4530
Fax: (21) 323 2746
Website: www.dnt.ro/users/tes

CLUJ NAPOCA
COMMUNITY ORGANISATIONS
Community Offices
25 Tipografiei Street
Telephone: (264) 11667

MIKVAOT
Cluj Napoca Mikvaot
16 David Fransisc Street

RESTAURANTS
Kosher Restaurant
5 Paris Street
Telephone: (264) 596600
Email: comevcluj@upcmail.ro

SYNAGOGUES
Beth Hamidrash Ohel Moshe
16 David Fransisc Street

Sas Hevra
13 Croitorilor Street 400 162
Telephone: (264) 532 221
Fax: (264) 532 221
Website: www.bcucluj.ro/fil/f-stiud.html
Library of Jewish studies

Templul Deportatilor
21 Horea Street

CONSTANTA
COMMUNITY ORGANISATIONS
Jewish Community Office and Cultural Club
3 Sarmisagetuza Street
Telephone: (241) 611 598

SYNAGOGUES
Constanta Synagogue
3 Sarmisagetuza Street

Great Temple Synagogue
2 C.A. Rosetti Street
While the Great Temple Synagogue is still standing, it is clearly a very long time since it was used and in serious need of repair (starting with the caved-in roof). It is definitely not available for services or even for inspection other than from the street.

DOROHOI
COMMUNITY ORGANISATIONS
Community Office
95 Spiru Haret Street
Telephone: (31) 611 797

SYNAGOGUES
Great Synagogue
4 Piata Unirii Street

GALATI
COMMUNITY ORGANISATIONS
Community Office
9 Dornei Street
Telephone: (236) 413 662

RESTAURANTS
Kosher Restaurant
9 Dornei Street
Telephone: (236) 413 662

SYNAGOGUES
Meseriailor
11 Dornei Street

IASI (JASSY)
COMMUNITY ORGANISATIONS
Community Office
15 Elena Doamna Street
Telephone: (232) 114 414

MIKVAOT
Iasi Mikvaot
15 Elena Doamna Street

RESTAURANTS
Kosher Restaurant
15 Elena Doamna Street
Telephone: (232) 117 883

SYNAGOGUES
Schor
5 Sf. Constantin Street

ORADEA
COMMUNITY ORGANISATIONS
Community Office
4 Mihai Viteazu Street 410095
Telephone: (259) 434 843
Fax: (259) 434 843

RESTAURANTS
Kosher Restaurant
5 Mihai Viteazu Street
Telephone: (259) 431 383

SYNAGOGUES
Oradea Synagogue
4 Mihai Viteazu Street 410095
Telephone: (259) 434 843
Fax: (259) 434 843

PIATRA NEAMT
COMMUNITY ORGANISATIONS
Community Office
7 Petru Rares Street
Telephone: (33) 623 815

SYNAGOGUES
Leipziger
12 Meteorului Street

Old Baal Shem Tov
7 Meteorului Street
Old historical monument

RADAUTI
COMMUNITY ORGANISATIONS
Community Office
11 Aleea Primaverii, Block 14, Apt.1
Telephone: (30) 461 333

SYNAGOGUES
Radauti Synagogue
2, 1 Mai Street

Vijnitzer
49 Libertatii street

SATU MARE
Satu Mare is the Romanian name for the town
of Szatmar, where the famous Hassidic sect
originated. It is in the north west of Romania,
very near the border with Hungary. Before
World War One the town itself used to be in
Hungary.

COMMUNITY ORGANISATIONS
Comunitatea Evreilor
4/a Decebal Street 440006
Telephone: (261) 713 703
Fax: (261) 713 703
Email: jcsatumare@yahoo.com
Website: www.jewishcommunity.ro
Central organisation: Federatia Comumitatilor Evreiesti Din
Romania

SYNAGOGUES
Share Tora Sinagogue
4/a Decebal Street 440006
Telephone: (261) 713 703
Fax: (261) 713 703
Email: jcsatumare@yahoo.com
Website: www.jewishcomunite.ro

SFANTU GHEORGHE
TRAVEL AGENTS
International Tourism and Trade
Jozef Bem Str. 2, PO Box 152 520023
Telephone: (267) 316 375
Fax: (267) 351 551
Mobile Phone: 744 343 201
Email: itt@honoris.ro
Website: www.loveromania.com
Central organisation: National Association of Tourism
Agencies (NATA)

SIGHET
COMMUNITY ORGANISATIONS
Community Office
8 Basarabia Street

SYNAGOGUES
Sighet Synagogue
8 Basarabia Street

SUCEAVA
COMMUNITY ORGANISATIONS
Community Office
8 Armeneasca Street
Telephone: (30) 213 084

TIMISOARA
Tourist Information
5 Gh. Lazar Street
Telephone: (56) 132 813

MIKVAOT
Timisoara Mikvaot
55 Resita Street

RESTAURANTS
Kosher Restaurant
10 Marasesti Street
Telephone: (56) 136 924

SYNAGOGUES
Cetate
6 Marasesti Street

Fabric
2 Splaiul Coloniei

Iosefin
55 Resita Street

TIRGU MURES
COMMUNITY ORGANISATIONS
Community Office
10 Brailei Street
Telephone: (65) 115 001

SYNAGOGUES
Tirgu Mures Synagogue
21 Aurel Filimon Street

TUSHNAD
HOTELS
Kosher
Olt Hotel
c/o Interom Tours
Telephone: (972) 3924 6425
Fax: (972) 3579 1720

VATRA DORNEI
COMMUNITY ORGANISATIONS
Community Office
54 M Eminescu Street
Telephone: (30) 371 957

SYNAGOGUES
Vijnitzer
14 Luceafarul Street

RUSSIAN FEDERATION

In early Russian history Jews were not allowed to settle, and the few who did were later expelled by various Czars. After 1772, however, Russia acquired a large area of Poland, where lived a significant number of Jews. There were still restrictions against the Jews, but eventually they were allowed to settle in the 'Pale of Settlement', an area in the west of the Russian Empire. Between 1881 and 1914 2,000,000 Jews emigrated from the Empire, escaping from anti-semitism.

Jews were only allowed into Russia itself in the mid-nineteenth century, and by 1890 there were 35,000 Jews in Moscow. Most were expelled the following year. The community grew after the Second World War, drawing Jewish immigration from Belarus and Ukraine to cities such as Moscow and Leningrad. Birobidzhan was a failed experiment to give the Jews their own 'Autonomous District', and those who moved there (in the far east, near China) soon moved away. Under communism both religious practices and emigration were restricted, but since 1991 there has been a revival in Jewish learning. There are synagogues functioning in many cities, and there are now 100 Jewish schools. The major threat is still from anti-semitic right-wing groups, who are unfortunately increasing their activity.

GMT +2 to +12 hours
Country calling code: **(+7)**
Total population: **146,100.000**
Jewish population: **300,000**
Emergency telephone: **(police–02) (fire–01) (ambulance–03)**
Electricity voltage: **220**

ASTRAKHAN
Astrakhan Synagogue
30 Babushkin Street

BIROBIDJAN
Birobidjan, the size of Belgium, was created in 1934 as a Jewish homeland in the wilds of Siberia. It was not a success and was effectively terminated in the 1940s. There has, however, now been a resurgence of interest in what was known as the Jewish Autonomous District.
Birobidjan Synagogue
9 Chapaev Street, Khabarovsk Krai

BRYANSK
Bryansk Synagogue
Narodov Vostoka Street 82 Lermontov Street
Lubavitch
Synagogue of Bryansk
27a Uritskovo Street 241000
Telephone: (832) 445 515

CHELYABINSK
Synagogue of Chelyabinsk
Pushkina 6b
454091
Telephone: (351) 263 2468/4971/3419;265 9150
Fax: (351) 263 2468
Email: chabadural@mail.ru
Central organisation: Federation of Jewish communities of the C.I.S

DERBENT
Derbent Synagogue
94 Tagi Zade street

Lubavitch
Jewish Community of Derbent
23 Kandelaky Street 368600
Telephone: (8724) 021 731

EKATERINBURG
Ekaterinburg Synagogue
18/2 Kirov Street

IRKUTSK
Irkutsk Synagogue
17 Karl Liebknecht Street

KAZAN
The capital of Tatarstan, an autonomous Russian republic, has 10,000 Jews, an Ort school and its own Jewish newspaper.

Lubavitch
Synagogue of Kazan
15 Profsouznaya Street 420111
Telephone: (8432) 329 743

KHABAROVSK
JUDAICA
Judaica Shop
Frunze St 76-2 POB 77

KOSTRAMA
SYNAGOGUES
Lubavitch
Synagogue of Kostrama

16a Sennoi Peroulok 156026
Telephone: (942) 514 388

KRASNOYARSK
Synagogue of Krasnoyarsk
65 Surikova Street 660049
Telephone: (3912) 223 615
Fax: (3912) 440 137

KURSK
Kursk Synagogue
3 Bolshevitskaya Street

MAKHACHKALA
Makhachkala Synagogue
111 Yermoshkin Street

MOSCOW
Around 200,000 Jews now live in Moscow, and since the collapse of the USSR in 1991 the community has experienced a revival. The Choral Synagogue on Arkhipova Street, which was built in 1891 and was used during the Soviet regime, is again the focus of Jewish religious life. The Lubavitch movement has its own centre, and there has been an upsurge of interest in Jewish education.

CONTACT INFORMATION
Chief Rabbi of Moscow
Rabbi Pinchas Goldschmidt
Telephone: (095) 623 4288; 940 5556
Fax: (095) 623 4186
Website: www.keroor.ru
Central organisation: KEROOR

EMBASSY
Embassy of Israel
Bolshaya Ordinka 56
Telephone: (095) 230 6777
Fax: (095) 238 1346

KOSHER FOODS
Kosher Food
Spassoglinishevsky per., 10
Kosher Supermarket
Trifonovskaya St. 45
Telephone: (095) 926 8728; 681 5265

Moscow Kosher Food Centre
Archipova Street
Telephone: (095) 925 4601

LIBRARIES
Central Library
A Jewish literature reading hall opened in 2002. The hall holds the state Library's Jewish Literature collection.

RESTAURANTS
Dairy
Café Yael
2nd Vysheslavtsev Pereulok 5a 127018
Telephone: (095) 231 3028/2777
Fax: (095) 231 3025

Kosher Food
The Restaurant on Nikitskaya
Nikitskaya Street 47
Telephone: (095) 291 4045

Meat
Choral Synagogue Restaurant
14, 6 Bolshoi Spaniglovskaya Street, Apartment 6, Moscow Synagogue, Kitai Gorod, Kitai Gorod

King David Club
Bolshoi Spasoglinishchevsky per. (Arkhipova Street) 6, door code 77
Telephone: (095) 925 4601
Fax: (095) 924 4243
Supervision: Rabbi Pinchas Goldschmidt, Chief Rabbi of Moscow
This kosher food centre serves as a glatt kosher restaurant and a mini hotel. Catering services are available, as are lunchboxes.

Mekor Haim
16 Zvinigorodskaya
Telephone: (095) 144 3246

Na Monmartre
Vetoshny per., 9
Telephone: (095) 745 5230
Fax: (095) 745 5239
Supervision: Rabbi Berl Lazar
On the 5th floor of a modern shopping centre (the Frech Gallery Mall) near Redsquare.

Yonah Kosher Restaurant
2nd Vysheslavtsev Pereulok 5a 127018
Telephone: (095) 231 3028
Fax: (095) 231 3025

SYNAGOGUES
Lubavitch
Chabad Lubavitch
4 Novousushevsky Peroulok 103055
Telephone: (095) 218 0001
Fax: (095) 219 9707

Chabad Lubavitch Synagogue
6 Balshaya Bronya Street 103104
Telephone: (095) 202 4530

Fax: (095) 291 6483
Known as the Polyakov synagogue after the railway and banking family

Darkei Shalom Synagogue
1 Novovladikinsky Peroulok 103055
Telephone: (095) 903 0782
Fax: (095) 903 2218

Orthodox
Moscow Choral Synagogue
Bolshoi Spasoglinishchevsky per. (Arkhipova Street) 10
Telephone: (095) 924 2424

NALCHIK
Nalchik Synagogue
73 Rabochaya Street, corner Osetinskaya

NIZHNY NOVGOROD
Lubavitch
Nizhny Novgorod Synagogue
5a Gruzinskaya Street 603000
Telephone: (8312) 336 345
Fax: (8312) 303 759

NOVOSIBIRSK
Novosibirsk Synagogue
23 Luchezarnaya Street

Lubavitch
Synagogue of Novosibirsk
14 Koministisheskaya
Telephone: (3832) 210 698

PENZA
Penza Synagogue
15 Krasnaya Street

PERM
Perm Synagogue
Pushkin Street

ROSTOV NA DONU
Lubavitch
Synagogue of Rostov na Donu
18 Gazetny Peroulok 344007
Telephone: (8632) 624 759
Fax: (8632) 624 119

SACHKHERE
Sachkhere Synagogue
145 Sovetskaya Street 105 Tsereteli Street

SAMARA
Samara Synagogue
3 Chapaev Street

Lubavitch
The Samara Jewish Community Centre
84B Chapaevskaya St 443099
Telephone: (8462) 334 064
Fax: (8462) 320 242
The community center has a school, kindergarten, library, women's Mikveh, and a kosher lemihadrin kitchen

SARATOV
Saratov Synagogue
Posadskov Street

Saratov Synagogue
2 Kirpichnaya Street

Lubavitch
Synagogue of Saratov
208 Posadskovo Street 410005
Telephone: (8452) 249 592

ST PETERSBURG
With 100,000 Jews, St Petersburg is witnessing a similar Jewish revival to Moscow. There are opportunities to pray, learn and eat kosher. This was not the case before 1991 in the USSR. Americans and Israelis are the main motivators behind the revival, but St Petersburg Jewry is also eager to learn about religion, now that there is the freedom to do so.

Seven-Forty Restaurant
Bolshoy Sampsonievsky pr. 108
Telephone: (812) 246 3444
Opening hours 12pm to 11pm
except Mon: 13pm to 11pm

MIKVAOT
St Petersburg Mikvaot
2 Lermontovsky Prospekt
Telephone: (812) 714 4428
Website: jewsp.ru

RESTAURANTS
Lechaim
Lermontovskiy Avenue 2 190121
Telephone: (812) 572 5616

Yeshiva
24 Sayuza Petshatnikov
Telephone: (812) 110 8496

Meat
Shalom
8 Koli Tomchaka Street
Telephone: (812) 327 5475

SYNAGOGUES
The Grand Choral Synagogue of St. Petersburg
2 Lermontovsky Prospekt 190121
Telephone: (812) 337 2478
Fax: (812) 320 1329
Email: tourismsynagogue@mail.ru

The Synagogue is open daily 8.30am to 8pm. The daily services are held at the Small Synagogue at 9am. Shabbat services at 10am at the Grand Choral Synagogue. Mikvah is open on request, please call 812 713 6209. Tourism department open daily 9am to 7pm except Saturdays and Sundays. Guided tours by Synagogue and Jewish Museum, cantor concerts, Jewish city excursions.
TOURS
Zekher Avoteinu Jewish Tourist and Genealogical Agency
Nastavnikov Av., 26 1 318 195298
Telephone: (921) 945 0874
Fax: (812) 325 2264
Website: www.zekhera.hypermart.net
Can be contacted in the USA, telephone 01.718 236 6037

TULA
SYNAGOGUES
Tula Synagogue
15 Veresaevskaya Street

VLADIKAVKAZ
Vladikavkaz Synagogue
Revolutsiya Street

VOLGOGRAD
Chabad of Volgograd
Novorosiyskaya 43 400087
Telephone: (8442) 378 308

YEKATRINBURG
Lubavitch
Yekatrinburg Synagogue
118/93 Shekmana Street 620144
Telephone: (3432) 236 440
Fax: (3432) 293 054

SERBIA

GMT +1 hours
Country calling code: (+381)
Emergency telephone: (ambulance–94)

BELGRADE
COMMUNITY ORGANISATIONS
Federation of Jewish Communities in Serbia
7 Karlija Petra Street 71a/III, PO Box 30 11001
Telephone: 2624 359; 2621 837
Fax: 2626 674
Email: office@savezscg.org

MUSEUMS
Jewish Historical Museum
Kralja Petra Street 71a/1 11000
Telephone: 2622 634
Fax: 626 674
Website: www.jimbg.org
Open daily from 10am to 2pm

SYNAGOGUES
Belgrade Synagogue -Succat Shalom
Birjuzova Street 19
Telephone: 112 910 363
Fax: 112 626 674
Mobile Phone: 6374 90850
Email: rabahut@savezscg.org
Supervision: European Central Kashrut
Central organisation: Federation of Jewish Communities in Serbia
Services are held Friday evenings, Saturday mornings and evenings and Jewish holidays

TOURIST SITES
Jewish Cemetery
There are monuments here to fallen fighters and martyrs of Fascism and fallen Jewish soldiers in the Serbian army in the First World War. In 1990 a new monument to Jews killed in Serbia was erected by the Danube, in the pre war Jewish quarter Dorcol.

NOVI SAD
COMMUNITY ORGANISATIONS
The Jewish Community Novi Sad
Jevrejska 11 21000
Telephone: (21) 423 882; 661 5750
Fax: (21) 423 882
Email: jonovisad@sbb.co.yu
Central organisation: Federation of the Jewish Communities in Serbia

TOURIST SITES
Jewish Cemetery
There is a monument to the Jews who fell in the War and the victims of Fascism. The synagogue here is no longer open but it's reported to be extremely beautiful, and is currently being converted to a concert hall.

SUBOTICA
COMMUNITY ORGANISATIONS
Community Offices
Dimitrija Tucovica Street 13
Telephone: (24) 28483

TOURIST SITES
Subotica Synagogue
24000Telephone: (24) 670 970
Central organisation: Jewish Community Subotica
The Subotica Synagogue built in 1901 and considered one of the finest Art Nouveau buildings in Europe is currently being restored.

SINGAPORE

As Singapore developed into an important south-east Asian trading centre in the mid-nineteenth century, some Jewish traders from India and Iraq set up a community there in 1841. A synagogue was built in 1878, and another in 1904. By the time of the Japanese occupation in the Second World War the community had grown to 5,000, and included some eastern European Jews. The Japanese imprisoned the community and took their property. After the war emigration to Australia and the USA reduced numbers, but in recent years Israelis who work in the country and other Jews have moved in. Ninety per cent of the community are Sephardi.

David Marshall, who was a POW in Japan, returned to Singapore and in 1955 became Chief Minister.

One of the two synagogues is used regularly, and there is a mikvahh and a newsletter. The Sir Manasseh Meyer Community Centre is the hub of Jewish life. The Jewish community today is small and mainly composed of professionals.

Country calling code: (+65)
Total population: 3,737,00
Jewish population: 300
Emergency telephone: (police–999) (fire–999) (ambulance–999)
Electricity voltage: 220/240

COMMUNITY ORGANISATIONS
Jewish Welfare Board
Robinson Road, PO Box 474

CONTACT INFORMATION
Rabbi Abergel
238592Telephone: 737 9112
Website: www.singaporejews.com
Supervision: Orthodox Rabbinate of Singapore
Central organisation: Jewish Welfare Board
Contact for more detailed information on the community
and availability of kosher products. Mrs. Simcha Abergel
can be contacted for information on the mikvah

EMBASSY
Embassy of Israel
58 Dalvey Road S 1025
Telephone: 235 0966
Fax: 733 7008

SYNAGOGUES
Orthodox
Chesed El
2 Oxley Rise 238693
Telephone: 732 8832
Services Monday only, Shacharit and Mincha/Maariv

Maghain Aboth Synagogue
24/26 Waterloo Street 187950
Telephone: 337 2189
Fax: 336 2127
Website: www.singaporejews.org
Daily and Sabbat services are held, except for Monday
when services are held at Chesed El Synagogue. Because
Singapore has equatorial times, Mincha/ Maariv
commences at 6.45 pm throughout the year. Shacharit:
weekdays 7.30 am, Friday night Shabbat meal served after
evening service. Shabbat 9am. Every Shabbat, lunch is
served for the community. Breakfast is currently served
every morning after services. Mikvah is available for use.
For details please contact 737 9112 Rabbi Mordechai
Abergel. There are kosher meat, cheese, wine, and other
grocery items on sale at the synagogue.

SLOVAKIA

Slovakia has passed through the control of
various countries over the centuries, finally
gaining independence after the peaceful
splitting of Czechoslovakia in 1992. Before
1918 the region was part of Hungary, and
many in southern Slovakia, near the
Hungarian border still speak Hungarian.

In 1939 the Jewish population in the Slovak
area of Czechoslovakia numbered 150,000,
but the Hungarians occupied the south of
the country and assisted the Germans in
deporting Jews to Auschwitz and other
camps. Many survivors emigrated after the
war, but some remained and are now redis-
covering their Jewish heritage. Since independence, B'nai B'rith and Maccabi have
been established, but anti-semitism has re-
emerged. There are kosher restaurants in
Bratislava and Kosice, and Jewish education is available once more.

GMT +1 hours
Country calling code: (**+421**)
Total population: **5,383,000**
Jewish population: **5,000**
Emergency telephone: (**police–158**) (**fire–150**)
(**ambulance–155**)
Electricity voltage: **220**

BRATISLAVA
Known in German as Pressburg, Bratislava was
a key centre of Judaism when Slovakia was
under Hungarian rule before the First World
War. Bratislava was especially famous for the
number of Jewish scholars living there,
including the Chatam Sofer. The preserved
underground tomb of the Chatam Sofer and
other rabbis is now a place of pilgramage.

COMMUNITY ORGANISATIONS
**Central Union of Jewish Religious
Communities in the Slovak Republic**
Kozia ul. 21 81447
Telephone: (2) 5441 2167/8357
Fax: (2) 5441 1106

GUEST HOUSE
Chez David
Zamocka 13 81101
Telephone: (2) 5441 3824
Fax: (2) 5441 2642
Website: www.chezdavid.sk

MIKVAOT
Bratislava Mikvaot
Zamocka 13 81101
Telephone: (2) 5441 7829
Fax: (2) 5441 7814

MUSEUMS
The Museum of Jewish Culture
Zidovska Street 81101
Telephone: (2) 593 49142/3/4
Fax: (2) 593 49145
Website: www.slovak jewish heritage.org
Contact: Prof. Pavol Mest'an Dr. Sc.

Underground Mausoleum

Contains the graves of eighteen famous rabbis, including the Chatam Sofer. The key is available from the community office.

PENSION AND JEWISH RESTAURANT
Chez David
Zamocka 13 81101
Telephone: (2) 5441 3824/6943
Fax: (2) 5441 2642
Website: www.chezdavid.sk
Supervision: Rabbi Baruch Myers

SYNAGOGUES
Bratislava Synagogue
Heydukova 11 13
Services held Monday, Thursday and Saturday

GALANTA

MIKVAOT
Galanta Synagogue
Partizanska 907

SYNAGOGUES
Galanta Synagogue
Partizanska 907
Daily services held

KOSICE

RESTAURANTS
Meat
Community Centre
Zvonarska Ul 5, Kaschau 4001
Telephone: (55) 622 1047

SYNAGOGUES
Beth Hamidrash
Zvonarska Ul 5, Kaschau
Daily services held

Kosice Synagogue
Puskinova Ul 3, Kaschau

PIESTANY

CEMETERIES
Old Cemetery
Janosikova Ul 606

SYNAGOGUES
Piestany Synagogue
Hviezdoslavova 59
Shabbat and festival services held

TRNAVA

MONUMENT
Monument of Deportees
Halenarska Ul 32
In the courtyard of the former synagogue

SYNAGOGUES
Synagogue
Kapitulska Ul 7

SLOVENIA

Maribor was the centre for medieval Jewish life in what is now Slovenia. Expulsion followed after the Austrian occupation in the late Middle Ages, but in 1867 the Jews in the Austrian empire were emancipated and some returned to Slovenia. The community was never large. During the Second World War the members of the small Jewish community either escaped to Italy, fought with the Yugoslav partisans, or were deported.

After WW2, the Jewish Community of Slovenia was formed which was attached to the Federation of Yugoslav Jewish Communities until Slovenia's secession in 1991. In 1997, the first official Jewish Community office since WW11 was bought and the community activities increased, and in 1999 Rabbi Ariel Haddad was inaugurated as the first Chief Rabbi of Slovenia in history.

Today, Slovenian Jews gather for the major Jewish Holidays and Festivals, and there are lectures and dancing classes. A cultural and educational bulletin is published monthly and there is a Youth group, which organises Shabbatot, educational events and outings.

Traces of Jewish history are to be found in Lendava, and there is a restored (but non-functioning) synagogue in Maribor.

GMT +1 hours
Country calling code: (+386)
Total population: **1,987,000**
Jewish population: **Under 400 - 600**
Emergency telephone: **(police–93) (fire–92)
(ambulance–94)**
Electricity voltage: **220**

LJUBLJANA
The great majority of Slovene Jews live in the capital Ljubljana

COMMUNITY ORGANISATIONS
Jewish Community of Slovenia
Trzaska 2 1000
Telephone: (61) 426 9150
Fax: (61) 2521 836
Email: jss@siol.net
Website: www.jewishcommunity.si
Opening hours: Tuesday 5pm to 7pm, Friday: 9:30am to 12pm

SOUTH AFRICA

Although some believe that Jews were present in the country at around the time of the first European settlement in the area in the seventeenth century, the community only really began in the nineteenth century when religious freedom was granted. In 1836 the explorer Nathaniel Isaacs published 'Travels and Adventures in Eastern Africa', an important contemporary account of Zulu life and customs.

The year 1841 saw the first Hebrew Congregation in Cape Town, and the discovery of diamonds in the Transvaal later in the century prompted a wave of Jewish immigration.

The main immigration of Jews into South Africa occurred at the end of the nineteenth century, when many thousands left Eastern Europe, the majority from Lithuania (40,000 had arrived by 1910). Although the country did not officially accept refugees from the Nazis, about 8,000 Jews managed to enter the country after their escape from Europe.

Today the community is affluent and has good relations with the government. There is a South African Board of Deputies, and many international Jewish associations are present in the country. There are kosher

hotels and restaurants, and Jewish museums. Kosher wine is produced at the Zaandwijk Winery.

GMT +2 hours
Country calling code: (+27)
Total population: **43,336,00**
Jewish population: **80,000**
Emergency telephone: **(police–1011) (fire–1022)
(ambulance–10222)**
Electricity voltage: **220/250**

Eastern Cape
PORT ELIZABETH
MUSEUMS
Jewish Pioneers' Memorial Museum
Raleigh Street cnr Edward Street
Telephone: (41) 373 5197
Fax: (41) 374 3612
Open between 10am and noon every Sunday. The museum has a ramp for disabled access. It is also a National Monument . For further information visitors may phone Dr Sam Abrahams (41) 583 3671.

SYNAGOGUES
Summerstrand Hebrew Congregation
47 Brighton Drive, PO Box 1365 6000
Telephone: (41) 585 2678

Orthodox
Port Elizabeth Hebrew Congregation
Abraham Levy Centre, Barris Walk, Glendinningvale 6001
Telephone: (41) 373 1332
Fax: (41) 374 3612

Progressive
Temple Israel
Upper Dickens Street
Telephone: (41) 373 6642

Free State
BLOEMFONTEIN
RELIGIOUS ORGANISATIONS
United Hebrew Institutions
Community Centre, 1 Dickie Clark Street, PO Box 1152
Telephone: (51) 436 2207
Fax: (51) 436 6447
Mornings

SYNAGOGUES
Bloemfontein Synagogue
1 Dickie Clark Street, Dan Pienaar, PO Box 9300
Telephone: (51) 436 2207
Fax: (51) 436 6447
Mikvah also available

Gauteng

BRAKPAN

RELIGIOUS ORGANISATIONS

Brakpan Synagogue
cnr. Victoria Avenue and Cavendish
Telephone: (53) 832 5652
For further information phone Mr Waner, tel: (011) 740 0903

JOHANNESBURG

The largest city in South Africa also has the
largest Jewish community in the country. About
70% of the country's Jews live there (a
community of some 55,000) and the
headquarters of many of South African Jewry's
institutions are housed there. There are more
than fifty synagogues in the city.

BAKERIES

Brooklyn Bagel
Shop 7, Lyndhurst Discount Centre, cnr
Modderfontein & Pretoria Rds, Lyndhurst
Telephone: (11) 882 2474
Fax: (11) 882 8565
Supervision: Johannesburg Beth Din

Friends Bakery
53 Ridge Road, Glenhazel
Telephone: (11) 440 5094
Fax: (11) 440 5096
Supervision: Johannesburg Beth Din

Shirley's
114 William Road, Norwood
Telephone: (11) 728 0974
Fax: (11) 728 2807
Supervision: Johannesburg Beth Din

BED AND BREAKFAST

Kosher Bed and Breakfast
124 Third Avenue, Fairmount
Telephone: (11) 485 5006
Fax: (11) 485 5518
Supervision: Johannesburg Beth Din

BOOKSELLERS

Chadbad House books
Shop 224 Balfour Park Shopping Centre
Telephone: (11) 786 1561

House of Judaica
Glenhazel

Kollel Bookshop
107 Norwood Road, Norwood
Telephone: (11) 728 1822
Fax: (11) 728 1813

BUTCHERS

Bolbrand Poultry Shoppe
74 76 George Avenue, Sandringham 2192
Telephone: (11) 640 4080
Supervision: Johannesburg Beth Din

Gallo Manor Kosher Butchery
Morning Glen Shopping Centre, cnr. Braides &
Kelvin Sts, Gallo Manor
Telephone: (11) 802 3539
Fax: (11) 802 6546
Supervision: Johannesburg Beth Din

Gardens Kosher
cnr. Grant & 6th Avenue, Norwood 2052
Telephone: (11) 483 3357
Fax: (11) 728 1562
Supervision: Johannesburg Beth Din

Maxi Discount Kosher Butcher
74 George Avenue, Sandringham 2192
Telephone: (11) 485 1485/1486
Fax: (11) 485 2991
Supervision: Johannesburg Beth Din

Nussbaums
434 Louis Botha Avenue, cnr. Main St., Rouxville
Telephone: (11) 485 2303
Fax: (11) 640 4663
Email: nussbaums@telkomsa.net
Supervision: Johannesburg Beth Din

Rishon Balfour
Checker Balfour Park, cnr. Louis Botha & Athol Sts,
Highlands North
Telephone: (11) 786 9626
Fax: (11) 885 1996
Supervision: Johannesburg Beth Din

Trevors
Bramley Gardens Shopping Centre
Telephone: (11) 885 3663
Fax: (11) 887 9502
Supervision: Johannesburg Beth Din

DELICATESSEN

DJ's Deli
85c 3rd Percelia
Telephone: (11) 887 5756
milchik vleishikMehadrin

DELICATESSEN AND BAKERIES

Fegel's Kosher Delicatessan
Bramley Gardens Shopping Centre, Shop 1, 280
Corlett Drive
Telephone: (11) 887 9505/6
Fax: (11) 887 9507
Supervision: Johannesburg Beth Din
Hours: Friday, 7.30 am to 4.30 pm; Sunday, 8am to 1pm;
Monday to Thursday, 10am to 5pm

Feigel's Kosher Delicatessan
Shop 3, Queens Place, Kingswood Road, Glenhazel
2192
Telephone: (11) 887 1364
Supervision: Johannesburg Beth Din

Kosher King
74 George Avenue, Sandringham
Telephone: (11) 640 6234
Supervision: Johannesburg Beth Din
Hours: Monday to Thursday, 8.30 am to 5pm; Friday, 8am to 3pm; Sunday, 9am to 1 pm

Pick 'N' Pay
cnr. Grant Avenue & 6th Street, Norwood
Telephone: (11) 483 3357
Fax: (11) 728 1562
Supervision: Johannesburg Beth Din

Pie Works and Deli
Shop 35 Greenhill Road, Emmarentia 2195
Telephone: (11) 486 1502
Fax: (11) 486 0580
Supervision: Johannesburg Beth Din
Hours: weekdays, 8am to 5.30 pm; Friday to 4pm; Sunday 9am to 2pm

Shoshana's Bakery
Stan Tech House, cnr. Cross Road and Queens Square, Glenhazel
Telephone: (11) 85 1039
Supervision: Johannesburg Beth Din

The Pie Works
74 George Avenue, Sea Point, Sandringham 2192
Telephone: (11) 485 2447
Supervision: Johannesburg Beth Din
Hours: weekdays, 8am to 5pm; Friday, to 4pm; Sunday to 2pm

LIBRARIES
The Manfred Frysh Library (Kollel Library)
5 Water Lane, Orchards 2192
Telephone: (11) 728 1308
Fax: (11) 728 8597
Central organisation: Kollel Yad Shaul

MEDIA
Newspapers
The S.A. Jewish Report
Suite 175, Postnet X10039, Randburg 2125
Telephone: (11) 886 0162
Fax: (11) 886 4202
Email: carro@global.co.za
Website: www.sajewishreport.co.za

Periodicals
Jewish Affairs
2 Elray Street, Raedene, PO BoX 87557, Houghton 2041 2192
Telephone: (11) 645 2500
Fax: (11) 645 2559
Email: david@beyacha
Website: www.jewish.org.za
Quarterly journal of the South African Jewish Board of Deputies

Jewish Heritage
PO Box 3 7179 Birnham Park 2015
Telephone: (11) 880 1830
Jewish Tradition
PO Box 46559, Orange Grove 2119
Telephone: (11) 485 4865
Fax: (11) 640 7528
Email: tradition@uos.co.za
Publication of the Union of Orthodox Synagogues of South Africa

South African Jewish Observer
PO Box 29189, Sandringham 2131
Telephone: (11) 440 2206
Fax: (11) 786 8155
A publication of the Mizrachi Organisation of South Africa

MIKVA
Be'Chaya Ester
Sandler Road, Glenhazel
Telephone: (11) 485 1417
Chana-Chabad Sandton
Sandton
Telephone: (11) 440 3161

MIKVAOT
Glenhazel Mikvah (Be'er Rachel)
65 Nicholson Avenue, Glenkay 2192
Telephone: (11) 485 1555
Email: ravperez@netactive.co.za
Sandton Mikvah
211 Rivonia Road, Morningside
Telephone: (11) 883 4210

RELIGIOUS ORGANISATIONS
The Southern African Union for Progressive Judaism
357 Louis Botha Avenue, Highlands North
Telephone: (11) 640 6614
Union of Orthodox Synagogues of South Africa
58 Oaklands Road, Orchards 2192
Telephone: (11) 485 4865
Fax: (11) 640 7528
Email: info@uos.co.za
The office of the Chief Rabbi as well as the Beth Din are located at the same address and phone number

RESTAURANTS
Crepe Latte
Shop 23 Melrose Boulevard
Telephone: (11) 684 2020
Vleishick Restaurant 'Relish' (meat) next door
Divine Restaurant
430 Louis Botha Avenue, corner Main Street, Sydenham
Mobile Phone: 9861 567 437
Mooz Brothers
74 George Avenue, Sandringham

Telephone: (11) 485 5589
michik parev bakery

Dairy
DJ's
Morningside Shopping Centre, corner Rivonia &
Outspan Road
Telephone: (11) 883 2265

Michelo's
15 Northfield Avenue, Glenhazel
Telephone: (11) 885 1500

Next Door
Grant Avenue
Telephone: (11) 728 2577

Meat
Burger Box
17 Northfield Avenue, Glenhazel

Chop Chop Chinese
Balfour Park Shopping Centre
Telephone: (11) 440 8958

D.J's Take Away
Balfour Park Shopping Centre, Shop No. 232,
Balfour Park 2090
Telephone: (11) 440 1792
Supervision: Johannesburg Beth Din

Metzuyan
Shop No. 7, Shell Court, cnr. Craddock Avenue &
Baker Street, Rosebank 2196
Telephone: (11) 880 4153
Supervision: Johannesburg Beth Din
Hours: Sunday to Thursday 10am to 3pm; 6pm to 10pm;
Motzei Shabbat, 1 hour after Shabbat to 12am.

Soul
Upper Level, Balfour Park Shopping Centre, cnr.
Athol Road, Highlands North
Telephone: (11) 887 4960
Supervision: Johannesburg Beth Din

The Barrio
80 Grant Avenue
Telephone: (11) 728 2577

Parev & Milchik
Franjelicas
5 Long Avenue, Glenhazel
Telephone: (11) 887 7675
Fax: (11) 443 8271
Mobile Phone: 082 88 2468
Website: www.jewishweb.co.za

SYNAGOGUES

There are more than fifty synagogues in Johannesburg.
Please contact the appropriate Religious Organisation for
details (Page 208).

TOURS
African Kosher Safaris
PO Box 51380, Raedene 2124
Telephone: (11) 485 4635
Fax: (11) 485 4635
Mobile Phone: 27 82 924 6527
Email: yoni@aksafaris.com
Website: www.aksafaris.com
Supervision: Beth Din of Johannesburg
Central organisation: Rabbi Yoni Isaacson
Kosher tours, safaris and youth camps in Southern Africa
for all budget levels and interest groups: Chobe, Victoria
Falls, Cape Town, Garden Route, St Lucia Wetlands, Kruger
National Park, Blyde River Canyon etc.

African Safaris Experience
26 Kings Road, Bedfordview
Telephone: (11) 832 5652
Website: www.asesouthafrica.co.za

Information
Lion of Africa
PO Box 64189, Highlands North 2037
Telephone: (11) 640 1608
Fax: (11) 640 1608
Mobile Phone: (82)331 8412
Email: Lion2@roary.com
Website: www.roary.com

TOURS & SAFARIS
Celafrica Tours
7 Wallace Street,
Waverley,
2037
Telephone: (11) 887 5262
Fax: (11) 885 3097
Mobile Phone: +27 82 320 5525
Email: celeste@celafrica.com
Website: www.celafrica.com
The company specialises in kosher safaris and tours to
southern Africa
Mailing: PO Box 357, Highlands North,

KRUGERSDORP
SYNAGOGUES
Krugersdorp Synagogue
1 Cilliers Street, Monument
Telephone: (11) 954 1367
Fax: (11) 953 4905

PRETORIA
EMBASSY
Embassy of Israel
3rd Floor, Dashing Centre, 339 Hilda Street, Hatfield
Telephone: (12) 342 2693

KASHRUT INFORMATION
Pretoria Council of BOD
Telephone: (12) 344 2372
Fax: (12) 344 2059

KOSHER FOODS
Pick 'N' Pay
Brooklyn Square Mall, Middle Street, Muckleneuk
Telephone: (12) 346 8680
Kosher prepacked food under the Johannesburg Beth Din.

Spar
Groenkloof Plaza, George Stonar Drive, Groenkloof
Telephone: (12) 346 5555
Kosher food prepacked under the Johannesburg Beth Din.

MUSEUMS
Sammy Marks Museum
PO Box 4197, Old Brokhorstpruit 1
Telephone: (12) 802 1150
Fax: (12) 802 1292
Central organisation: NFI
Hours of opening: Tuesday to Sunday, 10am to 4pm.

RESTAURANTS
JAFFA Old Age Home
42 Mackie Street, Baileys Muckleneuk 181
Telephone: (12) 346 2006
Fax: (12) 346 2008
Website: www.jaffa.org.za
Hotel as well, prior booking necessary. Kosher catering, resident mashgiach. Kosher meals, both meat and dairy, available on request.

SYNAGOGUES
Orthodox
Adath Israel Centre
246 Schroder Stresst, Groenkloof
Telephone: (12) 460 7991
Fax: (12) 480 5911
Email: phc@netactive.co.za
Website: www.phc org.za

Progressive
Temple Menorah
315 Bronkhorst Street, New Muckleneuk, PO Box 1497
Telephone: (12) 467 296

SPRINGS
Springs Synagogue
40 Charterland Avenue, Selcourt
Telephone: (11) 818 2572

KwaZulu Natal

DURBAN
BED AND BREAKFAST
Beit Ya'akov
75 Windmill Road, PO Box 47314, Greyville 4023
Telephone: (31) 202 7275
Fax: (31) 202 7302
Run by family who are shomer mitzvot

BUTCHERS
Pick 'N' Pay
Musgrave Centre, Berea 4001
Telephone: (31) 201 4208
Bakery as well

COMMUNITY ORGANISATIONS
Council of KwaZulu Natal Jewry
44 Old Fort Road 4001
Telephone: (31) 335 4452
Fax: (31) 337 9600
Email: cknj@djc.co.za
Mailing address: PO Box 10797, Marine Parade 4056

Durban Jewish Club
44 Old Fort Road, Durban 4001
Telephone: (31) 335 4456
Fax: (31) 337 9600
Mailing address: PO Box 10797, Marine Parade 4056

RESTAURANTS
Café Shalom
Durban Hebrew Congregation, cnr. Essenwood & Silverton Roads
Telephone: (31) 201 5177
Fax: (31) 202 8925

Dairy
Great Synagogue
Cnr. Silverton & Essenwood Roads, PO Box 50044, Musgrave Road 4062
Telephone: (31) 302 1205
Fax: (31) 209 2925

SYNAGOGUES
Orthodox
Durban United Hebrew Congregation The Great Synagogue
Cnr. Essenwood & Silverton Roads, PO Box 50044, Musgrave Road 4062
Telephone: (31) 201 5177
Fax: (31) 202 8925

The Vryheid Memorial Shul
Cnr. Old Fort & Playfair Roads 4001
Telephone: (31) 201 5177
Fax: (31) 202 8925

Progressive
Durban Progressive Jewish Congregation
369 Ridge Road, PO Box 37020, Overport 4067
Telephone: (31) 208 6105
Fax: (31) 209 2429
Email: dpjc@sbsa.com

UMHLANGA
CONTACT INFORMATION
Chabad of Umhlanga
PO Box 474 4320
Telephone: (31) 561 2487
Email: chabadnc@global.co.za
Website: www.chabadnc.com

Open all hours. Regular minyanim especially Shabbat and Yomim Tovim. Ladies' mikvah twenty minutes away. Kosher hospitality. For kosher tours in Southern Africa contact Slomo.

Kosher self-catering accommodation

Northern Cape

KIMBERLEY

SYNAGOGUES

Orthodox

Griqualand West Hebrew Congregation
Corner Memorial Road and Synagogue Street, PO BOX 1601 8300 8301
Telephone: (53) 831 1051/2
Fax: (53) 832 3632
Mobile Phone: 082 331 6266
Email: ahorwitz@lantic.net
Central organisation: Union of Orthodox Synagogues of South Africa

Western Cape

CAPE TOWN

BAKERIES
Checkers
Gallaria Centre, Regent Road, Sea Point
Telephone: (21) 439 6159
Supervision: Cape Beth Din

Pick 'n' Pay
Adelphi Centre, Sea Point
Telephone: (21) 434 8987
Supervision: Cape Beth Din

BOOKSELLERS
Judaica Booksellers
72 Regent Road, Sea Point
Telephone: (21) 434 8619

M Beinkinstadt
38 Canterbury Street
Telephone: (21) 461 2431
Fax: (21) 465 4135

The Jewish Book Centre
Grove Avenue, Claremont
Telephone: (71) 683 9977

Jewish Learning Centre
Chabad Centre
20 S. Johns Road, Sea Point 8005
Telephone: (21) 434 3740
Fax: (21) 484 2821
Website: www.chabad.co.za
Supervision: Rabbi Mendel Popack

BUTCHERS
Claremont Kosher
150 Main Road, Claremont
Telephone: (21) 439 6909

Claremont Kosher Butchers and Deli
150 Main Road, Corner Oliver, Sea Point, Claremont 7800
Telephone: (21) 439 6909
Fax: (21) 439 6920
Supervision: Cape Beth Din
Can deliver to your door.

Pick 'N' Pay
Constantia Village
Telephone: (21) 794 5960
Supervision: Cape Beth Din.
Prepacked with Beth Din Hechser sign only.

Pick 'N' Pay
Main Road, Claremont
Telephone: (21) 683 2724
Supervision: Cape Beth Din
Prepacked with Beth Din hecher sign only

Pick 'N' Pay
Adelphi Centre, Main Road, Sea Point
Telephone: (21) 434 8987
Supervision: Cape Beth Din

COMMUNITY ORGANISATIONS
Cape Town Jewish Community Centre
87 Hatfield Street, Gardens 8001
Telephone: (21) 464 6700
Fax: (21) 461 5805
Email: sajbd2@ctjc.co.za

Coffee Time
Astra Centre incorporating Jewish Sheltered Employment Centre
20 Breda Street, Gardens 8001
Telephone: (21) 465 4200
Fax: (21) 465 4231
Email: jsec@iafrica.com
Website: www.jsec.org.za

DELICATESSEN
Goldies Deli
174 Main Road, Sea Point 8001
Telephone: (21) 434 1116
Fax: (21) 434 1116
Email: goldiesdeli@gmail.com
Website: www.goldiesdeli.co.za
Supervision: Cape Beth Din
Sit down deli and take away. Meat and pareve. Hours: Sunday to Thursday, 7am to 8pm; Friday, to 5pm.

Goldies Deli
174 Main Road, Sea Point
Telephone: (21) 434 1116
Email: goldiesdeli@gmail.com
Website: www.goldiesdeli.co.za
Supervision: Cape Beth Din

GROCERIES
Pick 'N' Pay
Centre Point Milnerton
Telephone: (21) 552 2057
Supervision: Cape Beth Din
Prepacked with Beth Din Hechser only

Butcher/Deli
Checkers
Galleria Centre, Regent Road, Sea Point
Telephone: (21) 434 5218
Supervision: Cape Beth Din

GROCERIES AND DELICATESSEN
Parev & Meat
Sea Point Superspar
Regent Road, Sea Point 8005
Telephone: (21) 439 0913
Email: shuagreen@gmail.com
Supervision: Cape Beis Din
We have a Parev and Meat Deli as well as a Pat Yisrael Bakery, our Deli is closed on Shabbat and all Festivals
We also have a Kosher Fish Shop and a Kosher aisle where we stock a wide range of Kosher imported products as well as the widest range of Kosher Wines in the Western Cape
We stock Mehadrin & Mehadrin Commission Meats as well as the only retailer to stock Chalav Yisrael Products
Hours: Winter: Sunday – Thursday 7am to 10pm and Fri 7am to 4pm Summer: Sunday – Thursday 7am to Mid night and Fri 7am to 4pm

LIBRARIES
Jacob Gitlin Library
Albow Centre, 88 Hatfield Street 8001
Telephone: (21) 462 5088
Fax: (21) 465 8671
Email: gitlib@netactive.co.za

MIKVAOT
Chabad Centre
20 S. Johns Road, Sea Point 8005
Telephone: (21) 434 3740
Fax: (21) 434 2821
Website: www.chabad.co.za
Supervision: Rabbi Mendel Popack

Mikvah Aaron
31 Arthur's Road, Sea Point 8005
Telephone: (21) 434 3148
Website: www.uos.co.za
Central organisation: Union of Orthodox Synagogues

MUSEUMS
Cape Town Holocaust Centre
88 Hatfield Street, Gardens 8001
Telephone: (21) 462 5553
Fax: (21) 462 5554
Email: admin@ctholocaust.co.za
Website: www.ctholocaust.co.za
Open Sunday to Thursday 10am to 5pm. Friday, 10am to 1pm

South African Jewish Museum
88 Hatfield Street, Gardens 8001
Telephone: (21) 465 1546
Fax: (21) 465 0284
Website: www.sajewishmuseum.co.za
Open Sunday to Thursday 10am to 5pm; Fridays, 10am to 2pm. Museum shop and café. Closed Saturdays, open Public Holidays.

RESTAURANTS
Dairy
Café Riteve
88 Hatfield Street, Gardens
Telephone: (21) 465 1594
Fax: (21) 465 5983
Email: caferiteve@norriecaterers.co.za
Website: norriecaterers.co.za
Supervision: Cape Beth Din

Meat
Avron's Place Restaurant & Grill
19/33 Regent Road, Sea Point
Telephone: (21) 439 7610
Fax: (21) 439 7599
Mobile Phone: 27825774890
Email: avronsplace@netactive.co.za
Supervision: Cape Beth Din
Delivery within 5km radius (Mr Deliver+27214399916)

Goldies Bakery & Deli
66 Regent Road, Sea Point
Telephone: (21) 439 0628
Supervision: Cape Beth Din

Kaplan Student Canteen
University of Cape Town
Telephone: (21) 650 2688
Fax: (21) 650 3064
Supervision: Cape Beth Din
Lunches, take away and orders. Meat and pareve. Open Monday to Friday. Closed December/January for varsity holidays and during summer vacation.

SYNAGOGUES
Chabad Centre
20 S. Johns Road, Sea Point 8005
Telephone: (21) 434 3740
Fax: (21) 434 2821
Email: reception@chabad.co.za
Website: www.chabad.co.za
Supervision: Rabbi Mendel Popack

Orthodox
Beit Midrash Morasha
31 Arthur's Road, Sea Point 8005
Telephone: (21) 434 8680
Fax: (21) 434 0314
Email: morasha@cybersmart.co.za

Camps Bay
14 Chilworth Road, Camps Bay 8005
Telephone: (21) 438 8082
Fax: (21) 438 0014
Email:

Cape Town Hebrew Congregation
84 Hatfield Street, Gardens
Telephone: (21) 465 1405
Fax: (21) 461 7659
Website: www.gardensshul.org

Cape Town Synagogue
Camp Road, Muizenberg 7950
Telephone: (21) 785 5611
Fax: (21) 785 5611

Claremont Wynberg Hebrew Congregation
Grove Avenue (at Morris Road),, Claremont 7708
Telephone: (21) 671 9006
Fax: (21) 683 3011
Email: info@clarewynshul.co.za
Website: www.clarewynshul.co.za
Mailing address: PO Box 23035 Claremont, Cape Townzip: 7735

Constantia Hebrew Congregation
93 Old Kendal Road, Constantia 7806
Telephone: (21) 713 1818
Fax: (21) 715 3110
Website: www.shul.org.za

Green & Sea Point Hebrew Congregation
10 Marais Road, Sea Point 8005
Telephone: (21) 439 7543
Fax: (21) 434 3760
Mobile Phone: 08257 89795
Website: www.maraisroadshul.com
Central organisation: Union of Orthodox Synagogues
Rabbi - Aharon Hayon
Executive Director - Ian H Maltz Esq

Sephardi Hebrew Congregation
Weizmann Hall, 65 Regent Road, Sea Point 8005
Telephone: (21) 439 1962
Fax: (21) 439 9620
Email: sephardi@tellcomsa.net

Wynberg Hebrew Congregation
1 Mortimer Road, Wynberg 7806
Telephone: (21) 797 5029
Fax: (21) 797 5029

Reform
Temple Israel
Upper Portswood Road, Green Point
Telephone: (21) 434 9721
Fax: (21) 434 2400

OUDTSHOORN
United Hebrew Institutions
291 Buitenkant Street
Telephone: (44) 272 3068
Fax: (44) 272 3068
There is a Jewish section in the C.P. Nel Museum

PAARL
Paarl Synagogue
Herzlia School
Telephone: 872 4087
For further information phone Mr Kaufman (083) 325 6603

SPAIN

Spain has an ancient connection with the Jews, and the term 'Sephardi' originates from the Hebrew word for Spain. Beginning in Roman times the Jews have suffered the usual cycle of acceptance and persecution, with a 'golden age' under the Islamic Moorish occupation which began in 711. Great Jewish figures arose from the Spanish community, such as Ibn Ezra and the Ramban. However, the situation changed when the Christians gained the upper hand, and blood libels began. In 1492, almost 100 years after a particularly violent period of persecution, the Jews were expelled from Spain. Many thousands were baptised but practised Judaism in secret *(the Conversos)*, and many were caught and burnt at the stake.

Jewish life began again in the nineteenth century. The Inquisition ended in 1834 and by 1868 Spain had promulgated religious tolerance. Synagogues could be built after 1909, and Spain accepted many thousands of Jewish refugees before and during the Second World War. Angel Sanz-Briz alone helped to save thousands of Hungarian Jews by issuing 'letters of protection' and entry visas.

There has been a recent immigration from North Africa, and the community today has a central body and synagogues in several towns (including Torremolinos and Malaga). Rambam's synagogue in Cordoba can be visited, and there are several other old synagogues throughout the country.

GMT +1 hours
Country calling code: (+34)
Total population: 39,270,000
Jewish population: 14,000
Emergency telephone: (police–092 or 091) (fire–080) (ambulance–092)
Electricity voltage: 220

ALICANTE
COMMUNITY ORGANISATIONS
Comunidad Israelita
Apdo. 189, Playa de San Juan 3540
Telephone: (96) 515 1572
Comunidad Jud'a
call Juan de Herrera 19
Contact: Armando Azubel

SYNAGOGUES
Alicante Synagogue
Vila Carlota, 15 Urb Montivoli, Villajoyosa

Reform
Synagogue
Belgravia Crescent

BARCELONA
The ancient community of the city lived in the area of the Calle (from the Hebrew Kahall) and the cemetery was in Montjuic (Mountain of the Jews). Most of the original tombstones are now in the Provincial Archaeological Museum.

BUTCHERS
Carniceria
Avenir 24
Telephone: (93) 200 3375
Supervision: Barcelona Rabanut

COMMUNITY ORGANISATIONS
Community Centre
Avenir 24 8071
Telephone: (93) 200 6148 or 8513
Kosher meals available on request
Comunidad Israelita de Barcelona
Avenir 24 08001
Telephone: (93) 200 6148
Fax: (93) 200 6148
Website: www.cibonline.org

KOSHER FOODS
Kosher Food Service
Telephone: (93) 439 9934
Supervision: Rabbi Libersohn
Mrs Libersohn 607 922 805

MIKVAOT
Barcelona Mikvaot
Avenir 24 8071
Telephone: (93) 200 6148/8513

RESTAURANTS
Meat and Parve
Barcelona Chabad
27 calle Joan Gamper 08036
Telephone: (93) 439 9934

Vegetarian
Self Naturista
Carrer de Santa Anna 11-17 08002
Telephone: (93) 318 2684
Fax: (93) 412 5413
Email: info@selfnaturista.com
Website: www.selfnaturista.com

SYNAGOGUES
Orthodox
Communidad Israelita de Barcelona
Avenir 24 8021
Telephone: (93) 200 8513
The first synagogue to be built in Spain since the Inquisition

Progressive
Communitat Jueva ATID de Catalunya
Castanyer 27, Bajos, Izquierda 8022
Telephone: (93) 417 3704
Fax: (93) 417 3704
Website: www.atid.freeservers.com

Reform
Comunidad Judia Bet Shalom
Perez Galdos, 23 08012
Mobile Phone: 696 810 863
Website: www.betshalom.cat
TOURS
Urban Cultours Project
Telephone: (93) 417 1191
Fax: (93) 417 1191
Website: www.urbancultours.com
Walk of the Calle (Jewish Quarter) by a Jewish American architect. Visits to other places of Jewish interest in Catalonia can also be arranged.

BENIDORM
KASHRUT INFORMATION
Benidorm Kashrut Information
Telephone: (96) 522 9360

SYNAGOGUE
Comunidad Israelita de Alicante
Calle de Berlin, Edificio Parque Loix 3500
Telephone: (96) 989 6279; 585 5418
Website: www.comisral.com
Services: Fridays and Holy-days. A communal seder is also held.
The community invites all congregants and guests to kiddush following the service.
Contact: Harvey Bourne

CORDOBA
TOURIST SITES
Ancient Synagogue
Calle de los Judios 20
This is an ancient synagogue built in 1315 and one of only three pre expulsion ones remaining. It was declared a national monument in 1985. Nearby, a statue of

Maimonides has been erected in the Plaza de Tiberiades (named to perpetuate the connection between his birthplce and where he is buried).

EL ESCORIAL
LIBRARIES
San Lorenzon Monastry

The library of the San Lorenzo Monastry contains a magnificent collection of medieval Hebrew Bibles and illuminated manuscripts. On the walls of the Patio of Kings, in the Palace of Philip II, are sculpted effigies of six Kings of Judah.

GIRONA
ORGANISATIONS
Patronat Call De Girona
8 Carrer de la Forca 17004
Telephone: (972) 216 761
Fax: (972) 214 618
Email: callgirona@ajgirona.org
Website: www.ajgirona.org/call

Jewish History Museum and Institute of Jewish Studies. Built where there was once a 15th century synagogue, in the heart of the Jewish neighbourhood. It comprises the Museum of the History of Jews and Nahmanides Institute for Jewish Studies. Open May to October: Monday to Saturday 10am to 8pm, Sunday and Bank Holidays 10am to 3pm; November to April: Monday to Saturday 10am to 6 pm, Sundays and Bank Holidays 10am to 3pm.

MADRID
About 3,500 Jews live in Madrid. A new synagogue was completed in 1968, and there is a community centre providing kosher food. The Prado has a number of paintings of Jewish interest.

BREAD
El Boutique de Pan
29 Murillo Street
Bread only

BUTCHERS
Elias Shoshanna
35 Calle Viriato
Telephone: (91) 446 7847
Fax: (91) 593 0668
Supervision: Harav Ben Dahan, Rabbi of the community.
Also restaurant

CELL PHONES
Cell Phone Rental in Spain and Europe
Mobile Phone: (34) 687 558 529
Email: spaincellphone@hotmail.com
Website: www.puertademadrid.es/rentacellphone
COMMUNITY CENTRE
Federacion de Comunides Jud'as de Espa-a
Miguel Ángel 7° C 28010
Telephone: (91) 700 1208
Fax: (91) 391 5717

Email: fcje@fcje.org
Website: www.fcje.org

COMMUNITY ORGANISATIONS
Community Centre
Calle Balmes 3 28010
Telephone: (91) 591 3131
Fax: (91) 594 1517

EMBASSY
Embassy of Israel
Calle Velasquez 150, 7th floor 28002
Telephone: (91) 411 1357

GIFT SHOP
Sefarad Handicrafts
Gran Via 54
Telephone: (91) 548 2577, 547 6142
Fax: (91) 548 2577
Jewish religious articles

KOSHER FOODS
Kosher Food Delivery in Madrid and all over Spain
Mobile Phone: (34) 607 716 642
Email: koteltravel@hotmail.com
Website: www.puertademadrid.es/jewishspain
Delivery in Madrid and Toledo
MIKVAOT
Madrid Mikvaot
Calle Balmes 3
Telephone: (91) 591 3131
Fax: (91) 594 1517

MUSEUMS
Museo Arquelogico
Calle de Serrano 13
Permanent exhibition of casts of Hebrew inscriptions from medieval buildings

RESTAURANTS
El Cortes Ingles
79 calle Raimundo Fernandez Villa Verde

La Escudilla
Santisima Trinidad 16
Telephone: (91) 445 7380

Kosher Meat & Sephardi Cuisine
Naomi Grill
Pensamiento, 25 28020
Telephone: (91) 5716923
Supervision: Rabanut of the Madrid Jewish Community
Take away and group reservations, closed on Friday night until Saturday night

Meat
Community Centre
Calle Balmes 3 28010
Telephone: (91) 591 3131
Fax: (91) 594 1517
Website: comjudiamadrid.org
For groups only

SYNAGOGUES
Conservative
Congregation Bet El
5 Calle Boix y Moer, 5
Telephone: (91) 662 3241
Website: www.bet-el.org

Orthodox
Madrid Synagogue
Calle Balmes 3
Telephone: (91) 591 3131
Fax: (91) 594 1517
The capital's first synagogue since the expulsion of Jews in 1492 was opened in December 1968. The building also houses the Community Centre, as well as mikvah, library, classrooms, an assembly hall and the office of the community.

TOURS
Jewish Heritage Tours in Spain - Toledo Private Tours
Madrid
Mobile Phone: 34 607 716 642
Email: koteltravel@hotmail.com
Website: www.puertademadrid.es/jewishspain

MALAGA
BUTCHERS
Carmiceria Kosher
Calle Somera 14 29001
Telephone: (95) 260 4201

MIKVAOT
Malaga Mikvaot
Calle Somera 12 29001

SYNAGOGUES
Malaga Synagogue
Alameda Principal, 47 20B 29001
Telephone: (95) 260 4094

TOURIST SITES
Statue
There is a statue of the eleventh century Hebrew poet Shlomo Ibn Gabirol, a native of Malaga, in the gardens outside the Alcazaba Castle, in the heart of the city.

MARBELLA
GROCERIES
Hipercor
El Corte Ingles, Section No 16, Puerto Banus
Telephone: (952) 826 649
Kosher poultry and wine

Mrs Jacqueline Ohayon
Telephone: (952) 282 6649
Kosher poultry and wine

MEDIA
Periodicals
Edificio Marbella 2000
Paseo Maritima
Focus
PO Box 145 29600
Telephone: (952) 859 395
Fax: (952) 765 783
Community journal

SYNAGOGUES
Orthodox
Beth El Marbella Jewish Community
Urbanizacion El Real, KM 184, Jazmines Str. 21
Telephone: (952) 859 395
Fax: (952) 765 783
Website: www.jewishmarbella.org
About two miles from the town centre to the east. Services: Friday (winter) 7pm, (summer) 8.30 pm; Shabbat morning & fesivals 10am. Mikveh, catering for all occasions. Kosher food available on request, rooms and apartments for rent.

SALAMANCA
RESTAURANTS
Vegetarian
El Trigal
Calle Libreros 20

SEVILLE
The first mention of a Jewish community in Seville was in the 4th century. In 1391 riots broke out and many synagogues were converted into churches. The most important of these and well worth visiting is the Church of Santa Maria la Blanca.

The Archives of the Indies holds an extensive collection of documents relating to both north and south America and include the account books of Luis de Santagel, a *Converso*, who financed Columbus and assisted Jews to leave the country in 1492.

SYNAGOGUES
Comunidad Judia De Sevilla
Calle Bustos Tavera 8 (Planta Baja) 41003
Telephone: (95) 421 0412 (answer machine)
Email: comunidadjudiadesevilla@hotmail.com

TOLEDO
Though it now has no established community, Toledo is the historical centre of Spanish Judaism. Well worth a visit are two ancient former synagogues. One is the El Transito (in Calle de Samuel Levi), founded by Samuel Levi, the treasurer of King Pedro I, in the 14th century. It has been turned by the Spanish Government into a museum of Sephardi culture. The other, now the Church of Santa

Maria la Blanca, is the oldest Jewish monument in Toledo, having been built in the 13th century. It stands in a quiet garden in what was once the heart of the Juderia, not far from the edge of the Tagus River. Also of interest is the house of Samuel Levi, in which El Greco, the famous painter, lived. The house is now a museum of his works.

Plaza de la Juderia, half-way between El Transito and Santa Maria la Blanca, was part of the city's two ancient Jewish quarters, where many houses and streets are still much as they were 500 years ago.

JUDAICA

Jewish Information Centre

Libreria & Judaica - Casa de Jacob - Jewish Information Centre
Calle del Angel 15 45002
Telephone: (925) 216 454
Fax: (925) 216 454
Email: libreria-judaica@casadejacob.com
Website: www.casadejacob.com;
www.jewishtoledo.com

Casa de Jacob is a Judaica (books, music, jewish items...) and the Jewish Information Centre of Toledo. We offer guided visits to the Synagogue of Samuel HaLevi and Jewish Quarter.

We also stock some canned kosher food and wines.

TORREMOLINOS

BAKERIES AND RESTAURANT

Kosher

Panaderia
c/Casablanca, 27 (Local 8) 29620
Telephone: (95) 238 8786
Mobile Phone: 67537 9735
Email: simon.b@wanadoopro.ma
Close to synagogue

HOTELS

N.CH Hotel
5, Plaza Gamba Alegre 29620
Telephone: (95) 238 3758
Fax: (95) 238 2724
Website: www.n chhotel.com

RESTAURANTS

Eithan Kosher Restaurant
Calle Conde Mieres 21
Telephone: (95) 205 3064

SUPERMARKET

Kosher Costa
Avineda Palma de Mallorca 29620
Telephone: (95) 237 3038
Products from Israel

Butchery

Kash & Cash
Calle Conde Mieres 21 29620
Telephone: (95) 205 8160
Fax: (95) 237 7527
Email: prosperedery@telefonica.net
Supervision: Rabbi Shaul Khalili

SYNAGOGUES

Beth Minzi
Avenida Palma de Mallorca, 59
29620
Telephone: (95) 237 7414
Fax: (95) 205 4114

Calle Skal La Roca is a small street at the seaward end of the San Miguel pedestrian precinct, almost opposite the Police Station. Sephardi and Ashkenazi services are held on Sabbath morning at 9.30 am and Friday evening services are held at 6.30 pm in winter and 8.30 pm in summer.

School

Rabbi Shaul Khalili
Av. Palma de Mallorca, 55 Local 14 29620
Telephone: (95) 237 7414
Fax: (95) 205 4114
Mobile Phone: 627 723 324
Email: sykhalili@telefonica.net
Website: www.jewish-torremolinos.org

Supervision: Rabbi of Torremolinos and his Mashgiach Nechsher of Dayan Chanoch Ehrentreu

Central organisation: Comunidad Israelita de Torremolinos

Shul: 59 Castillo San Luis (Palma de Mallorca St.)

Jewish after school daily - Talmud Torah Mikveh under hechsher of Rabbi

Under Meir Posen from London Dayan Ehrentreu is also involved when there is any change

For the Shechita Glatt Beis Yosef and under his instructions for all Kashrus matters

VALENCIA

RESTAURANTS

Vegetarian

Buffet Chino Veg
Conde Altea 46
Telephone: (96) 334 7061

La Lluna
San Ramon 23
Telephone: (96) 392 2146

SYNAGOGUES

Valencia Synagogue
Calle Asturias 7 4´
Telephone: (96) 334 3416
Services: Friday evening & festivals.

Conservative
Sinagoga Conservador Masorti La Javura
Calle Uruguay 59, pta 13 46007
Telephone: (96) 380 2129/6970
Email: lajavura@ya.com
Website: www.uscj.org/world/valencia
Supervision: ALBA TOSCANO
Central organisation: Masorti Olami European Region
Tours of medieval Jewish quarter. The synagogue is a room
completely refurbished as a synagogue with sefer torah,
aaron hakodesh, ner tamid and a modest but well-
catalogued judaica library in Spanish. kabalat Shabat
every Friday evening at 8pm. Intoduction to Judaism and
Hebrew language classes. All festivals are celebrated. Both
Rosh Hashana and Yom Kippur are held in the Hotel
Astoria-Palce (Valencia).
Orthodox Sephardi
Communidad Israelita de Valencia
Calle Ingeniero Joaquin Benlloch, 29, 1st Floor,
Apart #2 46006
Telephone: (96) 351 5676
Fax: (96) 352 7901
Email: civ@ctv.es
Supervision: Madrid Chief Rabbi Mr Moshe Bendahan.
Central organisation: Federacion de Comunida desJudias
de Espana
Opening hours: Every Friday, 8.30 pm, Jewish Holydays:
Morning 9.00 am, Evening 8.30 pm.

BALEARIC ISLANDS
GMT +1 hours
Country calling code: (+34)
Emergency telephone: (police–092) (fire–085)
(ambulance–061)

Majorca
Majorca's Jewish population today numbers
about 300, although fewer than 100 are
registered with the community. Founded in
1971, it was the first Jewish community in
Spain to be officially recognised since 1435.
The Jewish cemetery is at Santa Eugenia, some
12 miles from Palma.
Palma Cathedral contains some interesting
Jewish relics, including a candelabrum with
365 lights, which was originally in a synagogue.
In the Tesoro' room are two unique silver
maces, over 6 feet long, converted from Torah
rimonim brought from Sicily in 1493. The Santa
Clara Church stands on the site of another pre-
Inquisition synagogue. The Montezion Church
was, in the 14th century, the Great Synagogue.
In Calle San Miguel is the Church of San
Miguel, which also stands on the site of a
former synagogue. It is not far from the Calle de
la Plateria, once a part of the Palma Ghetto.

PALMA
COMMUNITY ORGANISATIONS
Communidad Israelita de Mallorca
Apartado Correos 389
Telephone: (971) 283 799

CANARY ISLANDS

Gran Canaria
LAS PALMAS
SYNAGOGUES
Las Palmas Synagogue
Ap. Correos 2142 35080
Telephone: (928) 823 1976

Tenerife
COMMUNITY ORGANISATIONS
Commundad Israelite de Tenerife
Telephone: (922) 247 296/246
KASHRUT INFORMATION
Tenerife Kashrut Information
General Mola 4, Santa Cruz, Holdings 38006
Telephone: (922) 274 157
Welcomes all Jewish visitors.

SRI LANKA
Islamic and Samaritan legend relates that
Adam came to the island after his expulsion from Eden and that Noah's Ark came
to rest there. Solid evidence for Jewish settlement was recorded about 1.000 years
ago by Muslim travellers. There was a
small Jewish community when the Dutch
took the island as a colony. This attracted
Jews from southern India to the island
because of the possibility of trade.

There was a plan put forward when the
island came under British rule for mass
Jewish immigration. The Chief Justice Sir
Alexander Johnston appeared to consider
the idea a serious one, but the British government did not act on it. A coffee estate
was founded in 1841 near Kandy by
European Jews.

There is no communal organization on the
island. The Sri Lankans appear supportive
of Israel, despite the government's official
pro-Arab stance. Diplomatic relations with
Israel were resumed in May 2000.

GMT +5 1/2 hours
Country calling code: (+94)
Total population: **18,552,000**
Jewish population: **Under 100**
Emergency telephone: **(police–43 3333)** **(fire–42 2222)** **(ambulance–42 2222)**
Electricity voltage: **230/240**

Suriname's Jewish community is very old. The first Jews settled here in the seventeenth century, escaping from persecution in Brazil. Later Jews came from Britain after the country passed into British hands. Suriname welcomed more Jewish refugees from the Caribbean and the country became a Dutch colony in 1668, bringing Sephardi Jews from Amsterdam. Eventually, half the white population in the country was Jewish, and there was a 'Jodensavanne' (Jewish savannah), where the Jews owned large sugar plantations. They called the plantations by Hebrew names and built a synagogue in 1685. The community began to decline in the nineteenth century. Recently, many have emigrated to Israel.

Today there are two synagogues in Paramaribo, the capital. The Ashkenazi synagogue, like the one in Curaçao, has a sandy floor which is symbolic of the 40 years in the desert, and was also said to have muffled the footsteps of the *Conversos* as they carried out their Judaism in secret.

GMT -3 hours
Country calling code: (+597)
Total population: **437,000**
Jewish population: **200**
Emergency telephone:
Electricity voltage: **110/220**

PARAMARIBO
KASHRUT INFORMATION
Paramaribo Kashrut Information
Commewijnestr. 21
Telephone: 400 236
Fax: 471 154

ORGANISATIONS
Suriname Jewish Community
Keizerstraat 82 84
Telephone: 400 236; 473 896
Fax: 102 380; 471 154

SYNAGOGUES
Sedek Ve Shalom
Herenstr. 20
The entire contents of this eighteenth century synagogue are currently on long term loan to the Israel Museum in Jerusalem. The building is now being used as an internet café.

Ashkenazi/Sefardi
Neveh Shalom
Keizerstraat 82
Telephone: 472 817

TOURIST SITES
Joden Savanah
Sights to see include the Joden Savanah (Jewish Savanah), one of the oldest Jewish settlements in the Americas

SWEDEN

Sweden was under the influence of the Lutheran church until the late eighteenth century, and was opposed to Jewish settlement. Aaron Isaac from Mecklenburg in Germany, a seal engraver, was the first Jew admitted into the country in 1774. The emancipation of Jews in Sweden was a slow process; Jews had limited rights, as they were designated a 'foreign colony'. After a gradual lifting of restrictions in the nineteenth century Jews were fully emancipated in 1870, although the right to hold ministerial office was closed to them until 1951.

The emancipation heralded the growth of the community, and many eastern European Jews found refuge in Sweden at the beginning of the twentieth century. The initial refusal to accept Jews fleeing the Nazis changed to sympathy as evidence for the Holocaust mounted, and in 1942 many Jews and other refugees were allowed into the country, followed, in 1943, by almost all of Danish Jewry. Sweden also accepted Hungarian, Czechoslovakian and Polish Jews after the war.

There is an Official Council of Jewish Communities in Sweden, and many international Jewish groups are represented. There are three synagogues in Stockholm, including the imposing Great Synagogue built in 1870. There are synagogues in other large towns. Although shechita is forbidden, kosher food is imported, and there are some kosher shops.

GMT +1 hours
Country calling code: (+46)
Total population: **8,847,000**
Jewish population: **16,000**
Emergency telephone: (police–112) (fire–112) (ambulance–112)
Electricity voltage: **220**

BORAS

COMMUNITY ORGANISATIONS
Jewish Organisation of Boras & Synagogue
Varbersgaven 21, Box 46 50305
Telephone: (33) 124 892
Fax: (33) 255 425
Email: s.rytz@vertextrading.se

GOTHENBURG

The Jewish Community of Gothenburg
Ostra Larmgatan 12 411 07
Telephone: (31) 109 400
Fax: (31) 711 9360
Email: kansli@judiskaforsamlingen.se
Website: www.judiskaforsamlingen.se

GROCERIES
Dr. Allards
Gata 4
Telephone: (31) 741 1545

SYNAGOGUES
Conservative
The Jewish Community of Gothenburg
Ostra Larmgatan 12 S-41107
Telephone: (31) 109 400
Fax: (31) 711 9360

Orthodox
Beith Tefilah
Storgatan 5
Telephone: (31) 711 7872
Website: www.welcome.to/minyan
Supervision: Chabad
Mikvah on the premises

MALMO

COMMUNITY ORGANISATIONS
Judiska Forsamlingen (Jewish Community)
Box 4198 20313
Telephone: (40) 611 8460
Fax: (40) 234 469
Email: jfm@algonet.se

GROCERIES
Kosher Food
Konsum Erikslust
Torupsgatan 2
Telephone: (40) 611 8460

MIKVAOT
Malmo Mikvaot
Kamrergatan 11
Telephone: (40) 118 860

SYNAGOGUES
Orthodox
Malmo Orthodox Synagogue
Foreningsgatan 34 Betaniaplan
Telephone: (40) 611 8460
Fax: (40) 234 469
The Moorish style building celebrated its centenary during 2003

STOCKHOLM

Stockholm has a number of Jewish facilities. In addition,the Raoul Wallenberg Park is worth a visit.

COMMUNITY ORGANISATIONS
Jewish Community Centre
Judaica House, Nybrogatan 19, PO Box 5053 10242
Telephone: (8) 5878 5800
Fax: (8) 5878 5870
Website: www.jfst.se

Jewish Community of Stockholm
Wahrendensdorffsgatan 3B, PO Box 7427 103 91
Telephone: (8) 5878 5800
Fax: (8) 5878 5858
Email: info@jfst.se
Website: www.jfst.se
Open Monday to Thursday 9am to 5pm, Friday 9am to 4pm (closed for lunch noon to 1pm)

EMBASSY
Embassy of Israel
Torstenssongatan 4, PO Box 14006 104 40
Telephone: (8) 663 1465
Fax: (8) 662 5301

GROCERIES
Kosherian Blecher & Co
Nybrogatan 19, PO Box 5053 102 42
Telephone: (8) 663 6580
Fax: (8) 663 6580
Mobile Phone: 46 70 7928316
Website: www.kosherian.se
Supervision: Orthodox Rabbi Stockholm
Kosher groceries. Also offers cooked meals such as burgers, sausages, meat sandwiches etc. delivery to groups, hotels

KASHRUT INFORMATION
Rabbi Meir Horden
Jewish Community House, Wahrendorffsgatan 3b, PO Box 7472 103 91
Telephone: (8) 5878 5800
Fax: (8) 5878 5858
Website: www.jf stockholm.org/centret/judendom/kosher
Rabbi Meir Horden supervises kashrut in Stockholm. Look

at www.jf stockholm.org/kosher for the latest updated information.

LIBRARIES
The Jewish Library
Wahrendorffsgatan 3, PO Box 7427 103 91
Telephone: (8) 5878 5834
Fax: (8) 5878 5858
Website: www.jf stockholm.org/biblioteket
The Raoul Wallenberg Room is on the premises, named after the Swedish diplomat who saved scores of thousands of Hungarian Jews from the Nazis, was arrested by the Russians in Budapest in 1945, and disappeared. Open to the public, it holds 25,000 books on Judaism, Jewish history, particularly Swedish Jewish history, and other Judaica. Sweden's largest collection of books in Yiddish.

MEDIA
Periodicals
Judisk Kronika
PO Box 5053 102 42
Telephone: (8) 660 3872
Fax: (8) 660 3892
Email: judisk.kronika@swipnet.se
Menorah
PO Box 5053 102 42, 102 42
Telephone: (8) 667 6770
Fax: (8) 663 7676
Website: www.menorah sweden.com

MIKVAOT
Community Centre
Judaica House, Nybrogatan 19 102 42
Telephone: (8) 5878 5800
Fax: (8) 5878 5870
Website: www.jfst.se
The Mikva is located in the Judaica House.

MONUMENT
The Holocaust Monument
Wahrendorffsgatan 3
The monument was opened in 1998 by King Carl Gustaf of Sweden, and records over 8,500 Holocaust victims who are relatives of Jews residing in Sweden

MUSEUMS
Jewish Museum
Halsingegatan 2 113 23
Telephone: (8) 310 143
Fax: (8) 318 404
Email: info@judista-museet.se
Website: www.judiska-museet.se
Arranges exhibitions about the history of Swedish Jewry and is open every day, except Saturday, between noon and 4pm

RESTAURANTS
Community Centre
Nybrogatan 19 102 42
Telephone: (8) 663 6580
Supervision: Rabbi Meir Horden

Kosher lunches at the Community Centre are available during the summer. Dinners can also be arranged at the Community Centre for groups. Contact Mr Ika Tankus, Tel: (8) 647 4475.

Lao Wai
Luntmakargatan 74
Telephone: (8) 673 7800
Supervision: Rabbi Meir Horden
Mino's Café
Tegnergatan 36
Telephone: (8) 307 742
Jewish North African Cuisine. All meat is said to be kosher but there is no kosher licence.

SYNAGOGUES
Masorti
Great Synagogue
Wahrendorffsgatan 3, PO Box 7427 103 91
Telephone: (8) 5878 5800
Fax: (8) 5878 5858
Website: www.jfst.se
Supervision: Kashrut by Orthodox Rabbi Meir Horden
Erected in 1876, Services: Monday and Thursday mornings, Friday evenings and Saturday morning. Open for tourists during Summer, Mon to Thu 11am and 1pm. Fri 11am.

Orthodox
Adat Jeshurun
Riddargatan 5, PO Box 5053 102 42
Telephone: (8) 679 2900
Fax: (8) 663 6580
Daily services: weekdays 7.45am, shabbat 9am, Sunday 8.30am. The interior originally comes from a synagogue in Hamburg which survived Kristallnacht in Germany.

Adat Jisrael
St. Paulsgatan 13 11846
Telephone: (8) 644 1995
Email: info@adatjisrael.se
Website: www.adatjisrael.se
Supervision: Rabbi Isak Nachman
Situated in an 18th century building it was renovated some 20 years ago. Daily Services: weekdays 7.30 am, Shabbat 9am, Sunday 8.15 am

UPPSALA
ORGANISATIONS
Jewish Students Club
Dalgatan 15
Telephone: (8) 125 453

SWITZERLAND

Swiss Jewry originated in medieval times and their history followed the standard course of medieval European Jewry: working as money-lenders and pedlars, attacked by the local population, who accused them of causing the Black Death, then resettling a few years afterwards, only to be subsequently expelled.

By the late eighteenth century, when the Helvetic Confederation was formed, there were three small communities. Freedom of movement was allowed, and full emancipation was granted in 1866. Theodor Herzl held the first World Zionist Conference in Basle in 1897.

Although Switzerland accepted some refugees from Nazism many were refused, and most of the new refugee Jewish population emigrated soon after the war. The community today has a central body and is made up of various factions, from ultra-Orthodox to Reform. The major towns have synagogues and kosher meat is imported. There are several hotels with kosher facilities. Over half of the community live in the German-speaking area, the French-speaking area has the second largest number, and a small population is found in the southern Italian-speaking area.

Switzerland elected its first Jewish (and first female) president, Ruth Dreifuss in1998. In 2001 it was reported that evidence had been found of an early Jewish presence in the country a ring bearing images of a menorah and a ram's horn dating from 200CE.

GMT +1 hours
Country calling code: (+41)
Total population: 7,085,000
Jewish population: 18,000
Emergency telephone: (police–117) (fire–118)
(ambulance–144)
Electricity voltage: 220

AROSA

HOTELS
Levin's Hotel Metropol
7050Telephone: (81) 378 8181
Fax: (81) 378 8161
Email: hotel@levinarosa.com
Website: www.kosherhotels.net
Supervision: Biale Rebbe Rav Rabinovitz
Mikva on premises, own kosher bakery

BADEN

CEMETERIES
Liebenfels
Telephone: (56) 222 4921
Mobile Phone: 079 415 5426
Open Sundays 10am to 4pm
KOSHER FOODS
Atrium Hotel Blume
Kurplatz 4 5400
Telephone: (56) 200 0200
Fax: (56) 200 0250
Website: www.blume-baden.ch
Prepacked kosher meals on request.

SYNAGOGUES
Israelitische Kultusgemeinde Baden
Parkstrasse 17 5400
Telephone: (56) 222 9446
Fax: (56) 222 9447
Website: www.ikgb.ch
Friday nights: Winter 6.30pm, Summer 7.30pm. Shabbat and Festivals: mornings 9.30am

BASLE

The Jewish community dates back to the beginning of the 12th century. This lasted for some two hundred years until the Jews had to flee from persecution. They returned in the 16th century and Basle became a centre for jewish printing.

Basle is of course famous for the first Zionist Conference of 1897. A plaque on the wall of the Concert Hall commemorates this event.

BAKERIES
Bakery Schmutz
Austrasse 53
Telephone: (61) 272 4765

BOOKSELLERS
Victor Goldschmidt
Mostackerstrasse 17 4051
Telephone: (61) 261 6191
Fax: (61) 261 6123
Email: vgb@econophone.ch
Website: www.victorgoldschmidt.ch

BUTCHERS
Juedische Genossenschafts Metzgerei
Friedrichstrasse 26 4055
Telephone: (61) 301 3493
Fax: (61) 301 6882
Supervision: Both Basel Rabbinates
Also sells groceries and wine. Open 7.30am to 12noon, 3pm to 6pm. Closed Monday morning and Friday afternoon.

GROCERIES
Koscher Laden
leimenstrasse 44 4051
Telephone: (61) 228 7155
Fax: (61) 228 7165
Email: k.l.trading@swissonline.ch
Hours: Monday to Thursday 10am to 12.30pm and 2pm to 8pm, Friday 9am to 3pm, Sunday 2pm to 6pm.

MIKVAOT
Basle Mikvaot
Eulerstr. 10 4051
Telephone: (61) 272 9548 Thannerstrasse 60
Telephone: (61) 301 2220
Mobile Phone: 07920 82365

MUSEUMS
Jewish Museum of Switzerland
Kornhausgasse 8 4051
Telephone: (61) 261 9514
Website: www.juedisches-museum.ch
Hours: Monday to Wednesday, 2pm to 5pm; Sunday, 11am to 5pm. Free entrance.

RESTAURANTS
Holbein Hof Cafe-Restaurant
Leimenstrasse 67 CH-4051
Telephone: (61) 270 6810
Fax: (61) 270 6800
Email: info@holbeinhof.ch
Website: www.holbeinhof.ch
Supervision: Basle Rabbinate IGB
Serves both meat and dairy
Meat

Restaurant Topas
Leimenstrasse 24 4051
Telephone: (61) 206 9500
Fax: (61) 206 9501
Website: www.restaurant-topas.ch
Supervision: Local rabbinical authority
Hours: 11.30am to 2pm Sunday to Friday, 6.30pm to 9pm Sunday to Thursday, Friday night, Shabbat lunch and holidays by reservation before 2pm of preceding day

SYNAGOGUES
Israelitische Religionsgesellschaft
Ahornstrasse 14
Telephone: (61) 301 4898
Rabbi, tel: (61) 302 1434

Orthodox
Israelitische Gemeinde Basel
Leimenstrasse 24 4003
Telephone: (61) 279 9850
Fax: (61) 279 9851
Email: nisenholz@igb.ch

BEL/BIENNE
Bel/Bienne Synagogue
Ruschlistrasse 3

Telephone: (32) 377 3619
Fax: (32) 377 3619

BERN
EMBASSY
Embassy of Israel
Alpenstrasse 32 3006
Telephone: (31) 356 3500
Fax: (31) 356 3556

SYNAGOGUES
Conservative Traditional
Synagogue & Community Centre
Kapellenstrasse 2
Telephone: (31) 381 4992
Fax: (31) 382 3861
Website: www.jgb.ch
Rabbi Dr Michael Leipziger, tel: (31) 381 7303

BREMGARTEN/AARGAU
CONTACT INFORMATION
Israelitische Cultusgemeinde
Werner Meyer Moses, Ringstrasse, 37 5620
Telephone: (56) 633 6626
Fax: (56) 633 6626

ENDINGEN
J. Bloch
Buckstr. 2 5304
Telephone: (56) 242 1546
Visits to the old synagogue and cemetery can be arranged

FRIBOURG
SYNAGOGUES
Fribourg Synagogue
9 Avenue de Rome
Telephone: (26) 322 1670

GENEVA
Originally Jews were not allowed to settle in Geneva itself but only the surrounding district. They had come from France in 1182. In 1490 however they were expelled.

After Geneva's annexation by France, at the end of the 18th century, Jews were allowed back in. They were not allowed civic rights until 1841.

BAKERIES
Mon Petit Boulanger Chen'
Rue des Eaux Vives 72
Telephone: (22) 736 7078
Fax: (22) 736 1730
Ask for kosher bread

BUTCHERS
Boucherie Kosher
Biton 21, rue de Montchoisi
Telephone: (22) 736 3168

EMBASSY
Permanet Mission of Israel to the United Nations
9 Chemin Bonvent, Cointrin 1216

MIKVAOT
Geneva Chabad
12, Avenue Théodore Weber 1208
Telephone: (22) 860 8613
Website: www.habadgeneve.ch
New Chabad Mikva now. by appointment only:
+41-76-386-86-12
RESTAURANTS
Meat
Le Jardin Rose
21 Avenue Dumas
Telephone: (22) 317 8910
Fax: (22) 317 8990
Only open for lunch but arrangements can be made so that lunches and dinners can be delivered to any hotel downtown

SYNAGOGUES
Orthodox
Beth Habad
12 rue du Lac
Telephone: (22) 736 3682
The Geneva Synagogue (Ashkenazi)
place de la Synagogue
Sephardi
Hekhal Haness
54 ter route de Malagnou
Telephone: (22) 736 9632

TOURIST SITES
Cathedrale St Pierre
Cour Saint-Pierre 1204
Telephone: (22) 311 7575
Fax: (22) 311 7573
There is an interesting stained glass window depicting Moses in the Chapelle des Macchabees

LA CHAUX DE FONDS
SYNAGOGUES
La Chaux De Fonds Synagogue
rue de Parc 63 2300
Telephone: (39) 231 794
Jews first came to the town from Alsace in 1777. The synagogue was built in 1896.

LAUSANNE
BUTCHERS
Kosher
Kolbo Shalom
7 avenue Juste Olivier
Telephone: (21) 312 1265

COMMUNITY ORGANISATIONS
Communauté Israélite de Lausanne
3 avenue Geogette 1001
Telephone: (21) 341 7240
Fax: (21) 341 7241
Website: www.cisrl.ch

MIKVAOT
Lausanne Mikvaot
1 avenue Juste Olivier
Telephone: (21) 617 5818

RESTAURANTS
Community Centre
3 avenue Geogette 1003
Telephone: (21) 341 7242
Serves lunches only, from 12pm to 2pm

SYNAGOGUES
Orthodox
Lausanne Orthodox Synagogue
1 avenue Juste Olivier
Telephone: (21) 320 9911

LENGNAU
CONTACT INFORMATION
Tourist Information
Telephone: (56) 241 1203
For visits to the old synagogue and cemetery

LUCERNE
BUTCHERS
Judische Metzgerei
Bruchstrasse 26
Telephone: (41) 240 2560

MIKVAOT
Lucerne Mikvaot
Bruchstrasse 51
Telephone: (41) 320 4750

SYNAGOGUES
Lucerne Synagogue
Bruchstrasse 51
Telephone: (41) 240 6400

LUGANO
GROCERIES
Koschere Lebensmittel erhaltlich bei
Frutor SA via Bagutti 4
Telephone: (91) 922 8522, 922 8540
Fax: (91) 923 9824

HOTELS
Hotel Dan
Via Fontana 1 6902
Telephone: (91) 985 7030
Fax: (91) 985 7031
Website: www.pibt.de/l/dan.htm
Supervision: Rabbinate Lugano's Jewish Community

MIKVAOT
Lugano Mikvaot
Via Maderno 11
Telephone: (91) 923 8952

SYNAGOGUES
Lugano Synagogue
Via Maderno 11
Telephone: (91) 923 5698

NEUKIRCH EGNACH

CENTRAL ORGANISATIONS
Vegetarian Society
Schweizerische Vereinigung fur Vegetarismus (SVV)
Bahnhofstr 52 9315
Telephone: (71) 477 3377
Fax: (71) 477 3378
Website: www.vegetarimus.ch
Can supply information on those who wish to eat vegetarian in Switzerland.

SCUOL

Hotel Scuol Palace
 7550Telephone: (081) 861 1200
Fax: (081) 861 1300
Email: info@scuolpalace.ch
Website: www.scuolpalace.com
Supervision: Agudat Ahim Zurich
Scuol is famous throughout Europe for its magnificent baths and medicinal springs.
Hotel Scuol Palace

ST GALLEN

SYNAGOGUES
St Gallen Synagogue
Frongartenstrasse 18
Telephone: (71) 223 5923

ST MORITZ

HOTELS
Bermann's Hotel Edelweiss
 7500Telephone: (81) 836 5555
Fax: (81) 833 5556
Supervision: Rabbi Rabbinowitz, Lugano

WINTERTHUR

SYNAGOGUES
Winterthur Synagogue
Rosenstrasse 5
Telephone: (52) 232 8136

YVERDON

CONTACT INFORMATION
Dr Maurice Ellkan
1400 Cheseaux noreaz
Telephone: (24) 425 1851

ZUG

RESTAURANTS
Restaurant Glashof
Baarerstrasse 41 6301
Telephone: (42) 221 248
Prepared kosher meals are available

ZURICH

Jews first arrived in Zurich in 1273. Over the following two centuries Jews were repeatedly expelled and allowed to return. There are five stained glass Chagall windows in the Fraumunster Church (located at Munsterhof Square) of which four are on themes from the Hebrew Bible.

BAKERIES
Bäckerei Bollag
Waffenplazstrasse 5, (near Bahnhof Enge) 8002
Telephone: (44) 202 3045
Fax: (44) 291 4684

BUTCHERS
Kol Tuv
8 Aemtlerstrasse
Telephone: (44) 454 1000

COMMUNITY ORGANISATIONS
Reform
Jüdische Liberale Gemeinde JLG Or Chadasch
Hallwylstrasse 78/ im hof 8004
Telephone: 043 322 01 14
Fax: 043 322 03 16
Email: info@jlg.ch
Website: www.jlg.ch

GROCERIES
Jelmoli Department Store
Seidengasse 1 8001
Telephone: (44) 220 4747
Has a large kosher section

Pick and Pay
Seestrasse 27 8002
Telephone: (44) 202 0805
Kosher section

The Co-op
Birmensdorfferstrasse 200 8055
Has a kosher section

HOTELS
Hotel Ascot
Tessinerplatz 9 8002
Telephone: (44) 208 1414
Fax: (44) 208 1420
Website: www.ascot.ch
Serves a kosher breakfast

Hotel Neufeld
Goldbrunnenplatz 8055
Telephone: (43) 960 7373
Fax: (43) 960 7374
Website: www.hotel-neufeld.ch
Serves a kosher breakfast

JUDAICA
Books & Bagels
Waffenplatzstrasse 11 CH-8002
Telephone: (44) 201 1120
Fax: (44) 201 3120
Email: info@booksnbagels.com
Website: www.booksnbagels.com
We are a one-stop-shop for everything about Jewish living including
Jewish literature, Seforim, Judaica items, Jewish educational toys, CDs,
DVDs, silver items and much more. While visiting, our customers can enjoy
our coffee and bagels corner which includes a selection of soups, salads and pastries. Open Monday to Thursday: open 8am to 7pm; Friday: till 2pm

MEDIA
Newspaper
Juedische Zeitung
Brandschenkestrasse 14 8002
Telephone: (44) 201 4617
Weekly religious newspaper

Periodicals
Jewish City Guide of Switzerland
Spectrum Press International, Im Tannegg 1,
Friesenbergstrasse 221 8055
Telephone: (44) 462 6411/6412
Fax: (44) 462 6462
Email: spectrumpress@bluewin.ch
Published quarterly in English and German, a guide to Jewish communities throughout Switzerland

Tachles, Revue Juive, Aufbau
JM Jüdische MedienAG 8027
Telephone: 044 206 4222
Fax: 044 206 4220
Email: redaktion@tachles.ch
Website: www.tachles.ch
The jewish magazines for Switzerland and Europe

MIKVAOT
Israelitische Religionsgesellschaft
Freigutstrasse 37 8002
Telephone: 044 201 4998
Appointment by phone between 9.00 am and 11.00 am.

RESTAURANTS
Restaurant Schalom
G. van Dijk, Lavaterstrasse 33 8002
Telephone: 044 283 2233
Fax: 044 283 2234
Supervision: Rabbi Rothschild
Club Savyon is part of the restaurant

Dairy
Fein & Schein
Schontalstrasse 14, corner/Ecke Hallwylstrasse
Telephone: (44) 241 3040
Fax: (44) 241 2112
Supervision: Rabbi Schoul Breisch

Pizzeria
Milk n'Honey
Zelgstrasse 1 8003
Telephone: 043 817 2525

SYNAGOGUES
Orthodox
Israel Religionsgesellschaft
Freigutstrasse 37 8002
Telephone: 044 201 6746

Israelitische Cultusgemeinde Zurich
Lavaterstrasse 33 8002
Telephone: 44 283 2200
Email: info@icz.org
Website: www.icz.org

Judische Gemeinde Agudas Achim
Erikastrasse 8 8003
Telephone: (44) 463 8033
Fax: (44) 463 8045

Minjan Machsikei Hadass
Anwandstrasse 60 8004
Telephone: (44) 241 3759
Fax: (44) 241 2668
Rabbi Mosche Chaim Schmerler

Minjan Wollishofen
Etzelstrasse 6 8038
Website: www.minjan.ch

Zurich Synagogue
Freigutstrasse 37
Telephone: (44) 201 4998

TAHITI

The first known Jew in Tahiti was Alexander Salmon, the son of a Rabbi from Hastings (England), who arrived in 1841 and later married the Queen's sister. No community developed however until the 1960s when refugees came from Algeria.

Emergency telephone:

TAHITI CITY
Tahiti Synagogue
121196 Temple Dorette Assael, rue Morenhouy,
Papette
Telephone: (689) 437 156
Fax: (689) 410 392
Email: Acispo@mail.pf

TAIWAN

The US Army brought the first Jews to Taiwan in the 1950s, when an American base was set up in the country. In the 1970s some Jewish businessmen began to work on the island, serving two- or three-year contracts with their companies. Most are Americans, although there are some Israelis and other nationalities. Services are held on Shabbat in a hotel, and there is a Jewish community centre.

GMT +98 hours
Country calling code: (+886)
Total population: 21,854,000
Jewish population: Under 100
Emergency telephone: (police–110) (fire–119) (ambulance–119)
Electricity voltage: 110

TAIPEI
Taipei Jewish Community
16 Min Tsu East Road, Second Floor
Telephone: (2) 2591 3565

COMMUNITY ORGANISATIONS
Taiwan Jewish Community Centre
37 Lane 315, Shihpai Road, Shihlin
Telephone: (2) 396 0159
Fax: (2) 396 4022
Services are held on most Friday evenings at 7.30 pm. Visitors should check in advance. All Holy Days and major festivals are celebrated.

SYNAGOGUES
Orthodox
Ritz Landis Hotel
41 Min Chuan East Road
Telephone: (2) 597 1234
Fax: (2) 596 9223
Shabbat and festival services are held here, also, when minyan is available. Weekday Services.

TAJIKISTAN

One of the former Soviet Republics, Tajikistan has a small Jewish population. After the fall of the Soviet Union, many Jews emigrated to Israel. The community is a mix of 40 per cent Bokharans and 60 per cent Soviet Jews from other parts of the former USSR who migrated to Tajikistan during the Second World War. The Bokharan Jews are believed to be descendants of Persian Jewish exiles. Dushanbe,

the capital, and Shakhrisabz are provided with synagogues, and Dushanbe also has a library.

GMT +5 hours
Country calling code: (+7)
Total population: 5,513,000
Jewish population: 1,500
Emergency telephone:
Electricity voltage: 220

DUSHANBE
Ashkenazi
Synagogue
Proletarsky Street

Bokharan
Dushanbe Synagogue
Nazyina Khikmeta Street 26

SHAKHRISABZ
Shakhrisabz Synagogue
23 Bainal Minal Street

THAILAND

Although the first confirmed presence of Jews in Thailand was in 1890, Thai Jewry really began with Jews escaping Russia and eastern Europe in the 1920s and 1930s, although most of them emigrated after 1945.

The present community arrived in the post-war period of the 1950s and 1960s. They came from Syria and Lebanon, and also from Europe and America. Some Israelis also came, and jewellery is an important source of trade with Israel. Another relatively large influx came in 1979 as Jews left Iran after the fall of the Shah.

Bangkok has Ashkenazi, Sephardi and Lubavitch synagogues. The community centre is based in the Ashkenazi synagogue. The Lubavitch synagogue offers several communual activities, including Seders at Passover, which have a large attendance.

GMT +7 hours
Country calling code: (+66)
Total population: 60,206,000
Jewish population: 250
Emergency telephone:
Electricity voltage: 220

BANGKOK
COMMUNITY ORGANISATIONS
Jewish Association of Thailand
Beth Elisheva Building, 121 Soi Sai Nam Thip 2,
Sukhumvit Soi 22
Telephone: (2) 663 0244
Email: rabbi@jewishthailand.com
Website: www.jewishthailand.com
Friday night and Shabbat services with Kiddush and
Shabbat meal. Holiday services. Call to confirm.

EMBASSY
Embassy of Israel
'Ocean Tower II' 25th floor, 75 Sukhumvit Soi 19,
Asoke Road 10110
Telephone: (2) 204 9200
Fax: (2) 204 9255

KASHRUT INFORMATION
Bankok Kashrut Information
Telephone: (2) 318 1577; 234 0606; 237 1697

RESTAURANTS
Ohr Menachem–Chabad House
96 Ram Buttri Rd., Kaosarn Road, Banglampoo
Telephone: (2) 282 6388
Fax: (2) 629 1153
Supervision: Rabbi Y. Kantor
Open 12 noon to 9pm daily. Bakery and store. Tel: (2) 629
2944/5.

SYNAGOGUES
Orthodox
Beth Elisheva
121 Soi Sai, Nam Thip 2, Sukhumvit Soi 22
Telephone: (2) 663 0244
Fax: (2) 663 0245
Mobile Phone: 6681 837 7618
Email: rabbi@jewishthailand.com
Friday night service at candle lighting time followed by
Shabbat meal. Shabbat services 10am with Kiddush and
Shabbat meal. Call to confirm.

Even Chen
Chao Phya Office Tower, 4th floor, Soi
Charoenkrung, 42/1 New Road (Silom Road area)
Fax: (2) 663 0245
Mobile Phone: 6681 837 7618
Email: rabbi@jewishthailand.com

Ohr Menachem –Chabad House
96 Ram Buttri Rd., Kaosarn Road, Banglampoo
102000
Telephone: (2) 629 2770
Fax: (2) 629 1153
Email: bkk@chabadthailand.com
Website: www.chabadthailand.com
Daily services: Friday evenings at sundown with Shabbat
meal, attracts young Jewish travellers

CHIANG MAI
Chiang Mai Synagogue
189/15 Chang Clan Road 50000
Telephone: (53) 279 015
Website: ww.chabadthailand.co.il
Restaurant, please contact for reservation

KOH SAMUI
Koh Samui synagogue
39/7 Chawang Beach, Moo 3 Bophut
Telephone: (077) 414 180
Fax: (077) 414 179
Restaurant: please contact for reservation and deliveries.

TUNISIA
There is written proof of ancient Jewish settlement in Carthage in the year 200CE, when the region was under Roman control. The community was successful and was left in peace. Under the Byzantine Empire conditions for the Jews worseed, but after the Islamic conquest the 'golden age' of Tunisian Jewry occurred. There was prosperity and many centres of learning were established. This did not continue into the Middle Ages, as successive Arab and Spanish invasions led to discrimination. Emancipation came from the French, but the community suffered under the Nazi-influenced Vichy government. After the war many emigrated to Israel or to France and the community is currently shrinking.

There are several synagogues in the country, together with kindergartens and schools. Tunisia is not as extreme in its attitude towards Israel as some Arab states, and there has been communication between the two countries at a high level. An Israeli Interest Bureau in Tunis acts as an unofficial embassy. The Bardo Museum in Tunis has an exhibition of Jewish ritual objects.

GMT +1 hours
Country calling code: (**+216**)
Total population: **9,215,000**
Jewish population: **1,500**
Emergency telephone: (**police–197**)
(**ambulance–190**)
Electricity voltage: **220**

TUNIS

COMMUNITY ORGANISATIONS
Community Offices
15 rue de Cap Vert
Telephone: (1) 282 496; 287 153

KASHRUT INFORMATION
Communautee Juive de Tunisie
15 rue de Cap Vert 1002
Telephone: (1) 832 469; 831 503
Fax: (1) 832 364

SYNAGOGUES
Grande
43 avenue de la Liberte

Lubavich Yeshiva
73 rue de Palestine
Telephone: (1) 791 429

TURKEY

There have been Jews in Turkey since at least the fourth century BCE, making Turkey one of the earliest Jewish communities. The fifteenth and sixteenth centuries were periods of major prosperity for the Jews of Turkey.

After the expulsion of the Jews from Spain in 1492, at a time when Jews were not tolerated in most of the Christian countries of Western Europe, what was then the Ottoman (Turkish) Empire was their principal land of refuge. The Sultan was reported to have said of the Spanish King: 'By expelling the Jews, he has impoverished his country and enriched mine'.

During the Second World War Turkey was neutral and accepted those Jews able to enter it.

GMT +2 hours
Country calling code: (+90)
Total population: **63,745,00**
Jewish population: **20,000**
Emergency telephone: (police–155) (fire–110)
(ambulance–11)
Electricity voltage: 220

ANKARA

EMBASSY
Embassy of Israel
Mahatma Gandhi Sok 85, Gaziosmanpasa
Telephone: (312) 446 3605
Fax: (312) 446 8071

ISTANBUL

In the 12th century Benjamin Tudela said of the city 'There is no city like her except Baghdad'. At that time it was one of the most important Jewish centres in the world.

Since 1949 the Jewish community has had autonomy in its own affairs.

COMMUNITY ORGANISATIONS
The Jewish Community of Turkey
Tunel Yemenici Sokak No 21 Beyoglu 34430
Telephone: (212) 293 8794
Fax: (212) 244 1980
Email: info@musevicemaati.com
Website: www.musevicemaati.com

EMBASSY
Consul General of Israel
Valikonag Caddesi No 73
Telephone: (212) 255 1040
Fax: (212) 255 1048

MUSEUMS
Zulfari Museum
Telephone: (212) 274 2607
Fax: (212) 274 2607
The museum contains material relating to the Jewish members of the Ottoman Parliament, physicians at the Imperial Court, diplomats, academicians, police officers and civil servants. Contact Mr H Ojalvo (212) 275 3944 for further information.

RELIGIOUS ORGANISATIONS
Chief Rabbinate
Yemenici Sokak 23, Beyoglu, Tunel 80050
Telephone: (212) 293 8794/5
Fax: (212) 244 1980

RESTAURANTS
Levi Restaurant
Tustempasamah Kalcin Sok, Cavustasa Han (2nd floor)
Telephone: (212) 512 1196

Meat
Carne Restaurant
Muallim Naci Cad. 17, Ortakoy
Telephone: (212) 260 8424

SYNAGOGUES
Askenazi Synagogue
Yusekkaldinm Sok No 37, Galata
Telephone: (212) 252 2157
Fax: (212) 244 2975

Beth Israel
Efe Sok No 4, Sisli
Telephone: (212) 292 0386
Fax: (212) 292 0385
Email: nevesalom@nevesalom.org
Website: www.nevesalom.org
Every day

Caddesbostan Synagogue
Tasmektep Sok, Gaoztepe
Telephone: (212) 356 5922
Every day

Etz Ahayim Synagogue
Muallim Naci Cad No 40 & 41, Ortakoy
Telephone: (212) 260 1896
Every day

Hemdat Israel synagogue
Izettin Sok No 65, Kadikoy
Telephone: (212) 336 5293
Every day

Hesed Leavraam Synagogue
Pancur Sok No 15, Buyukada
Telephone: (212) 382 5788
June to September including High HolyDays

Italian Synagogue
Sair Ziya Pasa Yokusu No 27, Karakoy, Galata
Telephone: (212) 293 7784
Fax: (212) 293 7784
Mobile Phone: 05326 907072

Neve Shalom Synagogue
Buyuk Hendek Cad. No:61,, Galata, Karakoy
Telephone: (212) 292 0386 PBX
Fax: (212) 292 0385
Website: www.neveshalom.org
By appointment only

IZMIR
COMMUNITY ORGANISATIONS
Jewish Community Council
Azizler Sokak 920/44, Guzelyurt
Telephone: (232) 421 1290
Fax: (232) 463 5225

SYNAGOGUES
Beth Israel
265 Mithatpasa Street, Karatas, Kanamursil District
Telephone: (232) 425 1628

Shaar Ashamayan
1390 Sokak 4/2, Bikur Holim

UKRAINE

The Ukraine has had a long and compli-
cated history, with areas of the present
country being under the rule of a number
of other countries, from Austria to
Romania. The history of the Jews who live
in the modern-day Ukraine is both long
and tragic. From settlement in Kiev in the
tenth century, before the concept of a
Ukrainian national identity had been
formed, the Jewish community grew and
was joined by many Jews from central

Europe. The Chmielnicki massacre of
1648, in which up to 100,000 were killed,
was the worst event to befall the Jews
before the Holocaust, and much destruction occurred in the west of the country.

Throughout the nineteenth century, the
Ukraine was mainly under Russian domi-
naton. After 1918 the Ukraine attempted to
become independent, and many Jews were
killed in the fighting. The Ukraine absorbed
some of south-eastern Poland in 1939 and,
after the German invasion of the Soviet
Union, the Jewish community suffered ter-
rible losses in the Holocaust.

Today, the Jewish community of Ukraine
is said to be the fourth largest in the world
(after the United States, Israel, and Russia)
and numbers 550,000 people.
Demographically, the Jews of Ukraine are
concentrated mainly in Kiev with 110,000
Jews, 60,000 in Dnepropetrovsk and 45,000
in Kharkov and Odessa. Western Ukraine,
however, has only a small remnant of its
former Jewish population, with Lvov and
Chernovtsy each having only about 6,000
Jews. There are now Jewish schools, and
kosher restaurants. There are many interesting places to visit including graves of
famous Hassidic masters and the monument to the Babi Yar massacre (located
near Kiev) and there are memorials erected
all over the country to commemorate events
that took place during the Holocaust.

GMT +2 hours
Country calling code: (+380)
Total population: **58,800,000**
Jewish population: **180,000**
Emergency telephone: (**police–02**) (**fire–01**)
(**ambulance–03**)
Electricity voltage: 220

BERDICHEV
MIKVAOT
Berdichev Mikvaot
4 Dzherzhinskaya Street
Telephone: (4143) 23938; 20222

SYNAGOGUES
Berdichev Synagogue
4 Dzherzhinskaya Street
Telephone: (4143) 23938; 20222
Kosher kichen on premises

BEREGOVO
Beregovo Synagogue
17 Sverdlov Street

BERSHAD
Bershad Synagogue
25 Narodnaya Street

CHERNIGOV
Chernigov Synagogue
34 Kommunisticheskaya Street

CHERNOVTSY
Chernovtsy Synagogue
24 Lukyana Kobylitsa Street
Telephone: (372) 54878

Synagogue
L.Kobylitzy Street 53 58000
Telephone: (372) 522 585
Fax: (372) 585 280

CHMELNITSY
Chmelnitsy Synagogue
58 Komminnestnaya Street

DNEPROPETROVSK
Synagogue of Dnepropetrovsk
7 Kotsubinskovo Street 320030
Telephone: (56) 342 120
Fax: (56) 342 137
Website: www.jew.dp.ua

DONETSK
Synagogue of Donetsk
Oktiabrskaya Street 36 83086
Telephone: (62) 345 0052
Fax: (62) 335 7725

IVANO FRANKIVSK
Synagogue of Ivano Frankivsk
Strachenih Street 7 76018
Telephone: (34) 222 3029
Fax: (34) 277 5304
Rabbi Rolesnik (34)222 3029/275 0594; (50) 463 1286 is
prepared to assit those doing historical or genealogical
research in the Western Ukraine (Galicia)

KHARKOV
Kharkov Synagogue
48 Kryatkovskaya Street
Website: www.kharkovejewish.com

**Orthodox Union Jewish Community of
Kharkov**
Sumskaya 45
Telephone: (577) 140 301
Fax: (577) 140 515
Mobile Phone: 3806 7570 0899

Synagogue of Kharkov
12 Pushkinskaya Street 310057
Telephone: (577) 313 526; 311 971; 316 031
Fax: (577) 452 140
Website: www.synagogue.kharkov.ua
Plans are under way to include a library, audiovisual room,
wedding hall, lecture rooms, sport and recreation room and
dormitories. Kosher food is available, and there is a Sunday
school, facilities to study and social programmes that take
place

KHERSON
Synagogue of Kherson
27 Gorkovo Street 325025
Telephone: (552) 223 334
Fax: (552) 325 367

KIEV
Kiev's central position at the crossroads of
Western Europe and central Asia attracted
Jewish settlers as early as the eighth century.
The usual unfortunate cycle of persecution and
resettlement then began.

In 1911 Kiev was the location of a modern blood
libel case 'the Beilis affair'.

Makabi Restaurant
Shota Rustaveli 15
Telephone: (44) 235 9437
Opening Hours: 09:00-23:00
except Sat Closed
Located next to the central synagogue.
CENTRAL ORGANISATIONS

Vaad
6 Kurskaya Street
Telephone: (44) 276 1214

EMBASSY
Embassy of Israel
Lesi Ukrainki 34, GPE S 252195

RESTAURANTS
Cimes Restaurant
Ihorivs'ka 5
Telephone: (44) 428 7579
Opening Hours:11am to midnight

Haifa Restaurant
Kostiantynivs'ka 57
Telephone: (44) 417 2512
Opening hours 1pm to 11.30pm
Offers Jewish and European cuisine

King David Restaurant
Esplanadna 24
Telephone: (44) 235 7436
Opening Hours:11am to 11pm
The restaurant is owned by the Central Synagogue, and all
profits go toward charity

Makabi Restaurant
Shota Rustaveli 15
Telephone: (44) 235 9437
Opening Hours: 9am to 11pm, closed on Saturday
Located next to the central synagogue.

SYNAGOGUES
The Central Synagogue
13 Shota Rustavely
Telephone: (44) 225 0246
Originally built in 1897 the synagogue was, under Soviet
rule, converted into a puppet theatre. Today it is both a
puppet theatre and a synagogue.

Orthodox
Galitzky Shul
97a Zhilanska Street
Telephone: (44) 494 7 1737

Podil Synagogue
29 Schekavitskaya Street
Telephone: (44) 463 7087
Fax: (44) 463 7088

Reform
Reform Congregation
7 Nemanskaya Street
Telephone: (44) 296 3961
Fax: (44) 295 9604

TOURIST SITES
Babi Yar Monument
Melnikova Street
The monument, in the form of a menorah was erected in
1991, fifty years after the two days on which 33,371 Jews
were murdered by the Nazis

Sholom Aleichem Statue
Near Basseynye Street
Shalom Aleichem (Shalom Rabinovitz) was born in 1859 in
Pereyaslav, near Kiev.

KORSTEN
SYNAGOGUES
Korsten Synagogue
8 Shchoksa Street

KREMENCHUG
Kremenchug Synagogue
50 Sverdlov Street

Synagogue
Kvartalnaya 3 39600
Telephone: (53) 679 3471
Fax: (53) 679 3470

LVIV
Situated on the edge of shifting imperial
boundaries, this city has been under Austrian,
Polish and Soviet control. It has had as many
names as its number of rulers, among them
Lwów in Polish and Lemberg in German. Now
called Lviv in Ukrainian, there are 6,000 Jews in

the city, once a major Jewish centre in Galicia.
A couple of synagogues are still functioning,
and a number of monuments have been erected
commemorating the Holocaust. Many Jews on
'Heritage tours' use the town as a base to
explore the region, and guides (generally
Yiddish-speaking) are available.

TOURIST INFORMATION
Beis A'aron V'Yisroel
4 Brativ Michnovskich Street 79018
Telephone: (322) 387 876
Email: bald@mail.lviv.ua, bald@ukrpost.ua
Kosher Restaurant (please order in advance).
Tourist information. mobile telephone 509 555 555

NIKOLAYEV
SYNAGOGUES
Synagogue of Nikolayev
13 Karl Libknechta Street 327001
Telephone: (512) 358 310
Fax: (512) 353 072

ODESSA
Chabad Shomrei Shabos
21 Osipovo Street 65125
Telephone: (48) 728 0770
Fax: (48) 249 6301
Email: secravv@shomrei.farlep.net
School Chabad: 13 Vodoprovodnaya St
Orphanage Chabad: 78 Kanatnaya St
Great Choral Synagogue
25 Evreyskaya Street 65045
Telephone: (48) 777 1189
Fax: (48) 2347 850
Website: www.tikvaodessa.org

SIMFEROPOL
JEWISH CENTRE
Chabad
Mironova 24, Crimea 95001
Telephone: (52) 510 773
Fax: (52) 510 773

SYNAGOGUES
Orthodox
Simferopol Synagogue
Krasna Znamyonaya 78
Telephone: (52) 510 773
Fax: (52) 510 773
Also has a mikvah, information on kosher matters is
available from main office

SLAVUTA
Slavuta Synagogue
Kuzovskaya Street 2
Telephone: (447) 925 452
The first edition of Tanya was printed here by the Shapira
family, whose tombs are in the cemetery

ZAPAROZHE

MIKVA

Mikva
Angolenko 3
Telephone: (617) 875252
Email: nachum@zp.ukrtel.net
School "Or-Avner" Borodinskaya str. 9-a ,
tel. (612) 127 040
It is possible to order Kosher food and Challa bread there.
Kindergarten Gogolia str. 157,
tel. (612) 638 995

SYNAGOGUES

Synagogue of Zaparozhe
22 Turgeneva Street 330063
Telephone: (612) 642 961

ZHITOMIR

Synagogue of Zhitomire
7 Malaya, Berdishevskaya Street 262001
Telephone: (412) 226 608
Fax: (412) 373 428

Jewish Day Schools & Dormitories
Synagogue
7 Malaya Berdichevskaya Street, 57 Chekhova
Street, 100B Tzutupy Street 10014
Telephone: (412) 226 608
Mobile Phone: 380 504631284
Email: office@chabad.zt.ua
Reb Ze'ev Wolf, disciple of Dov Baer, is buried in the
Smolanka cemetery. The synagogue makes kevarim tours
all over the Ukraine.

UNITED KINGDOM

There were probably individual Jews in England in Roman and (though less likely) in Anglo-Saxon times, but the first historical records of any organised settlement start after the Norman Conquest of 1066. Jewish immigrants arrived early in the reign of William the Conqueror, and important settlements came to be established in London (at a site still known as Old Jewry), Lincoln, and many other centres. In 1190 massacres of Jews occured in many cities, most notably in York. This medieval settlement was ended by Edward I's expulsion of the Jews in 1290, after which date, with rare and temporary exceptions, only converts to Christianity or secret adherents of Judaism could live in the country.

After the expulsion of the Jews from Spain in 1492 a secret *Converso* community became established in London, but the pres-
ent Anglo-Jewish community dates in practice from the period of the Commonwealth. In 1650 Menasseh ben Israel of Amsterdam began to champion the cause of Jewish readmission to England, and in 1655 he led a mission to London for this purpose. A conference was convened at Whitehall and a petition was presented to Oliver Cromwell. Though no formal decision was then recorded, in 1656 the Spanish and Portuguese Congregation in London was organised. It was followed towards the end of the seventeenth century by the establishment of an Ashkenazi community, which increased rapidly inside London as well as throwing out offshoots to a number of provincial centres and seaports. The London community, however, has always comprised the largest section of Anglo-Jewry.

Although Jews in Britain had achieved virtual economic and social emancipation by the early nineteenth century, they had not yet gained political emancipation. Minor Jewish restrictions were progressively removed, and Jews were admitted to municipal rights and began to win distinction in the professions.

During the 19th century British Jews diversified from those callings which had hitherto been regarded as characteristic.

There has always been a steady stream of immigration into Britain from Jewish communities in Europe, originally from the Iberian Peninsula and northern Italy, later from western and central Europe. The community was radically transformed by the large influx of refugees which occured between 1881 and 1914, the result of the greater persecution in the Russian Empire. The Jewish population rose from about 25,000 in the middle of the nineteenth century to nearly 350,000 by 1914. It also became far more dispersed geographically.

From 1933 a new emigration of Jews commenced, this time from Nazi persecution, and again many settled in this country. Since the end of the Second World War, and notably since 1956, smaller numbers of refugees have come from Iran, Arab countries and eastern Europe.

The United Kingdom is divided into the original counties rather than the newer administrative districts and urban authorities.

Country calling code: **(+44)**
Emergency telephone: **(police–999)** **(fire–999)** **(ambulance–999)**
Electricity voltage: **240**

Avon
BRISTOL

Bristol was one of the principal Jewish centres of medieval England. Even after the Expulsion from England in 1290 there were occasional Jewish residents or visitors. A community of *Conversos* lived here during the Tudor period. The next Jewish settlement in Bristol was around 1754, and its original synagogue opened in 1786. The present building dates from 1871 and incorporates fittings from the earlier building.

ORGANISATIONS
Hillel House
45 Oakfield Road, Clifton BS8 2BA
Telephone: (0117) 946 6589

RESTAURANTS
Vegetarian
Millwards Vegetarian Restaurant
40 Alfred Place, Kingsdown BS2 8HD
Telephone: (0117) 924 6026

SYNAGOGUES
Orthodox
Bristol Hebrew Congregation
9 Park Row BS1 5LP
Telephone: (0117) 942 2610
Services: Friday night at 183 Bishop Road BS7. Summer 7.45 pm, Winter 7.00 pm. Saturday at synagogue 9.45 am.

Progressive
Bristol & West Progressive Jewish Congregation
43 47 Bannerman Road, Easton BS5 0RR
Telephone: (0117) 954 1937
Website: www.bwpjc.org

Bedfordshire
AMPTHILL

BUTCHERS
Lewcopak Ltd
Doolittle Mill Farm, Steppingley Road
Supervision: Rabbinical Authority of the London Board for Shechita

Berkshire
MAIDENHEAD

SYNAGOGUES
Reform
Maidenhead Synagogue
Grenfell Lodge, Ray Park Road SL6 8QX
Telephone: (01628) 637 012
Fax: (01628) 675 893
Email: admin@maidenheadsynagogue.org.uk
Website: www.maidenheadsynagogue.org.uk
Services: Friday 8.30 pm; Saturday 10.30 am

READING

Liberal
Reading Liberal Jewish Community
2 Church Street RG1 2SB
Telephone: (0118) 375 3422
Website: www.fljc.org

Reading Liberal Jewish Community
2 Church Street RG1 2SB
Telephone: (0118) 375 3422
Website: www.rljc.org

Orthodox
Reading Synagogue
Goldsmid Road RG1 7YB
Telephone: (0118) 957 1018
Email: info@rhc.org.uk
Website: www.rhc.org.uk

Buckinghamshire
CHESHAM

Liberal
South Bucks Jewish Community
PO Box 391 HP5 1WB
Telephone: (01494) 431 885
Website: www.sbjc.org.uk

HIGH WYCOMBE

United
Wycombe Synagogue
c/o 33 Hampden Road HP13 6SZ
Telephone: (01494) 529 821

MILTON KEYNES

BUTCHERS
Gilbert's Kosher Foods
Kestral House, Mount Avenue MK1 1LJ
Telephone: (01908) 646 787
Fax: (01908) 646 788
Supervision: London Board of Shechita

SYNAGOGUES
Reform
Milton Keynes & District Reform Synagogue
1 Hainault Avenue, Giffard Park MK14 5PQ
Telephone: (01908) 617 790
Website: www.mkdrs.org

Cambridgeshire
CAMBRIDGE
COMMUNITY ORGANISATIONS
Cambridge University Jewish Society
33 Thompson's Lane CB5 8AQ
Telephone: (01223) 515 375
Website: www.cam.ac.uk/societies/cujs

The Cambridge University CULanu Centre
33 Bridge Street CB2 1UW
Telephone: (01223) 366 338
Fax: (01223) 366 338
The CULanu Centre organises, with the Cambridge University Jewish Society, a programme of education events, debates and socials. There are regular Friday night meals.

The Rohr Chabad House
37a Castle Street CB3 0AH
Telephone: (01223) 354 603
Website: www.cuchabad.org
Supervision: Rabbi Reuven and Rochel Leigh

GROCERIES
Student Canteen
3 Thompson's Lane CB5 8AQ
Telephone: (01223) 352 145
Website: www.cujs.org
There is a kosher canteen during term time serving lunch most weekdays, and Friday night and Shabbat meals.

KOSHER FOODS
Derby Stores
26 Derby Street CB3 9JE
Telephone: (01223) 354 391
Fax: (01223) 319 720
Website: www.localflavour.co.uk
Stocks a range of kosher food and wine; fresh bread products each Thursday lunchtime. Can purchase goods to order.

SYNAGOGUES
Cambridge Synagogue
Syn/Student Centre, 3 Thompson's Lane CB5 8AQ
Telephone: (01223) 354 783; 570 417
Website: www.ctjc.org.uk
Daily morning and evening service during term time. Friday evening, Saturday and Sunday morning during vacations. Other services by arrangement.

Reform
Beth Shalom Reform Synagogue
PO Box 756 CBS5 9WB
Website: www.beth shalom.org.uk

PETERBOROUGH
Orthodox Ashkenazi
Peterborough Hebrew Synagogue
142 Cobden Avenue PE1 2NU
Telephone: (01733) 571 282

Cheshire
CHEADLE
BUTCHERS
Hymark Kosher Meat Ltd
39 Wilmslow Road
Telephone: (0161) 428 3400
Supervision: Manchester Beth Din
Meat department only

DELICATESSEN
Hyman's Delicatessen
41 Wilmstow Road
Telephone: (0161) 491 1100
Fax: (0161) 491 1100
Supervision: Manchester Beth Din

SYNAGOGUES
Yeshurun Hebrew Congregation
Coniston Road, Gatley SK8 4AP
Telephone: (0161) 428 8242
Fax: (0161) 491 5265
Email: office@yeshurun.org.uk
Website: www.yeshurun.co.uk

HALE BARNS
BUTCHERS
Hymark of Hale
The Square
Telephone: (0161) 980 2836
Supervision: Manchester Beth Din

MIKVAOT
Naomi Greenberg South Manchester Mikvah
Hale Synagogue, Shay Lane
Telephone: (0161) 904 8296
Use is by appointment only

SYNAGOGUES
United
Hale and District Hebrew Congregation
Shay Lane, Hale Barns, Cheshire WA15 8PA
Telephone: (0161) 980 8846
Fax: (0161) 980 1802
Email: admin@hale-community.org.uk

Cornwall
PENZANCE
Jewish Cemetery
Disused, Grade II listed. Accompanied visits by appointment contact the Custodian through the Penlee Museum 01736 363 625 or the Town Clerk's Office 01736 363 405.

TRURO

SYNAGOGUES

Reform

Kehillat Kernow
Telephone: (01209) 719 672
Website: www.kehillatkernow.com
Contact: Owl Cottage, 11 Mill Road, Penponds TR14 0QH

Cumbria
GRASMERE

HOTELS

Vegetarian

Lancrigg Vegetarian Country House Hotel
Easedale LA22 9QN
Telephone: (01539) 435 317
Fax: (01539) 35058
Website: www.lancrigg.co.uk

RESTAURANTS

Green Valley and Vegetarian Restaurant at Lancrigg Country House
Lancrigg Vegetarian Country House Hotel, Easedale LA22 9QN
Telephone: (01539) 35317
Fax: (01539) 35058
Website: www.lancrigg.co.uk
International vegetarian cooking using fresh wholefood ingredients.
A wide variety of organically produced wines and beers available.
Caters for vegans and people with food allergies.

Devon
EXETER

In pre-Expulsion times Exeter was an important Jewish centre. Jews were first mentioned in 1181. After the resettlement a community was again established in 1728.

SYNAGOGUES

Exeter Hebrew Congregation
Synagogue Place, Mary Arches Street EX4 3BA
Telephone: (01392) 251 529
Email: admin@exetersynagogue.org.uk
Website: www.exetersynagogue.org.uk
Central organisation: Independent
The synagogue was built in 1763, and is a Grade II listed building with a beautiful interior. The historic cemetery in Magdalen Road dates from 1757.

PLYMOUTH

The congregation was founded in 1752 and a synagogue erected ten years later. This is now the oldest Ashkenazi synagogue building in England still used for its original purpose. It is a scheduled historical monument. In 1815 Plymouth was one of the most important centres of Anglo-Jewry.

LIBRARIES

Holcenberg Collection
Plymouth Central Library, Drake Circus PL4 8AL
Telephone: (01752) 305 907/8
Fax: (01752) 305 905
Website: www.plymouthlibraries.info
A Jewish collection of fiction and non fiction books, mainly lending copies.

RESTAURANTS

Vegetarian

Plymouth Arts Centre Vegetarian Restaurant
38 Looe Street PL4 0EB
Telephone: (01752) 202 616
Fax: (01752) 206 118
Website: www.plymouthac.org.uk
Hours: lunch, Monday to Saturday, 12 noon to 2pm; dinner, Tuesday to Saturday, 5pm to 8.30 pm. Light refreshments served from 10am.

SYNAGOGUES

Orthodox

Plymouth Hebrew Congregation
Catherine Street PL1 2AD
Telephone: (01822) 614 203
Website: www.plymouthsynagogue.com
Services: Friday, 6pm; Saturday, 10am. The congregation offers use of the minister's flat as holiday accommodation in return for conducting Orthodox Friday evening and Saturday morning services.

TORQUAY

Torquay Synagogue
Old Town Hall, Abbey Road TQ1 1BB
Telephone: (01803) 607 197
Also covering Brixham and Paignton. Services first Sabbath of every month and festivals, 10.30 am.

Dorset
BOURNEMOUTH

The Bournemouth Hebrew Congregation was established in 1905, when the Jewish population numbered fewer than 20 families. Today, the town's permanent Jewish residents number 3,500 out of a total population of some 15,000. During the holiday season, however, there are many more Jews in Bournemouth, as it is an extremely popular resort, with kosher hotels, guest houses and other holiday accommodation.

COMMUNITY ORGANISATIONS

Bournemouth & District Jewish Representative Council
2 Imperial Court, Ravine Road, Canford Cliffs, Poole BH13 7HX
Telephone: (01202) 701 011

DELICATESSEN
Kosher
The Deli
7 Holdenhurst Road BH8 8EH
Telephone: (01202) 292 800
Email: the deli@virgin.net

HOTELS
The Acacia Gardens Hotel
12 Manor Road, East Cliff BH1 3HU
Telephone: (01202) 553 127
Supervision: Manchester Beth Din

Kosher
Normandie Hotel
Manor Road, East Cliff BH1 3HL
Telephone: (01202) 552 246, reservation 291 770
Fax: (01202) 291 178
Website: www.thenormandiehotelSupervision:
Kedassia

MIKVAOT
Bournemouth Hebrew Congregation
Synagogue Chambers, Wootton Gardens BH1 1PW
Telephone: (01202) 557 443

RESTAURANTS
Falafel Restaurant (Kosher)
218 Holdenhurst Road BH8 8AX
Telephone: (01202) 552 277
Fax: (01202) 380 600
Website: www.kosherbournemouth.co.uk
Supervision: Bournemouth Hebrew Congregation
Take-away

The Arbory at The Acacia Gardens Hotel
12 Manor Road, East Cliff BH1 3HU
Telephone: (01202) 553127
Supervision: Manchester Beth Din

Glatt Kosher
Falafel
218 Holdenhurst Road BH8 8AX
Telephone: (01202) 552 277
Fax: (01202) 291 918
Website: www.kosherbournemouth.co.uk
Supervision: BHC

SUPERMARKET
Delicatessen
The Deli
7 Holdenhurst Road BH8 8EH
Telephone: (01202) 292 800
Fax: (01202) 589 911
Supervision: London Beth Dinn

SYNAGOGUES
Reform
Bournemouth Reform Synagogue
53 Christchurch Road BH1 3PN
Telephone: (01202) 557 736
Fax: (01202) 317 271

United
Bournemouth Hebrew Congregation
Synagogue Chambers, Wootton Gardens BH1 1PW
Telephone: (01202) 557 433
Fax: (01202) 557 578

Durham
DARLINGTON
Reform
Darlington Hebrew Congregation
13 Bloomfield Road
Telephone: (01325) 464 068

Essex
BARKINGSIDE
BAKERIES
Kosher
Sharon's Bakery
143 High Road Ig6
Telephone: (020) 8551 1212

BUTCHERS
La Boucherie
145 High Street IG6 2AJ
Telephone: (020) 8551 9977
Fax: (020) 8551 9977
Supervision: with the sanction of the Rabbinic Authority of
the London Board for Shechita

BUCKHURST HILL
SYNAGOGUES
Masorti
New Essex Masorti Synagogue
For address information please contact Shul office
Mobile Phone: Office:07922 090180 Rabbi:0560
2443326
Email: nemasorti@hotmail.com
Website: www.way2shul.org/
Supervision: The European Masort Bet Din
Central organisation: The Assembley of Masorti
Synagogues
Masorti (Conservative) Synagogue serving the Jewish
community of South West Essex and North East London

CHIGWELL
United
Chigwell Synagogue
Limes Avenue, Limes Farm Estate IG7 5NT
Telephone: (020) 8500 2451

COLCHESTER
Independent
**Colchester and District Jewish Community
Synagogue**
Fennings Chase, Priory Street CO1 2QG
Telephone: (01206) 545 992
Services every Friday at 8pm, on the High Holydays and
most festivals.

DAGENHAM
United
Barking & Becontree Synagogue
200 Becontree Avenue RM8 2TR
Telephone: (020) 8590 2737

HARLOW
Reform
Harlow Jewish Community
Harberts Road CM19 4DT
Telephone: (01279) 432 503
Website: www.harlowjewishcommunity.org.uk

HAROLD HILL
United
Harold Hill Synagogue
348 Trowbridge Road RM3 8YE
Telephone: (01708) 348904

HORNCHURCH
Elm Park Synagogue
Woburn Avenue RM12
Telephone: (01708) 449305

ILFORD
BAKERIES
Golan Bakery
388 Cranbrook Road IG2 6HW
Telephone: (020) 8554 8202
Supervision: London Beth Din

BUTCHERS
Ilford Kosher Meats
7 Beehive Lane IG1 3RG
Supervision: Rabbinical Authority of the London Board for Shechita

MIKVAOT
Ilford Mikvah Federation of Synagogues
463 Cranbrook Road IG2 6EW
Telephone: (020) 8554 8532
Correspondence to 367 Cranbrook Road, Ilford IG 1 4UQ.

SYNAGOGUES
Federation of Synagogues
Ilford Synagogue
14/16 Coventry Road IG1 4QR
Telephone: (020) 8554 5289
Fax: (020) 8554 7003
Email: basswitz@zwst.org

Liberal
Bet Tikvah Synagogue
129 Perrymans Farm Road, Barkingside IG2 7LX
Telephone: (020) 8554 9682
Email: bettikvah@talktalkbusiness.net
Website: www.bettikvah.org.uk
Central organisation: Liberal Judaism

Reform
South West Essex & Settlement Reform Synagogue
Oaks Lane, Newbury Park IG2 7PL
Telephone: (020) 8599 0936
Fax: (020) 8597 9164
Website: www.swesrs.org.uk

Sephardi
Eastern Jewry Community
Newbury Park Station, Newbury Park
Telephone: (020) 8809 4387

United
Clayhall
Sinclair House, Woodford Bridge Road IG4 5QR
Telephone: (020) 8551 6533
Fax: (020) 8551 9803
Website: www.Clayhallsynagogue.org.uk

Ilford Synagogue
22 Beehive Lane IG1 3RT
Telephone: (020) 8554 5969
Fax: (020) 8554 4543
Email: office@ilfordsynagogue.co.uk
Website: www.ilfordsynagogue.co.uk
www.ilfordshul.co.uk
Central organisation: United Synagogue
The largest synagogue in Essex is pleased to welcome visitors from the North East London and Essex areas.

Newbury Park
23 Wessex Close IG3 8SU
Telephone: (020) 8597 0958

YOUTH HOSTELS
Federation of Synagogues
Ohel Jacob Synagogue
1st Floor, rear of 476/478 Cranbrook Road IG2 2LE
Telephone: (020) 8550 4596

LOUGHTON
SYNAGOGUES
Loughton Synagogue
Borders Lane IG10 1TE
Telephone: (020) 8508 0303
Friday evening, 7pm; Saturday morning 9am

RAINHAM
FISH MONGERS
Scotch Smoke Salmon Ltd
Unit B3, Suttons Business Park
Supervision: Rabbinical Authority of the London Board for Shechita

REDBRIDGE
BUTCHERS
N. Goldberg
12 Claybury Broadway IG5 0BB
Telephone: (020) 8551 2828
Fax: (020) 8551 3524
Supervision: London Board for Shechita

DELICATESSEN
Brownstein's
523 Cranbrook Road, Gants Hill IG2 6HA
Telephone: (020) 8518 3001
Website: www.brownsteins.co.uk
Supervision: London Beth Din
Buffet & Kiddushim catered

ROMFORD
SYNAGOGUES
United
Romford Synagogue
25 Eastern Road, RM1
Telephone: (01708) 741 690

SOUTHEND ON SEA
Jews began settling in the area in the late 19th
century, mainly from the East End of London.
The first temporary synagogue was built in
1906. The Jewish population is 4,500.

BOOKSELLERS
Dorothy Young
21 Colchester Road SS2 6HW
Telephone: (01702) 331 218
Website: www.dorothyyoung.co.uk
Religious articles, Israeli giftware also stocked. Jewish
software ordered. Call for appointment.

SYNAGOGUES
Southend District Reform Synagogue
851 London Road, Westcliff-on-Sea SS0 9SZ
Telephone: (01702) 711 663
Fax: (01702) 475 809
Website: www.southendreform.co.uk

Independent
**Southend and Westcliff Hebrew
Congregation**
Finchley Road, Westcliffe-On-Sea SS0 8AD
Telephone: (01702) 344 900
Fax: (01702) 391 131
Email: swhc@btclick.com
Website: www.swhc.org.uk
Supervision: Beth Din

WOODFORD GREEN
TRAVEL AGENTS
Longwood Travel
3 Bourne Court, Southend Road IG8 8HD
Telephone: (020) 8551 4466
Fax: (020) 8551 5588

Gloucestershire
CHELTENHAM
SYNAGOGUES
Traditional
Cheltenham Hebrew Congregation
Synagogue Lane, St James Square GL50 3PU

Telephone: (01242) 578 893
Fax: (01242) 578 893
The congregation was founded in 1823 and the cemetery in
Elm Street (still in use) was established in 1824. The
synagogue is an outstanding smaller Regency building and
was consecrated in 1839. The architect was William Knight
and the building is listed with Grade II* status.

The congregation numbers some ninety to one hundred
members and services follow the traditional Ashkenazi
pattern. Services are held every Friday evening at 7p.m. and
on High Holy Days and other Festivals, together with a wide
range of social and cultural activities.

United
Cheltenham Synagogue
7 Loweswater Road GL51 5AZ
Telephone: (01242) 242 724

Greater Manchester
BURY
Bury Hebrew Congregation
Sunnybank Road, Sunnybank BL9 8ET
Telephone: (0161) 796 5062
Fax: (0161) 796 5062
Email: mirrelbhc@hotmail.co.uk
Website: www.buryhc.org.uk

MANCHESTER
The Manchester Jewish community is the
second largest in the United Kingdom,
numbering about 35,000. There was no
organised community until 1780. The present
Great Synagogue claims to be the direct
descendant of this earlier community. The
leaders of Manchester Jewry in those early days
came from the neighbouring relatively
important Jewish community of Liverpool. In
1871 a small Sephardi group from North Africa
and the Levant drew together and formed a
congregation, which extended to fill two
handsome synagogues. One has now been
turned into a Jewish museum.

BAKERIES
Hale Bakery
12 The Square, Hale
Telephone: (0161) 980 7473

State Fayre Bakeries
Unit 1, Empire Street M3
Telephone: (0161) 832 2911
Supervision: Manchester Beth Din

BREAD & CONFECTIONERY
Delicatessen
State Fayre
77 Middleton Road M8
Telephone: (0161) 740 3435
Supervision: Manchester Beth Din

BUTCHERS
Lloyd Grosberg (J. Kreger)
102 Barlow Road M20
Telephone: (0161) 445 4983
Supervision: Manchester Beth Din

BUTCHERS AND DELICATESSEN
Grocery
J.A. Hyman (Titanic) Ltd
123/9 Waterloo Road M8
Telephone: (0161) 792 1888
Website: www.titanics.co.uk
Supervision: Manchester Beth Din
Suppliers of meat and poultry, cooked meats and delicatessen products.

COMMUNITY ORGANISATIONS
Manchester Liberal Jewish Community
Friend's Meeting Place, 6 Mount Street M2 5NS
Fax: (0161) 0870 051 6277
Mobile Phone: 08709 917 327
Website: www.mljc.org.uk

HOTELS
Fulda's Hotel
144 Bury Old Road M7 4QY
Telephone: (0161) 740 4551
Fax: (0161) 795 5920
Website: www.here.at/fuldas.com
Supervision: Manchester Beth Din
Four star hotel open all year. Glatt kosher.

KASHRUT INFORMATION
Manchester Beth Din
MJCC, Bury Old Road M7 4QY
Telephone: (0161) 740 9711
Fax: (0161) 721 4249
Contact them to ensure that an establishment is still certified.

LIBRARIES
Central Library
St Peter's Square M2 5PD
Telephone: (0161) 234 1983; 234 1984
Large collection of Jewish books for reference and loan, including books on Hebrew. Contact the Social Sciences Library.

MUSEUMS
Manchester Jewish Museum
190 Cheetham Hill Road M8 8LW
Telephone: (0161) 834 9879; 832 7553
Fax: (0161) 834 9801
Website: www.manchesterjewishmuseum.com
Exhibitions, heritage trails, demonstrations and talks. Details of events available on request. Educational visits for school and adult groups must be booked in advance. Open Monday to Thursday, 10.30am to 4pm, Sunday 10.30am to 5pm. Admission charge. Contact Don Rainger.

RESTAURANTS
Antonio's Restaurant
JCLC, Corner Bury Old Road & Park Road
Telephone: (0161) 795 8911
Fax: (0161) 795 8911
Supervision: Manchester Beth Din
Open Monday to Thursday 5pm to 11pm. Winter 1.5 hours after Shabbat until 2pm.

SYNAGOGUES
Masorti
Manchester Masorti
57 Torkington Road, Gatley SK8 4PW
Telephone: (0161) 428 0087
Contact Lisa Barrett

Orthodox
United Synagogue
Meade Hill Road M8 4LR
Telephone: (0161) 7409586

Reform
Cheshire Reform Congregation Menorah Synagogue
198 Altrincham Road, Sharston M22 4RZ
Telephone: (0161) 428 7746
Fax: (0161) 428 0937
Website: www.menorah.org.uk
Manchester Reform Synagogue
Jackson's Row, Albert Square M2 5NH
Telephone: (0161) 834 0415
Fax: (0161) 834 0415
Website: www.mcr reform.org.uk

Sephardi
Sephardi Congregation of South Manchester
Queenston Road, West Didsbury M20
Telephone: (0161) 445 6300

United
Cheetham Hebrew Congregation
Jewish Cultural Centre, Bury Old Road M7 4QY
Telephone: (0161) 740 7788
Cheetham Hebrew Congregation
453 Cheetham Hill Road M8 9PA
Telephone: (0161) 740 7788
Heaton Park Hebrew Congregation
Ashdown, Middleton Road M8 4JX
Telephone: (0161) 740 4766
South Manchester Synagogue
Wilbrahim Road M14 6JS
Telephone: (0161) 224 1366

TRAVEL AGENTS
ITS: Israel Travel Service
427/430 Royal Exchange, Old Bank Street M2 7EP
Telephone: (0161) 839 1111
Fax: (0161) 839 0000
Mobile Phone: 07990 901 021
Email: all@itstravel.co.uk

Website: www.itstravel.co.uk
Freephone 0800 0181 839

PRESTWICH

BOOKSELLERS
B. Horwitz
20 King Edwards Buildings, Bury Old Road M7 4QJ
Telephone: (161) 740 5897
Open 9.30 am to 5.30 pm Monday to Friday; 10.00 am to
1.00 pm Sunday; 9.00 am to 2.00 pm Friday during winter.

B. Horwitz Judaica World
2 Kings Road M25 0LE
Telephone: (161) 773 4956
Fax: (161) 773 4956

BUTCHERS
Glatt Butchers
61 Bury Old Road M25 0FG
Telephone: (161) 773 2020
Supervision: Manchester Beth Din - Glat

Kosher Foods
49 Bury New Road M25
Telephone: (161) 773 1308
Supervision: Manchester Beth Din
Sells groceries as well.

Vidal's Kosher Meats
75 Windsor Road M25
Telephone: (161) 740 3365
Supervision: Manchester Beth Din

DELICATESSEN
Habers World
Kings Road M25 0FY
Telephone: (161) 798 7370
Fax: (161) 798 5654
Supervision: Manchester Beth Din

GROCERIES
Getzels
82 Kings Road
Telephone: (0161) 773 4400

KOSHER SUPERMARKET
Haber's World
Kings Road M25 0FY
Telephone: (161) 798 7370
Fax: (161) 798 5654
Supervision: Manchester Beth Din

MEDIA
Newspapers
Jewish Telegraph
Telegraph House, 11 Park Hill, Bury Old Road
M25 0HH
Telephone: (161) 740 9321
Fax: (161) 740 9325
Email: manchester@jewishtelegraph.com
Website: www.jewishtelegraph.com

Jewish Telegraph Group of Newspapers
Telegraph House, 11 Park Hill, Bury Old Rd
M25 0HH
Telephone: (797) 694 5210
Fax: (161) 740 5555
Email: liverpool@jewishtelegraph.com
Website: www.jewishtelegraph.com

MIKVAOT
**Manchester & District Mikva (Machzikei
Hadass)**
Sedgley Park Road M25
Telephone: (161) 773 1537; 795 2223

RESTAURANTS
Asher's
5 Kings Road
Telephone: (161) 773 1414
Supervision: Manchester Beth Din

Maccs Bistro
M/cr Maccabi, Brooklands, Bury Old Road
Telephone: (0161) 206 0040

Pagoda
38 Bury Old Road
Telephone: (0161) 798 7776

Meat
J.S. Kosher Restaurant
7 Kings Road M25 0LE
Telephone: (161) 798 7776
Supervision: Manchester Beth Din
Glatt Kosher

SYNAGOGUES
Orthodox
Higher Prestwich
445 Bury Old Road M25 1QP
Telephone: (161) 773 4800

Holy Law South Broughton Congregation
Bury Old Road M25 0EX
Telephone: (161) 740 1634; 721 4705
Fax: (161) 720 6623
Prestwich Hebrew Congregation
Bury New Road M25 9WN
Telephone: (161) 773 1978
Fax: (161) 773 7015
Email: office@shrubberies.org.uk

Sedgley Park (Shomrei Hadass)
Park View Road M25 5FA
Telephone: (161) 773 4828; 740 1969

SALFORD

BAKERIES
Brackman's
45 Leicester Road M7
Telephone: (0161) 792 1652
Supervision: Manchester Beth Din

BOOKSELLERS
Hasefer Book Store
18 Merrybower Road M7
Telephone: (0161) 740 3013
Fax: (0161) 721 4649

J. Goldberg
11 Parkside Avenue M7 0HB
Telephone: (0161) 740 0732

Jewish Book Centre
25 Ashbourne Grove M7 4DB
Telephone: (0161) 792 1253
Fax: (0161) 661 5505
Hours: Sunday to Thursday, 9am to 9.00 pm; Friday, 9am to
1pm.

BUTCHERS
Halberstadt Ltd
55 Leicester Road M7 4AS
Telephone: (0161) 792 1109
Supervision: Manchester Beth Din
Open full day Tuesday, Wednesday and Thursday. Open half
day Sunday, Monday and Friday. Only Glatt Beth Yosef Meat
Mehadrin Poultry. Electric doors/disabled ramp.

GROCERIES
Halperns Kosher Food Store
57 59 Leicester Road M7 4DA
Telephone: (0161) 792 1752;792 2992
Fax: (0161) 708 8881
Supervision: Manchester Beth Din

MIKVAOT
Manchester Communal Mikvah
Broome Holme, Tetlow Lane M7 0BU
Telephone: (0161) 792 3970
For appointments for Friday night and Yom Tov evenings:
740 4071; 740 5199. For tevilat kelim, 795 2272.

RESTAURANTS
Dairy
Brackman's Bakery & Coffee Shop
45 Leicester Road
Telephone: (0161) 792 1652
Supervision: Manchester Beth Din

SYNAGOGUES
Orthodox
Adass Yeshurun
Cheltenham Crescent M7 0FE
Telephone: (0161) 740 2745

Adath Yisroel Nusach Ari
Upper Park Road M7 0HL
Telephone: (0161) 740 3905

Congregation of Spanish and Portuguese
18 Moor Lane, Kersal M7 4WX
Telephone: (0161) 795 1212
Fax: (0161) 792 7406
Website: www.moorlane.org
Rabbi Avraham Hassan

Higher Crumpsall & Higher Broughton
Bury Old Road M7 4PX
Telephone: (0161) 740 1210

Kahal Chassidim Lubavitch
62 Singleton Road M7 4LU
Telephone: (0161) 740 3632
Fax: (0161) 795 7759
Email: avrohomjaffe@aol.com
Website: www.lubavitch.co.uk

Machzikei Hadass
17 Northumberland Street M7 0FE
Telephone: (0161) 792 1313
Fax: (0161) 792 8592

Manchester Great & New Synagogue
Stenecourt, Holden Road M7 4LN
Telephone: (0161) 792 8399
Fax: (0161) 792 1991
Website: www.stenecourt.com

North Salford
2 Vine Street M7 0NX
Telephone: (0161) 792 3278

Ohel Torah
132 Leicester Road M7 0EA
Telephone: (0161) 740 2568
Fax: (0161) 745 8876

Sephardi
Spanish & Portugese Synagogue
Moor Lane M7
Telephone: (0161) 795 1212
Fax: (0161) 795 1212

TRAVEL AGENTS
Goodmos Tours (Man) Ltd.
23 Leicester Road M7 0AS
Telephone: (0161) 792 7333
Fax: (0161) 792 7336

Hampshire
PORTSMOUTH & SOUTHSEA
The Portsmouth community was founded in
1746. Its first synagogue was in Oyster Row, but
the congregation moved to a building in
White's Row which it continued to occupy for
almost two centuries. A new building was
erected in 1936. The cemetery is in a street
which was once known as Jews' Lane

SYNAGOGUES
United
Synagogue Chambers
The Thicket, Southsea
Telephone: (023) 9282 1494

SOUTHAMPTON
LIBRARIES
Hartley Library
University of Southampton SO17 1BJ
Telephone: (023) 8059 2721

Fax: (023) 8059 3007
Houses both the Parkes Library and the Anglo Jewish
Archives

SYNAGOGUES

Reform

South Hampshire Reform Jewish Community
Suite 153, 151 High Street SO14 2BT
Mobile Phone: 0709 237 3918
Website: www.shrjc.com

United

Southampton Hebrew Congregation
Moordaunt Road, The Inner Avenue SO14 6GP
Services Saturday morning 10am

Hertfordshire
BOREHAMWOOD
BOOKSELLERS
Borehamwood Judaica
11 Croxdale Road WD6 4QD
Telephone: (020) 8381 5559

BUTCHERS

Kosher
Just Koshered
11 Croxdale Avenue WD6 4QD
Telephone: (020) 8381 5559

DELICATESSEN
Just Kosher
5-7 Croxdale Road WD6 4QD
Telephone: (020) 8207 5556

RESTAURANTS

Meat
Levi Luca
5 Shenley Road WD6 3HZ
Telephone: (020) 8905 1118SYNAGOGUES

SYNAGOGUES

United
Borehamwood & Elstree Synagogue
Croxdale Road WD6
Telephone: (020) 8386 5227

BUSHEY
BUTCHERS
J.D. Glass & Co
100 High Road, Bushey Heath WD2 3JE
Telephone: (020) 8420 4443
Supervision: London Board for Shechita

RESTAURANTS
The Kanteen
23-25 High Road WD23 1EE
Telephone: (020) 8950 0747

SYNAGOGUES

United
Bushey and District Synagogue
177–189 Sparrows Herne WD23 1AJ
Telephone: (020) 8950 7340
Fax: (020) 8421 8267

COCKFOSTERS
GROCERIES
The World of Kosher
25 Station Road EN4 0DW
Telephone: (020) 8441 3621

EAST BARNET
BUTCHERS
Kosher
La Boucherie
4 Cat Hill EN4 8JB
Telephone: (020) 8449 9215
Fax: (020) 8441 1848
Supervision: with the sanction of the Rabbinic Authority of
the London Board for Shechita

ELSTREE
SYNAGOGUES
Federation of Synagogues
Ohr Yisroel Synagogue
31/33 Theobold Street WD6 4RN
Telephone: (020) 8207 6265

Liberal
The Liberal Synagogue Elstree
Elstree High Street WD6 3EY
Telephone: (020) 8953 8889
Website: www.tlse.org.uk

HATFIELD
United
Potters Bar Synagogue
Meadowcroft, Great North Road, Bell Bar
Telephone: (01707) 656 202

HEMEL HEMPSTEAD
Morton House
Midland Road HD1 1RP
Telephone: (01923) 232 007

NEW BARNET
SYNAGOGUES
United
Barnet Synagogue
Eversleigh Road EN5 1ND
Telephone: (020) 8449 0145
Website: www.barnetsynagogue.org.uk

RADLETT
BUTCHERS
Ivor Silverman
257 Watling Street WD7 7LA
Supervision: Rabbinical Authority of the London Board for Shechita*Reform*

Radlett and Bushey Reform Synagogue
118 Watling Street WD7 7AA
Telephone: (01923) 856 110
Fax: (01923) 854 444
Website: www.rbrs.org.uk

United
Radlett Synagogue
22 Watling Street WD7 7PN
Telephone: (01923) 856 878
Fax: (01923) 856–698

SAWBRIDGEWORTH
BANQUETING SUITE
Manor of Groves
High Wych CM21 0JU
Telephone: (0870) 410 8833
Fax: (0870) 417 8833
Website: www.manorofgroves.com

SHENLEY
SYNAGOGUES
United
Shenley Synagogue
PO Box 205 WD7 9ZN
Telephone: (01923) 857 786
Website: www.shenleyunited.org

ST ALBANS
Masorti
St Albans Masorti Synagogue
PO Box 23 AL1 4PH
Telephone: (01727) 860 642
Website: www.e-sams.org

United
St Albans United Synagogue
Oswald Road AL1 3AQ
Telephone: (01727) 854 872
Email: info@stalbanssynagogue.org.uk
Website: www.stalbanssynagogue.org.uk
Central organisation: United Synagogue

WATFORD
Hemel Hempstead Synagogue
c/o Devreux Drive WD1 3DD
Telephone: (01923) 232007

Watford Synagogue
16 Nascot Road WD17 4YE
Telephone: (01923) 222 755
Fax: (01923) 222 755
Email: secretary@watfordsynagogue.org.uk

Website: www.watfordsynagogue.org.uk
Also covers Abbots, Langley, Carpenters Park, Croxley Garden, Garston, Kings Langley and Rickmansworth.

WELWYN GARDEN CITY
Welwyn Garden City Synagogue
Barn Close, Handside Lane AL8 6ST
Telephone: (01707) 322 443
Email: info@wgcshul.org.uk
Website: www.wgcshul.org.uk

Humberside
HULL
In Hull, as in other English ports, a Jewish community was formed earlier than in inland areas. The exact date is unknown, but it is thought to be the early 1700s. There were enough Jews in Hull to buy a former Roman Catholic chapel, damaged in the Gordon Riots of 1780, and turn it into a synagogue. Hull was then the principal port of entry from northern Europe, and most Jewish immigrants came through it. Both the Old Hebrew Synagogue in Osborne Street and the Central Synagogue in Cogan Street were destroyed in air raids during the Second World War.

Orthodox
Hull Hebrew Congregation
30 Pryme Street, Anlaby HU10 6SH
Telephone: (01482) 653 242; 653 398
Fax: (01482) 650282
Email: shalom.osdoba@gmail.com

Reform
Neve Shalom Reform Synagogue
Great Gutter Lane, West Willerby HU10 6DP
Telephone: (01482) 658 312
Fax: (01482) 835 864
www.beehive.thisishull.co.uk/hullreformsynagogue

Kent
BROMLEY
Bromley Reform Synagogue
28 Highland Road BR1 4AD
Telephone: (020) 8460 5460
Fax: (020) 8460 5460
Email: janet@bromleyshul.org.uk
Website: www.bromleyshul.org.net
Central organisation: Movement for Reform Judaism

CANTERBURY
TOURIST SITES
The Old Synagogue
King Street CT1 2ES
Telephone: (01227) 595 544
Fax: (01227) 595 589
The Old Synagogue, an Egyptian style building erected in 1847, stands in King Street and is now used by the Kings School for recitals.

MARGATE
SYNAGOGUES
United
Margate Hebrew Congregation
Godwin Road, Cliftonville CT9 2HA
Telephone: (01843) 223 219

RAMSGATE
Montefiore Mausoleum
Hereson and Honeysuckle Road

Montefiore Synagogue
Honeysuckle Road CT11
Telephone: (01843) 862 507

Reform
Thanet and District Reform Synagogue
293a Margate Road, CT12 6TE
Telephone: (01843) 851 164
Fax: (01843) 861 218
Email: TDRS@imsbvs.f9.co.uk
Website:www.jewishkent.org.uk/communities/than
et/thanet.html
Central organisation: Movement for Reform Judaism

ROCHESTER
Magnus Memorial Synagogue
366 High Street ME1 1DJ
Telephone: (01634) 847 665
Grade II listed building known as The Chatham Memorial
Synagogue.

Lancashire
BLACKPOOL
DELICATESSEN
The Deli
6 Station Road, Lytham St Annes
Telephone: (01253) 735 861

SYNAGOGUES
Reform
Blackpool Reform Jewish Congregation
40 Raikes Parade FY1 4EX
Telephone: (01253) 623 687
Fax: (01253) 317 003

United
United Hebrew Congregation
Synagogue Chambers, Leamington Road FY1 4HD
Telephone: (01253) 392 382

LANCASTER
BED AND BREAKFAST
Lancaster University Jewish Society
Interfaith Chaplaincy Centre, University of
Lancaster, Bailrigg Lane LA1 4YW
Telephone: (01524) 594 075
Jewish rooms and kosher kitchen. Contact Rev Malcolm
Wiseman.

SALE
SYNAGOGUES
United
Sale & District Hebrew Congregation
14 Hesketh Road M33 5FB
Telephone: (0161) 973 3013

SOUTHPORT
COMMUNITY ORGANISATIONS
Southport Jewish Representative Council
Telephone: (01704) 540 704
Fax: (01704) 540 704

SYNAGOGUES
Reform
New (Reform) Synagogue
Portland Street PR8 1LR
Telephone: (01704) 535 950

Southport Reform Synagogue
The Home, Princes Street PR8 1EG
Telephone: (01704) 535 950
Website: www.southportrefoem.co.uk

ST ANNES ON SEA
Orthodox
Synagogue
Orchard Road FY8 1PJ
Telephone: 721 831
Services 7.30am and 8pm

WHITEFIELD
BUTCHERS
Haydn's Kosher Meats
142 Park Lane M45 7PX
Telephone: (0161) 766 5091
Supervision: Manchester Beth Din
Hours: Sunday 8.30am to 1pm; Monday & Friday 8am to
1pm; Tuesday, Wednesday & Thursday 8am to 6pm

DELICATESSEN
Cottage Deli
83 Park Lane M45 7HL
Telephone: (0161) 766 6216
Supervision: Manchester Beth Din

MIKVAOT
Whitefield Mikvah
Park Lane M45 7PB
Telephone: (0161) 796 1054
Fax: (0161) 767 9453
Evenings only: 773 7830. Use is by appointment only.

SYNAGOGUES

Orthodox
Hillock Hebrew Congregation
Beverley Close, Ribble Drive M45 8LB
Telephone: (0161) 959 5663
Email: hillock.shul@atlworld.com
Mailing adddress is 13 Mersey Close, Whitefield,
Manchester, M45 8LB

Reform
**Sha'arei Shalom North Manchester Reform
Synagogue**
Elms Street M45 8GQ
Telephone: (0161) 796 6736
Fax: (0161) 796 6736
Website: www.shaareishalom.org.uk

United
Whitefield Hebrew Congregation
Park Lane M45 7PB
Telephone: (0161) 766 3732
Fax: (0161) 767 9453

Leicestershire
LEICESTER
There has been a Jewish presence here since
the Middle Ages, but the first record of a 'Jews'
Synagogue' dates from 1861 in the Leicester
Directory. In 2001 the Leicester City Council
finally renounced a ban on Jews living in the
city which was originally imposed in 1731.

LIBRARIES
Jewish Library and Bookshop
Community Hall, Highfield Street LE2 0NQ
Telephone: (0116) 212 8920

MIKVAOT
Leicester Mikva
Synagogue Building, Highfield Street LE2 1AD
Telephone: (0116) 270 6622
Email: rabbipink@btinternet.com
Website: www.jewishleicester.org
Supervision: Rabbi Posen

RESTAURANTS
Vegetarian
The Good Earth
19 Free Lane LE1 1JX
Telephone: (0116) 262 6260

SYNAGOGUES
Leicester Progressive Jewish Congregation
24 Avenue Road LE2 3EA
Telephone: (0116) 271 5584
Fax: (0116) 271 7571
Website: www.thisisleicestershire.co.uk
Central organisation: Liberal Judaism

United
Leicester Synagogue
Highfield Street LE2 1WZ
Telephone: (0116) 270 099
Mikvah on premises. Mailing address: PO Box 6836,
Leicester, LE2 1WZ

Lincolnshire
GRIMSBY
Orthodox
Sir Moses Montefiore Synagogue
Heneage Road DN32 9DZ
Telephone: (01472) 824 463
Fax: (01472) 824 463
Services every Friday 7.00 pm and all major festivals

KILLINGHOLME
COMMUNITY ORGANISATIONS
Lincolnshire Jewish Community
3 West End Road, Ulceby
Telephone: (01469) 588 951

LINCOLN
Lincoln was one of the centres of medieval
Jewry. One of England's oldest stone houses in
the city is known as Aaron the Jew's House.
The site of the Old Synagogue is remembered
now at Jews' Court. In the cathedral is a recent
token of ecclesiastical apology for the 13th
century incident of the blood libel, retold in
Chaucer. Jews returned to the area in the 19th
century. The current community is of very
recent date.

TOURIST SITES
Aaron the Jew's House
47 Steep Hill
Believed to be the home of Aaron of Lincoln (c1123–1186),
the most prominent Anglo Jewish financier of the time. A
Grade I listed building.

Jews Court
2 Steep Hill
Telephone: (01522) 521 337
Fax: (01522) 521 337
Email: slha@lincolnshirepast.org.uk
Website: www.lincolnshirepast.org.uk
Site of the pre Expulsion synagogue. A Grade I listed
building.

LONDON
Jews came to London with the Normans
following their conquest of England in 1066. A
Jewish area in London is first mentioned in
1128; known as 'the Jewish quarter', it was
situated around Old Jewry, a street in the City
of London close to the Bank of England. Nearby
to the west is the church of St Lawrence of
Jewry, and about one mile to the east is Jewry

Street. The community expanded, and until 1177 had the only Jewish cemetery in the country. Although there is now no evidence of early Jewish life, the remains of a mikveh were found in 2001 in Milk Street, close to Old Jewry. It is one of the earliest pieces of physical evidence of Jews in Europe and is the only identifiable structure that has survived from that Jewish community.

The community flourished as arrivals, including a number of scholars, came into the country. In 1194 it contributed a large sum towards the levy raised to ransom Richard I.

In due course anti-Jewish feeling developed, and Jews were expelled from the whole country in 1290. At that time the population was estimated to be around 500.

Until the resettlement the only Jews in London, apart from the converts to Christianity who lived in the Domus Conversorum, a home established for that purpose in New Street, now Chancery Lane, were rare occasional visitors. After the expulsion from Spain in 1492, however, services were held in the city in secret by groups of crypto-Jews.

In December 1656, with resettlement, the estimated 20 families then living in the country established a synagogue in Creechurch Lane (a plaque now commemorates this just under one mile east of the original settlement), and in the following year a cemetery was acquired.

Following the accession of William of Orange the number of Spanish and Portuguese Jews arriving from Holland increased. Included among these were merchants and brokers. As a result, in 1697 'Jew Brokers' were allowed to trade on the Royal Exchange. In due course Ashkenazi settlers arrived, establishing their own community in 1690.

During the 19th century both communities expanded. In 1835 David Salomons (1797–1873) was elected a sheriff of the city. In 1847 he became the first Jewish alderman and in 1855 the first Jewish Lord Mayor of the City of London. In 1851 he had been elected a Member of Parliament but was unable to take his seat as he refused to take the oath of allegiance 'on the true faith of a Christian'. After the oath was amended in 1858, he sat as a member from 1859 until his death. The first Jew to take his seat, however, was Lionel de Rothschild, some months earlier in 1858.

From the 1880s until controls on immigration were established by the 1905 Aliens Act, around 100,000, generally poor, Jews arrived from Russia, Poland and other eastern European countries both to avoid pogroms and as economic migrants.

A Reform community was established in 1840. Jews College (now London School of Jewish Studies) was established in 1855 and the Board of Guardians for the Relief of the Jewish Poor in 1859.

Jewish London is split into a number of areas. Central, the East End and the City, the traditional home of immigrants into England; North London, which contains Stamford Hill, the most Orthodox area; and the North-West where the majority of London Jews now live. The remaining parts of London, the South and the East, have communities but offer little interest to a visitor.

Central London

The Hebrew section of the British Library, situated in Euston, has a large collection of interest to all Jewish visitors to the city. There is a Holocaust Memorial Garden in Hyde Park in the centre of London.

The East End and the City

There is little remaining of Jewish life apart from the historical Jewish sites. Of particular interest is Bevis Marks Synagogue, which was built in 1701 and is almost a duplicate of the Spanish and Portuguese Great Synagogue in Amsterdam. It is the oldest synagogue in the country (some of the oak benches come from the original synagogue in Creechurch Lane). It is still almost exactly the same now as it was 300 years ago, and is still lit by candles. Also worth a visit is the Spitalfields Heritage Centre, devoted to the history of immigration into the country. It is on the site of Princelet Street Synagogue, originally a Huguenot family house.

North London

Stamford Hill is the centre of London Jewish hassidic life. It is full of shteibels and small Jewish shops. Also in Stamford Hill is the Jewish Military Museum. Nearby in Camden Town is the Ben Uri Art Gallery and the Jewish Museum dealing with Jews in Britain and throughout the world.

North-West

Apart from two restaurants in the West End of London, this is the place to go if one wishes to eat kosher. The area around Golders Green and Edgware abounds in restaurants of varying cuisine and quality. There is also a multitude of Jewish shops of many kinds.

South London

Visitors to London should endeavour to go to the Holocaust Exhibition at the Imperial War Museum in Lambeth. In addition to the exhibition itself, the Imperial War Museum has much of interest.

Currently, around three-quarters of the approximate 300,000 Jews living in Britain live in London.

CENTRAL

COMMUNITY ORGANISATIONS

Board of Deputies of British Jews
6 Bloomsbury Square WC1A 2LP
Telephone: (020) 7543 5400
Fax: (020) 7543 0010
Website: www.bod.org.uk
Representative body of the British Jewish Community

The Sephardi Centre
2 Ashworth Road, Maida Vale W9 1JY
Telephone: (020) 7266 3682
Fax: (020) 7289 5957

CONTACT INFORMATION

Jewish Community Information (JCI)
6 Bloomsbury Square WC1A 2LP
Telephone: (020) 7543 5421
Fax: (020) 7543 0010
Website: www.bod.org.uk
The basic information service for all aspects of the Jewish Community in Britain. Answerphone for messages

Jewish Memorial Council (Jewish Committee for H.M. Forces)
25 26 Enford Street, W1H 1DW
Telephone: (020) 7724 7778
Fax: (020) 7706 1710
Website: www.jmcouncil.org
Inquiries to Senior Jewish Chaplain

DEPARTMENT STORE

Selfridges
Kosher Deli Department, 400 Oxford Street
Telephone: (020) 7201 2020

EMBASSY

Consulate General of Israel
15a Old Court Place, Kensington W8 4QB
Telephone: (020) 7957 9500
Fax: (020) 7957 9577
Website: www.israel embassy.org.uk/london
Nearest tube station: High Street Kensington. Consular office hours: Monday to Thursday, 10.00 am to 1.15 pm; Friday, 10.00 am to 12.00 pm. Postal address: Consular Section, Embassy of Israel, 2 Palace Green, London W8 4QB

Embassy of Israel
2 Palace Green, Kensington W8 4QB
Telephone: (020) 7957 9500
Fax: (020) 7957 9555
Website: www.london.mfa.gov.il

KASHRUT INFORMATION

Sephardi Kashrut Authority
2 Ashworth Road, Maida Vale W9 1JY
Telephone: (020) 7289 2573
Fax: (020) 7289 7663
Website: www.sephardikashrut.org

LIBRARIES

University College London Library
Wilkins Building, Gower Street WC1E 6BT
Telephone: (020) 7679 2598
Fax: (020) 7679 7373
Email: library @ucl.ac.uk
Website: www.ucl.ac.uk/library/
The Jewish Studies Collection also includes the Mocatta Library, Altmann Library, William Margulies Yiddish Library and the Library of the Jewish Historical Society of England. See website for access information.

Wiener Library - Institute of Contemporary History
4 Devonshire Street W1W 5BH
Telephone: (020) 7636 7247
Fax: (020) 7436 6428
Website: www.wienerlibrary.co.uk
The world's oldest institution dedicated to the documentation of Nazi Germany and the Holocaust. The collection includes 60,000 books and pamphlets, periodicals, documents, videos and photographs as well as extensive press cuttings from 1933 onwards. Other subjects include 20th century Jewish history, antisemitism, exile and refugee studies, minorities, fascism, citizenship etc.

RELIGIOUS ORGANISATIONS

Liberal Judaism
The Montagu Centre, 21 Maple Street W1T 4BE
Telephone: (020) 7580 1663
Fax: (020) 7631 9838
Website: www.liberaljudaism.org

Spanish & Portugese Jews' Congregation
2 Ashworth Road, Maida Vale W9 1JY
Telephone: (020) 7289 2573
Fax: (020) 7289 2709
Email: howardmiller@spsyn.org.uk
Website: www.sandp.org.uk

RESTAURANTS

Glatt Kosher
Reubens
79 Baker Street W1M 1AJ
Telephone: (020) 7486 0035
Fax: (020) 7486 7079

Meat
Reubens
79 Baker Street W1M 1AJ
Telephone: (020) 7486 0035
Fax: (020) 7486 7079
Supervision: Sephardi Kashrut Authority
Open daily except for Shabbat; open Friday until two hours before sundown.

New York Deli & Restaurant
Zvika
8 Great Chapel Street, off Oxford Street
Telephone: (020) 7434 2733
Fax: (020) 7287 0954
Supervision: Sephardi Beth Din

SNACK BAR
Sue Harris Student Centre
B'nai B'rith Hillel Foundation, 1 2 Endsleigh Street
WC1H 0DS
Telephone: (020) 7388 0801
Fax: (020) 7380 6599
Website: www.ujshillel.co.uk
Supervision: London Beth Din
Hours: Monday to Thursday. Please phone for details of
summer months opening. Re opens for students and all
other visitors mid September.

SUPERMARKET
Sainsbury Local
Fetter Lane WC1
Telephone: (020) 7583 4274
DD's Kosher Sandwiches available

Sainsburys
Aviation House, 129 Kingsway, Holborn WC1 6NH
Telephone: (020) 7242 6320
DD's Kosher Sandwiches available

Sainsburys
33 Stratton Street, Mayfair W1X 5SN
Telephone: (020) 7499 8221
DD's Kosher Sandwiches available

Sainsburys
145 Tottenham Court Road W1
Telephone: (020) 7387 5802
DD's Kosher Sandwiches available

Sainsburys
15-17 Tottenham Court Road W1T 1BL
Telephone: (020) 7580 7820
DD's Kosher Sandwiches available

Tesco
158-164 Bishopgate EC2M 6LN
Telephone: (020) 7506 7300
DD's Kosher Sandwiches available

Tesco
2-4 Dean Street W1
Telephone: (020) 7707 8400
DD's Kosher Sandwiches available

Tesco Metro
Cabot Square, Isle of Dogs E14 4QT
Telephone: (020) 7506 7700

Tesco Metro
21-25 Bedford Street, Covent Garden WC2E 9EQ
Telephone: (020) 7853 7500

Tesco Metro
10/16 Goodge Street W1P 1FF
Telephone: (020) 7599 7400
DD's Kosher Sandwiches available

Waitrose
98/101 Marylebone High Street W1M 1DD
Telephone: (020) 7935 4787
DD's Kosher Sandwiches available

SYNAGOGUES
Federation of Synagogues
West End Great Synagogue
32 Great Cumberland Place W1H 7TN
Telephone: (020) 7724 8121
Fax: (020) 7723 4413

Liberal
Bei Klal Yisrael
PO Box 1828 W10 5RT
Telephone: (020) 8960 5750
Website: www.beit klal yisrael.org.uk

Ealing Liberal Synagogue
Lynton Avenue, Drayton Green W13 0EB
Telephone: (020) 8997 0528
Fax: (020) 8997 0528
Email: admin@ealinglibsyn.fsnet.co.uk
Website: www.ealingliberalsynagogue.org.uk

West Central Liberal Synagogue
21 Maple Street W1T 4BE
Telephone: (020) 7636 7627
Email: wcls@liberaljudaism.org
Website: www.wcls.org.uk

Reform
West London Synagogue
33 Seymour Place W1H 5AU
Telephone: (020) 7723 4404
Fax: (020) 7224 8258
Website: www.wls.org.uk

Sephardi
Spanish & Portuguese Synagogue
St James Gardens W11 4RB
Telephone: (020) 7603 7961
Fax: (020) 7603 9471
Email: admin@hollandparksynagogue.com

United
Central Synagogue
Great Portland Street, 36 Hallam Street W1N 6NW
Telephone: (020) 7580 1355
Fax: (020) 7636 3831
Email: administrator@centralsynagogue.org.uk

New West End Synagogue
St Petersburgh Place, Bayswater Road W2 4JT
Telephone: (020) 7229 2631
Fax: (020) 7229 2355
Email: nwes@newwestend.org.uk
Website: www.newwestend.org.uk

Western Marble Arch Synagogue
32 Great Cumberland Place W1H 7TN
Telephone: (020) 7723 9333
Fax: (020) 7224 8065
Website: www.marblearch.org.uk

TRAVEL AGENTS
West End Travel
Barratt House, 341 Oxford Street W1R 2LE
Telephone: (020) 7629 6299
Fax: (020) 7499 0865

EAST END & CITY

BAKERIES
J. Grodzinski & Daughters
170 Clapton Common E5 9AG
Telephone: (020) 8802 4166

BED AND BREAKFAST
Harold Godfrey Hillel House
25 Louisa Street, Stepney E1 4NF
Telephone: (020) 7790 9557
Summer accommodation in London. Twenty three rooms, self catering, separate meat and milk kitchens. Contact the warden at the above address for more information or to book a room.

DELICATESSEN
Munch Box
41 Greville Street EC1
Telephone: (020) 7242 5487
Supervision: London Beth Din

HOTELS
Kosher
Kadimah Hotel
146 Clapton Common, Stamford Hill E5 9AG
Telephone: (020) 8800 5960
Fax: (020) 8800 6237
Email: kadimahhotel@yahoo.com
Website: www.kadimahotel.com
Supervision: Kadassia
Newly refurbished, air conditioned, all rooms en suite

MEDIA
Internet
Brijnet
11 The Lindens, Prospect Hill, Waltham Forest E17 3EJ
Telephone: (020) 8520 3531
Website: www.brijnet.org

Newspapers
Jewish Chronicle
25 Furnival Street EC4A 1JT
Telephone: (020) 7415 1500
Fax: (020) 7405 9040
Website: www.thejc.com
Established 1841, worlds oldest and most influential Jewish weekly newspaper.

MUSEUMS
Museum of Immigration
19 Princelet Street E1 6QH
Telephone: (020) 7247 5352
Fax: (020) 7375 1490
Website: www.19princeletstreet.org.uk
A museum devoted to the history of immigration into Great Britain. Included in the site is Princelet Street Synagogue, a 1870 synagogue built onto a Grade II* listed Georgian town house.
Educational tours by prior arrangement only due to great demand.

NEWSPAPERS
Portman News Agency
32 Greville Street, Hatton Garden EC1N 8TB
Telephone: (020) 7831 7866
DD's Kosher Sandwiches available

RESTAURANTS
Meat
Bevis Marks The Restaurant
Bevis Marks EC3 5DQ
Telephone: (020) 7283 2220
Fax: (020) 7283 2221
Website: www.BevisMarksTheRestaurant.com
Supervision: Sephardi Kashrut Authority
Description Modern British but with some traditional Jewish Ashkenazi and Sephardi dishes

SANDWICH BAR
The Garden Sandwich Bar
32 Hatton Garden EC1
Telephone: (020) 7831 1022
Supervision: Kedassia
Mincha services from 1pm - every 20 minutes until 3pm. The heart of Hatton Garden Jewellery Emporium.

SUPERMARKET
Sainsburys
43-45 Fenchurch Street EC3 7AE
Telephone: (020) 7220 7956
DD's Kosher Sandwiches available

Tesco Metro
6-8 Eastcheap EC2
DD's Kosher Sandwiches available

Tesco Metro
776-780 Cheapside EC2
Telephone: (020) 7506 7600
DD's Kosher Sandwiches available

Waitrose
Canada Place, Canada Square, Canary Wharf E14
Telephone: (020) 7719 0300

SYNAGOGUES
Federation of Synagogues
East London Central Synagogue
30/40 Nelson Street E1 2DE
Telephone: (020) 7790 9809
Mobile Phone: 07983931178
Email: johnben4e@aol.com

Yavneh Synagogue
25 Ainsworth Road E9 7JE
Telephone: (020) 8530 5816

Congregation of Jacob Synagogue - Kehilas Yakov
351/353 Commercial Road E1 2PS
Telephone: (020) 7790 2874
Website: www.congregationofjacob.org
Fax: 0871 661 6774
Independent shul. Affiliated to Adath, Federation and Chesed Ve'emeth Burial societies

Fieldgate Street Great Synagogue
41 Fieldgate Street E1 1JU
Telephone: (020) 7247 2644

Leytonstone & Wanstead Synagogue
2 Fillebrook Road E11
Telephone: (020) 8539 0088

Springfield Synagogue
202 Upper Clapton Road E5 9DH
Telephone: (020) 8806 3167
Fax: (020) 8806 7434

Stamford Hill Beis Hamedrash
50 Clapton Common E5 9AL
Telephone: (020) 8800 7369

Waltham Forest Hebrew Congregation
140 Boundary Road E17
Telephone: (020) 8509 0775

Orthodox
Sandys Row Synagogue
4a Sandys Row E1 7HW
Mobile Phone: 07977 923118
Email: sandys.row@hotmail.co.uk
Website: www.sandysrow.org.uk
Independent Orthodox

Progressive
Woodford Progressive Synagogue
Marlborough Road George Lane E18 1AR
Telephone: (020) 8989 7619
Website: www.woodfordprogressive.org.uk

Reform
Sukkat Shalom Reform Synagogue
1 Victory Road, Wanstead E11 1UL
Telephone: (020) 8530 3345
Email: admin@sukkatshalom.org.uk
Website: www.sukkatshalom.org.uk

Sephardi
The Spanish and Portuguese Synagogue
Bevis Marks EC3 5DQ
Telephone: (020) 7626 1274
Fax: (020) 7283 8825

United
Hackney & East London Synagogue
Brenthouse Road, Mare Street E9 6QG
Telephone: (020) 8985 4600
Fax: (020) 8986 9507

Highams Park & Chingford
81a Maryborough Road E4
Telephone: (020) 8527 0937

TRAVEL AGENTS
Mozes Travel
Dunstan House, 14a St Cross Street EC1N 8XA
Telephone: (020) 7430 2230
Fax: (020) 7405 5049

YOUTH HOSTELS
Sephardi
Aden Jews Congregation
Clapton Common E5
Telephone: (020) 8806 1320

NORTH
Parkway Patisserie
326-328 Regents Park Road , Finchley N3
Telephone: (020) 8346 0344

BAKERIES
J. Grodzinski & Daughters
91 Dunsmure Road N16 5HT
Telephone: (020) 8802 4165

Kosher
Renbake Patisserie Ltd
Unit A, 8-10 Timber Wharf Road, Stamford Hill N16
Telephone: (020) 8800 2525

Sharon's Bakery
182-184 Stamford Hill N16 6QZ
Telephone: (020) 9769
Also at 154 Stamford Hill

Sharon's Bakery
2b Woodberry Down, Manor House N4 2TB
Telephone: (020) 8800 6705

The Cake Company
3 Fontayne Road N14 4QL
Telephone: (020) 8493 9944
Website: www.thecakecompany.co.uk

Woodberry Down Bakeries Ltd
2A Crowland Road, Seven Sisters N15 6UT
Telephone: (020) 8800 4230

BOOKSELLERS
Hebrew Book and Gift Centre
24 Amhurst Parade, Amhurst Park N16 5AA
Telephone: (020) 8802 0609
Fax: (020) 8802 0609
Website: www.hebrewbooks.co.uk

BUTCHERS
A. Perlmutter & Son
1-2 Onslow Parade, Hampden Square, Southgate N14 5JN
Telephone: (020) 8361 5441/2
Supervision: London Board of Shechita

Greenspans
9 11 Lyttelton Road N2 0DW
Telephone: (020) 8455 9921
Fax: (020) 8455 3484
Supervision: London Board of Shechita

Jack Schlagman
112 Regents Park Road, Finchley N3
Telephone: (020) 8346 3598
Supervision: London Board of Shechita

Mehadrin Meats
25 Belfast Road, Stamford Hill N16
Telephone: (020) 8806 0000
Fax: (020) 8880 0500
Supervision: Kedassia

CAFETERIA
Whistlestop Food and Wine
Kings Cross Station, Platform 8 N1
Telephone: (020) 7833 2444
DD's Kosher Sandwiches available

DELICATESSEN AND BAKERIES
Kosher
So Real
43c Oldhill Street, Stamford Hill N16 6LR

HOTELS
Crofts Court Hotel
44 Ravenscroft Avenue, Golders Green N11 8AY
Telephone: (020) 8458 3331
Fax: (020) 8455 9175
Website: www.croftcourthotel.co.uk
Supervision: Kedassia

KASHRUT INFORMATION
Joint Kashrus Committee–Kedassia (Union of Orthodox Hebrew Congregation)
140 Stamford Hill N16 6QT
Telephone: (020) 8800 6833
Fax: (020) 8809 7092

London Beth Din
735 High Road, Finchley N12 0US
Telephone: (020) 8343 6255/6256 (Kashrut hotline: 8343 6333)
Fax: (020) 8343 6254
Website: www.kosher.org.uk
Licenses caterers, bakeries, restaurants, food manufacturers, bonbonnieres, delis and shops. Kosher certifies food products and ingredients worldwide.
Publishes The Really Jewish Food Guide listing kosher approved food and drink. Offers a telephone and email kashrut information service.

National Council of Shechita Boards
Elscot House, Arcadia Avenue, Finchley N3 2JU
Telephone: (020) 8349 9160
Fax: (020) 8346 2209

MEDIA
Newspapers
Hamodia
113 Fairview Road N15 6TS
Telephone: (020) 8442 7777

MIKVAOT
Adath Yisroel Synagogue Mkikvah
40a Queen Elizabeth's Walk, Stamford Hill N16 0HH
Telephone: (020) 8802 2554

Craven Walk Mikvah
72 Lingwood Road, Stamford Hill N16
Telephone: (020) 8800 8555
Evening telephone number: (020) 8809 6279

Satmar Mikkvah
62 Filey Avenue, Stamford Hill N16
Telephone: (020) 8806 3961

Stamford Hill & District Mikvah
Margaret Road, Stamford Hill N16
Telephone: (020) 8806 3880; 8809 4064; 8800 5119

The Sternberg Centre for Judaism
80 East End Road, Finchley N3 2SY
Telephone: (020) 8349 2568
Fax: (020) 8349 5699
Website: www.refsyn.org.uk

Union of Orthodox Hebrew Congregations
140 Stamford Hill N16 6QT
Telephone: (020) 8802 6226

MUSEUMS
Jewish Military Museum and Memorial Room
AJEX House, East Bank, Stamford Hill N16 5RT
Telephone: (020) 8800 2844
Fax: (020) 8800 1117
Website: www.ajex.org.uk
Memorabilia, artefacts, medals, letters, documents, pictures and uniforms all illustrating British Jewry's contribution to the Armed Forces of the Crown from the Crimea to the present day. By appointment, Sunday to Thursday, 11am to 4pm.

RELIGIOUS ORGANISATIONS
Assembly of Masorti Synagogues
Alexander House, 3 Shakespeare Road N3 1XE
Telephone: (020) 8349 6650
Fax: (020) 8349 2743
Website: www.masorti.org.uk

The Movement for Reform Judaism
The Sternberg Centre for Judaism, 80 East End Road, Finchley N3 2SY
Telephone: (020) 8349 5640
Fax: (020) 8349 5699
Email: jewishjourism.org.ukneys@reformjuda
Website: www.reformjudaism.org.uk
Central body for Reform Synagogues around the UK. We offer several 'Jewish Journeys' to worldwide destinations of Jewish interest throughout the year.

Union of Orthodox Hebrew Congregations
140 Stamford Hill N16 6QT
Telephone: (020) 8802 6226

United Synagogue
Adler House, 735 High Road, Finchley N12 0US
Telephone: (020) 8343 8989
Fax: (020) 8343 6262
Website: www.unitedsynagogue.org.uk

RESTAURANTS
Dairy
Tasty Pizza
23 Amhurst Parade, Amhurst Park, Stamford Hill N16 5AA
Telephone: (020) 8802 0018
Supervision: London Beth Din, Kedassia

Dairy-Kosher
Orli Cafe
108 Regents Park Road N3
Telephone: (020) 8371 9222

Meat
The Burger Bar
110 Regents Park Road N3 3JG
Telephone: (020) 8731 1555

Uncle Shloime's
204 Stamford Hill, Stamford Hill N16
Telephone: (020) 8802 9355
Supervision: Kedassia

Middle Eastern & Iranian
Olive
224 Regents Park Road N3
Telephone: (020) 8343 3188

Pizza-Kosher
Tasti Pizza
23 Amhurst Parade, Amhurst Park N16 5AA
Telephone: (020) 8802 0018

SYNAGOGUES
Avahat Israel Wiznitz Synagogue
89 Stamford Hill N16 5TP
Telephone: (020) 8800 9359

Beth Hachsidim D'Gur
2–4 Lampard Grove N16
Telephone: (020) 8806 4333

Beth Hamedrash D'Chassidery Ryzin
33 Paget Road N16
Telephone: (020) 8800 7979

Beth Hamedrash Skver Synagogue
22 Dunsmure Road N16
Telephone: (020) 8800 8448

Northworld Road Synagogue
55–57 Ravendale Road N16
Telephone: (020) 8809 4256

Federation of Synagogues
Finchley Central Synagogue
2 Redbourne Avenue N3 2BS
Telephone: (020) 8346 1892
Email: finchleycentralsynagogue@yahoo.com

Machzikei Hadass Synagogue
1–4 Highfield Road NW11
Telephone: (020) 855 9815
Fax: (020) 8381 4305
Email: nornamandnaomi@tiscali.co.uk

Masorti
New North London Synagogue
The Manor House, 80 East End Road N3 2SY
Telephone: (020) 8346 8560
Fax: (020) 8346 9710
Separate seating

New Whetstone Synagogue
All Saints Art Centre, 122 Oakleigh Road North,
Whetstone N20
Contact: Ellis Slater 020 8445 2671

Orthodox
Beis Nadvorna Beth Hamedrash
45 Darenth Road N16 6ES
Telephone: (020) 8806 9590
Fax: (020) 8806 9590

Progressive
Finchley Progressive Synagogue
Hutton Grove N12 8DR
Website: www.fps.org

North London Progressive Community
Website: www.nlpjc.org.uk
Innovative, open-minded & diverse synagogue,
encouraging friendship, learning, prayer & social action.

Southgate Progressive Synagogue
75 Chase Road N14 4QY
Telephone: (020) 8886 0977
Email: office@sps.uk.com
Website: www.sps.uk.com

Reform
Finchley Reform Synagogue
Fallowcourt Avenue, Finchley N12 0BE
Telephone: (020) 8446 3244
Fax: (020) 8446 5980
Email: admin@frsonline.org
Website: www.frsonline.org

Southgate & District Reform Synagogue
120 Oakleigh Road North N20 9EZ
Telephone: (020) 8445 3400
Fax: (020) 8445 3737
Email: info@sdrs.org.uk
Website: www.sdrs.org.uk

Sephardi
Jacob Benjamin Elias Synagogue
140 Stamford Hill N16 6QT
Telephone: (020) 8809 4387
Fax: (020) 8809 4387

Persian Hebrew Congregation
East Bank, Stamford Hill N16 5RT
Telephone: (020) 8800 9261

United
Cockfosters & N Southgate
Old Farm Avenue, Southgate N14 5QR
Telephone: (020) 8886 8225
Fax: (020) 8886 8234
Email: office@ourshul.co.uk
Website: www.ourshul.co.uk

Finchley Synagogue
Kinloss Gardens N3 3DU
Telephone: (020) 8346 8551
Fax: (020) 8349 1579
Email: david@kinloss.org.uk
Supervision: London Beth Din

Finsbury Park Synagogue
220 Green Lanes N4 2JG
Telephone: (020) 8802 7004

Hampstead Garden Suburb Synagogue
Norrice Lea N2 0RE
Telephone: (020) 8455 8126; Youth: 8458 9123;
Care: 8455 0040
Fax: (020) 8201 9247
Email: office@hgss.org.uk
Website: www.hgss.org.uk

Muswell Hill Synagogue
31 Tetherdown N10 1ND
Telephone: (020) 8883 5925
Fax: (020) 8883 5925
Email: office@muswellhillsynagogue.org.uk
Website: www.muswellhillsynagogue.org.uk

New Synagogue
Victoria Community Centre, Egerton Road N16
Telephone: (020) 8800 6003

Palmers Green & Southgate Synagogue
New Southgate N11 2BN
Telephone: (020) 8881 0037

South Tottenham Synagogue
111–113 Crowland Road N15 6UR
Telephone: (020) 8880 2731
Email: admin@stsynagogue.org.uk

Woodside Park Synagogue
Woodside Park Road N12 8RZ
Telephone: (020) 8445 4236
Website: www.woodsidepark.org.uk

TRAVEL AGENTS

Peltours
11-19 Ballards Lane, Finchley N3 1UX
Telephone: (020) 8371 5200
Fax: (020) 8343 0579
Email: sales@peltours.com
Website: www.peltours.com

YOUTH HOSTELS
United
Highgate Synagogue
57 North Road N6 4BJ
Telephone: (020) 8340 7655

NORTH WEST
Mehadrin Meats
19 Russell Parade, Golders Green NW11 9NN
Telephone: (020) 8455 9992
Fax: (020) 8455 3777; 8599 0984

BAKERIES
Carmelli Bakeries Ltd
126-128 Golders Green Road, Golders Green
NW11 8HB
Telephone: (020) 8455 2074
Fax: (020) 8455 2789
Website: www.carmelli.co.uk
Supervision: London Beth Din, Kedassia

Crème de la Crème
5 Temple Fortune Parade, Bridge Lane NW11 1QN
Telephone: (020) 8458 9090
Supervision: Kedassia

Daniel's Bagel Bakery
12-13 Hallswelle Parade, Finchley Road, Golders
Green NW11 0DL
Telephone: (020) 8455 5826
Fax: (020) 8455 5826
Supervision: London Beth Din

David Bagel Bakery
38 Vivian Avenue, Hendon NW4 3XP
Telephone: (020) 8203 9995
Supervision: London Beth Din, Kedassia

Golden Brown
88 Golders green road NW11
Telephone: (020) 8209 9866

Hendon Bagel Bakery
55 57 Church Road, Hendon NW4
Telephone: (020) 8203 6919
Fax: (020) 8203 8843
Supervision: Kedassia

J. Grodzinski & Daughters
9 Northways Parade NW3 5EN
Telephone: (020) 7722 4944
Website: www.grodzinski.co.uk
Supervision: London Beth Din, Kedassia
Bakery and take away snacks

M & D Grodzinski
223 Golders Green Road, Golders Green NW11 9ES
Telephone: (020) 8458 3654
Fax: (020) 8905 5382
Supervision: London Beth Din, Kedassia

Mr Baker
119-121 Brent Street, Hendon NW4 2DX
Telephone: (020) 8202 6845
Supervision: The Federation of Synagogues Kashrus

Parkway Patisserie Ltd.
30a North End Road, Golders Green NW11
Telephone: (020) 8455 5026
Supervision: London Beth Din, Kedassia

Woodberry Down Bakery
47 Brent Street, Hendon NW4
Telephone: (020) 8202 9962
Supervision: London Beth Din, Kedassia

Kosher
Bonjour
84 Brent Street NW4
Telephone: (020) 8203 8848

Sharon's Bakery
106 Brent Street NW4
Telephone: (020) 8203 6623

The Bagel Place
10 Thornfield parade, Dollis Road NW7 1LN
Telephone: (020) 8922 9454

BAKERIES AND RESTAURANT
Dairy
CakeArt Ltd
2 Sentinel Square, Hendon NW4 2EL
Telephone: (020) 8202 2327
Fax: (020) 8202 8058
Email: cakes@cakearte.co.uk
Website: www.cakearte.co.uk
Supervision: London Beth Din

BED AND BREAKFAST
Orthodox
Kacenberg's Guest House
1 Alba Gardens, Near Alba Court, Golders Green NW11 9NS
Telephone: (020) 8455 3780/9238
Shabbat meals available. Strictly orthodox

BOOKSELLERS
J. Aisenthal
11 Ashbourne Parade, Finchley Road, Temple Fortune NW11 0AD
Telephone: (020) 8455 0501
Fax: (020) 8455 0501
Website: www.aisenthal.co.uk

Jerusalem the Golden
146a Golders Green Road, Golders Green NW11 8HE
Telephone: (020) 8455 4960
Fax: (020) 8203 7808

Joseph's Bookstore
1255 -1257 Finchley Road, Temple Fortune NW11 0AD
Telephone: (020) 8731 7575
Fax: (020) 8731 6699
Website: www.josephsbookstore.com
Regular programme of cultural events including The Society of Jewish Study, Cafe Scientifique, Jazz and Klezmer

Menorah Book and Gift Centre
16 Russell Parade, Golders Road NW11 9NN
Telephone: (020) 8458 8289
Fax: (020) 8731 8403

Steimatzky Hasifria
46 Golders Green Road NW11 8LL
Telephone: (020) 8458 9774
Fax: (020) 8458 3449
Website: www.steimatzkyuk.co.uk

Torah Treasures
4 Sentinel Square, Brent Street, Hendon NW4 2EL
Telephone: (020) 8202 3134
Fax: (020) 8202 3161
Seforim, Judica and gifts

BUTCHERS

Frohwein's Butchers
1095 Finchley Road, Temple Fortune NW11 0QH
Telephone: (020) 8455 9848
Fax: (020) 8731 8241
Supervision: Kedassia
Deli and cooked food available for weekends and Shabbat.
Full range of fresh meat and poultry.

Golders Green Kosher
132 Golders Green Road, Golders Green NW11 8HB
Telephone: (020) 8381 4450
Fax: (020) 8731 6450

M. Lipowicz
9 Royal Parade, Ealing W5
Telephone: (020) 8997 1722
Fax: (020) 8997 0048
Supervision: London Board of Shechita

Menachem's Glatt Kosher
15 Russell Parade, Golders Green Road, Golders
Green NW11 9NN
Telephone: (020) 8201 8629
Fax: (020) 8201 8629
Supervision: London Board of Shechita

Nissim Glatt Kosher
61 Brent Street NW4 2BA
Supervision: Rabbinical Authority of the London Board for
Shechita

BUTCHERS AND DELICATESSEN

Temple Fortune Kosher Deli
9 Hallswelle Parade, Finchley Road NW11 0DL
Supervision: Rabbinical Authority of the London Board for
Shechita

CAFETERIA

Whistlestop Food and Wine
Euston Railway Station, Platform 8, Station
Concourse NW1 2DY
Telephone: (020) 7387 4046
DD's Kosher Sandwiches available

Whistlestop Food and Wine
St. Pancras Station NW1 2RA
Telephone: (020) 7837 6624
DD's Kosher Sandwiches available

Whistlestop Food and Wine
Baker Street Underground Station NW1 5LD
Telephone: (020) 7486 2404
DD's Kosher Sandwiches available

CONTACT INFORMATION

The International Jewish Vegetarianism
Society
Bet Teva, 855 Finchley Road NW11 8LX
Telephone: (020) 8455 0692
Fax: (020) 8455 1465
The International Jewish Vegetarian Society was formed 35
years ago to promote vegetarianism from a Jewish
perspective.

DELICATESSEN

Kosher Deli at Sainsbury's O2 Centre
Finchley Road NW3 6LU
Telephone: (020) 7433 1493 ext: 258

Café/patisserie

Parkview
56 The Market Place, Hampstead Garden Suburb
NW11 6JP
Telephone: (020) 8458 1878
Fax: (020) 8455 3946

Kosher

Adafina
67 Abbey Road, St. Johns Wood NW8 0AE
Telephone: (020) 7624 2013
Fax: (020) 7624 2014
Email: info@adafina.co.uk
Website: www.adafina.co.uk
Supervision: SKA

Deli Express
6 Bell Lane, Hendon NW4 2AD

Deli Express
119 The Broadway, Mill Hill NW7 3TG

Just Kosher
34 Vivian Avenue, Hendon NW4 3 XP

Kennedy Leigh Deli
Kennedy Leigh Children & Family Centre, Edgworth
Close, Hendon NW4
Telephone: (020) 8457 4745

Manna Delicatessen
146 Brent Street, Hendon NW$ 2DR
Telephone: (020) 8201 7575

FISH MONGERS

Leveyuson
47a Brent Street, Hendon NW4
Telephone: (020) 8202 7834
Supervision: London Beth Din

Sam Stoller
28 Temple Fortune Parade, Finchley Road, Golders
Green NW11 0QS
Telephone: (020) 8455 1957; 8458 1429
Fax: (020) 8445 1957
Supervision: Sephardi Kashrut Authority

Kosher

Tuv and Taam
97 Brent Street, Hendon NW4
Telephone: (020) 8202 9952

GROCERIES

B Kosher
91 Bell Lane, Hendon NW4 2AS
Telephone: (020) 82020 1711
Fax: (020) 8202 1599

B Kosher
144 Brent Street
Telephone: (020) 3210 4000

Carmel Fruit Shop
40 Vivian Avenue, Hendon NW4
Telephone: (020) 8202 9587
Fresh fruit and vegetables as well as a good supply of
kosher products, cakes and biscuits.

Yarden
123 Golders Green Road, Golders Green NW11
Telephone: (020) 8458 0979
Website: www.victorgoldschmidt.ch
Free delivery on orders over £25. Hours: Sunday,
Wednesday, Thursday, 8am to 10pm; Monday, Tuesday, 8am
to 9 pm; Friday, 8am.

Delicatessen
Kosher Kingdom
7 Russell Parade, Golders Green Road NW11 9NN
Telephone: (020) 8455 1429
Fax: (020) 8201 8924
Email: info@kosherkingdom.co.uk
Supervision: London Beth Din

Frozen/Dairy
Kosher Paradise Food Shop
10 Ashbourne Parade, Finchley Road, Temple
Fortune NW11 0AD
Telephone: (020) 8455 2454
Fax: (020) 8731 6919
Email: kosher.paradise@ntlbusiness.com

Paperware disposables
Maxine's
20 Russell Parade, Golders Green Road, Golders
Green NW11 9NN
Telephone: (020) 8458 3102
Fax: (020) 8455 3632
Kedassia Deli. Deliveries.

GUEST HOUSE
Sharon Guest House
7 Woodlands Close, Golders Green
Telephone: (020) 8458 8531
Supervision: Although not officially supervised it is said to
be Shomer Shabbat Dati

HOTELS
Central Hotel
35 Hoop Lane, Golders Green NW11 8BS
Telephone: (020) 8458 5636
Fax: (020) 8455 4792
Private bathrooms and parking

King Solomon Palace Hotel
155-159 Golders Green Road NW11 9BX
Telephone: (020) 8201 9000
Fax: (020) 8201 9853
Email: info@kingsolomonhotel.com
Website: www.kingsolomonhotel.com
Supervision: London Beth Din

Yamor Suites
Golders Green
Fax: (020) 8455 4231
Mobile Phone: 07968 387 499
Website: www.yamor.com

KASHRUT INFORMATION
Federation of Synagogues Kashrus Board KF
65 Watford Way NW4 3AQ
Telephone: (020) 8202 2263
Fax: (020) 8203 0610
Email: info@kfkosher.org
Website: www.kfkosher.org

LIBRARIES
British Library, Asia, Pacific & Africa Collections - Hebrew Section
96 Euston Road NW1 2DB
Telephone: (020) 7412 7646
Fax: (020) 7412 7641/7870
Email: ilana.tahan@bl.uk
Website: www.bl.uk/collections/hebrew.html
The Hebrew section contains over 70,000 printed books,
3,000 manscripts and some 10,000 Genizah fragments.
Asian and African studies reading room open to holders of
readers' passes: Monday 10am to 5pm; Tuesday to
Saturday 9.30am to 5pm. Hebrew manuscripts on
permanent display in the treasures gallery of the library.
The Golden Haggadah and the Lisbon Bible are included in
the electronic ' Turning the Pages' programme
http://www.bl.uk/onlinegallery/ttp/ttpbooks.html

MEDIA

Listings

The Diary
32 Bell Lane NW4 2AD
Telephone: (020) 8922 5437
Fax: (020) 8922 8709

Newspapers

Jewish News
Unit 611 Highate Studios, 53-79 Highate Road,
Kentish Town NW5 1TL
Telephone: (020) 7692 6929
Fax: (020) 7692 6689
Website: www.totallyjewish.com

MIKVAOT

North West London Communal Mikvah
40/42 Golders Green Crescent NW11 8PD
Telephone: (020) 8457 5900;8731 9494
10A Shirehall Lane NW4, only open Yom Tiv and Friday
nights by appointment.

The New Central London Mikvah
21 Andover Place NW6 5ED
Telephone: (020) 7372 7237
By appointment only

MUSEUMS

Ben Uri Gallery, The London Jewish Museum of Art
108a Boundary Road, St Johns Wood NW8 0RH
Telephone: (020) 7604 3991

Fax: (020) 7604 3992
Email: info@benuri.org.uk
Website: www.benuri.org.uk
Supervision: Suzanne Lewis
Ben Uri Gallery, the London Jewish Museum of Art, is
Britain's oldest Jewish cultural organisation. Our mission
is to inform the widest public in Britain and abroad of the
life, work and contribution of British and European artists
of Jewish descent and their contemporaries. Open Monday
to Thursday 10am to 5.30pm, Sunday 12am to 4pm Friday
(summer) 10am to 5.30pm, Friday (winter) 10am to 3pm.
Closed Jewish Holy Days.

The Jewish Museum
Raymond Burton House, 129 -131 Albert Street,
Camden Town NW1 7NB
Telephone: (020) 7284 1997
Fax: (020) 7267 9008
Website: www.jewishmuseum.org.uk
The Museum's premises include a History Gallery,
Ceremonial Art Gallery and a Temporary Exhibitions
Gallery offering a varied programme of changing
exhibitions. The Museum has been awarded designated
status by the Museums and Galleries Commission in
recognition of its outstanding collections of Jewish
Ceremonial Art, which are amongst the finest in the world.

**The Museum is closed for renovations and will
reopen in late 2009.**

RESTAURANT/TAKEAWAY

Moroccan Glatt Kosher

Kinnor David
119 Golders Green Road NW11
Telephone: (020) 8455 7766
Supervision: Sephardi beth Din

RESTAURANTS

Beit Hamadras
105 Brent High Street Nw4
Telephone: (020) 8203 4567

Bloom's
130 Golders green Road NW4 2EL
Telephone: (020) 8455 1338
Website: www.blooms-restaurant.co.ukF

Fernando's
56 The Burroughs, Hendon NW4 4AN
Telephone: (020) 8203 5313

Hendon Park Cafe
Queens Road, Hendon

Dairy

Art 2 Heart
109a Golders Green, London NW11
Telephone: (020) 8201 9991
Supervision: London Beth Din

Bon Baguette
122 Golders Green Road, NW11 8HB
Telephone: (020) 8209 0232
Supervision: London Beth Din

Isola Bella Café
63 Brent Street, Hendon NW4 2EA
Telephone: (020) 8203 2000
Website: www.isolabellacafe.com
Supervision: London Beth Din of the Federation of
Synagogues, Sephardi Kashrut Authority

Milk n' Honey
124 Golders Green Road, Golders Green NW11 8HB
Telephone: (020) 8455 0664
Supervision: Kedassia
Vegetarian/dairy restaurant/coffee shop. Air conditioned.
Menus in English and Hebrew. Take away available.

Orli Café
96 Brent Street, Hendon NW4 2HH
Telephone: (020) 8203 7555
Supervision: Kedassia

Slice
8 Princes Parade NW11 9PS
Telephone: (020) 8458 9483
Website: www.slicepizza.co.uk
Supervision: The Federation of Synagogues Kashrus

Taboon
17 Russell Parade, Golders Green Road NW11 9NN
Telephone: (020) 8455 7451
Supervision: Sephardi Kashrut Authority, Kedassia

Dairy-Kosher

Armando
252 Golders Green Road NW11 9NN
Telephone: (020) 8455 8159

Cafe Royal
1047 Finchley Road NW11

Coby's
115a Gokders Green Road NW11 8HA
Telephone: (020) 3209 5049

Little Coffee and I
100a Hamilton Road NW11 9DY

Novellino
103 Golders green Road NW11
Telephone: (020) 8458 7273

Fish & Vegetarian

Cafe Also
1255–1257 Finchley Road, Temple Fortune
NW11 0AD
Telephone: (020) 8455 6890
Fax: (020) 8731 6699
Website: www.josephsbookstore.com

Fish-Kosher

La Dorado
134 Brent Street NW4
Telephone: (020) 8202 5592

Glatt Kosher

Chopstix
119 Golders Green Road NW11 8HR
Telephone: (020) 8455 7766

Kavanna
60 Vivian Avenue, Hendon NW4 3XH
Telephone: (020) 8202 9449

Italian

Francesca
155/9 Golders Green Road NW11 9BX
Telephone: (020) 8201 9005
Supervision: London Beth Din

Kosher

Cafe Mai Yim
1117 Finchley Road NW11 0QB
Telephone: (020) 8458 8030

London Jewish Cultural Centre
Ivy House
94-96 North End Road NW11 7SX

Meat

"86"
86 Brent Street, Hendon NW4
Telephone: (020) 8202 5575
Supervision: The Federation of Synagogues Kashrus

Amors Takeaway
8 Russell Parade, Golders Green NW11

Telephone: (020) 8458 4221
Supervision: Kedassia
Serves meat and fish

Dizengoff Kosher Fried Chicken
122 Golders Green Road, Golders Green NW11 8HB
Telephone: (020) 8209 0232
Supervision: Sephardi Kashrut Authority
Hours: Sunday to Thursday, 11am to midnight; Friday to
4pm; Saturday night one hour after shabbat until 4am.

Dizengoff Kosher Restaurant
118 Golders Green Road, Golders Green NW11 8HB
Telephone: (020) 8458 7003
Fax: (020) 8381 4902
Website: www.Dizengoffkosherrestaurant.co.uk
Supervision: Sephardi
Israeli-style grill

Folman's Restaurant
134 Brent Street NW4
Telephone: (020) 8202 5592
Supervision: London Beth Din

Kaifeng
51 Church Road, Hendon NW4 4DU
Telephone: (020) 8203 7888
Fax: (020) 8203 8263
Website: www.kaifeng.co.uk
Supervision: London Beth Din
Chinese Restaurant with take away and delivery service.
Free delivery with minimum order of £30. Hours: Sunday to

Thursday, 12.30 pm to 2.30 pm, 5.30 pm to 10.30 pm; open Saturday evening, September to April.

La Fiesta
235 Golders Green Road NW11 9PN
Telephone: (020) 8459 0444
Fax: (020) 8455 2003
Supervision: London Beth Din

Lemonade
87 Brent Street NW4
Telephone: (020) 8201 5222
Supervision: Sephardi Kashrut Authority

Marcus's
5 Hallswelle Parade, Finchley Road, Golders Green NW11 0DL
Telephone: (020) 8458 4670
Website: www.marcuss.co.uk
Supervision: London Beth Din

Sami's Restaurant
157 Brent Street, Hendon NW4 4DJ
Telephone: (020) 8203 8088
Fax: (020) 8203 1040
Supervision: Beth Din of the Federation of Synagogues
Glatt kosher Middle Eastern cuisine

Solly's
148a Golders Green Road, Golders Green NW11
Telephone: (020) 8455 0004
Supervision: London Beth Din

Solly's Exclusive
146-150 Golders Green Road, Golders Green NW11
Telephone: (020) 8455 2121
Supervision: London Beth Din

The White House Restaurant
10 Bell Lane, Hendon NW4
Telephone: (020) 8203 2427
Website: www.whitehouserestaurant.co.uk
Supervision: London Beth Din of the Federation of Synagogues, Sephardi Kashrut Authority

Meat-Kosher
Entrcote Bar
102 Golders Green Road NW11 8HB

Met Su Yan
134 Golders Green Road NW11 8HB
Telephone: (020) 8458 8088

Pita
98 Golders Green Road NW11 8HB
Telephone: (020) 8381 4080
Supervision: The Federation of Synagogues Kashrus

Sushi
Kyoto Sushi Bar
51 Brent Street

SUPERMARKET
Sainsburys
Euston Tower, Regents Park Road NW1
Telephone: (020) 7388 4082

DD's Kosher Sandwiches available

SYNAGOGUES
Avath Shalom Synagogue
Clifford Way NW10 1AN
Telephone: (020) 8452 8113

Saatchi Synagogue
21 Andover Place NW6 5ED
Telephone: (020) 7266 2026

Shomrei Hadath Synagogue
527a Finchley Road NW3 7BG
Telephone: (020) 7435 3765

Federation of Synagogues
Beis Hamedrash
65 Watford Way NW4 3AQ
Telephone: (020) 8202 2263
Fax: (020) 8203 0610
Email: info@federationofsynagogues.com
Website: www.federationofsynagogues.com

Netzach Israel Synagogue
281 Golders Green Road NW11 9JJ

Sinai Synagogue
54 Woodstock Avenue NW11 9RJ
Telephone: (020) 8455 6876

Aish Community
379 Hendon Way NW4 3LP
Telephone: (020) 8457 4444
Fax: (020) 8457 4445
Email: info@aish.org.uk
Website: www.aish.org.uk

Finchley Road Synagogue
4 Helenslea Avenue NW11
Telephone: (020) 8455 4305

Independent
Belsize Square Synagogue
51 Belsize Square NW3 4HX
Telephone: (020) 7794 3949
Email: office@synagogue.org.uk
Website: www.synagogue.org.uk

Liberal
The Liberal Jewish Synagogue
28 St John's Wood Road NW8 7HA
Telephone: (020) 7286 5181
Fax: (020) 7266 3591
Website: www.ljs.org

Masorti
New London Synagogue
33 Abbey Road, St Johns Woid NW8 0AT
Telephone: (020) 7328 1026
Fax: (020) 7372 4162
Email: office@newlondon.org.uk
Website: www.newlondon.org.uk
Central organisation: Association of Masorti Synagogues (AMS)

Orthodox

Brondesbury Park Synagogue
143-145 Brondesbury Park NW2 5JL
Telephone: (020) 8459 1083
Email: admin@bpark.org

Shomrei Hadath Synagogue
64 Burrard Road NW6 1DD
Telephone: (020) 7435 6906
Fax: (020) 7794 5557
Central organisation: Federation of Synagogues

Reform

Hendon Reform Synagogue
Danescroft Avenue, Hendon NW4 2NA
Telephone: (020) 8203 4168
Fax: (020) 8203 9385
Website: www.hendonreform.org.uk

North Western Reform Synagogue
Alyth Gardens, Temple Fortune NW11 7EN
Telephone: (020) 8455 6763
Fax: (020) 8731 8175
Website: www.alyth.org.uk

Shir Hayim - Hampstead Reform
Hashomer House, 37a Broadhurst Gardens NW6 3QT
Telephone: (020) 7794 8488
Website: www.shirhayim.org.uk
Central organisation: Movement for Reform Judaism
Small and friendly synagogue

Sephardi

Ohel David Eastern Synagogue
4-15 Broadwalk Lane, Golders Green Road NW11
Telephone: (020) 8455 3491
Website: www.oheldavid.co.uk

United

Dollis Hill Synagogue
Dollis Hill Lane NW2 6RJ
Telephone: (020) 8958 6777

Ealing Synagogue
15 Grange Road W5 5QN
Telephone: (020) 8579 4894
Fax: (020) 8567 2348
Email: ealingsynagogue@spitfireuk.net
Website: www.ealingsynagogue.com

Golders Green Synagogue
Dunstan Road NW11 8AE
Telephone: (020) 8455 2460
Fax: (020) 8731 9296

Hampstead Synagogue
Dennington Park Road NW6 1AX
Telephone: (020) 7435 1518
Fax: (020) 7431 8369
Email: admin@hampsteadshul.org.uk
Website: www.hampsteadshul.org.uk

Hendon Synagogue
18 Raleigh Close NW4
Telephone: (020) 8202 6924
Fax: (020) 8202 1720

Mill Hill Synagogue
Brockenhurst Gardens NW7 2JY
Telephone: (020) 8959 1137
Fax: (020) 8959 6484

South Hampstead Synagogue
20–22 Eton Villas, Eton Road NW3 4SG
Telephone: (020) 7722 1807
Fax: (020) 7586 3459
Email: rachel@southhampstead.org
Website: www.southhampstead.org

St Johns Wood Synagogue
37-41 Grove End Road, St John' Wood NW8 9NG
Telephone: (020) 7286 3838
Fax: (020) 7266 2123
Email: office@shuleinthewood.com
Website: www.shulinthewood.com
Central organisation: United Synagogue

TRAVEL AGENTS

Hotels Direct-Kosher Hotels & Cruises Worldwide
24 Green Walk NW4 2AJ
Telephone: (020) 8203 4482
Email: info@kosherhotels.co.uk
Website: www.kosherhotels.co.uk
Pesach, Shavuot, Sukkot
Summer, winter, cruises and tours

LestAir Services
80 Highfield Avenue, Golders Green NW11 9TT
Telephone: (020) 8455 9654
Fax: (020) 455 9654
Email: family.schleimer@ukgateway.net
Promoting Jewish Heritage Tours to the Czech Republic,
Poland, Hungary, Belarus, Latvia and Lithuania and can be
contacted for detailed information and guidance.

Travelink Group Ltd.
50 Vivian Avenue NW4 3XH
Telephone: (020) 8931 8000
Fax: (020) 8931 8877
Website: www.travelinkuk.com

YOUTH HOSTELS
United
Kingsbury Green Synagogue
Hool Close NW9 8XR
Telephone: (020) 8204 8089

SOUTH
CAFETERIA
Whistlestop Food and Wine
Victoria Station Concourse SW1V 1JU
Telephone: (020) 7976 5533
DD's Kosher Sandwiches available

KOSHER FOODS
Kosher Corner
42 St George's Road, Wimbledon SW19 4ED
Mobile Phone: 07754 744 039
Email: s@dubov.org
Website: www.chabadwimbledon.com

MIKVAOT
South London Mikvah
42 St George's Road, Wimbledon SW19 4ED
Telephone: (020) 8944 7149
Fax: (020) 8944 7563
Email: sarah@dubov.org

MUSEUMS
The Holocaust Exhibition
Imerial War Museum, Lambeth Road SE1 6HZ
Telephone: (020) 7416 5439
Fax: (020) 7416 5457
Website: www.iwm.org.uk
The exhibition covers two floors and uses original artefacts,
film, documents and photographs to tell the story of the
Holocaust. Rare and important historical material, some
lent by former concentration and extermination camp
inmates. Opening hours: 10am to 6pm.

SUPERMARKET
Tesco
17-25 Regent Street SW1Y 4LR
Telephone: (020) 7499 8896

SYNAGOGUES
Woolwich & District Synagogue
Anglesea Road SE18 6EG
Telephone: (020) 8854 6680

Liberal
South London Liberal Synagogue
Prentis Road SW16 1QB
Telephone: (020) 8767 4787
Email: office@southlondon.org
Website: www.southlondon.org
Reform
Wimbledon & District Synagogue
1 Queensmere Road, off Wimbledon Parkside
SW19 5QD
Telephone: (020) 8946 4836
Fax: (020) 8944 7790
Email: office@wimshul.org
Website: www.wimshul.org

United
Catford & Bromley
Crantock Road SE6 2QS
Telephone: (020) 8698 9496
Website: www.catfordsynagogue.org.uk

Chelsea Synagogue
Smith Terrace, Smith Street SW3 4DL
Telephone: (020) 7629 0196

South London Synagogue
45 Leigham Court Road SW16 2NF
Telephone: (020) 8677 0234
Fax: (020) 8677 5107

Merseyside
LIVERPOOL
There is evidence of an organised community
before 1750, believed to have been composed of
Sephardi Jews and to have had some
connection with the West Indies and with
Dublin, although some authorities believe they
were mainly German Jews. The largely
Ashkenazi community, who arrived later, were
to some degree intending to emigrate to the
USA and the West Indies but changed their
minds and stayed in Liverpool. By 1807 the
community had a building in Seel Street, the
parent of today's synagogue in Princes Road,
one of the handsomest in the country.

BOOKSELLERS
Liverpool Jewish Book & Gift Centre
Harold House, Dunbabin Road L15 6XL
Telephone: (0151) 223 303
Email: malcolm.turner@onetel.net
Full range of Jewish books, artefacts and gifts. Sundays
11am to 1pm.

CATERER
Marcos Catering with Distinction
Churchill House, Gaskill Road L24 9PF
Telephone: (0151) 722 1536; 486 6435
Email: marcoscatering@yahoo.co
Supervision: Liverpool Kashrut Commission

COMMUNITY ORGANISATIONS
Merseyside Jewish Representative Council
433 Smithdown Road L15 3JL
Telephone: (0151) 733 2292
Fax: (0151) 734 0212
Email: repcouncil@mjccshifrin.co.uk
Website: www.liverpooljewish.com

DELICATESSEN
Childwall Kosher Deli
256 Woolton road L16
Telephone: (0151) 722 3545
Supervision: Liverpool Kashrut Commission
Provides fresh Glatt kosher meat

Rosemans Delicatessen
20 Childwall Abbey Road L16
Telephone: (0151) 722 2584
Fax: (0151) 722 2584
Supervision: Liverpool Kashrut Commission

KASHRUT INFORMATION
Liverpool Kashrut Commission (inc. Liverpool Shechita Board)
c/o Shifrin House, 433 Smithdown Road L15 3JL
Telephone: (0151) 733 2292
Fax: (0151) 734 0212

KOSHER WINES
Drinks-on-Wheels
Telephone: (0151) 722 4920
Mobile Phone: 07957 160339
Email: drinkson wheels@talktalk.net
Supervision: Liverpool Kashrut Commission
Kosher wines and bar service available from Gary Goodman

MIKVA
Childwall Hebrew Congregation
Dunbabin Road L15 6XL
Telephone: (0151) 722 2079

RESTAURANTS
JLGB Centre
Telephone: (0151) 475 5825; 475 5671
Open Sunday, Tuesday, Thursday 6.30 pm to 11pm. Licensed bar. Take away service.

Kosher
The Liverpool Jewish Youth and Community Centre
Harold House, Dunbabin Road, Childwall L15 6XL
Telephone: (0151) 722 3303; 475 5825
Email: lynda-ljyc@btconnect.com
Supervision: Liverpool Kashrut Commission
Also does take away.

Vegetarian
Munchies Eating House
Myrtle Parade
Telephone: (0151) 709 7896

SYNAGOGUES
Lubavitch Foundation Liverpool
76 Beech Lane L18 3ER
Telephone: (0151) 729 0443
Fax: (0151) 729 0770
Email: lubliv@blueyonder.co.uk

Orthodox
Allerton Hebrew Congregation
Malcolm Malits Court, 207 Mather Avenue L18 9UB
Telephone: (0151) 724 4811
Email: allerton.syn@virgin.net

Childwall Hebrew Congregation
Dunbabin Road, L15 6XL
Telephone: (0151) 722 2079
Email: childwallhc@tiscali.co.uk

Orthodox Ashkenazi
Greenbank Drive Hebrew Congregatrion
Greenbank Drive L17 1AN
Telephone: (0151) 733 1417
Fax: (0151) 733 3862
Email: greenbankdrive@hotmail.com
This synagogue is not open for regular services

Reform
Liverpool Synagogue
28 Church Road North L15 6TF
Telephone: (0151) 733 5871

United
Liverpool Old Hebrew Congregation
Synagogue Chambers, Princes Road L8 1TG
Telephone: (0151) 709 3431
Fax: (0151) 709 4187
Email: lohcl@aol.com
Website: www.exobus.org
Grade II listed building. Guided tours available daily during the week. Pre booking essential. Other times by special arrangement.

SOUTHPORT
Orthodox
Southport Hebrew Congregation
The Synagogue, Arnside Road PR9 0QX
Telephone: (01704) 532 964
Fax: (01704) 532 964
Email: office@shcarnside.co.uk
Mikvah on premises

Middlesex
BUSH HILL PARK
United
Enfield & Winchmore Hill
53 Wellington Park Road EN1 2PG
Telephone: (020) 8363 2697
Fax: (020) 8363 2697

EDGWARE

Ivor Silverman Ltd.
4, Canons Corner HA8 8AE
Telephone: (020) 8958 2692

BAKERIES
J. Grodzinski & Daughters- Hot Bread Shop
6 Edgwarebury Lane HA8 7JZ
Telephone: (020) 8958 1205
Fax: (020) 8905 4874

Kosher
Bonjour
2 Canons Corner HA8 8AE
Telephone: (020) 8958 1321

Sharon's Bakery
11 Edgwarebury Lane HA8 8LH
Telephone: (020) 8958 4789
Supervision: London Beth Din, Kedassia

BOOKSELLERS
Gifts
Divrei Kodesh
13 Edgwarebury Lane HA8 8LH
Telephone: (020) 8958 1133
Fax: (020) 8958 1345
Email: enquiries@divreikodesh.co.uk
Website: www.divreikodesh.co.uk

Carmel Gifts
62 Edgware Way HA8 8JS
Telephone: (020) 8958 7632
Fax: (020) 8958 6226
Email: carmelgifts.co.uk
Website: www.carmelgifts.co.uk

BUTCHERS
Louis Mann & Son Ltd
21–23 Edgwarebury Lane HA8 8LH
Telephone: (020) 8958 5945
Supervision: Rabbinical Authority of the London Board for Shechita

R. Wolff
84 Edgware Way HA8 8JS
Telephone: (020) 8958 8454
Supervision: London Board of Shechita

DELICATESSEN
Kosher
Kosher Edge
Mowbray Parade, 64 Edgware Way HA8 8JS

Pelter Stores
82 Edgware Way
Telephone: (020) 8958 6910

FISH MONGERS
Nat Jacobs
7 The Promenade, Edgwarebury Lane HA8 7JZ
Telephone: (020) 8958 5585

Fax: (020) 8958 5770
Email: mail@nat-jacobs.co.uk

GROCERIES
Kosher Net
293 Hale Lane HA8 7AX
Telephone: (020) 8281 1656
Supervision: London Beth Din

Pelter Stores
82 Edgware Way HA8
Telephone: (020) 8958 6910
Supervision: Beth Din of the Federation of Synagogues

MEDIA
Directory
Jewish Year Book
Vallentine Mitchell, Suite 314, Premier House, 112
114 Station Road HA8 7BJ
Telephone: (020) 8952 9526
Fax: (020) 8952 9242
Email: jyb@vmbooks.com
Website: www.vmbooks.com
Annual directory of all information relating to the British Jewish Community

Newspapers
Essex Jewish News
Vallentine Mitchell, Suite 314, Premier House, 112
114 Station Road HA8 7BJ
Telephone: (020) 8952 9526
Fax: (020) 8952 9242
Email: info@vmbooks.com
Quarterly publication serving East London and Essex

MIKVAOT
Edgware & District Communal Mikvah
Edgware United Synagogue Grounds, 22 Warwick Avenue Drive HA8
Telephone: (020) 8958 3233
Fax: (020) 8958 4004

RESTAURANTS
Met Su Yan
1-2 The Promenade, Edgwarebury Lane
Telephone: (020) 8958 6840

Dairy Italian-Kosher
Tutti Gusti
90-92 High Street
Telephone: (020) 8951 0100

Dairy-Kosher
Francesca
311 Hale Lane HA8 7AX
Telephone: (020) 8905 0552

Orli Café
295 Hale Lane HA8 7AX
Telephone: (020) 8958 1555
Supervision: Kedassia

Kosher
Sababa (Glatt Mehadrin)
226 Station Road HA8 8AU
Telephone: (020) 8958 5557

Meat
Aviv
87 High Street
Telephone: (020) 8952 2484
Fax: (020) 8952 0200
Website: www.avivrestaurant.com
Supervision: Beth Din of the Federation of Synagogues

Kinneret
313 Hale Lane HA8 7AX
Telephone: (020) 8958 4955
Supervision: Beth Din of the Federation of Synagogues

Penashe Glatt BBQ Grill
60 Edgware Way (Mowbray Parade) HA8 8JS
Telephone: (020) 8958 6008
Website: www.penashe.co.uk

Ralphy's- New York Grill
32-34 Station Road HA8 7AB
Telephone: (020) 8952 6036

Meat-Kosher
Aviv Restaurant
87 High Street

SYNAGOGUES
Federation of Synagogues
Yeshurun Synagogue
Fernhurst Gardens, Stonegrave HA8 7PH
Telephone: (020) 8952 5167
Fax: (020) 8905 7439

Masorti
Edgware Masorti Synagogue
Stream Lane HA8 7YA
Telephone: (020) 8905 4096
Fax: (020) 8905 4333
Email: admin@edgwaremasorti.org
Website: www.edgwaremasorti.org

Kol Nefesh Masorti Synagogue
Brady Maccabi Community Centre, Manor Park
Crescent HA8 7NN
Mobile Phone: 0776 9807 356
Website: www.kolnefeshmasorti.org.uk
Central organisation: Assembly of Masorti Synagogues
Shabbat sevice every week at 9.30am. Services some Friday
nights at 6.30pm. (call for details). Egalitarian; Mixed
seating.
Children and youth activities

Reform
Edgware & District Reform Synagogue
118 Stonegrove HA8 8AB
Telephone: (020) 8238 1000
Fax: (020) 8905 4710
Email: admin@edrs.org.uk
Website: www.edrs.org.uk

United
Edgware United Synagogue
Parnell Close HA8 8YE
Telephone: (020) 8958 7508
Fax: (020) 8905 4449
Website: www.edgwareu.com

TRAVEL AGENTS
Peltours AMG Travel
70 Edgware Way HA8 8JS
Telephone: (020) 8958 3188
Fax: (020) 8958 8898

Sabra Travel Ltd.
9 Edgwarebury Lane, Edware HA8 8LH
Telephone: (020) 8958 3244/7

HARROW
SYNAGOGUES
Progressive
Harrow and Wembley Progressive Synagogue
326 Preston Road HA3 0QH
Telephone: (020) 8904 8581
Website: www.hwps.org

Reform
Middlessex New Synagogue
39 Bessborough Road HA1 3BS
Telephone: (020) 8864 0133
Fax: (020) 8864 5323
Email: admin@mns.org.uk
Website: www.mns.org.uk
Central organisation: Movement for Reform Judaism

Sephardi
David Ishag Synagogue
352-354 Preston Road HA3 0QJ
Telephone: (020) 8904 9402

HATCH END
BUTCHERS
Ivor Silverman Ltd.
358, Uxbridge Rd HA5 4HP
Telephone: (020) 8428 6564

SYNAGOGUES
Masorti
Hatch End Masorti
The Girl Guides HQ, The Car Park, Grimsdyke Road
Telephone: (020) 8866 0320
Regular Shabbat service every week, traditional service,
mixed and separate seating available

Reform
Kol Chai Hatch End Jewish Community
The Synagogue, 434 Uxbridge Road HA5 4RG
Telephone: (020) 8421 5482
Website: www.kolchai.org

HOUNSLOW

CAFE/PATISSERIE

Cafe Nero
Heathrow Airport, Terminal 1 Airside, Departures
(Duty Free Area) TW6 1AT
Telephone: (020) 8759 9444
DD's Kosher Sandwiches available

CAFETERIA

Bire Café
Heathrow Airport, Terminal 3 Arrivals
Telephone: (020) 8759 3607
DD's Kosher Sandwiches available

Whistlestop Food and Wine
Heathrow Airport, Terminal 1 Landside, Arrivals
TW6 1EW
Telephone: (020) 8897 3005
DD's Kosher Sandwiches available

SYNAGOGUES

United
Hounslow & Heathrow Synagogue
100 Staines Road TW18
Telephone: (020) 8894 4020

KENTON

Kenton Synagogue
Shaftesbury Avenue HA3 0RD
Telephone: (020) 8907 5959
Fax: (020) 8909 2677
Email: office@kentonsynagogue.org.uk
Website: www.kentonsynagogue.org.uk

NORTHWOOD

Liberal
Northwood & Pinner Liberal Synagogue
Oaklands Gate HA6 3AA
Telephone: (01923) 822592
Fax: (01923) 824454
Email: admin@npls.org.uk
Website: www.npls.org.uk
Northwood & pinner Liberal Synagogue is a fully inclusive
and welcoming environment for Jews, their family and
friends to express themselves in the light of Jewish
tradition and modernity.

United
Northwood Synagogue
21–23 Murray Road HA6 2YP
Telephone: (01923) 820004
Fax: (01923) 820020
Email: northwoodus@tiscali.co.uk

PINNER

Pinner Synagogue
1 Cecil Park HA5 5HJ
Telephone: (020) 8868 7204
Fax: (020) 8868 7011
Website: www.pinnersynagogue.com

RUISLIP

Ruislip Synagogue
Shenley Avenue HA4 6BP
Telephone: (01895) 622 059

STAINES

Orthodox
Staines & District Synagogue
Westbrook Road, South Street TW18 4PR
Telephone: (020) 8890 0016
Email: staines.synagogue@btinternet.com
Website:
http://www.btinternet.com/~staines.synagogue
Central organisation: Affiliated to the United Synagogue
Closest synagogue to Heathrow airport. Services every
Friday night at 6pm, 7pm during British Summer Time.
Shabbat service at 10am, Yomtov service times on request.

STANMORE

BUTCHERS

La Boucherie Express
78 The Broadway HA7 4AH
Telephone: (020) 8954 6020
Fax: (020) 8954 9700
Supervision: with the sanction of the Rabbinic Authority of
the London Board for Shechita

DELICATESSEN

Kosher
B'te A'von Fine Meals by Oberlander
121 Merrioh Avenue WD6 4QD
Telephone: (020) 8905 3232
Website: www.justkosher.co.uk

La Boucherie Express
78 The Broadway
Telephone: (020) 8954 6020

DELICATESSEN/TAKEAWAY

Steve's Deli
5 Canons Corner HA8 8AE
Telephone: (020) 8958 9446
Fax: (020) 8905 4700
Website: www.mrbutler.net
Supervision: London Beth Din
Freshly cooked deli food and hot food take away. Made on
premises.
Also Kosher Caterers Stephen Rosenhead Banqueting.

SYNAGOGUES

Orthodox
Belmont Synagogue
101 Vernon Drive HA7 2BW
Telephone: (020) 8426 0104
Fax: (020) 8427 2046

United
Stanmore & Canons Park Synagogue
London Road HA7 4NS
Telephone: (020) 7286 3838
Fax: (020) 7266 2123

WEMBLEY

BAKERIES

Kosher

Parkway Patisserie Ltd
204 Preston Road
Telephone: (020) 8904 7736

BUTCHERS

Kelman's Butchers
198 Preston Road HA9 9NQ
Supervision: Rabbinical Authority of the London Board for
Shechita

Kelman's Kosher Products
Unit 20 Stadium Business Centre, North End road
HA9 0AT
Supervision: Rabbinical Authority of the London Board for
Shechita

SYNAGOGUES

United

Wembley Synagogue
Forty Avenue HA9 8JW
Telephone: (020) 8904 6565
Fax: (020) 8908 2740
Email: office@wembleysynagogue.org

Norfolk
NORWICH
Norwich is the site of the first recorded blood
libel in Europe when, in 1144, William of
Norwich was found murdered. At that time
Jews were connected with the woollen and
worsted trades for which the city was then
famous. Resettlement took place in the early
18th century, and the present community was
established in 1813.

Progressive Jewish Community of East Anglia
C/o Frimette Carr NR2 3RA
Telephone: (01603) 714162

United

Norwich Synagogue
3a Earlham Road NR2 3RA
Telephone: (01603) 623 948

Northamptonshire
NORTHAMPTON
Northampton Synagogue
Overstone Road NN1 3JW
Telephone: (01604) 633 345
Services on Friday night

Nottinghamshire
NEWARK
HOLOCAUST MEMORIAL CENTRE
Beth Shalom
Laxton NG22 0PA
Telephone: (01623) 836 627

Fax: (01623) 836 647
Beth Shalom Holocaust Memorial Centre was conceived as
a place where some of the implications of the Holocaust
can be faced. It is an education centre where Jews and non
Jews work together to forge a united front against the
perils of anti Semitism and racism in society today.

NOTTINGHAM
Jews settled in Nottingham as early as medieval
times, and centres of learning and worship are
known to have existed in that period. The
earliest known record of an established
community dates from 1822 when a grant of
land for burial purposes was made by the
Corporation.
The synagogue in Shakespeare Street (originally
a Methodist Church) is a Grade II listed
building.

RESTAURANTS

Vegetarian

Maxine's Salad Table
56 Upper Parliament Street NG1 2AG
Telephone: (0115) 947 3622

SYNAGOGUES

Liberal

**Nottingham Progressive Jewish
Congregation**
Lloyd Street, Sherwood NG5 4BP
Telephone: (0115) 962 4761
Website: www.npjc.org.uk

United

Synagogue
Shakespeare Villas, Shakespeare Street NG1 4FQ
Telephone: (0115) 947 2004

Oxfordshire
OXFORD
There was an important medieval community
here, and the present one dates back to 1842.
The Oxford Synagogue and Jewish Centre,
opened in 1974, serves both the city and the
university. It is available for all forms of Jewish
worship.

Orthodox, Liberal, Masorti

Oxford Synagogue and Jewish Centre,
21 Richmond Road OX1 2JL
Telephone: (01865) 514 356
Email: sifo7i802@sneakemail.com
Website: www.oxfordsynagogue.org.uk

The Oxford Jewish Congregation is an orthodox
congregation that encourages other denominational
worship. So there are orthodox services every Friday
evening and Shabbat morning. On the second Shabbat of
every month, there is additionally a Liberal Service and on
the last Shabbat of every month there is additionally a
Masorti service. There are also occasional services for
women, conducted by women and occasional Friday

evening Masorti services. The kiddush on Shabbat morning after the services is attended by everyone - if the two services do not end at the same time everyone waits so that we can be together as one congregation! All denominations are equal members of the Oxford Jewish Congregation. Wide range of communal activities. A kosher meals service operates during term time.

Recently expanded and redeveloped Jewish Centre available for hire and functions.

Staffordshire
STOKE ON TRENT
Ashkenazi/Orthodox
Synagogue
Birch Terrace, Hanley ST1 3JN
Telephone: (01782) 616 417

Surrey
CROYDON
Federation of Synagogues
Croydon & District Synagogue
The Almonds, 5 Shirley Oaks Road CR0 8YX
Telephone: (020) 8662 0011

GUILDFORD
MUSEUMS
Guildford Museum
Castle Arch GU1 3SX
Telephone: (01483) 444 750
Fax: (01483) 532 391
Email: museum@guildford.gov.uk
Website: www.guildfordmuseum.co.uk

SYNAGOGUES
Orthodox
Guildford & District Synagogue
York Road GU1 4DR
Telephone: (01483) 576 470
Website:
www.geocities.com/guildfordjewishcommunity
Correspondence: Irene Black 11 Grasmere Close, Merrow
Guildford GU1 2TG

TOURIST SITES
Medieval Synagogue
Enquiries about the discovery of a medieval synagogue in the town may be addressed to the Guildford Museum

KINGSTON UPON THAMES
SYNAGOGUES
United
Kingston, Surbiton & District Synagogue
33–35 Uxbridge Road KT1 2LL
Telephone: (020) 8546 9370
Email: info@kingston-synagogue.org.uk
Website: www.kingston-synagogue.org.uk

LONG DITTON
Liberal
Kingston Liberal Synagogue
Rushett Road, Long Ditton KT7 0UX
Telephone: 8398 7400
Fax: 8843 2405
Website: www.kingstonls.org.uk

RICHMOND–ON–THAMES
United
Richmond Synagogue
Lichfield Gardens TW9 1AP
Telephone: (020) 8940 3526

SUTTON
Sutton Synagogue
14 Cedar Road SM2 5DA
Telephone: (020) 8642 5419
Email: suttsyn@tiscali.co.uk

WEYBRIDGE
Reform
North West Surrey Synagogue
Hovarth Close, Rosslyn Park, Oaklands Drive KT13 9QZ
Telephone: (01932) 855 400
Fax: (01932) 855 400
Website: www.reformjudaism.org.uk/nwss

Sussex (East)
BRIGHTON
The first known Jewish resident of Brighton lived here in 1767. The earliest synagogue was founded in Jew Street in 1789. Henry Solomon, vice-president of the congregation, was the first Chief Constable of the town. His brother-in-law, Levi Emanuel Cohen, founded the Brighton Guardian, and was twice elected president of the Newspaper Society of Great Britain. The town's Jewish population today is about 8,000.

MIKVAOT
Brighton and Hove Mikvaot
Prine Regent Swimming Pool Complex, Church Street BN1 1YA
Telephone: (01273) 321 919

ORGANISATIONS
Hillel House
18 Harrington Road BN1 6RE
Telephone: (01273) 503 450
Closed during summer vacation. Friday evening meals available.

RESTAURANTS
Vegetarian
Food for Friends
17 18 Price Albert Street, The Lanes
Telephone: (01273) 202 310
Fax: (01273) 774 171
Website: www.foodforfriends.com
Wai Kika Moo Kau Limited
42 Meeting House Lane
Telephone: (01273) 323 824

SYNAGOGUES
Reform
Brighton & Hove Reform Synagogue
Palmeira Avenue
Telephone: (01273) 735 343
Fax: (01273) 734 537
Website: www.bh rs.org

EASTBOURNE
Orthodox
Eastbourne Hebrew Congregation
22 Susans Road BN21 3TJ
Telephone: (01323) 484135
Email: lindron@hotmail.co.uk

Progressive
Eastbourne Progressive Jewish Congregation
JAYBIRDS, 39 Mountbatten Drive, Langney Point
BN23 6AX
Telephone: (01323) 725 650
Fax: (01323) 417 645
Email: epjcong@aol.com
Website: www.epjcong.org.uk
Erev Shabbat Services are held on the 2nd and 4th Friday of each month, at The Friends Meeting House, Wish Road, Eastbourne, commencing at 7pm.
A Chavurah supper is usually held before the service on the 4th Friday commencing at 5.30pm. For details tel; 01323 725650

HOVE
COMMUNITY ORGANISATIONS
Lubavitch Chabad House
15 Upper Drive BN3 6GR
Telephone: (01273) 321 919
Fax: (01273) 821 518

MEDIA
Newspapers
Sussex Jewish News
PO Box 2178 BN3 3SZ
Telephone: (01273) 220461
Email: editor@sussexjewishnews.com
Website: www.jewishsussex.com
Monthly magazine covering the Jewish community in Sussex (and more.)
Editor: Linda Freedman

RELIGIOUS ORGANISATIONS
Brighton and Hove Joint Kashrus Committee
c/o B.H.H.C., 31 New Church Road, Hove BN3 4AD
Telephone: (01273) 888 855
Fax: (01273) 888 810

SYNAGOGUES
Orthodox
Hove Hebrew Congregation
79 Holland Road, Hove BN3 1JN
Telephone: (01273) 732 035

West Hove Synagogue
31 Church Road, Hove BN3 4AD
Telephone: (01273) 888 855
Fax: (01273) 888 810

Progressive
Synagogue
6 Landsdowne Road BN3 1FF
Telephone: (01273) 737 223
Fax: (01273) 737 223
Email: bhps@freenetname.co.uk
Website:
www.brightonandhoveprosynagogue.org.uk
Central organisation: Liberal Judaism
Office hours: 9.00am to 1.00pm

Sussex (West)
GATWICK
CAFETERIA
Whistlestop Food and Wine
Gatwick Airport, South Terminal RH6 0NP
Telephone: (01293) 502050
DD's Kosher Sandwiches available

Tyne & Wear
GATESHEAD
A community with many schools, yeshivot and other training institutions.

BAKERIES
Stenhouse
215 Coatsworth Road NE8 1SR
Telephone: (0191) 477 2001
Fax: (0191) 478 4778
Mobile Phone: 07778148902
Supervision: Gateshead Kashrus Authority

BOOKSELLERS
J. Lehmann
28 30 Grasmere Street NE8 1TS
Telephone: (0191) 477 3523
Fax: (0191) 430 0555
Email: info@lehmanns.co.uk
Also has wholesale and mail order, Unit E, Rolling Mill Road, NE32 3DP. Tel: (0191) 430 0333

BUTCHERS
G.K. Butchers
187 -189 Coatsworth Road NE8 1SR
Telephone: (0191) 477 3109

MIKVAOT
Gateshead Mikvaot
180 Bewick Road NE8 1UF
Telephone: (0191) 477 3552

SYNAGOGUES
Orthodox
Gateshead Synagogue
138 Whitehall Road NE8 1TP
Telephone: (0191) 477 3012

Gateshead Synagogue
180 Berwick Road NE8 1UF

NEWCASTLE UPON TYNE
The community was established before 1831 when a cemetery was acquired. Jews have lived in Newcastle since 1775. There are about 1,200 Jews in the city today.

KASHRUT INFORMATION
Kosher Facility, United Hebrew Congregation
Lionel Jacobson House, Graham Park Road, Gosforth NE3 4BH
Telephone: (0191) 284 4402
Fax: (0191) 284 4402
Email: secretary@uhc-newcastle.org
Supervision: UHC

MEDIA
Newspapers
The North East Jewish Recorder
24 Adeline Gardens NE3 4JQ
Telephone: (0191) 285 1253
Website: www.northeastjewish.org.uk

MIKVAOT
Newcastle Upon Tyne Mikvaot
Graham Park Road NE3 4BH
Telephone: (0191) 284 0959

RESTAURANTS
Vegetarian
The Supernatural
2 Princess Square NE1 8ER
Telephone: (0191) 261 2730

SYNAGOGUES
Reform
Newcastle Reform Synagogue
The Croft, off Kenton Road NE3 4RF
Telephone: (0191) 284 8621
Website: www.nertamid.org.uk

United
United Hebrew Congregation
Graham Park Road, Gosforth NE3 4BH
Telephone: (0191) 284 0959
Email: secretary@uhc-newcastle.org
Mikva on premises

SUNDERLAND
Orthodox
Sunderland Hebrew Congregation
Ryhope Road SR2 7EQ
This Grade II listed building is not now in everyday use - it is being maintained due to the generosity of an American/Jewish charitable foundation for the 38 or so Jewish families still remaining resident in Sunderland.

West Midlands
BIRMINGHAM
This Jewish community is one of the oldest outside London, dating from at least 1730. Birmingham was a centre from which Jewish pedlars covered the surrounding country.

The first recorded synagogue was in The Froggery in 1780. There was a Jewish cemetery in the same neighbourhood in 1730. The synagogue of 1780 was extended in 1791, 1809 and 1827. A new and larger synagogue, popularly known as 'Singers Hill', opened in 1856. Today's Jewish population stands at about 2,300.

BOOKSELLERS
Lubavitch Bookshop
95 Willow Road B12 9QF
Telephone: (0121) 440 6673
Fax: (0121) 446 4199

DELICATESSEN
Gee's Butchers Ltd
75 Pershore Road, Edgbaston B5 7NX
Telephone: (0121) 440 2160
Fax: (0121) 440 2421
Email: geeskosherdeli@hotmail.co.uk
Website: www.gees-kosher-butchers.com
Supervision: Birmingham Rabbinic Board
Kosher butcher, baker and deli.

INFORMATION AND RESOURCE CENTRE
Israel Information Centre for the Midlands
Singers Hill, Ellis Street B1 1HL
Telephone: (0121) 643 2688
Fax: (0121) 643 2688
Hours of opening: 10am to 4pm Monday, Tuesday, Thursday or by appointment.

KASHRUT INFORMATION
Shechita Board
Singers Hill, Ellis Street B1 1HL
Telephone: (0121) 643 0884

MIKVAOT
Birmingham Central Synagogue
133 Pershore Road B5 7PA
Telephone: (0121) 440 4439
Fax: (0121) 440 5405
Mobile Phone: 07891 645 612

SYNAGOGUES
Orthodox
Birmingham Hebrew Congregation
Singers Hill, Ellis Street B1 1HL
Telephone: (0121) 643 0884
Fax: (0121) 643 5950

Central Synagogue
133 Pershore Road, Edgbaston B5 7PA
Telephone: (0121) 440 4044
Fax: (0121) 440 5405
Mobile Phone: 07725 642 373
Email: cjennings@centralshul.com
Website: www.centralshul.com

Progressive
Progressive Synagogue
4 Sheepcote Street B16 8AA
Telephone: (0121) 643 5640
Fax: (0121) 633 8372
Website: www.bps pro syn.co.uk

COVENTRY
The Jewish presence in Coventry dates back to 1775, if not earlier.

Orthodox
Coventry Hebrew Congregation
Barras Lane CV1 3BW
Telephone: (024) 7622 0168

Reform
Coventry Jewish Reform Community
24 Nightingale Lane, Canley Gardens CV5 6AY
Telephone: (024) 7667 2027

SOLIHULL
Orthodox
Solihull & District Hebrew Congregation
3 Monastery Drive B91 1DW
Telephone: (0121) 706 8736
Fax: (0121) 706 8736
Website: www.solihullshul.org
Services: Friday evening 6.30pm winter, 8pm summer, Saturday 9.45am, Sunday 9am

Wiltshire
SWINDON
Reform
Swindon Jewish Community
16 Dowling Street SN1 5QY
Telephone: (01793) 521 910

Yorkshire (North)
HARROGATE
Orthodox
Harrogate Hebrew Congregation
St Mary's Walk
Telephone: (01423) 871 713
Fax: (01423) 879 143
Email: philip.morris@ukgateway.net
Services: Saturday 9-30am,
Festivals 9-30am
First Friday evening in month Winter 6pm / Summer 7pm.

YORK
TOURS
Yorkwalk
3 Fairway, Clifton YO30 5QA
Telephone: (01904) 622 303
Fax: (01904) 656 244
Email: admin@yorkwalk.fsnet.co.uk
Website: www.yorkwalk.co.uk
The Jewish Heritage Walk, recalling the Jewish contribution to York's history. The walk finishes at Clifford's Tower, the site of a dreadful massacre in 1190.
For regular public walks ring or see website;private tours at any time'

Yorkshire (South)
SHEFFIELD
SYNAGOGUES
Reform
Sheffield Kehillat Shivah Harim
PO Box 675 S11 8TE
Mobile Phone: 0771 920 9259 (text and answerphone)
Email: info@shef-ref.co.uk
Website: www.shef-ref.co.uk
Supervision: food is non-meat, vegetarian
Central organisation: movement for Reform Judaism
Friday night or Shabbat morning servicesnormally 2-3 times a month - some festival services, celebrations and other events - High Holy day services - Communal Seder

United
Sheffield Jewish Congregation and Centre
Kingfield Synagogue, Brincliffe Crescent S11 8UX
Telephone: (0114) 258 8855
Website: www.sjcc.co.uk
There is a mikveh in the building. There is also a kosher restaurant and butcher on Thursday only.

Yorkshire (West)
BRADFORD
The Jewish community, although only about 140 years old, has exercised much influence on the city's staple industry: wool. Jews of German descent developed the export trade of wool yarns and fabrics.

Orthodox
Bradford Hebrew Congregation
Springhurst Road, Shipley BD18 3DN
Telephone: (01274) 581189
Fax: (01274) 374101
Services 10 am monthly on Shabbat Mevorachim, High
Holy Days & certain festivals.

Reform
Bradford Synagogue
7A Bowland Street, Manningham Lane BD1 3BW
Telephone: (01274) 728 925
Service Saturday 11am; Festivals, 6pm and 11am. A grade II
listed building, built in 1873 in the Moorish style.

LEEDS
The Leeds Jewish community dates only from
the 1820s, although a few Jews are known to
have lived there in the previous half-century.
The first synagogue was built in 1860.
The population, which peaked at around 20,000
in the 1920s, and was possibly the city which
had largest population of Jews in the country at
that time, is now less than 8,000.

BAKERIES
Chalutz Bakery
378 Harrogate Road LS17 6PY
Telephone: (0113) 269 1350
Supervision: Leeds Beth Din
Hours: Monday to Thursday , 8am to 6pm; Friday to one
hour before Shabbat; Saturday, from one hour after
Shabbat to 2pm Sunday.

BUTCHERS
Gourmet Foods
Sandhill Parade, 584 Harrogate Road LS17 8DP
Telephone: (0113) 268 2726
Supervision: Leeds Beth Din
Butcher and deli

CAFETERIA
Oasis Cafe
311 Stonegate Road
Telephone: (0113) 218 5888
Website: www.mazcc.co.uk
Supervision: Leeds Bet Din
Foyer of Marjorie & Arnold Ziff Community Centre
Fully licensed bar.
Opening times are Sun, Tue, Wed and Thu 10am to 10pm
and Mon 10am to 4.30pm for drinks, sandwiches, cakes,
pastries and light snacks. Fri from 10pm to 1pm.
A hot lunchtime menu is served daily: midday to 4pm (until
1pm on Fri) A children's menu is available Sun to Thu from
midday onwards.

COMMUNITY CENTRE
Marjorie & Arnold Ziff Community Centre
311 Stonegate Road LS17 6AZ
Telephone: (0113) 218 5888
Website: www.mazcc.co.uk
Mini Gymnasum, restaurant & cafe

Centre now provides a home for Makor Jewish Culture and
Resource Centre, the shaliach, JNF, WIZO.uk and the Leeds
Jewish Representative Council as well as LJHA and LJWB.

COMMUNITY ORGANISATIONS
Leeds Jewish Representative Council
c/o Shadwell Lane Synagogue LS17
Telephone: (0113) 269 7520
Publishes Year Book

DELICATESSEN
Kosher Food
The Kosherie
410 Harrogate Road LS17 6PY
Telephone: (0113) 268 2943
Fax: (0113) 269 6979
Email: kosherie1@btconnect.com
Supervision: Leeds Beth Din

LEISURE
Moor Allerton Golf Club
Coal Road, Wike LS17 9NH
Telephone: (0113) 266 1154
Fax: (0113) 268 0589
Email: info@magc.co.uk

LIBRARIES
Porton Collection
The Information Centre, Central Library, Calverley
Street LS1 3AB
Telephone: (0113) 247 8282
Fax: (0113) 395 1833
Email: businessandresearch@leedslearning.net
Website: www.leeds.gov.uk

MEDIA
Newspapers
Jewish Telegraph
1 Shaftsbury Avenue LS8 1DR
Telephone: (0113) 295 6000
Fax: (0113) 295 6006
Email: leeds@jewishtelegraph.com
Website: www.jewishtelegraph.com

RESTAURANTS
Hansa's Gujarati Restaurant
72 North Street LS2 7PN
Telephone: (0113) 244 4408
Website: www.hanasrestaurant.co.uk
Indian vegetarian restaurant

Meat
The Vine Restaurant
311 Stonegate Road
Telephone: (0113) 218 5888
Fax: (0113) 203 4915
Email: info@mazcc.co.uk
Website: www.mazcc.co.uk
Based in The Linton Room
Open on a Mon to Thu from 12pm until 2pm and until 1pm
on a Fri. To help our members who are more frail and need
more help with service, the period between 12pm and

12.30pm is reserved for them. However all visitors are welcome from 12.30pm onwards

Open on Tue, Wed and Thu evenings offering an Early Bird Menu from 5pm to6.30pm Dinner Menu from 6.30pm - 9pm A Sunday Deli Brunch menu is available from 11.30am to 2.30pm and an a la carte Sunday Dinner menu from 6pm to 9pm.

SYNAGOGUES

Beth Hamidrash Hagadol
399 Street Lane LS17 6HQ
Telephone: (0113) 269 2181
Fax: (0113) 237 0113
Email: office@bhhs.co.uk

Masorti
Leeds Masorti
Telephone: (0113) 29 45 112

Orthodox
Etz Chaim Synagogue
411 Harrogate Road LS17 7TT
Telephone: (0113) 266 2214
Fax: (0113) 237 1183
Website: www.etzchaim.co.uk
Information about kosher food and accommodation may be obtained here.
Registered office: 584 Harrowgate Road   LS17 8DP

Queenshill Synagogue
Marjorie and Arnold Ziff Community Centre, 311 Stonegate Road LS17 6AZ
Telephone: (0113) 268 7364
Mailing address: 49 Queenshill Drive, Moortown, LS17 5BG

Shadwell Lane Synagogue (United Hebrew Congregation)
151 Shadwell Lane LS17 8DW
Telephone: (0113) 269 6141
Fax: (0113) 269 6141
Website: www.uhcleeds.com

Shomrei Hadass
368 Harrogate Road LS17 6QB
Telephone: (0113) 268 1461

Orthodox   Ashkenazi
Chassidishe
c/o Donisthorpe Hall, Shadwell Lane LS17 6AW
Telephone: (0113) 268 6805
Open to non-residents
Contact; Mr Roy Powell Membership Secretary

Reform
Sinai Synagogue
Roman Avenue, off Street Lane LS8 2AN
Telephone: (0113) 266 5256
Fax: (0113) 266 1539
Email: info@sinaisynagogue.org.uk
Website: www.sinaisynagogue.org.uk

CHANNEL ISLANDS
Alderney
LONGEY
MEMORIAL
World War II Occupation Memorial
Corblets Road
There is a memorial to the victims of the Nazis during their occupation of the Channel Islands during the Second World War. It bears plaques in English, French, Hebrew and Russian.

Jersey
ST BRELADE
CONTACT INFORMATION
Mr M Morton
16 La Rocquaise, La Route des Genets, St Brelade JE3 8HY
Telephone: (01534) 742 819
Fax: (01534) 747 554
Honorary secretary of the Jersey Jewish Congregation

SYNAGOGUES
Jersey Jewish Congregation
La Petite Route des Mielles, St Brelade JE3 8FY
Telephone: (01534) 865 333
Fax: (01534) 861 431
Shabbat morning service 10.30am; Holy Days 7pm and 10am

NORTHERN IRELAND
BELFAST
There were Jews living in Belfast in the year 1652, but the present community was founded in 1869.

RESTAURANTS
Jewish Community Centre
49 Somerton Road BT15 4DD
Telephone: (028) 9077 7974
Website: www.belfastjewishcommunity.org.uk
Open by arrangement only. Please phone ahead. Both meat and dairy.

SYNAGOGUES
Orthodox
Belfast Synagogue
49 Somerton Road BT15 3LH
Telephone: (028) 9077 5013
Email: mendybrackman@hotmail.com
Website: www.belfastjewishcommunity.org.uk
Services: Saturday, Sunday, Monday & Thursday am Friday pm

Antrim
ORGANISATIONS
Vegetarian & Vegans Northern Ireland
66 Ravenhill Gardens BT6 8GQ
Telephone: (028) 9028 1640

SCOTLAND

Lothian
EDINBURGH
The Town Council and Burgess Roll minutes of 1691 and 1717 record applications by Jews for permission to live and trade in Edinburgh.

KASHRUT INFORMATION
Rabbi D Sedley
Telephone: (0131) 667 9360

RESTAURANTS
Vegetarian
Black Bo's
57-61 Blackfriars Street, EH1 1NB
Telephone: (0131) 557 6136

Henderson's
94 Hanover Street EH2 1DR
Telephone: (0131) 225 2131
Fax: (0131) 220 3542
Website: www.hendersonsofedinburgh.co.uk
Hours: 8am to 10.30pm, closed on Sundays. Adjoining Bistro is also vegetarian (open on Sunday).

Kalpna Restaurant
2/3 St Patrick Square EH8 9EZ
Telephone: (0131) 667 9890
Fax: (0131) 443 8782
Email: kalpnarestaurant@yahoo.com
Website: www.kalpna.co.uk
Hours: Lunch 11am to 2pm dinner 5.30pm to 11pm

SYNAGOGUES
Orthodox
Edinburgh Synagogue
4 Salisbury Road EH16 5AB
Telephone: (0131) 667 3144
Fax: (0131) 613 750
Email: secretary@ehcong.com

Progressive
Edinburgh Liberal Jewish Community
Email: eljc@liberaljudaism.org
Website: www.eljc.org

Fife
DUNDEE
Orthodox
Dundee Synagogue
St Mary Place DD1 5RB
Telephone: (01382) 223 557

DUNOON
Argyll & Bute Jewish Community
Telephone: (01369) 705 118

ST ANDREWS
CONTACT INFORMATION
Jewish Student's Society
c/o. Students' Union, University of St Andrews
KY16 9UY

Grampian
ABERDEEN
RESTAURANTS
Vegetarian
Lemon Tree Café
5 West North Street AB24 5AT
Telephone: (01224) 621 610
Fax: (01224) 630 888
12 noon to 4pm Tuesday to Sunday

SYNAGOGUES
Orthodox
Aberdeen Synagogue
74 Dee Street AB11 6DS
Telephone: (01224) 582 135
Fax: (01224) 642 749
Website: www.aberdeenhebrew.org.uk
A small friendly community

Strathclyde
GLASGOW
The Glasgow Jewish community dates back to 1823. The oldest synagogue building is the Garnethill Synagogue, now also the home of the Scottish Jewish Archives, which opened in 1879. The community grew rapidly from 1891 with many Jews settling in the Gorbals. In recent years the community has gradually spread southwards and is now mainly situated in the Giffnock and Newton Mearns areas.

BOOKSELLERS
Well of Wisdom
Giffnock Synagogue G46
Telephone: (0141) 577 8260
Fax: (0141) 620 0823
Jewish Artifacts

J & E Levingstone
47/55 Sinclair Drive G42 9PT
Telephone: (0141) 649 2962
Fax: (0141) 649 2962
Religious requisities also stocked

COMMUNITY ORGANISATIONS
Jewish Community Centre
222 Fenwick Road G46 6UE
Telephone: (0141) 577 8200
Fax: (0141) 577 8202
Website: www.j scot.org/glasgow

DELICATESSEN
Hello Deli
200 Fenwick Road G46
Telephone: (0141) 638 8267
Fax: (0141) 621 2290

Marlenes Kosher Deli
2 Burnfield Road G46 7QB
Telephone: (0141) 638 4383

Michael Morrison and Son
52 Sinclair Drive G42 9PY
Telephone: (0141) 632 0998
Fax: (0141) 632 6091
Not under official supervision. Stockist of many glatt kosher items. Will deliver to hotels.

GUEST HOUSE
Bed and Breakfast
Mrs A. Malcolm, 26 St Clair Avenue G46 7QE
Telephone: (0141) 638 3924
Kosher, but not supervised, 2 twin bedded rooms

MEDIA
Newspapers
Jewish Telegraph
May Terrace, Giffnock G46 6LD
Telephone: (0141) 621 442233/55
Fax: (0141) 621 4333
Email: glasgow@jewishtelegraph.com
Website: www.jewishtelegraph.com

MIKVAOT
Giffnock & Newlands Synagogue
Maryville Avenue G46 7NE
Telephone: (0141) 577 8250
Fax: (0141) 577 8252

SYNAGOGUES
Orthodox
Garnethill
129 Hill Street G3 6UB
Telephone: (0141) 332 4151
Email: eric.jacobs@ntlworld.com
Shabbat services 10am, Yomtov services 9.45am

Giffnock & Newlands Hebrew Congregation
Maryville Avenue G46 7NE
Telephone: (0141) 577 8250
Fax: (0141) 577 8252

Langside
125 Niddrie Road G42 8QA
Telephone: (0141) 423 4062

Netherlee & Clarkston
Clarkston Road at Randolph Drive G44
Telephone: (0141) 637 8206; 639 7194
Fax: (0141) 616 0743

Newton Mearns
14 Larchfield Court, Newton Mearns G77 5BH
Telephone: (0141) 639 4000
Fax: (0141) 639 4000

Email: office@nmhc.org.uk
Website: www.nmhc.org.uk
Reform
Glasgow New Synagogue Or Chadash
147 Ayr Road, Newton Mearns G77 6RE
Telephone: (0141) 639 4083
Fax: (0141) 639 4249
Website: www.gns.org.uk
Central organisation: RSGB

WALES

Glamorgan (South)
CARDIFF
MIKVAOT
Cardiff Mikvaot
Wales Empire Pool Building, Wood Street CF1 1PP
Telephone: (029) 2038 2296

RESTAURANTS
Vegetarian
Munchies Wholefood Co op
60 Crwys Road, Cathays CF2 4NN
Telephone: (029) 2039 9677

SELF CATERING
Student Accomodation
Hillel House CF2 5NR
Telephone: (029) 2022 8845
Self catering for students

SYNAGOGUES
Reform
Cardiff Reform Synagogue
Moira Terrace, Roath CF24 0EJ
Telephone: (029) 2049 1689
Email: info@cardiffreformsyn.org.uk
Website: www.cardiffreformsyn.org.uk

United
Cardiff United Synagogue
Cyncoed Gardens, Cyncoed Road CF23 5SL
Telephone: (029) 2047 3728
Fax: (029) 2047 3728
Website: www.cardiffunited.org.uk

Glamorgan (West)
SWANSEA
RESTAURANTS
Vegetarian
Chris's Kitchen
The Market SA1 3PE
Telephone: (01792) 643 455
Hours: 8.30 am to 5.30 pm Monday to Saturday

SYNAGOGUES
United
Swansea Hebrew Congregation
17 Ffynone Drive SA1 6DB
Telephone: (01792) 401 205

Gwynedd
LLANDUDNO
HOTELS
Vegetarian
Plas Madoc Vegetarian Guesthouse
60 Church Walks LL30 2HL
Telephone: (01492) 876 514
Website: www.vegetarianguesthouse.com
Vegetarian and vegan not kosher

SYNAGOGUES
Llandudno Synagogue
28 Church Walks LL30 2HL
Telephone: (01492) 572 549

Jewish Culture and History

Editors: Nadia Valman, Tobias Brinkmann
Deputy Editor: Tony Kushner *Reviews Editor*: Nathan Abrams

Jewish Culture and History is a refereed inter-disciplinary refereed journal which brings together the best of current research in Jewish social history with innovative work in Jewish cultural studies. The journal includes cutting-edge research by younger scholars as well as the work of established specialists. Together with research articles and book reviews, it regularly reproduces selected primary materials from archives, private collections and lesser-known resources for the study of Jewish culture and history.

The journal explores previously neglected areas of the Jewish experience in different cultures and from a range of different perspectives. Its interests include: popular culture, film and visual culture, music, media, cultural representations of Jews, Jewish/non-Jewish relations, Jewish literature in all languages, intellectual, social, political and cultural histories, historiography, gendered histories of Jews, class, consumption and lifestyles, and cultural geographies.

ISSN 1462-169X   Volume 11 2009
Three issues per year: Summer, Autumn, Winter
Individuals £45/$75   Institutions £150/$260

Holocaust Studies
A JOURNAL OF CULTURE AND HISTORY

Editors: Dr Tom Lawson, Dr James Jordan
Reviews Editor: Dr K. Hannah Holtschneider

Holocaust Studies: A Journal of Culture and History is an innovative and interdisciplinary journal bringing together the best of current research into the Nazi persecution and mass murder of the Jews and other Nazi genocides. The journal provides a forum for both younger and established scholars engaged in research at the cutting edge of contemporary Holocaust studies. The interests of the journal are broad and include the investigation of Nazi genocides as historical and social phenomena, their origins and their consequences. Further, the journal explores the issues of representation and memorialisation through the investigation of film, literature, testimony and public rituals. The geographical and chronological focus of the journal is also extensive. The journal looks forward to publishing work which considers the Nazi politics of destruction in a global context, including their continuing and wide-ranging legal, social, cultural and political repercussions.

ISSN 1359-1371   Volume 15 2009
Three issues per year: Summer, Autumn, Winter
Individuals £45/$75   Institutions £150/$260

UNITED STATES OF AMERICA

The first Jews came to what is now the United States of America in 1654. The ship had come from the West Indies and included 23 Jews from Brazil, attempting to escape the arrival of the Inquisition following Portugal's recapture of Brazil from the Dutch earlier that year. It is believed they thought they were travelling to Amsterdam in the Netherlands, rather than to New Amsterdam (as New York was then called). Within ten years, however, the community was moribund. The surrender of New Amsterdam to the British in 1664 brought substantial changes to the Jewish settlement as some restrictions to both civil and religious rights were lifted. In a few colonies they were even granted the right to vote.

Following the English takeover communities were established along the eastern coast, and by 1700 there were between 200 and 300 Jews in the country. At the time of the Revolution there were between 1,500 and 2,000 Jews and they served both in the Militia (which was compulsory) and as officers and soldiers. In the decades immediately before the Civil War, the Jewish population rose from 15,000 to 150,000 as a result of emigration, mainly from German areas. During that war Jews served on both sides with their respective communities.

Immigration was at its peak between 1880 and 1925 (when free emigration ended) and during this period the Jewish population grew from 280,000 to 4,500,000. Unfortunately, during the 1930s, only a small number of the Jewish refugees trying to escape from Germany were able to enter the USA. America's numerical position in world Jewry has declined, with its population being in 1948 as much as ten times the population of Israel, to its current approaching parity. The largest concentration by far has always been in New York.

Each of the main religious groups has its own association of synagogues and rabbis and, unlike many other countries, there is no central religious organisation. There is therefore no central supervision of kashrut. Instead there are many hashgachot issued by both individual local communal organisations and rabbis, as well as by companies who issue such certificates on a commercial basis. Travellers may always check with a local rabbi to ascertain the appropriate supervisory body in a relevant location.

Travellers should also be aware that, following a decision in the Brooklyn (New York) District Court in July 2000, discussions are under way in several other jurisdictions to prepare for the eventuality that New York's kosher laws may be rendered unconstitutional on appeal.

Country calling code: (+1)
Total population: **274,520,000**
Jewish population: **5,700,000**
Emergency telephone: (police–911) (fire–911) (ambulance–911)
Electricity voltage: **110/220**

Alabama

Jefferson County

BIRMINGHAM

COMMUNITY ORGANISATIONS
Birmingham Jewish Federation
3966 Montclair Road 35213
Telephone: (205) 803 0416

CONTACT INFORMATION
Rabbi Avraham Shmidman
3225 Montevallo Road 35223
Telephone: (205) 879 1664
Fax: (205) 879 5774
Email: kicongreg@aol.com

DELICATESSEN
Browdy's
2607 Cahaba Road 35223
Telephone: (205) 879 6411

MIKVAOT
Knesseth Israel
3100 Overton Road 35223
Telephone: (205) 879 1664
Fax: (205) 879 5774
Email: knessethisrael@msn.com
Website: www.knessethisraelcongregation.org

SYNAGOGUES

Conservative
Beth-El
2179 Highland Avenue 35205
Telephone: (205) 933 2740
Fax: (205) 933 2747

Orthodox
Knesseth Israel Congregation
3100 Overton Road 35223
Telephone: (205) 969 5913
Fax: (205) 969 5912
Email: office@kicongregation.org
Website: www.knessethisraelcongregation.org

Reform
Emanu-El
2100 Highland Avenue 35205
Telephone: (205) 933 8037

Madison County
HUNTSVILLE
SYNAGOGUES

Conservative
Etz Chayim
7705 Baily Cove Road 35802
Telephone: (256) 882 2918

Mobile County
MOBILE
Reform
Spring Hill Avenue Temple
1769 Spring Hill Avenue 36607
Telephone: (251) 478 0415

Montgomery County
MONTGOMERY
COMMUNITY ORGANISATIONS
Jewish Federation
PO Box 20058 36120
Telephone: (334) 277 5820

SYNAGOGUES

Conservative
Agudath Israel
3525 Cloverdale Road 36111
Telephone: (334) 281 7394

Orthodox
Etz Ahayem (Sephardi)
725 Augusta Road 36111
Telephone: (334) 281 9819

Reform
Beth Or
2246 Narrow Lane 36106

Alaska
ANCHORAGE
GROCERIES
Carr's Market
Diamond Boulevard and Seward Highway
Telephone: (907) 341 1020

SYNAGOGUES

Orthodox
Congregation Shomrei Ohr
1210 E. 26th 99508
Telephone: (907) 279 1200
Fax: (907) 279 7890
Email: lubavitchofak@gci.net

Reform
Beth Sholom
7525 E. Northern Lights Boulevard 99504
Telephone: (907) 338 1836
Fax: (907) 337 4013
Email: sholomalaska@aol.com
Website: www.frozenchosen.org

JUNEAU
Juneau Jewish Community
Telephone: (907) 463 4333

Arizona
Cochise County
SIERRA VISTA
Temple Kol Hamidbar
Po Box 908 85636
Telephone: (520) 458 8637 (ans. phone only)
Email: tkh85636@hotmail.com
Website: www.uahcweb.org/congs/az/tkh/

Maricopa County
CHANDLER
Conservative
Temple Beth Sholom of the East Valley
3400 N. Dobson Road, Chandler 85224
Telephone: (408) 897 3636
Fax: (408) 897 3633
Email: info@templebethsholomaz.org
Website: www.templebethsholomaz.org

PHOENIX
COMMUNITY ORGANISATIONS
Jewish Federation of Greater Phoenix
32 W. Coolidge, Suite 200 85013
Telephone: (602) 274 1800

Orthodox Rabbinical Council of Greater Phoenix
515 E. Bethany Home Road 85012
Telephone: (602) 277 8858
Fax: (602) 274 0713

Email: bethjoseph515@hotmail.com
Supervision: Rabbi David Rebibo

KASHRUT INFORMATION
Rabbi David Rebibo
Phoenix Vaad Hakashruth, 515 E. Bethany Home
Road. 85012
Telephone: (602) 277 8858
Fax: (602) 274 0713
Email: bethjoseph515@hotmail.com
Website: www.phoenixbethjoseph.org and click on
vaad

MEDIA
Newspapers
Jewish News of Greater Phoenix
1625 E. Northern Avenue, Suite 106 85020
Telephone: (602) 870 9470
Fax: (602) 870 0426
Email: editor@jewishaz.com
Website: www.jewishaz.com

Shalom Arizona
32 W. Coolidge, Suite 200 85013
Telephone: (602) 274 1800

RESTAURANTS
King Solomon's Pizza
4810 N. 7th Street
Telephone: (602) 870 8655

Meat
Segal's Kosher Foods
4818 N. 7th Street
Telephone: (602) 285 1515
Fax: (602) 277 5760
Email: segalkosh@aol.com
Supervision: Vaad Hakashrut of Phoenix

SYNAGOGUES
Conservative
Beth El Congregation
1118 W. Glendale 85021
Telephone: (602) 944 3359
Website: www.bethelphoenix.com

Orthodox
Congregation Beth Joseph
515 E. Bethany Home Road 85012
Telephone: (602) 277 8858
Website: www.phoenixbethjoseph.org
Supervision: Rabbi David Rebibo

Congregation Beth Shaarei Tzedek
7608 N. 18th Avenue 85021
Telephone: (602) 944 1133

Young Israel of Phoenix
745 E. Maryland Avenue, Ste. 120 85014
Telephone: (602) 265 8888

Reform
Temple Beth Ami
4545 N. 36th Street, No. 211 85018
Telephone: (602) 956 0805

Temple Chai
4545 East Marilyn Rd 85032
Telephone: (602) 971 1234

SCOTTSDALE
CAFETERIA
Scottsdale Café and Market
10211 N. Scottsdale Road 85253
Telephone: (480) 315 8333
Website: www.scottsdalecafe.com

MUSEUMS
Sylvia Plotkin Judaica Museum
10460 N. 56th Street 85253
Telephone: (480) 951 0323
Fax: (480) 951 7150
Website: www.spjm.org

SYNAGOGUES
Conservative
Beth Emeth of Scottsdale
5406 E. Virginia Avenue 85254
Telephone: (480) 947 4604

Har Zion
5929 E. Lincoln Drive 85253
Telephone: (480) 991 0720

Orthodox
Chabad of Scottsdale
10215 North Scottsdale Road 85253
Telephone: (480) 998 1410
Website: www.chabadofscottsdale.org

Reform
Temple Kol Ami
15030 N. 64th Street 85254
Telephone: (480) 951 9660
Fax: (480) 951 5231
Email: templekolami@aol.com

Temple Solel
6805 E. MacDonald Drive 85253
Telephone: (480) 991 7414
Fax: (480) 451 0829
Website: www.templesolel.org

SUN CITY
Beth Shalom of Sun City
12202 101st Avenue 85351
Telephone: (623) 977 3240
Fax: (623) 977 3214

SUN CITY WEST
Conservative
Beth Emeth Congregation of the Sun Cities & West Valley of Phoenix
13702 West Meeker Boulevard 85375
Telephone: (623) 584 7210
Fax: (623) 975 2976
Email: info@bethemethaz.org
Website: www.bethemethaz.org

TEMPE
COMMUNITY ORGANISATIONS
Tri City Jewish Community Center
1965 E. Hermosa Drive 85282
Telephone: (602) 897 0588

SYNAGOGUES
Orthodox
Chabad-Lubavitch Center
23 W. 9th Street 85281
Telephone: (602) 966 5163

Reform
Temple Emanuel
5801 Rural Road 85283
Telephone: (602) 838 1414

Pima County
TUCSON
BAKERIES
Nadine's Pastry Shoppe
4553 Broadway Boulevard
Telephone: (520) 326 0735

BUTCHERS
Grocer
Feig's Kosher Market & Deli
5071 E. 5th Street 85711
Telephone: (520) 325 2255
Fax: (520) 325 2978
Email: rgfeigs@yahoo.com
Website: www.feigskosher.com
Supervision: Rabbi R.Eisen
Full Service Deli

COMMUNITY ORGANISATIONS
Jewish Federation of Southern Arizona
3822 E. River Road 85718
Telephone: (520) 577 9393
Fax: (520) 577 0734

SYNAGOGUES
Conservative
Congregation Bet Shalom
3881 E. River Road 85718
Telephone: (520) 577 1171
Fax: (520) 577 8903
Supervision: Rabbi Leo M Abrami

Orthodox
Congregation Chofetz Chayim
5150 E. 5th Street 85711
Telephone: (520) 747 7780
Fax: (520) 745 6325
Email: ewbecker@flash.net
Young Israel of Tucson
2443 E. 4th Street 85710
Telephone: (520) 326 8362

Arkansas
Garland County
HOT SPRINGS
House of Israel
300 Quapaw Avenue 71901
Telephone: (501) 623 5821
Email: houseofi@hotsprings.net

Phillips County
HELENA
Reform
Temple Beth El
406 Perry Street 72342
Telephone: (501) 338 6654

Pulaski County
LITTLE ROCK
COMMUNITY ORGANISATIONS
Jewish Federation of Arkansas
425 N. University Avenue 72205
Telephone: (501) 663 3571

SYNAGOGUES
Reform
B'nai Israel
3700 Rodney Parham Road, 72212
Telephone: (501) 225 9700

Traditional
Congregation Agudath Achim
7901 W. 5th Street 72205
Telephone: (501) 225 1683
Website: www.lrsynagogue.org
Mikvah open to the Jewish community and visitors. To use mikvah call Synagogue office,

Union County
EL DORADO
Reform
Beth Israel
1130 E. Main Street

California
As the general population of California continues to increase, the Jewish community is growing as well. Places of worship abound,

from Eureka in the north to San Diego in the south, but the major part of the community lives in the Los Angeles metropolitan area.

OAKLAND
RESTAURANTS
Holy Land Restaurant
677 Rand Avenue 94610
Telephone: (510) 272 0535
Website: www.holylandrestaurant.com
Supervision: Rabbi Yehuda Dardik

RESEDA
RESTAURANTS
Pizza-Kosher
Brami's Pizza
17736 Sherman Way 91335
Telephone: (818) 342 0611
Supervision: Rabbinical Council of California

Rami's Pizza
17736 1/2 Sherman Way 91335
Telephone: (818) 642 0611
Israeli/Mexican

WOODLAND HILLS
RESTAURANTS
Meat
Laffa Fresh
22435 Ventura Boulevard
Supervision: Kosher LA

Alameda County
ALAMEDA
SYNAGOGUES
Reform
Temple Israel
3183 McCartney Road 94502
Telephone: (510) 522 9355
Fax: (510) 522 9356

BERKELEY
MIKVAOT
Mikvah Taharas Israel
2520 Warring Street, 94704-3111
Telephone: (510) 848 7221
Fax: (510) 217 3596
Email: kosher@norcalkosher.org
MUSEUMS
Judah L. Magnes Museum
2911 Russell Street 94705
Telephone: (510) 549 6950
Fax: (510) 849 3673
Website: www.judahmagnesmuseum.org

RESTAURANTS
Dairy
Noah's Bagels
1883 Solano Avenue
Telephone: (510) 525 4447
Supervision: The Vaad Kakashrus of Northern California.

SYNAGOGUES
Conservative
Netivot Shalom
1841 Berkeley Way 94708
Telephone: (510) 549 9447
Fax: (510) 549 9448
Website: www.netivotshalom.org

Egalitarian
Berkeley Hillel Foundation
2736 Bancroft Avenue 94704
Telephone: (510) 845 7793
Fax: (510) 845 7753

Jewish Renewal
Aquarian Minyan
P.O. Box 7224 94707
Telephone: (510) 981 2130

Kehilla
PO Box 3063 94703

Orthodox
Chabad House
2643 College Avenue 94704
Telephone: (510) 540 5824
Fax: (510) 849 0536
Email: office@chabadberkeley.org
Website: www. chabadberkeley.org
Supervision: Rabbi Yehuda Ferris

Congregation Beth Israel
1630 Bancroft Way 94703
Telephone: (510) 843 5246
Fax: (510) 843 5058
Email: office@cbiberkeley.org
Website: www.cbiberkeley.org

Reform
Congregation Beth El
1301 Oxford St. 94709-1424
Telephone: (510) 848 3988 ext. 211
Fax: (510) 848 9434
Email: frontoffice@bethelberkeley.org
Website: www.bethelberkeley.org

BEVERLY HILLS
RESTAURANTS
French-Kosher
A Cow jumped Over the moon
421 N Rodeo Drive 90210
Telephone: (310) 274 4269
Fax: (310) 274 4263
Email: info@acowonrodeo.com
Sandwiches, salads, crepes, pasta and fish

Orthodox
Beth Jacob
9030 Olympic Boulevard 90211
Telephone: (310) 278 1911
Fax: (310) 278 9186

Young Israel of North Beverly Hills
9350 Civic Center Drive, North Beverly Hills 90210
Telephone: (310) 203 0170

Orthodox Sephardi
Magen David
322 N. Foothill 90210

BURBANK
Conservative
Temple Emanu-El
1302 N. Glenoaks Boulevard 91504
Telephone: (818) 845 1734
Website: BTEE.ORG

CASTRO VALLEY
Reform
Shir Ami
4529 Malabar Avenue 94546
Telephone: (415) 537 1787

FREMONT
Temple Beth Torah
42000 Paseo Padre Parkway 94538
Telephone: (510) 656 7141
Website: www.bethtorah-fremont.org

OAKLAND
COMMUNITY ORGANISATIONS
Berkeley/Richmond JCC
1414 Walnut Street, Berkeley 94709
Telephone: (510) 848 0237
Fax: (510) 848 0170
Website: www.brjcc.org
Jewish Commnity Federation of the Greater Eastern Bay
300 Grand Avenue 94610
Website: www.jfed.org

DELICATESSEN
Holy Land Restaurant
677 Rand Avenue 94610
Telephone: (510) 272 0535
Website: www.holylandrestaurant.com
Supervision: Rabbi Yehuda Dardik

MIKVAOT
Beth Jacob Synagogue
3778 Park Boulevard 94610
Telephone: (510) 482 1147
Fax: (510) 482 2374
Email: office@bethjacoboakland.org
Website: www.bethjacoboakland.org

SYNAGOGUES
Conservative
Beth Abraham
327 MacArthur Boulevard 94610
Telephone: (510) 832 0936

Beth Sholom
642 Dolores, San Leandro 94577

Independent
B'nai Israel of Rossmoor
c/o Fred Rau, 2601 Ptarmigasn #3 , Walnut Greek 94595

Beth Chaim
PO Box 23632, Pleasant Hill 94577

Orthodox
Beth Jacob Synagogue
3778 Park Boulevard 94610
Telephone: (510) 482 1147
Fax: (510) 482 2374
Email: office@bethjacoboakland.org
Website: www.bethjacoboakland.org

Reform
Beth Emek
PO Box 722, Livermore 94550
Beth Hillel
801 Park Central, Richmond 94803
Temple Sinai
2808 Summit 94609
Telephone: (510) 451 3263

Contra Costa County
LAFAYETTE
Temple Isaiah
3800 Mt. Diablo Boulevard 94549
Telephone: (925) 283 8575
Fax: (925) 283 8355
Email: temple-isaiah@temple-isaiah.org
Website: www.temple-isaiah.org

WALNUT CREEK
COMMUNITY ORGANISATIONS
Contra Costa JCC
2071 Tice Valley Boulevard 94595
Telephone: (925) 937 0765

SYNAGOGUES
Conservative
Congregation B'nai Shalom Synagogue
74 Eckley Lane 94596
Telephone: (925) 934 9446
Fax: (925) 934 9450
Email: office@bshalom.org
Website: www.bshalom.org
As the largest Conservative synagogue in Contra Costa County, Congregation B'nai Shalom emphasises traditional judaism whilst welcoming new forms of

religious expression. We are a Conservative Congregation affiliated with the affiliated with the United Synagogue of Conservative Judaism.

Contra Costa Jewish Community Center
2071 Tice Valley Boulevard 94595

Orthodox
Chabad of Contra Costa
1671 Newell Avenue 94595
Telephone: (925) 837 4101
Email: info@chabadcoco.com
Website: www.chabadcoco.com

Reform
Congregation B'nai Tikvah
25 Hillcroft Way 94595
Telephone: (925) 933 5397

Fresno County
FRESNO
COMMUNITY ORGANISATIONS
Jewish Federation Office
1340 W. Heerndon, Suite 103 93711

SYNAGOGUES

Conservative
Beth Jacob
406 W. Shields Avenue 93705
Telephone: (209) 222 0664
Fax: (559) 222 0609
Email: bjfresno@sbcglobal.net

Reform
Temple Beth Israel
6622 N. Maroa Avenue 93704
Telephone: 432 3600

Humboldt County
EUREKA
Temple Beth El
Hodgson & T Streets, PO Box 442 , 3233 T Street 95502
Telephone: (707) 444 2846
Fax: (707) 444 2846
Email: bethel@reninet.com
Website: www.tbe-eureka.org

Kern County
BAKERSFIELD
Conservative
B'nai Jacob
600 17th Street 93301
Telephone: (661) 325 8017

Reform
Temple Beth El
2906 Loma Linda Drive 93305
Telephone: (661) 322 7607
Fax: (661) 322 7807

Email: kernjew@aol.com
Website: www.templebethelbakersfield.org

Los Angeles County
ARCADIA
Conservative
Congregation Shaarei Torah
550 S. 2nd Avenue 91006
Telephone: (818) 445 0810

CULVER CITY
TOURS OF JEWISH INTEREST
Kosher Expeditions
3821 Crestview Rd Ste 3 90232
Telephone: 800)923-2645 or (310)237-0122 or (404)634-9206
Fax: (770)234 5170
Email: info@kosherexpeditions.com
Website: www.kosherexpeditions.com
Kosher travel programs worldwide – history & heritage, adventure travel, student tours, cruising
World's only supervised kosher eco-lodge in Costa Rica
Office hours are 9am to 5pm

DOWNEY
SYNAGOGUES
Reform
Temple Ner Tamid
10629 Lakewood Boulevard 90241
Telephone: (310) 861 9276

ENCINO
BOOKSELLERS
Steimatzky

CAFETERIA
Kosher
Bonjour
16550 Ventura Boulevard 91436
Telephone: (818) 783 2727
Supervision: Rabbinical Council of California
Sushi, sandwiches

RESTAURANTS
Pizza-Kosher
Jerusalem Pizza
17942 Ventura Boulevard 91316
Telephone: (818) 758 9595
Supervision: Kehilla of Los Angeles
Dairy/Cholov Yisroel. 100% Yashsan flour.

SYNAGOGUES
Conservative
Valley Beth Shalom
15739 Ventura Boulevard 91316
Telephone: (818) 788 6000

Orthodox
Chabad House
4917 Hayvenhurst, 91346

Reform
Shir Chadash
17000 Ventura Boulevard

GARDENA
Conservative
Southwest Temple Beth Torah
14725 S. Gramercy Place 90249
Telephone: (310) 327 8734

GRANADA HILLS
COMMUNITY ORGANISATIONS
North Valley Center
16601 Rinaldi Street 91344

HOLLYWOOD
KASHRUT INFORMATION
Kosher Information Bureau
15365 Magnolia Boulevard, Sherman Oaks 91403
Telephone: (818) 762 3197 & 262 5351
Fax: (818) 766 8537
Email: eeidlitz@kosherquest.org
Website: www.kosherquest.org

LAKEWOOD
SYNAGOGUES
Conservative
Temple Beth Zion Sinai
6440 Del Amo Boulevard 90713
Telephone: (310) 429 0715

LONG BEACH
BAKERIES
Fairfax Kosher Market & Bakery
11196-98 Los Alamitos Boulevard 90720
Telephone: (562) 828 4492

COMMUNITY ORGANISATIONS
**Jewish Federation of Greater Long Beach &
W, Orange County**
3801 E. Willow Street 90815
Telephone: (562) 426 7601

MEDIA
Newspapers
Jewish Community Chronicle
3801 E. Willow Street 90815-1791

MIKVAOT
Long Beach Mikvah
3847 Atlantic Avenue 90807

SYNAGOGUES
Orthodox
Congregation Lubavitch
3981 Atlantic Avenue 90807
Telephone: (562) 596 1681
Young Israel of Long Beach
PO Box 7041 90807-0041
Telephone: (562) 527 3163
Reform
Temple Israel
338 E. 3rd Street 90812

LOS ANGELES
Los Angeles is America's, and the world's,
second largest Jewish metropolis, with a
Jewish population of around 600,000. Fairfax
Avenue and Beverly Boulevard together form
the crossroads of traditional Jewish life, while
a growing Orthodox enclave centers around
Pico and Robertson Boulevards.
Important note: Area telephone codes have
recently been split to 310 and 213 for central
Los Angeles. We have endeavoured in all cases
to correct our information, but cannot
guarantee the accuracy of those who did not
send in updates.

BAKERIES
Noah's New York Bagels
1737 Santa Rita Road #400, Pleasanton 94566
Telephone: (213) 485 1921
Supervision: California Rabbinical Council

Schwartz Bakery
441 N. Fairfax Avenue 90036
Telephone: (213) 653 1683
Fax: (213) 653 6142
Supervision: RCC

CAFETERIA
Kosher
Cafe Elite
7115 Beverley Boulevard 90036
Telephone: (323) 936 2861
Supervision: Rabbinical Council of California

COMMUNITY ORGANISATIONS
Board of Rabbis of Southern California
6505 Wilshire Boulevard, Suite 430 90048
Telephone: (213) 761 8600
Fax: (213) 761 8603

Jewish Federation of Greater Los Angeles
6505 Wilshire Boulevard 90048
Telephone: (213) 761 8000
Fax: (213) 761 8123
Website: www.jewishla.org

West Side Jewish Community Center
5870 W. Olympic Boulevard 90036
Telephone: (323) 938 2531
Fax: (323) 954 9175

Email: info@westsidejcc.org
Website: www.westsidejcc.org

DELICATESSEN
Pico Kosher Deli
8826 W. Pico Boulevard 90035
Telephone: (213) 273 9381
Fax: (213) 273 8476
Supervision: RCC

EMBASSY
Consul General of Israel
Suite 1700, 6380 Wilshire Boulevard 90048
Telephone: (213) 852 5523
Fax: (213) 852 5555
Website: www.israelemb.org/la

GROCERIES
Kosher food to go
PS Kosher Food Services
9786 West Pico Boulevard, 4th Floor, MOT
cafeteria 90035
Telephone: (310) 553 8804
Fax: (310) 553 8989
Mobile Phone: 001 310 717 2102
Website: www.pskosherfood.com
Supervision: RCC
Services for travellers. Glatt

HOSPITAL
Cedars Sinai Hospital
8700 Beverly Boulevard
Telephone: (213) 855 4797
Supervision: RCC

KASHRUT INFORMATION
Rabbi Yehudah Bukspan
6407 Orange Street 90048
Telephone: (323) 653 5083
Supervision: USK

MEDIA
Newspapers
Heritage Southwest Jewish Press
20201 Sherman Way, Ste., 204, Winetka 91306
Jewish Journal
Weekly publication, coming out on Fridays

MUSEUMS
Museum of Tolerance
9786 West Pico Boulevard 90035
Telephone: (310) 800 900 9036
Fax: (310) 553 4521
Website: www.museumoftolerance.com

Libraries
Museum of Tolerance (Beit Hashoah)
9786 West Pico Boulevard 90035
Telephone: (800) 553 8403
Website: www.wiesenthal.com;
www. museumoftolerance.com

ORGANISATIONS
Museum of Tolerance
Simon Wiesenthal Plaza, 9786 West Pico
Boulevard
Telephone: (310) 553 8403
Fax: (310) 772 7655
Website: www.museumoftolerance.com

RESTAURANTS
Dairy
Fish Grill
7226 Beverley Boulevard 90036
Telephone: (323) 937 7162

Nagila Pizza Restaurant
9411 W. Pico Boulevard
Telephone: (213) 788 0111

Pizza Delight
435 N. Fairfax Avenue
Telephone: (213) 655 7800

Pizza World
368 S. Fairfax Avenue
Telephone: (213) 653 2896

Italian-Kosher
Milk & Honey
8837 W. Pico Boulevard 90035
Telephone: (310) 858 8850
Supervision: Rabbinical Council of California

The Milky Way
9108 W Pico Boulevard 90035
Telephone: (310) 859 0004
Supervision: Kehilla of Los Angeles

Meat
Chick 'N Chow
9301 W. Pico Boulevard
Telephone: (213) 274 5595

Cohen Restaurant
316 E. Pico Boulevard 90015
Telephone: (213) 742 8888
Fax: (213) 742 0066
Supervision: RCC

Encino Grill & Wok
16340 Ventura Boulevard
Telephone: (213) 905 8622

Glatt Hut
9303 W. Pico Boulevard
Telephone: (213) 246 1900

Jeff's Gourmet Sausage Factory
8930 W. Pico Boulevard 90035
Telephone: (310) 858 8590
Fax: (310) 858 8138
Website: www.jeffsgourmet.com

Kabob & chinese Food
11330 Santa Monica
Telephone: (213) 914 3040

La Gondola Ristorante Italiano
6405 Wilshire Boulevard
Telephone: (213) 852 1915

Magic Carpet
8566 W. Pico Boulevard 90035
Telephone: (310) 652 8507
Fax: (310) 652 3568
Supervision: Kehillah of Los Angeles

Mr Pickles Deli
13354 Washington Boulevard
Telephone: (213) 822 7777

Nathan's Famous
9216 W. Pico Boulevard
Telephone: (213) 273 0303

Simon's La Glatt
446 N. Fairfax Avenue
Telephone: (213) 658 7730

Parve
Fish Place Restaurant
9340 W. Pico Boulevard
Telephone: (310) 858 8737
Supervision: Kehila kosher

Pizzerias
Pizza Delight
435 N. Fairgfax avenue 90036
Telephone: (213) 655 7800
Fax: (213) 655 1142
Suprvision: Kehillah of Los Angeles.

Shalom Pizza
8715 W. Pico Boulevard
Telephone: (213) 271 2255
Supervision: RCC

Pizza-Kosher
Bibi's Warmstone Bakery
8928 W Pico Boulevard 90035
Telephone: (310) 246 1788
Supervision: Kehilla of Los Angeles
Middle Eastern specialities,handmade baked goods

Brooklyn Pizza & Pasta
9228 W Pico Boulevard
Telephone: (310) 550 9992
Supervision: Kehilla of Los Angeles

Circa
90035Telephone: (310) 854 0592
Supervision: Rabbinical Council of California
Pasta, sandwiches and soup

Hill Street Pizza
448 S Hill Street #406 90013
Telephone: (213) 627 9990
Supervision: Rabbinical Council of California

Pizza Mayven
140 N La Brea Boulevard 90035
Telephone: (323) 857 0353

Supervision: Kehilla of Los Angeles
Dairy/Cholov Yisroel
Pizza World
365 S Fairfax Avenue 90035
Telephone: (323) 653 2896
Supervision: Kehilla of Los Angeles
Chalav Yisrael, Mexican. Delivers, takeaway or eat in.

Shalom Pizza
8715 W Pico Boulevard 90035
Telephone: (310) 271 2255
Take-Away

Glatt Kosher Subway
8948 Pico Boulevard 90035
Telephone: (310) 274 1222
Website: www.glattkoshersubway.com
Supervision: Kehiia Kosher of Los Angeles
Open late hours

SNACK BAR
Kosher
La Brea Bagel Company
7308 Beverley Boulevard 90036
Telephone: (323) 965 1287
Supervision: Kehilla of Los Angeles
17612 Ventura Boulevard 91316
Telephone: (818) 205 1650
Fax: (818) 708 2319
Email: stmla@earthlink.net
Website: www.stmus.com
Shop online for Hebrew books and CDs

SYNAGOGUES
Conservative
Adat Shalom
3030 Westwood Boulevard
Telephone: (213) 475 4985

Sinai Temple
10400 Wilshire Boulevard 90024
Telephone: (213) 474 1518
Fax: (213) 474 6801

Temple Beth Am
1039 S. La Cienega Boulevard 90035
Telephone: (213) 652 7353
Fax: (213) 652 2384
Email: betham@tbala.org
Website: www.tbala.org

Orthodox
Chabad House
741 Gayley Avenue, West Los Angeles 90025

Etz Jacob Congregation
7659 Beverly Boulevard 90036
Telephone: (323) 938 2619

Los Angeles Orthodox Synagogue
9317 West Pico Boulevard, Century City 90035
Telephone: (310) 273 6954
Fax: (310) 273 7103

Email: shuloffice@yicc.org
Website: www.yicc.org
Ohel David
7967 Beverley Boulevard
Young Israel of Los Angeles
660 N. Spaulding Avenue 90036
Telephone: (213) 655 0300
Fax: (213) 655 0322

Orthodox Sephardi
Kahal Joseph
1005 Santa Monica Boulevard 90025
Telephone: (213) 474 0559

Temple Tifereth Israel
10500 Wilshire Boulevard 90024
Telephone: (213) 475 7311
Fax: (213) 470 9238

Reconstructionist
Kehillat Israel
16019 Sunset Boulevard Pacific Palisades 90272
Telephone: (213) 459 2328
Fax: (213) 573 2098
Email: kihome@aol.com

Reform
Leo Baeck Temple
1300 N. Sepulveda Boulevard 90049
Telephone: (213) 476 2861

Stephen S. Wise Temple
15500 Stephen S. Wise Drive, Bel Air 90024
Telephone: (213) 476 8561
Fax: (213) 476 3587

Temple Akiba
5249 S. Sepulveda Boulevard Culver City 90230
Telephone: (213) 398 5783
Fax: (213) 398 1637
Website: www.temakiba

Temple Isaiah
10345 W. Pico Boulevard 90064

University Synagogue
11960 Sunset Boulevard 90049
Telephone: (213) 472 1255
Fax: (213) 476 3237

Wilshire Boulevard Temple
3663 Wilshire Boulevard 90010
Telephone: (213) 388 2401
Fax: (213) 388 2595

NORTH HOLLYWOOD
CAFETERIA
Bonjour
12453 Oxnard Street 91606
Telephone: (818) 506 7145
Supervision: Rabbinical Council of California
Sandwiches

RESTAURANTS
Pizza-Kosher
La Pizza
12515 Burbank Boulevard
Telephone: (818) 760 8198
Supervision: Rabbi Shelaim Furst

Pacific Kosher Pizza
12460 Oxnard Street
Telephone: (818) 760 0087
Supervision: Rabbinical Council of California
Dairy Cholov Yisroel

Sushi-Kosher
Le Sushi
12524 Burbank Boulevard 91607
Telephone: (818) 763 6600
Supervision: Rabbinical Council of California
Soup, Chinese
KASHRUT INFORMATION
The Kashrus Information Bureau
12753 Chandler Boulevard, N. Hollywood 91607
Telephone: (818) 262 5351
Fax: (818) 766 8537
Email: eeidlitz@kosherquest.org
Website: www.kosherquest.org
The Kosher Information Bureau is a worldwide kashrus information only organization. It produces a weekly fax/email update, quarterly magazine and has a book titled "Is It Kosher". At the website you can find travel information for western U.S.

MIKVAOT
Teichman Mikvah Society
12800 Chandler Boulevard
Telephone: (818) 506 0996

RESTAURANTS
Meat
Flora Falafel
12450 Burbank Boulevard, North Hollywood
Telephone: (818) 766 6567
Supervision: RCC

Golan
13075 Victory Boulevard
Telephone: (818) 763 5375

SYNAGOGUES
Orthodox
Shaarey Zedek
12800 Chandler Boulevard 91607
Telephone: (818) 763 0560

NORTHRIDGE
Conservative
Temple Ramat Zion
17655 Devonshire Avenue, Northridge
Telephone: (818) 360 1881

Orthodox
Young Israel of Northridge
17511 Devonshire Street 91325
Telephone: (818) 368 2221
Website: www.yion.org
Supervision: Rabbi Aharon Simkin
Central organisation: National Council of Young Israel
Only daily Minyan in N san Fernando Valley morning and evening

Reform
Temple Ahavat Shalom
11261 Chimineas Avenue, Northridge

PASADENA
Conservative
Pasadena Jewish Temple and Center
1434 North Altadena Drive 91107
Telephone: (626) 798 1161

POMONA
SYNAGOGUES
Reform
Temple Beth Israel
3033 North Towne Avenue Pomona CA
Telephone: (909) 626 1277

SAN FERNANDO VALLEY
BAKERIES
Continental Kosher Bakery
12419 Burbank Boulevard 91607
Telephone: (818) 762 5005
Website: www.continentalbakery.net
kashrut: OU Pareve

RESTAURANTS
Apropo Falafel
6800 Reseda Boulevard
Telephone: (818) 881 6608
Hadar Restaurant and Catering
12514 Burbank Boulevard 91607
Telephone: (818) 762 1155
Supervision: RCC

Meat
Sportsman Lodge
Sherman Oaks
Telephone: (818) 984 0202

Pizzerias
La Pizza
12515 Burbank Boulevard
Telephone: (818) 760 8198

SYNAGOGUES
Conservative
Beth Meir Congregation
11725 Moorpark, Studio City 91604
Telephone: (818) 769 0515
Fax: (818) 769 7127

Email: congbethmeier@sbcglobal.net
Website: www.congregationbethmeier.org
Temple B'nai Hayim
4302 Van Nuys Boulevard, Sherman Oaks 91403
Telephone: (818) 788 4664
Fax: (818) 788 4661
Email: tbh-accounting@sbcglobal.net

SANTA MONICA
Orthodox
Chabad House
1428 17th Street 90404
Telephone: (310) 453-3011
Email: thechabadnik@thechabadnik.org
Website: www.thechabadnik.org
Young Israel of Santa Monica
21 Hampton Avenue
Telephone: (310) 399 8514

Reform
Beth Shir Sholom
1827 California Avenue 90403
Telephone: (310) 453 3361
Fax: (310) 453 6827
Website: www.bethshirsholom.com

SHERMAN OAKS
RESTAURANTS
Dairy
Fish Grill
13628 Ventura Boulevard
Telephone: (818) 788 9896

TARZANA
BAKERIES
Unique Pastry Bakery and Café
18385 Ventura Boulevard 91356
Telephone: (818) 757 3100
Fax: (818) 757 3144

SYNAGOGUES
Reform
Temple Judea
5429 Lindley Avenue

VAN NUYS
COMMUNITY ORGANISATIONS
Valley Cities Center
13164 Burbank Boulevard 91401

VENICE
SYNAGOGUES
Orthodox
Pacific Jewish Center
Shul on the Beach 505 Ocean Front Walk, Venice Beach 90291
Telephone: (310) 392 8749

Fax: (310) 392 4557
Website: www.pjcenter.com

WEST HILLS
COMMUNITY ORGANISATIONS
West Valley Center
22622 Vanowen Street, 91307

SYNAGOGUES
Conservative
Shomrei Torah Synagogue
7353 Valley Circle, West Hills 91304
Telephone: (818) 346 0811
Fax: (818) 346 3956
Website: www.shomreitorahsynagogue.org

WHITTIER
Beth Shalom Synagogues Center
14564 E. Hawes Street 90604
Telephone: (310) 914 8744

Marin County
TIBURON
Congregation Kol Shafar
215 Blackfield Drive 94920
Telephone: (415) 388 1818

Monterey County
CARMEL
SYNAGOGUES
Reform
Congregation Beth Israel
5716 Carmel Valley Road 93923
Telephone: (831) 624 2015
Fax: (831) 624 4786
Email: shalomcbi@aol.com

VALLEY VILLAGE
CAFETERIA
Kosher
Cafe del Mar
12526 Burbank Boulevard
Telephone: (816) 487 8171
Supervision: Kehilla of Los Angeles

FISH MARKET
Fish in the Village
12450 Burbank Boulevard #B 91607
Telephone: (816) 769 0085
Supervision: Rabbinical Council of California

SYNAGOGUES
Conservative
Adat Ari El
12020 Burbank Boulevard, 91607 2198
Telephone: (816) 766 9426

Orange County
ANAHEIM
SYNAGOGUES
Conservative
Temple Beth Emet
1770 W. Cerritos Avenue 92804
Telephone: (714) 772 4720
Fax: (714) 772 4710
Website: tbe-anaheimoc.org
Supervision: Rabbi Mordecai Kieffer
Central organisation: United Synagogue for Conservative
Judaism Pacific Southwest Region

COSTA MESA
GIFT SHOP
The Golden Dreidle
1835 Newport Boulevard #A111 92627
Telephone: (714) 645 3878

IRVINE
COMMUNITY ORGANISATIONS
Jewish Federation Orange County
1 Federation Way, Suite 210 92603
Telephone: (949) 435 3484
Fax: (949) 435 3485
Email: info@jfoc.org
Website: www.jewishorangecounty.org

LAGUNA HILLS
DELICATESSEN
The Kosher Bite
23595 Moulton Parkway 92653
Telephone: (949) 770 1818
Website: www.kosherbite.com
Supervision: Rabinical Council of Orange County

TUSTIN
SYNAGOGUES
Conservative
Congregation B'nai Israel
655 S. "B" St 92680
Telephone: (714) 259 0655

WESTMINSTER
Reform
Temple Beth David
6100 Hefley Street, Westminster 92683
Telephone: (714) 892 6623
Fax: (714) 897 5306
Email: tbdavid@verizon.net
Website: www.templebethdavid.org

Riverside County
PALM SPRINGS
Conservative
Temple Isaiah
322 W. Alejo Road 92262
Telephone: (760) 325 2281

Orthodox
Chabad of Palm Springs
425 Avenue, Ortega
Telephone: (760) 325 0774

Desert Synagogue
1068 N. Palm Canyon Drive 92262
Telephone: (760) 327 4848
Fax: (760) 327 4848
Email: desertsynagogue@gmail.com
Website: www.desertshul.org
Central organisation: Orthodox Union
We are a Modern Orthodox shul that welcomes Jews of all backgrounds and levels of observance. We use the ArtScroll Siddur.
Shabbat services are at approximately candle-lighting time on Friday afternoon and at 9:15 Shabbat morning. Inquire about daily minyanim, Shabbat dinners at the shul, and home hospitality. We enjoy visitors!

Sacremento County
SACRAMENTO
COMMUNITY ORGANISATIONS
Jewish Federation of Sacramento
2351 Wyda Way 95825
Telephone: (916) 486 0906
Fax: (916) 486 0816
Website: www.jewishsac.org

MIKVAOT
Kenesset Israel Torah Center
1165 Morse Avenue 95864
Telephone: (916) 481 1159
Email: kitc.office@sbcglobal.net
Website: www.kitcsacramento.org

Sacramento Mikvaot
1024 Morse Avenue 95864
Telephone: (916) 481 1158

RESTAURANTS
Meat
Bob's Butcher Block
6436 Fair Oaks Boulevard, Carmichael Oaks Shopping Center
Telephone: (916) 482 6884

SYNAGOGUES
Conservative
Mosaic Law
2300 Sierra Boulevard 95825
Telephone: (916) 488 1122
Fax: (916) 488 1165
Website: www.mosaiclaw.org

Orthodox
Kenesset Israel Torah Center
1165 Morse Avenue 95864
Telephone: (916) 481 1159
Email: kitc.office@sbcglobal.net
Website: www.kitcsacramento.org

Reform
B'nai Israel
3600 Riverside Boulevard 95818
Telephone: (916) 446 4861
Fax: (916) 446 2875
Website: www.bnais.com

Beth Shalom
4746 El Camino Avenue 09608
Telephone: (916) 485 4478
Fax: (916) 485 0776
Email: office@cbshalom.org
Website: www.cbshalom.org

San Bernardino County
ONTARIO
Conservative
Temple Sholom
963 West 6th St 91762
Telephone: (909) 983 9661
Rabbi Gil Alchadeff

TRAVEL
Ontario Travel Bureau
Laurie Neuman van Esschoten Your Kosher Travel Specialists , 1044 West 4th Street 91762
Telephone: (909) 984 2761 or (800) 893 5617
Fax: (909) 984 2764
Email: laurie@ontariotravelbureau.com
Website: www.thewanderingjew.net

RANCHO CUCAMONGA
SYNAGOGUES
Chadbad of the Inland Empire (Lubavitch)
8710 Baker 91730
Telephone: (909) 949 4553
Rabbi Sholom Harlig

SAN BERNARDINO
Reform
Emanu-El
3512 N. E. Street 92405
Telephone: (909) 886 4818
Fax: (909) 883 5892
Email: cee@emanuelsb.org

San Diego County
BONITA
Orthodox
Beth Eliyahu Torah Center
5012 Central Avenue 91902
Telephone: (619) 472 2144
Fax: (619) 472 0718

CARDIFF BY THE SEA
Reform
Temple Solel
Evie's Place Gift Shop, 3575 Manchester Avenue 92007
Telephone: (760) 436 0654
Fax: (760) 436 2748
Email: giftshop@templesolel.net

CHULA VISTA
Conservative
Temple Beth Sholom
208 Madrona Street 91910
Telephone: (619) 420 6040
Website: www.uscj.org/pacsw/chulavista
Services Friday 7.30pm, Saturday 9.30am and holidays. Visitors welcome.

LA JOLLA
Congregation Beth El
8660 Gilman Drive, 92037
Telephone: (619) 452 1734

Orthodox
Congregation Adat Yeshurun
8625 La Jolla scenic Drive 92037
Telephone: (619) 535 1196
Fax: (619) 535 0037
Email: info@adatyeshurun.org
Website: www.adatyeshurun.org

POWAY
Chadbad of Poway
16934 Chabad Way 92064
Telephone: (858) 451 0455
Fax: (858) 637 0299
Email: chabad-poway@cox.net
Website: www.chabad.poway.com

Reform
Temple Adat Shalom
15905 Pomerado Road 92064
Telephone: (858) 451 1200

RAMONA
Etz Chaim
PO Box 1138 92065
Telephone: (760) 789 7393

SAN DIEGO
BAKERIES
Sheila's Café & Bakery
4577 Clairemont Drive 92117
Telephone: (619) 270 0251
Fax: (619) 274 5797
Website: www.sheilascafe.com

COMMUNITY ORGANISATIONS
United Jewish Federation of San Diego County
4950 Murphy Canyon Road, San Diego 92123
Telephone: (619) (858) 571 3444

Fax: (619) (858) 571 0701
Email: outreach@ujfsd.org
Website: www.jewishinsandiego.org
United Jewish Federation of San Diego County has served as the central address of San Diego County's Jewish community for more than 65 years. Today, the UJF provides the critical resources that bring food, refuge, health care, education and emergency assistance to thousands of San Diegans and 2 million Jews around the world.

MEDIA
Newspapers
San Diego Jewish World
PO Box 19363 92159
Telephone: (619) 265 0808
Fax: (619) 265 0850
Email: sdheritage@cox.net
Website: www.sdjewishworld.com
Daily news web site, San Diego and worldwide Jewish coverage

RESTAURANTS

Dairy
Aarons Glatt Kosher Market
4488 Convoy Street 92111
Telephone: (619) 636 7979
Fax: (619) 636 7980
Website: www.kosherfooddelivery.com

Sababa, Kosher Restaurant
7520 El Cajon Boulevard 92115
Telephone: (619) 337 1880
Fax: (619) 523 9963

Shmoozers Vegetarian & Pizzeria
6366 El Cajon Boulevard 92115
Telephone: (619) 583 1636
Fax: (619) 683 1635
Supervision: Vaad HaRabbanim of San Diego

Dairy Market
Lang's Premium Kosher Foods/Shmoozers Pizza
6165 El Cajon Boulevard #F 92155
Telephone: (619) 287 7306
Fax: (619) 582 1545
Website: www.kosherbread.com
Supervision: Vaad of San Diego

Meat
Sheila's Café & Bakery
4577 Clairemont Drive 92117
Telephone: (619) 270 0251
Fax: (619) 274 5797
Website: www.sheilascafe.com

SYNAGOGUES
Conservative
Congregation Beth Am
5050 Black Mountain Road 92130
Telephone: (619) 481 8454
Fax: (619) 481 6068
Email: betham@betham.com

Ner Tamid
16770 West Bernardo Drive, Suite A 92127
Telephone: (619) 592 9141
Fax: (619) 592 4889

Tifereth Israel Synagogue
6660 Cowles Mountain Boulevard 92119
Telephone: (619) 697 6001
Fax: (619) 697 1102
Website: www.tiferethisrael.com

Orthodox
Beth Jacob Synagogue
4855 College Avenue 92115
Telephone: (619) 287 9890
Fax: (619) 287 0578

Chabad
6115 Montezuma Road 92115
Telephone: (619) 265 0519
Fax: (619) 265 0346
Email: chabadhousesd@aol.com

Chabad of La Jolla
3813 Governor Drive, Suite N 92122
Telephone: (619) 455 1670
Fax: (619) 451 1443

Ohr Shalom
1260 Morena Boulevard, Suite 100 92100
Telephone: (619) 275 9299
Fax: (619) 275 2078

Young Israel Congregation of San Diego
7291 Navajo Road 92119
Telephone: (619) 589 1447
Email: youngisraelSD@yahoo.com
Website: www.yisd.info
Supervision: Rabbi Chaim Hollander

Reconstructionist
Congregation Dor Hadash
4858 Ronson Court, Suite A 92111
Telephone: (619) 268 3674
Fax: (619) 794 4087

Reform
Congregation Beth Israel of San Diego
9001 Towne Centre Drive 92124
Telephone: (619) 535 1111
Fax: (619) 535 1130
Website: www.cbisd.org

Temple Emanu El
6299 Capri Drive 92120
Telephone: (619) 286 2555
Fax: (619) 286 3176

San Francisco County

SAN FRANCISCO
BAKERIES
Noahs Bagels
3519 California Street, Willow Glen
Telephone: (415) 387 3874

COMMUNITY ORGANISATIONS
**Jewish Com. Fed. of San Francisco, the
Peninsula, Marin & Sonoma Counties**
121 Steuart Street 94105 94105
Telephone: (415) 777 0411
Fax: (415) 495 6635
Email: info@sfjcf.org
Website: www.sfjcf.org
Notes: Central organisation for fundraising, planning,
outreach and leadership development.

EMBASSY
Consul General of Israel
Suite 2100, 456 Mongomery Street 94104

GROCERIES
Israel's Kosher Market
5621 Geary Boulevard 94121
Telephone: (415) 752 3064
Fax: (415) 752 3016

Jacob's Kosher Meats
2435 Noriega street 94122
Telephone: (415) 564 7482

Kosher Nutrition Kitchen
Montefiore Senior Center, 3200 California Avenue
Supervision: Orthodox Rabbinical Council

Restaurant
Tel Aviv Strictly Kosher Meats
2495 Irving Street 94122
Telephone: (415) 661 7588
Fax: (415) 661 8258
Supervision: Orthodox Rabbinical Council

LIBRARIES
Holocaust Library & Research Center
601 14th Avenue 94118
Telephone: (415) 751 6040

MIKVAOT
Mikva
3355 Sacramento Street 94118
Telephone: (415) 921 4070

MUSEUMS
The Contemporary Jewish Museum
282 Second Street, Suite 200 94105
Telephone: (415) 543 8088
Fax: (415) 344 8815
Email: info@thecjm.org
Website: www.thecjm.org

RESTAURANTS
Meat
Sabra
419 Grant Avenue, Chinatown
Telephone: (415) 982 3656
Fax: (415) 982 3650
Supervision: Vaad Hakashrus of Northern California

This is It
430 Geary Street 94210
Telephone: (415) 749 0201

SYNAGOGUES
Conservative
Beth Israel Judea
625 Brotherhood Way 94132
Telephone: (415) 586 8833
Beth Sholom
1301 Clement Street 94118
Telephone: (415) 221 8736
Fax: (415) 221 3944
Email: info@bethsholomsf.org
Website: www.bethsholomsf.org
Bn'nai Emunah
3595 Taraval Street 94116
Telephone: (415) 664 7373
Fax: (415) 664 4209
Email: bnaiemunah@sbcglobal.net
Website: usjc.org/ncalif/sanfranbe
Congregation Ner Tamid
1250 Quintara street 94116
Telephone: (415) 661 3383
Fax: (415) 661 9041
Email: nertamidsf@sbcglobal.net

Orthodox
Adath Israel
1851 Noriega Street 94122
Telephone: (415) 564 5565
Anshey Sfard
1500 Clement Street 94118
Telephone: (415) 752 4979
Chevra Thilim
751 25th Avenue 94121
Telephone: (415) 752 2866
Fax: (415) 752 2019
Kenesseth Israel
873 Sutter Street 94109
Telephone: (415) 771 3420
Torat Emeth
768 27th Avenue 94121
Telephone: (415) 386 1830
Young Israel of San Francisco
1806 A Noriega Street 94122
Telephone: (415) 387 1774

Reform
Sha'ar Zahav
290 Dolores Street 94103
Telephone: (415) 861 6932
Fax: (415) 841 6081
Email: office@shaarzahav.org
Sherith Israel
2266 California Street 94115
Telephone: (415) 346 1720
Fax: (415) 673 9439
Temple Emanu-El
Arguello Boulevard & Lake Street 94118
Telephone: (415) 751 2535
Fax: (415) 751 2511

Email: mail@emanuelsf.org
Website: www.emanuelsf.org
Temple Emanu-El is an architecturally significant building based on the Haggia Sophia in Istambul with a dome that can be seen for miles. It was built in 1925 and features a fountained courtyard and a main sanctuary with exemplary artifacts including a museum quality ark and remarkable stained glass windows to symbolize fire and water, the two mystical elements of creation.
Tours available Tuesday-Thursday at 1:30 or by prior appointment by calling the temple.

Sephardi
Magain David
351 4th Avenue 94118
Telephone: (415) 752 9095

TOURIST INFORMATION
Jewish Community Information & Referral
121 Steuart Street, 5th Floor 94105
Telephone: (415) 777 4545
Fax: (415) 495 4897
Email: Info@JewishNfo.org
Website: www.sfjcf.org/resources
Central organisation: Jewish Community Federation
JCI&R provides free, confidential information and referrals to all inquiries, personalised assistance and a connection to communities in the Bay Area, the USA and Israel. JCI&R connects callers to programs, activities, community services, volunteer opportunities, organizations, synagogues, Jewish education and culture, holidays and special needs. It operates an outreach program to welcome newborns and newly adopted babies and their families into the Jewish community.

San Joaquin County
STOCKTON
Stockton is one of the oldest communities west of the Mississippi River, founded in the days of the California Gold Rush. Temple Israel was founded as Congregation Ryhim Ahoovim in 1850 and erected its first building in 1855.

SYNAGOGUES
Reform
Temple Israel
5105 N. El Dorado Street 95207
Telephone: (209) 477 9306

San Mateo County
BURLINGAME
Peninsula Temple Sholom
1655 Sebastian Drive 94010
Telephone: (415) 697 2266

DALY CITY
Conservative
B'nai Israel
1575 Annie Street 94015
Telephone: (415) 756 5430

SAN CARLOS
CONTACT INFORMATION
Jewish Travel Network
PO Box 283 94070
Telephone: (650) 368 0880
Fax: (650) 599 9066
Website: www.jewishtravelnetwork.com/

Santa Barbara County
SANTA BARBARA
SYNAGOGUES
Orthodox
Chabad of Santa Barbara
6047 Stow Canyon Road, Goleta 93117
Telephone: (805) 683 1544
Fax: (805) 683 1545
Email: rabbi@sbchabad.org
Website: www.sbchabad.org

Young Israel of Santa Barbara
1826 Cliff Drive 93109
Telephone: (805) 966 4565

Reform
Congregation B'nai B'rith
1000 San Antonio Creek Road 93111
Telephone: (805) 964 7869
Fax: (805) 683 6473

Santa Clara County
LOS GATOS
Congregation Shir Hadash
20 Cherry Blossom Lane 95032
Telephone: 358 1751
Fax: 358 1753
Email: office@shirhadash.org
Website: www.shirhadash.org
Central organisation: Union for Reform Judaism

PALO ALTO
COMMUNITY ORGANISATIONS
Albert L. Schultz Community Center
655 Arastradero Road 94306
Telephone: (650) 439 9400

GROCERIES
Garden Fresh
1245 W. El Camino Road, Mount View 94040
Telephone: (650) 961 7795

SYNAGOGUES
Orthodox
Palo Alto Orthodox Minyan
260 Sheridan Avenue 94306
Telephone: (650) 948 7498

Chadbad of Greater South Bay
3070 Louis Road 94303
Telephone: (650) 424 9800

Fax: (650) 493 3425
Email: chabad1@pacbell.net
Website: www.chabadgsb.com

SAN JOSE
BOOKSELLERS
Alef Bet Judaica
1410-0 Winchester Boulevard Los Gatos 95032
Telephone: (408) 370 1818
Fax: (408) 725 8269

COMMUNITY ORGANISATIONS
Jewish Federation of Greater San Jose
14855 Oka Road, Los Gatos 95030
Telephone: (408) 358 3033
Fax: (408) 356 0733

MIKVAOT
Mikvah Society of San Jose
1670 Phantom Avenue 95125
Telephone: (408) 371 9548 for appointments; 264 3138 for info
Fax: (408) 264 3139
Email: bergman.d@sbcglobal.net

SYNAGOGUES
Conservative
Congregation Beth David
19700 Prospect Road, Saratoga 95070
Telephone: (408) 257 3333
Fax: (408) 257 3338
Email: admin@beth-david.org
Website: www.beth-david.org

Congregation Emeth
PO Box 1430, Gilroy 95021
Telephone: (408) 847 4111

Congregation Sinai
1532 Willowbrae Avenue 95125-4450
Telephone: (408) 264 8542
Fax: (408) 264 4316

Orthodox
Almaden Valley Torah Center
1422 Helmond Lane 95118
Telephone: (408) 445 1770
Fax: (408) 267 9812
Mobile Phone: 408 375 7770
Email: rabbi770@sbcglobal.net
Website: www.rabbi770.com

Am Echad Community
1504 Meridian Avenue 95125
Telephone: (408) 267 2591
Email: info@amechad.org
Website: www.amechad.org

Reform
Temple Beth Sholom
2270 Canoas Garden Avenue 95125
Telephone: (408) 978 5566

Temple Emanu-El
1010 University Avenue 95126
Telephone: (408) 292 0939

Torah Orthodox Sephardic
Ahabat Torah
1537-A Meridian Avenue 95125
Telephone: (408) 266 2342
Fax: (408) 264 3139
Email: ahavastorahsj@aol.com
Website: www.ahava.org
Torah Orthodox Sephardic Congregation

SAN RAFAEL
Reform
Rodef Sholom
170 N. San Pedro Road 94903
Telephone: (415) 479 3441

SUNNYVALE
CATERERS
Kosher Catering
1030 Astoria Drive 94087
Telephone: (408) 739-5949
Supervision: VAAD Hakashrus of Northern California "
Sunnyvale California 94087
 Delivery available.

SYNAGOGUES
Bar Yohai sefardic Minyan
1030 Astoria Drive 94087
Website: www.baryohai.org

Solano County

VALLEJO
Unaffiliated
Congregtion B'nai Israel
1256 Nebraska Street 94590
Telephone: (707) 642 6526

Sonoma County

SANTA ROSA
Conservative
Beth Ami
4676 Mayette Avenue 95405
Telephone: (707) 360 3000
Fax: (707) 360 3003
Website: www.bethamisr.org

Reform
Congregation Shomrei Torah
2600 Benett Valley Road 95404
Telephone: (707) 578 5519
Fax: (707) 578 3967
Email: shomrei@shomreitorah.org

Ventura County

THOUSAND OAKS
Conservative
Temple Etz Chaim
1080 E. Janss Road 91360
Telephone: (805) 497 6891
Fax: (805) 497 0086
Email: info@templeetzchaim.org
Website: www.templeetzchaim.org

VENTURA
COMMUNITY ORGANISATIONS
Jewish Community Centre
259 Callens Road 93004
Telephone: (805) 647 4181

SYNAGOGUES
Reform
Temple Beth Torah
7620 Foothill Road 93004
Telephone: (805) 647 4181

Yolo County

DAVIS
Davis Jewish Fellowship
1821 Oak Avenue 95616
Telephone: (916) 758 0842

Colorado

Arapahoe County

GREENWOOD VILLAGE
OUTREACH SYNAGOGUES
Orthodox
Aish/Ahavas Yisroel; a Center for Jewish Outreach
9550 E. Belleview Avenue 80111
Telephone: (303) 220 7200
Website: www.aishdenver.com
Outreach centre and full service synagogue. Daily minyanim and classes. Shabbos hospitality.

Boulder County

BOULDER
COMMUNITY ORGANISATIONS
Boulder JCC
3800 Kalmia Avenue 80301
Telephone: (303) 998 1900
Fax: (303) 998 1965
Email: linda@boulderjcc.org
Website: www.boulderjcc.org

ORGANISATIONS
Lubavitch of Boulder County
4740 Table Mesa Drive Unit B
80303
Telephone: (303) 494 1638
Fax: (484) 208 3860
Email: lubavbldr@cs.com
Website: www.lubavitchofboulder.org

SYNAGOGUES
Hillel Foundation
2795 Colorado Avenue, University of Colorado
Telephone: (303) 442 6571

Conservative
Congregation Bonai Shalom
1527 Cherryvale Road, 80303
Telephone: (303) 442 6605
Fax: (303) 442 7545
Website: www.bonaishalom.org

Orthodox
Chabad Lubavitch of Boulder
4900 Sioux Drive 80303
Telephone: (303) 494 1638
Email: lubavbldr@cs.com
Website: Lubavitchofboulder.org

Reform
Congregation Har Hashem
3950 Baseline Road 80303
Telephone: (303) 499 7077
Jewish Renewal Community of Boulder
5001 Pennsylvania 80303
Telephone: (303) 271 3541

Denver County
DENVER
BAKERIES
The Bagel Store
942 South Monaco 80224
Telephone: (303) 388 2648
Supervision: Vaad Hakashrus of Denver

COMMUNITY ORGANISATIONS
Allied Jewish Federation of Colorado
300 S. Dahlia street 80246
Telephone: (303) 316 6491
Website: jewishcolorado.org
Jewish Family & Children's Service
1355 S. Colorado Boulevard 80222
Telephone: (303) 759 4890
Fax: (303) 759 5998
Email: jfs@jewishfamilyservice.org
Website: www.jewishfamilyservice.org

GROCERIES
Auerbach's
4810 Newport Street
Telephone: (303) 289 4521

Cub Foods
1985 Sheridan Boulevard, Edgewater
Telephone: (303) 232 8972
King Soopers
890 S. Monaco Parkway
Telephone: (303) 333 1535
6470 East Hampden Avenue
Telephone: (303) 758 1210
Safeway
7150 Leetsdale Drive (& Quebec)
Telephone: (303) 377 6939
640 E. Yale (& Monaco)
Telephone: (303) 691 8870

KASHRUT INFORMATION
Scoll K Vaad Hakashrus of Denver
1350 Vrain 80204
Telephone: (303) 595 9349

MEDIA
Newspapers
Intermountain Jewish News
1177 Grant Street 80203
Telephone: (303) 861 2234
Fax: (303) 832 6942
Email: email@ijn.com

MIKVAOT
Mikvah of Denver
1404 Quitman 80204
Telephone: (303) 893 5315

RELIGIOUS ORGANISATIONS
Synagogue Council of Greater Denver
Po Box 102732 80250
Telephone: (303) 759 8484

RESTAURANTS
Meat
East Side Kosher Deli
499 South Elm St.
Telephone: (303) 322 9862
Full-scale meat restaurant, with an
attached grocery store and fresh-cooked take-out counter.
The take-out food, at least, is under the supervision of the
Vaad Hakashrus of Denver.
Jeff's Diner
731 Quebec Street 80220
Telephone: (303) 333 4637

Pizzeria
Pete's Kosher Pizza
5606 E. Cedar Avenue 80204
Telephone: (303) 255 5777

SYNAGOGUES
Conservative
Beth Shalom
2280 East Noble Place, Littleton 80121
Telephone: (303) 794 6643

Hebrew Educational Alliance (HEA)
3600 South Ivanhoe Street 80237
Telephone: (303) 758 9400
Fax: (303) 758 9500
Email: info@headenver.org

Rodef Shalom
450 S. Kearney 80224
Telephone: (303) 399 0035
Fax: (303) 399 7623
Website: www.rodef shalom.org

Orthodox
Bais Medrash Kehillas Yaakov
295 S. Locust Street 80222
Telephone: (303) 377 1200
Fax: (303) 355 6010

Congregation Zera Abraham
1560 Winona Court 80204
Telephone: (303) 825 7517

Reform
Beth Shalom
2280 E. Noble Place 80121
Telephone: (303) 794 6643

Temple Micah
2600 Leyden street 80207
Telephone: (303) 388 4239
Fax: (303) 377 4816
Email: office@micahdenver.org
Website: www.micahdenver.org

Temple Sinai
3509 South Glencoe street 80237
Telephone: (303) 759 1827
Fax: (303) 759 2519
Email: mail@sinaidenver.org
Website: www.sinaidenver.org

Traditional
B.M.H. BJ Congregation
560 S. Monaco Parkway 80224
Telephone: (303) 388 4203
Fax: (303) 388 4210

El Paso County
COLORADO SPRINGS
Conservative & Reform
Temple Shalom
1523 E. Monument street 80909
Telephone: (719) 634 5311
Fax: (719) 447 9385
Email: Tshalom@qwest.net
Website: www.templeshalom.com

Jefferson County
EVERGREEN
Reconstructionist
Congregation Beth Evergreen
PO Box 415 80439
Telephone: (303) 670 4294

Fax: (303) 670 6930
Email: shalom@bethevergreen.org
Website: www.bethevergreen.org
Set in the pines overlooking scenic Elk Meadow, thirty minutes from Denver, Congregation Beth Evergreen offers inclusive, warm welcoming services and programs in an intimate atmosphere. We are committed to fostering community by offering opportunities ffor meaningful worship, the pursuit of spirituality and lifelong Jewish education.

Pueblo County
PUEBLO
Conservative
United Hebrew Congregation
106 W. 15th street 81003
Telephone: (719) 544 9897; 583 8303

Reform
Temple Emanuel
1325 Grand Avenue 81003
Telephone: (719) 544 6448
Email: mikeaa@coloradobluesky.org

Connecticut
Fairfield County
BRIDGEPORT
COMMUNITY ORGANISATIONS
Jewish Center for Community Services of Eastern Fairfield County
4200 Park Avenue 06604
Telephone: (203) 372 6567
Fax: (203) 374 0770

MEDIA
Radio
WVOF Radio
c/o Fairfield University, Fairfield 06430
Telephone: (203) 254 4111

RELIGIOUS ORGANISATIONS
Va'ad of Fairfield County
1571 Stratfield Road, Fairfield 06432
Telephone: (203) 372 6529

RESTAURANTS
Cafe Shalom
c/o Abel, Community Center
Telephone: (203) 372 6567

SYNAGOGUES
Conservative
B'nai Torah
5700 Main Street, Trumbull 06611

Rodeph Sholom
2385 Park Avenue 06604
Telephone: (203) 334 0159
Fax: (203) 334 1411
Email: cong.rodeph.sholom@snet.net
Website: www.rodephsholom.com

Orthodox
Agudas Achim
85 Arlington Street 06606

Bikur Cholim
Park & Capitol Avenue 06604
Telephone: (203) 336 3383
Email: jbm@ou.org
Website: www.ou.org

Reconstructionist
Congregation Shirei Shalom
Po Box 372, Monroe 06468

Reform
Temple B'nai Israel
2710 Park Avenue 06604
Telephone: (203) 336 1858
Fax: (203) 367 7889
Email: welcome@congregationbnaiisrael.org

DANBURY
COMMUNITY ORGANISATIONS
Jewish Federation
69 Kenosia Avenue 06810
Telephone: (203) 792 6353
Fax: (203) 748 5099
Email: info@thejf.org
Website: www.thejf.org

SYNAGOGUES
Conservative
Congregation B'nai Israel
193 Clapboard Ridge Road 06811
Telephone: (203) 792 6161

Orthodox
Chabad
9 Golden Heights Road 06811
Telephone: (203) 790 4700

Reform
United Jewish Center
141 Deer Hill Avenue 06810
Telephone: (203) 748 3335

FAIRFIELD
BAKERIES
Carvel Ice Cream Bakery
1838 Black Rock Turnpike
Telephone: (203) 384 2253
Supervision: Vaad Hakashrus of Fairfield County

MIKVAOT
Mikveh Israel of Fairfield
1326 Stratfield Road 06825
Telephone: (203) 374 2191
Fax: (203) 373 7378

SYNAGOGUES
Conservative
Congregation Beth El
1200 Fairfield Woods Road, Fairfield 06825
Telephone: (203) 374 5544
Fax: (203) 374 4962
Email: congbethel@aol.com
Website: www.uscj.org/ctvalley/fairfield

Orthodox
Congregation Ahavath Achim
1571 Stratfield Road, Fairfield 06825
Telephone: (203) 372 6529
Fax: (203) 373 0647

STAMFORD
COMMUNITY ORGANISATIONS
United Jewish Federation of Greater Stamford, New Canaan and Darien
1035 Newfield Avenue, Suite 200 06905 2591
Telephone: (203) 321 1373
Fax: (203) 322 3277
Email: office@ujf.org
Website: www.ujf.org

DELICATESSEN
Delicate Essen at the JCC
1035 Newfield Avenue 06902
Telephone: (203) 322 0944
Fax: (203) 322 5160
Supervision: Vaad Hakashrus of Fairfield County.

SYNAGOGUES
Orthodox
Young Israel of Stamford
69 Oak Lawn Avenue 06905
Telephone: (203) 348 3955

WESTPORT
Synagogue Westport
215 Post Road West 06880
Telephone: (203) 226 6901

Hartford County

HARTFORD
COMMUNITY ORGANISATIONS
Jewish Federation of Hartford
333 Bloomfield Avenue , Suite C 06117
Telephone: (860) 232 4483
Fax: (860) 232 5221
Email: info@jewishhartford.org
Website: www.jewishhartford.org

KASHRUT INFORMATION
Kashrut Commission
162 Brewster Road 06117
Telephone: (860) 563 4017

MEDIA
Guide
All Things Jewish
333 Bloomfield Avenue 06117
Telephone: (860) 232 4483

MIKVAOT
Mikva
61 Main Street 06119

SYNAGOGUES
Conservative
Beth El
2626 Albany Avenue, West Hartford 06117

Beth Tefilah
465 Oak Street, East Hartford 06118

Emanuel synagogue
160 Mohegan Drive, West Hartford 06117
Telephone: (860) 236 1275
Fax: (860) 231 8890

Orthodox
Agudas Achim
1244 N. Main Street, West Hartford 06117

Beth David Synagogue
20 Dover Road, West Hartford 06117
Telephone: (860) 236 1241

Teferes Israel
27 Brown Street, Bloomfield 06002

United Synagogue of Greater Hartford
840 N. Main S., West Hartford 06117

Reform
Temple Sinai
41 W. Hartford Road, Newington 06011

MANCHESTER
Conservative
Temple Beth Sholom
400 Middle Turnpike E. 06040
Telephone: (603) 643 9563
Fax: (603) 643 9565
Email: riplavin@sbcglobal.net
Website: www.myshul.org

NEW BRITAIN
B'nai Israel Conservative Synagogue
265 W. Main Street, 06051
Telephone: (860) 224 0479

Orthodox
Tephereth Israel
76 Winter Street 06051

NEWINGTON
Conservative
Congregation B'nai Sholom
26 Church Street Newington 06111 4401
Telephone: (860) 667 0826

Website: www.cbsnewington.org
Conservative, Egalitarian synagogue: "Where evryone knows your name"

WEST HARTFORD
BOOKSELLERS
The Judaica Store
31 Crossroads Plaza 06117
Telephone: (860) 236 9956
Fax: (860) 236 9956

SYNAGOGUES
Orthodox
Young Israel of West Hartford
2240 Albany Avenue 06117
Telephone: (860) 233 3084
Fax: (860) 232 5850
Email: westhartfordrav@aol.com
Website: www.youngisraelwh.org

Reform
Congregation Beth Israel
701 Farmington Avenue 06119
Telephone: (860) 233 8215
Fax: (860) 523 0223
Email: bethisrael@cbict.org
Website: www.cbict.org

Middlesex County
MIDDLETOWN
Conservative
Adath Israel
48 Church Street, 06457
Telephone: (860) 346 4709

New Haven County
MERIDEN
SYNAGOGUES
Conservative
B'nai Abraham
127 E. Main Street, 06450
Telephone: (203) 235 2581
Fax: (203) 235 2582

NEW HAVEN
COMMUNITY ORGANISATIONS
Jewish Federation of Greater New Haven
360 Amity Road, Woodbridge Ct. 06525
Telephone: (203) 387 2424

CONTACT INFORMATION
Young Israel House at Yale University
c/o Joseph Slifka Center, 80 Wall Street 06511
Telephone: (203) 432 1134
Fax: (203) 432 8690
Website: www.yale.edu/slifka/org/yihy.html
For Jewish life at Yale

DELICATESSEN
The Westville
1460 Whalley Avenue 06515
Telephone: (203) 397 0839

GROCERIES
Westville Kosher Meat Market
95 Amity Road 06525
Telephone: (203) 389 1723

LIBRARIES
Center Cafe & Jewish Library
360 Amity Road 06525
Telephone: (203) 387 2424

MIKVAOT
New Haven Mikvah Society
86 Hubinger Street 06511
Telephone: (203) 387 2184
Email: amhack@sbcglobal.net

RESTAURANTS
Dairy
Claire's Gourmet Vegetarian Restaurant & Caterer
1000 Chapel Street 06510
Telephone: (203) 562 3888
Supervision: Rabbi David Avigdor

SYNAGOGUES
Conservative
Beth El Keser Israel
85 Harrison Street 06515
Telephone: (203) 389 2108

Orthodox
Beth Hamedrosh Westville
74 West Prospect Street 06515
Telephone: (203) 389 9513
Fax: (203) 389 9514
Email: westvilleshul@sbcglobal.net
Website: www.westvilleshul.org

Congregation Bikur Cholim Sheveth Achim
112 Marvel Road 06515
Telephone: (203) 387 4699
Email: bikurcholim@comcast.net

Yeshiva of New Haven
765 Elm Street, New Haven 06511
Telephone: (203) 777 2200
Fax: (203) 777 7198
Email: info@yeshivanewhaven.org
Website: www.yeshivanewhaven.org

WATERBURY
COMMUNITY ORGANISATIONS
Jewish Communities of Western CT, Inc.
73 Main Street, South Woodbury 06798
Telephone: (203) 263 5121
Fax: (203) 263 5143

WOODBRIDGE
LIBRARIES
Department of Jewish Education Library
360 Amity Road 06525
Telephone: (203) 387 2424 ext. 330
Fax: (203) 387 1818
Email: library@jewishnewhaven.org
Website: www.jewishnewhaven.org/
Central organisation: Dept. of Jewish Education of the Jewish Federation of Greater New Haven
Judaic Library open to the public. Collection includes books and A/V materials (DVD, VHS, CD, Audio-cassette) for all ages. Special emphasis on Jewish customs and ceremonies, Israel, Holocaust, Bible studies, women in Judaism, and materials for children and young adults.

New London County
NEW LONDON
COMMUNITY ORGANISATIONS
Jewish Federation of Eastern Connecticut
28 Channing Street 06320
Telephone: (860) 442 8062
Fax: (860) 443 4175
Email: jfischer@jfec.com
Website: www.jfec.com

SYNAGOGUES
Conservative
Congregation Beth El
660 Ocean Avenue 06320
Telephone: (860) 442 0418
Website: www.bethel-nl.org

NORWICH
SYNAGOGUES
Orthodox
Brothers of Joseph
Broad & Washington Avenues.   06360
Telephone: (203) 887 3777

Delaware
Kent County
DOVER
Conservative
Congregation Beth Sholom of Dover
PO Box 223 19903
Telephone: (302) 734 5578

New Castle County
NEWARK
Reconstructionist
Temple Beth El
101 Possum Park Rd 19711
Telephone: (302) 366 833

WILMINGTON
COMMUNITY ORGANISATIONS
Jewish Community Center
101 Garden of Eden Road 19803
Telephone: (910) 478 5660
Fax: (910) 478 6068

SYNAGOGUES
Conservative
Beth Shalom
18th Street and Baynard Boulevard 19802

Orthodox
Adas Kodesh Shel Emeth
Washington Boulevard & Torah Drive 19802
Telephone: (302) 762 2705
Fax: (302) 762 3236
Website: www.akse.org

Reform
Beth Emeth
300 W. Lea Boulevard 19802
Telephone: (302) 764 2393
Fax: (302) 764 2395

District of Columbia
WASHINGTON
RESTAURANTS
Kosher
Eli's Restaurant
1253 20th Street NW 20036
Telephone: (202) 785 4314
Email: sina118@hotmail.com
Website: www.elisdc.com
Supervision: Va'ad Hakashrut of Washington
Sun to Thu 10am to 9pm; Fri 10am to 2.30pm, closed Sat nights

District of Columbia County
DELICATESSEN
Hunan Deli
H Street
Telephone: (202) 833 1018

Posins Bakery & Deli
5756 Georgia Avenue
Telephone: (202) 726 4424

EMBASSY
Embassy of Israel
3514 International Drive 20008
Telephone: (202) 364 5500
Fax: (202) 364 5423

MEDIA
Newspapers
The Jewish Week
1910 "K" Street 20006

MUSEUMS
B'nai B'rith Klutznick National Jewish Museum
1640 Rhode Island Avenue 20036
Telephone: (202) 857 6583
Fax: (202) 857 1099
Email: eberman@bnaibrith.org
Website: www.BBlnet.org

Jewish Historical Society of Greater Washington
 20001Telephone: (202) 789 0900
Fax: (202) 789 0485
Email: info@jhsgw.org
Website: www.jhsgw.org
Also the Lillian & Albert Small Jewish Museum. Monday to Thursday open by appointment.

Lillian & Albert Small Jewish Museum
701 3rd Street N.W. 20001
Telephone: (202) 789 0900
Fax: (202) 789 0485
Email: info@jhsgw.org
Website: www.jhsgw.org
Central organisation: Jewish Historical Society of Greater Washington
Hours: Sunday to Thursday open by appointment

National Museum of American Jewish Military History
1811 R. Street N.W 20009
Telephone: (202) 265 6280
Fax: (202) 462 3192
Website: www.nmajmh.org

Smithsonian Institute
The National History Building, 10th & Constition Avenues N.W. 20001

The National Portrait Gallery
F Street between 7th & 8th Streets

United States Holocaust Memorial Museum
100 Raoul Wallenberg Place. S.W. 290024 2150
Telephone: (202) 488 0400, group tours
phone:(202) 488 0419
Fax: (202) 488 2606
Email: group_visit@ushmm.org
Website: www.ushmm.org
Notes: Hours: 10am to 5.30pm. The Museum is accessible to people with disabilities. The permanent exhibition recommended for visitors eleven years and older, presents a comprehensive history of the Holocaust through artefact, photographs, films and eyewitness testimonies. There are other changing special exhibitions and a special exhibition designed for children and families.

RESTAURANTS
JCC Cafe
1559 16th Street at Q 20036
Telephone: (202) 387 3246
Fax: (202) 387 3248
Email: info@jcccafe.com
Website: www.jcccafe.com
Supervision: Va'ad Hakashrut of Washington
Hours: Sun to Thu 11am to 8pm

TOURIST SITE
John F. Kennedy Center
2700 "F" Street

New Castle County
CONTACT INFORMATION
Eruv in Georgetown
Telephone: (202) 338 ERUV

PLANTATION
Temple Kol Ami Emanu-El
8200 Peters Road
Telephone: (954) 472 1988
Website: www. kolami-emanuel.com
Religious School, Day School, Early Childhood Center.
Services: Friday night, Saturday morning and every Jewish
Holiday and Holy Day.

SUNRISE
RESTAURANTS
Blue Star Cafe n Grill
7794A NW 44 Street
Telephone: (954) 749 4150

Broward County
DEERFIELD BEACH
SYNAGOGUES
Orthodox
Young Israel of Deerfield Beach
202 Century Boulevard 33442
Telephone: (954) 571 3904
Fax: (954) 571 5234

FORT LAUDERDALE
KOSHER FOOD
O K Gourmet
3515 Galt Ocean Drive 33308
Telephone: (954) 564 6511
Meat/Fish restaurant, kosher market and deli

MIKVAOT
Mikveh/Young Israel of Hollywood Ft Lauderdale
3291 Stirling Road 33312
Telephone: (954) 963 3952
Fax: (954) 962 5566

RESTAURANTS
Amore' Ristorante
8067 West Oakland Park Boulevard, Sunrise
Telephone: (954) 749 6888
Supervision: Glatt kosher

SYNAGOGUES
Orthodox
Temple Ohel B'nai Raphael
4351 West Oakland Park Boulevard 33313
Telephone: (954) 733 7684

Young Israel of Hollywood/Ft Lauderdale
3291 Stirling Road 33312
Telephone: (954) 966 7877
Fax: (954) 9625566
Website: www.yih.org
Sephardi
B'nai Sephardim
3670 Stirling Road, Ft Lauderdale

HALLANDALE
RESTAURANTS
Dairy
Fressers at Tierra Mar
1960 S. Ocean Drive
Telephone: (954) 889 0075

Meat
Kosher World
514 41st Street
Telephone: (954) 532 2210

Pita Loca South Beach Israeli Restaurant
601 Collins Avenue, Suite #5
Telephone: (954) 673 3388
Website: www.pitaloca.8m.com

SYNAGOGUES
Conservative
Hallandale Jewish Center
416 N.E. Eighth Avenue 33009
Telephone: (954) 454 9100

Orthodox
Congregation Levi Yitzchok Lubavitch
1295 E. Hallandale Beach Boulevard. 33009
Telephone: (954) 458 1877
Fax: (954) 458 1651

HOLLYWOOD & VICINITY
COMMUNITY ORGANISATIONS
Jewish Federation of South Broward
2719 Hollywood Boulevard. 33020
Telephone: (954) 921 8810

JUDAICA
Holyland Judaica
5650 Stirling Road, Hollywood 33021
Telephone: (954) 964 4288
Fax: (954) 964 0189
Email: holylandjudaica@aol.com

KOSHER FOOD
Ilana's Cookies
5650 Stirling Road, Hollywood
Telephone: (954) 963 6130

RESTAURANTS
Dairy
Sara's
3944 N. 6th Avenue 33021
Telephone: (954) 986 1770

Meat
Pita King
5650 Stirling Road 33021
Telephone: (954) 985 8028

Pizzerias
JP Bistro
5650 Stirling Road 33021
Telephone: (954) 964 6811

SYNAGOGUES
Conservative
B'nai Aviv
1410 Indian Trace, Weston 33326

Century Pines Jewish Center
13400 S.W. 10 Street, Pembroke Pines 33027
Telephone: (954) 431 3300

Temple Beth Ahm Israel
9730 Stirling Road 33024
Telephone: (954) 431 5100

Temple Judea of Carriage Hills
6734 Stirling Road 33021
Telephone: (954) 987 0026

Orthodox
Chabad of Southwest Broward
11251 Taft Street, Pembroke Pines

Congregation Ahavat Shalom
315 Madison Street, PO Box 220918 33022 0918
Telephone: (954) 922 4544
Fax: (954) 922 4523
Email: beachshul@beachshul.org
Website: www.beachshul.org

Young Israel of Pembroke Pines
13400 S.W. 10 Street, Pembroke Pines

Reform
Temple Beth El
1351 S. 14 Avenue 33020
Telephone: (954) 920 8225
Fax: (954) 920 7026

Temple Beth Emet
4807 South Flamingo Road, Cooper City, Pembroke Pines
Telephone: (954) 680 1882

Temple Solel
5100 Sheridan Street, Hollywood 33021
Telephone: (954) 989 0205

PEMBROKE PINES
Orthodox
Young Israel of Pembroke Pines
13400 SW. 10th Street 33027
Telephone. (954) 433 8666

ROCKLEDGE
COMMUNITY ORGANISATIONS
Jewish Federation of Brevard
108A Barton Avenue
Telephone: (321) 636 1824

TAMARAC
SYNAGOGUES
Orthodox
Young Israel of Taramac
8565 W. McNab Road 33321
Telephone: (954) 726 3586

Columbia County
LAKE CITY
GROCERIES
Lake City Jewish & Kosher Center/Brevard Kosher Zone
750 Woodlands Terrace 32055
Telephone: (386) 344 5099
Fax: (386) 719 9569
Email: bkz3@hotmail.com
Supervision: Various orthodox supervisions

Duval County
JACKSONVILLE
COMMUNITY ORGANISATIONS
Jacksonville Jewish Federation
8505 San Jose Boulevard. 32217
Telephone: (904) 448 5000

MIKVAH
Etz Chaim
10167 San Jose Boulevard. 32257
Telephone: (904) 262 3565

ORGANISATIONS
Community Kosher Nutrition Program
5846 Mt Carmel Terrace 32216
Telephone: (904) 737 9075
Website: www.jfcsjax.org
Central organisation: Jewish Family and Community Services
Lunch program for Mt. Carmel Gardens residents. Additional in house programs "Kosher Kart" program supplying meals to homebound patrons. Kosher catering for community events or personal needs.

SYNAGOGUES
Orthodox
Eitz Chaim Synagogue
10167 San Jose Boulevard 32217
Telephone: (904) 262 3565

Escambia County
PENSACOLA
Conservative
B'nai Israel
1829 N. 9th Avenue, PO Box 9002 32513
Telephone: (850) 433 7311
Fax: (850) 435 9597

Reform
Temple Beth El
800 N. Palafox Street 32501
Telephone: (850) 438 3321

Flagler County
PALM COAST
Conservative
Temple Beth Shalom
40 Wellington Drive 32164
Telephone: (386) 445 3006
Fax: (386) 445 3006
Email: hakol@bellsouth.net
Central organisation: United Synagogue of America

Hillsborough County
TAMPA
COMMUNITY ORGANISATIONS
Tampa Jewish Federation
13009 Community Campus Drive 33625-4000
Telephone: (813) 264 9000
Fax: (813) 265 8450
Email: info@jewishtampa.com
Website: www.jewishtampa.com

MIKVAOT
Bais Tefilah
14908 Pennington Road 33624
Telephone: (813) 963 2317

SYNAGOGUES
Conservative
Congregation Rodeph Sholom
2713 Bayshore Boulevard. 33629
Telephone: (813) 837 1911
Fax: (813) 832 4168
Website: www.rsholom.org

Kol Ami
3919 Moran Road 33618
Telephone: (813) 962 6338

Orthodox
Bais Menachem Chabad
613 South Melville Avenue 33606
Telephone: (813) 504 4432
Email: bmchabad@gmail.com
Website: www.chabadofcentralflorida.com
The shul of downtown Tampa

BaisTemple David
2001 Swann Avenue 33606
Telephone: (813) 251 4300
Fax: (813) 466 8770
Email: rabbilrivkin@hotmail.com

Hebrew Academy
14908 Pennington Road 33624
Telephone: (813) 963 0706

Young Israel of Tampa
2001 Swann Ave 33606
Telephone: (813) 832 3018
Website: www.youngisraeloftampa.org

Young Israel Tampa
5205 E. 131 Avenue 336
Telephone: (813) 832 3018
Email: youngisraeltampa@hotmail.com
Website: www.youngisraeloftampa.org

Reform
Schaarai Zedek
3303 Swann Avenue 33609
Telephone: (813) 876 2377

Temple Shalom
4630 Pine Ridge Road 34119
Telephone: (813) 455 3030
Fax: (813) 455 4361
Website: www.naplestemple.org

Lee County
FORT MEYERS
Temple Beth El
16225 Winkler Road Ext 33908
Telephone: (941) 433 0018

Leon County
TALLAHASSEE
Conservative
Congregation Shomrei Torah
4858 Kerry Forest Parkway 32309
Telephone: (850) 893 9674
Fax: (850) 893 9674
Email: administrator@shomreitorahonline.org
Website: www.shomreitorahonline.org

Manatee County
VERNO BEACH
Reform
Temple Beth Shalom
365 43rd Avenue 32968
Telephone: (772) 569 4700
Fax: (772) 569 4701

Miami-Dade County
MIAMI / MIAMI BEACH
EMBASSY
Consul General of Israel
Suite 1800, 100N Biscayne Boulevard 33132

GIFTS, JUDAICA
Art Gallery
Tamar
459 41st Street 33140
Telephone: (305) 535 8888
Fax: (305) 535 8831
Email: tamarjudaica@yahoo.com
Distinctive judaica, gifts, books, art and music

GROCERIES
Butcher
The New Kosher World
518 W. 41st Street, 1672 N.E. 164 Street 33140
Telephone: (305) 532 2210
Fax: (305) 332 8816

HOTELS
Saxony Hotel
3201 Collins Avenue, Miami Beach 33140
Telephone: (305) 538 6811
Supervision: National Kashruth

MEDIA
Directory
Jewish Life in Dade County
4200 Biscayne Boulevard. 33137
Telephone: (305) 576 4000
Website: www.jewishmiami.org

Radio
Shalom South Florida (WAXY 790 AM)

MIKVAOT
B'nai Israel & Greater Miami Youth Synagogue Mikveh
16260 S. W. 288th Street, Naranja 33033
Telephone: (305) 264 6488

Congregation and Mikvah Adas Dej
225 37th Street 33140
Telephone: (305) 674 8204

Daughters of Israel
2530 Pinetree Drive 33140
Telephone: (305) 672 3500
Fax: (305) 534 1592
Mail only: 2850 Prairie Avenue, Miami Beach, Florida 33140

Rabbi Meisel's Mikveh
Washington Av. & 2nd Street 33139
Telephone: (305) 673 4641

Shul of Bal Harbour Mikvah
9540 Collins Avenue, Surfside 331545
Telephone: (305) 868 1411
Email: info@theshul.org

MUSEUMS
Jewish Museum of Florida
301 Washington Avenue, Miami Beach 33139 6965
Telephone: (305) 672 5044
Fax: (305) 672 5933

Email: mzerivitz@aol.com
Website: www.jewishmuseum.com
Site comprised of two former synagogues, restored by the Museum, and connected with a glass-domed café. Core exhibit, MOSAIC, depicts nearly 250 years of Jewish Life in Florida. Museum open Tuesday-Sunday, 10am to 5pm; Cafe open Tuesday to Friday and Sun 10am to 5pm closed Civil & Jewish Holidays; free on Saturdays. Wheelchair accessible and parking in vicinity

RELIGIOUS ORGANISATIONS
Young Israel Southern Regional Office
173575 NE 7th Avenue 33162
Telephone: (305) 770 3993

RESTAURANTS
Dairy
Bagel Time
3915 Alton Road 33140
Telephone: (305) 538 0300
Supervision: Star K

Gitty's Hungarian Kitchen
6565 Collins Avenue, Sherry Frontenac Hotel 33141
Telephone: (305) 865 4893

Milky Way
530 41st Street
Telephone: (305) 534 4144

Meat
Europa Grill
5445 Collins Avenue
Telephone: (305) 993 3924

Jerusalem Peking
4299 Collins Avenue, Miami Beach
Telephone: (305) 522 2263

Mexico Bravo
16850 Collins Avenue, Sunny Isles Beach
Telephone: (305) 945 1999
Supervision: Star K

Original Pita Hut
530 41st Street
Telephone: (305) 534 4144/531 6090

Shalom Tokyo Steak House
5101 Collins Avenue, Miami Beach
Telephone: (305) 866 6039

Pizzerias
Shemtov's Pizza
514 41st Street 33140
Telephone: (305) 538 2123
Supervision: Star K

SYNAGOGUES
Orthodox
The Shul of Bal Harbor, Bay Harbor & Surfside
9540 Collins Avenue 33154
Telephone: (305) 868 1411
Email: info@theshul.org

Young Israel of Miami Beach
4221 Pine Tree Drive 33140
Telephone: (305) 538 9462
Fax: (786) 363 4293
Email: youngisraelmb@aol.com
Central organisation: NCYI

NORTH MIAMI / NORTH MIAMI BEACH

MIKVAOT
Mikveh Jovita Cojab
1054 N.E. Miami Gardens Drive 33179
Telephone: (305) (305) 949 9650
Fax: (305) (305) 653 6757
Email: morajudi@comcast.net

RESTAURANTS
Mexico Bravo
16850 Collins Aveue, Sunny Isles Beach
Telephone: (305) 945 1999

Dairy
The Noshery
Saxony Hotel, 3201 Collins Avenue 33140
Telephone: (305) (305) 538 6811

Yummy Miami
18090 Collins Avenue
Telephone: (305) 466 1010

Meat
China Kikar Tel Aviv
5005 Collins Avenue 33140
Telephone: (305) 866 3316

Giuliani's Café
3439 NE 163rd Street North Miami Beach
Telephone: (305) 940 8141

Kosher World
514 41st
Telephone: (305) 532 2263

Shalom Haifa
18533 W. Dixie Highway
Telephone: (305) 945 2884
Fax: (305) 936 1811

Subrific
1688 NE Street
Telephone: (305) 946 7811

Thai Treat
2176 123rd Street
Telephone: (305) 892 1118

The New Kosher World
1123 NE 163rd Street 33162
Telephone: (305) 944 7726

Wing Wan II
1640 N.E. 164 Street 33162
Telephone: (305) 945 3585

Pizzerias
Jerusalem Pizza
761 N.E. 167 Street 33162
Telephone: (305) 653 6662

Sarah's Kosher Pizza
2214 N.E. 123rd Street 33181
Telephone: (305) 891 3312

Sarah's Kosher Pizza
1127 N.E. 163 Street 33162
Telephone: (305) 948 7777

SYNAGOGUES
Orthodox
Young Israel of Greater Miami
990 N.E. 171st Street 33162

Young Israel of Sky Lake
1850 N.E. 183rd Street 33179
Telephone: (305) 945 8712/8715

Young Israel of Sunny Isles Beach
17395 North Bay Road, Sunny Isles Beach 33160
Telephone: (305) 935 9095
Fax: (305) 692 1600
Email: YoungIsraelofsib@bellsouth.net
Website: www.youngisraelsib.com

PINECREST
Young Israel of Kendall
7880 SW 112th Street 33156
Telephone: 232 6833
Fax: 232 6418
Email: yikendall@aol.com

Monroe County

KEY WEST
Conservative
B'nai Zion
750 United Street 33040 3251
Telephone: (305) 294 3437

Orange County

ORLANDO
COMMUNITY ORGANISATIONS
Jewish Federation of Greater Orlando
851 N. Maitland Avenue, Maitland 32751
Telephone: (407) 645 5933
Fax: (407) 645 1172

DELICATESSEN
Market Place Deli, Hyatt Orlando
6375 W. Bronson Highway
Telephone: (407) 396 1234

GROCERIES
Amira's Catering and Speciality
1351 E. Altamonte, Altamonte Springs
Telephone: (407) 767 7577

HOTELS
Quality Inn Kosher Hotel
4944 W. 192 Orlando Kissimmee 34746
Telephone: (407) 787 3400
Fax: (407) 397 1116
Website: www.kosherinflorida.com

MIKVAOT
Mikvah Yisrael
708 Lake Howell Road 32751
Telephone: (407) 644 2362
Fax: (407) 644 0545
Email: devorahleah@aol.com
Central organisation: Chabad of Greater Orlando

RESTAURANTS
Glatt Kosher
The Lower East Side Restaurant & Shul
8548 Palm Parkway , Lake Buena Vista 32836
Telephone: (407) 465 0565
Fax: (407) 238 6427
Mobile Phone: 407 230 8721
Email: orlandoisus@earthlink.net
Website: www.kosherorlando.com
Supervision: Orthodox Rabbinical Vaad ORV of central Florida
Hotels and Villas with Food Package,Shul, dine-in, take out, conventions. open all year, special Shabbos Programs.

SYNAGOGUES
Conservative
Congregation Beth Shalom
13th & Center Streets, Leesburg 32748
Telephone: (407) 742 0238

Congregation Ohev Shalom
5015 Goddard Avenue 32804
Telephone: (407) 298 4650

Congregation Shalom (Williamsburg)
11821 Soccer Lane, c/o Sydney Ansell 32821-7952

Congregation Shalom Aleichem
PO Box 424211, Kissimmee 34742 4211

Southwest Orlando Jewish Congregation
11200 S. Apopka- Vineland Road 32836
Website: www.sojc-orlando.org

Temple Israel
4917 Eli Street 32804
Telephone: 647 3055

Orthodox
Congregation Ahavas Yisrael/Chabad
708 Lake Howell Road, Maitland 32751
Telephone: (407) 644 2500
Fax: (866) 379 4913
Email: rabbidubov@aol.com
Website: www.chabadorlando.com
Supervision: RCF

Reform
Congregation of Liberal Judaism
928 Malone Drive 32810
Telephone: (407) 645 6444
Fax: (407) 645 3368
Website: www.crjorlando.org
Supervision: RCF

Palm Beach County

BOCA RATON
COMMUNITY ORGANISATIONS
Jewish Federation of South Palm Beach County
9901 Donna Klein Boulevard 33428 1788
Telephone: (561) 852 3100

JUDAICA
Holyland Judaica
Del Mar Shopping Village, 7080 Beracasa Way
Telephone: (561) 367 8277

MIKVAOT
Boca Raton Synagogue
7900 Montoya Circle 33433
Telephone: (561) 394 5854

RESTAURANTS
Dairy
Campus Café
Cultural Arts Building, 9801 Donna Klein
Boulevard 33428 1788
Telephone: (561) 852 3200 ext. 4103
Supervision: Jewish Federation of South Pam Beach Coun

Eilat Café
6853 SW 18th Street, Wharfside Shopping Center 33428 1788
Telephone: (561) 368 6880

Jon's Place
22191 Powerline Road (outhwest corner Palmetto & Powerline
Telephone: (561) 338 0008

My Favourite Café
3369 Sheridan Street
Telephone: (561) 965 0111

Meat
Café Haifa
2901 N. Federal Highway 33431
Telephone: (561) 955 8500

City Grill
Delmar Shopping Village, 7158 N. Beracasa Way 33434
Telephone: (561) 417 8936

Jerusalem
8255 International Drive
Telephone: (561) 248 9494
Website: www.jerusalemglatt.com
Supervision: Rabbi Konig

Jerusalem Grill
19635 US Highway 411, Boca Plaza Greens 33428
Telephone: (561) 470 1120

Sagi's Falafel Armon
22767 State Road 7 33428
Telephone: (561) 477 0633

RESTAURANTS AND DELICATESSEN
Ben's Kosher Delicatessen
9942 Clint Moore Road 33496
Telephone: (561) 470 9963
Fax: (561) 470 4963
Email: info@bensdeli.net
Website: www.bensdeli.net
Supervision: Supervised

SYNAGOGUES
Conservative
Beth Ami Congregation
1401 N.W. 4th Avenue 33432
Telephone: (561) 347 0031
Fax: (561) 393 5326
Email: bethamicong@aol.com

Orthodox
Boca Raton Synagogue
7900 Montoya Circle 33433
Telephone: (561) 394 5732
Fax: (561) 394 0180
Website: www.brsweb.org

Young Israel of Boca Raton
7200 Palmetto Circle North 33433
Telephone: (561) 391 3235
Fax: (561) 391 5509
Email: yiboca@bellsouth.net

Reform
Congregation B'nai Israel
2200 Yamato Road 33431
Telephone: (561) 241 8118

DELRAY BEACH
GROCERIES
Meat Market
Oriole Kosher Market, 7345 West Atlantic Avenue
33446

SYNAGOGUES
Conservative
Temple Anshei Shalom of West Delray
Oriole Jewish Center, 7099 W Atlantic Avenue
33446
Telephone: (561) 495 1300
Fax: (561) 498 9766

Temple Emeth
5780 W. Atlantic Avenue 33446

Orthodox
Anshei Emuna
16189 Jog Road 33446
Telephone: (561) 499 9229
Fax: (561) 637 9289
Supervision: Orthodox Union membership

Reform
Temple Sinai of Palm Beach County
2475 W. Atlantic Avenue 33445
Telephone: (561) 276 6161
Fax: (561) 276 3485
Website: www.TempleSinaiPBC.org

PALM BEACH
Conservative
Temple Emanu-el of Palm Beach
190 N. County Road 33480
Telephone: (561) 832 0804
Email: lisa@tepb.org

Orthodox
Palm Beach Synagogue
120 N. County Road, PO Box 1028 33480
Telephone: (561) 838 9002
Fax: (561) 838 5356
Email: pbsynagogue@bellsouth.net
Website: www.pbos.org

PALM CITY
Conservative
**Treasure Coast Jewish Center Congregation
Beth Abraham**
3998 S.W. Leighton Farms Avenue 34990
Telephone: (407) 287 8833

WEST PALM BEACH
COMMUNITY ORGANISATIONS
Jewish Federation of Palm Beach County
4601 Community Drive 33417
Telephone: (561) 478 0700
Fax: (561) 478 9696

Pinellas County
CLEARWATER
Jewish Federation of Pinellas County
13191 Starkey Road, Suite 8, Largo 33773 1438
Telephone: (727) 530 3223
Website: www.jfedpinellas.org

SYNAGOGUES
Conservative
Beth Shalom
1325 S. Belcher Road 33764
Telephone: (727) 531 1418
Fax: (727) 531 0798

Orthodox
Chabad Lubavitch Mada
1374 Druid Road 33756
Telephone: (727) 474 3663
Email: clearwaterjew@gmail.com

Reform
B'nai Israel
1685 S. Belcher Road 34624
Telephone: (727) 531 5829

Temple Ahavat Shalom
1575 Curlew Road, Palm Harbor 34683
Telephone: (727) 785 8811
Fax: (727) 785 8822

ST. PETERSBURG
DELICATESSEN
Jo-El's Delicatessen & Marketplace
2619 23rd Avenue N 33713
Telephone: (727) 321 3847
Fax: (727) 327 0682

GROCERIES
Jo-El's Specialty Foods
2619 23rd Avenue N. 33713
Telephone: (727) 321 3847
Fax: (727) 327 0682
Supervision: Rabbi Jacob Luski
All Kosher products

SYNAGOGUES
Conservative
Beth Shalom
1844 54th Street S. 33707
Telephone: (727) 3380

Congregation B'nai Israel of St. Petersburg
300 58th Street North 33710
Telephone: (727) 381 4900
Fax: (727) 344 1307
Email: rabbissec@cbistpete.org
Website: www.cbistpete.org

Reform
Temple Beth-El
400 Pasadena Avenue S. 33707
Telephone: (727) 347 6136
Fax: (727) 343 8982
Email: info@templebeth-el.com
Website: www.templebeth-el.com

Polk County
LAKELAND
Conservative
Temple Emanuel
600 Lake Hollingsworth Drive 33803
Telephone: (813) 682 8616

Sarasota County
SARASOTA
COMMUNITY ORGANISATIONS
Sarasota Manatee Jewish Federation
580 S. McIntosh Road 34232-1959
Telephone: (941) 371 4546
Fax: (941) 378 2947

SYNAGOGUES
Conservative
Temple Beth Shalom
1050 South Tuttle Avenue 34237
Telephone: (941) 955 8121

St. Johns County
ST AUGUSTINE
The First Congregation Sons of Israel
161 Cordova Street 43084

St. Lucie County
FORT PIERCE
Reform
Temple Beth El Israel
4600 Oleander Drive 34982
Telephone: (407) 461 7428

VOLUSIA COUNTY
DAYTONA BEACH
COMMUNITY ORGANISATIONS
Jewish Federation of Volusia & Flagler Counties
470 Andalusin Avenue, Ormond Beach 32174
Telephone: (904) 672 0294
Fax: (904) 673 1316

SYNAGOGUES
Conservative
Temple Israel
1400 S. Peninsula Drive 32118
Telephone: (386) 252 3097
Fax: (386)255 4333
Email: templeisraeloffice@cfl.rr.com

Reform
Temple Beth El
579 N. Nova Road, Ormond Beach 32174
Telephone: (904) 677 2484

Georgia
Chatham County
SAVANNAH
COMMUNITY ORGANISATIONS
Savannah Jewish Federation
5111 Abercorn Street 31405
Telephone: (912) 355 8111

Fax: (912) 355 8116
Email: sharon@savj.org
Website: www.savj.org

CONTACT INFORMATION
Rabbi Avigdor Slatus
5444 Abercorn Street 31405
Telephone: (912) 354 7721
Fax: (912) 354 9923
Email: bbjsynagogue@bellsouth.net
Website: www.bbjsynagogue

GUEST APARTMENTS
Buckingham South
5450 Abercorn Street 31405
Telephone: (912) 355 5550
Fax: (912) 353 7373
Supervision: Rabbi Avigdor Slatus

SYNAGOGUES
Conservative
Agudath Achim
9 Lee Boulevard. 31405
Telephone: (912) 352 4737
Fax: (912) 352 3477
Email: agudatha@aol.com
Website: agudath-achim.com

Orthodox
B'nai B'rith Jacob
5444 Abercorn Street 31405
Telephone: (912) 354 7721
Fax: (912) 354 9923
Email: bbjsynagogue@bellsouth.net
Website: www.bbjsynagogue.com

Reform
Mickve Israel
Bull & Gordon Streets 31401
Telephone: (912) 233 1547

Clarke County
ATHENS
Congregation Children of Israel
Dudley Drive 30606
Telephone: (404) 549 4192

Decatur County
DECATUR
RESTAURANTS
Meat
Twelve Oaks Barbecue
1451 Scot Boulevard.
Telephone: (404) 377 0120

Fulton County
ATLANTA
BED AND BREAKFAST
All Seasons Kosher Bed & Breakfast
1300 Carolyn Drive, Toco Hills 30329
Telephone: (404) 633 9560
Email: savtapaula@gmail.com
Located within the eruv and within walking distance of
Orthodox Synagogue or accessible by public transport.
Free parking. Indoor smoking restrictions apply. No pets
are allowed. For availability, rate information and
reservations contact PAULA 404 633 9560

COMMUNITY ORGANISATIONS
Jewish Federation
1753 Peachtree Road, NE 30309
Telephone: (404) 873 1661

EMBASSY
Consul General of Israel
Suite 440, 1100 Spring Street, NW 30309 2823

HOTELS
Bed & Breakfast Atlanta
1608 Briarcliff Road, Suite 5 30306
Telephone: (404) 875 0525
Website: www.bedandbreakfast.com

KASHRUT INFORMATION
Atlanta Kashrut Commission
1855 La Vista Road, N.E. 30329
Telephone: (404) 634 4063
Website: www.kosheratlanta.org
Orthodox

RESTAURANTS
Dairy
Wall Street Pizza
2470 Briarcliff Road 30329
Telephone: (404) 633 2111
Supervision: Atlanta Kasrut Commission

Glatt Kosher Chinese
Chai Peking
2205 La Vista Road, N.E. (inside Kroger) 30329
Telephone: (404) 327 7810
Fax: (404) 634 7848
Website: www.chaipeking.com
Supervision: Atlanta Kasrut Commission

Meat
Off Broadway Restaurant
Off Broadway, 2166 Briarcliff Road 30329
Telephone: (404) 633 9288; 329 0888
Mobile Phone: (404) 663-0228
Website: www.bijancatering.com
Supervision: Atlanta Kasrut Commission
Catering - hotel delivery (770) 457 4578

Vegetarian
Broadway Café
2168 Briarcliff Road, off Broadway 30329
Telephone: (404) 329 0888
Fax: (404) 329 9888
Supervision: Atlanta Kasrut Commission
Vegetarian and dairy specialities. Glatt kosher full service dining, wine and beer.

SYNAGOGUES
Conservative
Ahavath Achim
600 Peachtree Battle Avenue 30327
Telephone: (404) 355 5222
Fax: (404) 352 2831
Website: www.aasynagogue.org
Supervision: USCJ

Orthodox
Anshi S'Fard
1324 North Highland Avenue, N.E. 30306
Telephone: (404) 874 4513

Congregation Beth Jacob
1855 La Vista Road NE 30329
Telephone: (404) 633 0551
Fax: (404) 320 7912
Email: admin@bethjacobatlanta.org
Website: www.bethjacobatlanta.org
Beth Jacob's mission is to follow and teach Orthodox Judaism in an environment of acceptance, warmth and mutual respect so that all Jews can grow and practise at their own pace.

Young Israel of Toco Hills
2074 La Vista Road, Toco Hills 30329
Telephone: (404) 315 1417
Fax: (404) 315 1433
Email: yitocohills@gmail.com
Website: www.yith.org

Reform
Temple Sinai
5645 Dupree Drive, N.W. 30327
Telephone: (404) 252 3073

The Temple
1589 Peachtree Road
Telephone: (404) 873 1731

Sephardi
Ner Hamizrach
1858 La Vista Road, N.E. 30329
Telephone: (404) 315 9020

Macon County
MACON
Conservative
Sha'arey Israel
611 First Street 31201
Telephone: (478) 745 4571
Fax: (478) 745 5892
Website: www.csimacon.org

Reform
Beth Israel
892 Cherry street 31201
Telephone: (478) 745 6727

Muscogee County
COLUMBUS
Conservative
Shearith Israel
2550 Wynnton Road 31906
Telephone: (706) 323 1443

Reform
Temple Israel
1617 Wildwood Avenue 31906
Telephone: (706) 323 1617
Website: www.ga003.urj.net

Richmond County
AUGUSTA
BAKERIES
Sunshine Bakery
1209 Broad Street 30902

DELICATESSEN
Parti-Pal
Daniel Village 30904

Strauss
965 Broad Street 30902

SYNAGOGUES
Orthodox
Adas Yeshuron
935 Johns Road, Walton Way 30904
Telephone: (404) 733 9491

Illinois
BUFFALO GROVE
BAKERIES
Kosher
Shalom Bakery
1165 N Arlington Heights Drive
Telephone: (847) 808 9300
Fax: (847) 808 8403
Supervision: CRC
Hours: Mon to thu 6am to 6pm; Fri 6am to 2 hours before Shabbat. Closed Shabbat

CONFECTIONERY
Long Grove Confectionery Co.
333 Lexington Drive 60089
Telephone: (847) 459 3100
Supervision: CRC
Hours: Mon to Sat 9.30am to 5.30pm; Sun 11am to 4pm

EVANSTON

RESTAURANTS

Chinese-Kosher

Tein Li Chow
2485 Howard
Telephone: (847) 328 4642
Fax: (847) 328 5957
Supervision: OU/CRC
Hours: Sun to Thu 11am to 9pm; Fri 10am to 3pm. Closed
Shabbat

Take-Away
Now We're Cookin' Grill
710 Central Street 60035
Telephone: (847) 432 7310

Champaign County
CHAMPAIGN-URBANA

COMMUNITY ORGANISATIONS
Champaign-Urbana Jewish Federation
503 E. John Street 61820
Telephone: (217) 367 9872
Email: cujf@shalomcu.org
Website: www.shalomcu.org

SYNAGOGUES

Reform
Sinai Temple
3104 Wndsor Road 61821
Telephone: (217) 352 8140

Cook County
CHICAGO

BAKERIES
North Shore Bakery
2919 w Touhy Avenue 60645
Telephone: (773) 262 0600
Fax: (773) 262 3641
Supervision: crc
Hours: Sun 6am to 4pm; Mon to Wed 6am to 6pm; Thu
6am to 7pm; Fri 6am to 1½ before Shabbat. Closed
Shabbat.

Tel Aviv Kosher Bakery
2944 W Devon Avenue 60659
Telephone: (773) 764 8877
Fax: (773) 764 8854
Supervision: OU
Hours: Sun to Wed 6am to 6pm; Thu 6am to 8pm; Fri 6am
to 1hour before Shabbat. Closed Shabbat.

BUTCHERS
Argyle Kosher Meat Market
4465 W Lawrence 60630
Telephone: (773) 794 0303
Supervision: Rabbi H Gross
Hours Sun to Thu 8am to 6pm; Fri 8am to sundown.
Closed Shabbat

Ebner's Kosher Meat Market
2649 W Devon Avenue 60659
Telephone: (773) 274 0430; 764 1446
Supervision: Rabbi H Gross
Hours: Mon to Thu 7am to 5pm; Fri 7am to 2pm. Closed
Shabbat and Sun.

Good Morgan Fish
2948 W Devon Avenue 60659
Telephone: (773) 764 8115
Supervision: CRC
Hours: Sun 8am to 2pm; Mon to Thu 8am to 8pm; Fri 8am
to 2pm. Closed Shabbat.

Robert's Fish on Devon
2916 W Devon Avenue 60659
Telephone: (773) 761 3424
Supervision: CRC
Hours: Mon to Thu 7am to 5pm; Fri 7am to 2pm. Closed
Shabbat and Sunday.

BOOKSELLERS
Chicago Hebrew Book Store
2942 W. Devon 60659
Telephone: (312) 973 6636
Fax: (312) 973 6465

Rosenblum's World of Judaica, Inc.
2906 W. Devon Avenue 60659
Telephone: (773) 262 1700
Fax: (773) 262 1930
Email: avi@alljudaica.com
Website: www.alljudaica.com
Toll free 800 626 6536

Spertus Shop
Spertus Institute of Jewish Studies, 610 S.
Michigan Avenue 60605
Telephone: (312) 322 1768 Toll Free 888 322 1740
Fax: (312) 913 0083
Email: bariff_shop@spertus.edu
Website: www.spertus.edu

DELICATESSEN
Best's Kosher Outlet Store
1000 W Pershing Road 60609
Telephone: (773) 650 6338
Fax: (773) 650 9046
Website: www. bestkosherfoods.com
Supervision: Rabbi H Small & Rabbi H Kaufman
Hours: Sun 8am to 3pm; Mon to Thu 7am to 5pm; Fri 7am
to before Shabbat. Closed Shabbat.

Kol Tuv Kosher Foods
2938 W Devon Avenue 60659
Telephone: (773) 764 1800
Fax: (773) 764 0130
Supervision: Mosdos Machzikei hadas
Hours: Sun 9am to 7pm;Mon to Wed 8am to 9pm; Thu
8am to 11pm; Fri 8am to 2 hours before Shabbat. Closed
Shabbat

Moshe's New York Kosher
2900 W Devon Avenue 60659
Telephone: (773) 338 3354
Fax: (773) 338 9010
Supervision: CRC
Hours: Sun 8am to 6pm; Mon to thu 9am to 7pm; Fri 8am to 2 hours before Shabbat. Shabbat closed.

Romanian Kosher Sausage
7200 N. Clark 60626
Telephone: (773) 761 4141
Supervision: Orthodox Union

EMBASSY
Consul General of Israel
Suite 1308, 111 East Wacker Drive 60601

MIKVAOT
Bnei Ruven
6350, N. Whipple 60659
Telephone: (312) 743 4282

MUSEUMS
Spertus Museum
Spertus Institute of Jewish Studies , 610 S. Michigan Avenue 60605
Telephone: (312) 322 1747
Fax: (312) 922 3934
Email: musm@spertus.edu
Website: www.spertus.edu
Housed in a newly completed revolutionary, environmentally-sustainable building.Highlights include a series of special changing exhibitions, and an interactive Children's Center. There is a kosher cafe and a gift and bookshop. Wireless Internet available throughout the building. Public programming includes lectures, performance, comedy, and film. For hours, admission, parking, and program information, visit www.spertus.edu. Museum Hours: Sunday-Wednesday 10 am - 6 pm, Thursday 10 am - 7 pm, Friday 10 am - 3 pm. Closed Saturday, and public and Jewish holidays. Free museum admission for everyone every Tuesday from 10 am - 12 noon and every Thursday from 3 - 7 pm.

RESTAURANTS
Dairy
Jerusalem Kosher Restaurant
3014 W. Devon 60659
Telephone: (312) 262 0515
Supervision: OK

Dairy-Kosher
Tel Aviv Kosher Pizza & Dairy Restaurant
6349 N Carolina 60659
Telephone: (773) 764 3776
Supervision: CRC
Hours: Sun to Thu 11am to 11pm; Fri 11am to 2pm (4pm summer); Sat one hour after Shabbat until 1am.
Mexican, Israeli and vegetarian dishes.

Israeli -Kosher
Taboun Grill
6339 N Carolina
Telephone: (773) 381 2606
Supervision: CRC
Hours: Sun to Thu 11am to 11pm; Fri 11am to two hours before sundown; Sat two hours after sundown until midnight.

Meat
Great Chicago Food & Beverage Co.
3149 W. Devon 60659
Telephone: (312) 465 9030
Fax: (312) 465 9011
Email: gcfbken@aol.com
Supervision: Chicago Rabbinical Council

Mi Tsu Yun Kosher Chinese Restaurant
3010 W. Devon 60659
Telephone: (312) 262 4630
Fax: (312) 262 4835
Supervision: Chicago Rabbinical Council

Shallots
2324 N. Clark Street 60614
Telephone: (312) 755 5205
Website: www.shallots-chicago.com

SANDWICH BAR
Dairy-Kosher
B.B's Bagels
2835 W Touhy Avenue 60645
Telephone: (773) 761 8805
Fax: (773) 761 8807
Website: www.bbsbagels.com
Supervision: CRC
Hours: Sun 7.30am to 4pm; Mon to Thu 6.30am to 7pm; Fri 6.30am to 3 hours before Shabbat. Closed Shabbat.

Kosher
Bartlett Hall Food Court
University of Chicago, 5640 s University Street 60714
Telephone: (773) 834 8450
Supervision: CRC

SNACK BAR
Dairy-Kosher
Dunkin' Donuts
3132 W Devon Avenue 60659
Telephone: (773) 262 4561
Fax: (773) 262 4561
Supervision: CRC
Open 24 hours daily

SYNAGOGUES
Conservative
Anshe Emet Synagogue
3751 North Broadway 60613-4104
Telephone: (312) 281 1423
Fax: (312) 281 2813
Website: www.ansheemet.org

Orthodox
K.I.N.S. of West Rogers Park
2800 W. North Shore Avenue 60645
Telephone: (312) 761 4000
Fax: (312) 761 4959

Lake Shore Drive Synagogue
70 E. Elm Street 60611
Telephone: (312) 337 6811

Young Israel of Chicago
4931 North Kimball Street 60625
Telephone: (312) 338 6380

Young Israel of West Rogers Park
2706 West Touhy Avenue 60645
Telephone: (312) 743 9400
Email: youngisraelwrp@yahoo.com
Website: www.youngisraelwrpCentral
organisation: National Council of Young Israel
Traditional

Chicago Loop Synagogue
16 S. Clark Street 60603
Telephone: (312) 346 7370
Fax: (312) 346 9791
Website: www.chicagoloopsynagogue.org

NORTHBROOK
Orthodox
Young Israel of Northbrook
3545 Walters Road 60062
Telephone: (847) 480 9462
Fax: (847) 205 1967

SKOKIE
BAKERIES
Chaim's Kosher Bakery
4964 Dempster Street 60077
Telephone: (847) 675 1005
Fax: (847) 675 0028
Website: www.chaimkosher.com

Kosher
Breadsmith
3327 W Dempster 60076
Telephone: (847) 673 5001
Fax: (847) 673 5502
Supervision: CRC
Hours:Mon to Thu 7.30am to 7pm;Fri 7am to 5pm, 2pm
Autumn and Winter. Sun 8am to 5pm. Closed Shabbat.

CAFETERIA
Dairy-Kosher
Main Street Pizza and Ice Cream Bar
4209 Main Street
Telephone: (847) 568 9920
Supervision: CRC
Hours: Sun to Thu 11am to 8pm; Fri 11am to 2pm; Sat one
hour after Shabbat until midnight.

Italian-Kosher
Da'Nali's Cafe
4032 W Oakton 60076
Telephone: (847) 677 2782
Fax: (847) 677 2807
Website: www. danaliscafe.com
Central organisation: CRC
HoursSun Noon to 9pm; Mon to Thu 11am to 9pm; Fri
11am to 2pm; Shabbat one and a half hours after
sundown to 1am. Brick oven pizza and pasta.

CONFECTIONERY
Kosher
Zelda's Sweet Shoppe
4113 W Main Street 60076
Telephone: (847) 679 0033
Fax: (847) 679 0030
Website: www.zeldas.net
Supervision: CRC
Hours: Sun 11am to 4pm; Mon to Wed 10am to 6pm; Thu
10am to 8pm; Fri 8am to 5pm.

DELICATESSEN
Carvel
4041 W Dempster 60076
Telephone: (847) 675 8177
Supervision: CRC
Hours: Winter: Mon to Fri 2pm to 10pm; Sat 11am to
midnight; Sun 11am to 10pm. Summer: Mon to Fri 11am
to 11pm;Sat/Sun 11am to 1am.

Hungarian Kosher Foods
4020 W Oakton
Telephone: (847) 674 8008
Fax: (847) 674 6256
Supervision: CRC
Hours: Sun 8am to 6pm; Mon to Thu 8am to 9pm; Fri 8am
to 3pm. Closed Shabbat

Illinois Nut & Candy
3745 W Dempster 60076
Telephone: (847) 677 5777
Website: www.illinoisnut.com
Supervision: CRC
Hours: Sun 11am to 3pm; Mon to Fri 9am to 6pm, until
1½ before Shabbat in the winter. Closed Shabbat.

Webkosher
7324 N Lawndale 60076
Telephone: (847) 932 5674
Website: www.webkosher.com
Delivers certified kosher food to your door.

JUDAICA
Hamakor Gallery Ltd.
4150 Dempster Street 60076
Telephone: (847) 677 4150
Fax: (847) 677 4160
Email: gallery@jewishsource.com
Website: www.jewishsource.com

KOSHER FOOD
Dairy
Malibu Pizza and Pasta
3355 W. Dempster 60076
Telephone: (847) 675 2847
Email: gcfbken@aol.com
Supervision: Cholov Yisroel under the cRc
Live music and a "Girls night out" every month

MEDIA
Newspapers
Chicago Jewish Star
PO Box 268 60076
Telephone: (847) 674 7827
Fax: (847) 674 0014
Email: chicago-jewish-star@mcimail.com

RESTAURANTS
Dairy
Bagel Country
9306 Skokie Boulevard. 60077
Telephone: (847) 673 3030
Fax: (847) 673 4040
Supervision: Chicago Rabbinical Counci

Da'Nali's
4032 W. Oakton 60076
Telephone: (847) 677 2782
Supervision: Chicago Rabbinical Council

Italian-Kosher
Slice of Life
4120 W Dempster 60076
Telephone: (847) 674 2021
Fax: (847) 674 2036
Supervision: CRC
Hours Sun 10.30am to 9pm; Mon to Thu 11.30am to 9pm;
Fri 11.30am to 3pm (2pm in the winter). Sat half hour
after Shabbat until 12.30am

Meat
Hy Life
4120 W. Dempster, Skokie 60076
Telephone: (847) 674 2021
Supervision: Chicago Rabbinical Council

Ken's Diner
3353 W. Dempster 60076
Telephone: (847) 679 4030
Fax: (847) 679 0687
Email: gcfbken@aol.com
Supervision: Chicago Rabbinical Council
A 1950's Diner. All Glatt Kosher

Meat-Kosher
Hy Life Bistro
4120 W Dempster 60076
Telephone: (847) 674 2021
Supervision: CRC
Hours: Sun toThu 5pm to 9pm

Ken's Diner
3353 W Dempster
Telephone: (847) 679 2850
Website: www.kensdiner.com
Supervision: CRC
Hours: Sun to Thu 11am to 9pm; Fri 11am to 2pm. Closed
Shabbat

Shallotts Bistro
4741 Main Street 60076
Telephone: (847) 677 DINE
Fax: (847) 677 3420
Supervision: CRC
Hours: Mon to Thu 12pm to 2pm for lunch, 5pm to
8.30pm for dinner. Open Sat nights in the winter.

Vegetarian
Mysore Woodlands
2548 Devon Avenue 60659
Telephone: (847) 338 8160
Fax: (847) 338 8162
Supervision: CKA

SANDWICH BAR
Dairy-Kosher
Bagel Country
9306 N Skokie Boulevard 60077
Telephone: (847) 673 3030
Fax: (847) 673 4040
Website: www.bagelcountry.com
Supervision: CRC
Hours: Sun 7am to 7.30pm; Mon to Thu 6.30am to
7.30pm; Fri 6.30am to 2pm (2.30pm Summer). Open Sat
nights in the fall.

Meat-Kosher
The Sandwich Club
4507 W Oakton 60076
Telephone: (847) 677 6020
Fax: (847) 677 5692
Supervision: CRC
Hours: Sun to Thu 11am to 8pm; Fri 11am to 2pm. Closed
Shabbat

SYNAGOGUES
Orthodox
Young Israel of Skokie
3740 W. Dempster 60076
Telephone: (847) 329 0990

Lake County
HIGHLAND PARK
BAKERIES
Kosher
Breadsmith
664 Central Avenue 60035
Telephone: (847) 432 3330
Supervision: CRC
Hours: Mon to Fri 7am to 5.30pm; closed Shabbat and
Sunday.

BUTCHERS
Kosher Marketplace at Jewel
1600 Deerfield Road 60035
Telephone: (847) 579 0872
Supervision: OU Mashgiach Tmidei. Hours: Sun to Wed
8am to 8pm
Kosher deli and meat/fish dept.
Hours: Sun to Wed 8am to 8pm; Thu 8am to 9pm; Fri 7am
to to 3 hrs before Shabbat. Closed Shabbat

Shaevitz Kosher Meats and Deli
712 Central Avenue 60035
Telephone: (847) 432 8334
Supervision: Rabbi H Gross
Hours: Sun 8.30am to 4pm; Mon to Thu 8.30am to 6pm;
Fri 8.so am to 3pm. Closed Shabbat.

DELICATESSEN
Now We're Cooking Grill
710 Central 60035
Telephone: (847) 432 7310
Supervision: Chicago Kashrut Association Inc.

SYNAGOGUES
Conservative
North Surburban Synagogue Beth El
1175 Sheridan Road 60035
Telephone: (847) 432 8900
Website: www.nssbethel.org

Peoria County
PEORIA
Orthodox
Agudas Achim
5614 North University Street 61614
Telephone: (309) 692 4849
Fax: (309) 692 7255

Reform
Anshai Emeth
5614 North University Street 61614
Telephone: (309) 691 3323

Rock Island County
ROCK ISLAND
COMMUNITY ORGANISATIONS
Jewish Federation of the Quad Cities
209 18th Street 61201
Telephone: (309) 793 1300
Fax: (309) 793 1345

Sangamon County
SPRINGFIELD
SYNAGOGUES
Conservative
Temple Israel
1140 West Governor Street 62704

Telephone: (217) 546 2841
Fax: (217) 726 9857
Email: temple-israel@sbcglobal.net
www.shalomspringfield.org/community/Israel.html

Winnebago County
ROCKFORD
COMMUNITY ORGANISATIONS
Jewish Federation of Greater Rockford
1500 Parkview Avenue 61107
Telephone: (815) 399 5497

SYNAGOGUES
Conservative
Ohave Sholom
3730 Guildford Road 61107
Telephone: (815) 226 4900

Reform
Temple Beth El
1203 Comanche Drive 61107
Telephone: (815) 398 5020

Indiana
Allen County
FORT WAYNE
Conservative
B'nai Jacob
7227 Bittersweet Moors Drive 46814
Telephone: (219) 672 8459

Reform
Congregation Achduth Vesholom
5200 Old Mill Road 46807
Telephone: (219) 260 744 4245
Fax: (219) 260 744 4246
Email: office@templecav.org
Website: www.templecav.org

Delaware County
MUNCIE
Temple Beth El
525 W. Jackson Street, cnr. Council Street 47305
Telephone: (765) 288 4662
Website: www.soalafayette.org

Greene County
HIGHLAND
COMMUNITY ORGANISATIONS
Jewish Federation of North West Indiana
2939 Jewett Street, Highland 48322-3005
Telephone: (219) 661 0840

Lake County
EAST CHICAGO
SYNAGOGUES
Orthodox
B'nai Israel
3517 Hemlock Street 46312

GARY
Reform
Temple Israel
601 N. Montgomery Street 46403
Telephone: (219) 938 5232

HAMMOND
Temple Beth-El
6947 Hohman Avenue 46324
Telephone: (219) 932 3754

Conservative
Beth Israel
7105 Hohman Avenue 46324
Telephone: (219) 931 1312

WHITING
Orthodox
B'nai Judah
116th Street & Davis Avenue 46394
Telephone: (219) 659 0797

LaPorte County
MICHIGAN CITY
Reform
Sinai Temple
2800 S. Franklin Street 46360
Telephone: (219) 874 4477
Fax: (219) 874 4190
Email: sinaitemple@sbcglobal.net

Marion County
INDIANAPOLIS
COMMUNITY ORGANISATIONS
Jewish Federation of Greater Indianapolis
6705 Hoover Road 70002-4826
Telephone: (317) 888 2209

SYNAGOGUES
Conservative
Congregation Shaarey Tefilla
5879 Central Avenue 46220-2509
Telephone: (317) 253 4591
Website: www.shaareytefilla.org
Tot Shabbat services are held on the first Friday evening
of each month and monthly Friday Night Live or Saturday
Morning Awake, family orientated services led by our
elementary school aged children.

Conservative/Reconstructionist
Beth-El Zedek
600 W. 70th Street 46260
Telephone: (317) 253 3441
Website: www.bez613.org

Orthodox
B'nai Torah
6510 Hoover Road 46260
Telephone: (317) 253 5253
Fax: (317) 253 5459

Etz Chaim Sephardic Congregation
6939 Hoover Road 46260
Telephone: (317) 251 6220
Website: www.etzchaimindy.org

Reform
Indianapolis Hebrew Congregation
6501 N. Meridian Street 46260
Telephone: (317) 255 6647

Monroe County
BLOOMINGTON
Orthodox
Chabad House
516 E. 17th Street 47408
Telephone: (8112) 332 6784

Reform
Congregation Beth Shalom
3750 E. Third 47401
Telephone: (8112) 334 2440

Porter County
VALPARAISO
Conservative
Temple Israel
Po Box 2051 46383

St. Joseph County
SOUTH BEND
COMMUNITY ORGANISATIONS
Jewish Federation of St. Joseph Valley
3202 Shalom Way 46615
Telephone: (574) 233 1164
Fax: (574) 288 4103
Email: dbartongrant@thejewishfed.org
Website: www.thejewishfed.org

CONTACT INFORMATION
Rabbi Y. Gettinger
Hebrew Orthodox Congregation, 3207 S. High
Street 46614
Telephone: (574) 291 4239
Fax: (574) 291 9490

KASHRUT INFORMATION
Hebrew Orthodox Congregation
3207 S. High Street 46614
Telephone: (574) 291 4239
Fax: (574) 291 9490
Rabbi Yisrael Gettinger

SYNAGOGUES
Conservative
Sinai
1102 E. Laselle Street 46617
Telephone: (574) 234 8584
Fax: (574) 234 6856
Website: www.uscj.org/midwest/southbend

Orthodox
Hebrew Orthodox Congregation
3207 S. High Street 46614
Telephone: (574) 291 4239
Fax: (574) 291 9490

Reform
Beth El
305 W. Madison Street 46601
Telephone: (574) 234 4402

Tippecanoe County
LAFAYETTE
Orthodox
Sons of Abraham
661 N. 7th Street 47901
Telephone: (317) 742 2113

WEST LAFAYETTE
Reform
Synagogue West Lafayette
620 Cumberland Street 47906
Telephone: (765) 463 3455
Fax: (765) 463 4650

Vanderburgh County
EVANSVILLE
Conservative
Temple Adath B'nai Israel
3600 E. Washington Avenue 47715
Telephone: (812) 477 1577
Fax: (812) 477 1577
Email: tabi@evansville.net

Vigo County
TERRE HAUTE
DELICATESSEN
Kosher Meats & Sandwiches
410 W. Western Avenue 71301
Telephone: (812) 445 9367
Fax: (812) 445 9369

Iowa
Allamakee County
POSTVILLE
SYNAGOGUES
Orthodox
Synagogue Postville
440 South Lawlor Street
Telephone: (319) 863 3013

Des Moines County
DES MOINES
COMMUNITY ORGANISATIONS
Jewish Federation of Greater Des Moines
910 Polk Boulevard 50312
Telephone: (515) 277 6321
Fax: (515) 277 4069
Email: jcrc@dmjfed.org
Website: jewishdesmoines.org

DELICATESSEN
The Nosh
800 First Street 70898
Telephone: (515) 291 5895

SYNAGOGUES
Conservative
Tifereth Israel
924 Polk Boulevard. 50312
Telephone: (515) 255 1137

Orthodox
Beth El Jacob
954 Cummins Parkway 50312
Telephone: (515) 274 1551
Website: www.betheljacob.org

Reform
Temple B'nai Jeshurun
5101 Grand Avenue 50312
Telephone: (515) 274 4679
Fax: (515) 274 2072
Website: www.templebnaijeshurun.org

Dubuque County
DUBUQUE
Beth El
475 W. Locust Street 52001
Telephone: (563) 583 3483

Johnson County
IOWA CITY
Conservative & Reform
Agudas Achim Congregation
602 E. Washington Street 52240
Telephone: (319) 337 3813
Fax: (319) 337 6764

Email: jennifer@agudasachimic.org
Website: www.agudasachimic.org

Linn County
CEDAR RAPIDS
Reform
Temple Judah
3221 Lindsay Lane S.E. 52403
Telephone: (319) 362 1261

Scott County
DAVENPORT
Temple Emanuel
12th Street & Mississippi Avenue 52803

Webster County
FORT DODGE
Conservative
Fort Dodge Conservative Synagogue
501 N. 12th Street 50501
Telephone: (515) 572 8925

Woodbury County
SIOUX CITY
Congregation Beth Shalom
815 38th Street 51104
Telephone: (712) 255 1990
Fax: (712) 258 0619

Orthodox
United Orthodox
Nebraska & 14th Street 51105
Telephone: (712) 255 4455

Kansas
Douglas County
LAWRENCE
Lawrence Jewish Community Center
917 Highland Drive 66046
Telephone: (785) 841 7636
Email: ljcc@sunflower.com
Website: www.lawrencejcc.org

Johnson County
OVERLAND PARK
BUTCHERS
Jacobsons Strictly Kosher Foods
5200 West 95th Street 70115
Telephone: (913) 897 8246

MEDIA
Newspapers
Kansas City Jewish Chronicle
7373 W 107th Street 66212
Telephone: (913) 648 4620

Email: chronicle@sunpublications.com
Website: www.kcjc.com

SYNAGOGUES
Congregation Beth Shalom
14200 Lamar Avenue 66223
Telephone: (913) 647 7279
Website: www.bethshalomkc.org

Orthodox
Congregation Beth Israel Abraham & Voliner
9900 Antioch 66212
Telephone: (913) 341 2444
Fax: (913) 341 2467
Kehilath Israel Synagogue
10501 Conser 66212
Telephone: (913) 642 1880
Fax: (913) 642 7332

Reform
Congregation Beth Torah
6100 W. 127th Street 66209
Telephone: (913) 498 2212

PRAIRE VILLAGE
Conservative
Ohev Sholom
5311 W. 75th Street 66208
Telephone: (913) 642 6460
Fax: (913) 385 9962
Email: rabbiscott@sbcglobal.net

Sedgwick County
WICHITA
GROCERIES
Dillon's
21st Street & Rock Road 70002
Telephone: (316) 828 2125
Fax: (316) 828 2827
Dillon's
13th Street & Woodlawn Street 70002
Telephone: (316) 888 2010
Fax: (316) 888 2014
Website: www.koshercajun.com
Foodbarn
Woodlawn & Central Streets 68154
Telephone: (316) 334 8200
The Bread Lady
20205 Rock Road, Suite 80 67208
SYNAGOGUES
Reform
Congregation Emanu-El
7011 E. Central Street 67206
Telephone: (316) 685 5148

Traditional
Hebrew Congregation
1850 N. Woodlawn 67208
Telephone: (316) 685 1339

Shawnee County
TOPEKA
COMMUNITY ORGANISATIONS
Topeka Lawrence Jewish Federation
4200 Munson Street 70002
Telephone: (785) 828 2125
Fax: (785) 828 2827

SYNAGOGUES
Reform
Temple Beth Sholom
4200 SW Munson Avenue 66604-1879
Telephone: (785) 272 6040
Fax: (785) 272 1565
Email: pmf4200@aol.com
Website: www.templebethsholomtopeka.org

Kentucky
Fayette County
LEXINGTON
COMMUNITY ORGANISATIONS
Central Kentucky Jewish Federation
1050 Chinoe Road, #302 40502
Telephone: (859) 268 0672
Fax: (859) 268 0775
Email: ckjf@jewishlexington.org
Website: www.jewishlexington.org

SYNAGOGUES
Conservative
Lexington Havurah
685 Shasta Circle 40503
Telephone: (859) 223 1299

Ohavay Zion
2048 Edgewater Ct. 40502
Telephone: (859) 266 8050
Fax: (859) 268 3357
Email: ozslex@windstream.net
Website: www.ozs.org

Reform
Adath Israel
124 N. Ashland Avenue 40502
Telephone: (859) 269 2979
Fax: (859) 269 7347

Jefferson County
LOUISVILLE
COMMUNITY ORGANISATIONS
Jewish Community Federation
3630 Dutchmans Lane 40205
Telephone: (502) 451 8840

Fax: (502) 458 0702
Email: jfed@iglou.com
Website: www.jewishlouisville.org
We publish an annual "Guide to Jewish Louisville" that is available free upon request. It includes detailed information about all aspects of our Jewish community. We also publish a bi-weekly newspaper, "Community", and every four weeks, we publish "The Silver Lining" for seniors.

SYNAGOGUES
Conservative
Adath Jeshurun
2401 Woodbourne Avenue 40205
Telephone: (502) 458 5359
Fax: (502) 451 5634
Website: www.adathjeshurun.com

Knesseth Israel
2531 Taylorsville Road 40205
Telephone: (502) 459 2780

Orthodox
Anshei Sfard
3700 Dutchman's Lane 40205
Telephone: (502) 451 3122
Fax: (502) 451 3123
Website: www.ansheisfard.com

Reform
Temple Shalom
4615 Lowe Road 40220
Telephone: (502) 458 4739
Fax: (502) 451 9750
Email: rsmiles@pipeline.com
Central organisation: Union for Reform Judaism
The Temple
5101 Brownsboro Road 40241
Telephone: (502) 423 1818
Website: www.uahcweb.org/ky/thetemple

McCracken County
PADUCAH
Temple Israel
330 Joe Clifton Drive, PO Box 1141 42001
Telephone: 442 4104

Louisiana
Caddo Parish
SHREVEPORT
Conservative
Agudath Achim
9401 Village Green Drive 71115
Telephone: (318) 797 6401
Fax: (318) 797 6402

Reform
B'nai Zion
245 Southfield Road 71105
Telephone: (318) 861 2122

East Baton Rouge Parish
BATON ROUGE
COMMUNITY ORGANISATIONS
Jewish Federation of Greater Baton Rouge
PO Box 80827 66207
Telephone: (504) 648 3880

SYNAGOGUES
Reform
B'nai Israel
3354 Kleinert Avenue 70806
Telephone: (504) 343 0111
Beth Shalom
9111 Jefferson Highway 70809
Telephone: (504) 924 6773

Lafayette County
LAFAYETTE
Temple Sholom
603 Lee Avenue, PO Box 53711 70505
Telephone: (317) 234 3760

Orleans County
NEW ORLEANS
COMMUNITY ORGANISATIONS
Jewish Federation of Greater New Orleans
3500 N. Causeway Boulevard., Suite 1240,
Metairie 66204

DELICATESSEN
Kosher Cajun Deli & Grocery
3519 Severn Street, Metairie or 3520 N. Hullen
Street, Metairie 70002
Telephone: (504) 888 2010
Fax: (504) 888 2014
Website: www.koshercajun.com
Supervision: Louisianna Kashrut Committee

GROCERIES
Touro Infirmary
1401 Foucher Street 63146

MEDIA
Newspapers
The Jewish News
Goldring-Woldenberg Jewish Community Campus,
Harry & Jeanette Weinberg Building, 3747 West
Esplanade Avenue, Metairie 70002
Telephone: (504) 780 5614
Fax: (504) 780 5601

MIKVAOT
Beth Israel
7000 Canal Boulevard. 64114

Chabad of Louisiana
7037 Freret Street 70118
Telephone: (504) 866 5164
Fax: (504) 861 7709
Email: info@chabadneworleans.com
Website: www.chabadneworleans.com

RESTAURANTS
Kosher
Casablanca
3030 Seven Avenue, Metairie 70002
Telephone: (504) 888 2209
Fax: (504) 888 5605
Email: casa3030@aol.com
Website: www.kosherneworleans.com
We are the only kosher fine dining restaurant in the state
of Louisiana. We specialize in Moroccan & Middle Eastern
Cuisine.

Meat
Casablanca
3030 Severn Avenue, Metairie
Telephone: (504) 888 2209
Fax: (504) 888 5605
Website: www.kosherneworleans.com
Supervision: Lubavitch Shechita & Chabad

Creole Kosher Kitchen
115 Chartres Street
Telephone: (504) 529 4120
Supervision: Beth Israel Congregation

SYNAGOGUES
Orthodox
Anshe Sfard
2230 Carondelet Street 70130
Telephone: (504) 522 4714
Website: www.anshesfard.com

Chabad House (Chabad of Louisiana)
7037 Freret Street 70118
Telephone: (504) 866 5164
Fax: (504) 861 7709
Email: info@chabadneworleans.com
Website: www.chabadneworleans.com/tourist

Rapides County
ALEXANDRIA
CONTACT INFORMATION
Jewish Welfare Federation
Telephone: (318) 445 9367

GROCERIES
Home Hospitality
Dr & Mrs B Kaplan
100 Park Place 71301
Telephone: (318) 445 9367
Fax: (318) 445 9369
Mobile Phone: 318 730 0337
Email: judithkaplan@cox.net

LIBRARIES
Meyer Kaplan Memorial Library (Judiaca)
c/o B'nai Israel, 1908 Vance Street 66604
Telephone: (318) 445 9367

SYNAGOGUES
Reform
Gemiluth Chassodim
2021 Turner Street 71301
Telephone: (318) 445 3655

Traditional
B'nai Israel
100 Park Place 71301
Telephone: (318) 445 9367
Mailing Address: c/o Meyer Kaplan, 211 Fourth Street
~30119 Alexandria, Louisianna, 71301

Maine
Androscoggin County
AUBURN
COMMUNITY ORGANISATIONS
Lewiston Auburn Jewish Federation
74 Bradman Street 04210
Telephone: (207) 786 4201
Fax: (207) 786 4202
Email: temple6359@aol.com

SYNAGOGUES
Conservative
Congregation Beth Abraham
Main Street & Laurel Avenue 04210
Telephone: (207) 783 1302

Temple Shalom
74 Bradman Street 04210
Telephone: (207) 786 4201
Fax: (207) 786 4202
Email: temple6359@aol.com

Cumberland County
PORTLAND
BUTCHERS
Penny Wise Super Market
182 Ocean Avenue 55812
Telephone: (503) 724 8857

COMMUNITY ORGANISATIONS
Jewish Fed.-Com. Council of Southern Maine
57 Ashmont Street 55907
Telephone: (503) 288 7500

MIKVAOT
Shaarey Tphiloh
76 Noyes Street 55416
Telephone: (503) 381 3410

SYNAGOGUES
Conservative
Temple Beth El
400 Deering Avenue 04103
Telephone: (503) 774 2649

Orthodox
Shaarey Tphiloh
76 Noyes Street 04103
Telephone: (503) (207) 773 0693
Email: office@shaareytphiloh.org
Website: www.shaareytphiloh.org
Modern Orthodox welcoming community in handsome 1950's building.

Kennebec County
AUGUSTA
Reform
Temple Beth El
PO Box 871, Woodlawn Street 04330
Telephone: (404) 622 7450

Knox County
ROCKLAND
Conservative
Adas Yoshuron
Willow Street
Telephone: (207) 594 4523

Penobscot County
BANGOR
RESTAURANTS
Bagel Central
33 Central Street 04401
Telephone: (207) 947 1654
Supervision: Beth Abraham Rabbi Fred Neble

SYNAGOGUES
Conservative
Congregation Beth Israel
144 York Street 04401
Telephone: (207) 945 3433
Fax: (207) 945 3840

Orthodox
Beth Abraham
145 York Street 04401
Telephone: (207) 942 8093
Email: rabbi@jewishbangor.com
Website: www.jewishbangor.com

York County
OLD ORCHARD BEACH
KASHRUT INFORMATION
Eber Weinstein
187 E. Grand Avenue, PO Box 163 04064
Telephone: (207) 934 2973

Mobile Phone: 450 8043
Email: ebbbw@yahoo.com
Website: www.cbisrael.com

SYNAGOGUES

Orthodox

Congregation Beth Israel
49 East Grand Avenue, PO Box 213 04064
Telephone: (207) 934 2973
Email: cbisrael@lycos.com
Website: www.cbisrael.com
Open daily in summer, Shabbos morning in winter.
Contact Eber(207) 450 4083 or Neal Weinstein (207) 934 2173

Maryland

Bethesda, Bowie, Chevy Chase, Gaithersburg, Greenbelt, Hyattsville, Kensington, Laurel, Lexington Park, Olney, Potomac, Rockville, Silver Spring & Wheaton and Temple Hills are all part of Greater Washington, DC.

COLLEGE PARK

DELICATESSEN

Kosher

Sabra Deli
University of Maryland Hillel, 7612 Mowatt Lane 20740
Telephone: (301) 403 1607 Direct line to kitchen
Fax: (301) 422 4455
Website: www.hillelmd.org
Hours: Lunch Mon to Thu 11.30am to 1.30pm; Fri 11am to 1pm
Dinner Mon to Thu 5pm to 6.45pm; Fri Shabbat dinner following services

RESTAURANTS

Pita Plus
4425-4427 Lehigh Road 20740
Telephone: (301) 864 5150
Fax: (301) 864 2028
Email: dlm235@aol.com
Website: www.pitaplusmd.com
Supervision: Va'ad Hakashrut of Washington
Hours: Sun to Thu 11am to 9.30pm; Fri 10am to 3pm; Sat open for private parties after sunset

Goldberg's Bagels
4824-26 Boiling Brook Parkway 20852
Telephone: (301) 816 9229
Hours: Sun 7am to 4pm; Mon to Wed 7am 3pm; Thu open until 7pm; Fri open until 3pm(Summer) 2pm (Winter).

RESTAURANTS

Royal Dragon Kosher Restaurant
4832 Boiling Brook Parkway 20852
Telephone: (301) 468 1922
Supervision: Va'ad Hakashrut of Washington
Hours: Sun to Thu 11.30am to 9pm, Fri 11.30am to 2pm

Pizza-Kosher

Mama Leah's Gourmet Pizza
4836 Boiling Brook Parkway 20852
Telephone: (301) 770 1781
Fax: (301) 770 1783
Email: jgautieri@mamaleahspizza.com
Website: www.mamaleahspizza.com
Hours: Mon/Tue 11am to 8pm; Fri 11am to 2.30pm (winter 2pm); Sat 1 hr after Shabbat until 11.30.

Allegany County

CUMBERLAND

SYNAGOGUES

Conservative

Beth Jacob
1 Columbia street 21502
Telephone: (301) 777 3717

Reform

B'Er Chayim
107 Union Street 21502
Telephone: (301) 722 5688
Website: www.berchayim.org

Anne Arundel County

ANNAPOLIS

Conservative

Congregation Kol Shalom
1909 Hidden Meadow Lane 21401
Telephone: (410) 266 6006
Email: office@kolshalomannapolis.org
Website: www.kolshalomannapolis.org

Orthodox

Congregation Knesseth Israel
1125 Spa Road 21403
Telephone: (410) 263 3924

Reform

Temple Beth Shalom
1461 Baltimore-Annapolis Boulevard 21012

Baltimore County

BALTIMORE

BAKERIES

Alder's Bakery
1860D Reisterstown Road
Telephone: (410) 653 1119

Dunkin Donuts
1508 Reisterstown Road 21208
Telephone: (410) 653 8182
Supervision: Rabbi Salfer

Dunkin Donuts
7000 Reisterstown Road 21215
Telephone: (410) 764 6846
Fax: (410) 764 6846
Supervision: Rabbi Salfer

Goldman's Kosher Bakery
6848 Reisterstown Road, Fallstaff Shopping Center
21215
Telephone: (410) 358 9625
Fax: (410) 358 5859
Website: www.goldmanskosherbakery.com and
www.goldmansbakery.com
Supervision: Star-K of Baltimore
All products are Pareve, Pas Yisroel and Yoshon. Packaged
dairy products are available and are Star-K, Cholov
Yisroel.

Pariser's Kosher Bakery
6711 Reisterstown Road 48104
Telephone: (410) 995 3276

Schmell & Azman Kosher Bakery
1351 Lamberton Drive 48075
Telephone: (410) 559 5005/06

Schmell-Azman
7006 Reisterstown Road 21215
Telephone: (410) 484 7373
Supervision: Star K

BUTCHERS
Shlomo Meat & Fish Market
4135 Amos Avenue, (Menlo Industrial Park) 21215
Telephone: (410) 358 9633

Wasserman & Lemberger
7006-D Reisterstown Road 20208
Telephone: (410) 486 4191

COMMUNITY ORGANISATIONS
Associated Jewish Community Federation of Baltimore
101 W. Mount Royal Avenue 55416
Telephone: (410) 926 3829
Fax: (410) 920 2184
Email: office@kenessethisrael.org
Website: www.jirs.info

Jewish Information and Referral Service
5750 Park Heights Avenue 48075
Telephone: (410) 466 4636
Fax: (410) 664 0551
Email: cordetroit@hotmail.com
Website: www.jirs.info

DELICATESSEN
Knish Shop
508 Reisterstown Road 21208
Telephone: (410) 484 5850

Liebes Kosher Deli Carry Out
607 Reisterstown Road 211208
Telephone: (410) 653 1977
Glatt Kosher, Sunday to Wednesday 8.30 am to 6.00 pm.

GROCERIES
Seven Mile Market
4000 Seven Mile Lane 21208
Telephone: (410) 653 2000; 2002
Supervision: Star K

Shlomo's Kosher Meat and Fish Market
506 Reisterstown Road 21208
Telephone: (410) 602 7888
Supervision: Vaad Hakashrut of Baltimore, and Kashrut of
Greater Washington
We deliver orders in the Baltimore area

Wasserman & Lemberger
706-D Reisterstown Road 48237
Telephone: (410) 443 2425

KASHRUT INFORMATION
Star-K Kosher Certification
122 Slade Avenue, Suite 300 21208
Telephone: (410) 484 4110
Fax: (410) 653 9294
Email: star-k@star-k.org
Website: www.star-k.org
Supervision: Rabbi Moshe Heinemann

MIKVAOT
Mikva of Baltimore Inc.
3207 Clarks Lane 21215
Telephone: (410) 764 1448
Supervision: Vaad Hababanim of Baltimore
Full service, 20 prep room, 2 mikva pods, appointments
not necessary, call for hours

MUSEUMS
The Jewish Museum of Maryland
15 Lloyd Street 21202
Telephone: (410) 732 6400
Fax: (410) 732 6451
Email: info@jewishmuseummd.org
Website: www.jewishmuseum.org

RESTAURANTS
Café Shalom
2401 West Belvedere Avenue 21215
Telephone: (410) 601 5000 ext 3971
Fax: (410) 601 6312
Supervision: Orthodox Union

Goldberg's Bagels
708 Reisterstown Road
Telephone: (410) 415 7001
Supervision: Star-K

Krispy Kremes
10021 Reisterstown road (nr. Painters Mill Road)
Telephone: (410) 356 2655
Supervision: Star-K

Mama Leah's Pizza
1852 Reisterstown Road
Telephone: (410) 653 7600
Supervision: Star-K.

Dairy
Caramel's Pizza & Ice Cream
700 Reisterstown Road
Telephone: (410) 486 2365
Supervision: Star-K.

Milk and Honey Bistro
Commercecentre, 1777 Reisterstown Road
Telephone: (410) 484 3544
Supervision: Star-K.

Meat
David Chu's China Bistro
7105 Reisterstown Road 21215
Telephone: (410) 602 5008
Fax: (410) 602 3570
Supervision: Star-K.

Kosher Bite
6309 Reisterstown Road 48502
Telephone: (410) 767 5922
Fax: (410) 767 9024
Email: fjf@tm.net

Royal Restaurant
7006 Reisterstown Road 21208
Telephone: (410) 661 1000

Szechuan Dynasty
1860C Reisterstown Road
Telephone: (410) 602 1817

The Brasserie
Pomona Square Shopping Center, 1700
Reisterstown Road 50265

Pizzeria
Tov Pizza
6313 Reisterstown Road
Telephone: (410) 358 5238
Website: www.tovpizza.com
Supervision: KOF-K

SYNAGOGUES
Baltimore Hebrew Congregation
7401 Park Heights Avenue 21208-5490
Telephone: (410) 764 1587, ext. 225
Fax: (410) 764 7948

TOURS OF JEWISH INTEREST
Holocaust Memorial
Gay & Lombard Sts. 51105
Telephone: (410) 258 0618

KEMP MILL
SYNAGOGUES
Kemp Mill Synagogue
11910 Kemp Mill Road
Telephone: (301) 593 0966

Montgomery County
BETHESDA
COMMUNITY ORGANISATIONS
United Jewish Appeal Federation of Greater Washington
7900 Wisconsin Avenue 48034

CHEVY CHASE
SYNAGOGUES
Conservative
Ohr Kodesh
8300 Meadowbrook Lane 20815
Telephone: (301) 589 3880
Fax: (301) 495 4801
Email: JKiewe@ohrkodesh.org

Reform
Temple Shalom
8401 Grubb Road 20815
Telephone: (301) 587 2273

GAITHERSBURG
Conservative
Kehilat Shalom
9915 Apple Rdge Road 20886
Telephone: (301) 869 7699
Fax: (301) 977 7870
Email: mail@kehilatshalom.org
Website: www.kehilatshalom.org

KENSINGTON
Reform
Temple Emanuel
10101 Connecticut Avenue 20895
Telephone: (301) 942 2000
Fax: (301) 942 9488
Website: www.templeemanuelmd.org

OLNEY
Conservative
B'nai Shalom
18401 Burtfield Drive 20832
Telephone: (301) 774 0879

POTOMAC
Har Shalom
11510 Falls Road 20854
Telephone: (301) 299 7087
Email: shalom@harshalom.org
Website: www.harshalom.org
Orthodox
Beth Sholom Congregation and Talmud Torah
11825 Seven Locks Road 20854
Telephone: (301) 279 7010
Fax: (301) 279 5815
Website: www.bethsholom.org

Young Israel Ezras Israel of Potomac
11618 Seven Locks Road 20854
Telephone: (301) 299 2827
Website: www.yieip.org

ROCKVILLE

GROCERIES - DELI

Butcher
KosherMart
4860 Boiling Brook Parkway 20852
Telephone: (301) 468 0400
Fax: (301) 468 0408
Website: www.koshermart.com
Supervision: Rabbinical Council of Greater Washington
Restaurant, caterer

CAFETERIA
Cafe S.K. - Hebrew Home
6105 Montrose Road 20852
Telephone: (301) 770 8346
Website: www. hebrew-home.org
Supervision: Va'ad Hakashrut of Washington
Hours: Mon to Fri 11.30am to 2pm; Sun 11.30am to 4pm.
Dinner only served Sunday night.

GROCERY

Meat Dairy Bakery
Koshermart
184 Rollins Avenue
 20852
Telephone: (301) 468 4840
Website: www.koshermart.com
Supervision: Rabbinical Council of Greater Washington
RESTAURANTS

Kosher
Moti's Grill and Restaurant
4860 Boiling Brook Parkway 20852
Telephone: (301) 468 0400
Fax: (301) 468 0408
Email: moti@koshermart.com
Website: www.koshermart.com
Supervision: Rabbinical Council of Greater Washington
Hours: open 11am, except Sat, until 8pm; Mon /Tue until
9pm; Wed/Thu until 2.30pm (2pm winter). Sat open 1 hr
after Shabbat until 11.30pm.
Reservations welcomed

Meat
Royal Dragon
4840 Boiling Brook Parkway
Telephone: (301) 468 1922

Pizzeria
Siena's Pizzeria
11417 Woodglen Drive
Telephone: (301) 770 7474

Take outor Dine in
Moti's Falafel Stand
184 Rollins Avenue 20852
Telephone: (301) 468 4840
Supervision: Rabbinical Council of Greater Washington

SYNAGOGUES
Conservative
B'nai Israel
6301 Montrose Road 20852
Telephone: (301) 881 6550
Fax: (301) 881 6221
Tikvat Israel
2200 Baltimore Road 20851
Telephone: (301) 762 7338
Fax: (301) 424 4399
Website: www.tikvatisrael.org

Orthodox
Magen David Sephardic Congregation
11215 Woodglen Drive 208752
Telephone: (301) 770 6818
Fax: (301) 881 0498
Email: magendavid@mdscbe.org
Website: www.magendavidsynagogue.com

Reform
Temple Beth Ami
14330 Travilah Road 20850
Telephone: (301) 340 6818
Fax: (301) 738 0094

SILVER SPRING

BAKERIES
Kosher Pastry Oven
2521 Ennalls Avenue
Telephone: (301) 946 0159

Schmell and Azman
Kemp Mill Shopping Center, Arcola Avenue
Telephone: (301) 593 4785

The Wooden Shoe Pastry Shop
11301 Georgia Avenue 20902
Telephone: (301) 942 9330

Virtuoso
11230a Lockwood Avenue 50901
Telephone: (301) 593 6034

BOOKSELLERS
Elli-Chai's One Stop Judaica Shop
2305 University Boulevard West, Wheaton 20901
Telephone: (301) 933 1800
Fax: (301) 933 7466
Email: onestopjudaicashop@hotmail.com
Website: www.onestopjudaicashop.com

The Jewish Bookstore
11252 Georgia Avenue 40502
Telephone: (301) 268 0672
Fax: (301) 268 0775
Email: ckjf@jewishlexington.org

GROCERIES
Shalom
2309 University Boulevard 21215
Telephone: (301) 764 1448
Fax: (301) 578 0018

Shaul & Hershel Meat Market
Telephone: (301) 949 8477

MIKVAOT
Mikva
8901 Georgia Avenue 46322
Telephone: (301) 972 2251
Fax: (301) 972 4779

RESTAURANTS
Dairy
Ben Yehuda Pizza
Kemp Mill Shopping Center, off Arcola Avenue
20902
Telephone: (301) 681 8900
Fax: (301) 681 8999
Website: ben-yehuda-pizzia.com
Will deliver to tour groups throughout the area

The Nut House
11419 Georgia Avenue 20902
Telephone: (301) 942 5900
Hours: Sun to Thu 11am to 9pm, Fri 11am to 1hr before
sundown; Sa 1hr after Havdalah to 1.30am

Kosher
Max's
2319 University Boulevard 20902
Telephone: (301) 949 6297
Fax: (240) 290 5133
Email: contactus@the shalomgroup.com
Website: www.theshalomgroup.com
Supervision: Va'ad Hakashrut of Washington
Hours: Sun to Thu 11am to 9pm, Fri 11am to 2.30pm
(winter until 2pm).
Prepared foods: Wed and Thu 11am to 8pm, Fri 8am to
2.30pm.

SYNAGOGUES
Conservative
Har Tzeon-Agudath Achim
1840 University Boulevard W 20902

Shaare Tefila Congregation
10881 Lockwood Drive 20901
Telephone: (301) 593 3410
Fax: (301) 593 3860
Email: info@shaaretefila.org
Website: www.shaaretefila.org

Orthodox
Silver Spring Jewish Center
1401 Arcola Avenue 46614
Telephone: (301) 291 4239
Fax: (301) 291 9490

South-East Hebrew Congregation
10900 Lockwood Drive 20902

Woodside Synagogue Ahavas Torah
9001 Georgia avenue 20910
Telephone: (301) 587 8252; 565 5005
Email: information@wsat.org

Website: www.wsat.org
Supervision: Members of the OU and Capitol K
Young Israel of White Oak
PO Box 10613, White Oak 20914
Telephone: (301) 369 1531
**Young Israel Shomrai Emunah of Greater
Washington**
1132 Arcola Avenue 20902
Telephone: (301) 593 4465
Fax: (301) 593 2330
Email: office@yise.org
Website: www.yise.org

Prince George's County
BOWIE
Conservative
Nevey Shalom
12218 Torah Lane 20715
Telephone: (301) 262 9020
Fax: (301) 262 9015
Email: neveyshalom@maxinter.net

Reform
Bowie Reform Synagogue
2901 Mitchelville Road 20716
Telephone: (301) 249 2424

GREEN BELT
Conservative
Mishkan Torah
Westway and Ridge Road 20770
Telephone: (301) 474 4223

HYATTSVILLE
Beth Torah Congregation
6700 Adelphi Road 20782
Telephone: (301) 927 5525
Fax: (301) 927 5526
Email: bethtorah@starpower.net
Website: www.bethtorah.ws

LAUREL
Reconstructionist
Oseh Shalom
8604 Briarwood Drive 20708
Telephone: (301) 498 5151

TEMPLE HILLS
Conservative
Shaare Tikva
5405 Old Temple Hills Road 20748
Telephone: (301) 894 4303

St. Mary's County
LEXINGTON PARK
Beth Israel Congregation
PO box 1683, 21780 Bunker Hill Drive 20653
Telephone: (301) 862 2021

Email: bethisraelsyna@geocities.com
Website: www.geocities.com/bethisraelsyna

Washington County
HAGERSTOWN
Reform
B'nai Abraham
53 E. Baltimore Street 21740
Telephone: (301) 733 5039

Wicomico County
SALISBURY
Conservative
Beth Israel Beth Israel Congregation
600 Camden Ave 21801
Telephone: (410) 742 2564
Fax: (410) 742 2697
Email: Salisrab@verizon.net
Website: www.bethisraelsalisbury.org

Worcester County
POCOMOKE
Temple Israel
3rd Street 21851

Massachusetts
Barnstable County
CAPE COD
SYNAGOGUES
Orthodox
Beth Israel of Onset Cape Cod Synagogue
cnr. of Onset Avenue & Locust Street, PO Box 24,
Onset 02558
Telephone: (781) 784 7153
Email: elimhauser@yahoo.com
Website: www.capecodshul.org

EAST FALMOUTH
Reform
Falmouth Jewish Congregation
7 Hatchville Road 02536
Telephone: (508) 540 0602
Fax: (508) 540 8094
Website: www.falmouthjewish.org

HYANNIS
Cape Cod Synagogue
145 Winter Street 02601
Telephone: (508) 775 2988

Berkshire County
NORTH ADAMS
Congregation Beth Israel
53 Lois Street MA 01247
Telephone: (413) 663 5830
Website: www.cbiweb.org

PITTSFIELD
COMMUNITY ORGANISATIONS
Jewish Federation of the Berkshires
196 South Street 01201
Telephone: (413) 442 4360
Website: www.jewishberkshires.org

Bristol County
ATTLEBORO
SYNAGOGUES
Reconstructionist
Agudas Achim Congregation
901 N. Main Street 02703
Telephone: (508) 222 2243
Website: www.shamash.org/jrf/agudasma

EASTON
Traditional
Temple Chayai Shalom
238 Depot Street 02334
Telephone: (508) 238 6385

FALL RIVER
COMMUNITY ORGANISATIONS
Fall River Jewish Community Council
Room 377, 56 N. Main Street 21201
Telephone: (508) 727 4828

SYNAGOGUES
Conservative
Beth El
385 High Street 02720
Telephone: (508) 674 9761

Orthodox
Adas Israel
1647 Robeson Street 02720
Telephone: (508) 674 9761
Fax: (508) 678 3195

NEW BEDFORD
COMMUNITY ORGANISATIONS
Jewish Federation of Greater New Bedford
467 Hawthorn Street, N. Dartmouth 20902
Telephone: (508) 942 5900

SYNAGOGUES
Conservative
Tifereth Israel
145 Brownell Avenue 02740
Telephone: (508) 997 3171
Fax: (508) 997 3173

Orthodox
Ahavath Achim
385 County Street 02740
Telephone: (508) 994 1760

Fax: (508) 994 81286
Email: rabbibarry@aol.com
Website: www.members.aol.com/rabbibarry

Dukes County
VINEYARD HAVEN
Reform
Martha's Vineyard Hebrew Center
Center Street 02568
Telephone: (508) 693 0745

Essex County
ANDOVER
Temple Emanuel
7 Haggett's Pond Road 01810
Telephone: (978) 470 1356
Fax: (978) 470 1783
Email: info@templeemanuel.net
Website: www.templeemanuel.net

BEVERLY
Conservative
B'nai Abraham
200 E. Lothrop Street 01915
Telephone: (978) 927 3211
Fax: (978) 922 5281
Website: www.templebnaiabraham.com

GLOUCESTER
Ahavat Achim
86 Middle Street 01930
Telephone: (978) 281 0739

HAVERHILL
Orthodox
Anshe Sholom
427 Main Street 01830
Telephone: (508) 372 2276

Reform
Temple Emanu-El
514 Main Street 01830
Telephone: (508) 373 3861

LAWRENCE
COMMUNITY ORGANISATIONS
Jewish Community Council of Greater Lawrence
580 Haverhill Street 20910
Telephone: (913) 565 3737

SYNAGOGUES
Orthodox
Anshai Sholom
411 Hampshire Street 01843
Telephone: (913) 683 4544

LYNN
Ahabat Sholom
151 Ocean Street MA 01902
Telephone: (781) 593 9255
Fax: (781) 593 9255
Website: www.ahabatsholom.org
Anshai Sfard
150 South Common Street 01905
Telephone: (617) 599 7131

MARBLEHEAD
Conservative/Masorti
Temple Sinai
1 Community Road 01945
Telephone: (617) 631 2763

Orthodox
Orthodox Congregation of the North Shore
4 Community Road 01945
Telephone: (617) 598 1810

Reform
Temple Emanu-El
393 Atlantic Avenue 01945
Telephone: (617) 631 9300

NEWBURYPORT
Conservative
Congregation Ahavas Achim
Washington & Olive Streets 09150
Telephone: (508) 462 2461

PEABODY
Temple Ner Tamid
368 Lowell Street 001960
Telephone: (508) 532 1293
Fax: (508) 532 0101
Email: audrey368@aol.com
Website: www.templenertamid.org

Independent
Congregation Tifereth Israel
Pierpont Street 01960
Telephone: (508) 531 8135

Reform
Beth Shalom
489 Lowell Street 01960
Telephone: (508) 535 2100

Traditional
Congregation Sons of Israel
Park & Spring Streets 01960
Telephone: (508) 531 7576

SALEM
Conservative
Temple Shalom
287 Lafayette Street 01970
Telephone: (508) 741 4880

Fax: (508) 741 4882
Email: dottie@templeshalomsalem.org
Website: www.templeshalomsalem.org

SWAMPSCOTT

Congregation Shirat Hayam of the North Shore
55 Atlantic Avenue 01907
Telephone: (781) 599 8005
Fax: (781) 599 1860
Email: csh@shirathayam.org
Website: www.shirathayam.org

Temple Israel
837 Humphrey Street 01907
Telephone: (617) 595 6635
Fax: (617) 595 0033
Website: www.templeisraelswampscott.org

Franklin County

GREENFIELD

Temple Israel
27 Pierce Street 01301
Telephone: (413) 773 5884

Hampden County

HOLYOKE

Sons of Zion
378 Maple Street 01040
Telephone: (413) 534 3369

Orthodox
Rodphey Sholom
12800 Northampton Street 01040
Telephone: (413) 534 5262

LONGMEADOW

MIKVAOT
Mikveh Association
1104 Converse MA 2558
Telephone: (413) 295 9820

SYNAGOGUES
Conservative
Congregation B'nai Jacob
2 Eunice Drive 01106
Telephone: (413) 567 0058

Orthodox
Beth Israel
1280 Williams Street 01106
Telephone: (413) 567 3210

Lubavitcher Yeshiva Synagogue
1148 Converse St 01106
Telephone: (413) 567 8665
Email: lyaadmin@comcast.net
Website: www.lya.org

SPRINGFIELD

COMMUNITY ORGANISATIONS
Jewish Community Center
1160 Dickinson Street 02607
Email: blev@springfieldjcc.org
Website: www.springfieldjcc.org

GROCERIES
Waldbaum's Food Mart
355 Belmont Avenue 2368
Telephone: (413) 961 4929

RESTAURANTS
Vi's Coffee Shoppe
Jewish Community Center, 1160 Dickinson Street 01108
Telephone: (413) 739 4715
Fax: (413) 739 4747
Email: agoldsmith@springfieldjcc.org

SYNAGOGUES
Orthodox
Congregation Kodimoh
124 Sumner Avenue 01108
Telephone: (413) 781 0171
Fax: (413) 737 8002

Kesser Israel
19 Oakland Street 01108
Telephone: (413) 732 8492

Reform
Temple Sinai
1100 Dickinson Street 01108
Telephone: (413) 736 3619

Hampshire County

AMHERST

Reconstructionist
Jewish Community of Amherst
742 Main Street 01002
Telephone: (413) 256 0160
Fax: (413) 256 1588
Email: info@j-c-a.org
Supervision: Star-K.

NORTHAMPTON

Conservative
B'nai Israel
253 Prospect Road 01060
Telephone: (413) 584 3593

Middlesex County

ACTON

Independent
Beth Elohim
10 Hennessy Drive 07120
Telephone: (978) 263 8610

AYER
Congregation Anshey Sholom
Cambridge Street 01432
Telephone: (508) 772 0896

BELMONT
Reform
Beth El Temple Center
2 Concord Avenue 02478
Telephone: (617) 484 6668
Website: www.uahc.org/ma/betc

BURLINGTON
Temple Shalom Emeth
14-16 Lexington Street 01803
Telephone: (718) 272 2351
Fax: (718) 272 2351
Website: www.shalom-emeth.org

CAMBRIDGE
KASHRUT INFORMATION
Harvard Hillel
Harvard University, 52 Mount Auburn Street 21202
Telephone: (617) 732 6400
Fax: (617) 732 6451

RESTAURANTS
Kosher Restaurant
52 Mount Auburn Street 02138
Telephone: (617) 495 4695
Fax: (617) 864 1637
Email: linda@hillel.harvard.edu
Website: www.hillel.harvard.edu

Dining hall: 5.00-7.00pm Sunday-Thursday; Shabbat dinner; Shabbat lunch 12.15pm. Open during Harvard University academic calendar only. Lunch and dinner during the High Holidays and Passover. Open to the public, weekday meals no reservation, all other meals require reservation. For further information contact Linda Mulligan, ext. 221 or email Linda

Meat
MIT Hillel Kosher Kitchen
40 Massachusetts Avenue 02139
Telephone: (617) 253 2982
Fax: (617) 253 3260
Email: hillel@mit.edu
Website: web.mit.edu/dining/locations/kosher.html
Supervision: Vaad Harabonim of Massachusetts

SYNAGOGUES
Orthodox
Chabad
38 Banks Street 02138
Telephone: (617) 547 6124
Email: info@chabadharvard.org

Harvard University Hillel
52 Mount Auburn Street 01238
Telephone: (617) 495 4695
Fax: (617) 864 1637

Email: linda@hillel.harvard.edu
Website: www.hillel.harvard.edu
Traditional
Temple Beth Shalom of Cambridge
8 Tremont Street 02139
Telephone: (617) 864 6388
Fax: (617) 864 0507
Website: www.tremontstreetshul.org

CHELMSFORD
Reform
Congregation Shalom
Richardson Road 01824
Telephone: (978) 251 8090

EVERETT
Traditional
Tifereth Israel
34 Malden Street 02149
Telephone: (617) 387 0200

FRAMINGHAM
RESTAURANTS
Meat
Rami's of Framington
341 Cochituate Road 01701
Telephone: (508) 370 3577

SYNAGOGUES
Conservative
Temple Beth Sholom
50 Pamela Road 01701
Telephone: (508) 877 2540
Fax: (508) 877 8278
Website: www.beth-sholom.org

Orthodox
Chabad House
74 Joseph Road 01701
Telephone: (508) 877 5313
Fax: (508) 877 5313

Reform
Beth Am
300 Pleasant Street 01701
Telephone: (508) 872 8300
Fax: (508) 872 9773
Email: tempbetham@

Temple Beth Am
100 Pleasant Street 01701
Telephone: (508) 872 8300
Website: www.templebetham.org

HOLLISTON
Conservative
Temple Beth Torah
2162 Washington Street 01746
Telephone: (508) 429 6268

Fax: (508) 429 7729
Email: tbt@bethtorah.org

LEXINGTON
Temple Emunah
9 Piper Road 02421
Telephone: (781) 861 0300
Fax: (781) 861 7141
Email: abell@emunahlex.org
Website: www.templeemunah.org
Supervision: Rabbi David G. Lerner
Central organisation: United Synagogue of Conservative Judaism
Conservative, egalitarian

Orthodox
Chabad Center
9 Burlington Street 02173
Telephone: (859) 863 8656

Reform
Temple Isaiah
55 Lincoln Street 02173
Telephone: (859) 862 7160

LOWELL
MIKVAOT
Lowell Mikvaot
48 Academy Drive
Telephone: (978) 933 1800

SYNAGOGUES
Conservative
Temple Beth El
105 Princeton Boulevard 01851
Telephone: (978) 453 7744

Orthodox
Montefiore Synagogue
460 Westford Street 20902
Telephone: (978) 649 4425

Reform
Temple Emanuel of Merrimack Valley
101 W. Forest Street 01851
Telephone: (978) 454 1372
Email: info@temv.org
Website: www.temv.org

MALDEN
Conservative
Ezrath Israel
245 Bryant Street 02148
Telephone: (781) 322 7205

Orthodox
Congregation Beth Israel
10 Dexter Street 02148
Telephone: (781) 322 5686
Fax: (781) 322 6778
Email: director@bethisraelmalden.com
Website: ww.betisraelmalden.com

Young Israel of Malden
45 Holyoke Street 02148
Telephone: (781) 961 9817

Reform
Tifereth Israel
539 Salem Street 02148
Telephone: (781) 322 2794

Traditional
Agudas Achim
160 Harvard Street 02148
Telephone: (781) 322 9380

MARLBORO
Conservative
Temple Emanuel
150 Berlin Road 01752
Telephone: (508) 485 7565

MEDFORD
Temple Shalom
475 Winthrop Street 02155
Telephone: (781) 396 3262
Fax: (781) 393 4864
Email: office@templeshalommedford.org
Website: www.templeshalommedford.org

MELROSE
Reform
Temple Beth Shalom
21 E. Foster Street 02176
Telephone: (617) 665 4520

NATICK
Conservative
Temple Israel
145 Hartford Street 01760
Telephone: (508) 650 3521 ext. 100
Fax: (508) 655 3440
Email: office@tiofnatick.org
Website: www.tiofnatick.org

NEWTON
COMMUNITY ORGANISATIONS
Jewish Community Center of Greater Boston
333 Nahanton Street 20902
Telephone: (617) 946 1041

KASHRUT INFORMATION
Synagogue Council of Massachusetts
1320 Centre Street Suite 306 02459
Telephone: (617) 244 6506
Synagogue Council of Massachusetts

RESTAURANTS
Rosenfeld Bagels
1280 Centre Street, Newton Center 02459
Telephone: (617) 527 8080

SYNAGOGUES
American Jewish Historical Society
160 Herrick Road 02459
Telephone: (617) 559 8880
Orthodox
Beth El Atereth Israel
561 Ward Street 02459
Telephone: (617) 244 7233
Fax: (617) 588 5296.
Email: congbethel@rcn.com
Central organisation: Union of Orthodox Jewish
Congregation of North America.
Congregation B'nai Jacob (Zvhil-Mezbuz Rebbe)
955 Beacon Street
Telephone: (617) 227 8200
Fax: (617) 227 8420
Email: info@rebbe.org
Website: www.rebbe.org
Supervision: Grand Rabbi Y. A. Korff (Zvhil-Mezbuz Rebbe)
Shaarei Tefila
35 Morseland Avenue 02459
Telephone: (617) 527 7637

SOMERVILLE
Independent
B'nai Brith of Somerville
201 Central Street 02145
Telephone: (617) 625 0333
Email: tbb@templebnaibrith.org
Website: www.templebnaibrith.org

SUDBURY
Congregation B'nai Torah
225 Boston Post Road (Rt. 20), PO Box 273,
Sudbury MA 01776
Telephone: (978) 443 2082

Reform
Congregation Beth El
105 Hudson Road 01776
Telephone: (978) 443 9622
Fax: (978) 443 9629
Email: secretary@bethelsudbury.org
Website: www.bethelsudbury.org

WAKEFIELD
Conservative
Temple Emanuel
120 Chestnut Street 01880
Telephone: (781) 245 1886
Website: www.geocities.com/temple_emanuel

WALTHAM
Beth Israel
25 Harvard Street 02154
Telephone: (617) 894 5146

WAYLAND
Reform
Temple Shir Tikva
141 Boston Post Road 01778
Telephone: (508) 358 9992
Fax: (508) 358 9994
Email: clergy@shirtikva.org
Website: www.shirtikva.org

WINCHESTER
Temple Shir Tikvah
PO Box 373 01890
Telephone: (617) 792 1188

Norfolk County
BROOKLINE
BAKERIES
Catering by Andrew
402 Harvard Street 02446
Telephone: (617) 731 6585
Fax: (617) 232 3788
Email: cbandrew@aol.com
Supervision: Vaad Harabonim of Massachusetts
Kupel's
421 Harvard Street
Telephone: (617) 566 9528

GROCERIES
Beacon Kosher
1706 Beacon Street
Telephone: (617) 734 5300

JUDAICA
Israel Book Shop, Inc.
410 Harvard Street 02446
Telephone: (617) 566 7113
Fax: (617) 566 0006
Email: info@israelbookshop.com
Website: www.israelbookshop.com

JUDAICA
Kolbo Fine Judaica
437 Harvard Street 02446
Telephone: (617) 731 8743

RESTAURANTS
Dairy
Café Eilat
406 Harvard Street 02446
Telephone: (617) 277 7770
Website: www.cafe-eilat.com
Supervision: Vaad Harabbanim Rabbi Hommoui
Pizza, pasta, fish and Mexican
Meat
Rami's
324 Harvard Street 02446
Telephone: (617) 738 3577

Rubin's Kosher Deli and Restaurant
500 Harvard Street 02146
Telephone: (617) 731 8787

Ruth's Kitchen
401 Harvard Street 02446
Telephone: (617) 484 4110

Taam China
423 Harvard Street
Telephone: (617) 264 7274

SYNAGOGUES

Conservative

Kehillath Israel
384 Harvard Street 2146
Telephone: (617) 277 9155

Meat

Shalom Hunan
92 Harvard Street 02445-46
Telephone: (617) 731 9778

Orthodox

Beth Pinchas (Bostoner Rebbe)
1710 Beacon Street 02146
Telephone: (617) 734 5100
Fax: (617) 739 0163

Congregation Lubavitch
100 Woodcliff Road 02467
Telephone: (617) 469 5000
Fax: (617) 469 0089
Website: www.congregationlubavitch.org

Young Israel Brookline
62 Green Street 02446
Telephone: (617) 734 0276
Fax: (617) 734 7195
Email: office@yibrookline.org
Website: www.yibrookline.org

Reform

Ohabei Shalom
1187 Beacon Street 2446
Telephone: (617) 277 6610
Email: dberman@ohabei.org
Website: www.ohabei.org

Temple Sinai
50 Sewall Avenue, Coolidge Corner 02146
Telephone: (617) 277 5888

Sephardi

Sephardic Congregation of New England - Beth Abraham
18 Williston Road 02445
Telephone: (617) 308 0602
Website: www.bethabraham.net

CANTON
Conservative
Beth Abraham
1301 Washington Street 02021
Telephone: (781) 828 5250

Reform

Temple Beth David of the South Shore
1060 Randolph Street 02021
Telephone: (781) 828 2275
Fax: (781) 821 3997
Email: info@templebethdavid.com
Website: www.templebethdavid.com

HOLBROOK
Conservative
Temple Beth Shalom
95 Plymouth Street 02343
Telephone: (617) 767 4922

MILLIS
Ael Chunon
334 Village Street 02054
Telephone: (508) 376 5984

MILTON
Temple Shalom
180 Blue Hill Avenue 02186
Telephone: (617) 698 3394
Fax: (617) 696 9265
Email: office@templeshalomonline.org
Website: www.templeshalomonline.org

Orthodox

B'nai Jacob
100 Blue Hill Parkway 02187
Telephone: (617) 698 0698
Supervision: Rabbi Nathan Korff.

NEEDHAM
Conservative
Temple Aliyah
1664 Central Avenue 02492
Telephone: (781) 444 8522
Website: www.templealiyah.com

Reform

Temple Beth Shalom
670 Highland Avenue 02494
Telephone: (781) 444 0077
Fax: (781) 449 3274
Email: tbshalom@tbsneedham.org
Website: www.tbsneedham.org

NORWOOD
Conservative
Temple Shaare Tefilah
556 Nichols Street, P.O. Box 662 02062
Telephone: (781) 762 8670
Fax: (781) 762 8670
Email: rabbi@tst@norwoodlight.com
Website: www.templeshaaretefilah.org

RANDOLPH

BOOKSELLERS
Davidson's Hebrew Book Store
1106 Main Street 4130

SYNAGOGUES
Orthodox
Young Israel - Kehillath Jacob of Mattapan & Randolph
374 N. Main Street, PO Box 880 02368
Telephone: (781) 986 6461

STOUGHTON

BAKERIES
Ruth's Bake Shop
987 Central Street 02072
Telephone: (781) 344 8993
Supervision: Vaad Harabonim of Massachusetts

SYNAGOGUES
Conservative
Adhavath Torah Congregation
1179 Central Street 02072
Telephone: (781) 344 8733
Fax: (781) 344 4315

WELLESLEY HILLS

Reform
Beth Elohim
10 Bethel Road 02181
Telephone: (617) 235 8419

WESTWOOD

Beth David
40 Pond Street 02090
Telephone: (617) 769 5270

Norfolk County

QUINCY

Conservative
Temple Beth El
1001 Hancock Street 02169
Telephone: (617) 479 4309

Orthodox
Beth Israel
33 Grafton Street, PO Box 690388 02269-0388
Telephone: (617) 472 6796

SHARON

HOTELS
Sharon Woods Inn
80 Brook Road 02067
Telephone: (781) 784 9401
Fax: (781) 784 2411
Email: kctova@yahoo.com

MIKVAOT
Chevrat Nashim
9 Dunbar Street 4103
Telephone: (781) 773 0693

RELIGIOUS ORGANISATIONS
Eruv Society
Telephone: (781) 997 7471

SYNAGOGUES
Conservative
Adath Sharon
18 Harding Street 02067
Telephone: (781) 784 2517

Temple Israel
125 Pond Street 02067
Telephone: (781) 784 3986
Fax: (781) 784 0719

Orthodox
Chabad Center
101 Worcester Road 02067
Telephone: (781) 784 8167

Young Israel of Sharon
100 Ames Street 02067
Telephone: (781) 784 6112
Fax: (781) 784 7758
Website: www.yisharon.org

Reform
Temple Sinai
25 Canton Street 02067
Telephone: (781) 784 6081
Fax: (781) 784 2616
Website: www.temple-sinai.com

Plymouth County

BROCKTON

Conservative
Temple
479 Torres Street 02401
Telephone: (508) 583 5810

Orthodox
Agudas Achim
144 Belmont Avenue 02301
Telephone: (508) 583 0717

HINGHAM

Reform
Congregation Sha'aray Shalom
1112 Main Street, Hingham, MA 02043
Telephone: (781) 749 8103
Fax: (781) 740 1480
Email: cssadm@aol.com
Website: http://www.shaaray.org

HULL
Conservative
Temple Beth Sholom
600 Nantasket Avenue 02045
Telephone: (617) 925 0091
Fax: (617) 925 9053
Email: templebethhull@aol.com
Website: www.tbshull.com
Temple Israel of Nantasket
9 Hadassah Way 02045
Telephone: (617) 925 0289

ONSET
HOTELS
Bridge View Hotel
12 S. Water Street 20814
Telephone: (508) 652 6480

PLYMOUTH
SYNAGOGUES
Reform
Congregation Beth Jacob
Synagogue on Pleasant Street, Community Center
on Court Street, PO Box 3284 02361
Telephone: (508) 746 1575

Suffolk County
BOSTON
Office of the Chaplain, City of Boston
15 School Street
Telephone: (617) 227 8200
Fax: (617) 227 8420
Email: info@rebbe.org
Website: www.rebbe.org
Supervision: Grand Rabbi Y. A. Korff (Zvhil-Mezbuz Rebbe)

EMBASSY
Consul General of Israel
1020 Statler Office Boulevard 02116

KASHRUT INFORMATION
The Kashruth Commission
177 Tremont Street 02111
Telephone: (617) 426 2139
Fax: (617) 426 6268
Email: rabbi@kvh613.org
Supervision: kosher and certification

MEDIA
Guide
Jewish Guide to Boston and New England
15 School Street 02108
Telephone: (617) 367 9100
Fax: (617) 367 9310

Newspapers
The Jewish Advocate, Inc.
15 School Street 02108
Telephone: (617) 367 9100
Fax: (617) 367 9310
Website: www.thejewishadvocate.com
Supervision: Star-K.
Boston Jewish Times
15 School Street 02108
Telephone: (617) 484 3544
Supervision: Star-K.

RELIGIOUS ORGANISATIONS
Rabbinical Council of New England
177 Tremont Street 02111
Telephone: (617) 426 2139
Fax: (617) 426 6268
Email: tshanok@kvh613.org

RESTAURANTS
Dairy
Kosher Restaurant
50 Milk Street 21208
Telephone: (617) 486 4191

SYNAGOGUES
Orthodox
Chabad House
491 Commonwealth Avenue 02215
Telephone: (617) 424 1190
Fax: (617) 266 5997
Email: rsp@chabadboston.org
Website: www.chabadboston.org
The Boston Synagogue (at Charles River Park)
55 Martha Road 02114
Telephone: (617) 523 0453
Zvhil-Mezbuz Beis Medrash (Zvhil-Mezbuz Rebbe)
15 School Street 02108
Telephone: (617) 227 8200
Fax: (617) 227 8420
Email: info@rebbe.org
Website: www.rebbe.org
Supervision: Grand Rabbi Y. A. Korff (Zvhil-Mezbuz Rebbe)
Reform
Temple Israel
Longwood Avenue & Plymouth Street 02215
Telephone: (617) 566 3960
Fax: (617) 731 3711
Website: www.tisrael.org

BRAINTREE
Conservative
Temple Bnai Shalom
41 Storrs Avenue 02184
Telephone: (781) 843 3687

BRIGHTON
MIKVAOT
Daughters of Israel
101 Washington Street, (located just off
Commonwealth Avenue) 02135
Telephone: (617) 782 9433

SYNAGOGUES
Conservative
Temple B'nai Moshe
1845 Commonwealth Avenue 02135
Telephone: (617) 254 3620
Fax: (617) 254 3620
Website: www.templebnaimoshe.org

Orthodox
Chai Odom
77 Englewood Av. 02135
Telephone: (617) 734 5359
Website: www.chaiodom.org

Congregation Kadimah-Toras Moshe
113 Washington Street 02135
Telephone: (617) 254 1333

Lubavitch Shul and Mikvah of Brighton
239 Chestnut Hill Avenue 02135
Telephone: (617) 782 8340
Fax: (815) 377 2444

Talner Congregation Beth David
64 Corey Road 02135
Telephone: (617) 232 2349

HYDE PARK
Conservative
Temple Adas Hadrath Israel
28 Arlington Street 02136
Telephone: (617) 364 2661

REVERE
DELICATESSEN
Myer's Kosher Kitchen
168 Shirley Avenue 4103
Telephone: (617) 773 7254

SYNAGOGUES
Independent
Temple B'nai Israel
1 Wave Avenue 02151
Telephone: (617) 284 8388

Orthodox
Ahavas Achim Anshei Sfard
89 Walnut Way 02151
Telephone: (617) 289 1026

Tifereth Israel
43 Nahant Avenue 02151
Telephone: (617) 284 9255

WEST ROXBURY
Reconstructionist
Hillel B'nai Torah
120 Corey Street 02132
Telephone: (617) 323 0486
Fax: (617) 327 8338
Email: office@templehbt.org
Website: www.templehbt.org
Supervision: www.templehbt.org
Central organisation: Reconstructionist (JRF)

WINTHROP
Conservative
Tifereth Israel
93 Veterans Road 02152
Telephone: (617) 846 1390

Orthodox
Tifereth Abraham
283 Shirley Street 02152
Telephone: (617) 846 5063

Worcester County
ATHOL
Conservative
Temple Israel
107 Walnut Street 01331
Telephone: (978) 249 9481

CLINTON
Independent
Shaarei Zedek
Water Street 01510
Telephone: (978) 365 3320

LEOMINSTER
Conservative
Congregation Agudat Achim
268 Washington Street 01453
Telephone: (508) 534 6121
Fax: (508) 534 6121
Email: debbie@agudat-achim.org

MILFORD
Temple Beth Shalom
55 Pine Street 01757
Telephone: (508) 473 1590
Website: www.templebethshalom.com

WESTBOROUGH
Reform
Congregation B'nai Shalom
117 E. Main street, PO Box 1019 01581-6019
Telephone: (508) 366 7191

WORCESTER

COMMUNITY ORGANISATIONS

Jewish Community Centre of Worcester
633 Salisbury Street
Telephone: (508) 756 7109

Jewish Federation
633 Salisbury Street 01609
Telephone: (508) 756 1543

CONTACT INFORMATION

Agudath Israel of America Hachnosas Orchim Committee
69 S. Flagg Street 01602
Telephone: (508) 754 3681
Mrs Reuven Fischer

Rabbi Hershel Fogelman
22 Newton Avenue 2138
Telephone: (508) 495 4696
Fax: (508) 864 1637
Email: linda@hillel.harvard.edu

MIKVAOT

Mikva
Huntley Street 2151

SYNAGOGUES

Conservative
Beth Israel
15 Jamesbury drive
Telephone: (508) 756 6204
Website: www.bethisraelworc.org

Orthodox
Young Israel of Worcester
889 Pleasant Street 01602
Telephone: (508) 754 3681

Reform
Temple Emanuel
280 May Street
Telephone: (508) 755 1257
Website: www.temple-emanuel.org

Temple Sinai
661 Salisbury Street
Telephone: (508) 755 2519

Michigan

FARMINGTON HILLS

MUSEUMS

Library-Archive
Holocaust Memorial Center Zekelman Family Campus
28123 Orchard Lake Road 48334-3738.
Telephone: (248) 553 2400
Fax: (248) 553 2433.
Email: info@holocaustcenter.org
Website: www.holocaustcenter.org

We are the first free standing Holocaust Museum in the United States. The Center is made up of the Museum of European Jewish History, Holocaust Museum and International Institute of the Righteous. We also have an extensive Library-Archive. Check out our website and you will learn about our activities. The Museum is open to the public and free of charge.

Berrien County

BENTON HARBOR

SYNAGOGUES

Conservative
Temple B'nai Shalom
2050 Broadway 49022
Telephone: (212) 925 8021

Genesee County

FLINT

COMMUNITY ORGANISATIONS

Flint Jewish Federation
619 Wallenberg Street 48502
Telephone: (810) 767 5922

SYNAGOGUES

Conservative
Congregation Beth Israel
5240 Calkins Road 48532
Telephone: (810) 732 6310
Fax: (810) 732 6314
Email: cbiflint@tir.com
Website: www.uscj.org/michigan/flint/

Orthodox
Chabad House
5385 Calkins 48532
Telephone: (810) 230 0770

Reform
Temple Beth El
501 S. Ballenger Highway 48532
Telephone: (810) 232 3138

Ingham County

EAST LANSING

Conservative & Reform
Shaarey Zedek
1924 Coolidge Road 48823

LANSING

Reconstructionist
Kehillat Israel
2014 Forest Road 48910-3711
Telephone: (517) 882 0049
Website: www.kehillatisrael.net
Supervision: Rabbi Michael Zimmerman

Jackson County
JACKSON
Reform
Temple Beth Israel
801 W. Michigan Avenue 49202
Telephone: (517) 784 3862

Kalamazoo County
KALAMAZOO
Conservative
Congregation of Moses
2501 Stadium Drive 49008
Telephone: (616) 342 5463

Kent County
GRAND RAPIDS
Congregation Ahavas Israel
2727 Michigan Street N.E. 49506
Telephone: (616) 949 2840
Website: www.ahavasisraelgr.org

Orthodox
Chabad House of Western Michigan
2615 Michigan Street N.E. 49506
Telephone: (616) 957 0770
Email: rabbiyyw@chabadwm.com
Website: www.chabadwm.com

Reform
Temple Emanuel
1715 E. Fulton Street 49503
Telephone: (616) 459 5976

Oakland County
BLOOMFIELD HILLS
COMMUNITY ORGANISATIONS
Jewish Federation of Metr. Detroit
6735 Telegraph Road, PO Box 2030 48303-2030
Telephone: (248) 642 4260
Website: www.thisisfederation.org

OAK PARK
MIKVAOT
Mikvah Israel
15116 W. Ten Mile Road, Oak Park 48237
Telephone: (248) 967 5402

Oakland County
SOUTHFIELD
GROCERIES
One Stop Kosher
25155 Greenfield Road, W Ten Mile Road
Telephone: (248) 569 5000

KASHRUT INFORMATION
Council of Orthodox Rabbis of Greater Detroit
16947 W. Ten Mile Road 1602
Telephone: (248) 755 1257

MEDIA
Newspapers
Jewish News
Franklin Road, Southfield 1970
Telephone: (248) 745 4222
Fax: (248) 741 7507
Email: mail@jfns.org

RELIGIOUS ORGANISATIONS
Kashrut Information
Council of Orthodox Rabbis of Detroit
25881 Greenfield Road #32 48075
Telephone: (248) 559 5005/5006
Fax: (248) 559 5202
Email: cordetroit@sbcglobal.net

RESTAURANTS
Dairy
Jerusalem Pizza
26025 Greenfield, Southfield 48034
Telephone: (248) 552 0088
Fax: (248) 552 0087

Meat
Unique Kosher
25270 Greenfield
Telephone: (248) 967 1161

SYNAGOGUES
Orthodox
Young Israel of Southfield
27705 Lahser Road 48034
Telephone: (248) 358 0154
Fax: (248) 358 0154
Email: rabg@aol.com

WEST BLOOMFIELD
RELIGIOUS ORGANISATIONS
Jewish Community Center of Metr. Detroit
6600 W. Maple Road, W. Bloomfield 2111
Telephone: (248) 426 2139
Fax: (248) 426 6268

SYNAGOGUES
Orthodox
Young Israel of West Bloomfield
6111 West Maple Road, Suite 408 48322
Telephone: (248) 661 4182

Saginaw County
SAGINAW
Conservative
Temple B'nai Israel
1424 S. Washington Avenue 48601
Telephone: (517) 753 5230

Reform
Congregation Beth El
100 S. Washington Avenue 48607
Telephone: (517) 754 5171

Van Buren County
SOUTH HAVEN
Unaffiliated
First Hebrew Congregation
249 Broadway 49090
Telephone: (269) 637 1603
Email: lazarcha@aol.com

Washtenaw County
ANN ARBOR
COMMUNITY ORGANISATIONS
Jewish Federation of Washtenaw County
2939 Birch Hollow Drive 48108
Telephone: (734) 6770100
Fax: (734) 677 0109
Email: info@jewishannarbor.org
Website: www.jewishannarbor.org

MIKVAOT
Chabad House
715 Hill 48104
Telephone: (734) 995 3276

SYNAGOGUES
Orthodox
Ann Arbor Orthodox Minyan
1429 Hill Street 48104
Telephone: (734) 994 5822

Wayne County
DETROIT
ORGANISATIONS
Machon L'torah (The Jewish Network of Michigan)
W. Ten Mile Road 1851
Telephone: (313) 459 9400

Minnesota
MINNEAPOLIS
SYNAGOGUES
Orthodox
Congregation Bais Yisroel
4221 Sunset Blvd. 55416
Telephone: (952) 926-7867

Fax: (952) 926-2936
Email: baisline@baisyisroel.org,
Website: www.baisyisroel.org
Supervision: Rabbi Moshe Tuvia Lieff

Hennepin County
GROCERIES
Fishman's Kosher Market
4100 Minnetonka Boulevard St Louis Park 55416
Telephone: (612) 926 5611

MIKVAOT
Mikva for Women
4624A Minnetonka Boulevard 55416
Telephone: (952) 926 0276

RESTAURANTS
Dairy
Calypso Coffee Co.
3238 W. Lake Street 55416

SYNAGOGUES
Orthodox
Congregation Bais Yisroel
4221 Sunset Boulevard, St. Louis Park 55416
Telephone: Office - (952) 926 7867
Fax: (952) 926 2936
Email: office@baisyisroel.org
Website: www.baisyisroel.org
HaRav Moshe Tuvia Lieff

ST LOUIS PARK
COMMUNITY ORGANISATIONS
Sabes Jewish Community Center
4330 Cedar Lake Road S. 55416
Telephone: (952) 381 3400
Fax: (952) 381 3401
Website: www.sabesjcc.org
SYNAGOGUES
Orthodox
Kenesseth Israel Congregation
4330 W. 28th Street , 55416
Telephone: (952) 920 2183
Fax: (952) 920 2184
Mobile Phone: 952 2509376
Email: rabbi@kenessethisrael.org
Website: www.kenessethisrael.org
Louis County
DULUTH
COMMUNITY ORGANISATIONS
Jewish Federation & Com. Council
1602 E. 2nd Street 1108
Telephone: (218) 737 4313

SYNAGOGUES
Conservative & Reform
Temple Israel
1602 E. 2nd Street 55812
Telephone: (218) 724 8857

Orthodox
Adas Israel
302 E. Third Street 55802
Telephone: (218) 722 6459

Olmsted County
ROCHESTER
HOME HOSPITALITY
Lubavitch Bais Chaya Moussia Hospitality Center
730 2nd Street S.W. 55902
Telephone: (507) 288 7500
Fax: (507) 286 9329
Email: rabbigreene@chabadrochestermn.com
Website: www.chabadrochestermn.com

SYNAGOGUES
Reform
B'nai Israel Synagogue
621 SW 2nd Street 55902
Telephone: 288 5825
Email: bnaisrael@aol.com

Ramsey County
ST PAUL
GROCERIES
L'Chaim
655 Snelling Avenue 1002
Telephone: (612) 256 0160
Fax: (612) 256 1588
Website: www.j-c-a.org

RESTAURANTS
Dairy
Old City Cafe
1571 Grand Avenue
Telephone: (612) 291 6240

Mississippi
Adams County
NATCHEZ
SYNAGOGUES
Reform
B'nai Israel
Washigton & S. Commerce Streets, PO Box 2081 39120

Jackson County
JACKSON
Congregation Beth Israel
5315 Old Canton Road 39211
Telephone: (517) 956 6215

Lee County
TUPELO
Conservative
Tupelo Synagogue
Marshall & Hamlin Streets 38801
Telephone: (601) 842 9169

Leflore County,
GREENWOOD
Orthodox
Ahavath Rayim
Market & George Streets, PO Box 1235 38935-1235
Email: joe_erber@hotmail.com
We hold services the first Friday night of each month as there are only about 12 congregants left.

Washington County
GREENVILLE
Reform
Hebrew Union Congregation
504 Main Street 38701
Telephone: (662) 332 4153

Missouri
Buchanan County
ST JOSEPH
Conservative
Temple B'nai Sholem
615 S. 10th Street 64501
Telephone: (816) 279 2378
Fax: (816) 361 4495

Jackson County
KANSAS CITY
RESTAURANTS
Sensations
1148 W. 103 Street
Telephone: (816) 424 0191

SYNAGOGUES
Reform
The New Reform Temple
7100 Main 64114
Telephone: (816) 523 7809
Fax: (816) 523 2454
Email: nrt7100@aol.com
Website: website: www.nrtkc.org
A Friendly medium size Classical reform Congregation. Join us for Shabbat services Fridays led by Rabbi Jacques Cukierkorn at 6pm

Mississippi County
JEFFERSON CITY
Temple Beth El
238 East High Street 65101
Telephone: (573) 635 8727

St. Louis County
ST LOUIS
BAKERIES
Schnuck's Nancy Ann Bakery
Olive & Mason
Telephone: (314) 569 0727
Fax: (314) 569 1723

BUTCHERS
Diamant's Kosher Meat Market
618 North & South Road
Telephone: (314) 712 9624

Simon Kohn's Kosher Meat & Deli
10405 Old Olive Street, St Louis, MO 63141
Telephone: (314) 569 0727
Website: http://www.kohnskosher.com

Sol's Kosher Meat Mart
8627 Olive Street
Telephone: (314) 721 9624

COMMUNITY ORGANISATIONS
Jewish Federation of St Louis
12 Millstone Campus Drive, St Louis, Missouri 63146
Telephone: (314) 432 0020
Fax: (314) 432 1277
Email: jfedstl@jfedstl.org
Website: www.jewishinstlouis.org
Founded in 1901, Jewish Federation is the central fundraising and planning organisation for the 60,000 member St Louis Jewish Community. The Federation supports 47 local, national and international human and social service organisations.

LIBRARIES
The Brodsky Jewish Community Library
12 Millstone Campus Drive 63146
Telephone: (314) 442 3720
Fax: (314) 432 6150
Email: brodsky-library@jfedstl.org
Website: www.brodskylibrary.org
The Saul Brodsky Jewish Community Library is the St. Louis community's central and comprehensive source for Judaica. Established in 1983 through the generosity of the Saul Brodsky family and with the continued support of the Jewish Federation of St. Louis and the St. Louis community, the Brodsky Library has become one of the finest Judaic libraries in the midwest and an invaluable Jewish resource for the community.

MIKVAOT
Mikvah
4 Millstone Campus 63146
Telephone: (314) 569 2770 ext.14
Fax: (314) 569 2774

MUSEUMS
Holocaust Museum and Learning Center
12 Milestone Campus Drive 63146
Telephone: (314) 432 0020
Fax: (314) 432 1277
Website: www.hmlc.org

RELIGIOUS ORGANISATIONS
The Vaad Hoeir (United Orthodox Jewish community of St Louis)
4 Millstone Campus
Telephone: (314) 569 2770
Fax: (314) 569 2774
Website: www.ovkosher.org

RESTAURANTS
Meat
Diamant's
618 North & South Road
Telephone: (314) 291 6050

Simon Kohn's
10405 Old Olive Street 63141
Telephone: (314) 560 0727
Website: http://www.kohnskosher.com

SYNAGOGUES
Young Israel of St Louis
8101 Delmar Boulevard 63130
Telephone: (314) 727 1880
Fax: (314) 727 2177

Montana
Cascade County
GREAT FALLS
Reform
Aitz Chaim
1015 1st Avenue North, Suite 304 59401
Telephone: (406) 322 2705
Fax: (406) 761 3601
Email: aitzchaim@gmail.com
Website: http://mt002.urj.net
We are in the middles of changing phone numbers. Please send all communications via email

Christian County
BILLINGS
Congregation Beth Aaron
1148 N. Broadway 59101
Telephone: (406) 248 6412

Missoula County
MISSOULA
Har Shalom
PO Box 7581 59807
Telephone: (406) 549 9595
Email: toba@bigsky.net
Website: www.har-shalom.org

We are a small synagogue without a building of our own but we meet every Saturday morning for Torah study at the Missoula Public Library from 10am to noon. Visitors are welcome.

Nebraska

Douglas County

OMAHA
COMMUNITY ORGANISATIONS
Jewish Federation of Omaha
333 S. 132nd Street
Telephone: (402) 993 9977

MIKVAOT
Com. Mikva
323 S. 132nd Street
Telephone: (402) 334 8200
Fax: (402) 334 1330
Email: jkatzman@jewishomaha.org
Website: www.jewishomaha.org
Supervision: Rav Ha'machsher, Rabbi Jonathan Gross
Central organisation: Jewish Federation of Omaha

SYNAGOGUES
Conservative
Beth El Synagogue
14506 California Street 68154
Telephone: (402) 492 8550
Fax: (402) 492 8520
Email: exec@bethel-omaha.org
Website: www.bethel-omaha.org

Orthodox
Beth Israel
1502 N. 52nd Street 68104
Telephone: (402) 556 6288

Beth Israel Synagogue
12604 Pacific Street, Omaha, NE 68104
Telephone: (402) 556 6288

Reform
Temple Israel
7023 Cass Street 68132
Telephone: (402) 556 6536
Fax: (402) 556 6189
Email: tisrael@templeisraelomaha.com
Website: www.templeisrael-ne.org

Lincoln County

LINCOLN
Conservative
Congregation Tifereth Israel
3219 Sheridan Boulevard 68502
Telephone: (402) 423 8569
Fax: (402) 423 0178

Reform
South Street Temple B'nai Jeshurum
20th & South Streets 68502
Telephone: (402) 423 8004

Nevada

Clark County

LAS VEGAS
DELICATESSEN
Casba Glatt Kosher
2845 Las Vegas Boulevard.
Telephone: (702) 791 3344

Rafi's Place
6135 West Sahara 89102
Telephone: (702) 253 0033

Sara's Place
4972 S. Maryland

MIKVAOT
Mikvaot
1260 S. Arville
Telephone: (702) 259 0770 ext 8

RESTAURANTS
Meat
Haifa Restaurant
855 E. Twain
Telephone: (702) 791 1956

Las Vegas Kosher Deli
3317 L.V. Boulevard S.
Telephone: (702) 892 9080

Shalom Hunan
4850 W. Flamingo Road
Telephone: (702) 871 3262
Fax: (702) 871 3083
Supervision: Chabad of southern Nevada

SYNAGOGUES
Conservative
Temple Emanu El
4925 South Torrey Pines Drive 89118
Telephone: (702) 254 3270

Orthodox
Chabad of Southern Nevada
1261 S. Arville
Telephone: (702) 877 4700
Email: chabadlv@aol.com
Website: www.chabadlv.org

Chabad of Summerlin
2640 Regatta Drive
Telephone: (702) 855 0770
Fax: (702) 433 0770
Email: chabadofsummerlin@yahoo.com
Website: www.chabadofsummerlin.com

Congregation Or-Bamidbar
2991 Emerson Avenue
Telephone: (702) 369 1175

Young Israel of Las Vegas
9590 West Sahara 89117
Telephone: (702) 360 8909
Website: www.aish.combranches/las_vegas

Reform
Adat Ari El
4675 W Flamingo Road #2 89103
Telephone: (702) 221 1230
Affiliated with Union Reform Judaism

Temple Beth Am
9001 Hillpointe Road
Telephone: (702) 254 5110

Temple Bett Emet
St. Andrew Lutheran Church , 8901 Del Webb
Boulevard Sun City
Telephone: (702) 243 5781

Lander County
HENDERSON
Congregation Ner Tamid
2920 North Green Valley Parkway #521 89014
Telephone: (702) 733 6292
Website: www.lvnertamid.org

Washoe County
RENO
Temple Sinai
3405 Gulling Road 89503
Telephone: (775) 747 5508
Fax: (775) 747 1911
Email: temple.sinai@pyramid.net
Website: www.templesinai-reno.com

New Hampshire
Grafton County
BETHLEHEM
HOTELS
Arlington Hotel
1848 Main St 03574
Telephone: (603) 869 3353

MIKVAOT
Machzikei Hadas
Lewis Hill Road 03574
Telephone: (603) 869 3336

SYNAGOGUES
Conservative
Bethlehem Hebrew Congregation
Strawberry Hill, P.O. Box 524 03574
Telephone: (603) 869 5465
Email: bethlehemsynagogue.org

Orthodox
Machzikei Hadas
Lewis Hill Road 03574
Telephone: (603) 869 3336

Hillsborough County
MANCHESTER
COMMUNITY ORGANISATIONS
Jewish Federation of Greater Manchester
698 Beech Street 03104
Telephone: (603) 627 7679
Fax: (603) 627 7963

MEDIA
Newspapers
The Reporter
698 Beech Street 03104
Telephone: (603) 627 7679

SYNAGOGUES
Orthodox
Lubavitch
7 Camelot Drive 03104
Telephone: (603) 647 0204

Reform
Adath Yeshurun
152 Prospect Street 03104
Telephone: (603) 669 5650

Merrimack County
CONCORD
Temple Beth Jacob
67 Broadway 03301
Telephone: (603) 228 8581

Rockingham County
PORTSMOUTH
Conservative
Temple Israel
200 State Street 03801
Telephone: (603) 436 5301
Fax: (603) 436 5328
Email: office@templeisraelnh.org
Website: www.templeisraelnh.org

New Jersey
LAKEWOOD
KOSHER FOOD
Euro Cut Inc /LaBruiye Meals
520 James Street, Unit 1C
Telephone: (732) 905 1555
Website: www.labruitemeals.com

UNION
SYNAGOGUES
Orthodox
Elmora Hills Minyan
961 Magic Avenue
Supervision: haRav Elazar M. Teitz

Atlantic County
ATLANTIC CITY
RESTAURANTS
Meat
Jerusalem
6410 Ventnor Ave, Ventnor 08406
Telephone: (609) 822 2266
Supervision: Rabbi Abraham Spacirer

RESTAURANTS
Glatt Kosher
Sharis Glatt Kosher Steakhouse
6821 Black Horse Pike, Egg Harbor Township
Telephone: (609) 272 6556

SYNAGOGUES
Conservative
Beth El
500 N. Jerome Ave, Margate 08406

Beth Judah
700 N Swarthmore Avenue, Ventor 08406
Telephone: (609) 822 7116
Fax: (609) 822 4654
Email: congbethjudah@aol.com

Community Synagogue
Maryland & Pacific Avs 08401
Telephone: (609) 345 3282

Orthodox
Chelsea Hebrew Congregation
4001 Atlantic Av 08401
Telephone: (609) 345 0825

Rodef Shalom
3833 Atlantic Av 08401
Telephone: (609) 345 4580

Reform
Beth Israel
2501 Shore Rd, Northfield 08225
Telephone: (609) 641 3600

Temple Emeth Synagogue
8501 Ventnor Av, Margate 08402
Telephone: (609) 822 4343

Bergen County
BERGENFIELD
BUTCHERS
Take out & Deli
Glatt World
89 Newbridge Road 07621
Telephone: (201) 439 9675
Fax: (201) 439 0342
Email: glattworld@gmail.com
Supervision: RCBC

DELICATESSEN
Foster Village Kosher Delicatessen & Catering
469 S. Washington Avenue 07621
Telephone: (201) 384 7100
Fax: (201) 384 0303
Supervision: Quality Kashrut Supervisory Service

SYNAGOGUES
Conservative
Congregation Beth Israel of Northern Valley
169 N. Washington Avenue 07621
Telephone: (201) 384 3911
Website: www.uscj.org/njersey/bergenfield

ELMWOOD PARK
COMMUNITY ORGANISATIONS
Elmwood Park Jewish Center
100 Gilbert Avenue
Telephone: (201) 797 7320/797 9749

ENGLEWOOD
GROCERIES
Kosher By the Case & Less
255 Van Norstrand Avenue 07631
Telephone: (201) 568 2281
Fax: (201) 568 5681
Supervision: RCBC

MIKVAOT
Mikva
89 Huguenot Avenue
Telephone: (201) 567 1143

RESTAURANTS
Meat
Sol & Sol
34 E Palisade Avenue 07631
Telephone: (201) 541 6880
Supervision: Kashrut Committee of Bergen County

SYNAGOGUES
Conservative
Temple Emanu-el
147 Tenafly Road 07631
Telephone: (201) 567 1300

Orthodox
Ahavath Torah
240 Broad Avenue, NJ 07631
Telephone: (201) 568 1315
Fax: (201) 568 2991
Email: egorlyn@ahavathtorah.org
Website: www.ahavathtorah.org
Supervision: Rabbinical Council of Bergen County
Central organisation: Member of Orthodox Union

Shomrei Emunah
89 Huguenot Avenue, between Broad and Grand
Avenues 07631
Telephone: (201) 567 9420
Email: shomreiemunah@verizon.net
Website: www.shomreiemunahnj.org
Mikvah on premises
Fax: Att. Robert Lunzen (212) 644 3792

FAIR LAWN
BAKERIES
New Royal Bakery
19-09 Fair Lawn Avenue 07410
Telephone: (201) 796 6565
Fax: (201) 796 8501
Supervision: RCBC

BUTCHERS
Food Showcase
24-28 Fair Lawn Avenue 07410
Telephone: (201) 475 0077
Superviosion: RCBC

RESTAURANTS
Dairy
J.C. Pizza of Fairlawn
14-20 Plaza Road 07410
Telephone: (201) 703 0801
Supervision: RCBC

SYNAGOGUES
Orthodox
Bris Arushon
22-24 Fairlawn Avenue 07410
Telephone: (201) 791 7200

FORT LEE
BUTCHERS
**Blue Ribbon Self-Service Kosher Meat
Market**
1363 Inwood Terrace 07024
Telephone: (201) 224 3220
Fax: (201) 224 7281

DELICATESSEN
Al's Kosher Deli
209 Main Street 07024
Telephone: (201) 461 3044
Supervision: Quality Kashrut Supervisory Service

SYNAGOGUES
Conservative
Jewish Community Center of Fort Lee
1449 Anderson Avenue 07024
Telephone: (201) 947 1735
Fax: (201) 947 1530

Orthodox
Young Israel of Fort Lee
1610 Parker Avenue 07024
Telephone: (201) 592 1518
Fax: (201) 592 8414
Email: yiftlee@gmail.com
Website: www.yiftlee.org

HACKENSACK
COMMUNITY ORGANISATIONS
**Jewish Federation of Community Services of
Bergen County**
170 State Street 07601

SYNAGOGUES
Conservative
Temple Beth El
280 Summit Avenue 07601
Telephone: (201) 342 2045

HASBROUCK
Reform
Temple Beth Elohim
Bourlevard & Charlton Aves
Telephone: (201) 393 7707

MAHWAH
Temple Beth Haverim
280 Remjo Valley Road
Telephone: (201) 512 1983

PARAMUS
BUTCHERS
Harold's Self-Service Kosher Meat
67-A E. Ridgewood Avenue
Telephone: (201) 262 0030

COMMUNITY ORGANISATIONS
Jewish Center of Paramus
304 Midland Avenue
Telephone: (201) 262 7691

SYNAGOGUES
Conservative
Jewish Community Center of paramus
E-304 Midland Avenue 07652
Telephone: (201) 262 7691
Website: www.uscj.org/njersey/paramus

RIDGEWOOD
Temple Israel
475 Grove Street
Telephone: (201) 444 9320

RIVER EDGE
Reform
Temple Sholom
385 Howland Avenue 07661
Telephone: (201) 489 2463
Fax: (201) 489 0775
Website: www.uahcweb.org/nj/tsholomre/

TEANECK
BAKERIES
Butterflake Bake Shop
448 Cedar Lane 07666
Telephone: (201) 836 3516
Fax: (201) 836 3056
Supervision: RCBC

Gruenebaum Bakeries
477B Cedar Lane 07666
Telephone: (201) 839 3128

Korn's Bakery
1378 Quenn Anne Road 07666
Telephone: (201) 833 0114

Sammy's New York Bagels
1443 Queen Anne Road 07666
Telephone: (201) 837 0515
Fax: (201) 837 9733
Supervision: Kof-K

BOOKSELLERS
Zoldan's Judaica Center
406 Cedar Lane 07666
Telephone: (201) 907 0034

BUTCHERS
Glatt Express
1400 Queen Anne Road 07666
Telephone: (201) 837 8110
Fax: (201) 837 0084
Supervision: RCBC

DELICATESSEN
Kosher
Chopstix
172 West Englewood Avenue 07666
Telephone: (201) 833 0200
Fax: (201) 833 8326
Email: chopstixusa@yahoo.com
Website: www.chopstixusa.com
Supervision: RCBC

JUDAICA
Books
Judaica House
478 Cedar Lane 07666
Telephone: (201) 801 9001
Fax: (201) 801 9004
Email: mail@judaicahouse.net
Website: www.jewishbookdistributors.com
www.jewishbookdistributors.com

MIKVAOT
Mikveh
1726 Windsor Road 07666
Telephone: (201) 837 8220

RESTAURANTS
Dairy
Jerusalem Pizza
496 Cedar Lane 07666
Telephone: (201) 836 2120
Fax: (201) 836 2261
Supervision: RCBC

Plaza Pizza & Restaurant
1431 Queen Anne Road 07666
Telephone: (201) 837 9500
Fax: (201) 836 2261
Supervision: RCBC

Shelly's
482 Cedar Lane
Telephone: (201) 692 0001
Fax: (201) 692 1890
Supervision: RCBC

Meat
Hunan Teaneck
515 Cedar Lane 07666
Telephone: (201) 692 0099
Fax: (201) 692 1907
Supervision: RCBC

Noah's Ark
493 Cedar Lane 07666
Telephone: (201) 692 1200
Fax: (201) 692

SYNAGOGUES
Conservative
Congrtation Beth Shalom
354 Maitland Avenue 07666
Telephone: (201) 833 2620
Fax: (201) 833 2620
Email: bsteaneck@aol.com
Website: www.uscj.org/njersey/teaneckcbs

Orthodox
Congregation Beth Aaron
950 Queen Anne Road 07666
Telephone: (201) 836 6210
Fax: (201) 836 0005
Website: www.bethaaron.org

Congregation Bnai Yeshurun
641 W. Englewood Avenue 07666
Telephone: (201) 836 8916
Fax: (201) 836 1888
Email: bnaiyeshurun@aol.com
Website: www.bnaiyeshurun.org

Rinat Yisrael
389 W. Englewood Avenue 07666
Telephone: (201) 837 2795
Email: office@rinat.org

Roemer Synagogue
Whittier School, W. Englewood Avenue 07666

Reform
Congregation Beth Am
1148 Converse Street 01106
Telephone: (201) 413 567 8665
Fax: (201) 410 567 2233

Temple Emeth
1666 Windsor Rd 07666
Telephone: (201) 833 1322
Fax: (201) 833 4831
Website: www.emeth.org

Traditional
Jewish Center of Teaneck
70 Sterling Place 07666
Telephone: (201) 833 0515
Fax: (201) 833 0511
Email: execdir@aol.com
Website: www.jewishcenterofteaneck.org
Also with alternative;Orthodox Mechitza service, Shira
Hadasha service, Family service

TENAFLY
Reform
Temple Sinai of Bergen County
1 Engle Street 07670
Telephone: (201) 568 3035
Fax: (201) 568 6095
Website: www.uahc.org/congs.nj/nj009

WASHINGTON TOWNSHIP
Temple Beth Or
56 Ridgewood Rd
Telephone: (201) 664 7422

WYCKOFF
Temple Beth Rishon
585 Russell Ave
Telephone: (201) 891 4466
Fax: (201) 891 0508

Burlington County
BURLINGTON
Conservative
B'nai Israel
212 High Street
Telephone: (201) 858 9052

CINNAMINSON
Temple Sinai
2101 New Albany Road 08077
Telephone: (609) 829 0658
Fax: (609) 829 0310
Email: tsoffice@snip.net
Website: www.uscj.org/njersey/cinnaminson

WILLINGBORO
Reform
Adath Emanu-El
299 John F. Kennedy Way 08046
Telephone: (609) 871 1736

Cumberland County
BRIDGETON
SYNAGOGUES
Conservative
Congregation Beth Abraham
330 Fayette Street 08302
Burlington

SYNAGOGUES
Conservative
B'nai Israel
212 High Street 08332
Telephone: (718) 386 0406

Camden County
CHERRY HILL
BUTCHERS
Cherry Hill Kosher Market
907 W. Marlton Pike 08002
Telephone: (856) 428 6663

COMMUNITY ORGANISATIONS
Torah Education at Cherry Hill
25 Lantern Lane 08002
Website: www.teach613.org

SYNAGOGUES
Orthodox
Young Israel of Cherry Hill
817 Cooper Landing Road 08002
Telephone: (856) 667-1979
Email: president18@yicherryhill.org
Website: www.yicherryhill.org

DELICATESSEN
Leo's Deli
J.C.C. 1301 Springdale Road
Telephone: (856) 424 4444 Ext 158
Supervision: Tri-County Vaad

MIKVAOT
Sons of Israel
720 Cooper Landing Road 08002
Telephone: (856) 667 3515
Email: officemgr@SonsIsrael.com
Website: www.sonsofisrael.org

RESTAURANTS
Meat
Maxim's Restaurant
404 Route 70
Telephone: (856) 428 5045

SYNAGOGUES

Conservative

Beth El
2901 W. Chapel Avenue 08002
Telephone: (856) 667 1300

Beth Shalom
1901 Kresson Road 08003
Telephone: (856) 751 6663

Congregation Beth Tikva
115 Evesboro-Medford Road, Marlton,

Orthodox

Congregation Sons of Israel
720 Cooper Landing Road 08002
Telephone: (856) 667 9700

Reform

Congregation M'kor Shalom
850 Evesham Road
Telephone: (856) 424 4220
Fax: (856) 424 2890

Temple Emmanuel
1101 Springdale Road

HADDONFIELD
BUTCHERS
Sarah's Kosher Kitchen
63 Ellis Road

Cumberland County

BRIDGETON
SYNAGOGUES
Conservative
Congregation Beth Abraham
330 Fayette Street 08302

VINELAND
COMMUNITY ORGANISATIONS
Jewish Federation of Cumberland County
1063 East Landis Avenue, Suite B 08360-3785
Telephone: (856) 696 4445
Fax: (856) 696 3428

SYNAGOGUES

Conservative
Beth Israel
1015 E. Park Avenue 08630
Telephone: (856) 691 0852

Orthodox
Ahavas Achim
618 Plum Street 08360
Telephone: (856) 691 2218

Synagogue
321 Grape Street 08360
Telephone: (856) 692 4232
Fax: (856) 691 4985

Essex County

LIVINGSTON
RESTAURANTS
Dairy
Jerusalem Restaurant
99-101 West Mt Pleasant Avenue 07039
Telephone: (973) 533 1424
Fax: (973) 533 9275
Supervision: Vaad Hakashrus of the Council of Orthodox
Rabbis Metrowest

Meat
Moshavi
515 S. Livingston Avenue 07039
Telephone: (973) 740 8777
Supervision: Vaad Hakashrus of the Council of Orthodox
Rabbis Metrowest

SYNAGOGUES

Conservative
Temple Beth Shalom
193 E. Mt Pleasant Avenue 07039
Telephone: (973) 992 3600

Independent
Temple B'Nai Abraham
300 East Northfield Road 07039
Telephone: (973) 994 2290
Fax: (973) 994 1838
Email: tbainfo@tbanj.org
Website: www.tbanj.org

Orthodox
Etz Chaim Synagogue
1 Lafayette Drive 07039
Telephone: (973) 597 1655

Synagogue of the Suburban Torah Center
85 W Mount Pleasant Avenue 07039
Telephone: (973) 994 2620/0122
Fax: (973) 535 3898
Email: admin@suburbantorah.org
Website: www.suburbantorah.org

Reform
Temple Emanu-el of West Essex
264 W. Northfield Road 07039
Telephone: (973) 992 5560

MAPLEWOOD
BOOKSELLERS
Skybook
1923 Springfield Avenue 07040
Telephone: (973) 763 4244/4245

SHORT HILLS
SYNAGOGUES
Reform
B'Nai Jeshurun
1025 South Orange Avenue 07078
Telephone: (973) 379 1555
Fax: (973) 379 4345
Email: info@tbj.org
Website: www.tbj.org

WEST CALDWELL
DELICATESSEN
David's Deco-Tessen
555 Passaic Avenue 07006
Telephone: (973) 808 3354
Fax: (973) 808 5806
Email: davidsdecotessen@aol.com
Supervision: Rabbi Herman Savitz (Conservative)

WEST ORANGE
GROCERIES
Gourmet Galaxy
659 Eagle Rock Avenue 07052
Telephone: (973) 736 0060
Supervision: Vaad Hakashrus of the Council of Orthodox
Rabbis Metrowest

JUDAICA
Lubavitch Center of Essex County
456 Pleasant Valley Way 07052
Telephone: (973) 731 0770
Fax: (973) 731 6821

KOSHER FOOD
Chinese
Chopstix
478 Pleasant Valley Way
Telephone: (973) 324 8000
Fax: (973) 243 1332
Website: www.chopstixusa.com
Supervision: Vaad Hakashrus of Metro West

RESTAURANTS
Meat
Eden Wok
478 Pleasant Valley Way 07052
Telephone: (973) 243 0115
Fax: (973) 243 1332
Supervision: Vaad Hakashrus of the Council of Orthodox
Rabbis Metrowest

Pleasantdale Kosher Meat
470 Pleasant Valley Way 07052
Telephone: (973) 731 3216

SYNAGOGUES
Conservative
B'Nai Shalom
300 Pleasant Valley Way 07052
Telephone: (973) 731 0160
Fax: (973) 731 1160
Email: bnai@aol.com

Orthodox
Congregation Ahawas Achim B'nai Jacob and David
700 Pleasant Valley Way 07052
Telephone: (973) 736 1407
Fax: (973) 736 8006

Essex County,
SOUTH ORANGE
GROCERIES
Zayda's Super Value Meat Market & Deli
309 Irvington Avenue 07079
Telephone: (973) 762 1812

SYNAGOGUES
Conservative
Oheb Shalom Congregation
170 Scotland Road 07079
Telephone: (973) 762 7067

Reform
Temple Sharey Tefilo-Israel
432 Scotland Road 07079
Telephone: (973) 763 4116

Hudson County
BAYONNE
COMMUNITY ORGANISATIONS
Jewish Community Centre
1050 Kennedy Blv 07002
Telephone: (201) 436 6900

SYNAGOGUES
Conservative
Temple Emanuel
735 Kennedy Boulevard 07002
Telephone: (201) 436 4499

Orthodox
Ohab Sholom
1016-1022 Avenue C 07002

Ohav Zedek
912 Avenue C 07002
Telephone: (201) 437 1488

Uptown Synagogue
49th Street & Avenue C 07002

Reform
Temple Beth Am
111 Avenue B 07002
Telephone: (201) 858 9052

JERSEY CITY

Orthodox
Congregation Mount Sinai
128 Sherman Avenue 07307
Telephone: (201) 222 3445
Email: MtSinai@gmail.com
Website: www.mtsinai.net

WEST NEW YORK
Congregation Shaare Zedek
5308 Palisade Avenue 07093
Telephone: (201) 867 6859

Mercer County
LAWRENCEVILLE
Young Israel of Lawrenceville
2556 Princeton Pike 08648
Telephone: (609) 883 8833
Website: www.yiol.com

PRINCETON

Conservative
The Jewish Center of Princeton
435 Nassau Street 08540
Telephone: (609) 921 0100
Fax: (609) 921 7531
Email: info@thejewishcenter.org
Website: www.thejewishcenter.org

TRENTON

COMMUNITY ORGANISATIONS
Jewish Federation of Mercer & Bucks Counties
999 Lower Ferry Road 08628
Telephone: (609) 883 5000

Middlesex County
COLONIA
SYNAGOGUES
Conservative
Ohev Shalom
220 Temple Way 07067
Telephone: (908) 388 7222

CRANBURY
Jewish Congregation of Concordia
c/o Club House 08512
Telephone: (609) 655 8136

EAST BRUNSWICK
BUTCHERS
East Brunswick Kosher Meats
1020 State Highway 18 08816
Telephone: (908) 257 0007

SYNAGOGUES
Conservative
East Brunswick Jewish Center
511 Ryders Lane 08816
Telephone: (732) 257 7070
Fax: (732) 257 9630
Website: www.ebjc.org

Reform
Temple B'nai Shalom
Fern & Old Stage Road, PO Box 957 08816
Telephone: (732) 251 4300

EDISON
COMMUNITY ORGANISATIONS
Jewish Community Center of Middlesex County
1775 Oak Tree Road 8820
Telephone: (732) 494 3232
Fax: (732) 548 2850

SYNAGOGUES
Conservative
Beth El
91 Jefferson Boulevard 08817
Telephone: (732) 985 7272

HIGHLAND PARK
GROCERIES
Berkley Bakery
405 Raritan Avenue 08904
Telephone: (732) 220 1919

Kosher Catch
239 Raritan Avenue
Telephone: (732) 572 9052

MIKVAOT
Park Mikva
112 S. 1st Avenue 08904
Telephone: (732) 249 2411

SYNAGOGUES
Conservative
Highland Park Conservative Temple & Center
201 S. 3rd Avenue 08904
Telephone: (732) 545 6482
Fax: (732) 246 3100

Orthodox
Congregation Ahavas Achim
216 S. 1st Avenue 08904
Telephone: (732) 247 0532
Fax: (732) 247 6739

Email: info@ahavasachim.org
Website: www.ahavasachim.org
Supervision: Rabbi Steven Miodownik
Congregation Etz Ahaim (Sephardi)
230 Denison Street NJ 08904
Telephone: (732) 247 3839
Fax: (732) 545 3191
Email: info@etzahaim.org
Website: www.etzahaim.org
Supervision: Rabbi David Bassous
Sephardic Synagogue welcomes all Jews

JAMESBURG
Rossmoor Jewish Congregation Meeting Room
Telephone: (609) 655 0439

METUCHEN
Conservative
Neve Shalom
250 Grove Avenue 08840
Telephone: (732) 548 2238
Fax: (732) 548 2238
Email: neve.shalom@verizon.net
Website: www.neveshalom.net

NEW BRUNSWICK
Orthodox
Chabad House Friends of Lubavitch
170 College Avenue 08901
Telephone: (732) 296 1800
Fax: (732) 828 6890
Website: www.chabad.rutgers.edu
Central organisation: Chabad-Lubavitch

Congregation Poile Zedek
145 Neilson Street, PO Box 166 08903
Telephone: (732) 545 6123
Fax: (732) 545 0394
Email: admin@poilezedek.org
Website: www.poilezedek.org
Congregation Poile Zedek is an Orthodox Ashkenazic synagogue. We offer daily morning, Shabbat and holiday services, and are committed to Torah education and community service. Centrally located, we are just a few short blocks from New Jersey Transit, major highways, and the New Brunswick Hyatt. In 1995 our beautiful building was placed on the National Register of Historic Places.

NORTH BRUNSWICK
Conservative
Congrgation B'nai Tikvah
1001 Finnegans Lane 08902
Telephone: (732) 297 0696
Fax: (732) 297 2673
Email: office@bnaitikvah.org
Website: www.bnaitikvah.org

Reform
Anshe Emeth Memorial Temple
222 Livingston Avenue 08901
Telephone: (732) 545 6484
Fax: (732) 745 7448
Website: www.aemt.net

OLD BRIDGE
Conservative
Ohav Shalom
3018 Bordertown Avenue 08859
Telephone: (201) 727 4334

PERTH AMBOY
Beth Mordechai
224 High Street 08861
Telephone: (732) 442 2431

Orthodox
Shaarey Teflioh
15 Market Street 08861
Telephone: (732) 826 2977

SPOTSWOOD
Reform
Monroe Township Jewish Center
11 Cornell Avenue 08884
Telephone: (201) 251 1119

Middlesex County

SOUTH RIVER
COMMUNITY ORGANISATIONS
Jewish Federation of Greater Middlesex County
230 Old Bridge Turnpike 08882
Telephone: (732) 432 7711
Fax: (732) 432 0292
Email: info@jf-gmc.org
Website: www.JewishMiddlesex.org

SYNAGOGUES
Traditional
Congregation Anshe Emeth of South River
88 Main Street 08882
Telephone: (732) 257 4190
Fax: (732) 254 8819
Website: www.members.home.net/ebweiss

Monmouth County

ABERDEEN
Orthodox
Young Israel of Aberdeen - Cong. Bet Tefilah
479 Lloyd Road 07747
Telephone: (732) 583 6262
Mobile Phone: 347 276 5708
Email: Rabbi@yiaberdeen.com
Website: www.yiaberdeen.com
Supervision: Rabbi Chaim Lobel

Central organisation: National Council Young Israel Affilliate

The Young Israel of Aberdeen - Congregation Bet Tefilah is an orthodox synagogue serving Greater Aberdeen. Led by Rabbi Chaim Z. Lobel, the Young Israel provides daily minyanim, classes, and special events.

BELMAR
SYNAGOGUES
Orthodox
Sons of Israel Congregation
PO Box 298 07719
Telephone: (973) 681 3200

BRADLEY BEACH
SYNAGOGUES
Orthodox
Congregation Agudath Achim
301 McCabe Avenue 07720
Telephone: (973) 774 2495

DEAL
RESTAURANTS
Pizzerias
Jerusalem II Pizza
106 Norwood Avenue 07723
Telephone: (732) 531 7936

SYNAGOGUES
Orthodox
Ohel Yaacob Congregation
6 Ocean Avenue, PO Box 225 07723
Telephone: (732) 531 0217/2405

Synagogue
128 Norwood Avenue 07723
Telephone: (732) 531 3200

FREEHOLD
RESTAURANTS
Fred and Murry's
Pond Road Shopping Center, Route 9 07728
Telephone: (732) 462 3343
Website: www.fredandmurrys.com

SYNAGOGUES
Traditional
Agudath Achim/Freehold Jewish Center
Broad & Stokes Streets 07728
Telephone: (732) 462 0254
Fax: (732) 462 6868
Email: freeholdjc@gmail.com
Website: www.freeholdjewishcenter.com

RUMSON
Conservative
Congregation B'nai Israel
Hance & Ridge Roads 07760
Telephone: (908) 842 1800

Morris County
MORRIS PLAINS
DELICATESSEN
Jonathan's Deli Restaurant
2900 Route 10 West 07950
Telephone: (973) 539 6010

MORRISTOWN
KASHRUT INFORMATION
Rabbinical College of America
226 Sussex Avenue 07960
Telephone: (973) 267 9404

MIKVAOT
Mikvah Bais Chana, Sarah Esther Rosenhaus Mikvah Institute
93 Lake Road 07960
Telephone: (973) 292 3932
Email: vallevue@verizon.net

SYNAGOGUES
Conservative
Morristown Jewish Center
177 Speedwell Avenue 07960
Telephone: (973) 538 9292
Website: www.mjcby.org

Orthodox
Congregation Ahavath Yisrael
9 Cutler Street 07960
Telephone: (973) 267 4184
Fax: (973) 898 1711
Email: sofernj@aol.com

Congregation Levi Yitzchok
226 Sussex Avenue 07960
Telephone: (973) 984 6326

PARSIPPANNY
DELICATESSEN
Arlington Kosher Deli, Restaurant & Caterers
Arlington Shopping Center, 744 Route 46W 07054
Telephone: (973) 335 9400

RANDOLPH
SYNAGOGUES
Orthodox
Mount Freedom Jewish Center
1209 Sussex Turnpike 07970
Telephone: (781) 895 2100

WHIPPANY
COMMUNITY ORGANISATIONS
United Jewish Federation of Metrowest
901 Route 10   07981
Telephone: (973) 884 4800
Fax: (973) 884 7361

MEDIA
Newspaper
The New Jersey Jewish News
901 Route 10 07981
Telephone: (973) 887 8500
Fax: (973) 887 4152

Ocean County
LAKEWOOD
BAKERIES
Gelbsteins Bakery
415 Clifton Avenue 08701
Telephone: (732) 363 3636
Supervision: Orthodox
Lakewood Heimishe Bakeshop
225-2nd Street 08701
Telephone: (732) 905 9057
Supervision: Orthodox

BOOKSELLERS
Torah Treasures
254-2nd Street 08701
Telephone: (732) 901 1911
Fax: (732) 905 6482

BUTCHERS
Shloimy's Kosher World
23 E. County Line Road 08701
Telephone: (732) 363 3066

COMMUNITY ORGANISATIONS
Jewish Federation of Ocean County
301 Madison Avenue 08701
Telephone: (732) 363 0530
Fax: (732) 363 2097
Email: ocjf@optonline.net
Website: www.jewishoceancounty.org

KASHRUT INFORMATION
KCC - Cashrus Council of Lakewood
Telephone: (732) 901 1888

MIKVAOT
Congregation Mikvah Tahara
1101 Madison Avenue 08701
Telephone: (732) 370 1666

RESTAURANTS
Dairy
Bagel Nosh
380 Clifton Avenue 08701
Telephone: (732) 363 1115
Fax: (732) 363 5745
Email: info@bagelnoshnj.com
Central organisation: Kashrus Council of Lakewood

Meat
R & S Kosher Restaurant and Deli
416 Clifton Avenue 08701

Telephone: (732) 363 6688
Supervision: Kashrus supervision: Lakewood Satmar Dayan
Yum Mee Glatt
116 Clifton Avenue 08701
Telephone: (732) 886 9688
Pizzeria
Pizza Plus
241 4th Street 08701
Telephone: (732) 367 0711
Supervision: Orthodox

SYNAGOGUES
Conservative
Congregation Ahavat Shalom
1075 Forest Avenue 08701
Telephone: (732) 363 5190
Website: www.uscj.org/njersey/lakewood

Orthodox
Beth Medrashe Govoha
617 Private Way (Sixth Street) 08701
Telephone: (732) 367 1060
Kol Shimson
323 Squamkum Road 08701
Telephone: (732) 901 6680
Sons of Israel
Madison Avenue & 6th Street 08701
Telephone: (732) 364 2800

Passaic County
CLIFTON
COMMUNITY ORGANISATIONS
Jewish Federation of Greater Clifton-Passaic
199 Scoles Avenue 07012
Telephone: (973) 777 7031
Fax: (973) 777 6701
Email: planned.giving@verizon.net

MEDIA
Newspaper
Jewish Community News
199 Scoles Avenue 07012

RESTAURANTS
Jerusalem II Pizza
224 Brook Avenue 07055
Telephone: (973) 778 0960

SYNAGOGUES
Conservative
Clifton Jewish Center
18 Delaware Street 07011
Telephone: (973) 772 3131

Reform
Beth Shalom
733 Passaic 07012
Telephone: (973) 773 0355

PASSAIC

DELICATESSEN
B&Y Kosher Korner Inc.
200 Main Avenue 07055
Telephone: (973) 777 1120

SUPERMARKET
Kosher Konnection
200 Main Avenue 07055
Telephone: (973) 777 1120
Fax: (973) 777 4991

SYNAGOGUES
Orthodox
Young Israel of Passaic-Clifton
200 Brook Avenue
Telephone: (973) 778 7117

PATERSON
Conservative
Temple Emanuel
151 E. 33rd Street 07514
Telephone: (973) 684 5565

WAYNE

COMMUNITY ORGANISATIONS
Jewish Federation of New Jersey
1 Pike Drive 07470
Telephone: (973) 595 0555

SYNAGOGUES
Conservative
Shomrei Torah
30 Hinchman Avenue 07470
Telephone: (973) 694 6274

Reform
Temple Beth Tikvah
950 Preakness Avenue 07470
Telephone: (973) 595 6565
Fax: (973) 595 8192

Somerset County
SOMERSET
Conservative
Temple Beth El
1945 Amwell Road 08873
Telephone: 873 2325

Union County
CLARK
Temple Beth O'r
111 Valley Road 07066
Telephone: (732) 381 8403
Fax: (732) 381 1389
Email: tbethor@gmail.com
Website: www.bethorbethtorah.org

CRANFORD
CONTACT INFORMATION
Rabbi Hoffberg
Telephone: (201) 276 9231

SYNAGOGUES
Conservative
Temple Beth El Mekor Chayim
338 Walnut Avenue 07016
Telephone: (908) 276 9231
Fax: (908) 276 6570
Email: office@tbemc.org

ELIZABETH
BAKERIES
The Elizabeth Kosher Bakery
187 Elmora Avenue 07202
Telephone: (908) 289 4424
Supervision: haRav Elazar M. Teitz

CATERERS
Majestic Kosher Caterers
Barry Wacholder
Telephone: (908) 353 2680
Supervision: haRav Elazar M. Teitz

Platinum Caterers
Larry Seidman
Telephone: (908) 577 8309
Supervision: haRav Elazar M. Teitz

GROCERIES
Elizabeth One Stop Kosher
155 Elmora Avenue 07202
Telephone: (908) 354 0448
Fax: (908) 354 0449
Website: haRav Elazar M. Teitz

Kosher supermarket
Glatt Star
157 Elmora Avenue, 155 Elmora Avenue 07202
Telephone: (908) 354 6777/0448
Fax: (908) 354 0449
Email: 1stopkosher@myway.com
Website: njkosher.com
Supervision: haRav Elazar M. Teitz

RESTAURANTS
Dairy
Dunkin' Donuts
186 Elmora Avenue 07202
Supervision: haRav Elazar M. Teitz

Meat
New Kosher Special
163 Elmora Avenue 07202
Telephone: (908) 353 1818
Supervision: haRav Elazar M. Teitz

Pizzerias
Jerusalem Restaurant
150 Elmora Avenue 07202
Telephone: (908) 289 4810
Supervision: haRav Elazar M. Teitz

MIKVA
Mathilda Goldflies Mikvah
35 North Avenue 07208
Telephone: (908) 352 5048
Fax: (908) 289 5245
Email: emunah18@aol.com
Newly renovated Mikvah

Shabbas Tov Mikva
JEC Elmora Building, 330 Elmora Avenue 07208
Telephone: (908) 352 5048
Supervision: haRav Elazar M teitz
Press*2 then leave a message for Friday or Yomtov night appointments

SYNAGOGUES
Orthodox
Adath Israel
1391 North Avenue 07208
Telephone: (908) 354 7318; 355 4851
Fax: (908) 289 5245
Website: www.theJEC.org
Ashkenaz and Eidot Mizrach Minyanim. Closest synagogue to Newark International Airport.

Adath Jeshurun
200 Murray Street 07202
Supervision: haRav Elazar M. Teitz

Bais Medrash/Kollel
Yeshiva Be'er Yitzchak, 1391 North Avenue 07208
Telephone: (908) 355 6058
Bais Yitzchak
153 Bellevue Street 07202
Telephone: (908) 354 4789

Jewish Educational Center
330 Elmora Avenue 07208
Telephone: (908) 355 4850
Website: www.thejec.org
Supervision: haRav Elazar M. Teitz
Rabbi Avrohom Herman ext. 104. Rav including Minyan Sephardim and Teen Minyanim.

Jewish Educational Center Synagogue
330 Elmora Avenue 07208
Telephone: (908) 355 4850
Fax: (908) 289 5245
Website: www.thejec.org
Several daily and Shabbat Minyanim

HILLSIDE
Congregation Sinai Torath Chaim
1531 Maple Avenue 0705
Telephone: (908) 923 9500

Shomrei Torah Ohel Yosef Yitzchok
910 Salem Avenue 07205
Telephone: (908) 289 0770
Fax: (908) 289 9422

LINDEN
Conservative
Mekor Chayim Suburban Jewish Center
Deerfield Road & Academy Terrace 07036
Telephone: (908) 925 2283

Orthodox
Congregation Anshe Chesed
1000 Orchard Terrace at St George Avenue 07036
Telephone: (908) 486 8616
Fax: (908) 486 8888

PLAINFIELD
United Orthodox Synagogue
526 W. 7th Street 07063
Telephone: (908) 755 0043

Reform
Temple Sholom
815 W. 7th Street 07063
Telephone: (908) 756 6447

RAHWAY
Conservative
Temple Beth Torah
1389 Bryant Street 07065
Telephone: (609) 576 8432

ROSELLE
MEDIA
Guide
Shalom Book
843 St Georges Avenue 07203
Telephone: (908) 298 8200
Fax: (908) 298 8220

SCOTCH PLAINS
COMMUNITY ORGANISATIONS
Jewish Federation of Central New Jersey
1391 Martine Avenue
Telephone: (908) 889 5335/351 5060
Fax: (908) 889 5370
Website: www.jewishjerseycentral.org

SYNAGOGUES
Conservative
Congregation Beth Israel
18 Shalom Way, 1920 Cliffwood Street 07076
Telephone: (908) 889 1830
Fax: (908) 889 5523
Website: www.cbinj.org

UNION
Beth Shalom
2046 Vauxhall Road 07083
Telephone: (908) 686 6773

Temple Israel
2372 Morris Avenue 07083
Telephone: (908) 686 2120

VAUXHALL
RESTAURANTS
Meat
Mosaica
2933 Vauxhall Road
Telephone: 206 9911

WESTFIELD
SYNAGOGUES
Reform
Temple Emanu-El
756 E. Broad Street 07090
Telephone: (908) 232 6770
Fax: (908) 233 3959
Email: cshane@tewnj.org
Website: www.tewnj.org

Warren County
WARREN
Temple Har Shalom
104 Mount Horeb Road 07059-5529
Telephone: (732) 356 8777
Fax: (732) 356 0580

New Mexico
Bernalillo County
ALBUQUERQUE
COMMUNITY ORGANISATIONS
Jewish Federation of Greater Albuquerque
5520 Wyoming Boulevard N.E 87109
Telephone: (505) 821 3214
Website: www.jewishnewmexico.org

KASHRUT INFORMATION
JFGA
Telephone: (505) 821 3214

MEDIA
Newspaper
The Link
5520 Wyoming Boulevard 87109
Telephone: (505) 821 3214

SYNAGOGUES
Conservative
Congregation B'nai Israel
4401 Indian School Road 87110
Telephone: (505) 266 0155

Fax: (505) 268 6136
Website: www.bnaiisrael-nm.org
Orthodox
Chabad of New Mexico
4000 San Pedro 87110
Telephone: (505) 880 1181

Dona Ana County
LAS CRUCES
Reform
Temple Beth-El
3980 Sonoma Springs Avenue (on Sonoma Ranch)
, PO Box 1029 88004
Telephone: (575) 524 3380
Fax: (575) 5521 8111
Email: TempleBethEl@swwn.net
Website: www.nm002.urj.net/
Supervision: Rabbi Paul Citrin

Los Alamos County
LOS ALAMOS
Conservative
Los Alamos Jewish Center
2400 Canyon Road 87544
Telephone: (505) 662 2440

Sandoval County
RIO RANCHO
Reform
Rio Rancho Jewish Center
2009 Grande Boulevard 87124
Telephone: (505) 892 8511

Santa Fe County
SANTA FE
Orthodox
Chabad Jewish Center
242 West S. Mateo (corner Galisteo)
Telephone: (505) 983 2000
Fax: (505) 983 2055
Website: www.chabadsf.com

Pardes Yisroel
1307 Don Diego Avenue 87505
Telephone: (505) 986 1603
Website: www.pardes-yisroel.org/py/

Reform
Congregation Beit Tikvah
PO Box 2112 87504
Telephone: (505) 820 2991
Fax: (505) 820 2991
Email: rap1818@aol.com
Website: www.beittikva.org

Temple Beth Shalom
205 E. Barcelona Road 87505
Telephone: (505) 982 1376
Fax: (505) 983 7446
Email: nfo@sftbs.org
Website: www.sftbs.org

New York State

New York City encompasses so much territory and so much activity that it can sometimes be easy to forget that there is also a whole state named New York. The Empire State stretches from New York City in the south to the Canadian border at Quebec and Ontario provinces in the north; from the New England border with Connecticut, Massachusetts and Vermont in the east to Pennsylvania and the Great Lakes of Erie and Ontario in the southwest and west.

Within this 50,000 square mile expanse lie metropolis, suburb, small town, large city, village, vast state parks and preserves, seashores, islands, high mountains and rolling foothills, and abundant natural wilderness.

To New York City residents, anything outside the five boroughs (Manhattan, Queens, Brooklyn, the Bronx, and Staten Island) is either upstate or Long Island. But within those areas are numerous large and thriving Jewish communities. The cities of Buffalo, Rochester, Binghamton, Syracuse, and Schenectady, the suburban counties of Westchester and Rockland, and the Long Island counties of Nassau and Suffolk count hundreds of thousands of Jews among its residents.

Jewish settlement began in New York in early September 1654 when twenty-three Sephardic and Ashkenazi Jews disembarked at the harbour of New Amsterdam from the French ship St Catherine. They had escaped the Spanish Inquisition in Recife, Brazil to settle in the Dutch colony. Though Governor Peter Stuyvesant forbade their admission to his jurisdiction, the travellers' protests to his bosses at the Dutch West India Company were accepted and the Jews were allowed to settle. Ten years later, in 1664, four British men-of-war appropriated New Amsterdam in the name of King Charles II of England, who, in turn, made a gift of it to his brother, James, Duke of York. Hence the name, New York.

Jewish immigration was sparse for the next 150 years, but it increased dramatically, especially in New York City between 1880 and 1924, as more than two million Jews made their way to 'der goldene medinah' (the golden door) from eastern and central Europe.

From that original group of twenty-three Jews in 1654, some made their way up the Hudson River

as far as Albany (now the state capital). Two of them, Asser Levy and Jacob de Lucena, became Hudson River traders and also dealt in real estate in the Albany and Kingston areas. South of Albany, in nearby Newburgh, Jewish merchants established a trading post in 1777, but no Jewish community existed there until 1848.

New York's first Jewish community outside of New York City was the town of Sholom in the Catskill mountains in Ulster county. Founded by twelve families, it no longer exists. The oldest existing community is Congregation Beth El, founded in 1838 in Albany and later merged with Congregation Beth Emeth.

Westchester (just north of New York City) county's present Jewish population of close to 150,000 dates from 1860.

Rockland

Southeast of the Catskills, in Rockland county just north of New York City, are a number of communities with large Hasidic and Orthodox populations. New Square, a corruption of the name Skvir, was founded by the Skvirer Hasidim and is incorporated as a separate village within the town of Ramapo. With such an administrative and legal designation, New Square has its own zoning rules, its own village council, its own mayor, etc., and is run on strictly orthodox precepts. Monroe, Monsey and Spring Valley have very large Orthodox and Hasidic communities. Though observant Jews are predominant, these communities are also home to non-Jews and less-observant Jews. There are a number of villages in the area which have been incorporated with the express purpose of keeping Orthodox and Hasidim out, through regulations such as zoning to prevent synagogues from being built too close to residences and through the prohibition of having a synagogue in one's house.

Albany County

ALBANY

GROCERIES
Price Chopper Market
1892 Central Avenue 12205
Telephone: (518) 456 2970
Supervision: Vaad Hakashruth
Full service kosher department.

JEWISH STUDENT CENTER
Shabbos House
State University of New York, 316 Fuller Road
Telephone: (518) 438 4227
Email: shabbos@albany.net
Website: www.shabboshouse.com
Also a synagogue.

MIKVAOT
Mikvaot
340 Whitehall Road
Telephone: (518) 437 1303

SYNAGOGUES
Conservative
Ohav Shalom
New Krumkill Road 12208
Telephone: (518) 489 4706

Temple Israel
600 New Scotland Avenue 12208
Telephone: (518) 438 7858
Fax: (518) 482 5762
Email: timain@templeisraelalbany.org
Website: www.templeisraelalbany.org

Kosher Vegetarian
Chabad-Lubvitch Center of the Capital District
122 Main Avenue 12208
Telephone: (518) 482 5281
Fax: (518) 482 6330
Email: rabbirubin@saratogachabad.com
Website: www.saratogachabad.com

Orthodox
Beth Abraham-Jacob
380 Whitehall Road 12208
Telephone: (518) 489 5819/5179
Fax: (518) 489 5179
Mobile Phone: r5187275566 rabbi moshe e bomze
Email: mbomzer@aol.com

Shomray Torah
463 New Scotland Avenue 12208
Telephone: (518) 438 8981

Reform
B'nai Sholom
420 Whitehall Road 12208
Telephone: (518) 482 5283
Email: office@bnaisholom.albany.ny.us
Website: www.bnaisholom.albany.ny.us

Beth Emeth
100 Academy Road 12208
Telephone: (518) 436 9761
At this 160-year-old congregation, Rabbi Isaac Mayer Wise, founder of American Reform Judaism, served when he first arrived in the United States.

Daughters of Sarah Senior Community
180 Washington Avenue Extension 12203
Telephone: (518) 456 7831
Fax: (518) 456 1563
Email: info@daughtersofsarah.org
Website: www.daughtersofsarah.org
Traditional service, Saturday 9.15 am. Reform service, Friday 3 pm. Traveller's advisory and kosher facility.

DELMAR
Orthodox
Chabad House of Delmar
109 Elsmere Avenue 12054
Telephone: (518) 439 8280

Reconstructionist
Reconstructionist Havurah of the Capital District
98 Meadowland Street 12054
Telephone: (518) 439 5870

Broome County
BINGHAMTON
MIKVAOT
Beth David Synagogue
39 Riverside Drive 13905
Telephone: (607) 722 1793
Fax: (607) 722 7121
Email: bethdavidrabbi@aol.com

SYNAGOGUES
Community Center
500 Clubhouse Road 13903
Telephone: (607) 724 2417

Conservative
Temple Israel
Deerfield Place, Vestal 13850
Telephone: (607) 723 7461

Reform
Temple Concord
9 Riverside Drive 13905
Telephone: (607) 723 7355

VESTAL
COMMUNITY ORGANISATIONS
Jewish Federation of Broome County
500 Clubhouse Road 13850
Telephone: (607) 724 2332
Fax: (607) 724 2311

MEDIA
Newspaper
The Reporter
500 Clubhouse Road 13850
Telephone: (607) 724 2360
Fax: (607) 724 2311
Email: reporter@aol.com

Chemung County
ELMIRA
SYNAGOGUES
Orthodox
Shomray Hadath
Cobbles Park 14905
Telephone: (607) 732 7410

Reform
B'nai Israel
Water & Guinnip Streets 14905
Telephone: (607) 734 7735

Columbia County
HUDSON
Conservative
Anshe Emeth
240 Jolsen Boulevard 12534
Telephone: (518) 828 9040

Delaware County
FLEISCHMANNS
HOTELS
Kosher
Oppenheimer's Regis
PO Box 700, Fleischmanns 12430
Telephone: (845) 254 5080
Fax: (845) 254 4399
Email: kurtopp@aol.com
Supervision: Rabbinate of K'hal Adas Jeshurun, NYC
Open from Pesach to Succos. Off-season: Fax (732) 367 5417.

Dutchess County
BEACON
SYNAGOGUES
Conservative
Hebrew Alliance
55 Fishkill Avenue 12508
Telephone: (845) 831 2012

POUGHKEEPSIE
COMMUNITY ORGANISATIONS
Jewish Community Center of Dutchess County
110 Grand Avenue   12603
Telephone: (845) 471 0430

SYNAGOGUES
Conservative
Temple Beth El
118 Grand Avenue 12603
Telephone: (845) 454 0570
Website: www.uscj.org/empire/poughktb

Orthodox
Shomre Israel
18 Park Avenue 12603

Reform
Vassar Temple
140 Hooker Avenue 12601
Telephone: (845) 454 2570

Erie County
BUFFALO
COMMUNITY ORGANISATIONS
Jewish Federation of Greater Buffalo
787 Delaware Avenue 14209
Telephone: (716) 886 7750
Fax: (716) 886 1367

DELICATESSEN
Tops Kosher Deli
Cnr of North Bailey and Maple Road
Telephone: (716) 615 0076

GROCERIES
Grocers
Corner of North Bailey and Maple Road
Telephone: (716) 515 0075

MEDIA
Guide
Shalom Buffalo
787 Delaware Avenue 14209
Telephone: (716) 886 7750
Fax: (716) 886 1367

Newspaper
Buffalo Jewish Review
15 Mohawk Street 14203
Telephone: (716) 54 2192

MIKVAOT
Mikva
1248 Kenmore Avenue 14216
Telephone: (716) 632 1531

MUSEUMS
Benjamin & Dr. Edgar R. Cofeld Judaic Museum of Temple Beth Zion
700 Sweet Home Road 14226
Telephone: (716) 836 6565
Fax: (716) 831 1126
A collection of more than a thousand Judaic artifacts dating from the tenth century to the present. There are unique Ben Shahn stained glass windows in the building.

SYNAGOGUES
Conservative
Hillel of Buffalo
Campus Center for Jewish Life, 520 Lee Entrance, The Commons/Suite #204, Amherst 14228
Telephone: (716) 639 8361

Temple Beth El of Greater Buffalo
2368 Eggert Road, Tonawanda 14150
Telephone: (716) 836 3762
Fax: (716) 836 3764
Email: templebethel@juno.com
Website: http://bethelbuffalo.uscjhost.net

Temple Shaarey Zedek
621 Getzville Road 14226
Telephone: (716) 838 3232
Fax: (716) 835 6154
Email: office@tszbuffalo.org
Website: tszbuffalo.org

Orthodox
B'nai Shalom
1675 N. Forest Road 14221
Telephone: (716) 689 8203

Beth Abraham
1073 Elmwood Avenue 14222
Telephone: (716) 874 4786

Chabad House
3292 Main Street, & N. Forest Road
14214 & 14068
Telephone: (716) 688 1642

Saranac Synagogue
85 Saranac Avenue 14216
Telephone: (716) 876 1284
Daily Minyan.

Young Israel of Greater Buffalo
105 Maple Road, Williamsville 14221
Telephone: (716) 634 0212

Reconstructionist
Temple Sinai
50 Alberta Drive, Amherst 14226
Telephone: (716) 834 0708
Fax: (716) 838 2597

Reform
Beth Am
4660 Sheridan Drive 14221
Telephone: (716) 633 8877
Fax: (716) 633 8952
Email: rabbif@aol.com

Congregation Havurah
6320 Main Street 14221
Telephone: (716) 874 3517

Temple Beth Zion
805 Delaware Avenue 14209
Telephone: (716) 886 7150
Fax: (716) 831 1126
Website: www.tbz.org

Traditional
Kehilat Shalom
700 Sweet Home Rd 14226
Telephone: (716) 885 6650

Essex County
LAKE PLACID
Lake Placid Synagogue
2307 Saranac Avenue, Post Office Box 521 12946-0521.
Telephone: (518) Answering machine: 523 3876
Website: www.lakeplacidsynagogue.org
Tel: (518) 891 3458 for times of servic

Fulton County
GLOVERSVILLE
Community Center
28 E. Fulton Street 12078

Conservative
Knesseth Israel
34 E. Fulton Street 12078
Telephone: (518) 725 0649

Monroe County
ROCHESTER
DELICATESSEN
Bagel bakery
Brownstein's Deli and Bakery
1862 Monroe Avenue 14618
Telephone: (585) 422 2770
Supervision: Rabbi Henry Hyman
Strictly kosher - takeout only

Brighton Donuts
Monroe Avenue
Telephone: (585) 716 271 6940

COMMUNITY ORGANISATIONS
Jewish Community Federation
441 East Avenue 14607
Telephone: (585) 585 461 0490
Fax: (585) 585 461 0912
Email: mcohen@jewishrochester.org
Website: www.jewishrochester.org

DELICATESSEN
Fox's Kosher Restaurant and Deli
3450 Winton Place 14623

MEDIA
Newspaper
Jewish Ledger
2525 Brighton-Henrietta Town Line R 14623

RESTAURANTS
Meat
Jewish Home of Rochester Cafeteria
2021 S. Winton Road 14618

SYNAGOGUES
Conservative
Temple Beth Hamedrash-Beth Israel
1369 East Avenue 14610
Telephone: (585) (585) 244 2060
Email: bhbi@frontiernet.net
Website: www.bhbirochester.org

Orthodox
Congregation Beth Sholom
1161 Monroe Avenue 14620
Telephone: (585) (585) 473 1625
Website: www.bethsholomrochester.com

Montgomery County
AMSTERDAM
Conservative
Congregation of Sons of Israel
355 Guy Park Avenue 12010
Telephone: (518) 842 8691

Nassau County
BALDWIN
RESTAURANTS
Ben's Kosher Delicatessen
933 Atlantic Avenue 11510
Telephone: (516) 868 2072
Fax: (516) 868 2062
Email: info@bensdeli.net
Website: www.bensdeli.net
Supervision: Supervised
Kosher catering

CARLE PLACE
Ben's Kosher Delicatessen
59 Old Country Rd. 11514
Telephone: (516) 742 3354
Fax: (516) 742 3296
Email: info@bensdeli.net
Website: www.bensdeli.net
Supervision: Supervised
Kosher catering

GREAT NECK
BUTCHERS
Great Neck Glatt
501 Middle Neck Road 11023
Telephone: (516) 773 6328
Supervision: Vaad Harabonim of Queens

MEDIA
Newspapers
Long Island Jewish Week
98 Cutter Mill Road 11020
Telephone: (516) 773 3679

Long Island Jewish World
115 Middle Neck Road 11021
Telephone: (516) 829 4000

MIKVAOT
Mikvaot
26 Old Mill Road 11023
Telephone: (516) 487 2726

RESTAURANTS
Dairy
Kings Kosher Pizza
605 Middle Neck Road 11023
Telephone: (516) 482 0400
Fax: (516) 482 0405
Supervision: Star K

Meat
Bistro Grill
132 Middle Neck Road
Telephone: (516) 829 4428

Chattanooga
37 Cuttermill Road
Telephone: (516) 487 4455

Colbeh
75 N. Station Plaza
Telephone: (516) 466 8181
Supervision: Kof-K

Danny's
624 Middle Neck Road
Telephone: (516) 487 6666

Hunan
507 Middle Neck Road
Telephone: (516) 482 7912
Supervision: Vaad Rab. of Queens

GREENVALE
RESTAURANTS AND DELICATESSEN
Ben's Kosher Delicatessen
140 Wheatley Plaza 11548
Telephone: (516) 621 3340
Fax: (516) 621 2178
Email: info@bensdeli.net
Website: www.bensdeli.net
Supervision: Supervised
Kosher catering

LAWRENCE
RESTAURANTS
Dairy
Dairy Review
143 Washington Avenue
Telephone: (508) 295-7417
Supervision: Vaad HaKashrus of the Five Towns

LONG BEACH
MIKVAOT
Mikva
Sharf Manor, 274 W. Broadway 11561
Telephone: (310) 431 7758

SYNAGOGUES
Conservative
Beth Shalom of Long Beach and Lido
700 E. Park Avenue 11561
Telephone: (310) 432 7464

Orthodox
Temple Beth El
570 W. Walnut Street 11561
Telephone: (310) 432 1678

WEST HEMPSTEAD
MIKVAOT
Mikva
775 Hempstead Avenue 11552
Telephone: (516) 489 9358

RESTAURANTS
Meat
Wing Wan
248 Hempstead Avenue
Telephone: (516) 482 7912

WOODMERE
KASHRUT INFORMATION
Vaad HaKashrus of the Five Towns
859 Peninsula Boulevard., Woodmere 11598
Telephone: (516) 569 4536
Fax: (516) 295 4212

SYNAGOGUES
Orthodox
Young Israel of North Woodmere
634 Hungry Harbor Road, 11581
Telephone: (516) 791 5099

New York County

NEW YORK CITY
Nowhere in the United States is there a city richer in Jewish heritage than New York. From the city's beginnings as a Dutch trading post in the 17th century up to the present day, Jews have flocked to New York, made it their home, and left an indelible mark on the city's heritage, language, culture, physical structure, and day-to-day life. There are more Jews in the New York metropolitan area than in any other city in the world, and more than in any country except Israel. So, without a great deal of effort, just being in this largest urban Jewish community in history affords you the opportunity to be a tourist without concern about the ease of observing kashrut and Shabbat.

New York City is the largest Jewish community in the world outside Israel. The estimated Jewish population of New York City proper is just over one million. Another million or so live in the immediate suburbs, which include not only New York, but also New Jersey and Connecticut. Roughly one-third of American Jews live in and around New York City and virtually every national Jewish organization has its headquarters here.

New York City neighbourhoods with large Jewish populations are the upper west and upper east sides of Manhattan (modern Orthodox and secular Jewish), Borough Park, Williamsburg (Orthodox and Hasidic) and Brighton Beach (Russian) in Brooklyn, Forest

Hills (Israelis and Russians), Kew Gardens, Kew Garden Hills (Orthodox) in Queens, Riverdale in the Bronx, and Staten Island.

In this largest urban Jewish community in history, the Jewish traveller is overwhelmed with choices of where to eat, where to find a minyan, what to see of Jewish interest and so on. And the variety of kosher restaurants makes choosing a pleasure: Chinese, Moroccan, Italian (both meat and dairy), traditional European, Indian, Japanese and seafood.

Though Jews from numerous countries of origin live together throughout New York's Jewish communities, many groups tend to congregate in their own neighbourhoods or sections of neighbourhoods.

Ever since the fateful year of 1654 Jews have been coming to New York City. Sometimes a few, sometimes more, and sometimes by the boatload, as was the case between 1880 and 1924 when some two million Jews entered the United States. And though one might argue cause and effect, New York City is still the commercial, intellectual and financial center of the country.

Synagogues
Hundreds if not thousands of synagogues, chavurot and shtiblech lie within the city, representing the myriad expressions of Judaism: Orthodox, Hasidic, Conservative, Reform and Reconstructionist.

The 1,300-seat, Moorish-style Central Synagogue (Reform) at 652 Lexington Avenue in Manhattan reopened its doors in October 2001, three years after a devastating fire. It is the city's oldest synagogue on an original site and is an official New York City landmark; the oldest Ashkenazi congregation, founded in 1825, is Bínai Jeshrun (Conservative) at 270 West 89th Street; Shearith Israel, the Spanish and Portuguese synagogue on Central Park West at 70th Street, is one of the oldest congregations in the United States and originated with those 23 refugees from the Spanish Inquisition in Brazil in 1654. The present building still has religious items from the earliest days of the congregation and its small chapel is representative of the American colonial period; Temple Emanu-El (Reform) at Fifth Avenue and 65th Street is not only the city's largest, but the world's largest synagogue. The congregation was founded in 1848 and the building, built in 1929, can seat over 2,000 people; the Fifth Avenue synagogue at 5 East 62nd Street was, until early 1967, presided over by the then Rabbi Dr Immanuel Jakobovits, who later became the Chief Rabbi of Great Britain and the Commonwealth; the Park East synagogue at 163 East 67th Street, on the very fashionable Upper East Side, was founded in 1890 and is a historic landmark. Kehilath Jeshurun (Orthodox), 125 East 85th Street, is a popular option if you are on the Upper East Side. On the Upper West Side, Lincoln Square Synagogue (Orthodox), 200 Amsterdam Avenue at 69th Street, and Ohab Zedek (Orthodox), 118 West 95th Street, are both very popular options. Visitors may be interested in a late 9 am minyan on the Upper West Side at 303 W.91st East between West End Avenue and Riversdale Drive.

Libraries, Museums, and Institutes of Learning

New York's newest educational research center and one of the country's most important resources for Jewish scholarship opened in October 2000 and is located at 15 West 16th Street. The centre is a partnership of five major institutions of Jewish scholarship: American Jewish Historical Society, American Sephardi Federation, Leo Baeck Institute, Yeshiva University Museum and YIVO Institute for Jewish Research. The combined collections and the professional staff of these five institutions create an opportunity for an unparalleled comprehensive study of modern Jewish history. The Jewish Museum (Fifth Avenue and 92nd Street, 212-423-3200) has been in existence since 1904. Under the auspices of the Conservative Jewish Theological Seminary, the museum has permanent and changing exhibits and programmes and an excellent collection of Jewish ritual and ceremonial objects.

The library at the Jewish Theological Seminary (3080 Broadway at 122nd Street, 212-678-8000) houses one of the greatest collections of Judaica and Hebraica in the world. Its holdings include a rare manuscript by Maimonides (the Rambam).

Other libraries with large Judaica collections are at Yeshiva University (212-960-5400), the Judaica Collection at the New York Public Library (212-340-0849), New York University (212-998-1212), Columbia University (212-854-1754), the House of Living Judaism at Temple Emanu-El (212-744-1400) and the Leo Baeck Institute (212-744-6400). Inquire at each one individually as to availability of the collections.

One of New York's living museums is the Eldridge Street Synagogue (14 Eldridge Street, 212-219-0888). At over 100 years old, the Eldridge Street synagogue is a ghost of its former splendour. But, in its heyday at the turn of the century, it was among the busiest synagogues on the Lower East Side, and the first built for that purpose by New York's eastern European Jews. An official New York City landmark, and listed on the National Register of Historic Places, the synagogue is an

ongoing restoration project. The synagogue functions as a museum and has a whole host of programmes.

In the same neighbourhood and sociologically related is the Lower East Side Tenement Museum (97 Orchard Street, 212-431-0233). Contrary to popular opinion, the word tenement does not mean slum housing, but a particular building design devised to house the masses of immigrants who came to New York in the latter part of the 19th century. Tenements are five- or six-storey walk-up buildings distinguished by narrow entry halls and a central air shaft. Each floor contained four apartments. Toilet facilities, located in the hallway, were shared by all the residents. Baths were taken at numerous local public bath houses. The museum, located in a restored tenement built in 1863, shows visitors what tenement life was like via a model apartment. In addition, actors in period dress present 90-minute shows in a small theatre. This is how the vast majority of Jews lived when they first came to New York City.

Ellis Island National Monument (212-269-5755) was once the point of entry for Jews and other immigrants. Some five million Jews came to the United States between 1850 and 1948 and most were processed through immigration at Castle Garden (the present ferry ticket office) or, after 1890, Ellis Island.

Neighbourhoods and areas of historical interest

Manhattan

The Lower East Side has physically changed very little in over a century. Cramped tenements and crowded, dirty streets have always characterised the area. But for the absence of vendors calling out 'I cash clothes' one can get a pretty good idea of what life looked like for Jews newly arrived in New York City from eastern European countries, although it is difficult to imagine the strangeness of a new language or being away from home for the first time.

Although the Lower East Side is not as Jewish as it once was and many Jewish shops have closed, it is appropriate that historical jaunts in New York begin in its tangle of streets and alleys. For the ancestors of some 80 per cent of American Jews, this was the first piece of America they saw. Now other immigrant groups call the Lower East Side home. Settlement houses such as the Henry Street Settlement and the Educational Alliance on East Broadway once served the Jewish immigrant population in their need to learn English and become Americanised. Still in existence, they provide services to current residents, Jewish and non-Jewish alike.

Many Jews still do business in the neighbourhood and the area is full of historic buildings, Jewish shops, foodstores and stores selling all manner of ritual items (kipot, taliltot, tefilin, siddurim, etc.). Look along Essex, Orchard, Grand, Rivington, Hester and Canal streets.

One of the best guidebooks for this area (as well as the rest of New York City) is the 'AIA [American Institute of Architects] Guide to New York City' by Elliot Willensky and Norval White. An organization called Big Onion Walking Tours gives Lower East Side tours and they are worth a telephone call (212-439-1090).

You may notice that a number of churches on the Lower East Side used to be synagogues. They were re-consecrated as churches when the Jewish community dwindled. But in many cases you still can tell which were synagogues. Look for things like Stars of David on building cornerstones, darkened mezuzah shaped areas on doorposts, and shadows of Stars of David on building facades. They are quite evident if you look.

Synagogues of note in the area are the Bialystoker synagogue (7 Wilet Street); Beth Midrash HaGadol (60 Norfolk Street); First Roumanian American Congregation (89 Rivington Street); and the Eldridge Street Synagogue (14 Eldridge Street).

The only kosher winery in Manhattan is Schapiro's kosher Winery (126 Rivington Street, 674-4404), founded in 1899. Call for tour information.

Along Second Avenue below 14th Street you can still see the remnants of the scores of Yiddish theatres that once lined the street. Note particularly the movie theatre on Second Avenue at 12th Street, currently the City Cinemas Village East. In the upper level auditorium you can get an idea of what the place looked like when stars like Molly Picon and Boris Tomeshevsky held forth on the stage.

Forty-seventh Street between Fifth Avenue and Avenue of the Americas is the diamond centre. Some 75 per cent of all the diamonds which enter the United States pass through here. As this is overwhelmingly a Jewish and Hasidic business, the street is bustling with diamond dealers concluding deals in the open market atmosphere that is pervasive. Most deals are made with a handshake. There are a number of kosher restaurants up and down the block and on the mezzanines of office buildings.

Historical Cemeteries

Manhattan

Shearith Israel Cemeteries

Vestiges of early Jewish settlement in New York can be gleaned from the remnants of the community's first cemeteries. The following three are owned by New York's oldest congregation, Shearith Israel, the Spanish Portuguese Synagogue.

First: Shearith Israel Graveyard: 55 St. James Place (between Oliver and James St), the first Jewish cemetery in New Amsterdam, was consecrated in 1656 and was located near the present Chatham Square. Its remains were moved to this location. It contains the remains of Sephardic Jews who emigrated from Brazil.

Second: Cemetery of the Spanish and Portuguese Synagogue (1805–1829): 72–76 West 11th Street, just east of Sixth Avenue on the south side of the street.

Third: Cemetery of the Spanish and Portuguese Synagogue (1829–1851): 98–110 West 21st Street, just west of Sixth Avenue on the south side of the street.

Brooklyn

Green-Wood Cemetery (Fifth Avenue and Fort Hamilton Parkway, Brooklyn) contains the graves of many prominent Jewish figures.

Queens

Fourth Cemetery of the Spanish and Portuguese Synagogue: Cypress Hills Street and Cypress Avenue, Queens. The beautiful chapel and gate were built in 1885.

Arts and Entertainment

As American entertainment is largely a secular Jewish enterprise, one need not look very far for Jewish references in plays and musicals. However, there are some dedicated Jewish theatrical companies and venues: the Jewish Repertory Company (212-831-2000); the American Jewish Theater (212-633-1588); the YM & YWHA (212-427-6000) has several outstanding lecture series, some with specific Jewish themes. For other events of Jewish interest consult one of the weekly listings magazines such as Time Out New York or New York Magazine, or the Sunday Arts & Leisure section of the New York Times. Jewish newspapers with events listings are Jewish Week, Forward and Jewish Press, all available at most newsstands.

Jewish Neighbourhoods of Interest outside Manhattan

Brooklyn

Williamsburg was for many years the centre of Hasidic life in New York City. But in the last decade many rebbes and their followers have moved to the suburbs, particularly Rockland county. However, a trip to Williamsburg is still worthwhile.

Boro Park is almost completely Orthodox and is a world apart from the rest of the city.

Crown Heights is populated by Hasidim of many sects, but particularly the Lubavitch, whose world headquarters is at 770 Eastern Parkway. The neighbourhood is not totally Jewish and there are often clashes (sometimes violent) between the Caribbean residents and Jewish residents.

New Jersey

Many towns in northern and central New Jersey are less than 40 minutes travel time by either car or public transport from Manhattan, and as such are part of metropolitan New York. They are: Bayonne, Clifton, Elizabeth, Englewood, Fairlawn, Hackensack, Hoboken, Jersey City, Newark, Passaic, Teaneck, Union and West New York.

Restaurants

By law in New York State, the selling of non-kosher food as kosher is a punishable fraud. Administered by the kosher Law Enforcement Section of the New York State Department of Agriculture, heavy penalties are imposed on violators. An Orthodox rabbi oversees the operation. Businesses selling kosher food must display proper signage, indicating under whose hashgacha they operate, and establishments which sell both kosher and non-kosher food must display that as well, with a sign in block letters no smaller than four inches high.

In July 2000 a Federal Judge ruled that this law violated the First Amendment. In September 2002 there was a further stay of this ruling pending appeal.

'The Kosher Directory', issued by the Union of Orthodox Jewish Congregations, lists foods and services which bear the symbol. It is available for a charge by calling 212-563-4000. Other reliable kashruth insignias also exist.

Note that kosher packaged foods, including bread, meat, fish, cake, biscuits and virtually anything you can think of, are widely available in supermarkets throughout the New York metropolitan area. Many foodstores, especially on the Upper West Side of Manhattan and in Jewish neighbourhoods in Brooklyn and Queens, sell fresh kosher prepared meals as well.

BRONX

RESTAURANTS

Second Helping
3532 Johnson Avenue 10463
Telephone: (718) 548 1818
Supervision: Vaad Harabonim of Riverdale
Take-out food only; Glatt kosher.

Yeshiva University: Bronx Center
Eastchester Rd & Morris Park Avenue 10461
Telephone: (718) 430 2131

Dairy

Main Event
3708 Riverdale Avenue, Riverdale 10463
Telephone: (718) 601 6246
Fax: (718) 601 0008
Supervision: Rabbi Jonathan Rosenblatt, Riverdale Jewish Center

Meat

Riverdelight
3534 Johnson Avenue, Riverdale 10463
Telephone: (718) 543 4270
Fax: (718) 543 7545
Email: uallon@aol.com
Website: www.riverdelight.com
Supervision: Vaad Harabonim of Riverdale
Glatt kosher. Grill, deli, Sushi,open salad bar, and Middle-Eastern cuisine

BROOKLYN

HOTELS

Midwood Suites
1078 East 15 S
Telephone: (718) 253 9535
Fax: (718) 253 3269
Email: shalom@midwoodsuites.com

Scharf's Ateret of Midwood
1410 East 10th Street 11230
Telephone: (718) 998 5400
Fax: (718) 645 8600
Email: ateretavoth@aol.com
Daily Minyon. Under strict Hashgocha. Cholov Yisroel/Glatt Kosher

The Crown Palace Hotel
570-600 Crown Street
Telephone: (718) 604 1777
Glatt kosher.

LIBRARIES

Levi Yitzhak Library
305 Kingston Avenue 11213

MUSEUMS

The Chasidic Art Institute
375 Kingston Avenue

RESTAURANTS

Dairy

Bella Luna
557 Kings Highway
Telephone: (718) 376 2999

Chapp-u-Ccino
4815 12th Avenue
Telephone: (718) 633 4377
Supervision: Rabbi Amrom Roth

Fontana Bella
2086 Coney Island Avenue
Telephone: (718) 627 3904
Supervision: Rabbi Gornish

Gio Caffe
448 Avenue P
Telephone: (718) 375 5437

Milk 'N Honey
5013 10 Avenue
Telephone: (718) 871 4319
Fax: (718) 871 4297
Supervision: Rabbi Friedlander

Sunflower Café
1223 Kings Highway, cor. E. 13th Street
Telephone: (718) 336 1340
Supervision: Rabbi Gornish

Tea For Two Café
547 Kings Highway
Telephone: (718) 998 0020
Supervision: Rabbi Gornish

Wendy's Plate
434 Avenue U
Telephone: (718) 376 3125
Fax: (718) 871 4297
Supervision: Rabbi Friedlander

Broadway's J-2 N.Y.C. Pizza
926 3rd Avenue 11232
Telephone: (718) 768 7437
Fax: (718) 768 6802
Email: flyingpizzas@flyingpizzas.com
Website: www.flyingpizzas.com
Fast food - groups and tours welcome

Meat

1st Jerusalem Steak House
533 Kings Highway
Telephone: (718) 336 5115

47th St. Kosher Restaurant
274 47th Street , (off 3rd Avenue)
Telephone: (718) 492 2000
Fax: (718) 492 4199

A-Kosher Delight
4600 13th Avenue
Telephone: (718) 435 8500
Fax: (718) 435 1669

Bamboo Garden
904 Kings Highway
Telephone: (718) 375 8501
Supervision: Rabbi Yisroel P. Gornish

Cancun
448 Avenue P.
Telephone: (718) 375 4916
Supervision: Vaad Harabonim of Flatbush

Chap-A-Nosh Plus
1424 Elm Avenue
Telephone: (718) 627 0072
Fax: (718) 645 6336
Supervision: Rabbi G. Reisman

China Glatt
4413 13th Avenue
Telephone: (718) 438 2576

Dougies
4310 18th Avenue between McDonald Avenue &
E. 2nd Street Off Ocean Parkway
Telephone: (718) 686 8080
Supervision: Udvar Kashruth of America

Essex on Coney
1359 Coney Island Avenue
Telephone: (718) 253 1002
Supervision: Vaad Harabonim of Flatbush

Fuji Hana
512 Avenue. U
Telephone: (718) 336 3888
Supervision: Vaad Harabonim of Flatbush

Glatt-a-la-Carte
5123 18th Avenue
Telephone: (718) 438 6675
Fax: (718) 438 6675
Email: info@glattalacarte.com
Website: www.glattalacarte.com
Supervision: R'Yechiel Babad

Jerusalem Steak House II
1316 Avenue M
Telephone: (718) 376 0680

Kaosan
1387 Coney Island Avenue
Telephone: (718) 252 6969

Kineret Steak House
521 Kings Highway, Bet. E. 2nd - E. 3rd Sts
Telephone: (718) 336 8888
Supervision: Kehilah Kashruth

McFleishig's
5508 16th Avenue
Telephone: (718) 435 2779
Supervision: Rabbi Babad, Tartikover

Olympic Pita
1419 Coney Island Avenue, Bet. J & K
Telephone: (718) 258 6222
Fax: (718) 258 3106
Supervision: Kehilah Kashrus

Shang-Chai
2189 Flatbush Avenue
Telephone: (718) 377 6100

Tokyo of Brooklyn
2954 Avenue U., off Nostrand Avenue
Telephone: (718) 891 6221
Supervision: Kehilah Kashrus

Yunkee
1424 Elm Avenue, (corner. E. 15th/St & Avenue M)
Telephone: (718) 627 0072
Fax: (718) 645 6336
Supervision: Rabbi G. Reisman

SYNAGOGUES
Orthodox
Lubavitch Movement
770 Eastern Parkway, 11213
Telephone: (718) 774 4000
Fax: (718) 774 2718
Email: hq@lubavitch.com
Website: www.lubavitch.com

Lubavitch Movement
770 Eastern Parkway 11213
Telephone: (718) 774 4000
Fax: (212) 774 2718
Email: info@lubavitch.com
Website: www.lubavitch.com
Central organisation: Lubavitch World Headquarters

LONG ISLAND
CEDARHURST
BAKERIES
Zomick's Bake Shop
444 Central Avenue,
Telephone: (516) 569 5520
Supervision: Vaad HaKashrus of the Five Towns

BOOKSELLERS
Judaica
530 Central Avenue
Telephone: (516) 295 4343

Judaica Plus
530 Central Avenue
Telephone: (516) 295 4343

RESTAURANTS
Dairy
Ruthie's Kosher Dessert and Dairy Café
560A Central Avenue
Telephone: (516) 569 1818
Supervision: Vaad HaKashrus of the Five Towns

Meat
Burger Express
140 Washington Ave
Telephone: (516) 295 2040
Supervision: Supervised

K Roasters
72 Columbia Avenue
Telephone: (516) 791 5100
Vaad Hakashrus of the Five Towns

K.D.'s El Passo BBQ
546 Central Avenue
Telephone: (516) 569 2920
Supervision: Supervised

King David Delicatessen
550 Central Avenue 11516
Telephone: (516) 569 2920
Vaad Hakashrus of the Five Towns

Wok Tov
594 Central Avenue
Telephone: (516) 295 3843
Fax: (516) 295 3865
Vaad Hakashrus of the Five Towns

LAWRENCE
BAKERIES
Tasty Heimish Bakery
343 Central Avenue,
Telephone: (508) 569 5551/5552

RESTAURANTS
Dairy
Primavera
Telephone: (508) 374 5504
Supervision: Supervised

Meat
Burger Express
140 Washington Avenue
Telephone: (508) 374 1714
Supervision: Vaad HaKashrus of the Five Towns

Cho-Sen Island
367 Central Avenue
Telephone: (508) 374 1199
Supervision: Vaad HaKashrus of the Five Towns

Traditions
302 Central Avenue
Telephone: (508) 295 3630

SYOSSET
COMMUNITY ORGANISATIONS
Conference of Jewish Organisations of Nassau County
North Shore Atrium, 6900 Jericho Turnpike 11791
Telephone: (516) 364 4477
Fax: (516) 921 5092

WESTHAMPTON BEACH
RESTAURANTS
Beach Bakery Café
112 Main Street 11978
Telephone: (631) 288 6552
Supervision: Rabbi Ariel Konstantyn

SYNAGOGUES
Orthodox
Hampton Synagogue
154 Sunset Avenue 11978
Telephone: (631) 288 0534

WOODBURY
RESTAURANTS AND DELICATESSEN
Meat
Ben's Kosher Delicatessen
7971 Jericho Turnpike 11797
Telephone: (516) 496 4236
Fax: (516) 496 4354
Email: info@bensdeli.net
Website: www.bensdeli.net
Supervision: Supervised
Kosher catering Tone Rubin+ 47 91332575

MANHATTAN
BAKERIES
H & H Bagels
2239 Broadway at 80th Street 10024
Telephone: (212) 595 8000
Fax: (212) 799 6765
Supervision: K-of-K

BOOKSELLERS
Gifts, Judaica
J. Levine Judaica
5 West 30th Street 10001
Telephone: (212) 695 6888
Fax: (212) 643 1044
Email: sales@levinejudaica.com
Website: www.LevineJudaica.Com
The World's Oldest Judaica Store now in its 5th
generation

EMBASSY
Consul General of Israel
800 Second Avenue 10017
Telephone: (718) 499 5400
Fax: (212)499 5555

JUDAICA
Eichler's of Manhattan
62 West 45th Street
Telephone: 1 877 EICHLERS
Website: www.EICHLERS.com

LIBRARIES
Butler Library of Colombia University
Broadway at 116th Street 10027
Has some 6,000 Hebrew books and pamphlets, plus 1,000
manuscripts and a Hebrew psalter printed at Cambridge
University in 1685 and used by Samuel Johnson at the
graduation of the first candidates for bachelor's degrees.

The Jewish Division of the New York Public Library
Fifth Avenue at 42nd Street 10018
Telephone: (212) 930 0601
Fax: (212) 642 0141
Email: freidus@nypl.org
Has 125,000 volumes of Judaica and Hebraica, along with
extensive microfilm and bound files of Jewish
publications, one of the finest collections in existence.

MUSEUMS
Center for Jewish History
15 West 16th Street 10011
Telephone: (212) 294 8301
Fax: (212) 294 8302
Website: www.cjh.org
The Center has brought together the following five
institutes to create the largest single repository for Jewish
history in the Diaspora: American Jewish Historical
Society, American Sephardi Federation, Leo Baeck
Institute, Yeshiva University Museum and YIVO Institute
for Jewish Research. It has over 500,000 volumes and
over 100 million documents. A wide variety of exhibitions
illustrate the diversity of Jewish art, history and culture.
Tours are available and there is a kosher dairy cafe open
Monday to Thursday 9.15 am to 4.30 pm and Sunday
11.00 am to 4.30 pm.

Lower East Side Tenement Museum
91 Orchard Street 10002
Telephone: (212) 431 0233 ext. 235
Fax: (212) 431 0402
Website: www.tenement.org
The tenement museum is open to visitors by guided tours
only.
Visitors to the Museum tour carefully restored tenement
apartments and learn about the lives of actual past
residents.

The House of Living Judaism
5th Avenue and 65th Street
Frequently shows paintings and ritual objects. Twelve
marble pillars symbolise the Twelve Tribes.

The Jewish Museum
1109 Fifth Avenue 10128
Telephone: (212) 423 3200
This is one of the outstanding museums in the city and a
'must' not just for Jewish visitors but for all interested in
art. The permanent display consists of one of the finest
collection of Jewish ritual and ceremonial art in the world,
along with notable paintings and sculptures.

The Library of the Jewish Theological Seminary
3080 Broadway at 122nd Street 10027
Telephone: (212) 678 8975
Fax: (212) 678 8891
Email: shmintz@jtsa.edu
The Library of the Jewish Theological Seminary is one of
the world's premier research libraries of Judaica and
Hebraica. More than a thousand years of written history
are to be found within the library's 375,000 rare books,
40,000 Genizah fragments and thousands of rare

documents and prints. The remarkable treasures represent scholarship in the areas of Bible, liturgy, rabbinics, kabbala, philosophy and history. Throughout the year, exhibitions featuring selected pieces from the collection, showcase the library's treasures. Sundays, 10am to 5pm; Monday through Thursday, 9am to 6pm; Fridays, 9am to 2pm; closed Saturday.

The Museum of Jewish Heritage—A Living Memorial to the Holocaust
36 Battery Place 10280
Fax: (212) 437 4341
Website: www.mjhnyc.org
A living memorial to the Holocaust.

Theological Seminary of America
Fifth Avenue & 92nd Street 10028
An outstanding museum, with permanent displays of Jewish ritual and ceremonial art, along with notable paintings and sculptures.

ORGANISATIONS

UJA-Federation Resource Line
130 E. 59th Street 10022
Telephone: (800) 852 3337
Fax: (212) 888 7538
Email: resourceline@ujafedny.org
Website: www.ujafedny.org

RESTAURANTS

Yeshiva University: Main Center
500 W. 185th Street 10033-3201
Telephone: (212) 960 5248
Fax: (212) 960 0070

Dairy

American Café
160 Broadway
Telephone: (212) 732 1426

Bagels & Co.
1428 York Avenue, cnr. E. 76th Street
Telephone: (212) 717 0505
Supervision: New York Kosher

Broadway's Jerusalem 2
1375 Broadway, at 38th Street 10018
Telephone: (212) 398 1475
Fax: (212) 398 6797
Email: n.y.pies@.com
Supervision: OU
Chalav Yisruel, Prs Yisruel. Home of the N.Y. Flying Pizza Pies. Visit the 'Jewish Wall of Fame', 7.00 am to 12.00 pm. Saturday nights to 2.00 am.

Café 18
8 East 18th Street, Bet. 5th and Broadway
Telephone: (212) 620 4182

Cafe Roma Pizzeria
175 W. 90th Street
Telephone: (212) 875 8972

Diamond Dairy Kosher Lunchonette
4 W. 47th Street 10036
Telephone: (212) 719 2694

On the gallery overlooking the diamond & jewelry exchange. Hours: Monday to Thursday, 7:45am to 4.45pm; Friday, to 2pm. Homemade food.

EEE's Bakery & Café
105 East 34th Street, Between Park and Lexington Avenues
Telephone: (212) 686 3933
Fax: (212) 686 3786
Email: david@eeescafe.com
Website: www.eeescafe.com
Supervision: Orthodox Kosher Labs

Gusto va Mare
237 E. 53rd Street
Telephone: (212) 583 9300
Supervision: Organised Kashrut

Mike's Bistro
228 W, 72nd Street, Bet. B'way and West End Avenue
Telephone: (212) 875 9020
Supervision: Organised Kashrut

Mom's Bagels of NY
240 West 35th Street 10001
Telephone: (212) 494 0440
Fax: (212) 494 0402
Supervision: Kof-K
Chulov Yisruel

My Most Favorite Dessert
120 West 45th Street
Telephone: (212) 997 5130
Fax: (212) 997 5046
Supervision: OU
Chalav Yisrael.

Va Bene
1589 Second Avenue 10028
Telephone: (212) 517 4448
Fax: (212) 517 2258
Supervision: OU
Chalav Yisrael Italian restaurant.

Vegetable Garden
48 East 41st Street, (Bet. Mad & Park)
Telephone: (212) 883 7668

Indian Vegetarian

Saffron
81 Lexington Avenue 10016
Telephone: (212) 696 5130
Fax: (212) 696 5146

Kosher Vegetarian

Great American Health Bar
35 W. 57th Street
Telephone: (212) 355 5177
Website: www.greatamericantogo.com

Meat
A-Kosher Delight
1359 Broadway
Telephone: (212) 563 3366
Fax: (212) 268 9352

Abigael's Grill and Caterers
9 East 37th Street 10016
Telephone: (212) 725 0130
Fax: (212) 725 3577
Supervision: Kof-K
Glatt kosher.

Abigael's on Broadway
1407 Broadway, at 39th Street 10018
Telephone: (212) 575 1407
Fax: (212) 869 0666
Website: www.abigaels.com
Supervision: Kof-K
Glatt kosher. Lunch Monday to Friday 12pm to 3pm.
Dinner Sun to Thursday 5pm to 10pm.
Open Saturday nights October to April.

Cafe Classico
35 West 57th Street
Telephone: (212) 355 5411
Website: www.57thstreetkosher.com
Glatt kosher.

Colbeh
43 West 39 St, (Mid Town)
Telephone: (212) 354 8181

Deli Kasbah
2553 Amsterdam Avenue
Telephone: (212) 568 4600

Domani Ristorante
1590 First Avenue, Bet. 82nd-83rd Street
Telephone: (212) 717 7575/7557
Supervision: Organised Kashrut

Eden Wok
127 W. 72 Street 10023
Telephone: (212) 787 8700
Fax: (212) 787 9801
Supervision: OU

Essex on Coney Downtown
17 Trinity Place
Telephone: (718) 809 3000

Estihana
221 W. 79 Street 10024
Telephone: (212) 501 0393
Fax: (212) 501 0458
Website: www.estihana.com
Japanese cuisine, glatt kosher, Asian, bistro

Glatt Dynasty
1049 Second Avenue, East 55th & East 56th Street
10022
Telephone: (212) 888 9119
Fax: (212) 888 9163
Supervision: Kof-K
Glatt kosher.

Haikara
1016 2nd Avenue 10022
Telephone: (212) 355 7000
Supervision: OU

Il Patrizio
206 East 63rd Street, between 2nd and 3rd
Avenues
Telephone: (212) 980 4007
Supervision: OU

Jasmine
11 East 30 Street, between Madison and 5th
Avenues
Telephone: (212) 251 8884
Supervision: Vaad l'Kashrut Badatz Sepharadic
Glatt kosher Persian and Middle Eastern cuisine. Open
Sunday to Friday, for lunch and dinner.

Jewish Theological Seminary Dining Hall
3080 Broadway at 122nd Street 10027
Telephone: (212) 678 8822
Open September through to July (closed August) for
breakfast and lunch: 7.30am to 10am; 11am to 2pm.
Strictly kosher, Shomer Shabbat.

Kasbah Restaurant
251 W. 85th Street
Telephone: (212) 496 1500
Fax: (212) 496 2273
Supervision: Circle K
Hours: Sunday to Thursday, 12pm to 11pm. American and
Mediterranean food.

Kosher Delight
1359 Broadway (37th Street)
Telephone: (212) 563 3366

Kosher Deluxe
10 W. 46th St, (Off 5th Avenue)
Telephone: (212) 869 6699

Le Marais
150 W. 46th Street 10036
Telephone: (212) 869 0900
Fax: (212) 869 1016
Email: lemaraisat46@hotmail.com
Website: www.lemarais.net
Supervision: OU
Glatt kosher. Hours: Sunday to Thursday, 12 pm to 12am;
Friday, to 3pm; Saturday, October to May, one hour after
sundown to 1am.

Le Marais 2
15 John Street
Telephone: (212) 285 8585
Fax: (212) 791 3280
Supervision: Organised Kashrut

Levana
141 West 69th Street 10023
Telephone: (212) 877 8457
Fax: (212) 595 7522
Email: info@levana.com
Website: www.levana.com
Supervision: Orthodox Union
Glatt kosher.

Mendy's
Rockfeller Center, 30 Rockfeller Plaza
Telephone: (212) 262 9600

Mendy's West
208 West 70th Street 10023
Telephone: (212) 877 6787
Supervision: OU

Mr Broadway
1372 Broadway, (Bet. 37 & 38 St)
Telephone: (212) 921 2152

Penguin
258 W. 15th Street, Bet. 7-8 Avenue
Telephone: (212) 255 3601
Supervision: Vaad Hakashrus

Pita Express
1470 2nd Avenue (77th Street)
Telephone: (212) 249 1300
Glatt kosher.

Prime Grill
60 East 49th Street
Telephone: (212) 692 9292
Fax: (212) 883 8752

Second Avenue Delicatessen-Restaurant
156 2nd Avenue, corner 10th Street
Telephone: (212) 677 0606
Fax: (212) 477 5327
Hours:Sunday to Thursday 7.30am to 12am. Friday andSaturday 7.30am-3am.

Shallots
550 Madison Avenue 10022
Telephone: (212) 833 7800
Email: shallotsny.com
In the Sony Plaza Atrium. Between 55th and 56th Sts

The Box Tree
250 East 49th Street
Telephone: (212) 758 8320

Wolf & Lamb Steakhouse
10 E. 48th Street, Nr Rockerfeller Ctr., Between 5th & Madison 10017
Telephone: (212) 317 1950
Fax: (212) 317 0159
Supervision: Organised Kashrut

Tevere
155 E. 84 Street
Email: info@teverekitchen.com
Website: www.teverenyc.com
Supervision: OU
Italian steakhouse from Rome

Organic
Caravan of Dreams
405 East 6th Street, Bet. 1st Avenue & Avenue A
Telephone: (212) 254 1613
Supervision: Orthodox Rabbinical

Vegetarian
Maharani Restaurant
156 W. 29 Street (between 6 & 7 Avenue)
Telephone: (212) 868 0707/2211

Quintessence
566 Amsterdam Avenue
Telephone: (212) 501 9700 or (646) 654 1823

RESTAURANTS AND DELICATESSEN

Meat
Ben's Kosher Delicatessen
209 West 38th Street 10018
Telephone: (212) 398 2367
Fax: (212) 398 3354
Email: info@bensdeli.net
Website: www.bensdeli.net
Supervision: Supervised
Hours: 11am to 9.
Kosher catering

SYNAGOGUES

Conservative
Binai Jeshrun
270 West 89th Street, NY 10010
Telephone: (212) 787 7600

Park Avenue Synagogue
50 East 87th Street, NY   10128
Telephone: (212) 369 2600
Fax: (212) 410 7879
Email: dlincoln@pasyn.org

United Synagogue of America
155 Fifth Avenue, NY 10010
Telephone: (212) 533 7800
World Council of Synagogues can be found at the same location.

Orthodox
Agudat Israel World Organization
84 William Street, NY 10038
Telephone: (212) 797 9600
Fax: (212) 269 2843

Fifth Avenue Synagogue
5 East 62nd Street, NY, 10021
Telephone: (212) 838 2122
Fax: (212) 319 6119
Email: info@5as.org
Website: www.5as.org

Kehilath Jeshurun
125 East 85th Street, NY 10028
Telephone: (212) 427 1000

Lincoln Square
220 Amsterdam Avenue at 69th Street, NY, 10023
Telephone: (212) 874 6100
Fax: (212) 877 4065
Email: info@lss.org
Website: www.lss.org
Supervision: Orthodox Union
See website for our mission and vision

National Council of Young Israel National Office
3 West 16th Street, NY 10011
Telephone: (212) 929 1525
Fax: (212) 727 9526
Email: nyci

Ohab Zedeck
118 West 95th Street, NY 10025
Telephone: (212) 749 5150

Park East
163 East 67th Street, NY 10021
Telephone: (212) 737 6900
Fax: (212) 570 648

Union of Orthodox Jewish Congregations of America
333 Seventh Avenue, NY 10001
Telephone: (212) 563 4000
Fax: (212) 613 8333

Union of Orthodox Jewish Congregations of America
11 Broadway 10004
Telephone: (212) 563 4000
Fax: (212) 564 9058
Email: info@ou.org
Website: www.ou.org

Progressive
World Union for Progressive Judaism
838 Fifth Avenue, NY 10021
Telephone: (212) 650 4090
Fax: (212) 650 4090
Email: 5448032

Reform
Central Synagogue
652 Lexington Avenue, NY, 10022
Telephone: (212) 838 5122

Temple Emanuel-El
1 East 65th Street, NY, 10023
Telephone: (212) 744 1400
Fax: (212) 570 0826
Website: www.emanuelnyc.org

Sephardi
Shearith Israel
2 West 70th Street, NY, 10023

Union of Sephardi Congregations
8 West 70th Street, NY 10023
Telephone: (212) 873 0300

THEATRE
Jewish Repertory Theatre
c/o Midtown YMHA, 344 E. 14th Street
Telephone: (212) 505 2667; 674 7200

QUEENS
BUTCHERS
Herskowitz Glatt Meat Market
164-08 69th Avenue, Hillcrest 11365
Telephone: (718) 591 0750
Fax: (718) 591 0750
Supervision: Vaad Harabonim of Queens

DELICATESSEN
Berso Foods
64-20 108th Street, Forest Hills 11375
Telephone: (718) 275 9793
Supervision: Vaad Harabonim of Queens
Take-out only.

Meal Mart
72-10 Main Street, Flushing 11367
Telephone: (718) 261 3300
Fax: (718) 261 3435
Supervision: Vaad Harabonim of Queens & Rabbi Teifelbaum
Catering and take out.

RESTAURANTS
Ben's Best Deli Restaurant
96-40 Queens Boulevard, Rego Park 11374
Telephone: (718) 897 1700
Fax: (718) 997 6503
Email: bensbest@worldnet.att.net
Website: www.bensbest.com

Dairy
Habustan Mediterranean Cuisine
188-202 Union Turnpike, Jamaica Estate

Kosher Corner Dairy
73-01 Main Street, Kew Gardens Hills
Telephone: (718) 263 1177

Zen Pavillion
251-15 Northern Boulevard, Little Neck
Telephone: (718) 281 1500

Meat
Burger Nosh
69-48 Main Street, Kew Gardens Hills
Telephone: (718) 520 1933

Cho-Sen Garden
64-43 108th Street, Forest Hills 11375
Telephone: (718) 275 1300
Supervision: Vaad Harabonim of Queens
Chinese food.

Colbeh
68-34 Main Street, Flushing
Telephone: (718) 268 8181
Supervision: Kof-K

Da Mikelle II
102-39 Queens Boulevard, Forest Hills
Telephone: (718) 997 6166

Dougie's
73-27 Main Street, Kew Gardens Hills
Telephone: (718) 793 4600
Fax: (718) 793 9003
Supervision: Vaad Harabonim of Queens

Glatt Kosher International Restaurant
JFK Airport, Terminal 4, 3rd floor, Forest Hills
Telephone: (718) 751 4787
Supervision: Vaad Harabonim of Queens

Glatt Wok Express
190-11 Union Turnpike, Jamaica 11366
Telephone: (718) 740 1675
Supervision: Vaad Harabonim of Queens
Chinese food. Take-away service available.

Hapisgah Steakhouse
147-25 Union Turnpike, Flushing
Telephone: (718) 380 4449
Fax: (718) 591 7099
Website: www.hapisgah.com
Supervision: Vaad Harabnim of Queens

La France
111-08 Queens Boulevard
Telephone: (718) 520 6488

Pita House
98-102 Queens Boulevard, Bet. 66-67th Avenue,
Flushing
Telephone: (718) 897 4829
Supervision: Rabbi David Katz

Vegetarian
Budda Bodai
42-96 Main Street, Flushing
Telephone: (718) 939 1188
Supervision: Rabbi Mayer Steinberg

STATEN ISLAND
KASHRUT INFORMATION
Directory
Organised Kashrus Laboratories
PO Box 218, Brooklyn
Telephone: (718) 851 6428
Including the Circle K trademark.

Niagara County
NIAGARA FALLS
COMMUNITY ORGANISATIONS
Jewish Federation of Niagara Falls
c/o of Beth Israel
Telephone: (716) 284 4575

SYNAGOGUES
Conservative
Beth Israel
College & Madison Avenues 14305
Telephone: (716) 285 9894

Reform
Beth El
720 Ashland Avenue 14301
Telephone: (716) 282 2717
Call for time of services.

Oneida County.
UTICA
COMMUNITY ORGANISATIONS
**Jewish Community Federation of the
Mohawk Valley**
2310 Oneida Street, 13501
Telephone: (315) 733 2343
Fax: (315) 733 2346
The Federation supports the Jewish Community Center.

SYNAGOGUES
Conservative
Temple Beth El
1607 Genesee Street 13501
Telephone: (315) 724 4751

Orthodox
Congregation Zvi Jacob
112 Memorial Parkway 13501
Telephone: (315) 724 8357

Reform
Temple Emanu-El
2710 Genesee Street 13502
Telephone: (315) 724 4177

Onondaga County
SYRACUSE
Orthodox
Young Israel Shaarei Torah of Syracuse
4313 E. Genesee Street 13214
Telephone: (315) 446 6194
Fax: (315) 446 7936

Ontario County
GENEVA
Reform
Temple Beth El
755 South Main Street 14456
Telephone: (315) 789 2945
Email: rosenfield@hws.edu
Website: http://www.templebethelgenevany.org

Orange County
NEWBURGH
KASHRUT INFORMATION- KOSHER
Agudas Israel
290 North Street 12550
Telephone: (845) 562 5604
Email: agudasisrael@aol.com

Supervision: Unit
Central organisation: United Synagogue of Conservative Judaism

MUSEUMS
Gomez Mill House
Millhouse Road, Marlboro 12542
Telephone: (845) 236 3126
Website: www.gomez.org
Oldest Jewish residence now maintained as a museum.

WEST POINT
SYNAGOGUES
United States Military Academy Jewish Chapel
Building 750 10096
Telephone: (845) 938 2766
Fax: (845) 446 7706
With a local community of over 200 the Chapel was designed by the firm responsible for the United Nations building and the Lincoln Center

Queens County
BAYSIDE
QUEENS
RESTAURANTS AND DELICATESSEN
Meat
Ben's Kosher Delicatessen
Bay Terrace Shopping Center, 211-37 26th Avenue 11360
Telephone: (718) 229 2367
Fax: (718) 229 3066
Email: info@bensdeli.net
Website: www.bensdeli.net
Supervision: Supervised
 Kosher catering

Rensselaer County
TROY
MIKVAOT
Troy Chabad Center
2306 15th Street 12180
Telephone: (518) 274 5572

SYNAGOGUES

Conservative
Temple Beth El
411 Hoosick Street 12180
Telephone: (518) 272 6113
Fax: (518) 272 6151
Website: www.templebetheloftroy.org

Reform
Congregation Berith Shalom
167 3rd Street 12180
Telephone: (518) 272 8872
Fax: (518) 272 8984

Rockland County
HAVERSTRAW
Orthodox
Congregation Sons of Jacob
37 Clove Avenue 10927
Telephone: (845) 429 4644

MONSEY
BAKERIES
Bubba's Bagels
Wesley Hills Plaza, Wesley Hills 10952
Telephone: (845) 362 1019
Supervision: Va'ad Harabonim of Greater Monsey

DELICATESSEN
Sammy's Bagels
421 Route 59 10952
Telephone: (845) 356 3030

HOME HOSPITALITY
Mendel & Margalit Zuber
32 Blauvelt Road, 10952
Telephone: (845) 425 6213
The Zuber's write 'Anyone wishing to spend a Shabbat or Yom Tov with us is more than welcome. We are Lubavitch Chasidim, glatt kosher.'

RESTAURANTS
Mehadrin Restaurant
82 Route 59 10952

Dairy
Al di La
455 Route 306, Wesley Hills 10952
Telephone: (845) 354 2672
Supervision: Va'ad Harabonim of Greater Monsey
Italian/Dairy. Cholov Yisrael.

Chai Pizza
94 Route 59 10952
Telephone: (845) 356 2135
Jerusalem Pizza & Restaurant
190 Route 59 10952
Telephone: (845) 426 1500
Kol Tov Pizza
118 Rte 59

Meat
Glat Wok
106 Route 59
Telephone: (845) 426 3600
Kyo Sushi and Steak
419 Rte 59
Telephone: (845) 371 5855

SYNAGOGUES

Orthodox

Young Israel of Monsey and Wesley Hills Inc
58 Parker Boulevard 10952
Telephone: (845) 362 1838

NEW CITY

DELICATESSEN
Steve's Deli-Bake
179 South Main Street   10956
Telephone: (845) 634 8749

GROCERIES
M&S Kosher Meats
191a South Main Street 10956
Telephone: (845) 638 9494

SYNAGOGUES

Conservative
New City Jewish Center
47 Old Schoolhouse Road 10956
Telephone: (845) 634 3619
Website: www.uscj.org/metny/newcity/index.html

Reform
Temple Beth Sholom
228 New Hempstead Road 10956
Telephone: (845) 638 0770
Fax: (845) 638 1696
Website: www.templebethsholom.info

ORANGEBURG

Conservative
Orangetown Jewish Center
8 Independence Avenue   10962
Telephone: (845) 359 5920

SPRING VALLEY

DELICATESSEN
GPG Deli
Main Street 10977

RESTAURANTS

Catering
Eli's Bagel Shop
58 N. Myrtle Avenue 10977
Telephone: (845) 425 6166
Fax: (845) 356 0442
Hours: Sunday - Thursday 6.30am to 5pm. Friday 6.30am to 2pm. Open Motzei Shabbos from after Succos until Pesach. Catering and platters for all occasions. Under the Hashgocha of Rabbi Mordechai Ungar / Machon L'kashrus. We have available an elegant dining hall with accommodations for up to 100 guests, with a meat or dairy menu.

Dairy
Sheli's Café and Pizza
126 Maple Avenue 10977
Telephone: (845) 426 0105

Fax: (845) 362 5004
Supervision: Rabbi Breslaver

SYNAGOGUES

Orthodox
Young Israel of Spring Valley
23 Union Road
Telephone: (845) 356 3363

SUFFERN

Bais Torah
89 West Carlton Road 10901
Telephone: (845) 352 1343
Fax: (845) 352 0841

Saratoga County

CLIFTON PARK

Conservative
Beth Shalom
Clifton Park, Center Road 12065
Telephone: (518) 371 0608

SARATOGA SPRINGS

Conservative
Shaare Tefilah
84 Weibel Avenue 12866
Telephone: (518) 584 2370

Orthodox
Chabad-Lubavitch Center of the Capital District
130 Circular Street 12866
Telephone: (518) 584 7702
Mobile Phone: 518 526 0773
Email: Rabbirubin@saratogachabad.com
Website: www.Saratogachabad.com
Central organisation: National Chabad
See website for Upstate Tourist Kosher, Minyan & Mikva services, Daily Lake George Minyan in August

Congregation Mikveh Israel
26 Lafayette Street 12866
Telephone: (518) 584 6338, (718) 972 7179, (917) 804 1014
Services in July & August. Kosher food available

Orthodox Minyan
510 1/2 Broadway 12866
Telephone: (518) 437 1738

Schenectady County

SCHENECTADY

Agudat Achim
2117 Union Street 12309
Telephone: (518) 393 9211

Orthodox
Beth Israel
2195 Eastern Parkway 12309
Telephone: (518) 377 3700
Fax: (518) 370 4769

Reform
Gates of Heaven
852 Ashmore Avenue 12309
Telephone: (518) 374 8173

Suffolk County
COMMACK
COMMUNITY ORGANISATIONS
Suffolk Council of Jewish Organizations
74 Hauppauge Road 11725
Telephone: (631) 462 5826
Email: info@suffolkcojo.org
Website: www.lijewishlinks.org
Publishes "Suffolk Jewish Directory".

RESTAURANTS
Meat
Pastrami 'N Friends
110a Commack Road 11725
Telephone: (631) 499 9537

SYNAGOGUES
Orthodox
Young Israel of Commack
40 Kings Park Road 11725
Telephone: (631) 543 1441
Fax: (631) 543 1482
Email: rwizman@optonline.net

DIX HILLS
TOURIST INFORMATION
Jewish Genealogy Society of Long Island
37 Westcliff Drive 11746-5627
Telephone: (631) 549 9532
Email: info@jgsli.org
Website: www.jgsli.org
Offers assistance to Jewish travellers on their New York or US roots.

MONROE
SYNAGOGUES
Reform
Temple Beth-El
Monroe Temple of Liberal Judaism, 314 N. Main Street 10950
Telephone: (845) 783 2626
Website: www.monroetemplebeth-el.org

Sullivan County
LOCH SHELDRAKE
RESTAURANTS
Meat
Kikar Tel Aviv
Vacation Village
Telephone: (845) 434-0600

SYNAGOGUES
Orthodox
Young Israel of Vacation Village
PO Box 1014 12759
Telephone: (845) 436 8359

MONTICELLO
HOTELS
Kutsher's Country Club
Kutshers Road 12701
Telephone: (845) 794 6000
Fax: (845) 794 0157
Email: kutshers@warwick.net
Daily services.

MIKVAOT
Mikva
16 North Street 12701
Telephone: (845) 794 6757
Summer: opens at sunset for two hours. Winter: by appointment only.

SYNAGOGUES
Orthodox
Landfield Avenue Synagogue
18 Landfield Avenue 12701
Telephone: (845) 794 8470
Daily services.

Reform
Temple Sholom
Port Jervis & Dillon Roads 12701
Telephone: (845) 794 8731
Daily services.

Sullivan County.
WOODRIDGE
HOTELS
The Lake House Hotel
Lake House Road
Telephone: (845) 434 7800
Glatt kosher. Chalav Yisrael products only. Open Pesach to Succot.

Tompkins County
ITHACA
SYNAGOGUES
Conservative
Temple Beth El
402 N. Tioga Street 14850
Telephone: (607) 273 5775
Fax: (607) 273 5804
Email: rabbi@tbeithaca.org
Website: www.tbeithaca.org

Orthodox
Young Israel of Cornell
106 West Avenue 14850
Telephone: (607) 272 5810

Ulster County
ELLENVILLE
MIKVAOT
Congregation Ezrath Israel
Rabbi Herman Eisner Square 12428
Telephone: (845) 647 4472
Fax: (845) 647 4472
Email: ezrathisrael@verizon.net
Website: ezrathisrael.org
Supervision: Rabbi Yechiel Babad
Mikvah - call for hours.

Warren County
GLEN FALLS
SYNAGOGUES
Conservative
Shaaray Tefila
68 Bay Street 12801
Telephone: (518) 792 4945

Reform
Temple Beth El
3 Marion Avenue 12801
Telephone: (518) 792 4364
Website: www.templebethel-online.org

Westchester County
HARRISON
Orthodox
Young Israel of Harrison
207 Union Avenue 10528
Telephone: (914) 777 1236

MOUNT VERNON
Brothers of Israel
116 Crary Avenue 10550
Telephone: (914) 667 1302
Fax: (914) 667 0278

Fleetwood Synagogue
11 East Broad Street 10552
Telephone: (914) 664 7643
Fax: (914) 664 7643
Email: shul@fleetwoodsynagogue.org
Website: www.fleetwoodsynagogue.org

NEW ROCHELLE
RESTAURANTS
Eden Wok
1327 North Avenue 10804
Telephone: (914) 637 9363

Fax: (914) 637 9371
Supervision: Vaad of Westchester

SYNAGOGUES
Conservative
Bethel
Northfield Road

Orthodox
Congregation Anshe Sholom
50 North Avenue 10805
Telephone: (914) 632 9220
Fax: (914) 632 8182
Email: asnewroch@aol.com
Young Israel of New Rochelle
1228 North Avenue 10804
Telephone: (914) 777 1236
Contact Rabbi on 835-5581

Reform
Temple Israel
1000 Pine Brook Boulevard 10804

PEEKSKILL
Conservative
First Hebrew Congregation
1821 E. Main Street 10566
Telephone: (914) 739 0500

PORT CHESTER
RESTAURANTS
Vegetarian
Green Symphony
427 Boston Post Road 10573
Telephone: (914) 937 6537

Vegetarian Kosher
Vegetarian Kosher
427 Boston Post Road
Telephone: (914) 937 6537

SYNAGOGUES
Conservative
Kneses Tifereth Israel
575 King Street 10573
Telephone: (914) 939 1004

SCARSDALE
Orthodox
Young Israel of Scarsdale
1313 Weaver Street 10583
Telephone: (914) 636 8686
Fax: (914) 636 1209
Website: www.yisny.org/

Orthodox Sephardi
Magen David Sephardic Congregation
1225 Weaver Street, P O B 129H 10583
Telephone: (914) 633 3728
Fax: (914) 633 3728
Email: mitchser@aol.com

WHITE PLAINS
Conservative
Temple Israel Center
280 Old Mamaroneck Road, at Miles Avenue 10605
Telephone: (914) 948 2800
Fax: (914) 948 4755

Orthodox
Hebrew Institute of White Plains
20 Greenridge Avenue 10605
Telephone: (914) 948 3095
Fax: (914) 949 4676
Email: office@hiwp.org
Website: www.hiwp.org
Young Israel of White Plains
135 Old Mamaroneck Road, 10605
Telephone: (914) 683 YIWP
Website: www.yiwp.org

Reconstructionist
Bet Am Shalom
295 Soundview Avenue 10606
Telephone: (914) 946 8851

Reform
Jewish Community Center
252 Soundview Avenue 10606
Telephone: (914) 949 4717

YONKERS
Conservative
Agudas Achim
21 Hudson Street 10701

Orthodox
Lincoln Park Jewish Center
323 Central Park Avenue 10704
Telephone: (914) 965 7119
Website: www.lpjc.org

Reform
Temple Emanu-El
306 Rumsey Road 10705
Telephone: (914) 963 0575

North Carolina
Buncombe County
ASHEVILLE
SYNAGOGUES
Conservative
Congregation Beth Israel
229 Murdock Avenue 28804
Telephone: (704) 252 8431

Reform
Beth Ha-Tephila
43 N. Liberty Street 28801
Telephone: (704) 253 4911

Cumberland County
FAYETTEVILLE
Conservative
Beth Israel Congregation
2204 Morganton Road 28303
Telephone: (910) 484 6462

Durham County
DURHAM
COMMUNITY ORGANISATIONS
Durham Chapel Hill Jewish Federation and Community Council
205 Mt. Bolus Road, Chapel Hill 27514
Telephone: (919) 967 6916

KASHRUT INFORMATION
Dr Ed Halperin
c/o Duke University Medical centre
Email: halpe001@mc.duke.edu

SYNAGOGUES
Conservative
Beth El
1004 Watts Street 27701
Telephone: (919) 682 1238

Reform
Judea Reform Congregation
1955 Cornwallis Road 27705
Telephone: (919) 489 7062
Fax: (919) 489 0611
Email: infobox@judeareform.org

Guilford County.
GREENSBORO
COMMUNITY ORGANISATIONS
Greensboro Jewish Federation
5509 C West Friendly Avenue 27410-4211
Telephone: (336) 852 5433

SYNAGOGUES
Conservative
Beth David
804 Winview Drive 27410
Telephone: (336) 294 0007
Fax: (336) 294 7011
Email: info@bethdavidsynagogue.org
Website: www.bethdavidsynagogue.org

Henderson County
HENDERSONVILLE
Reform
Agudas Israel Congregation
505 Glasgowln 28739
Telephone: (828) 693 9838

Email: agudasisraelnc@bellsouth.net
Website: www.agudasisraelsynagogue.org

Mecklenburg County

CHARLOTTE

COMMUNITY ORGANISATIONS
Jewish Federation
5007 Providence Road 28226
Telephone: (704) 366 5007

DELICATESSEN
The Kosher Mart & Delicatessen
Amity Gardens Shopping Center, 3840 E.
Independence Boulevard 28205
Telephone: (704) 563 8288
Fax: (704) 532 9111
Email: koshermartusa@mindspring.com
Website: www.koshermartusa.com

LIBRARIES
Levine-Sklut Jewish Library and Resource Center
5007 Providence Road, Suite 107 28226
Telephone: (704) 944 6763
Fax: (704) 362 4171
Email: library@shalomcharlotte.org
Website: www.jewishcharlotte.org

MEDIA
Newspaper
Charlotte Jewish News
Telephone: (704) 366 5007

MIKVA
Mikvah-Congregation Ohr HaTorah /Chabad
6500 Newhall Road 28270
Telephone: (704) 366 3984
Email: sardis@earthlink.net

MIKVAOT
Lubavitch Educational Center-Congregation Ohr HaTorah
6619 Sardis Road 28270
Telephone: (704) 366 3984
Fax: (704) 362 1423
Website: www.ohrhatorahnc.org

SYNAGOGUES
Conservative
Temple Israel
4901 Providence Road
Telephone: (704) 362 2796
Fax: (704) 362 1098
Email: templeisraelnc.org
Website: www.templeisraelnc.org

Orthodox
Congregation Ohr HaTorah /Chabad
6619 Sardis Road 28270
Telephone: (704) 366 3984

Fax: (704) 362 1423
Email: sardis@earthlink.net
Website: www.ohrhatorahnc.org
Central organisation: Chabad-Lubavitch

Reform
Temple Beth-El
5101 Providence Road 28207
Telephone: (704) 366 1948

New Hanover County

WILMINGTON

Conservative
B'nai Israel congregation
2601 Chestnut Street 28405
Telephone: (910) 762 1117

Reform
Temple Emanuel
201 Oakwood Drive 27103
Telephone: (302) 722 6640

Temple of Israel
1 South 4th Street 28401
Telephone: (302) 0000

Wake County

RALEIGH

GROCERIES
Eshel Kosher Market
5540 Atlantic Springs Road
Telephone: (919) 872 7757

MIKVAOT
Congregation of Sha'arei Israel
7400 Falls of the Neuse Road 27615
Telephone: (919) 847 8986

SYNAGOGUES
Conservative
Beth Meyer
504 Newton Road 27615
Telephone: (919) 848 1420

Orthodox
Congregation of Sha'arei Israel - Lubavitch
7400 Falls of the Neuse Road 27615
Telephone: (919) 847 8986
Fax: (919) 847 3142

Reform
Temple Beth Or
5315 Creedmoor Road 27612
Telephone: (919) 781 4895
Fax: (919) 781 4697
Email: tempbethor@aol.com
Website: www.templebethor-raleigh.org

North Dakota
Burleigh County
BISMARK
Bismark Hebrew Congregation
703 North Fifth Street 58103
Telephone: (701) 258 3572

Cass County
FARGO
Temple Beth El
809 11th Avenue S 58103
Telephone: (701) 232 0441

Ohio
Cuyahoga County
CLEVELAND
For further information about the facilities located in and around Cleveland visit the following website
www.clevelandjewishnews.com/source

BAKERIES
Breadsmith
9708 Kenwood Road, Blue Ash 45242
Telephone: (216) 791 8817

BUTCHERS
Tibor's Glatt Meat Market
2185 S. Green Road, S. Euclid 44121
Telephone: (216) 381 7615
Fax: (216) 381 5215

COMMUNITY ORGANISATIONS
Jewish Community Federation of Cleveland
1750 Euclid Avenue 44115
Telephone: (216) 566 9200
Fax: (216) 861 1230
Email: info@jcfcleve.org
Website: www.jewishcleveland.org

DELICATESSEN
Unger's Kosher Market and Bakery
1831 S. Taylor Road, Cleveland Heights 44118
Telephone: (216) 321 7176

MEDIA
Newspaper
Cleveland Jewish News
23880 Commerce Park, Suite 1 44122
Telephone: (216) 454 8300
Website: www.clevelandjewishnews.com

MIKVAOT
Charlotte Goldberg Community Mikvah of the Park Synagogue
3300 Mayfield Road, Cleveland Heights 44118
Telephone: (216) 371 2244 ext 198
Fax: (216) 321 0639

K'hal Yereim Synagogue
1771 S. Taylor Road, Cleveland Heights 44118
Telephone: (216) 321 5855

Mikva
Cleveland Heights
Telephone: (216) 387 1040

MUSEUMS
Park Synagogue
3300 Mayfield Road 44118

RESTAURANTS
Dairy
Issi's Place
14431 Cedar Road F, South Euclid 44121
Telephone: (216) 291 9600

Meat
Abba's Market and Grille
13937 Cedar Road, S. Euclid 44121
Telephone: (216) 321 5660

Contempo Cuisine
13898 Cedar Road, University Heights 44118
Telephone: (216) 397 3520
Fax: (216) 397 3523

Empire Kosher Kitchen
2234 Warrensville Center Road, University Heights
Telephone: (216) 691 0006

Ruchama's Singapore
2172 Warrensville Center Road, University Heights 44118
Telephone: (216) 321 1100

SYNAGOGUES
Orthodox
Congregation Shomre Shabbos
1801 S. Taylor Road, Cleveland Heights 44118
Telephone: (216) 371 0033

K'hai Yereim
1771 S. Taylor Road, Cleveland Heights 44118
Telephone: (216) 321 6855

CLEVELAND/BEACHWOOD
Young Israel of Greater Cleveland
2463 South Green Road, 44122
Telephone: (216) 382 5740
Fax: (216) 382 8722
Email: office@yigc.org
Website: www.yigc.org

Franklin County
COLUMBUS
RESTAURANTS
Dairy
Sammy's New York Bagels
40 N. James Road 43213
Telephone: (614) 246 0426
Fax: (614) 246 0427

Email: sammysbagel@msn.com
Website: www.sammysbagels.net
Supervision: Vaad Ho-ir of Columbus

SYNAGOGUES
Conservative
Agudas Achim Synagogue
2767 E. Broad Street 43209
Telephone: (614) 237 2747
Email: info@agudasachim.org
Website: www.agudasachim.org
Supervision: OU
We strive to be a place of prayer, learning and fun for
young and old alike. Our new state-of-the-art facility is
the spiritual home for over 500 families. We welcome you
to join us!
Orthodox
Congregation Ahavas Sholom
2568 E. Broad Street 43209
Telephone: (614) 252 4815
Email: ahavas@beol.net
Website: www.ahavas-sholom.org

Beachwood Kehilla
Telephone: (216) 556 0010
Fax: (216) 595 0989
Email: info@beachwoodkehilla.org
Website: www.beachwoodkehilla.org
Daily 6.30am;Sunday, public holidays 7.30am; Shabbat:
Friday evening at sunset; Saturday morning 9am; Saturday
afternoon at sunset.

Green Road Synagogue
2437 South Green Road 44122
Telephone: (216) 381 4757
Fax: (216) 381 5059
Email: Office@GreenRoadSynagogue.org
Website: www.GreenRoadSynagogue.org
Orthodox congregation with Shabbat Youth Programs,
NCSY, and Aish Shabbat class.

Reform
Anshe Chesed Fairmount Temple
23737 Fairmount Boulevard
Telephone: (216) 464 1330
Fax: (216) 464 3628
Email: mail@fairmounttemple.org
Website: ww.fairmounttemple.org

Hamilton County
CINCINNATI
BAKERIES
Just Desserts
6964 Plainfield Road 45236
Telephone: (513) 793 6627

COMMUNITY ORGANISATIONS
Jewish Community Center of Cincinnati
7420 Montgomery Road 45236
Telephone: (513) 761 7500
Website: www.jcc-cinci.com

Jewish Federation
1811 Losantiville, Suite 320 45237
Telephone: (513) 351 3800

DELICATESSEN
Bilkers
7648 Reading Road 45237

LIBRARIES
**Hebrew Union College-Jewish Institute of
Religion**
Klau Library, 3101 Clifton Avenue 45220-2488
Telephone: (513) 487 3279
Fax: (513) 221 0519
Email: klau@huc.edu
Website: www.huc.edu/libraries
The Klau Library is one of the most comprehensive Jewish
libraries in the world. It contains: 465,000 printed
volumes, and some 2,500 manuscript codices. Special
collections include many thousands of pages of archival
documents, Jewish Americana, music, and extensive
microforms. It also houses the American Jewish Periodical
Center, which preserves American Jewish periodicals and
newspapers on microfilm. More than 875 titles, with over
12,000,000 pages, are available in the Center.

MEDIA
Newspaper
American Israelite
906 Main Street 45202

MIKVAOT
Kehelath B'nai Israel
1546 Beaverton Avenue 45237
Telephone: (513) 761 5260

RESTAURANTS
Dairy
Dunkin' Donuts
9385 Colerain Avenue 45231
Telephone: (513) 385 0930

Marx Hot Bagels
9701 Kenwood Road, Blue Ash 45242
Telephone: (513) 891 5542
Fax: (513) 891 1063

Meat
Pilder's Deli
4070 East Galbraith Road 45236
Telephone: (513) 792 9961

SYNAGOGUES
Conservative
**Northern Hills Synagogue - Congregation
B'nai Avraham**
5714 Fields Ertel Road 45249
Telephone: (513) 931 6038
Fax: (513) 530 2002
Email: berniceu@fuse.net
Website: www.nhs-cba.org

Orthodox
Downtown Synagogue
Bartlett Building, 36 E. Fourth, 7th Floor 45202
Telephone: (513) 241 3576

Golf Manor Synagogue
6442 Stover Avenue 45237
Telephone: (513) 531 6654

Sephardic Beth Shalom
Manss Avenue, PO Box 37431 45222
Telephone: (513) 793 6936

Reform
Isaac M. Wise Temple
8329 Ridge Road 45236
Telephone: (513) 793 2556

Lorain County
LORAIN
Conservative
Agudath B'nai Israel
1715 Meister Road 44053
Telephone: (216) 282 3307

Lucas County
TOLEDO
B'nai Israel
2727 Kenwood Boulevard. 43606
Telephone: (419) 531 1677

Orthodox
Congregation Etz Chayim
3852 Woodley Road 43606
Telephone: (419) 473 2401
Fax: (419) 474 1880
Website: www.etzchayimtoledo.org

Reform
The Temple-Congregation Shomer Emunium
6453 Sylvania Avenue 43560
Telephone: (419) 883 3341

Mahoning County
YOUNGSTOWN
COMMUNITY ORGANISATIONS
Youngstown Area Jewish Federation
505 Gypsy Lane 44501
Telephone: (330) 746 3251

MIKVAOT
Children of Israel
3970 1/2 Logan Way 44505
Telephone: (330) 759 2167

SYNAGOGUES
Conservative
Ohev Tzedek-Shaarei Torah
5245 Glenwood Avenue 44512
Telephone: (330) 758 2321
Fax: (330) 758 2322
Email: ot20@zoominternet.net

Temple El Emeth
3970 Logan Way 44505
Telephone: (330) 759 1429

Reform
Rodef Sholom
Elm Street & Woodbine Avenue 44505
Telephone: (330) 744 5001

Montgomery County
DAYTON
BAKERIES
Rinaldo's Bakery
910 West Fairview Avenue 45406
Telephone: (937) 274 1311
Supervision: Rabbi Hillel Fox, Beth Jacob Congregation.

COMMUNITY ORGANISATIONS
Jewish Federation of Greater Dayton
4501 Denlinger Road 45426
Telephone: (937) 854 4150

HOME HOSPITALITY
Shomrei Emunah
1706 Salem Avenue 45406
Telephone: (937) 274 6941

MEDIA
Newspaper
Dayton Jewish Observer
4501 Denlinger Road 45426
Telephone: (937) 854 4150
Fax: (937) 854 2850
Email: dayjobs@aol.com
The Dayton Jewish Advocate
Telephone: (937) 854 4150 ext. 118

MIKVAOT
Mikva
556 Kenwood Avenue 45406
Telephone: (937) 275 1436

SYNAGOGUES
Orthodox
Beth Jacob Congregation
7020 North Main Street 45415
Telephone: (937) 274 2149
Fax: (937) 274 9556
Email: bethjacob1@aol.com
Website: www.bethjacobcong.org
Supervision: Rabbi Hillel Fox, Beth Jacob Congregation

Stark County
CANTON
COMMUNITY ORGANISATIONS
Jewish Community Federation
2631 Harvard Avenue 44709
Telephone: (781) 452 6444

SYNAGOGUES
Conservative
Shaaray Torah
423 30th Street N.W 44709
Telephone: (781) 492 0310

Orthodox
Agudas Achim
2508 Market Street N. 44704
Telephone: (781) 456 8781

Reform
Temple Israel
333 25th Street N.W 44709
Telephone: (330) 455 5197
Fax: (330) 455 5268
Email: templeisrael@neo.rr.com
Website: www.templeisraelcanton.org

Summit County
AKRON
COMMUNITY ORGANISATIONS
Jewish Community Board of Akron
750 White Pond Drive 44320
Telephone: (330) 869 2424
Fax: (330) 867 8498
Email: mary_dean@jewishakron.org
Website: www.jewishakron.org

MIKVAOT
Mikva
Telephone: (330) 867 6798

SYNAGOGUES
Conservative
Beth El
464 S. Hawkins Avenue 44320
Telephone: (330) 864 2105
Fax: (330) 864 9398
Email: bethel@neo.rr.com
Website: www.bethahabah.org

Orthodox
Anshe Sfard Synagogue
646 N.Revere Road 44333
Telephone: (330) 867 7292
Fax: (330) 867 7719

Reform
Temple Israel
133 Merriman Road 44303
Telephone: (330) 762 8617
Website: www.templeisraelakron.org

Warren County
WARREN
Conservative
Beth Israel Temple Center
2138 E. Market Street 44483-6104
Telephone: 395 3877
Fax: 394 5918
Email: bethisrael1@juno.com

Oklahoma
Oklahoma County
OKLAHOMA CITY
BAKERIES
Ingrid's Kitchen
2309 N.W. 36th Street 73112

KASHRUT INFORMATION
Chabad House
6401 Lenox Avenue 73116
Telephone: (405) 810 1770

SYNAGOGUES
Conservative
Emanuel Synagogue
900 N.W. 47th Street 73106
Telephone: (405) 528 2113

Reform
Temple B'nai Israel
4901 N. Pennsylvania Avenue 73112
Telephone: (405) 848 0965

Tulsa County
TULSA
COMMUNITY ORGANISATIONS
Jewish Federation of Tulsa
2021 E. 71st Street 74136
Telephone: (918) 495 1100
Fax: (918) 495 1220
Email: federation@jewishtulsa.org
Website: www.jewishtulsa.org

KASHRUT INFORMATION
Chabad
6622 S. Utica Avenue 74136
Telephone: (918) 492 4499
Email: ChabadTulsa@sbcglobal.net
Website: Chabad.org

MEDIA
Newspaper
Tulsa Jewish Review
2021 E. 71st Street 74136
Telephone: (918) 495 1100

MIKVAOT

Congregation B'nai Emunah
1719 S. Owasso 74120
Telephone: (918) 583 7121
Fax: (918) 747 9696
Email: thenicepeople@tulsagogue.com
Website: www.tulsagogue.com

Mikva Shoshana - Chabad
6622 So. Utica Avenue 74136
Telephone: (918) 493 7006
Email: chabadtulsa@sbcglobal.net
Contact: Etel Weg tel: (918) 493 7006

MUSEUMS

The Sherwin Miller Museum of Jewish Art
2021 East 71st Street South 74136
Telephone: (918) 492 1818
Fax: (918) 492 1888
Email: info@jewishmuseum.net
Website: www.jewishmuseum.net

SYNAGOGUES

Conservative

Congregation B'nai Emunah
1719 S. Owasso 74120
Telephone: (918) 583 7121
Fax: (918) 747 9696

Orthodox

Chabad House
6622 S Utica Avenue 74136
Telephone: (918) 492 4499; 493 7006
Fax: (918) 492 4499

Reform

Temple Israel
2004 E. 22nd Place 74114
Telephone: (918) 747 1309
Fax: (918) 747 3564
Email: office@templeisraeltulsa.com
Website: www.templetulsa.com

Oregon

Jackson County

ASHLAND

Temple Emek Shalom-Rogue Valley Jewish Community
PO Box 1107 1800 East Main Street 97520
Telephone: (541) 488 2909
Fax: (541) 482 5076
Email: TEShalom@mind.net
Website: www.emekshalom.org
Central organisation: Union for Reform Judaism

Lane County

EUGENE

Reconstructionist
Temple Beth Israel
42 W. 25th Avenue 97405
Telephone: (541) 485 7218
Website: www.tbieugene.org

Marion County

SALEM

Beth Shalom
1795 Broadway NE 97303
Telephone: (508) 362 5004

Temple Beth Shalom
1795 Broadway, NE 97303
Telephone: (508) 362 5004

Multnomah County

PORTLAND

COMMUNITY ORGANISATIONS
Jewish Federation of Portland
6680 S.W. Capitol Highway 97219
Telephone: (503) 245 6219
Fax: (503) 245 6603
Email: federation@jewishportland.org
Website: www.jewishportland.org

GROCERIES
Albertson's
5415 SW Beaverton Hillsdale Highway 97221
Telephone: (503) 246 1713

MIKVAOT
Ritualarium
1425 S.W. Harrison Street 97219
Telephone: (503) 224 3409

MUSEUMS
Oregon Jewish Museum
310 NW Davis Street 97209
Telephone: (503) 226 3600
Fax: (503) 226 1800
Email: museum@ojm.org
Website: www.ojm.org

RESTAURANTS
Mittleman Jewish Community Center (Kosher restaurant)
6651 S. W. Capitol Highway 97219
Telephone: (503) 244 0111

SYNAGOGUES
Conservative
Congregation Neveh Shalom
2900 SW Peaceful Lane 97239
Telephone: (503) 246 8831
Fax: (503) 246 7553

Email: frothstein@nevehshalom.org
Website: www.nevehshalom.org

Orthodox
Ahavath Achim
3225 S.W. Barbur Boulevard 97201
Telephone: (503) 775 5895

Kesser Israel
136 S.W. Meade Street 97201
Telephone: (503) 222 1239

Shaare Torah
920 N.W. 25th Avenue 97210
Telephone: (503) 226 6131
Fax: (503) 226 0241
Website: www.shaarietorah.org

Reform
Temple Beth Israel
1972 NW Flanders 97209
Telephone: (503) 222 1069

Pennsylvania

Allegheny county

MCKEESPORT

SYNAGOGUES
Conservative
Tree of Life-Sfard
Cypress Avenue 15131
Telephone: (412) 673 0938

Orthodox
Gemilas Chesed
1400 Summit Street, White Oak 15131
Telephone: (412) 678 9859

Reform
B'nai Israel
536 Shaw Avenue 15132
Telephone: (412) 678 6181

PITTSBURGH

BAKERIES
Pastries Unlimited
2119 Murray Avenue 15217
Telephone: (412) 521 6323

BOOKSELLERS
Pinskers Judaica Center
2028 Murray Avenue 15217
Telephone: (412) 421 3033;1 800 JUDAISM (1 800
583 2476)
Fax: (412) 421 6103
Email: info@judaism.com
Website: www.judaism.com

COMMUNITY ORGANISATIONS
United Jewish Federation of Greater Pittsburgh
234 McKee Place 15213
Telephone: (412) 681 8000
Fax: (412) 681 3980
Email: jcohan@ujfpittsburgh.org
Website: www.ujfpittsgburgh.org

GROCERIES
Brauner's Emporium
2023 Murray Avenue 15217

MEDIA
Newspaper
Pittsburgh Jewish Chronicle
5600 Baum Boulevard 15206
Telephone: (412) 687 1000
Fax: (412) 687 5119
Email: news@pittchron.com
Website: www.pittchron.com

MIKVAOT
Mikva
2336 Shady Avenue 15217
Telephone: (412) 422 7110
Supervision: Rabbi Shimon Silver

MUSEUMS
Holocaust Center of the United Jewish Federation of Greater Pittsburgh
5738 Darlington Road 15217
Telephone: (412) 421 1500
Fax: (412) 422 1996
Email: ebnaveh@ujfpittsburgh.org
Website: www.holocaustcenterpgh.org
Library and resource centre

RESTAURANTS
Meat
Greenberg's Kosher Poultry
2223 Murray Avenue 15217

Platters Restaurant
2020 Murray Avenue 15217
Telephone: (412) 422 3370

Prime Kosher
1916 Murray Avenue 15217
Telephone: (412) 421 1015

SYNAGOGUES
Conservative
Ahavath Achim
500 Chestnut Street, Carnegie 15106
Telephone: (412) 279 1566

Beth El of South Hills
1900 Cochran Road 15220
Telephone: (412) 561 1168

Beth Shalom
Beacon & Shady Aenues 15217
Telephone: (412) 421 2288

New Light
1700 Beechwood Boulevard 15217
Telephone: (412) 421 1017

Parkway Jewish Center
300 Princeton Drive 15235
Telephone: (412) 823 4338
Website: www.parkwayjewishcenter.com

Tree of Life
Wilkins & Shady Avenuess 15217
Telephone: (412) 521 6788
Fax: (412) 521 7846

Orthodox
B'nai Emunoh Congregation
4315 Murray Avenue 15217
Telephone: (412) 521 1477

Beth Hamedrash Hagodol - Beth Jacob Congregation
709 Forbes Avenue 15219
Telephone: (412) 471 4443
Fax: (412) 281 1965

Bohnei Yisroel
6401 Forbes Avenue 15217
Telephone: (412) 521 6047

Kether Torah
5706 Bartlett Street 15217
Telephone: (412) 521 9992

Poale Zedeck
6318 Phillips Avenue 15217
Telephone: (412) 421 9786
Fax: (412) 421 3383
Email: mil313@aol.com
Website: www.pzonline.com

Shaare Tefillah
5741 Bartlett Street 15217
Telephone: (412) 521 9911

Shaare Torah
2319 Murray Avenue 15217
Telephone: (412) 421 8855

Torath Chaim
728 North Negley Avenue, PO Box 5133 15206
Telephone: (412) 521 4060
Contact Person is Joe Berger (412 521-4060)

Young Israel of Greater Pittsburgh
5831 Bartlett Street 15217-1636
Telephone: (412) 421 7224

Reconstructionist
Dor Hadash
PO Box 8223 15217
Telephone: (412) 422 5158
Email: dh15217@verizon.net
Website: www.dorhadash.net

Reform
Rodef Shalom
4905 5th Avenue 15213
Telephone: (412) 621 6566
Fax: (412) 621 5475
Email: herzog@rodefshalom.org

Temple David
4415 Northern Pike, Monroeville 15146

Temple Emanuel of South Hills
1250 Bower Hill Road 15243
Telephone: (412) 279 2600

Temple Sinai
5505 Forbes Avenue 15217
Telephone: (412) 421 9715

Traditional
Young Peoples Synagogue
6404 Forbes Av. 15217
Telephone: (412) 521 1440
Website: www.youngpeoples.org
Traditional service, all volunteer synagogue, separate seating.

Berks County
READING
COMMUNITY ORGANISATIONS
Jewish Federation
1700 City Line Street 19604
Telephone: (610) 921 2766

SYNAGOGUES

Conservative
Kesher Zion Synagogue
1245 Perkiomen Avenue 19602
Telephone: (610) 375 1352
Email: kzrabbi@entermail.net

Orthodox
Shomrei Habrith
2320 Hampden Boulevard 19604
Telephone: (610) 921 0881
Fax: (610) 685 3866
Email: lipsker@aol.com
Website: www.l-chaim.org
Supervision: Rabbi Yosef Lipsker

WYOMISSING
Reform
Reform Congregation Oheb Sholom
555 Warwick Drive, Wyomissing 19610
Telephone: (610) 375 6034
Fax: (610) 375 6036
Email: office@ohebsholom.org
Website: www.ohebsholom.org

Bucks County
BENSALEM
MIKVAOT
Bucks County Mikveh
2454 Bristol Road 19020
Telephone: (215) 891 5565
Fax: (215) 752 2340
Supervision: Rabbi Moshe Travitsky

SYNAGOGUES
kehillas B'nai Shalom
2446 Bristol Road 19020
Telephone: (215) 752 5032
Fax: (215) 752 2340
Supervision: Rabbi Moshe Travitsky   Orthodox

Cambria County
JOHNSTOWN
COMMUNITY ORGANISATIONS
United Jewish Federation of Johnstown
700 Indiana Street 15905
Telephone: (814) 536 0647

SYNAGOGUES
Conservative
Beth Sholom Congregation
700 Indiana Street 15905
Telephone: (814) 536 0647

Dauphin County
HARRISBURG
COMMUNITY ORGANISATIONS
United Jewish Community of Greater Harrisburg
100 Vaughn Street 17110
Telephone: (717) 236 9555

GROCERIES
Bakeries Giant Food Store and Weis Market
Linglestown Road
Quality Kosher
7th Division Street 17110

KOSHER FOOD
Norman Gras Catering
3000 Green Street 17110-1234
Telephone: (717) 234 2196
Fax: (717) 234 3943
Email: normangras@aol.com

SYNAGOGUES
Conservative
Beth El
2637 N. Front Street 17110
Telephone: (717) 232 0556

Chisuk Emuna
5th & Division Streets 17110
Telephone: (717) 232 4851
Fax: (717) 232 7950

Orthodox
Kesher Israel
2945 N. Front Street 17110
Telephone: (717) 238 0763

Reform
Ohev Sholom
2345 N. Front Street 17110
Telephone: (717) 233 6459

HERSHEY
SNACK BAR
Meat
Central PA's Kosher Mart
Hershey Park
Telephone: (717) 392 1503

Erie County
ERIE
SYNAGOGUES
Conservative
Brith Sholom Jewish Center
3207 State Street 16508
Telephone: (814) 454 2431
Fax: (814) 452 0790

Reform
Temple Anshe Hesed
930 Liberty Street 16502
Telephone: (814) 454 2426
Fax: (814) 454 2427

Lackawanna County
SCRANTON
BUTCHERS
Blatt's Butcher Block
420 Prescott Avenue 18510
Telephone: (570) 342 3886
Fax: (570) 342 9711
Supervision: Rabbi Fine and Rabbi Herman of Scranton Rabbinate

COMMUNITY ORGANISATIONS
Jewish Federation of Northeastern Pennsylvania
601 Jefferson Avenue 18510
Telephone: (570) 961 2300
Fax: (570) 346 6147
Email: jfednepa@epix.net

MUSEUMS
Houdini Museum Tour and Magic Show
1433 N. Main 18508
Telephone: (570) 342 5555
Website: www.houdini.org

SYNAGOGUES
Conservative
Temple Israel
Gibson Street & Monroe Avenue 18510
Telephone: (570) 342 0350
Fax: (570) 342 7250
Email: tiscran@epix.net

Orthodox
Beth Shalom
Clay Avenue at Vine Street , 1025 Vine St 18510
Telephone: (570) 346 0502
Fax: (570) 346 8800
Email: bethshalom2@aol.com
Supervision: Rabbi Yisroel Brotsky

Congregation Machzikeh Hadas
600 Monroe Avenue 18510
Telephone: (570) 342 6271
Email: info@ohavzedek.org
Website: www.ohavzedek.org

Ohev Zedek
1432 Mulberry Street 18510
Telephone: (570) 343 2717

Reform
Temple Hesed
Lake Scranton 18505
Telephone: (570) 344 7201

Lancaster County
LANCASTER
COMMUNITY ORGANISATIONS
Jewish Community Alliance of Lancaster
2120 Oregon Pike 17601
Telephone: (717) 569 7352
Fax: (717) 569 1614
Email: ljcc@lancasterjcc.org
Website: www.lancasterjcc.org

SYNAGOGUES
Conservative
Beth El
1836 Rohrerstown Road 17601
Telephone: (717) 581 7891
Fax: (717) 581 7870
Email: tbelancaster@verizon.net

Orthodox
Degel Israel
1120 Columbia Avenue 17603
Telephone: (717) 397 0183
Fax: (717) 509 6188
Email: ourkehilla@mail.com
Website: www.ourkehilla.com

Reform
Temple Shaarei Shomayim
N. Duke & James Streets 17602
Telephone: (717) 397 5575

Lehigh County
ALLENTOWN
COMMUNITY ORGANISATIONS
Jewish Federation of Lehigh Valley
702 22nd Street 18104
Telephone: (610) 821 5500
Fax: (610) 821 8946
Email: shalom@jflv.org
Website: www.jewishlehighvalley.org
Supervision: Lehigh Valley Kashrut Commission
Kosher food available

MIKVAOT
Mikva
1834 Whitehall Street 18104
Telephone: (610) 776 7948

RESTAURANTS
Meat
Glatt Kosher Community Center
702 N. 22nd Street 18104
Telephone: (610) 435 3571

SYNAGOGUES
Conservative
Temple Beth El
1702 Hamilton Street 18104
Telephone: (610) 435 3521

Orthodox
Congregation Agudas Achim
625 North Second Street 18102
Telephone: (610) 432 4414

Congregation Sons of Israel
2715 Tilghman Street 18104
Telephone: (610) 433 6089
Fax: (610) 433 6080
Email: torczyner@gmail.com
Website: www.sonsofisrael.net

Reform
Congregation Keneseth Israel
2227 Chew Street 18104
Telephone: (610) 435 9074
Email: congki@enter.net

BETHLEHEM
Conservative
Congregation Brith Sholom
Macada & Jacksonville Roads 18017
Telephone: (603) 866 8009

Orthodox
Agudath Achim
1555 Linwood Street 18017
Telephone: (603) 866 8891

Luzerne County
HAZELTON

Conservative
Agudas Israel
77 N. Pine Street 18201
Telephone: (717) 455 2851

Reform
Beth Israel
98 N. Church Street 18201
Telephone: (717) 455 3971

WILKES-BARRE

COMMUNITY ORGANISATIONS
Jewish Federation of Greater Wilkes Barre & Community Center
60 S. River Street
Telephone: (570) 822 4146
Fax: (570) 824 5966

SYNAGOGUES
Conservative
Temple Israel
236 S. River Street 18702
Telephone: (570) 824 8927

Orthodox
Ohav Zedek
242 S. Franklin Street 18701
Telephone: (570) 825 6619
Fax: (570) 825 6634
Email: info@ohavzedek.org
Website: www.ohavzedek.org

Reform
B'nai B'rith
408 Wyoming Street, Kingston 18704

Lycoming County
WILLIAMSPORT

Conservative
Ohev Sholom
Cherry & Belmont Streets 17701
Telephone: (717) 322 4209

Reform
Beth Ha-Sholom
425 Center Street 17701
Telephone: (717) 323 7751

Mercer County
SHARON

Temple Beth Israel
840 Highland Road 16146
Telephone: (781) 346 4754
Fax: (781) 981 4424

Montgomery County
BALA CYNWYD

BOOKSELLERS
Rosenberg Hebrew Book Store
144 Montgomery Avenue 19004
Telephone: (610) 667 9299
Fax: (610) 667 4810

JUDAICA
Wines
Rosenberg Judaica & Wines
144 Montgomery Avenue 19004
Telephone: (610) 667 9299
Fax: (610) 667 4810

RESTAURANTS
Chinese
Yi-Tzi Peking
145 Montgomery Avenue
Telephone: (484) 562 9489
Supervision: Community Kashrus of Greater Philadelphia

Dairy
Cafe Shira
134 Bala Avenue
Telephone: (610) 664 5574
Supervision: Community Kashrus of Greater Philadelphia

ELKINS PARK

BAKERIES
Rolings
7848 Montgomery Avenue
Telephone: (215) 635 5524
Supervision: Community Kashrus of Greater Philadelphia

ELKINS PARK

Orthodox
Young Israel of Elkins Park
7715 Montgomery Avenue 19027
Telephone: (215) 635 3152
Email: host@yiep.org
Website: www.yiep.org

TOURIST INFORMATION
Beth Sholom
8231 Old York Road 19027
Telephone: (215) 887 1342
Fax: (215) 887 6605
Website: www.bethsholomcongregation.org

POTTSTOWN

SYNAGOGUES

Conservative

Congregation Mercy & Truth
575 N. Keim Street 19464
Telephone: (610) 326 1717

Northampton County

EASTON

B'nai Abraham
16th & Bushkill Streets
Telephone: (508) 258 5343

Reform

Temple Covenant of Peace
1451 Northampton Street 18042
Telephone: (610) 253 2031
Fax: (610) 253 7973
Email: tcop@verizon.net
Website: www.urj.org/congs/pa/pa610
Central organisation: Union of Reform Judaism

Philadelphia County

ELKINS PARK

MUSEUMS

Temple Judea Museum of Reform Congregation Kenesseth Israel
8339 Old York Road 19027
Telephone: (215) 887 2027; 887 8700
Fax: (215) 887 1070
Email: tjmuseum@kenesethisrael.org
Website: www.kenesethisrael.org

Central organisation: Council of American Jewish Museums Collection ranges from historic Judaica to contemporary Jewish art. The museum presents an active schedule of changing original exhibitions.

PHILADELPHIA

BAKERIES

Arthur's Bakery
Academy Plaza, Red Lion and Academy Roads 19114
Telephone: (2i5) 637 9146
Supervision: Rabbinical Assembly

Best Cake Bakery
7594 Haverford Avenue 19151
Telephone: (2i5) 878 1127
Supervision: Community Kashrus of Greater Philadelphia

Dante's Bakery
Richboro Centre, Bustleton and Second Street Pikes, Richboro 18954
Telephone: (2i5) 357 9599
Supervision: Rabbinical Assembly

Hesh's Eclair Bake Shoppe
7721 Castor Avenue 19152
Telephone: (2i5) 742 8575
Supervision: Vaad Hakashruth

Hutchinson's Classic Bakery
13023 Bustleton Pike 19116
Telephone: (2i5) 676 8612
Supervision: Rabbinical Assembly

Kaplan's New Model Bakery
901 North 3rd Street 19123
Telephone: (2i5) 627 5288
Supervision: Rabbi Solomon Isaacson

Lipkin and Sons Bakery
8013 Castor Avenue 19152
Telephone: (2i5) 342 3005
Supervision: Rabbi Abraham Novitsky

Moish's Addison Bakery
10865 Bustleton Avenue 19116
Telephone: (2i5) 469 8054
Supervision: Rabbinical Assembly

Rilling's Bakery
2990 Southampton Road 19154
Telephone: (2i5) 698 6171
Supervision: Rabbinical Assembly

Viking Bakery
39 Cricket Avenue, Ardmore 19003
Telephone: (2i5) 642 9227
Supervision: Rabbi Joshua Toledano

Weiss Bakery
6635 Castor Avenue 19149
Telephone: (2i5) 722 4506
Supervision: Community Kashrus of Greater Philadelphia

Zach's Bakery
6419 Rising Sun Avenue 19111
Telephone: (2i5) 722 1688
Supervision: Rabbinical Assembly

BOOKSELLERS

Gratz College
Old York Road and Melrose Avenue, Melrose Park 19027
Telephone: (2i5) 635 7300
Fax: 635 7320

Jerusalem Israeli Gift Shop
7818 Castor Avenue 19152
Telephone: (2i5) 342 1452

Rosenberg Hebrew Book Store
409 Old York Road, Jenkintown 19046
Telephone: (2i5) 884 1728; 800 301 8608

BUTCHERS

Aries Kosher Meats
6530 Castor Avenue 19149
Telephone: (2i5) 533 3222
Supervision: Vaad Hakashruth

Best Value Kosher Meat Center
8564 Bustleton Avenue 19152
Telephone: (2i5) 342 1902
Supervision: Rabbi Dov Brisman

Bustleton Kosher Meat Market
6834 Bustlton Avenue 19149
Telephone: (2i5) 332 0100
Supervision: Rabbi Shalom Novoseller

Glendale Meats
7730 Bustleton Avenue 19152
Telephone: (2i5) 725 4100
Supervision: Vaad Hakashruth

Main Line Kosher Meats
75621 Haverford Avenue 19151
Telephone: (2i5) 877 3222
Supervision: Vaad Hakashruth

Simons Kosher Meats and Poultry
6926 Bustleton Avenue 19149
Telephone: (2i5) 624 5695
Supervision: Vaad Hakashruth

Wallace's Krewstown Kosher Meat Market
8919 Krewstown Road 19115
Telephone: (2i5) 464 7800
Supervision: Vaad Hakashruth

CONTACT INFORMATION
Jewish Information and Referral Service
2100 Arch Street, 7th Floor 19103
Telephone: (2i5) 832 0821
Fax: (2i5) 832 0833
Email: lroth@philafederation.org
Website: www.jewishphilly.org
Central organisation: JEWISH FEDERATION OF GREATER
PHILADELPHIA

EMBASSY
Consul General of Israel
230 South 15th Street 19102
Telephone: (2i5) 546 5556
Website: www.israelemb.org/pa

ERUV
Center City Eruv Corporation
44 North 4th Street 19106
Telephone: (2i5) 922 5446
Fax: (2i5) 922 1550
Email: info@mikvehisrael.org
Website: www.mikvehisrael.org

GROCERIES
Best Value Kosher Meat Center
8564 Bustleton Avenue 19152
Telephone: (2i5) 342 1902
Supervision: Community Kashrus of Greater Philadelphia

R & R Produce & Fish
7551 Haverford Avenue
Telephone: (2i5) 878 6269
Supervision: Community Kashrus of Greater Philadelphia

RESTAURANTS
Dairy
Espresso Cafe
7814 Castor Avenue
Telephone: (2i5) 745 0130
Supervision: Community Kashrus of Greater Philadelphia

Meat
Aroma Grill
10183 Veler Road
Telephone: (2i5) 677 7401
Supervision: Community Kashrus of Greater Philadelphia

Holy Land Grill
7628 Castor Avenue
Telephone: (2i5) 725 7000
Supervision: Community Kashrus of Greater Philadelphia

Vegetarian
Mamas
18 South 20th Street
Telephone: (2i5) 751 0477
Supervision: Community Kashrus of Greater Philadelphia

HISTORIC SITE
Mikveh Israel Cemetery
8th and Spruce Streets 19107
Telephone: (2i5) 922 5446

The Frank Synagogue
Albert Einstein Medical Center, Old York and Tabor
Roads 19141
Telephone: (2i5) 456 7890

JUDAICA & JEWELRY
Bala Judaica and Jewelry Center
222 Bala Avenue, Bala Cynwyd 19004
Telephone: (610) 664 1303
Fax: (610) 664 4319
Email: jewishweddings@msn.com

KASHRUT INFORMATION
Board of Rabbis of Greater Philadelphia
2100 Arch Street 3rd Floor 19103
Telephone: (2i5) 832 0675

Community Kashrus of Greater Philadelphia
7505 Brookhaven Road 19151
Telephone: (2i5) 871 5000

Ko Kosher Service
5871 Drexel Road 19131
Telephone: (610) 696 0408
Fax: (610) 696 9249
Email: amiel@kokosher.org
Website: www.ko-kosher-service.org
Central organisation: Adas Harabonim of Philadelphia

Rabbinical Assembly
United Synagogue of Conservative, Judaism, 1510
Chestnut Street 19102
Telephone: (2i5) 563 8814

Rabbinical Council of Greater Philadelphia
44 North 4th Street 19106
Telephone: (2i5) 922 5446
Fax: (2i5) 922 1550
Email: info@mikvehisrael.org
Website: www.mikvehisrael.org

Vaad Hakashruth and Beth Din of Philadelphia
1147 Gilham Street 19111
Telephone: (2i5) 725 5181
Fax: (2i5) 725 5182

LIBRARIES

Annenberg Research Institute
420 Walnut Street 19106
Telephone: (2i5) 238 1290

Mordecai M Kaplan
1299 Church Road, Wyncote 19095
Telephone: (2i5) 576 0800 ext 232
Fax: (2i5) 576 8163
Email: kaplanlibrary@rrc.edu
Website: www.rrc.edu
Central organisation: Reconstructionist Rabbinical College

Philadelphia Jewish Archives Center
Balch Institute for Ethnic Studies, 18 South 7th
Street 19106
Telephone: (2i5) 925 8090

Talmudical Yeshivah Library
6063 Dexel Road 19131
Telephone: (2i5) 477 1000
Fax: (2i5) 477 5065

Temple University
Paley Library, 13th Street and Berks Mall 19122
Telephone: (2i5) 787 8231

The Free Library of Philadelphia
Central Library, Logan Square 19103
Telephone: (2i5) 686 5392
Website: www.library.phila.gov

Tuttleman Library
Gratz College, Mandell Education Campus, 7605
Old York Road, Melrose Park 19027
Telephone: (2i5) 635 7300 ext. 169
Fax: (2i5) 635 7320
Email: libraryinfo@gratz.edu

University of Pennsylvania
Van Pelt Library, 3420 Walnut Street 19104
Telephone: (2i5) 898 7556

MEDIA

Newspapers

Jewish Exponent
Jewish Publishing Group, 2100 Arch Street 19103
Telephone: (2i5) 832 0700
Fax: (2i5) 832 0786
Email: dalpher@jewishexponent.com

Jewish Post
P.O.Box 442, Yardley 19067
Telephone: (2i5) 321 3443

Jewish Times
Jewish Publishing Group, 103A Tomlinson Road,
Huntingdon Valley 19006
Telephone: (2i5) 938 1177

Mir
P.O. Box 6162 19115
Telephone: (2i5) 934 5512

Periodicals

Inside Magazine
Jewish Publishing Group, 2100 Arch Street 19103
Telephone: (2i5) 893 5797

Jewish Quarterly Review
420 Walnut Street 19106
Telephone: (2i5) 238 1290
Email: jqroffice@sas.upenn.edu

Shofar Magazine
P.O. Box 51591 19115
Telephone: (2i5) 676 8304

Radio

Meridian
Telephone: (2i5) 962 8000

Radio & TV

Barry Reisman Show
Telephone: (2i5) 365 5600

Bucks County Jewish Life
Telephone: (2i5) 949 1490

Comcast Cablevision of Philadelphia
4400 Wayne Avenue 19140
Telephone: (2i5) 673 6600

Pulse
WSSJ, Camden
Telephone: (2i5) 365 5600

MEMORIAL

Monument to the Six Million Jewish Martyrs
16th Street and the Benjamin Franklin Parkway
19103
Telephone: (2i5) 832 0655
Fax: (2i5) 933 6974

MIKVAOT

Mikveh Association of Philadelphia (Ardmore)
Torah Academy, Wynnewood and Argyle Roads,
Ardmore 19003
Telephone: (2i5) 642 8679

Mikveh association of Philadelphia (Northeast Branch)
7525 Loretto Avenue, Philadelphia 19111
Telephone: (2i5) 745 3334

MUSEUMS

Balch Institute for Ethnic Studies
18 South 7th Street 19106
Telephone: (2i5) 925 8090

Borowsky Gallery
Jewish Community Centers of Greater,
Philadelphia, 401 South Broad Street 19147
Telephone: (2i5) 545 4400
Email: www.gershmany.org

Fred Wolf Jr Gallery
Jewish Community Centers of Greater,
Philadelphia, 10100 Jamison Avenue 19116
Telephone: (2i5) 698 7300

Holocaust Awareness Museum
Gratz College, Mandell Education Campus, 7601
Old York Road, Melrose Park 19027
Telephone: (2i5) 635 6480

National Museum of American Jewish History
Independence Mall East, 55 North 5th Street
19106-2197
Telephone: (2i5) 923 3811
Fax: (2i5) 923 0763
Email: nmajh@nmajh.org
Website: www.nmajh.org

Rosenbach Museum & Library
2008-2010 Delancey Place 19103
Telephone: (2i5) 732 1600
Fax: (2i5) 545 7529
Email: info@rosenbach.org
Website: www.rosenbach.org
One of the true cultural treasures of Philadelphia, the Rosenbach Museum & library offers public exhibitions and programs throughout the year. The museum was founded by the legendary book dealer A.S.W. Rosenbach, his brother and business partner Philip, with an outstanding collection of rare books, manuscripts, furniture, and art. The Rosenbach is a historic house, museum and world-renowned research library. Visitors enjoy a uniquely imaginative and intimate experience touring the 1865 town house and changing exhibitions.

RESTAURANTS

Dairy
Cherry Street Chinese Vegetarian
1010 Cherry Street 19107
Telephone: (2i5) 923 3663
Supervision: Rabbinical Assembly

Pizzerias
Holyland Pizza
8010 Castor Avenue
Telephone: (2i5) 725 7444

Shalom Pizza
7598a Haverford Avenue
Telephone: (2i5) 878 1500

SYNAGOGUES

Philadelphia Congregation Rodeph Shalom
615 North Broad Street 19123
Telephone: (2i5) 627 6747

Conservative
Congregation Beth El
21 Penn Valley Road, Fallsington, Levittown 19054
Telephone: (2i5) 945 9500

Ohev Shalom
2 Chester Road, Wallingford 19086
Telephone: (2i5) 874 1465
Email: www.uscj.org/delvlly/wallingford

Tiferet Bet Israel
1920 Skippack Pike, Blue Bell 19422
Telephone: (2i5) 275 8797

Orthodox
Young Israel of Oxford Circle
6427 Large Street 19149
Telephone: (2i5) 743 2848

Young Israel of the Main Line
273 Montgomery Ave, Bala-Gynwyd 19004
Telephone: 610 667 3255

Orthodox Sephardi
Congregation Mikveh Israel
44 North Fourth Street 19106
Telephone: (2i5) 922 5446
Fax: (2i5) 922 1550
Email: info@mikvehisrael.org
Website: www.mikvehisrael.org

Reform
Congregation Rodeph
615 North Broad Street
Telephone: (2i5) 627 6747

Temple Shalom
Edgley Road, off Mill Creek Pkwy., Levittown 19057
Telephone: (2i5) 945 4154

THEATRE
Theatre Ariel/Habima Ariel
PO Box 0334, Merion Station 19066
Telephone: (2i5) 567 0670

TOURS OF JEWISH INTEREST
American Jewish Committee Historic Tour
117 South Seventeenth Street, Suite 1010
Telephone: (2i5) 665 2300

Rhode Island
Bristol County
BARRINGTON
SYNAGOGUES
Reform
Temple Habonim
165 New Meadow Road 02806
Telephone: (401) 245 6536

Kent County
WARWICK
Conservative
Temple Am David
40 Gardiner Street 02888
Telephone: (401) 463 7944

Newport County
MIDDLETOWN
Temple Shalom
223 Valley Road 02842
Telephone: (401) 846 9002
Fax: (401) 682 2417

NEWPORT
HOTELS
Admiral Weaver Inn
28 Weaver Avenue 02840
Telephone: (401) 849 0051
Website: www.kosherbedandbreakfast.com

TOURS OF JEWISH INTEREST
Touro Synagogue
85 Touro Street 02840
Telephone: (401) 847 4794
Fax: (401) 847 8121

Providence County
CRANSTON
SYNAGOGUES
Conservative
Temple Torat Yisrael
330 Park Avenue 02905
Telephone: 785 1800

Reform
Temple Sinai
30 Hagan Avenue 02920
Telephone: 942 8350

PROVIDENCE
COMMUNITY ORGANISATIONS
Jewish Federation of Rhode Island
130 Sessions Street 02906
Telephone: (401) 421 4111
Rhode Island Jewish Historical Association
Telephone: (401) 863 2805

KASHRUT INFORMATION
Brown University-RISD Hillel
80 Brown Street 02906
Telephone: (401) 863 2805
Vaad Hakashrut
Telephone: (401) 621 9393

MEDIA
Periodical
L'Chaim
130 Sessions Street 02906
Telephone: (401) 421 4111

MIKVAOT
mikva
401 Elmgrove Avenue 02906
Telephone: (401) 751 0025

MUSEUMS
Rhode Island Holocaust Memorial Museum
401 Elmgrove Avenue 02906
Telephone: (401) 861 8800

SYNAGOGUES
Conservative
Temple Emanu-El
99 Taft Avenue 02906
Telephone: (401) 331 1616

Orthodox
Beth Sholom
275 Camp Avenue 02906
Telephone: (401) 621 9393
Fax: (401) 331 9393

Congregation Sons of Jacob
24 Douglas Avenue 02908
Telephone: (401) 274 5260

Mishkon Tfiloh
203 Summit Avenue 02906
Telephone: (401) 521 1616

Shaare Zedek
688 Broad Street 02907
Telephone: (401) 751 4936

Reform
Beth El
70 Orchard Avenue 02906
Telephone: (401) 331 6070

WOONSOCKET
Conservative
Congregation B'nai Israel
224 Prospect Street 02895
Telephone: (401) 762 3651
Fax: (401) 767 5243
Website: www.shalom-cbi.org

Washington County
NARRAGANSETT
Congregation Beth David
Kingstown Road 02882
Telephone: (401) 846 9002

WESTERLY
Orthodox
Congregation Shaare Zedek
Union Street 02891
Telephone: (401) 596 4621

South Carolina
Charleston County
CHARLESTON
BAKERIES
Ashley Bakery
1662 Savannah Highway 29407
Telephone: (843) 763 4125
Cookie Bouquet
280 W. Coleman Road
Telephone: (843) 881 0110

COMMUNITY ORGANISATIONS
Jewish Federation and Community Center
1645 Raoul Wallenberg Boulevard, PO Box 31298
29416
Telephone: (843) 571 6565
Fax: (843) 556 6206

DELICATESSEN
Nathan's Deli
1836 Ashley River Road 29407
Telephone: (843) 556 3354

SYNAGOGUES
Orthodox
Brith Sholom Beth Israel
182 Rutledge Avenue
Telephone: (843) 577 6599
Fax: (843) 577 6699
Email: sholomsc@aol.com
Website: www.bs-bi.com

Reform
Kahal Kadosh Beth Elohim
90 Hasell Street 29401
Telephone: (843) 723 1090
Fax: (843) 723 0537
Email: office@kkbe.org
Website: www.kkbe.org
Supervision: Ken Davidson
Notes: Dating from 1749, it is the birthplace of Reform
Judaism in the United states, the second oldest
synagogue building in the country, and the oldest
surviving Reform Synagogue in the world. It has been
designated as a national historic landmark

Georgetown County
GEORGETOWN
CEMETERIES
Old Cemetry

Horry County
MYRTLE BEACH
RESTAURANTS
Jerusalem Kosher Restaurant
1007 Withers Drive
Telephone: (803) 946 6650

SYNAGOGUES
Conservative
Temple Emanuel
406 65th Avenue N 29577
Telephone: (803) 449 5552

Orthodox
Beth El
401 Highway 17 N., 56th Avenue 29577
Telephone: (803) 449 3140
Chabad Lubavitch
2803 N. Oak Street 29577
Telephone: (803) 448 0035
Fax: (843) 626 6403
Mobile Phone: 843 385 2238
Email: daizenman@hotmail.com
Website: www.chabadmb.com
Supervision: Rabbi Yossi Naparstek

Richland County
COLUMBIA
COMMUNITY ORGANISATIONS
Columbia Jewish Federation
4540 Trenholm Road, Cola 29206
Telephone: (803) 787 2023

DELICATESSEN
Groucho's
Five Points 29205

SYNAGOGUES
Conservative
Beth Shalom
5827 North Trenholm Road 29206
Telephone: (803) 782 2500
Fax: (803) 782 5420
Email: bethshalom@bellsouth.net
Website: www.bethshalomcolumbia.org

Reform
Tree of Life Congregation
6719 North Trenholm Road 29206
Telephone: (803) 787 2182
Fax: (803) 787 0309

Email: tolcong@bellsouth.net
Website: www.tolsc.org

South Dakota
Brown County
ABERDEEN
Conservative
Congregation B'nai Isaac
202 North Kline Street 57401
Telephone: (605) 225 7360

Pennington County
RAPID CITY
Reform
Synagogue of the Hills
417 N. 40th Street 57702
Telephone: (605) 348 0805

Tennessee
Anderson County
OAK RIDGE
Conservative
Jewish Congregation of Oak Ridge
101 W. Madison Lane 37830
Telephone: (423) 482 3581

Davidson County
NASHVILLE
COMMUNITY ORGANISATIONS
Jewish Federation of Nashville and Middle Tennessee
801 Percy Warner Boulevard 37205
Telephone: (615) 356 3242

MIKVAOT
Sherith Israel
3600 West End Avenue 37205
Telephone: (615) 292 6614
Fax: (615) 463 8260
Email: RabbiSaul@SherithIsrael.com
Website: www.sherithisrael.com

RESTAURANTS
Vegetarian
Grins
Schulman Centre, Corner of 25th Avenue S. and Vanderbilt Place
Telephone: (615) 322 8571
Fax: (615) 777 2233
Supervision: Sherith Israel

SYNAGOGUES
Conservative
West End Synagogue
3814 West End Avenue 37205
Telephone: (615) 269 4592
Fax: (615) 269 4695
Email: office@westendsyn.org
Website: www.westendsyn.org

Reform
The Temple
5015 Harding Road 37205
Telephone: (615) 352 7620

Hamilton County
CHATTANOOGA
COMMUNITY ORGANISATIONS
Jewish Community Federation
5326 Lynnland Terrace 47311
Telephone: (423) 894 1317

SYNAGOGUES
Conservative
B'nai Zion
114 McBrien Road 37411
Telephone: (423) 894 8900

Orthodox
Beth Sholom
20 Pisgah Avenue 37411
Telephone: (423) 894 0801

Reform
Mizpah Congregation
923 McCallie Avenue 37403
Telephone: (423) 267 9771
Fax: (423) 267 9773
Email: mizpah@mizpahcongregation.org
Website: www.mizpahcongregation.org
Siskin Museum of Religious Artifacts
1101 Carter Street 37402
Telephone: (423) 648 1700
Fax: (423) 648 1780

Shelby County
MEMPHIS
COMMUNITY ORGANISATIONS
Jewish Federation and Community Center
6560 Poplar Avenue 38138
Telephone: (901) 767 7100

DELICATESSEN
Kroger Kosher Deli
540 S. Mendenhall
Telephone: (901) 683 8846

Schnuck's Kosher Deli
799 Truse Parkway
Telephone: (901) 682 2989

KASHRUT INFORMATION
Vaad Hakehilloth of Memphis
Memphis Orthodox Jewish Community Council, PO
Box 41133 38104
Telephone: (901) 767 2263

MIKVAOT
Anshei Sphard
120 E. Yates Road
Telephone: (901) 682 6302

Baron Hirsch Congregation
400 South Yates Road 38120
Telephone: (901) 683 7485
Website: www.baronhirsch.org

SYNAGOGUES
Orthodox
Anshei Sephard-Beth El Emeth
120 E.Yates Road N. 38117
Telephone: (901) 682 1611

Baron Hirsch Congregation
400 South Yates Road 31820
Telephone: (901) 683 7485
Fax: (901) 680 7990
Email: general@baronhirsch.org
Website: www.baronhirsch.org

Young Israel of Memphis
531 S. Yates 38120
Telephone: (901) 761 6060
Fax: (901) 761 6060
Email: jmilevsky@gmail.com

Reform
Temple Israel
1376 E. Massey Road
Telephone: (901) 761 3130

Texas
SAN ANTONIO
Chabad Lubavitch of South Texas
14535 Blanco Road 78216
Telephone: (210) 492 1085
Fax: (210) 493 9460
Email: rabbiblock@chabadsa.com

Bexar County
COMMUNITY ORGANISATIONS
Jewish Federation of San Antonio
12500 NW Military Highway 78231-1871
Telephone: (210) 302 6960
Fax: (210) 408 2332
Website: www.jfsatx.org

MUSEUMS
Holocaust Memorial
12500 N W Military Highway 78231-1871
Telephone: (210) 302 6807
Fax: (210) 408 2332
Email: cohenm@jfsatx.org
Website: www.jfsatx.org

SYNAGOGUES
Conservative
Agudas Achim
16550 Huebner Road 78248
Telephone: (210) 479 0307
Fax: (210) 479 0295
Email: info@agudas-achim.org

Orthodox
Rodfei Sholom
3003 Sholom Boulevard 78230
Telephone: (210) 493 3557
Fax: (210) 492 0629
Email: rodfei@sbcglobal.net
Website: www.ou.org

Reform
Temple Beth El
211 Belknap Place 78212
Telephone: (210) 733 9135
Fax: (210) 737 8946
Website: www.beth-elsa.org

Dallas County
DALLAS
COMMUNITY ORGANISATIONS
Jewish Federation of Greater Dallas
7800 Northaven Road 75230
Telephone: (214) 369 3313
Fax: (214) 369 8943
Email: contact@jfgd.org
Website: www.jewishdallas.org

HOTELS
The Westin Galleria, Dallas
13340 Dallas Parkway
Telephone: (972) 934 9494
Fax: (972) 450 2979
Email: meetings.01052@westin.com

MIKVAOT
Mikvah Association
5640 McShan 75230
Telephone: (214) 776 0037

RELIGIOUS ORGANISATIONS
DATA
5840 Forest Lane 75230
Telephone: (214) 987 3282
Fax: (214) 987 1764
Email: data@datanet.org
Website: www.datanet.org

SITE
Zaide Reuven's Esrog Farm
Telephone: (972) 931 5596
Email: esrog@esrogfarm.com
Website: www.esrogfarm.com

SYNAGOGUES

Orthodox
Chabad of Dallas
7008 Forest Lane 75230
Telephone: (214) 361 8600
Fax: (214) 361 8680
Website: www.chabadcenters.com/dallas

Ohr HaTorah
12800 Preston Road
Telephone: (214) 404 8980

Shaare Tefilla
6131 Churchill Way, off Preston Road 75230
Telephone: (214) 661 0127
Fax: (214) 661 0150

Reform
Temple Emanu-El
8500 Hillcrest Road 75230
Telephone: (214) 706 0000
Fax: (214) 706 0025
Website: www.tedallas.org

Sephardi
Magen David Congregation
7314 Campbell Road 75248
Telephone: (214) 386 7166

El Paso County

EL PASO

COMMUNITY ORGANISATIONS
Chabad Lubavitch
6615 Westwind Drive 79912
Telephone: (915) 584 8218
Website: www.chabadelpaso.com

MUSEUMS
El Paso Holocaust Museum and Study Center
401 Wallenberg Drive 79912
Telephone: (915) 833 5656
Website: www.flash.net/~epholo.com

SYNAGOGUES

Conservative
B'nai Zion
805 Cherry Hill Lane 79912
Telephone: (915) 833 2222

Reform
Sinai
4408 N. Stanton Street 79902
Telephone: (915) 532 5959

Harris County

BAYTOWN

SYNAGOGUES
Unaffiliated
K'nesseth Israel
100 W. Sterling, PO Box 702 77522
Telephone: (281) 424 5829
Email: donte@hal-pc.org

HOUSTON

BAKERIES
Three Brothers Bakery
4036 S. Braeswood 77025
Telephone: (713) 666 2551
Fax: (713) 666 9313
Email: orders@3brothersbakery.com
Website: www.3brothersbakery.com
Supervision: Houston Kashruth Association
Full line scratch kosher bakery. Transfat free. Large variety
of pareve & dairy products.

BAKERIES
Kroger's
S. Post Oak   77096
Telephone: (713) 721 7691
Supervision: Houston Kashruth Association

New York Bagel Shop
9724 Hillcroft 77096
Telephone: (713) 723 5879
Supervision: Houston Kashruth Association

Randall's Bakery
Supervision: Houston Kashruth Association

BUTCHERS
Kroger's
S. Post Oak   77096
Telephone: (713) 721 7691
Supervision: Houston Kashruth Association

COMMUNITY ORGANISATIONS
Jewish Federation of Greater Houston
5603 S. Braeswood Boulevard. 77096
Telephone: (713) 729 7000
Fax: (713) 721 6232
Website: www.houstonjewish.org

EMBASSY
Consul General of Israel
Suite 1500, 24 Greenway Plaza 77046

GROCERIES
Albertson's
S. Braeswood
Telephone: (713) 271 1180
Supervision: Houston Kashruth Association

JEWISH CENTER
**TORCH - Torah & Outreach Resource Center
of Houston**
10103 Fondren Rd, Suite 425 77096
Telephone: (713) 721 6400 x101 (office)
Fax: (713) 721 6900
Mobile Phone: (832) 452-2288
Email: torch@torchweb.org
Website: www.torchweb.com

KASHRUT INFORMATION
Houston Kashrut Association
9001 Greenwillow 77096
Telephone: (713) 723 3850

MIKVAOT
Chabad Lubavitch Center
10900 Fondren Road 77096
Telephone: (713) 777 2000
United Orthodox Synagogues
4221 S. Braeswood Boulevard 77096
Telephone: (713) 723 3850

RESTAURANTS
Dairy
Saba's Mediterranean
9704 Fondren
Telephone: (713) 270 7222
Supervision: Houston Kashruth Association

Meat
Nosher's at the Jewish Community Centre
5601 S. Braeswood 77096
Telephone: (713) 729 3200
Supervision: Houston Kashruth Association

Vegetarian
Madras Pavilion
3910 Kirby Drive 77098
Telephone: (713) 521 2617
Supervision: Houston Kashruth Association

Wonderful Vegetarian Restaurant
7549 Westheimer 77063
Telephone: (713) 977 3137
Supervision: Houston Kashruth Association

SYNAGOGUES
Conservative
Beth Yeshurun
4525 Beechnut Street 77096-1896
Telephone: (713) 666 1881
Fax: (713) 666 7767
Email: ldorfman@bethyeshurun.org
Website: www.bethyeshurun.org
B'rith Shalom
4610 Bellaire Boulevard 77401
Telephone: (713) 667 9201
Congregation Shaar Hashalom
16020 El Camino Real 77062
Telephone: (713) 488 5861

Fax: (713) 488 3561
Email: stuartfederow@hotmail.com
Website: www.shaarshalom.org
Orthodox
Chabad Lubavitch of Houston
10900 Fondren Road 77096
Telephone: (713) 777 2000
United Orthodox Synogogues
9001 Greenwillow 77096
Telephone: (713) 723 3850
Website: www.uosh.org
Young Israel of Houston
7823 Ludinton Road 77071
Telephone: (713) 729 0719
Website: www.youngisraelofhouston.org

Orthodox Sephardic
Congregation Beth Rambam
11333 Braesridge Boulevard 77071
Telephone: (713) 723 3030
Fax: (713) 723 0399
Email: congbethrambam@aol.com

Reform
Beth Israel
5600 N. Braeswood Boulevard 77096
Telephone: (713) 771 6221
Fax: (713) 771 5705
Website: www.Beth-Israel.org

Congregation Emanu-El
1500 Sunset Boulevard 77005
Telephone: (713) 529 5771
Fax: (713) 529 0703
Email: emanuelhouston.org
Website: www.emanuel.org

Congregation for Reform Judaism
801 Bering Drive 77057
Telephone: (713) 782 4162

Jewish Community North
5400 Fellowship Lane 77379
Telephone: (713) 376 0016
Mobile Phone: 832 257 1200
Email: office@cjcn.org
Website: www.cjcn.org

Jefferson County

BEAUMONT
Temple Emanuel
1120 Broadway 7740
Telephone: (409) 832 6131

Lubbock County

LUBBOCK
GROCERIES
Albertson's
Telephone: (806) 794 6761

Lowe's Supermarket
82nd & Slide Road

SYNAGOGUES
Reform
Congregation Shaareth Israel
6928 83rd Street 79424
Telephone: (806) 794 7517
Fax: (806) 550 4139,
Email: monty.strauss@ttu.edu

Nueces County
CORPUS CHRISTI
Temple Beth El
4402 Saratoga Street 78413
Telephone: (361) 857 8181

Potter County
AMARILLO
Temple B'nai Israel
4316 Albert Street 79106
Telephone: (806) 352 7191
Email: bnaiisrael@nts-0nline.net
Website: tx019

Tarrant County
ARLINGTON
Congregation Beth Shalom
1210 Thannisch Drive 76011
Telephone: (817) 860 5448
Email: bethshalom.org

FORT WORTH
MEDIA
Newspaper
Texas Jewish Post
3120 South Freeway 76110
Telephone: (817) 927 2831
Fax: (817) 429 0840
Email: news@texasjewishpost.com
Website: texasjewishpost.com
Dallas Location:
7920 Beltline Road #680
Dallas, TX 75254
Ph. 972-458-7283
Fx: 972-458-7299

Travis County
AUSTIN
COMMUNITY ORGANISATIONS
Jewish Federation and Community Center of Austin
7300 Hart Lane 78731
Telephone: (512) 331 1144
Fax: (512) 331 7059

SYNAGOGUES
Conservative
Agudas Achim
7300 Hart Lane 78731
Telephone: (512) 735 8400
Congregation Beth El
8902 Mesa Drive 78759
Telephone: (512) 346 1776
Fax: (512) 233 004
Email: difriedman@aol.com

Orthodox
Action Community Kollel
6807 Thorncliffe Unit B
Telephone: (512) 340-0899
Tiferet Israel Congregation
7300 Hart Lane 78731
Telephone: (512) 340 0899
Email: rabbi@tiferetaustin.org
Website: www.tiferetaustin.org
Daily and Shabbat Services. Daf Yomi. Kosher information and schedules on website

Reform
Temple Beth Israel
3901 Shoal Creek Boulevard. 78756
Telephone: (512) 454 6806

Waco County
WACO
Conservative
Agudath Jacob
4925 Hillcrest Drive 76710
Telephone: (254) 772 1451
Fax: (254) 772 2471
Website: www.agudath-waco.org

Reform
Rodef Sholom
1717 N. New Road 76707
Telephone: (254) 754 3703
Fax: (254) 754 5538

Utah
Salt Lake County
SALT LAKE CITY
DELICATESSEN
Kosher on the Go
1575 S. 1100 East
Telephone: (801) 463 1786

SYNAGOGUES
Chabad
Chabad Lubavitch of Utah
1760 South 1100 East 84105
Telephone: (801) 467 7777

Fax: (801) 486 7526
Email: rabbi@jewishutah.com
Website: www.jewishutah.com

Reconstructionist
Chavurah B'yachad
Jubilee Center, 309 East 100 South 84111
Telephone: (801) 596 8996

Reform
Congregation Kol Ami
2425 E. Heritage Way 84109
Telephone: (801) 484 1501
Fax: (801) 484 1162
Website: www.conkolami.org

Vermont

Chittenden County.

BURLINGTON

Conservative
Ohavi Zedek
188 N. Prospect Street 05401
Telephone: 802 864 0218
Fax: 802 864 0219
Email: office@ohavizedek.com
Website: www.ohavizedek.com

Orthodox
Ahavath Gerim
corner Archibald & Hyde Streets 05401
Telephone: 862 3001

SOUTH BURLINGTON

Reform
Temple Sinai
500 Swift Street 05403
Telephone: (802) 862 5125
Fax: (802) 652 1073

Washington County

MONTPELIER

Congregation Beth Jacob
10 Harrison Avenue 05602
Telephone: (802) 229 9429

Virginia

FALLS CHURCH

Reform
Temple Rodef Shalom
2100 Westmoreland Street 22043
Telephone: (703) 532 2217

HAMPTON

Conservative
Rodef Sholom
318 Whealton Road, Hampton 23666
Telephone: (757) 826 5894

Traditional
B'nai Israel
3116 Kecoughtan Road, Hampton 23661
Telephone: (757) 772 0100

NORFOLK

COMMUNITY ORGANISATIONS
United Jewish Federation of Tidewater
5000 Corporate Woods Drive, Suite 200, , Virginia
Beach 23462
Telephone: (757) 965 6100
Fax: (757) 965 6102
Email: info@ujft.org
Website: www.jewishVA.org

DELICATESSEN AND RESTAURANT
Meats
The Kosher Place
738 W. 22nd Street 23517
Telephone: (757) 623 1770
Website: www.kosherplacecafe.com
Supervision: Vaad Hakashrus of Tidewater
The Kosher Place is a combination grocery/butcher/deli and
restaurant. Fleishig and Pareve entrees are available from a
full deli menu as well as daily restaurant lunch and dinner
specials. Catering and Shabbos meal packages are also
featured. Call for seasonal hours. Only Deli is offered on
Mondays and Tuesdays when they close at 6pm.

HOTELS
Sheraton Norfolk Waterside Hotel
777 Waterside Drive 23510
Telephone: (757) 622 6664

KASHRUT INFORMATION
Vaad Hakashrus of Tidewater
PO Box 11082 23517
Telephone: (757) 627 7358
Fax: (757) 627 8544
Email: mostsky@hotmail.com
Website: www.vaadoftidewater.com

MIKVAOT
B'nai Israel Congregation
420 Spotswood Avenue 23517
Telephone: (757) 627 7358
Fax: (757) 627 8544
Email: office@bnaiisrael.org
Website: www.bnaiisrael.org
Supervision: Va'ad Hakashrus of Tidewater

SYNAGOGUES
Conservative
Beth El
422 Shirley Avenue 23517
Telephone: (757) 625 7821
Fax: (757) 627 4905
Email: office@bethelnorfolk.com

Temple Israel
7255 Granby Street 23505
Telephone: (757) 489 4550

Orthodox
B'nai Israel
402 Spotswood Avenue 23517
Telephone: (757) 627 7358

Reform
Ohef Sholom
Stockley Gdns at Raleigh Avenue 23507
Telephone: (757) 625 4295

The Commodore Levy Chapel
Frazier Hall, Building C-7 (inside Gate 2), Norfolk
US Navy Station
Telephone: (757) 444 7361
Fax: (757) 444 7362

RICHMOND
COMMUNITY ORGANISATIONS
Jewish Community Federation
5403 Monument Avenue 23226
Telephone: (804) 288 0045
Website: www.jewishrichmond.org

HOTELS
The Farbreng-Inn Kosher Retreat Center
212 N Gaskins Road 23233
Telephone: (804) 740 2000
Fax: (804) 750 1341
Email: info@chabadofva.org

MIKVAOT
Congregation Kol Emes (Young Israel of Richmond)
4811 Patterson Avenue 23226
Telephone: (804) 353 3831
Fax: (804) 288 4381
Email: kolemes@yahoo.com
Website: http://www.kolemes.org
A warm, heimishe shul where everyone is welcome - always love to welcome guests.

MUSEUMS
Beth Ahabah Museum & Archives
1109 W. Franklin Street 23220
Telephone: (804) 353 2668
Fax: (804) 358 3451
Email: bama@bethahabah.org

SYNAGOGUES
Conservative
Or Atid
501 Parham Road 23229
Telephone: (804) 740 4747

Orthodox
Kenesseth Beth Israel
6300 Patterson Avenue 23226
Telephone: (804) 288 7953
Fax: (804) 673 9558

Young Israel of Richmond
4811 Patterson Avenue 23226
Telephone: (804) 353 5831

Reform
Or Ami
9400 N. Huguenot Road 23235
Telephone: (804) 272 0017

Albemarle County
CHARLOTTESVILLE
The Hillel Jewish Center
The University of Virginia, 1824 University Circle 22903
Telephone: (804) 295 4963

Reform
Congregation Beth Israel
301 E. Jefferson Street 22902
Telephone: (434) 295-6382
Fax: (434) 296-6491
Website: www.cbicville.org
Phone: (434) 295-6382
Fax: (434) 296-6491

Alexandria County
ALEXANDRIA
Conservative
Agudas Achim Congregation
2908 Valley Drive 22302
Telephone: (703) 998 6460
Fax: (703) 998 5843

Reform
Beth El Hebrew Congregation
3830 Seminary Road 22304
Telephone: (318) 370 9400
Fax: (318) 370 7730

Arlington County
ARLINGTON
Conservative
Congregation Etz Hayim
2920 Arlington Boulevard. 22204
Telephone: (703) 979 4466
Fax: (703) 979 4468

Email: office@etzhayim.net
Website: www.etzhayim.net

Danville County
DANVILLE
Reform
Temple Beth Sholom
Sutherlin Avenue
Telephone: (804) 792 3489

Fairfax County
FAIRFAX
Conservative
Congregation Olam Tikvah
3800 Glenbrook Road 22031
Telephone: (703) 425 1880

Princess Anne County
VIRGINIA BEACH
MEDIA
Newspapers
Southeastern Virginia Jewish News
5029 Corporate Woods Drive, Suite 225 23462
Telephone: (757) 671 1600
Fax: (757) 671 7613
Email: news@ujft.org
Website: www.jewishva.org

Periodical
Southeastern Virginia Jewish News & RENEWAL Magazine
5041 Corporate Woods Drive #150 23462-4381
Telephone: (757) 671 1600
Fax: (757) 671 7613
Email: news@ujft.org
Website: www.jewishva.org

SYNAGOGUES
Conservative
Kempsville Conservative
952 Indian Lakes Boulevard. 23464
Telephone: (757) 495 8510
Website: www.uscj.org/seabd/virginiabeach/

Temple Emanuel
25th Street 23451
Telephone: (757) 428 2591

Orthodox
Chabad Lubavitch
533 Gleneagle Drive 23462
Telephone: (757) 499 0507

Reform
Beth Chaverim
3820 Stoneshore Road 23452-7965
Telephone: (757) 463 3226
Fax: (757) 463 1134

Warwick County
NEWPORT NEWS
BAKERIES
Brenner's Warwick Bakery
240 31st Street 23607
Supervision: Va'ad Hakashrut

COMMUNITY ORGANISATIONS
United Jewish Community of the Virginia Peninsula
2700 Spring Road 23606
Telephone: (757) 930 1422

MIKVAOT
Adath Jeshurun
12646 Nettles Drive 23606
Telephone: (757) 930 0820

SYNAGOGUES
Reform
Temple Sinai
11620 Warwick Boulevard 23601
Telephone: (757) 596 8352

Washington
BELLVUE
Chassidic Orthodox
Congrgation Beis Menachem-Lubavitch
Eastside torah Center, 1837 156th Avenue N.E., Suite 303 98007
Telephone: (425) 957 7860
Fax: (425) 957 0524
Email: eastsidechabad@earthlink.com
Website: www.chabadbellvue.org
Services Monday through Friday at 7am, Sunday at 9am. Shabbat and Holidaysat 9.30am Call rabbi Farkash (425) 641 9474 for more information.

SEATTLE
Orthodox
Bikur Cholim-Machzikay Hadath Congregation
5145 S. Morgan Street 98118
Telephone: (206) 721 0970
Fax: (206) 723 0679
Email: rabbimyk@bcmhseattle.org
Daily Services: Shacharis: Sundays 7.30 and 9am, Monday and Thursday 6.40 and 7.40am, Tuesday, Wednesday and FRiday 6.50 and 7.45am. Public Holidays 7.30 amd 9am. Minch, 10 minutes before sunset, with Maariv following. Please contact Synagogue for times of other services.

Orthodox Chassidic
Congregation Shaarei Tefilah-Lubavitch
6250 43rd Avenue NE 98115
Telephone: (206) 527 1411; 547 6498
Fax: (206) 524 1856
Please call (206) 527 1411 for times of services.

Sephardic Orthodox
Congregation Ezra Bessaroth
5217 S Brandon Street 98118
Telephone: (206) 722 5500
Fax: (206) 725 8985
Services: Friday sundown, Saturday 8,30am. Please contact for further information.

Grays Harbor County
ABERDEEN
Conservative
Temple Beth Israel
1219 Spur Street 98520
Telephone: (732) 533 3784

King County
MERCER ISLAND
COMMUNITY ORGANISATIONS
Stroum Jewish Community Center of Greater Seattle
Mercer Island Facility, 3801 E. Mercer Way 98040
Telephone: (206) 232 7115
Fax: (206) 232 7119
Email: info@sjcc.org
Website: www.sjcc.org

MUSEUMS
Community Center
3801 E. Mercer Way 98040
Telephone: (206) 232 7115

SEATTLE
BAKERIES
Bagel Deli
340 15th Avenue E. 98112
Telephone: (206) 322 2471
Email: djoneswa@earthlink.net

COMMUNITY ORGANISATIONS
Jewish Federation of Greater Seattle
2031 3rd Avenue 98121
Telephone: (206) 443 5400

Stroum Jewish Community Center of Greater Seattle
Northend Facility, 8606 35th Avenue NE 98115
Telephone: (206) 526 8073
Fax: (206) 526 9958
Website: www.sjcc.org

Washington Association of Jewish Communities
2031 3rd Avenue 98121

JEWISH STUDENT CENTRE
Hillel, Foundation for Jewish Campus Life at the University of Washington
4745 17th Avenue N.E 98105
Telephone: (206) 527 1997

Fax: (206) 527 1999
Website: www.hilleluw.org

KASHRUT INFORMATION
Va'ad HaRabanim of Greater Seattle
5305 52nd Avenue S 98118-2502
Telephone: (206) 760 0805
Fax: (206) 725 0347
Email: vaadinfo@seattlevaad.org
Website: www.seattlevaad.org

MEDIA
Periodical
The Jewish Transcript
2031 3rd Avenue 98121
Telephone: (206) 441 4553
Fax: (206) 441 2736

RESTAURANTS
Panini Grill
2118 NE 65 Street
Telephone: (206) 522 2730

Dairy
Leah's Deli
65 Street between 21st and 22nd
Telephone: (206) 524 3870

Vegetarian
Bamboo Garden
364 Roy Street, near Seattle Center 98109
Telephone: (206) 282 6616
Fax: (206) 284 2775
Email: bamboogarden@aol.com
Website: www.bamboogarden.net
Certified Kosher: Va'ad HaRabanim of Greater Seattle

Teapot Vegetarian House
125 E. 15th Avenue
Telephone: (206) 325 1010

Spokane County
SPOKANE
COMMUNITY ORGANISATIONS
Jewish Community Council
37 West 39th Avenue 99203
Telephone: (509) 838 4261

SYNAGOGUES
Conservative
Temple Beth Shalom
1322 East 30th Avenue 99203
Telephone: (509) 747 3304

Thurston County.
OLYMPIA
Progressive
Temple Beth Hatfiloh
201 8th Avenue, SE 98501
Telephone: (360) 754 8519

Fax: (360) 528 2046
Email: tbh@callatg.com
Website: www.bethhatfiloh.org

West Virginia
Cabell County
HUNTINGTON
SUPERMARKET
Conservative & Reform
B'nai Sholom
949 10th Avenue 25701
Telephone: (304) 522 2980

Kanawha County
CHARLESTON
SYNAGOGUES
Reform
Temple B'nai Israel
2312 Kanawha Boulevard 25311
Telephone: (304) 342 5852
Fax: (304) 342 8612

Traditional
Congregation B'nai Jacob
1599 Virginia Street East 25311
Telephone: (304) 346 4722
Fax: (304) 344 4167
Email: wvrabbi@chater.net
Website: www.bnaijacob.com

Wisconsin
MADISON
COMMUNITY ORGANISATIONS
Jewish Experience of Madison Campus Kollel
341 State Street 53703
Website: www.jemadison.com
Jewish Experience of Madison Campus Kollel
341 State Street 53703
Website: www.jemadison.com

Dane County
Jewish Experience of Madison Campus Kollel
341 State Street 53703
Website: www.jemadison.com
Madison Jewish Community Council
6434 Enterprise Lane 53179-1117
Telephone: (608) 278 1808
Fax: (608) 278 7814
Email: mjcc@mjcc.net
Website: www.jewishmadison.org
Among the major programms sponsored by MJCC are:
Camp Shalom, the oldest day campm in Dane County; our

early childhood program, The Hilde L. Mosse Gan Hayeled Preschool; the Midrasha Hebrew High school, our supplementary program of Jewish and Hebrew studies;and our monthly reporter Madison Jewish News. MJCC owns and operates the Irwin A. & Robert D. Goodman Jewish Community Campus in Verona which includes the Goodman Aquatic Center operated jointly with the MSCR. The pool is open to the public at specified hours. The year-round facilities at the 154 acre Goodman Campus are available for rental.

SYNAGOGUES
Conservative
Beth Israel Center
1406 Mound Street 53711
Telephone: (608) 256 7763
Fax: (608) 256 9434
Email: office@bethisraelcenter.org
Website: www.bethisraelcenter.org

Orthodox
Chabad House
1722 Regent Street , 223 W Gilman Street 53726
Telephone: (608) 231 3450; 257 1757
Fax: (608) 231 3790
Email: rabbi@chabadofmadison.com
Website: www.chabadofmadison.com

Reform
Beth El
2702 Arbor Drive 53711
Telephone: (608) 238 3123

Milwaukee County
MILWAUKEE
COMMUNITY ORGANISATIONS
Coalition for Jewish Learning
6401 North Santa Monica Boulevard 53217
Telephone: (414) 962 8860

MEDIA
Directory
Wisconsin Jewish Chronicle
1360 N. Prospect Avenue 53202
Telephone: (414) 390 5888
Website: www.jewishchronicle.org

Newspaper
Wisconsin Jewish Chronicle
1360 N. Prospect Avenue 53202
Telephone: (414) 390 5888
Website: www.jewishchronicle.org

RESTAURANTS AND DELICATESSEN
Meat
Kosher Meat Klub - Emes Kosher Catering
4731 West Burleigh 53210
Telephone: (414) 449 5980
Fax: (414) 449 5985
Mobile Phone: 414 403 3621
Email: emeskoshercatering@yahoo.com

Supervision: WIS-K Rabbi B Z Twerski
Retail kosher store with a complete line of dairy, fish, grocery, meat products
Take out services available from the deli.

SYNAGOGUES
Orthodox
Beth Jehudah
3100 North 52nd Street 53216
Telephone: (414) 442 5730
Website: www.bethjehudah.org

Congregation Anshai Leibowitz
2415 West Mequon Road 53092
Telephone: (414) 512 1195

Ozaukee County
MEQUON
Agudas Achim Chabad
2233 West Mequon Road 53092
Telephone: 242 2235
Fax: 242 9516
Email: info@chabadmequon.org
Website: www.chabadmequon.org
Central organisation: The Peltz Center for Jewish Life
We serve every aspect of Jewish life in the Mequon area, a synagogue, pre-school, Hebrew school, teen center, senior programs etc.

Sheboygan County
SHEBOYGAN
Traditional
Temple Beth El
1007 North Avenue 53083
Telephone: (920) 452 5828

Wyoming

Laramie County
CHEYENNE
Unaffiliated
Mount Sinai
2610 Pioneer Avenue , P.O. Box 1012 82003
Telephone: (307) 634 3052
Email: info@mtsinaicheyenne.org
Website: www.mtsinaicheyenne.org

LARAMIE
Reform
Laramie JCC
PO Box 202 82073
Telephone: (307) 760 9275
Website: www.uahc.org/wy/wy001

Natrona County
CASPER
Classic Reform

Temple Beth-El
Jewish Community Association of Casper, 4105 S. Poplar, PO Box 50933 82605
Telephone: (307) 237 2330
Fax: (307) 472 6839
Email: utopialtd@aol.com
Website: www.jewishcasper.org

HAWAII

Hawaii
KONA
SYNAGOGUE
Reform
Kona beth Shalom Kailua
Telephone: (808) 322 4192/6004

Maui
KIHEI
SYNAGOGUE
Congrgation Gan Eden
PO Box 555, Kihei Road 96753
Telephone: (808) 879 9221
Fax: (808) 874 8570

Oajhu
HONOLULU
GROCERIES
Down To Earth
King's Street, Near University Avenue
Foodland Supermarket Beretania
1460 South Beretania Street

Deli Grocery /Takeout
Marzal's Kosherland
55 North King Street ~ 13 96817
Telephone: (808) 848 1700
Supervision: Chabad of Hawaii
Will deliver Shabbat meals to your hotel room on Fridays. Can also do deliveries of meals on other days. Small grocery as well.

SYNAGOGUES
Conservative
Congregation Sof Ma'arav
2500 Pali Highway 96817
Telephone: (808) 595 3678

Reform
Temple Emanu El
2550 Pali Avenue 96817
Telephone: (808) 595 7521

WAIKIKI
SYNAGOGUE
Orthodox
Chabad
Hawaiian Monarch Hotel, Nieu Street

URUGUAY

After the *Conversos* in the sixteenth century, there was no known Jewish community in Uruguay until the late nineteenth
century when the country served as a stop-
over on the way to Argentina. The Jewish
population rose in the twentieth century,
with immigration from the Middle East and
eastern Europe. A synagogue was opened
by 1917. Despite restrictive immigration
laws imposed against European Jews fleeing Nazism, 2,500 Jews managed to enter
the country between 1939 and 1940.
Further Jewish immigration followed from
Hungary and the Middle East in the post-
war period.

There are many Jewish organisations functioning in Uruguay, including Zionist and
women's organisations. Kosher restaurants
exist in Jewish institutions, and there are a
number of synagogues.

GMT -3 hours
Country calling code: **(+598)**
Total population: **3,221,000**
Jewish population: **25,000**
Emergency telephone: **(police–999) (fire–999)**
(ambulance–999)
Electricity voltage: **220**

MONTEVIDEO
With approximately 10,000 families in the
capital of Uruguay, Montevideo contains almost
all of the country's Jewish community. There is
a Museum of the Holocaust in Montevideo, and
near the Teatro Solis opera house stands a
Golda Meir monument. An Albert Einstein
monument can be found in Rodo Park.

COMMUNITY ORGANISATIONS
Beit Jabad
Avenida Brasil 2704, CP 111300
Telephone: (2) 709 3444; 708 5169
Fax: (2) 711 3696
Email: rabino.shemtov@jabad.org.uy
Website: www.jabad.org.uy
Central organisation: Lubavitch

Comite Central Israelita Del Uruguay
Rio Negro 1308, P.5 11100
Telephone: (2) 901 6057; 902 9195
Fax: (2) 900 6562
Website: www.cciu.org.uy

EMBASSY
Embassy of Israel
Bulevar Artigas 1585 89 11 200
Telephone: (2) 400 4164
Fax: (2) 409 5821
Email: info@montevideo.mfa.gov.il
Website: www.montevideo.mfa.gov.il
GROCERIES
**Mercadito Casher – Meat, Dairy, Vegetarian,
Parve**
Ellauri 696
Telephone: (2) 707 5360
Supervision: Local Rabbinate
Glatt/non Glatt, Cholov Yisael. Opening times: Monday to
Friday, 9am to 1pm and from 4pm to 8pm.

Yavne
Cavia 2800
Telephone: (2) 908 7869
Fax: (2) 707 0866

HOTELS
Kosher Restaurant
Best Western Armon Suites
2885 21st September Road 11300
Telephone: (2) 712 4120
Fax: (2) 712 4117
Website: www.armonsuites.com.uy

MEDIA
Newspapers
Semanario Hebreo
Soriano 875/201
Telephone: (2) 925 311
Spanish language weekly, editor also directs daily Yiddish
radio programme

MIKVAOT
Beit Jabad
Auda, Brasil 2704
Telephone: (2) 709 3444
Email: jabad@chasque.net
Website: www.jabad.org.uy

MUSEUMS
Centro Recordatorio del Holocausto
Canelones 1084, P.3 11100
Telephone: (2) 622 7223
Fax: (2) 622 7223
First museum of the Shoah in South America

RESTAURANTS
Kasherisssimo
Camacua 623
Telephone: (2) 915 0128

Fax: (2) 208 1536
Supervision: Chief Rabbi Yosef Bitton
The restaurant is situated in the Hebraica Macabi building.

SYNAGOGUES
Comunidad Israelita Hungara
Durazno 972
Telephone: (2) 900 8456
Fax: (2) 900 8456

Social Isralite Adat Yeshurun
Alarcon 1396

Ashkenazi
Comunidad Israelita de Uruguay
Canelones 1084, Piso 1
Telephone: (2) 902 5750
Fax: (2) 902 5740

Conservative
Nueva Congregation Israelita
Wilson Ferreira Aldunate 1168
Telephone: (2) 902 6620
Fax: (2) 902 0589

Orthodox
Vaad Ha'ir

Canelones 828
Telephone: (2) 900 6106
Fax: (2) 711 7736
Mobile Phone: marebis *Sephardi*
Comunidad Israelita Sefardi
Buenos Aires 234, 21 de Setiembre 3111
Telephone: (2) 710 179

Templo Sefardi
de Pocitos L. Franzini 888

TOURIST SITES
Memorial to Golda Meir
Reconquista y Ciudadela

UZBEKISTAN

The ancient Jewish community in this central Asian republic is believed to have originated from Persian exiles in the fifth century. The Jews were subject to harsh treatment under the various rulers of the region, but still managed to become important traders in this area, which straddled the route between Europe and China and the Far East. In the late Middle Ages Jewish weavers and dyers were asked to help in the local cloth industry, and Bukhara became a key Jewish city after it became the capital of the country in the 1500s. Once the area had been incorporated into the Russian Empire in 1868, many Jews

from the west of the Empire moved into Uzbekistan. A further influx occurred when Uzbekistan was used to shelter Jews during the Nazi invasion of the Soviet Union, and many subsequently set up home there.

The original Bukharan Jews are generally more religious than the Ashkenazim who entered the area in the nineteenth and twentieth centuries. There are Jewish schools in the area, and although there is no central Jewish organisation, there are many Jewish bodies operating on separate levels for the Ashkenazim and the Bukharans.

GMT +5 hours
Country calling code: (+998)
Total population: **21,206,000**
Jewish population: **15,000**
Emergency telephone: **(police–03) (fire–03) (ambulance–03)**
Electricity voltage: **220**

ANDIZHAN
SYNAGOGUES
Andizhan Synagogue
7 Sovetskaya Street

BUKHARA
Bukhara Synagogue
20 Tsentrainaya Street

KATTA KURGAN
Katta Kurgan Synagogue
1 Karl Marx Alley

KERMINE
Kermine Synagogue
36 Narimanov Street

KOKAND
Kokand Synagogue
Dekabristov Street, Fergan Oblast

MARGELAN
Margelan Synagogue
Turkilskaya Street, Fergan Oblast

NAVOY
Navoy Synagogue
36 Narimanov Street

SAMARKAND
3,000 Jews live in Samarkand. Many are Bukharan and live in the special mahala, the quarter designated for Jews.

Samarkand Synagogue
18 Esayva Street
Synagogue Gumbaz
2 i Llyazarov Proezd 1
Telephone: (66) 223 0978; 235 7862; 233 1145
Fax: (66) 233 4640

TASHKENT
COMMUNITY ORGANISATIONS
Jewish Community of Uzbekistan
2nd Mirobadskaya 15/17 100015
Telephone: (71) 153 5114
Fax: (71) 1206 4318
Email: jewish@jewish.uz
Website: www.jewish.uz
Supervision: Rabbi David Gurevitch, Chairman Roman Bensman
CONTACT INFORMATION
Lubavitch in Uzbekistan & Asia
30 Balakiereva Street (Shohjahon tor –kuchasi), 15
Second Mirobad Street 100100
Telephone: (71) 253 9640: 252 5978
Fax: (71) 120 6431
Email: gurevitchabad@jewishuz.org
Website: www.jewishhuz.com
Central organisation: Lubavitch
EMBASSY
Embassy of Israel
16A Shakhrisabz Street, 5th Floor
Telephone: (71) 152 911
Fax: (71) 152 1378

SYNAGOGUES
Central Synagogue Beit Menachem
2 ya Kunaeva Street 15/17 700015
Telephone: (71) 152 59 78, 256 51 14
Fax: (71) 120 64 31

Ashkenazi
Tashkent Ashkenazi Synagogue
77 Chempianov Street

Orthodox
Tashkent Orthodox Synagogue
9 Sagban Street 700100

Sephardi
Kotel Levi Yitzchok
Shcolave 911 700100
Tashkent Sephardi Synagogue
3 Sagban Street
Telephone: (71) 40 0768

VENEZUELA

Settlement in Venezuela began in the early nineteenth century from the Caribbean. The Jews were granted freedom early (between 1819 and 1821), which encouraged more settlement. The community at that time was not religious. At the beginning of the twentieth century some Middle Eastern Jewish immigrants organised a central committee for the first time. The powerful influence of the Catholic Church meant few Jews were accepted as immigrants in the pre-war rush to escape Nazi Europe.

After the war however, the community began to expand, with arrivals from Hungary and the Middle East. The successful oil industry and the excellent Jewish education system attracted immigrants from other South American countries.

Today most Jews live in Caracas, the capital. Fifteen synagogues serve the country. The Lubavitch movement is present and maintains a yeshivah. Caracas has a Jewish bookshop and a weekly Jewish newspaper. Venezuela has an expanding Jewish community, in contrast to many of its South American neighbours. The oldest Jewish cemetery in South America, in Coro, with tombstones dating from 1832, is still in use today.

GMT -4 hours
Country calling code: **(+58)**
Total population: **22,777,000**
Jewish population: **22,000**
Emergency telephone: **(ambulance–545 4545)**
Dr. 02 483 7021
Electricity voltage: **220**

CARACAS
The first real Jewish settlement in the city dates from 1880, although there is mention of them being in the territory in the early 18th century. The present community is basically Sephardi.

BAKERIES
Pasteleria Kasher
Avenida Los Proceres
Telephone: (2) 515 086

BOOKSELLERS
Liberia Cultural Maimonides
Avenida Altamira Edif. Carlitos PB, (near Avenida Galapen), San Bernardino
Telephone: (2) 551 6356
Fax: (2) 552 9127

COMMUNITY ORGANISATIONS

Chabad Lubavitch
9na. Trans. Altamira final de Ae Luis Roche Altamira
Telephone: (2) 264 0711
Fax: (2) 264 7011
Website: www.jabadve.com

Chabad Lubavitch
Avenue J Washington QTA Lore No. 8
Telephone: (2) 552 0044
Fax: (2) 552 2184

CONTACT INFORMATION

Chabad Lubavitch Centre
Apartado 5454 1010A
Telephone: (2) 523 887

DELICATESSEN

La Belle Delicatesses
Avenida Bogotá, Edif Santa Maria, Local 2, Los Caobos
Telephone: (2) 781 7204
Fax: (2) 781 7182
Kosher delicatessen and mini market, restaurant and take away

EMBASSY

Embassy of Israel
Avenida Francisco de Miranda, Centro Empresarial Miranda, 4 Piso Oficina 4 D, Apartado Postal Los Ruices 70081
Telephone: (2) 239 4511/4921
Fax: (2) 239 4320

MEDIA

Newspapers
Nuevo Mundo Israelita
Avenida Marques del Toro 9, Los Caobos

MIKVAOT

Shomrei Shabbat Association Synagogue
Avenida Anauco, San Bernardino
Telephone: (2) 517 197

Union Israelita de Caracas Synagogue & Community Centre
Avenida Marques del Toro 9, San Bernardino
Telephone: (2) 552 8222
Fax: (2) 552 7628

SYNAGOGUES

Ashkenazi
Great Synagogue of Caracas
Avenida Francisco Javier Ustariz, San Bernardino
Telephone: (2) 511 869

Shomrei Shabat Associacion Synagogue
Avenida Anauco, San Bernardino
Telephone: (2) 517 197

Union Israelita de Caracas Synagogue & Community Centre
Avenida Marques del Toro 9, San Bernardino
Telephone: (2) 552 8222
Fax: (2) 552 7628
If notified in advance, they can arrange kosher lunches, there is also a meat snack bar open in the evening

Sephardi
Bet El
Avenida Cajigal, San Bernardino
Telephone: (2) 522 008

Keter Tora
Avenida Lopez Mendez, San Bernardino

Shahare Shalom
Avenida Bogota, Quinta Julita, Los Caobos 1050
Telephone: (2) 782 6755
Fax: (2) 782 6755
Email: isaacsananes@hotmail.com
SHAHARE SHALOM

Tiferet Yisrael
Avenida Mariperez, Los Caobos
Telephone: (2) 781 1942

MARACAIBO

COMMUNITY ORGANISATIONS

Associación Israelita de Maracaibo
Calle 74 No 13 26
Telephone: (61) 70333

PORLAMAR

SYNAGOGUES

Or Meir
Calle Carnevali, Margarita Island
Telephone: (95) 634 433
Mikva on premises

VIETNAM

GMT +7 hours
Country calling code: **(+84)**
Total population: **85,200,000**
Emergency telephone: **(police–13) (fire–14) (ambulance–15)**

HO CHI MINH CITY

SYNAGOGUES

Chabad House
121/137 Le Loi Street, Ben Nghe District 1
Telephone: (8) 821 8055
Mobile Phone: (+84) 090916770
Email: chabadvietnam@gmail.com

VIRGIN ISLANDS (USA)

Jews first began to settle on the island in 1655, taking advantage of liberal Danish rule. They were mainly traders in sugar cane, rum and molasses, and by 1796 a synagogue had been founded. The Jewish population of 400 made up half of the islands' white community in 1850. There have been three Jewish governors. One was Gabriel Milan, the first governor who was appointed by King Christian of Denmark.

The community began to shrink after the Panama Canal was opened in 1914, and by 1942 only 50 Jews remained. Since 1945 the community has expanded again, with families arriving from the US mainland.

GMT -4 hours
Country calling code: (+1 340)
Total population: **115,000**
Jewish population: **300**
Emergency telephone: **(police–911) (fire–911) (ambulance–911)**
Electricity voltage: **911**

ST THOMAS
Hebrew Congregation of St Thomas
PO Box 266 VI 00804
Telephone: 774 4312
Fax: 774 3249
Website: www.onepaper.com/synagogue
Located on 16A & B Crystal Gade, Charlotte Amalie. Open to visitors: Monday to Friday 9am to 4pm. Services schedule: Friday 6.30 pm, Saturday 10am.

ZAMBIA

The Jewish community began in the early twentieth century, with cattle ranching being the main attraction for Jewish immigrants. The community grew, and the copper industry was developed largely by Jewish entrepreneurs. With refugees from Nazism and a post-war economic boom, the Jewish community in the mid-1950s totalled 1,200. The community declined after independence in 1964.

Today the Council for Zambian Jewry (founded in 1978) fulfils the role of the community's central body.

GMT +2 hours
Country calling code: (+260)
Total population: **9,715,000**

Jewish population: **Under 100**
Emergency telephone: **(police–999) (fire–999) (ambulance–999)**
Electricity voltage: **220**

LUSAKA
COMMUNITY ORGANISATIONS
Council for Zambian Jewry
PO Box 30089 10101
Telephone: (211) 229 556
Fax: (211) 223 798
Email: ceo@galaunia.co.zm

SYNAGOGUES
Lusaka Hebrew Congregation
Chachacha Road, POB 30020 10101
Telephone: (211) 229 190
Fax: (211) 221 428
Mobile Phone: 9585 7565
Central organisation: African Jewish Congress

ZIMBABWE

Jews were among the earliest pioneers in Zimbabwe. The first white child born there (April 1894) was Jewish. The first synagogue in Zimbabwe (formerly Rhodesia) was set up in 1894, in a tent in Bulawayo. In 1897 a Jew was elected as the first mayor of Bulawayo. The first Jews came from Europe (especially Lithuania), and they became involved in trade and managing hotels. They were joined in the 1920s and 1930s by Sephardis from Rhodes. Some senior politicians in the country were Jewish, including one prime minister.

The 1970s saw the turbulent transition to Zimbabwe, and many Jews emigrated to escape the unrest. The community is now mainly Ashkenazi, with an important Sephardi component. Harare has both an Ashkenazi and a Sephardi synagogue; Bulawayo has a Ashkenazi synagogue. There are community centres and schools, in both the towns, although the latter have many local, non-Jewish pupils.

GMT +2 hours
Country calling code: (+263)
Total population: **12,294,000**
Jewish population: **900**
Emergency telephone: **(police–999) (fire–999) (ambulance–999)**
Electricity voltage: **220/240**

BULAWAYO
Orthodox
Bulawayo Hebrew Congregation
PO Box 337, Sinai Centre, Corner Coghlan Avenue
and Bailey Road
Telephone: (9) 78726; 259698
Fax: (9) 65535
Email: hms@netconnect.co.zw
Website: www.zjc.org.il
Supervision: Rabbi David Alima,rabbiChevra Kadishah,
Jewish Old Age Home and other charities

HARARE
COMMUNITY ORGANISATIONS
Zimbabwe Jewish Board of Deputies
PO BOX 1954
Telephone: (4) 702 507
Fax: (4) 702 506
Hours of opening 8.30am to 12noon

SYNAGOGUES
Harare Hebrew Congregation
Milton Park Jewish Centre, Lezard Avenue, PO Box
342
Telephone: (4) 798 683
Fax: (4) 798 463

Sephardi Congregation
54 Josiah Chinamano Avenue, PO Box 1051
Telephone: (4) 722 899

Kosher Fish in Europe

CYPRUS

Antzouva(Anchovy)
Bacceliaos (Cod) Barbouni
(Pike) Cephalos (Perch)
Glossa (Sole) Lavraki (Bass)
Sardella (Pilchard) Scoumbri
(Mackerel) Tonos(Tuna)
Tsipoura (Bream)

CZECH REPUBLIC Ancovicka
(Anchovy) Belicka (Roach)
Kambala (Brill) Kapr(Carp)
Lin (Tench)
Losos (Salmon) Makrela
(Mackerel) Okoun (Perch)
Parmice (Mullet) Platejs (Dab)
Platyz (Plaice)
Plotice (Sole)
Prazama (Bream) Pstruh
(Trout) Sardinka (Sardine) Sled
(Herring)
Sprota (Sprat)
Stika (Pike)
Treska (Haddock) Tunak(Tuna)

DENMARK

Aborre (Perch)
Ansjos (Anchovy)
Bars (Bass)
Brasen (Bream) Brisling (Sprat)
Geode (Pike) Helleyflynder
    (Halibut)
Hvilling (Whiting)
Ising (Dab)
Karpe (Carp) Knurhane
(Gunard)
Kuller (Haddock) Kulmule
(Hake)
Laks (Salmon)
Lange (Ling)
Lubbe (Pollack) Makrel
(Mackerel) Multe (Mullet)
Orred (Trout) Rodspaette
(Plaice) Sardin (Sardine)
Sild (Herring)

Skalle (Roach) Skrubbe
(Flounder) Slethvarre (Brill)
Suder (Tench)
Torsk (Cod)
Tun fisk (Tuna) Tunge
(Sole)

FRANCE

Aiglefin (Haddock) Anchois
(Anchovy) Bar Commun (Bass)
Barbue (Brill)
Breme (Bream) Brochet (Pike)
Cabillaud (Cod)
Carpe (Carp)
Carrelet (Plaice) Daurade
(Bream) Epirlan (Smelt)
Flet (Flounder)
Fletan (Halibut) Gardon
(Roach) Grondin (Gunard)
Hareng (Herring)
Lieu Jaune (Pollack) Limande
(Dab)
Lingue (Ling) Maquereau
    (Mackerel)
Merlan (Whiting) Merlu
(Hake)
Mulet (Mullet) Perche
(Perch) Pilchard (Pilchard)
Plie (Plaice)
Sardine (Sardine) Saumon
(Salmon) Sole (Sole)
Sprat (Sprat) Tanche
(Tench) Thon (Tuna)
Truite (Trout)

GERMANY

Barsch (Perch)
Brasse (Bream) Flunder
(Flounder) Forelle (Trout)
Glattbutt (Brill)
Hecht (Pike)
Heilbutt (Halibut) Hering
(Herring) Kabeljau (Cod)
Knurrhahn (Gunard) Lachs
(Salmon)

Leng (Ling)
Makrele (Mackerel) Meerasche
(Mullet) Pilchard (Pilchard)
Plotze (Roach)
Pollack (Pollack) Sardelle
(Anchovy) Sardine (Sardine)
Scharbe (Dab) Schellfisch
(Haddock) Schlei (Tench)
Scholle (Plaice) Seebarsch
(Bass) Seehecht(Hake)
Seezunge (Sole) Sprotte (Sprat)
Thun (Tuna) Weissfisch (Carp)
Wittling (Whiting)

GREECE

Antjuga (Anchovy) Bakaliaros
(Cod) Chematida
(Flounder) Chromatida (Dab)
Gados (Haddock)
Giavros(Anchovy) Glinia
(Tench)
Glossa (Sole)
Glossaki (Plaice) Hippoglossa
(Halibut) Kaponi (Gunard)
Kephalos (Mullet) Kyprinos
(Carp) Lavraki (Bass)
Lestia (Bream) Papalina (Sprat)
Pentiki (Ling)
Perca chani(Perch) Pestropha
(Trout)
Pissi (Brill)
Regha (Herring) Romvos (Brill)
Sardella (Pilchard) Sardine
(Sardine) Scoumbri (Mackerel)
Solomos (Salmon) Tonnos
(Tuna)
Tourna (Pike)
Tsironi (Roach)

ITALY

Acciuga (Anchovy) Aringa
(Herring) Asinello (Haddock)
Brama (Bream)
Carpa (Carp)
Cefalo (Mullet) Halibut

(Halibut) Limanda (Dab)
Luccio (Pike) Maccerello
(Mackerel) Merlano (Whiting)
Merluzzo Bianco (Cod)
Merluzzo Giallo

(Pollack)
Molva (Ling) Nasello
(Hake)
Passera (Plaice) Passera
Pianuzza
(Flounder)
Pesce (Perch)
Pesce Capone
(Gunard)
Rombo Liscio (Brill) Salmone
(Salmon) Sardina (Sardine)
Sogliola (Sole)
Spigola (Bass)
Spratto (Sprat) Tinca (Tench)
Tonno (Tuna) Triotto (Roach)
Trota (Trout)

NETHERLANDS
Aaldoe (Mullet) Ansjovis
(Anchovy)
 Baars (Perch) Blankvoorn
(Roach) Bot (Flounder) Brasem
(Bream)
Forel (Trout)
Griet (Brill)
Harder (Mullet) Haring
(Herring)
Heek (Hake)
Helibot (Halibut) Kabeljauw
(Cod) Karper(Carp)
Leng (Ling)
Makree (Mackerel) Pelser
(Sardine)
Poon (Gunard)
Salm (Salmon)
Sardien (Sardine) Schar(Dab)
Schelvis (Haddock) Schol
(Plaice)
Snoek (Pike)
Sprot (Sprat)
Tong (Sole)
Tonijn (Tuna)

Wijting (Whiting) Witte koolvis
(Pollack) Zeebaars (Bass)
Zeelt (Tench)

PORTUGAL
Alabote (Halibut) Anchova
(Anchovy) Arenque (Herring)
Arinca (Haddock) Atum (Tuna)
Bacalhau (Cod) Badejo
(Pollack) Biqueirao (Anchovy)
Carpa (Carp)
Donzela (Ling) Espadilha
(Sprat) Linguado (Sole)
Lucio (Pike)
Perca (Perch)
Pescada (Hake) Petruca
(Flounder) Robalo (Bass)
Rodovalho (Brill) Ruivaca
(Roach)
Ruivo (Gunard) Salmao
(Salmon) Sarda (Mackerel)
Sardinha (Sardine) Sargo
(Bream)
Solha (Plaice)
Solhao (Dab)
Tainha (Mullet) Tenca(Tench)
Truta (Trout)

SPAIN
Abadejo (Pollack) Anchoa
(Anchovy)
Arenque (Herring) Atun (Tuna)
Bacalao (Cod) Bermejuela
(Roach) Boqueron (Anchovy)
Caballa (Mackerel) Carpa
(Carp)
Eglefino (Haddock) Espadin
(Sprat) Halibut (Halibut)
Lenguado (Sole) Limanda
(Dab)
Lisa (Mullet) Lubina (Bass)
Lucio (Pike) Maruca (Ling)
Merlan (Whiting) Merluza
(Hake) Perca (Perch)
Platija (Flounder) Remol
(Brill) Rubios (Gunard)
Salmon (Salmon) Sardina
(Sardine) Solla (Plaice)

Tenca (Tench) Trucha
(Trout)

TURKEY
Alabalik (Trout) Bakalyaro
(Whiting) Berlam (Hake)
Caca (Sprat)
Civisiz kalkan (Brill) Derepissi
(Flounder) Dil baligi (Sole)
Gelincik (Ling)
Hamsi (Anchovy) Kadife baligi
(Tench) Kefal (Mullet) Kirlangic
(Gunard) Kizilgoz (Roach)
Levrek (Bass)
Morina (Cod)
Palatika (Sprat)
Pisi baligi (Dab)
Ringa (Herring) Sardalya
(Sardine) Sardayalo (Pilchard)
Sazan (Carp)
Som baligi (Salmon) Tahta
baligi (Bream) Tatlisu levregi
(Perch) Ton baligi (Tuna)
Turna baligi (Pike) Uskumru
(Mackerel)

UNITED KINGDOM
Anchovy
Barbel
Bass
Bloater
Bonito
Bream
Brill
Brisling
Buckling
Carp
Coalfish
Cod
Coley
Dab
Dace
Flounder
Fluke
Grayling
Gurnard
Haddock
Hake

Halibut
Herring
Hoki
John Dory
Keta Salmon Kipper
Ling
Mackerel
Megrim
Mock
Halibut
Mullet Grey
Mullet Red
Norway Haddock

Parrot Fish
Perch
Pike
Pilchard
Plaice
Pole
Pollack
Redfish
Roach
Saithe
Salmon
Sardine
Shad

Sild
Smelt
Snapper
Snoek
Sole Dover
Sole Lemon
Sprat
Tench
Tilapia
Trout
Tuna (Tunny) Whitebait
Whiting
witch

Kosher Fish outside Europe

AUSTRALIA

Anchovy
Baramundi
Barracouta
Barracuda
Blue Eye
Blue Grenadier
Bream
Butterfly-fish
Cod
Coral Perch
Duckfish
Flathead
Flounder
Garfish
Groper
Gurnard
Haddock
Hake
Harpuka
Herring
Iewfish
John Dory
Lemon Sole
Mackerel
Morwong
Mullet
Murray Cod
Murray Perch
Orange Roughy
Perch

Pike
Pilchard
Red Emperor
Redfin
Salmon
Sardine
Sea Perch
Shad
Sild
Snapper
Tailor
Tasmanian
Trumpeter
Terakiji
Trevally
Trout Tuna:
    Albacore, Bluefin
    North bluefin
    South bluefin
    Skipjack (striped)
    Yellowtan
Whiting
Yellowtail

CANADA

Albacore
Anchovy
Bass
Boston Bluefish
Carp
Cisco

Cod
Flounder
Goldeye
Haddock
Hake
Halibut
Herring
Mackerel
Orange Roughy
Perch
Pickerel
Pike
Pollock
Pompano
Salmon
Sardine
Silverside
Smelt
Snapper
Sole
Sunfish
Tarpon
Trout
Tuna

CARIBBEAN

Bonito
Grouper
Kingsish
Mullet
Muttonfish

Pompano
Roballo
Smelt
Snapper Red/Yellow
Spanish Mackerel
Trout
Tuna

HONG KONG

Anchovy
Bigeyes
Carp
Crevalles
Croakers
Giant Perch
Grey Mullet
Grouper
Japanese Sea Perch
Leopard Coral Trout
Pampano
Pilchard
Red Sea Bream
Round Herring
Sardine
Scad
Whitefish

NEW ZEALAND

Hoki
John Dory
Kingfish

Mackerel
Mullet
Orange Roughy
Perch
Piper
Salmon
Smooth Black
Snapper
Sole
Southern Whiting
Terakihi
Trevally
Trout

SOUTH AFRICA
Albacore Tuna
Albacore
Butterfish
Carp
Euthynnus Tuna
Haddock
Herring
Kabeljou
Kingklip
Maas Banker
Mackerel

Pilchards
Salmon
Sardines
Seventy Four
Skipjack Tuna
Snoek
Sole
Steembras
Stock fish
Stump Nose
Tongol Tuna
Trout
Yellowfin Tuna

UNITED STATES OF AMERICA
Albacore
Alewife   Smelts
Amberjack
Anchovies
Angelfish
Barb
Barracouta
Barracuda
Bass
Bigeyes
Black Cod
Blackfish

Blueback
Bluefish
Bluegill
Bonito
Bream
Brill
Capelin
Carp
Cero
Char
Chub
Cisco
Coalfish
Cod
Crevalle
Dab
Flounders
Fluke
Gag
Grayling
Grouper
Haddock
Hake
Halibert
Herrings
John Dory
Kingfish
Mackeral
Mahi Mahi

Merluccio
MulletParrotfish
Perch
pike
Pilchard
Plaice
Pollock
Pomfrets
Red Snappers
Roach
Saithe
Salmon
Sardine
Shad
Sierra
Skipjack
Smelt
Snapper
Sole
Sprat
Tench
Tilapia
Trout
Tuna
Wahoo
Whitefish
Whiting
Yellowtail

Jewish Calendar

2009 (5769-5770)

Fast of Esther	Monday	March 9th
Purim	Tuesday	March 10th
First Day Pesach	Thursday	April 9th
Second Day Pesach	Friday	April 10th
Seventh Day Pesach	Wednesday	April 15th
Eighth Day Pesach (Yizkor)	Thursday	April 16th
Holocaust Memorial Day	Tuesday	April 21st
Israel Independence Day	Wednesday	April 29th
Lag B'Omer	Tuesday	May 12th
First Day Shavout	Friday	May 29th
Second Day Shavout (Yizkor)	Saturday	May 30th
Fast of Tammuz	Thursday	July 9th
Fast of Ab	Thursday	July 30th
First Day Rosh Hashanah	Saturday	September 19th
Second Day Rosh Hashanah	Sunday	September 20th
Fast of Gedaliah	Monday	September 21st
Yom Kippur (Yizkor)	Monday	September 28th
First Day Succot	Saturday	October 3rd
Second Day Succot	Sunday	October 4th
Shemini Atseret (Yizkor)	Saturday	October 10th
Simchat Torah	Sunday	October 11th
First Day Chanukah	Saturday	December 12th

2010 (5770-5771)

Fast of Esther	Thursday	February 25th
Purim	Sunday	February 28th
First Day Pesach	Tuesday	March 30th
Second Day Pesach	Wednesday	March 31st
Seventh Day Pesach	Monday	April 5th
Eighth Day Pesach (Yizkor)	Tuesday	April 6th
Holocaust Memorial Day	Sunday	April 11th
Israel Independence Day	Monday	April 19th
Lag B'Omer	Sunday	May 2nd
First Day Shavout	Wednesday	May 19th
Second Day Shavout (Yizkor)	Thursday	May 20th
Fast of Tammuz	Tuesday	June 29th
Fast of Ab	Tuesday	July 20th
First Day Rosh Hashanah	Thursday	September 9th
Second Day Rosh Hashanah	Friday	September 10th
Fast of Gedaliah	Sunday	September 12th
Yom Kippur (Yizkor)	Saturday	September 18th
First Day Succot	Thursday	September 23rd
Second Day Succot	Friday	September 24th
Shemini Atseret (Yizkor)	Thursday	September 30th
Simchat Torah	Friday	October 1st
First Day Chanukah	Thursday	December 2nd

Index

Charleston (WV)	408	Columbia (SC)	398	Deauville	72
Charlotte	382	Columbus (GA)	313	Decatur	312
Charlottesville	405	Columbus	383	Debrecen	128
Chateauroux	72	Commack	299	Deerfield Beach	304
Chatham	41	Compiegne	68	Degania Alef	139
Chattanooga	399	Concord	346	Delft	182
Cheadle	235	Constanta	197	Delmar	361
Chelles	74	Copenhagen	60	Delray Beach	310
Chelmsford (MA)	333	Coquitlam	37	Denmark	60
Cheltenham	239	Cordoba (Argentina)	5	Denver	398
Chelyabinsk	200	Cordoba (Spain)	214	Derbent	200
Chemnitz	113	Corfu	122	Des Moines	320
Chernigov	231	Cork	133	Desswffy	128
Chernovtsy	231	Corsica	108	Detroit	342
Cherry Hill	350	Corpus Christi	403	Dieuze	68
Chesham	234	Costa Mesa	291	Dijon	68
Chevy Chase	327	Costa Rica	54	District of Columbia	303
Cheyenne	409	Coventry	271	Dix Hills	379
Chiang Mai	228	Cracow	190	Dnepropetrovsk	231
Chicago	314	Cranbury	353	Dominican Republic	62
Chigwell	237	Cranford	357	Donetsk	231
Chile	49	Cranston	397	Dorohoi	197
Chimkent	166	Crete	122	Dortmund	113
China	50	Creteil	74	Dover	302
Chisinau	174	Croatia	54	Downey	285
Chmelnitsy	231	Croydon	269	Dresden	113
Choisy-le-Roi	74	Cuba	56	Druskininkai	169
Christchurch	184	Cuernavaca	172	Dublin	133
Chula Vista	293	Culver City	285	Dubrovnik	55
Cincinnati	384	Cumberland	325	Dubuque	320
Cinnaminson	350	Cuneo	156	Duluth	342
Clark	357	Curaçao	183	Dundee	275
Clearwater	310	Curitiba	30	Dunkirk	68
Clermont-Ferrand	102	Cusco	188	Dunoon	275
Cleveland	383	Cyprus	56	Durban	210
Cleveland/Beachwood	383	Czech Republic	57	Durham	381
Clichy-sur-Seine	74			Dushanbe	227
Clifton	356	**D**		Dusseldorf	114
Clifton Park	378				
Clinton	339	Dagenham	238	**E**	
Cluj Napoca	197	Dallas	400		
Coblenz (Koblenz)	113	Daly City	295	East Barnet	243
Cochabamba	27	Damacor	183	East Brunswick	353
Cochin	130	Dan	139	East Chicago	319
Cockfosters	243	Danbury	300	East Falmouth	330
Colchester	237	Danville	406	East Lansing	340
College Park	325	Darlington	237	Eastbourne	270
Cologne	113	Daugavpils	168	Easton (MA)	330
Colmar	68	Davenport	321	Ecuador	62
Columbia (SC)	400	Davis	297	Edam	182
Colombia	53	Dayton	385	Edgware	265
Colonia	353	Daytona Beach	311	Edinburgh	275
Colorado	297	Dead Sea	139	Edison	353
Colorado Springs	299	Deal	355	Edmonton	36

Khabarovsk	200	Lake City	305	Little Rock	282
Khamasa	130	Lake Placid	363	Liverpool	263
Kharkov	231	Lakeland	311	Livorno	157
Kherson	231	Lakewood (CA)	286	Ljubljana	206
Kibbutz Harduf	148	Lakewood (NJ)	356	Llandudno	277
Kibbutz Yotvata	149	Lancaster (PA)	391	Loch Sheldrake	379
Kiel	116	Lancaster (UK)	245	Lod	149
Kiev	231	Landau	116	Lodz	192
Kihei	409	Lansing	340	Lohamei Hagetaot	149
Killingholme	246	Laramie	409	London (Canada)	41
Kimberley	211	Larissa	122	London (UK)	246
Kingston (Canada)	41	Larnaca	57	Central	248
Kingston (Jamaica)	165	Las Cruces	359	East End and City	250
Kingston Upon Thames	269	Las Palmas	218	North	251
Kislunhalas	128	Las Vegas	345	North West	254
Kitchener	41	Latvia	167	South	263
Klaipeda	169	Launceston	10	Long Beach (CA)	286
Knokke	26	Laurel	329	Long Ditton	269
Kobe	165	Lausanne	224	Long Island	370
Kobersdorf	15	Lawrence (KS)	321	Longney	274
Koh Samui	228	Lawrence (MA)	331	Longmeadow	332
Kokand	411	Lawrence (NY)	370	Lorain	385
Kolkata	131	Lawrenceville	353	Lorient	72
Kona	409	Le Blanc Mesnil	76	Los Alamos	359
Konstanz	116	Le Chesnay	76	Los Angeles	286
Korazim	149	Le Havre	72	Los Gatos	296
Korbin	22	Le Kremlin-Bicetre	76	Loughton	238
Korsten	232	Le Mans	72	Louisiana	322
Kosice	205	Le Perreux Nogent	76	Louisville	322
Kostrama	200	Le Raincy	76	Lowell	334
Kowloon	53	Le Vesinet	77	Lubbock	402
Krasnoyarsk	200	Leeds	273	Lubeck	116
Krefeld	116	Legnica	192	Lublin	192
Kremenchug	232	Leicester	246	Lucerne	224
Krugersdorp	209	Leiden	182	Lugano	224
Kuba	19	Lengnau	224	Luneville	69
Kursk	200	Leominster	339	Lusaka	414
Kutaisi	109	Les Lilas	77	Luxembourg	170
Kyrgyzstan	167	Levallois Perret	77	Luxembourg City	170
		Lexington (KY)	322	Lviv	232
L		Lexington (MA)	334	Lynn	331
		Lexington Park	329	Lyon	103
La Ciotat	103	Liberec	58		
La Courneuve	76	Libourne	107	**M**	
La Garenne-Colombes	76	Liege	26		
La Jolla	293	Liepaja	168	Maagan	149
La Paz	27	Lille	69	Maastricht	182
La Rochelle	111	Lima	188	Maayan Harod	149
La Serena	49	Limoges	107	Macedonia	170
La Seyne-sur-Mer	103	Lincoln (NE)	345	Macon (France)	104
La Varenne St-Hilaire	76	Lincoln (UK)	246	Macon (GA)	313
La Chaux de Fonds	224	Linden	359	Mad	128
Lafayette (CA)	284	Linz	15	Madison	408
Lafayette (IN)	320	Lisbon	194	Madrid	215
Laguna Hills	291	Lithuania	168	Magdeburg	116

Mahanayim	149	Mexico	171	Mozir	22
Mahwah	348	Mexico City	172	Mulheim	117
Maidenhead	234	Miami/Miami Beach	306	Mulhouse	69
Maine	324	Michelstadt	116	Mumbai	131
Mainz	116	Michigan	340	Muncie	318
Maisons Alfort	77	Michigan City	319	Munich	117
Majorca	218	Middletown (CT)	301	Myanmar	178
Mako	128	Middletown (RI)	397	Myrtle Beach	398
Makhachkala	200	Mikulov	58		
Malaga	216	Milan	158	**N**	
Malden	334	Milford	339		
Malmo	220	Millis	336	Nagykanizsa	129
Malta	171	Milton	336	Nagykoros	129
Manaus	29	Milton Keynes	234	Nahariya	149
Manchester (CT)	301	Milwaukee	408	Nairobi	167
Manchester (NH)	346	Minden	117	Nalchik	201
Manchester (UK)	239	Minneapolis	342	Namibia	178
Manhattan	371	Minnesota	342	Nancy	69
Manila	189	Minsk	22	Nantes	72
Mantua	157	Miskolc	128	Naples	159
Maplewood	351	Mississauga	42	Narragansett	397
Maputo	177	Mississippi	343	Nashville	399
Maracaibo	413	Missoula	344	Nassau	20
Marbella	216	Missouri	343	Natchez	343
Marblehead	331	Mobile	280	Natick	334
Marburg an der Lahn	116	Modena	159	Navoy	411
Margate	245	Moghilev	22	Nazareth	150
Margelan	411	Mogi Das Cruzes	32	Nebraska	345
Marignane	104	Moldova	174	Needham	336
Marlboro	334	Monaco	175	Negev	150
Marrakech	176	Monchengladbach	117	Nepal	178
Marseilles	104	Moncton	40	Netanya	150
Martinique	171	Monroe	379	Netherlands	178
Maryland	325	Mons	26	Neuilly	78
Massachusetts	330	Monsey	377	Neukirch-Egnach	225
Massy	77	Montana	344	Neustadt	118
Maui	409	Montauban	107	Nevada	345
McKeesport	388	Montbeliard	69	Neve Tzedek	151
Meaux	77	Monte Carlo	175	New Barnet	243
Medellin	53	Monterrey	174	New Bedford	330
Medford	334	Montevideo	410	New Britain	301
Meknes	177	Montgomery	280	New Brunswick	354
Melbourne	10	Monticello	379	New City	378
Melilla	171	Montpelier	404	New Delhi	131
Melrose	334	Montpellier (France)	105	New Hampshire	346
Melun	77	Montreal	46	New Haven	301
Memphis	399	Montreuil	78	New Jersey	346
Menton	105	Montrouge	78	New London	302
Merano	157	Morocco	175	New Mexico	359
Mercer Island	407	Morris Plains	3551	New Orleans	323
Meriden	301	Morristown	355	New Rochelle	380
Merlebach	69	Moscow	200	New York City	365
Metuchen	354	Moshav Shoresh	149	New York State	360
Metz	69	Mount Vernon	380	New Zealand	184
Meudon-La-Foret	78	Mozambique	177	Newark (DE)	302

Porto Alegre	31	Regina	48	Saginaw	342
Portsmouth (NH)	346	Rehovot	151	Saint Denis	97
Portsmouth &		Reims	69	Saint Germain	97
Southsea (UK)	242	Rennes	72	Saint John	40
Portugal	193	Reno	346	Saint-Avold	70
Postville	320	Reseda	283	Saint-Die	70
Poti	109	Revere	339	Saint-Etienne	106
Potomac	327	Rezhitsa	168	Saint-Fons	106
Pottstown	393	Rhode Island	396	Saint-Laurent-du-Var	106
Poughkeepsie	362	Rhodes	122	Saint-Louis	70
Poway	293	Riccione	159	Saint-Ouen-L'Aumône	97
Prague	58	Richmond (Canada)	37	Saint-Quentin	70
Prairie Village	321	Richmond (VA)	405	Salamanca	216
Prestwich	241	Richmond Hill	43	Sale	245
Pretoria	209	Richmond on Thames	269	Salem (MA)	331
Princeton	353	Ridgewood	348	Salem (OR)	387
Providence	397	Riga	168	Salford	241
Pueblo	299	Rijeka	55	Salgotarjan	129
Puerta Vallarta	174	Rio Rancho	359	Salisbury	330
Puerto Rico	195	Ris-Orangis	97	Salt Lake City	403
Pune	132	River Edge	349	Salvador	29
		Roanne	106	Salzburg	16
Q		Rochester (MN)	343	Samara	201
		Rochester (NY)	363	Samarkand	411
Qatzrin	151	Rochester (UK)	245	San Antonio	400
Quebec City	48	Rock Island	318	San Bernardino	292
Queens	375	Rockford	318	San Carlos	296
Quincy	337	Rockland	324	San Diego	293
Quito	63	Rockledge	305	San Fernando Valley	290
		Rockville	328	San Francisco	294
R		Roissy-En-Brie	97	San Jose (CA)	296
		Romania	195	San Jose (Costa Rica)	54
Ra'anana	151	Rome	159	San Juan-Santurce	195
Rabat	177	Romford	239	San Pedro Sula	124
Radauti	198	Rosario	5	San Rafael	297
Radlett	244	Roselle	358	San Salvador	64
Rahway	358	Rosh Hanikra	152	Santa Barbara	296
Rainham	238	Rosh Pina	152	Santa Cruz	27
Raleigh	382	Rosny-Sous-Bois	97	Santa Fe	359
Ramat Gan	151	Rostov-na-Donu	201	Santa Monica	290
Ramat Hanegev	151	Rotterdam	182	Santa Rosa	297
Ramat Hasharon	151	Rouen	72	Santiago	49
Ramat Yohanan	151	Rousse	35	Santo Andre	32
Ramona	293	Ruislip	267	Santo Domingo	62
Ramsgate	245	Rumson	355	Santos	32
Rancho Cucamonga	292	Russian Federation	199	Sao Caetano do Sul	32
Randolph (MA)	337	Rzeszow	192	Sao Jose dos Campos	32
Randolph (NJ)	355			Sao Paulo	32
Rapid City	399	**S**		Sarajevo	28
Reading (PA)	389			Sarasota	311
Reading (UK)	234	Saarbrucken	118	Saratoga Springs	378
Rechitza	22	Sachkhere	201	Saratov	202
Recife	30	Sacramento	292	Sarcelles	97
Redbridge	238	Safed	152	Sarrebourg	70
Regensburg	118	Safi	177	Sarreguemines	70

Index to Advertisers

Please complete and return Jewish Travel Guide form to us by 1 September 2009

Please reserve the following advertising space in

Jewish Travel Guide 2010:

	Black and White	Colour	
☐ Full Page	£500	£850	181 x 115 mm
☐ Half Page	£295	£425	91 x 115 mm
☐ Quarter Page	£175	£275	45 x 115 mm

(*UK advertisers please note that the above rates are subject to VAT*)

Special positions by arrangement. Colour only available in either front or back colour section.

☐ **Please insert the attached copy (If setting is required a 10% setting charge will be made.)**

☐ **Copy will be forwarded from our Advertising Agents *(see below)***

Contact Name: _____

Advertisers Name: _____

Address for invoicing: _____

_____

Tel: _____ Fax: _____

Signed: _____ Title: _____

VAT No: _____

Date: _____

Agency Name (if applicable): _____

Address: _____

_____

Tel: _____ Fax: _____

advertisements set by the publisher will only be included if they have been signed and approved by the advertiser.

To the Advertising Department
Jewish Travel Guide
Vallentine Mitchell Publishers
Suite 314, Premier House, 112-114 Station Road, Edgware, Middlesex HA8 7BJ
Tel. No.: +44(0)20 8952 9526   Fax: +44(0)20 8952 9242
Email: info@vmbooks.com   www.vmbooks.com

Update for Jewish Travel Guide 2009

Readers are asked kindly to draw attention to any omissions or errors. If errors are discovered, it would be appreciated if you could give appropriate up-to-date information referring to the appropriate page, and send this form to the Editor at the address below.

We prefer you to email any changes to **jtg@vmbooks.com** or to fax them to **+44 (0)20 8952 9242**

With reference to the following entry:

Page:

Country:

Entry should read:

Email essential

Signed: _____ Date _____

Name (BLOCK CAPITALS) _____

Address: _____

_____

Telephone: _____

Fax: _____

The Editor
Jewish Travel Guide
Vallentine Mitchell Publishers
Suite 314, Premier House, 112-114 Station Road, Edgware, Middlesex HA8 7BJ
Tel. No.: +44(0)20 8952 9526   Fax: +44(0)20 8952 9242
Email: jtg@vmbooks.com   www.vmbooks.com

Jewish Year Book 2009

The Jewish Year Book 2009 is a comprehensive directory of communal institutions and organisations, covering all aspects of British Jewish society and cultural and religious activities, together with details of their leading personalities. It offers an extensive guide to the primary organisations of the Jewish communities of the world and a substantial survey of Israel and its organisations having associations with British Jewry, including a list of Israel's overseas embassies and missions.

From the reviews

> *'In a Jewish world that at times seems mired in uncertainty and chaos, it is reassuring to greet the latest version of the enduring symbol of stability and durability that is* The Jewish Year Book ... *It presents a portrait of the current state of Jewish life in the British Isles, with fact-filled glimpses of Jewish communities world-wide. It is a trove of information, logically organized and clearly set forth.'*

> *Jack E. Friedman*, Jerusalem Post

Please send me____copies of the *Jewish Year Book 2009* at the price of £35.00 hardback

❏ I enclose a cheque for £ _____ made payable to **Vallentine Mitchell**

Postage and packing is £2.50 for the first book and £1.50 for each subsequent book in the UK. Please add $5.50 and $1.50 for each subsequent book in North America. Rest of World: £3.50 first book, £1.50 each subsequent book. Airmail rates upon request. VAT registration No: GB 232 7273 75.

Please charge my   ❏ Visa   ❏ Mastercard   ❏ American Express

Card Number: _____   Issue No: _____

Expiry date: _____   Sec. No: _____

Name: _____   Signature: _____

Address: _____

_____

_____

Tel: _____   Fax: _____

E-mail: _____